An extraordinary encounter with a Native American visionary draws young Englishwoman Celia Gunn into a tribal struggle for cultural sovereignty and spiritual wholeness. *A Twist in Coyote's Tale* is the true-life account of six years spent working alongside the Arrow Lakes Indian Band in the spectacular valleys of British Columbia, Canada, and the dramatic Interior Plateau country of Washington State, USA. Celia's inspiring personal journey entwines with the renascence of the Arrow Lakes people and traces her own spiritual awakening in the midst of a living shamanic tradition.

Celia Gunn (Sun and Moon in Taurus, Gemini rising) is a Northumbrian-born writer now living in the West Country of England. Since her North American experience she has written two novels, *A Dark Wind* and *The Fourth Gateway*. She continues to pursue a lifelong interest in the mysteries of reality, and with her husband enjoys exploring and researching the mystical landscape of Wessex: stone circles, medieval churches, crop formations and landscape zodiacs. Currently Celia is working on the biography of an elder of the Western Mystery tradition and a novel about ancient North America. When not planning her writing on long dog-walks, she can most often be found tending her beautiful chakric woodland garden.

A Twist in Coyote's Tale is a remarkable and incredibly truthful revelation of the author's inner life while she participated in the recent awakening and empowerment of the Arrow Lakes people during the time they returned the bones of their ancestors to their central sacred site at Vallican, in south-eastern British Columbia. I could not put *Coyote's Tale* down because as the prophesized deep awakening unfolded for the Arrow Lakes people, Celia Gunn touched depths in her psyche that few ever dare explore. The issue of our times is the healing of each human on the planet, so that each person can honor Earth. In North America, the healers are the indigenous people because they are the keepers of the sacred sites; Celia has truly honored their ways and has found her own inner peace. Filled with exceedingly important detail about this ancient people, it also reads like a novel, so enjoy this wonderful story!

Barbara Hand Clow, author of *The Mayan Code: Time Acceleration and Awakening the World Mind*, is a Cherokee teacher and an International Mayan Elder.

Other titles by the author

A Dark Wind
The Fourth Gateway

Other titles by Archive Publishing

Journey in Depth: A Transpersonal Perspective
The Fires of Alchemy: A Transpersonal Viewpoint
A Twist in Coyote's Tale
The Dark Moon
Performing the Dreams of your Body

Other titles distributed by Archive

Working with Others
Forging the Future Together

A Twist in Coyote's Tale

CELIA M GUNN

Celia M Gunn

with love for Kate
n Greg with wolf~

ARCHIVE publishing

CHICHESTER ENGLAND

2006

First published in Great Britain by
ARCHIVE PUBLISHING
Chichester   England

Designed for Archive Publishing by Ian Thorp

© 2006 Celia M Gunn

A CIP Record for this book is available from
the British Cataloguing in Publication data office

ISBN-13 978-0-9542712-4-4 (Hardback)
ISBN-10 0-9542712-4-6
ISBN-13 978-0-9542712-5-1 (Paperback)
ISBN-10 0-9542712-5-4

Printed and bound in England by
CROMWELL PRESS
Trowbridge Wiltshire

CONTENTS

Dedicated to the Sinixt First Nation/Arrow Lakes People

For my children, Sivan, Natalie and Nicolas; so that they may know

You want my young men to do whiteman's work? Then how can they dream? And without singing and drumming the dream, where is the wisdom? Where is the future of the people?

After Smohalla, Dreamer-Prophet of the
mid-Columbia River, c.1880

The carryover soul memory dominated the moment.

Mary Summer Rain, Phoenix Rising

Memory and experience are the truest sources of power.

Robert Holdstock, Ancient Echoes

TWO COYOTE TALES

In the long-ago time, when the plant, animal, bird and mineral people were placed on the earth by the Creator and given extraordinary powers, Old Man Coyote was feeling lonely; he had no-one to talk to. "The others are too busy," he complained to the Creator. "They have no time to visit with me. I want a people of my own, so I may watch over them."

To form the new people, Coyote filled a parfleche with good red soil, but Mountain Goat added white soil to the red as a trick and the Creator breathed life into two races.

"What strengths will these new two-leggeds have?" Coyote asked the Creator. "What guidance will they have?"

Coyote went to the plant, animal, bird and mineral persons. "Those who take pity on the two-legged ones and provide sustenance for them will bring these new people into the Order of Creation by this sacrificial giveway," he told them. "Communicate with the humans through their Sumix [sacred power] in song, dream and vision. In this way, they will be endowed with a spiritual power."

***

Coyote and the Spirit-Chief had a power contest. Unable to move a mountain except when the Spirit-Chief wanted him to, Coyote was defeated. He was taken to an island in the ocean, where he lived in exile with his wife and four children.

But when the world changes again in 2000, Coyote will come back.

Eneas Seymore, of Sinixt/Arrow Lakes descent.

RED CLOUD

All-encompassing, the drumbeat; pervasive, insistent.

The mist-filled clearing is pale with first light; hunched by the sacred fire sits a lone drummer, a shadowy figure.

He gets up, begins to walk in my direction, the throb of his drum filling my head, my whole being, compelling me to walk down the low-ridge to meet him.

The mist eddies, swirls; beyond, darkness like the edge of the world. Unseen, encircling trees rustle, whisper....

Shocking-red, the drummer's jacket; raven-black, the hair flowing thick and loose over his shoulders; hollow-cheeked, hawk-like, his face is dark, lined. Ageless.

So close we could touch. I know, yet do not know him....

His coppery face a mask-like grimace, almost a sneer, the Native American thrusts the drum and stick towards me, jerking them at me, imperatively challenging: "You take the drum! Now, you call the people!"

Stumbling backwards, I shake my head, waving my hands in negation. "No! I've never drummed! I don't know how!"

Hands pushing at thin air, I woke up, my heart pounding. It took a few moments to remember where I was; pulling back the curtain from the window of my camper-van, I looked outside. The early-morning mist was gone and the clearing was bright with sunlight; a thin blue wraith of smoke curled over the sacred fire. Nobody was to be seen. As my heart calmed, an excited curiosity began to replace the feeling of panic. My dreams were often vivid but this one carried an immediacy new to me.

Had I been told this powerful dream would herald an intense involvement with a group of Native American people that would profoundly affect my life and being for the next six years and beyond, I doubt I would have believed it, even though I sensed something special was going on.

It was summer solstice; I was camped at the Rebirth of Mother Earth Medicine Wheel Gathering, near the Arrow Lakes in south-eastern British Columbia, Canada. A Native American-led gathering was a new experience for my three children and me; unsure what it might involve, the previous afternoon I had chosen a campsite on the periphery of the growing encampment.

At the time unaware of the significance of the year, 1987,[1] I had been sensing something in my inner planes beginning to actively seek expression. A month before, visiting a friend in

---

1   According to Jose Arguelles, the year of the Harmonic Convergence, signifying a global spiritual awakening and part of the Great Count of the Mayan Calendar which ends at the winter solstice of 2012. I believe this is not a prediction of the end of the world but a crossroad for human consciousness, whose choice of direction the Maya could not foresee. It is a prophecy to be found in cultures around the globe. (See Geoff Stray, *Beyond 2012: Catastrophe or Ecstasy.*)

Toronto and missing my children on Mother's Day, I had joined in a Mother Earth Day celebration taking place on Algonquin Island, one of a small string of jewels a short ferry-ride from the harbour. Under the soft blue, lightly-feathered sky of a warm May day, watched over by the slim, commanding presence of the telecommunications tower, several hundred people – singles, couples, families; Rastafarians, Hare Krishna devotees, punks, rockers, bikers, musicians, poets, artists, craftspeople, environmentalists, old and new hippies and a throng of children – danced, sang and drummed together, peddled handcrafted wares, shared ideas and food, and filled the day with laughter and creativity.

A single mother, I had been inspired by the harmonious, colourful experience and sense of an extended family, and wanted to find something similar for my own little family. Only a few days after returning home to Vernon in the North Okanagan area of British Columbia, a two-line announcement in a local advertising rag had caught my eye: a "Native-led Rebirth of Mother Earth Medicine Wheel Gathering" was taking place at Edgewood the following month, just a couple of hours' drive away. The reference to Mother Earth seemed to continue a theme; "Native-led" and whatever a "Medicine Wheel" might be further spiced my interest, for despite a life-long interest in the Native American way of life and having lived in Canada for twelve years, I had only recently befriended a Native family.

The day before leaving for the gathering, I had had a sense of needing to be alone in nature and for the first time since moving there, climbed up into the hilly ranch-land above our home. It was a hot, windless day; after a three-hour ascent through coarse tufted grass and scratchy sage-brush I reached a massive rocky outcropping overlooking the city and stopped to rest. It was not the hazed overview of the valley that held me there for the next timeless period, but an incredible sight that at first made me think I was suffering heat-stroke. Like spots before my eyes, several large birds were gliding lazily on outspread wings, just beyond the cliff-edge. Twelve, I counted, fleetingly wondering if a dying creature were somewhere below. But these were no vultures – their sleek heads gleamed white. They were eagles, bald eagles; effortlessly, majestically coasting the invisible currents above a blue-grey-green checkerboard. Drawn in by their grace and beauty, I had felt myself weaving in among them. Never had I seen anything like it.

Native American traditional wisdom teaches that the natural world communicates with us; that encounters and experiences with birds, animals, trees, wind, water, the mineral kingdom, all carry message and meaning. Everything has spirit, and spirit speaks to spirit. While aware of the concept, my understanding was limited, but I knew it was no accident that I had been witness to such an awesome sight. Only in hindsight did I recognise it as a synchronous precursor of what I was unknowingly about to become part of: a gathering of eagles.

The following day, a two-hour drive over the Monashee mountains in the heat of early afternoon and a further one-hour sidetrack into the village of Edgewood, where a couple of amused locals, clearly accustomed to this mistake, sent us back up to the main highway to a turnoff marked by balloons, had left me feeling less confident. The track was rough; billowing clouds of dust chased us as we rattled over a cattle-grid and past hayfields, more turnoffs, woods, with no sign of any human activity. I had been about to give up when I noticed a small hand-painted sign: a rainbow-crowned "Rebirth of Mother Earth", pointing out a narrow, rutted track almost hidden among the trees, and gratefully turned off into the shade to crawl along a green tunnel for a few hundred feet. Then the track burst out into a clearing.

All my misgivings had fled. Before me lay a dreamlike vision: an immense, sun-filled meadow speckled with wildflowers, edged with freshly-greened young trees and protectively enclosed by dark, thickly-forested mountain slopes. Bright and unexpected, a crescent of tipis graced the far side of the clearing, causing a painful twist in my chest and bringing tears to my eyes. Following the track round the edge of the clearing, I found it hard to take my eyes off the tipis. Coloured streamers dangled from the top of the poles, which opened out like a fan; the heavy canvas covers were hitched up at the base, exposing thick woody ankles. Separate from the crescent and situated where it would receive shade much of the day from the only trees in the meadow, two towering pines, stood a small tipi. Down one side swooped a beautifully hand-painted golden eagle, wings outspread, fierce yellow beak agape and black claws wide; on the other reared a brown horse, black mane and tail flying. Red and yellow lines snaked round the base and yellow hand-prints climbed over the entrance, which yawned darkly open.

Scattered in the shade of the surrounding trees were a few tents, less than I had anticipated, which had made me wonder if there was much interest in this kind of event. Thinking I would simply observe what went on, I set up our little camp in the shade on a small rise behind the tipis, well back from the main area. Hot and restless after the long drive, my kids clamoured to go swimming so we set off to find Whatshan Lake, which I had noted crudely sign-posted on a fork in the trail about a half-mile back.

As I slowly drove back down the little ridge, a robust, elderly Native man wearing black-framed glasses appeared from among the trees to the right, striding down the bank towards my moving vehicle, one hand raised in what seemed like greeting. Thick, iron-grey braids framed his round, weathered face, bright with a smile that matched his size. Something about him made me stop, turn off the engine and get out, and we met in front of my vehicle. Taking my hand, he shook it firmly and began to speak, a flow of words in a language I'd never heard before. His hand was large, the skin warm, dry, rough. Then to my surprise, still talking, he opened his arms, smiled broadly and enfolded me in an enveloping hug.

It had felt uncannily comfortable, and the unfamiliar resonance of his words had a beguiling elegance. Breathing in the musky, smoky aroma of the rough wool of the red plaid lumberjacket pressed against my cheek, part of me wondered at how easily I had allowed this elderly Native stranger such intimacy. Then he grasped me gently by the tops of my arms and held me at arm's length, smiling, still talking away. Sunlight glinted off his glasses; liquid, warm brown pools, his eyes gazed into mine.

It was as if he knew me, but how could that be?

"Thank you," I said when at last his words fell away. "I don't know your language so I can't understand your words, but you've made me feel very welcome. This is a beautiful place, I'm happy to be here. We're just going to cool off in the lake." Not knowing if he understood, I indicated three little faces watching impatiently from the van. He smiled and spoke again briefly, his breath sweet as dry grass crushed in the sun, then stepped back and waved us on our way.

If this was how Native people welcomed newcomers, I had thought, I need not feel uneasy about being here.

Whatshan Lake had appeared accessible only through a private campground. Exploring further, another turnoff took us up along a narrow, winding gravel road through a tunnel of greenery. Crossing a rickety old bridge, far below I glimpsed a creek; something told me to check it out and we found a faint, steep trail leading down into the narrow little ravine. A couple of minutes of scrambling upstream brought us to a perfect swimming-place: enclosed by high, sheer rock-walls, a pool fed by the silvery threads of a waterfall lacing the far rock-face. It was not very large – I could swim the perimeter in a few minutes – but its ice-cold, shadowy greenness hinted at glacier-source and great depth. Above, the filtered, flickering light of the lowering sun played through the greenery. Peaceful yet poised, the atmosphere pervading this wild and secret place whispered of enchantment.

By the time we returned to the gathering-place, a motley collection of tents had appeared, looking like exotic blue, orange, green and silver beetles foraging under the trees. Strung out alongside the track were cars, campers, converted buses; the buzz and hum of new arrivals continued as daylight fled. The atmosphere was charged with a feeling of festivity; the colourful clothing everyone seemed to be wearing reminded me of the hippy-sixties. Children swarmed everywhere, happily running round and shrieking. The busiest area was a communal kitchen, set up in an old barn on one side of the clearing, one of many dilapidated lean-tos and outhouses. I learned the site had used to host an annual barter fair.

Central to it all, somehow oblivious, stood the tipis: massive, mystical guardian-elders, eerily aglow, their hearth fires an erratic heart-flutter in the darkness.

As evening progressed, round the sacred fire in the middle of the meadow gathered a growing group of people, drumming and chanting Native American songs which continued long into the night, as soothing to sleep as waves washing upon the shore.

Then early in the morning, the slow, solid thump of a drumbeat had gently roused me. Drowsily wondering if the drumming had gone on all through the night, I'd raised myself on an elbow and looked out the window of my camper. It was barely light; early-morning mist enveloped the clearing, shrouding the tipis, which were haunted by ethereal, pale-blue wisps of smoke. By the sacred fire sat a figure, a lone drummer, swaying to his beat.

How appropriate to welcome the dawning of a new day this way, I had thought; I should get up and join him, to set the tone for the day.

Lying back, I had promptly fallen asleep again, to be taken into the most vivid and intense dream I had ever experienced.

"Take the drum, call the people." What people? It made no sense, the people were already here. Anyway, I had refused. Because of embarrassment, panic…. I found myself wishing I could go back, accept the drum and see what happened next. Perhaps a Native person could help me with the meaning of this powerful dream.

Within a couple of hours, I realised there seemed to be very few Native people around and anyone with any air of authority was busy organising the day's activities. By late morning a number of workshops had been posted. Putting my dream aside, I chose to start with the basics by attending a workshop explaining the Medicine Wheel.

This turned out to be led by a non-Native woman but she seemed to know her subject, teaching not only the symbolic meaning of the Wheel and the four directions but also how to use it as a divinatory tool. As an intriguing conclusion, she also told us how coming into contact with the Native American way of life had profoundly affected the way she had since chosen to live.

In the afternoon, I chose to take the kids to the hand-fasting of a couple who had met at a previous gathering. Dressed in a white cotton shift, a young blonde woman held the hand of a bearded, long-haired young man draped in a crimson blanket, and they waited in the centre of a circle of witnesses until joined by a striking figure, Chief Wobay Kitpou. A Native elder, small and heavy-set, he had risen to the occasion and was wearing a slightly-askew buffalo headdress, many ostentatious pieces of silver and turquoise jewellery, moccasins, and a loincloth tied tightly beneath his heavy, naked belly. After the ceremony, the couple retired into a tipi and after a couple of raunchy jokes, the chief amused us with a string of stories and songs.

Back at our camper, we were eating when it struck me that it had become strangely quiet, like the stillness before a storm. The clearing seemed oddly deserted. Then two people hurried into the biggest tipi, another rushed out and within minutes brought back an older, bearded man with cropped grey hair. Something was wrong, seriously wrong; I could feel it. A few minutes later a young woman wearing a long, tie-dyed skirt and a loose white blouse came hurrying by, wisps of ash-blonde hair straggling across her face, caught in the wetness on her cheeks. I waved her to stop. "What's going on?"

Her face was pale and blotchy, her eyes red and puffy. "He's gone!" She wailed like a banshee: "O-o-h, he's go-o-ne."

"Who's gone, what do you mean?"

"O-o-oh, Red Cloud...." She waved an arm blindly towards the tipis below us. "No-o-o, no-o-o, he can't-" She broke off, seemed to come back into herself. "They're down there now, trying to revive him." Her mouth reformed into the "o" of an incipient wail.

I had no idea who she was talking about but the image of an aged body being abusively thumped and jolted back to a life already departed flashed powerfully, distastefully, into my mind's eye. "Why don't they allow him the dignity of his departure? Surely he knows when it's his time to leave?"

The words were out of my mouth before I thought, but they seemed to have a calming effect. The young woman looked at me properly for the first time. "You're right. He would know." She turned away and headed slowly down towards the tipis.

Feeling calm and detached – as I might, given the death of someone I didn't know – I watched a knot of people gather at the tipi. About twenty minutes later an ambulance came rolling across the meadow and parked beside it, looking oddly out of place. Watching felt intrusive, macabre, but I couldn't turn away. Within minutes, a stretcher bearing a deathly-still form draped in white was carried out of the tipi and loaded into the vehicle.

For a long time after the ambulance had left, the entire camp seemed frozen. Curiosity eventually drove me down to the tipis where I chanced on the young blonde woman again and tentatively asked: "This Red Cloud – it was a heart-attack? Who was he?"

"Founder of the Rebirth gathering ... visionary." She stared at me, clearly appalled by my ignorance. "You must have seen him around. The Native elder with the glasses and the red jacket." Tears brightened her eyes. "God, he cared so much about Mother Earth. He'd even pick up other people's cigarette stubs from the ground and put 'em in his pocket. He hated littering.... He had a stroke awhile back, lost English, but his Native tongue, he kept that."

She was describing the red-jacketed Native elder who had hugged me so warmly less than twenty-four hours earlier. I was speechless.

Not until late that night when I lay reflecting on the fullness of a day of Medicine Wheel teachings; laughter and joy at the hand-fasting; Native songs and stories; and the sudden shock of death and the slow, despondent pipe ceremony that had later taken place at the Medicine Wheel, did the hawk of perception strike like a sudden shaft of sunlight.

In my dream, the drummer had been wearing a red jacket. As had the Native elder into whose warm hug I had bent like a willow, in whose demeanour I had sensed an underlying recognition. Who turned out to be the founder of the gathering. Yet physically there seemed little resemblance between the two men. Was there a connection?

A shiver ran icily through my body. Viewing death as a natural step in the journey of the spirit, the collective grief had brushed over me like the touch of a feather, but now I began to feel the loss. How would I ever find out why Red Cloud had singled me out and so warmly greeted me? It had been more than a welcome; he had barely stopped talking. What had he been saying? Into the darkness of the night I sent out my questions: had it been Red Cloud, visionary, who appeared in my dream-state with the challenge, the order? What did it mean to take the drum, call the people? What was it I had turned down?

The next day dawned bright and clear: the last day of the gathering, although the sacred fire would be kept alive for a full seven days and a core group camped there for a moon. The mood was subdued and there were no more workshops but it seemed the gathering would continue; other Native Americans seemed to appear out of nowhere and "Native-led" became an extraordinary reality, touching me personally and inspiring me to become directly involved with the gathering.

Something more profound than I could ever imagine had been set in motion. The personal vision – communication between an individual and the Creator – of a spiritual Native elder and the gathering he brought into manifestation as a result of that vision would have a fundamental and permanent effect on many lives, bringing forward issues on levels both personal and political that had long called for redress. His life-purpose fulfilled, red-jacketed Red Cloud passed over into the spirit-world at the nascence of a far-reaching turn of events which he had in effect seeded: a magical process of renascence on the inner, personal and outer, group levels.

UNDER THE SKIN

Sometimes it seemed it was only the memory of the Medicine Wheel gathering, a glowing sustaining light, which kept me going through the chain of trying events over the following few weeks: my elderly VW camper off the road for over two months with a broken transmission, a replacement proving difficult to locate and afford; our bicycles stolen; a pernicious health problem; a supposed friend letting me down badly. Burn-out from almost six years of over-zealous commitment to the principles of co-operative living was also a factor, but my attempts to move were frustrated by the lack of a vehicle. It was like being in a logjam; feeling powerless, battered and bruised, one day in late August I finally caved in, began to cry and found myself unable to stop. Never having experienced such lack of self-control, I retreated to bed to nurse a flood of emotionality and self-pity. It was the first time my children had seen me like this; as a single parent I had always steeled myself to be a tower of strength for them. Now they took over, comforting me with little pats and words I had often given them.

Eventually emptied, exhausted and ashamed of such a display of weakness, I sent them off to play. Left alone in a benumbed state, all I was feeling began to tumble from my lips like the ranting of a mad-woman. Part prayer, part plea, with all my heart I called for renewal of the hope, the sense of purpose I had felt the last day of the gathering – dream within a dream it now seemed: the drama, the sense of mystery and magic; and an encounter with another striking Native American, which had affected me more than I realised.

The following day, shaky and weak, I called in sick at the fitness centre where I worked and was mixing some new music for my classes when the doorbell rang. I heard one of my kids open the door. There was a short silence, then Sivan, the oldest, rushed into the living-room. Her stage-whisper was breathless, as if she'd run a mile: "You'll never guess who it is!"

Strangely detached, my mind took an unaccountably imaginative leap and I coolly responded: "Bob ... from the gathering?" And then could only gently shrug and shake my head as she asked with a puzzled little frown: "How did you know?"

I had no idea, nor why this Native American I had briefly met over two months ago should come calling.

Two silhouettes stood in the doorway. Breathless from the fluttering in my solar plexus, I held out my hand in welcome. Bob's hand, slim, smooth and warm, grasped mine firmly. His eyes were hidden by the same sunglasses he had worn at the Rebirth gathering; a wide smile creased his cheeks as he inclined his head slightly in greeting and again his memorable, rich, almost lazy drawl delighted my ears: "Hey there, how ya doin'? We almost didn't make it." He laughed. "Found your place okay. We drove in but I didn't see your 'bus'. Thought you wasn't home so we turned an' we was almost gone when I seen your boy, runnin' out the house. Remembered him from Edgewood."

Giving silent thanks to my son, I gushed: "Come in, come in. I'll make coffee. We're going to eat soon; you're welcome to join us."

Stepping over the threshold, Bob indicated the young man shyly grinning behind him, hands tucked in his jean pockets. "This here's Virgil, one of my boys – one of the good 'uns! We was on our way to take him to his school ... real good school, in Washington State. Thought we'd make a trip of it."

Recollecting Bob had told me he was from an American Reservation in that state, I shook the boy's strong, broad hand, a little taken aback by his size. Slight and slim, Bob was about my height but Virgil, who looked to be fourteen or fifteen, was showing indications of impending height and a powerful build. His t-shirt, with a picture of a colonial soldier standing guard above the words "Washington, D.C.", was stretched tightly across a muscled chest and broad shoulders; as he stepped inside, I could see he would soon tower over his father.

A faint, evocative fragrance accompanied them: wood-smoke, transporting me to another place, another time. A gaggle of little neighbourhood children, my two younger ones among them, stared silently from the drive, and for a moment I saw through their eyes: entering my "little twentieth-century box" as Bob would later call it, a classically handsome representative of the Native American race: smooth tanned skin, high brow and prominent cheekbones, dark eyes and cleft chin, gleaming slim black braids immaculately secured with leather ties, and a large, pale jade-coloured claw on a leather thong at his throat; a striking contrast to my blonde hair and blue eyes, the red dress I happened to be wearing.

Leading the way into the living-room, I recalled some of the things Bob had told me at the gathering and casually remarked over my shoulder: "I remember you saying you travel a lot through your ancestral lands but Vernon is kind of a long way from there. And from Washington State.... How come you're over this far west?"

"I came because you called."

My heart gave a sudden thud. Everything seemed to stop although my body kept moving, step by automatic step. For I had indeed "called", with all my heart and strength, only the day before. But not by phone. And not him specifically, I was sure. Yet the day following my "dark night of the soul", the response to my prayer seemed to have uncannily arrived in the shape of this person. How on earth could he have "heard" my call? At the gathering, he had said that if I ever needed help, I need only call, he was only a few hours away, but I had taken for granted he meant by conventional means, through the wires. Although I had witnessed him doing something extraordinary and sensed he was somehow special. Who – or what – was he? How – and why – should he have "heard"? And in what way could he ever help me?

In time, I would look back on this stage as analogous to the transitional period of labour, Bob as a kind of midwife. Then small and sleepy, the city of Vernon in the picturesque North Okanagan had been a perfect location to raise small children alone, and the housing co-operative had not only provided a secure, affordable roof over our heads but satisfied my principles about land-ownership. After six years in the big city, I had never regretted leaving Vancouver, where both my daughters had been born. Lately, however, I had been feeling as if Vernon – my son's birthplace – were trying to squeeze me out, even as it grew larger.

As in a dream, I busied myself in the kitchen. It was partially open to the living-room and I could hear Bob chatting easily with Sivan, then eleven, who was opening up to him in a way I did not recognise. My other two little ones then came in and I heard their childish voices in response to his. This was surprising and pleasing, for all three children were reserved and wary of the men who occasionally appeared in my life. Bob's tone was warm and light, sometimes gently teasing, in what I was to learn is the natural Native manner that instinctively stops short of offence. I noticed how he waited until they took their accustomed places at the table before seating himself and his son and only when they had all taken food did he serve himself. Natalie, then six, insisted on sitting next to him and finally asked her burning question: "Can you show me how to turn into an animal?"

"Natalie!" I chided. Where had she got such a notion?

He just chuckled and turned to the awed child. "Not me. But some of them ways're still known to the old folk."

As I washed up, Bob came into the kitchen. "Better get some coffee brewin'." He smiled. "We got a lo-o-t of talkin' to do. Could take all night. Then me 'n' Virgil, we gotta be on our way, first light."

To my ears, the eliding vowel sounds were a delightful signature of Bob's way of speaking, played over many times in my mind since our encounter. Intrigued, I settled Virgil in the television room, which doubled as a guest room, with a stack of videos and dressed the two younger children in jeans and sweaters so they could play outside. A delicately-scented, welcome respite from the heat of a summer's day in the Okanagan – classed as semi-desert – early evening also heralds the arrival of mosquitoes and their irritating agenda. Then I made coffee, wondering what on earth we could have to talk about that would take all night.

It turned out to be like a university course crammed into six or seven hours, with short breaks to get the children bathed and to bed, and make fresh coffee, again and again, although I had no need for any stimulant; I had never felt so alert, so alive. Nor had I ever found it so easy to remember so much; everything Bob proceeded to tell me seemed to blaze itself like a fiery brand into my memory. In a way, it was like being reminded of something I already knew, a sort of re-collecting. The wealth of information and depth of insight into the Native American way of life that Bob encapsulated throughout that timeless, scintillating night was a priceless gift, one I would increasingly appreciate during the ensuing years: a foundation of vitally-pertinent knowledge that would serve me in many ways.

"I been travellin' the lands of my ancestors, an' one of the things I learned: when I say 'my people', it's not just the people I come from," he began, sitting down at the other end of the couch. "It's the people I meet – somethin' about them just fits. We visit, an' we find we hold a lotta things in common, an' we respect each other, don't matter where they come from. I call these people, 'the people of my heart'. That's what I mean when I say 'my people'. Over that way," a wave of his arm indicated the south-east, "in the place they call Grand Forks, my uncle used to have land there. There's a people live there now ... come over from Russia, they told me, round the turn of the century. Maybe you heard of 'em; they call themselves Doukhobors. There's others I met that live over near Castlegar an' in the Slocan Valley."

The names were not unfamiliar to me. A year earlier I had made a trip through south-eastern British Columbia, and had learned of the people who had built the unique cubed wooden houses that peppered the Kettle Valley region.

"I visit with these folk. They sure know how to make a man feel welcome. Good food, an' they always feed you up a storm. Man, I get so full I can hardly move! An' they like to visit; they never make you feel like you have to leave."

His smile and soft drawl were like a caress. Hoping he felt that way in my home, I reflected how I would not want this handsome, gentle-spoken man to leave, either.

"Yeah, they sure know a lo-o-t about hospitality." The long vowel sound slid through me, smooth as a snake. "That's what it's like among us Indians, kinda like an unwritten law of hospitality. You share the best you got, treat your guest like a king. Then you know when you go visit, you get treated the same way. Why," he smiled broadly, "in the old days, I heard they'd even share their wife! Not," his soft, rolling chuckle tumbled like water over pebbles, "that I'd take anything for granted!"

A fluttering commenced in my stomach. Was this some kind of veiled proposition? "Well, I can see the point," I smiled wryly. "Might liven up a dull marriage. And improve the gene pool. As long as the wife had a say!"

Our eyes met then, and held for a long breathless moment. His were dark, warm, dancing. Powerful surges of a hot and heavy, dizzying feeling pulsed through me.

"In our way," he said, a little nod accompanying his words, his eyes still on mine, "the woman always gits her say. An' usually her way! Least that's how I'm told it was in the old days, an' it hasn't changed all that much since then. Women always made 'most all the decisions."

Was there a double meaning? Or was I reading between the lines when there was nothing there? Struggling to contain my trembling, calm my thudding heart, I absorbed the information and tried to stay on track. Was he saying that his was a matriarchal people? But what about the "people of my heart"? The silence stretched out of time while a tumult of thoughts and emotions vied for my shaky attention. My eyes dropped to the ostentatious brass belt-buckle at his waist: a cowboy astride a bucking bronco. When I looked up again, Bob was gazing out the window.

Wisps of cloud tinged with hints of peach and apricot feathered the deepening blue sky; the faint voices of children at play drifted through the open window.

"Them Doukhobors, I got a re-al respect for them people," he resumed. "They work hard, put up all their own food. Pretty near self-sufficient. They respect the land, an' they know how to care for it, just like the Indian did. They burn off the old dead growth, just like my ancestors did when it got too thick in the forest. To keep it clear for the game, an' feed the earth. You should see them old folk tellin' the fire to go this way, that way." Gracefully, his hand swept from side to side. "They respect their elders, an' they listen to 'em.... They got their own religious beliefs. An' they been at odds with the government.

"They remind me of the Indians an' what's all been done to us. They suffered religious persecution an' had their kids taken away from them just like the Indian did. An' they got some kind of an agreement with the government, kind of like a treaty I guess, but they're still havin' to fight for their rights. Same old story, the government never can stick to no treaty!" He broke off and stared into space. When he resumed, his voice was tight. "There was nothin' wrong with them treaties. Nothin', 'cept they never stuck to even a one of them! Ev'ry single one was broken." His eyes flashed black with anger. "They never once kept their word, not spoken or written!" A pause, then his voice softened: "Your word rides on your breath ... your breath, breathed into you by the Creator. My ancestors didn't know what it meant, to break your word ... lie about spirit...."

A prickling crawled over the top of my head. It was the most beautiful way of describing integrity, and so simple. A sigh escaped from deep within me.

"When the Europeans came, they was met with peace in our heart. The trappers – some of 'em took Indian wives an' learned the ways to live good, live right. But more came, an' more.... Started pushin' the Indian people round: 'go here, don't go there' ... on the land the Creator give us! Priests, sayin' the Indian ways was no good. Think of it; some of their ways must've been real strange to the Indian ... men in black skirts. But we believe: 'live and let live'. We don't tell people how to live or what to believe; that's not the Indian way. The only way's the Creator's, and we was given the right to choose our own path....

"The settlers; the military. They brought diseases, alcohol." Emotion broke his voice and he jumped to his feet, strode across the room and threw open the door to the fading light. A subtle scent of damp clay earth, of drying grasses and pine – the unique aroma of the Okanagan – breathed into the room. Quietly, Bob spoke to the darkening sky: "It didn't even have to be no war. Those diseases: smallpox, influenza, even the common cold.... Back then, Indians was a strong and healthy people. They bathed in the creek all year round, even in winter. An' they used the sweat-lodge. Body and spirit were strong....

"Qu'il-tsin ... in my language, sweat-lodge."

The first word I had heard in his mother-tongue: essentially a holy-word. Feeling privileged, I tried to echo it and he smiled as we bounced the half-swallowed sound back and forth.

"They didn't know disease," he continued. "They lived out in the open, travellin' the trails an' waterways of their fathers an' their fathers before them. Huntin' the game that ran the forests and valleys, fishin' the lakes an' rivers. Gatherin' roots an' berries. Plants grew here like in a garden, like the Eden in your Bible.... Eatin' natural foods put here by the Creator, an' not," his voice twisted, "processed white-poison handed out by the government." He shook his head. "They went with the natural order of things, risin' with the light, to bed with the dark ... unless.... You heard of tipi-creepin'?" Throwing back his head, he laughed.

The term was self-explanatory, making me grin and feign nonchalance as a rush of trembling warmth again flooded my body.

"We're the red race, you know! We're a red-blooded people!" Then he sighed deeply. " ... They was tuned to the rhythms of the seasons an' their world revolved round that rhythm. They'd scatter in the summer accordin' to age an' ability, in preparation for the drawin'-in of winter, then come back together 'n' share. A life of sharin'. A simple way of life.... Sure, they must have known hard times and hunger, but a life of huntin' an' fishin' ... the mountains, the lakes ... the water clean, the air pure.... Hell, when work is play, that's when you're really living!"

Filing this great truth away, I thought how rare it was to think of a job as play, to be able to really live, in modern society.

"Kept their numbers small. They had natural ways to do that. Reckon there was never more than about two, three thousand of us Arrow Lakes people at any one time."

The name of his people had been a constant in my mind since he had told it to me at the gathering, when I had wondered if they had been named for the great lake system of the region or vice versa.

"I was told there was twelve clans," he continued, "each about two hundred strong. Kum-sin'kin, that's 'clan'. They had a strong an' stern tradition an' it was strictly adhered to. They knew 'bout livin' in balance; what they'd learned over time, watchin' those first teachers: the plants, the birds, the animals. Leave enough of the roots an' berries so's there'd be enough for the other creatures, enough that they'd grow back for the next year. Not take too many deer an' never the does, else there'd be a shortage of deer-meat after. Leave enough fish so's they'd spawn for the next year. Not stay too long in one place so's it'd get polluted, the game hunted out or learn to stay away." His tone changed and a small crease appeared in his brow. "Then came those times of great change. When those European sicknesses hit 'em, their bodies never had no time to build up a resistance. The old ones an' the little ones, they'd be the ones that got sick an' died first."

Aware of the tragic decimation of Native peoples since European contact, it struck me like a hammer-blow that I was sitting with a descendant of the few survivors of my ancestors' contamination. Great plagues had swept through historic Europe; in turn, black deaths had been inflicted on the New World. A sense of disgust at my race bubbled up in me.

Bob got up, paced back and forth, the subject clearly painful as a raw wound, his anger showing white as bone: "There was Indian doctors but there'd never been anythin' like this. Indian doctors'd've been helpless against this great evil: people dyin' by the tens, hundreds; looks like the medicine man lost his power – the white man had the new and powerful magic...." His distracted gaze seemed to be reaching back to the horror of those times. "No matter what the medicine man tries, everythin' he knows ... people fallin' sick an' dyin' like flies. His power gone, maybe he's already dead himself.... Families left to rot in the lodge where they died; no-one able to carry out the traditions for them, their last rites....

"The whole fabric of their lives was torn apart. You can see how they'd fall into superstition. So much useless ... lost ... forgotten in the face of this evil.... Like Spirit deserted 'em ... foundation ripped out from under."

His face was a pale, hard mask, his eyes obsidian. My chest ached painfully with a deep empathy that was closer to the bone than I could have imagined.

"They say the white man gifted 'em blankets purposely infected with smallpox. Eighty per-cent died, that's what the records say. I gotta degree in Native American history – I read the books, studied what's been written. Four out of five, an' there wasn't that many in the first place.... The settlers, when they come, they just had to push a little, the Indian was already on the edge. The ones that survived was herded onto the poorest pieces of land signed by the government, got given some farmin' tools an' were left to get on with it.

"The way my ancestors passed for thousands of years – the lands where we was put by the Creator – got split by an imaginary line, an' my forebears was told to belong one side or the other."

I realised he was talking about the International Boundary.

"The ones on the south side was put into a concentration camp they called the Colville Reservation, along with remnants of other tribes. Thirteen non-treaty tribes, some of 'em traditional enemies. Hoped we'd be at each other's throats, I guess, finish off the job for them.... Then they even took back half of that land, an' white folks're still buying it up."

As it happened, I had recently learned about a fundamental difference between Reservations in the United States and Reserves in Canada. I had made an enquiry about renting a house on the Okanagan Band Reserve on the west side of Okanagan Lake near Vernon and learned that while non-Native people could obtain a lease to build there, they could never own the freehold. In the States, Reservation land can be sold to non-Natives.

"They took the little ones away from their families to the mission schools," Bob continued tersely, sitting down again. "Priests and nuns whipped their language, their way of life, their identity out of 'em. They wasn't allowed to come back, they lost touch with their parents and their grandparents. If disease hadn't already killed 'em off, the ones that remembered the old ways.... There's many ways to destroy a people; you don't have to go in an' murder 'em all outright.... Those kids grew up without a family, not knowin' a mother or a father. They never learned, so how could they do it in their own turn? An' people wonder why our kids today are in such trouble. Parents don't know how to parent, to discipline, how to say 'no', so kids don't know how to discipline themselves, how to say 'no' to themselves.... Believe me, I know what I'm talkin' about – I got seventeen children!" he announced with a sudden grin.

I was taken aback. Despite him having arrived with a son, I found it hard to think of him as someone's husband.

Taking a deep breath, Bob clenched his fists and stared out into the dark velvet of the sky. "An' if I want to walk the land of my grandfathers this side of the line, or bring my kids here, first I have to give white people pieces of paper to prove I am who I say I am, an' that I have the right to be here. A piece of paper that says I have the right to hunt an' fish in my own ancestral lands! An' they have the right to turn me away." He shook his head, and plunged back into history: "They took away a people's whole way of life. Stopped the salmon comin' up the Columbia when they built the dams, the Grand Coulee, the Chief Jo; took away the staple of the Indian's way of life. They say the chief of the Sanpoil, he died of a broken heart when he saw the waters risin'.... What the white man does, because he's afraid of the dark! Places where we gathered our food drowned, an' our villages, our burial-grounds.... Well, least our ancestors are safe under there from those archaeologists! They can't dig 'em up an' stick 'em in no museum now!"

In the silence that followed, I felt an echo of the feeling that had surged up in me when he had told me at the Medicine Wheel gathering about human remains having been dug up from an ancestral burial-ground and taken to a museum. The strength of my reaction – raw outrage – had shocked me; until then I had never given much consideration to the meaning of old bones on display at a museum. If anything, I thought of them impersonally, as a discarded shell.

"Alcohol, drugs," he muttered, bringing my attention back. "There's many ways to get us to do ourselves in. You ever been to a Reservation? It's not a pretty place."

I thought about the Canadian Reserve I had only recently visited: the Okanagan Band Reserve, which I would learn was relatively well-managed and prosperous. The Native neighbour I had recently befriended, whose children were favoured playmates of my children (because, as Natalie put it, "They're always so nice") was of Okanagan descent; when her mother died she had returned to live on the Reserve and I had begun to visit her there. Her partner, a big, quiet, thoughtful and well-read man originally from Germany, had told me about a generation of Germans who had a powerful feeling for the Native American life-way, which he believed stemmed from romantic teachings during his childhood in Germany and the influence of a series of books by Adolf Hungry Wolf, which in turn would explain the preponderance of German visitors at Native American gatherings. Then I recalled a Sunday excursion some nine years earlier: driving along the north shore of the Fraser River in North Vancouver, I had passed a series of run-down, ramshackle dwellings lined up along the highway at the foot of the misted mountains, their yards filled with junk. A sense of depressed desolation had hung over that little Reserve.

Since emigrating from Israel to Canada in 1975 with my then-husband, my life had been wrapped up in work, children, and the collapse of my marriage. Not even seeing for myself the conditions under which Native people lived had woken me to the terrible truth of the high standard of living I was enjoying. Now my eyes were being opened to the fact that it was built on the back of the rape and repression of the indigenous peoples and the unsustainable extraction of natural resources.

"In the old way," Bob continued, "the village was the political entity, anything bigger was unknown. Villages'd co-operate with each other, an' groups would share tasks. A council of six elders – women, I was told – oversaw decision-making. But the government set up a system of tribal councils, with elected officials. 'Elect your own representatives! Do it our way! An experiment,' they told us. Well, I don't want to speak badly of those elected people. But while some people genuinely want to help others, there's always some that want status, power. A tribal council violates our constitution and by-laws by not consultin' with the elders before important decisions are made."

But elders are the guiding force, I instinctively wanted to say.

"But we're not stupid!" His voice was tight. "If there was no treaties made, we're still a sovereign nation! We haven't forgotten our hereditary lineage. Nothin' to do with elections, nothin' to do with white men's pieces of paper! But I guess the plan is for enough time to pass that the lines get forgot....

"But we haven't. An' we won't go away. We've not only survived, we're comin' back. We're gettin' us a white-man education. There's Indian teachers, lawyers. We're comin' back! An' Ol' Man Coyote – he's back, an' he'll play one of his little tricks. The white man's tables'll be turned on himself – he'll be his own heyoka!"

We sat in silence as the storm of his emotions passed over. I hadn't heard the word heyoka before but it was easy to guess: it was about us – white people – doing ourselves in with our own cleverness. Ol' Man Coyote I knew to be the trickster, teaching us whether or not we want to learn; the cosmic joker who shows us the foolishness of believing we know what we are doing; the wild card.

It was like being in a dream: incredible, and wonderful, to be sitting in companionable silence in my home with a handsome Native American. Growing up in England, my fascination – if that's what it can be called – with the race had been part of my make-up for as long as I could remember. Childhood games of cowboys and Indians – I had always wanted to be the "red Indian", a scout, and still carried the scar on my eyebrow, a mark gained clearing the way for the others. I had read everything about them I could find in our small local library; and watching cowboy movies, I always rooted for the Indian. Like most people, my knowledge was a second- or third-hand, Hollywood-embossed mix of truth and illusion coloured by my own romantic imaginings. Now the truth was being set before me. More than ever I felt the pain of being part of the race that was clearly still perpetrating genocide upon what I viewed as a great and noble race; labelled a stone-age culture, yet highly civilised by the only standard that mattered in my eyes: the extent to which they communicated with, co-operated with and utilised nature without precipitating drastic ecological change. Clearing my throat, I said: "I often feel so ashamed of the race I've been born to. The arrogance, insensitivity, cruelty-"

To my surprise, Bob laughed. "Oh, don't mind me! I get riled up easy! Anyway, don't you remember? We had a contract. We thought it'd be of more use to have you in a white skin this time round!"

LAUGHING THUNDER

Totally taken aback, I forgot my useless apologies. Not only did Bob, a Native American, seem to be taking reincarnation, a concept I had thought of as Buddhist, for granted, but he was implying that prior to a life being taken up, some kind of spirit-agreements were made about what was supposed to happen in it. It was an appealing idea but a huge leap for me. That we might live many lives was something I had only recently begun to take seriously and I had not got as far as imagining that a life might be planned for in advance of taking it up. Although once I thought about it, I realised most people feel a sense of some deep purpose, some special thing to do in their life. Where would such an idea come from?

And who was this "we"? From the way he had said it, it was not just he and I who had got together in spirit to make these arrangements; others were involved. Unless, with his teasing tone, he was joking. The thought darkened my elation. Was it all just romantic New Age yearnings?

Thrilled and torn at the same time, I escaped to make fresh coffee and see the children to bed; mundane tasks which let me put the whole issue to the back of my mind, where it sat, titillating and somehow comforting.

"Good to see a woman, carin' for her little ones," Bob said as I returned. His voice took on a soft, caressing tone: "You're a mother. I envy you. You carried those little ones; they came through you into the world. You carry life.... Life is sacred an' only through a woman can life come into the world. Only a woman has that power, to bring life into the world. Man is here to provide for that life, protect it. But only a woman can carry it. Woman holds the intelligence of life."

I didn't really understand the last bit, but his words reminded me of the Medicine Wheel gathering and the first time I had seen him.

The evening after Red Cloud's death, I had learned that a pipe ceremony was being conducted at the Medicine Wheel. Strange to say, it was the first I had heard of the great construct, marked out by stones, which lay in a neighbouring clearing and by the time we got there the ceremony was underway, buried in the midst of an immense circle of people – perhaps the entire encampment. From the periphery, I could make out a small, grey-haired elder and several others in the centre but barely see what was going on or hear a word. The children became restless; I picked some yarrow and was showing them how to rub it on their skin as a defence against mosquitoes when I sensed a kind of shift, a subtle change in atmosphere.

The pipe ceremony seemed to have ended. A slight figure with long, black hair, wearing blue jeans, a brown waistcoat and Apache boots, was now speaking; the way he stood and his graceful gesticulations reinforced my impression that he was Native American but I couldn't remember having seen him that day. Tantalising snatches about the sacredness of the planet and of woman reached my ears, something I had never heard before from a man, which rekindled in me a light of optimism about the future, an innate sense – or I would not have had children – that had been eclipsed by the seeming downward spiral the world was riding. Later, I would find out that almost every woman there had immediately fallen in love with this speaker.

Bob got up and walked slowly across the room, his eyes seeming to look beyond the confines of the walls. "The Creator gifted woman with the right an' the ability to carry life. We all come onto the Earth through a woman, no other way. You got to respect that; how can you live, an' not respect what that means, not respect your mother? But you see it all around. Women treated bad. Right from when they're just little 'uns. Used, abused; I seen how people treat even their own mothers.... I don't know how they can live with themselves when they treat their own mothers like that! The one that bore them, brought them into the world."

Never having felt positive about being a woman – a seeming impediment, a handicap, in our society – I felt a little caged bird in my chest begin to sing.

"They treat Mother Earth the same way. Like any mother, She gives her children everythin', all they need: nourishment, shelter, comfort, beauty. She don't ever ask for nothin' back. But her children – they take an' take, more'n they ever need, without respect. An' they hide it away for themselves, forget the teachin's 'bout sharin'. They even end up buryin' food, an' burnin' it. They tear into their Mother, rip Her up, strip Her ... poison the Mother that gives them life. They never think 'bout balance, 'bout givin' back.

"They try an' control Her, manipulate Her, change the way She is. They think they know better than the Creator how She should be! Treat Her like an enemy, somethin' to be feared, 'stead of the paradise She is.... Well, now She lies bleedin' under their feet. An' you can be sure, like any good mother, She knows when to say, 'No'! An' when She says, 'No', we'll all hear Her! We'll all feel Her then!" Pausing, he took a deep breath. "But here I go again, ain't no use gettin' all riled up."

As Bob sat down again on the other end of the couch from me and took a drink of coffee, I closed my eyes. Only too aware of my race's fear of raw nature, its self-arrogated dominion over the natural world, its need to control and subjugate the earth, its greed to wrench wealth from her bowels, all as foreign to the soul of the traditional Native American as our polluting technology, I didn't know what to say. Then the thought struck me: how would Mother Earth say "No"? Through the prophesised Earth Changes?

Before I could ask, he resumed: "They say my people came from the north. I read what the scientists wrote. But it's not that way – we came from the south." His words carried the weight of authority. "Remember. Remember what I'm telling you: we came from the south. All the old ones tell us this....

"I don't know why it all went wrong, how we forgot what we all knew one time. One time, people knew how to walk gently on Mother Earth, in balance. I was told we had it right once – must've been the golden times some people speak of." He laughed wryly, as I recalled reading about a Golden Age, a Golden Dawn. "But who'm I to question the ways of the Creator? For some reason we fell off the path. All those old teachin's, they got lost, hidden away. Or messed up, contaminated....

"They say now that a woman in her time of the month is unclean. A woman'd go off to the moon-lodge for four days – people started thinkin' it was because she was unclean, she'd contaminate the food or other things. But the way I was told, she went off because it was her time of power. How could they forget that? An' once you know that, how can you not see it? Ev'ry moon, a woman bleeds an' there it is: the outward show of her creative power, far greater than anything a man could have. Maybe the men got jealous – that old poison – or maybe they just got afraid. Maybe it was the priests polluted the teachin'." He sighed deeply. "Woman went off for those four days so's not to be round the men, not handle their food ... an' especially not their medicine things! The power of her moon-cycle was so strong, it'd upset the balance; she'd knock their medicine right out the picture!" Tipping back his head, he laughed, then continued: "Her female relations'd take over her work an' she'd go be with the other women in the moon-lodge. 'Sisters in the moon', I heard them called...." He grinned in a shy sort of way. "Guess they kinda knew how to time it to be in there together."

"Sounds a great idea to me," I smiled. "I'd certainly appreciate four days with no responsibilities for home and family, especially at that time of the month! That's one tradition we should bring back at once!" Embarrassed that it had sounded like I was working with him, I quickly added: "And you're right about those 'sisters': that happened when I worked in the same room with five other women for almost two years, and three of us who were close friends...." I broke off, realising this might be an embarrassing subject for him. But his words had cast new light on a terribly misjudged condition and I could not resist excitedly adding: "I never thought to look at it this way. Right from the start, that time was an embarrassing inconvenience. Like a sickness. God, at school, we all even called it 'the Curse'."

Bob did not look at me and continued as if I had not spoken: "That's why a woman always walked a little behind the man. He'd be like a shield. If she walked in front of him, her power would knock him over! Like an eclipse...." he mused. "An' then when a woman don't bleed no more, she becomes an elder. The creative energy stops its outward flow, turns inward. Held inside, it becomes wisdom. An' them women elders'd be in that moon-lodge, sharin' with the younger ones, passin' it all on: how to be with a man, how to raise a family.... Just as they'd learned it from their elders."

I was impressed. Viewed with such distaste and negativity by contemporary society, menopause and old age were bathed in a wholesome new light.

"You know I like to tease," he continued. "Them old women'd say: 'Don't tease. You never know the threshold for another.' A man might tease his wife, meanin' no harm, but don't see she's finding it hurtful. She gets resentful an' there you go, the beginnin' of bad relations, maybe the beginnin' of the end. An' the little 'uns – you gotta be re-eal careful with little 'uns. They live in the now; they don't understand teasin' but they can sense when they're bein' belittled an' it don't do their hearts no good. It's a real fine line." Folding his arms across his chest, he sighed and leaned back, looking toward the window. "I been tellin' you all this woman stuff. It's not my place to do that. You gotta meet with some of the old ladies I know. They're good people. My mother, she knows the old ways. It was 'cause of her that I went to that gatherin'. She told me to go. I wasn't interested, but she calls me an' says: 'They're practisin' medicine in our ancestors' lands an' no-one asked permission. You go on up there an' see what they're up to.' I didn't want to go, not one bit, but I always end up doin' what my ma tells me, so I went in the end."

Intrigued, I found I could not ask how she had known.

"It was strange," he mused, "the way that old fella, the one that passed over...."

"Red Cloud?"

"Yeah. Red Cloud. He didn't know Manny 'n' me for anyone but Arrow Lakes and he greeted us like we was some long-lost relatives and says: 'At last, you finally got here.'"

That this might have significance and that there might be a connection between Bob's reception and my own warm welcome passed me by at the time.

"When did you get there?" I asked.

"Afternoon of the Saturday. Next thing I knew, he'd passed over."

Later, I would be told of the rest of the circumstances: after meeting Bob, Red Cloud had sent his partner, Tiger Lily, off for a walk, then gave away his T-shirt, eating-dish, ring and other personal items, returned to his tipi and succumbed to the heart-attack.

"An' then they was askin' me to do the eulogy," Bob continued, "which was strange, 'cause I knew nothin' about him."

This I remembered well, for it had been when my so-called observer position had seemed to come adrift. Having heard about the ceremony in advance and wanting to see and hear everything this time, I had taken the children to the site of the sacred fire early, as surrealistically-long shadows fingered across the meadow. Beyond the silver birch, jagged-toothed granite peaks glowed rose-gold as a large, solemn circle of witnesses formed round the fire. Accompanied by another Native man, the speaker who had caught my attention at the pipe ceremony the previous evening appeared on the opposite side of the circle. My breath caught in my throat: the two men looked like they might have stepped in from the previous century, or out of a movie about Apaches. They sat down cross-legged on the grass as the grey-haired, bespectacled elder who'd led the pipe ceremony shuffled forward on the arm of a young, attractive blonde. Not his daughter, I could tell, but found it hard to believe she might be the partner of such a bent, skinny, grizzled old man with the most impressive beak of a nose. He had led a workshop on alpha and beta brain-waves the previous day, something which seemed to me rather odd for a Native elder to be teaching.

Even from where I was sitting, the elder's words were but a mumble as he packed the ceremonial pipe and raised it to the sky before having it lit by his companion. Four times he drew on the pipe, blowing the smoke in each of the cardinal directions. Then it was passed reverently round the circle, each person either drawing on it or touching it to either shoulder in turn, as I did in mine.

When the pipe ceremony came to a slow, meditative end, the handsome Native man stood up and approached the sacred fire, his exotic appeal a dynamic contrast to the elder's. Like the previous evening, he was wearing jeans, a navy-blue shirt, a dark leather waistcoat and tanned, knee-high Apache boots. Gracefully he carried himself, his back straight, his step light. Hooked behind his ears, two slim, shining black braids fell over his chest. Only the sunglasses detracted from the overall effect.

His companion remained sitting. Not good-looking in the conventional sense, his weathered, dark features were strangely attractive: truly primitive, in the meaning of "first". His face was broad, the nose wide and flat, lips full; the lines carved into brow, cheeks and jaw whispered of millennia, of suffering, of ancient wisdom. Flowing over his shoulders, his hair was thick, blue-black and cut in spikes on top. He could have come from the pages of National Geographic: ageless, timeless.

Speaking of his respect for the vision of the founder and the importance of gatherings that brought people of different races together in respect and harmony for the healing of the planet, the Native man in sunglases eloquently spun a vision of the sacredness of woman, of Mother Earth and our responsibility as human beings. Some of it I had heard the evening before, but this time I began to feel light and tingly, as if I might melt in the earth. Eventually his words flowed to an end and he stood in silent meditation for some time, etched in memorable stillness against the delicate greenery of the silver birch. There was a long, dark, narrow feather in his right hand, held close against his leg: flight feather of an eagle, I guessed.

Placing his other hand on his hip, he raised the feather to point into the glowing embers of the sacred fire, his lips moving soundlessly. Then he slowly raised both arms, open to the deepening heavens, and stood as if frozen, head tilted back, arms widespread, feather dramatically extended. His chest heaved as he took a slow, deep breath; the words that passed his lips were directed skyward, as if following the path directed by the feather. The soft flow of alien sounds, a guttural catch, made me shiver. Perhaps at some level I knew it was the first time in many, many decades that the ancient language of these lands had been uttered in this sacred place.

With a swift, controlled movement, he pointed the feather down at the sacred fire, his left arm still raised, hand open to the sky. The stream of words fell away until his lips moved soundlessly, then with a slight flourish of the feather he lowered both arms and moved clockwise one quarter round the fire, and repeated the ritual. No-one moved – I barely breathed – as he prayed through the remaining three directions.

As his words sank away for the last time, a breeze snatched at the edge of the crescent of birch, turning the leaves silver-bellied up to dance, trembling. Gaining in strength, it trailed round the clearing in a clockwise direction, causing the young trees to rustle and whisper. Then it dropped, and with its passing I realised what an unnatural wind it had been. Not a breeze or a gust announcing a change in the weather, but a breath like the passing of a spirit.

Sitting beside me, Sivan grasped my hand. "Mum, did you see that? Did you see what happened? Every time he pointed the feather at the fire, the smoke went in the direction he pointed! Did you see?"

I had seen but it had not registered. My whole body prickled as I whispered back: "Yes, I saw."

Nor could I forget. Feeling compelled to personally express my appreciation for the inspiration and sense of hope I felt his words had given me, I had looked out for the Native man but not until a couple of hours later did I find him, sitting with a group of people I realised were the organisers of the gathering. Waiting until there was a gap in their dialogue – several minutes at least – I managed to catch his eye.

Or did he catch mine?

"Sorry to intrude, but I just wanted to thank you for your words today, which helped me enormously." Glancing at the others, I felt chilled by their looks. "Please excuse me." Turning away, I found I was trembling.

Behind me, I heard him say: "Think we're done here." Suddenly, the Native man was beside me. "Come an' sit with me awhile."

Numbly accompanying him as he led the way to the grassy rise overlooking the tipis, the meadow and the sacred fire, I had hardly been able to believe what was happening. Nor was the next intense half-hour any less dreamlike as we sat side-by-side and he told me how he regularly travelled the lands of his ancestors, and described their extent and how his people had been forced onto the Colville Reservation in Washington State. The geography was unfamiliar to me; I had never heard of most of the places he mentioned. In fact, my ears were buzzing so loudly I could barely hear him at all; my face was burning so I did not dare look at him and I was trembling with a sort of combined pride (which I did not like) and amazement at being so singled out … and something else I could not name.

And there it was, sitting on a little bench of land overlooking the encampment of the catalytic Rebirth of Mother Earth Medicine Wheel Gathering that – almost in passing – I first heard about the issue that would galvanise so much on the inner and outer planes over the following years: "Over that way," his arm had gracefully indicated the Selkirks, "in the Slocan Valley, some of my ancestors was even dug up, stuck in a museum." He shook his head as if in disbelief. "How can they continue their spiritual walk? Their bones have to return to dust in the place from which they sprung, else they wander the earth, lost, unable to take the next step on their path…."

Something in my chest had twisted and spread like fire, rising hot and choking into my throat. Not heartburn; I had never felt anything like it and was reduced to making a sympathetic noise. For several minutes we sat in silence, while for my part I tried to rationalise the unexpected reaction, the deep feeling, I realised, of outrage....

Had this ever been explained to the museum officials? Someone had to tell them, they would give them back; spiritual beliefs would be respected, surely. I stole a swift look at my new-found companion, who was gazing over the clearing, perhaps beyond. His profile imprinted itself on my whirling mind, the red bandanna round his throat a punctuation mark. "Gotta get back to those others, I guess," he said quietly.

Watching his graceful walk carrying him away, and totally unaware of the profound and far-reaching effect this personal exchange would have upon me, I had felt a chill, a strange sense of emptiness. I did not even know his name.

The nebulous but intense feelings sparked by that first personal encounter had since grown into a kind of steady, burning longing, and on being again with Bob in the immediacy of my home, listening to his words, they were being fanned into fierce life.

"Yeah, my mother, she sent me to that place," Bob continued. "She knows the old ways, speaks the language. She's Lakes. Me, I'm half Lakes, half Coeur d'Alene."

"What is the name of your people?" I asked.

"We call ourselves Lakes Indians. Some call us Arrow Lakes Indians." He laughed. "Last count, we had about fourteen names! You'll see us called 'Senatcheggs' in that place, Edgewood. They got a plaque there that says we're extinct! An' a totem pole. A totem pole.... Guess they watched a few too many movies! But we're still here, more'n they'd guess…."

On a single track, I persisted: "Your people's name for yourselves, in your own language?"

Obligingly, he enunciated a word that I could only reproduce as a sorry shadow of the half-swallowed sound. I tried to sound it out: "sin-eye-kst", the half-swallowed sound of central syllable reminiscent of the Hebrew letter "ayin". Bob added that it was their name for the Dolly Varden, the char that inhabit the high, clean lakes in the area, and that a tribe might be named for its most important resource.

The following year, I would visit the plaque and totem pole at the small community of Edgewood on the banks of the Upper Arrow Lake. Financed by B.C. Hydro at the time of the construction of the Hugh Keenleyside Dam at Castlegar, which created the great body of water that the Arrow Lakes have become on this section of the Columbia River, the plaque was intended as a tribute, a dedication to the drowned villages and lands of the " ... Senatcheggs, now extinct", the " ... Lakes Tribe of Indians ... who made the Arrow Lakes their home". Carved by a local, the totem pole was intended to represent their fishing, hunting and gathering life-style; sitting at the top is Coyote, their "mythological god". Despite ensuing events and many requests for the record to be set straight, to the best of my knowledge both plaque and pole are still there at time of writing.

"Well, you don't seem very extinct to me." I only just managed to hold back from touching him in jest. And even though I had a sense that my next question might be forward, I was simultaneously so vitalised and comfortable that I felt I could ask him anything. It was as if I had known him for a long time, or from long ago and we were renewing this earlier acquaintance. "I must ask you – and I hope it's not bad manners – what's your name? Your Indian name, I mean, in your own language?"

"A label to hang on a cage of bones...." Thrilled by the kind of poetic language that feeds my soul, I barely heard the next alien sound. He repeated it: "Kee'ha-hes'ke'."

The "h" was aspirated like the "ch" in the Scottish "loch"; the final sound seemed swallowed. After trying it out, I asked what it translated to.

"My grandfather," he smiled, "he named me for the time I was born. The time of the laughing thunder. That's what it means: Laughing Thunder."

SILVER-STRANDED WEB

Being told his – to me – real name was like a most wonderful gift; as far as my deeper feelings were concerned, he was not and never had been a "Bob". "Laughing Thunder" was poetry to my soul: elemental name, powerfully elemental man.

"It was a happy time for the people, the time of the laughing thunder," he continued. "In the spring they'd hear it an' know it for the time the salmon would be entering the river, beginning their long journey up from the sea. They'd hear the thunder: Boom-boom-boom-boomm," his voice imitated a diminishing cadence of rolling thunder, "an' know food was on its way, times of plenty ahead.... A good time to be born."

A strange sense of inevitability made me press him further: "So, in the spring, your birthday. What date, exactly?"

Somehow I was not surprised to learn his date of birth was the same as mine, except I had followed him into the world eleven years later.

Eleven I knew to be a powerful destiny number, but what about the sharing of a birthday? Hadn't I read somewhere that according to astrology it was not auspicious for a relationship? But what was I thinking? Married men had always been taboo to me. There was no denying a powerful attraction, but beneath my turmoil was a sense it was on a level other than physical, and deeper than the feeling of connectedness I often experienced with Taurean men. Later, I would learn that if two people have common traits, a shared birthday basically facilitates understanding and agreement.

The passage of almost a half-century was belied by his smooth, unlined face, lithe body, hair black as night. Revelling in what I saw as an amazing, powerful birth-connection, I impetuously tucked my chilled bare feet under the warmth of his thigh. "What an amazing coincidence," I said breathlessly. "I like having been born at that time of year."

He nodded absently, not seeming to notice the new intimacy of our position. "Our story ... the story of the people, it's like the Salmon story. Like Salmon, Ti-tigh, we leave the ocean – the spirit-world – and enter the great river. The great river we call life." He placed his palms together as if in prayer. "Like Salmon, we struggle upstream, meetin' up with obstacles – shallows, rapids, waterfalls, great boulders...." His hands punctuated his words with snaking, leaping movements. "We leap forward, fall back; like Salmon, battered and bruised, we push ourselves on, over, round....

"Where the water's slow, pooling, then Salmon rests and gathers strength for the next tough passage. In the same way, we get our quiet an' peaceful times, like little vacations, though I reckon there seems to be less 'n' less of 'em in these times of change! But we're pulled, like by a magnet, back to the source. Like Salmon, we can sense it, almost smell it...." Fine nostrils flared, eyes closed, he tilted back his handsome head. "Followin' the most subtle an' irresistible scent, carried on the currents ... calling us back to where we come from. Back to the source.

"We are the Salmon Story."

Enchanted by the powerful allegory, I imagined the magnificent great fish: a strong, vital force; a silver flash up tumbling falls; a sparkling spray of water thrusting through churning rapids; almost invisible, resting in clear backwaters. My own bruises were forgotten in the vibrancy of the refined energy suffusing my body and I wondered at how at ease I felt with this man I barely knew: Laughing Thunder, born of a different race, culture, religion.

"Some day," he began anew, "I'm gonna set up somethin' like that gathering. But it won't be the same; I'll do it in a traditional way. Whole families together. I don't like to see the little ones shunted off separate from their family. I see them out there all together, granma an' granpa too, learning how to live in a simple way, sharin' an' learning the old ways....

"There's so much to be learned from the elders. In the old way, they was the ones who raised the children. 'Kids shouldn't be raisin' kids!' they'd say and send the parents off to do their thing: hunting, gathering ... finding themselves. The grandparents raised the grandchildren."

"Interesting teaching," I could not help remarking. "Nowadays they're too busy jetting off to Florida or playing golf. At least in my race.... Would you take over the Medicine Wheel gathering, involve those people?" The idea of a truly traditional camp had sparked my interest.

"Got my own ideas where to set up," he said. "Been checking it out. On the Arrow Lakes, near a place called Renata. We'll get set up on a piece of land there. We been negotiating with the folk there.... Them people at Edgewood, they can go on doin' what they're doin'. They're doin' it how they see fit, but it's not the way I'd do it."

"So if they're not doing it right, don't you find it offensive? Why not show them, help them?" I asked.

Shrugging, he said: "It's not for me to do that. Who knows what's right for them? Like I say, they're running it how they want." He chuckled. "I can only look at the shape of their heads an' love 'em!"

All are equal in the Eye of God was what he was saying, essentially, but in a much lighter way. Little did I know how soon these words would become a sort of grounding mantra for me.

"We all're at the place we need to be," Bob continued. "It's a certain type of person gets attracted to these things. When they're at the right level, they'll find their way to the traditional people. In the meantime, some of them intellectuals, an' them space cadets," he laughed wryly, "an' them that challenge the traditional teachings, they'll find folk like that old man – Grey Wolf or whatever he calls himself – he's like a red herring, a cushion for the elders. When you get to the traditional people, you don't go arguin' with them about the teachings."

So the old man who had led the pipe ceremonies was called Grey Wolf, and that was how he was seen by Laughing Thunder. Having little idea of what he meant, I remained silent.

"But one thing I don't like is how they treat that place they call the 'hippie hole'. Swimmin' there naked. That place was sacred to my people."

I knew he meant the secret, deep pool we had found the first afternoon, after Red Cloud's welcome, and wondered if swimming there had been a sort of baptism or initiation.... I also remembered the intrusion of some youthful members of the gathering who had stripped off and rowdily horsed around in the nude, breaking the peaceful sanctity of the place and embarrassing my children so we had to leave.

"An' the sweats," he continued. "There was some things went down there.... Us Arrow

Lakes, we sweat different to how they set it up, but when they asked me to lead a sweat, how could I say no? I seen the size of their need. So many people showed."

I nodded, not because I understood what he meant about the set-up but because I had been one of over fifty people who had shown up for that sweat, the first after Red Cloud's death. It would have been my first experience of the ceremony and although I had little idea of what to expect, I had been intent on it ever since the announcement about who would be leading it. The sweat-lodge could only accommodate twenty at capacity, "double-packed", as he had called it, and as we all stood around waiting for what would happen next, he had quietly said that those who really needed to be there would know who they were. Without understanding why, I had been one of those who turned away, and had sweated later with an all-women's group led by a non-Native woman.

"The energies in a sweat-lodge," Bob said quietly, "you have to know people're there for a cleansin', a renewal. It's a powerful spiritual experience, the heat, the dark, the prayers.... People come in an' pour all the garbage out of themselves. You gotta have a leader that knows what's going on an' how to handle it." His voice lowered. "I was told some women in their moon came in, even though they was told.... We had to go back an' clean it up."

I knew he meant spiritually and on reflection realised this was an example of what he meant about challenging traditional teachings. Habituated prejudices and the interpretation of modern science have each in their own way obliterated the symbolic meaning of woman's monthly flow of blood. While feminists – perhaps most modern women – might feel slighted at being prohibited from a sweat in their moon-time, I thought that if they appreciated the meaning of moon-time power, they might spare the men. In time, I would understand that traditional customs lose their meaning when they are taken out of their spiritual context, and that a taboo is a spiritual statement which might also have practical relevance; breaking it causes disharmony, sometimes because of an off-balance response.

Darkness had long fallen. The house was still, hushed. I renewed the coffee, moving as in a dream-world, beyond need or even thought of sleep. Bob got up to stretch. "You ever been over that way?"

I knew where he meant. "Two years ago a friend took me over to visit some people in Burton, on the Upper Arrow Lake. It's pretty wild over there. Rained most of the time." I recalled vast, sombre, leaden, white-capped waters; massive, soaring, naked peaks; drifting mists pierced with dark spikes of evergreen; most of all, an oppressive loneliness pervading the long, narrow valley, which did not seem to invite habitation. "The people I met lost their organic garlic crop two years in a row. It rotted in the ground. They were about to move away."

"Wasn't always that way there. Creatin' a big body of water changes the weather, attracts more water. Rains more there now than it used to. You can see where the orchards've rotted in the ground. The old folks that stayed'll tell you 'bout it.... Guess those people didn't feel so good, bein' told they had to move on. Compensation don't give you no roots."

I thought how terribly aware of that he must be and fleetingly wondered if the sense of desolation was because of the uprooting of people. At the time, neither of us had any idea that an Arrow Lakes Indian Reserve had once existed almost directly across the lake from that small community.

"It's drier, warmer, down where my ranch is." Bob spoke more lightly as he sat down again and to my surprise and delight, took hold of one of my feet and began to rub it into warmth. The contact was electric; I had a hard time keeping my equilibrium. "It's in the mountains. But I got no power, no runnin' water. Don't want 'em neither. An' probably wouldn't get 'em; never been much good 'bout settlin' bills!"

"There's certain things about twentieth-century life I like too much to give up. Like hot baths, and my stereo," I laughed, despite basically agreeing with him about public utilities.

"Plenty of ways to have those things without payin' through the nose, and no pollution. There's people I know found ways to make the wind, the sun, even a little creek work for 'em. I'd like for you to meet some of these people."

My heart sang; the tingling sensation in my foot suffused my whole body. There would be more, then; this was an on-going connection.... Was it about an alternative community? Was this the beginning of something I had held in my heart since my teens: the creation of a sustainable, non-invasive, co-operative community? Only with an element I had never before considered: Native and non-Native people working together? As soon as the thought hit me, I wondered how I had ever imagined it would be possible without the knowledge, experience and wisdom of the First People.

"The Arrow Lakes was used for hunting an' fishin'; people lived at the mouths of creeks," Bob continued after a while. I wanted to talk about the idea of a community but instinctively felt I should go with his flow. "Next valley over to the east, the Slocan's not so wild and steep, not so hard for a people to cling to. There was bigger settlements there, all the way down to where the Slocan meets the Kootenay, up far's Kootenay Lake an' down where it joins with the Columbia, an' on down past Trail ... you know, where that operation, Cominco, sure creates a God-almighty pollution!"

Wondering where this was leading, I nodded. I barely knew the area, rivers or towns, but the great blight on the landscape, the zinc and fertiliser plant Cominco, largest of its kind in North America, had inscribed itself on my memory: a massive, ugly sprawl of dull-grey and bright-orange, rusting labyrinthine pipes, storage vats, flues, spewing chimneys and floodlights, seen under a deceptive icing-sugar sprinkle of snow en route to Alberta the previous year. Apparently in the 1950s it looked like an atom bomb had been dropped on the area; the devastating effect of the pollution is still evident in the stunted growth of trees and high local incidence of stomach cancer. Upstream, north of Castlegar on the Lower Arrow Lake lies another noisome eyesore, Celgar pulp mill. I knew that fish pulled out downriver from these two behemoths are too tainted to eat but had yet to learn how, in the short space of fifty years, one of the principal rivers in the world has been killed.

Bob's words recovered a quiet intensity: "North end of the Arrow Lakes there's a place called Arrowhead, where my grandfather's buried. I got to find his restin'-place, an' make sure it's taken care of. Else how can I face him, when I cross over the other side? How can I look him in the eye, when he asks me if I took care of his restin'-place?"

His hands had stopped massaging; again the air seemed charged with a strange electricity, an imminence.

"When I find my grandfather's restin'-place an' take care of it," he continued. "When my own bones lie there.... Then I can proceed on to the next level. I know I'm ready for the next stage; I'm completin' my purpose in this life. Then I'll proceed on to the next level. Not just me – all the rest of the soul-family'll get pulled up an equal amount. An' everyone else. The actions of the one affects the rest. We don't get the opportunity to do that too often but it's a responsibility at these times of great changes. We got the choice as well as the chance to make the leap."

Spellbound by his words as much as the thrill of his hand resting on my foot, into my mind's eye came the image of Salmon, approaching a mighty fall of water – the greatest spout yet encountered – and as he was sucked into the cauldron of waters boiling at its foot, my mind yawned open, a great mouth of darkness within which gleamed a bright hook of understanding to which I could not put words. Every cell in my body seemed to be sparking. I had never heard anyone talk like this, but in a deep, inner place, I recognised, understood, assimilated ... a natural, profound knowing-without-thinking that left me trembling on the outer as well as the inner.

"I reckon we'll get it right. It's about time!" Bob said with a chuckle, reeling me back in. "There'll be enough of the 'heart people', them that care about living in right relation with each other and the land. Don't matter the colour of skin or what belief they follow, they want the same things in life: get set up on a piece of land, be self-sufficient, live peacefully with themselves, each other, the land.... Learnin' from what was good in the old ways, takin' what's good from the new. No polluting technologies, there's plenty inventions around already if only they was allowed to come out.... A place where the little ones like yours can grow up healthy, strong an' free; where they can run wild a little, stretch their wings. The elders teaching them, showing them their place in the order of things, so's they know who they are an' where they come from. Then they'll know where they're goin'...."

"Clean air, clean water ... I always say, if you take care that the water is clean, then everything else'll fall into place.... Doin' it together, not in separateness, where a person grows lonely an' fearful and acts from that place. A community maturin' in co-operation. If you enhance what helps others, then it's easier for them others to adapt. We've all gotta change. From survival of the fittest to continuity of the most useful and co-operative.... Nothin' to do with government. Soon enough, that whole world that's been set up – it's gonna come tumblin' down round our ears...."

Words failed me; this was exactly how I thought, these were my ideals.

After some reflective moments, he continued: "My ancestors, they got overrun too. I was told the old ways was already lost, we fell off the path, before the white man came. But we can learn from them. We been through it before and it's comin' round again. Creator's giving us another chance to get it right."

My mind was spinning. Not only was he speaking of the prophesised time of great changes almost upon us, about which I had only recently learned, but of a way of life long in my heart. Was it at last the time for the blossoming of a whole new way of being and living, beyond race, colour, creed; in peace and harmony, in balance with ourselves, each other and our beautiful planet? A way to break free from the bleak reflection of the fear-based cultural values of western society; a destiny calling on the highest sense of spirit, of love, forgiveness, tolerance, respect and appreciation for the life we have been gifted, in all its myriad forms? In those exquisitely scintillating moments, I was convinced I had finally met someone who envisioned a meaningful option to the present horror of destroying everything on the planet that did not serve the paranoid needs of a species that had forgotten its origins; someone who saw a practical way forward.

This new way of life would shine like a light. A new, higher consciousness, one of conscientiousness, compassion, co-operation, would be birthed. And then perhaps the headlong rush into doom would wind down, even stop. There was no need for any devastating Earth Changes if we made the changes ourselves.

Utterly thrilled to hear the articulation of deeply-held personal beliefs, dreams and ideals after years of attempts at such a way of life, I was ready to join with whatever Bob proposed. Experience of communal life in England, a kibbutz in Israel in my idealistic early twenties and the housing co-operative had convinced me that the only way co-operative living might succeed, would be if survival were the bottom line. But with the elective participation of committed people of two races, anything was possible.

Had I been aware of the time-span Bob had in mind, I might not have thrown myself in so wholeheartedly. Imagining it would take about five years to set up such a community and all we had to do was pull together some like-minded, committed people and settle on ancestral Arrow Lakes territory, out in the wilds (I fantasised we would set up a sort of psychic barrier so Big Brother wouldn't notice), some four tumultuous years later, expressing my frustration that our Salmon-story seemed to be running up too many side-streams, I was set straight: "I see things fifty years down the line." A wide, flat sweeping motion of Bob's hand encompassed a half-century. "But aren't you learning a lot?"

By then I had learned so much I felt my head might burst.

Looking back, I wonder at my naiveté. Yet had I been less of a romantic dreamer, less propelled by an unconscious need to "belong" to something cohesive, something with meaning, I might not have got involved with what happened next at all. And perhaps what followed was not so much about creating an ideal community as about the raising of consciousness. Perhaps there are those capable of making a fantastic, giant (salmon-like) leap in consciousness in these powerful times of change, one beyond the scope of our limited imagination; one which would, as Bob had intimated, quantitatively and qualitatively elevate the collective consciousness.

"An' I know who'll be there," Bob resumed, bringing me back to the room, "because when I look into a man's eyes, I see deep into his soul. I see all what's layin' there. I know what's movin' him."

Self-consciousness covered me like a blanket. Seemingly aware of the effect of his words, he laughed and said: "I better stay on track! Like I said, we've a lot of ground to cover." Getting up, he stretched and swept his arm in an eastward direction. " ... That valley I spoke of, the Slocan. You know," he chuckled, "they call it 'The Valley', like it's the only one.... There's a lot of good people live there. Maybe you'd like it over there. It's cleaner, the water, the air. There's less people live there. But it's cooler. An' more rain than over this way."

"That's okay by me." Why was I responding as if I had to reassure him that I would like it? "I used to like the dry and hot weather here, especially after Vancouver, which may be picturesque but you pay a price for living at the foot of mountains: greyness, the rain.... It got pretty oppressive at times, especially once I learned about the acid rain. But we've been here five years and the Okanagan summers seem to be getting hotter and hotter. Sivan – my eldest – recently said the sun sort of stings her skin. I feel it, too. Makes me wonder what they haven't told us about the ozone-layer, the greenhouse effect...."

Initially I had loved the Okanagan, an easily-accessed landscape of sparsely-treed, gentle-sloped, grassy hills dotted with wild sage, scrubby Oregon grape and lanky sumac, which blazed into life in spring with yellow bursts of wild sunflowers before softening into a blue haze of wild lupins; the long, hot summers, dramatically punctuated with loud, wild thunderstorms; the warm air redolent with the distinctive dry, sweet scent of baked clay earth and crushed pine needles; the golden grasslands of late summer; the lakes, Okanagan and Kalamalka, the former named for the indigenous people, the latter meaning "many-coloured". Even the winter, while colder than at the coast, was relatively dry and temperate. However, just as I had welcomed the changeable weather in Vancouver after almost four years of living with the relentless burnt-ochre of the desert, the cloudless skies and blazing sun that comprise eight months of the year in Jerusalem, I was again yearning for moist air, the breath of forests. And some isolation.

"Look where I came from originally," I added, perplexed by my seeming need to reassure him. "England's pretty notorious for rain, and the North-East, where I grew up, never got very warm. Anyway," I finished firmly, "I'd welcome the change; it's getting too hot for us here." Considering the burn-out I was feeling, this was true in more ways than one.

Bob swept his arm in an arc which encompassed my living-room and said with a wry smile: "Take a lot to get you moved!"

Not for the first time I felt embarrassed about my material possessions. What I owned was average for a family of four and I felt it was important to have an attractive environment for growing sensibilities. Various pieces of furniture had already proven useful as an investment against financial uncertainty, but I would have preferred to live more simply. "A five-ton truck'd get me anywhere!" I laughed, knowing I would walk away from it all if he said the word; except for my children and the camper-van. Which, I remembered, was laid up.

"What do you do?"

Taken aback by this new tack, I hesitated. It was difficult to know how to respond. Mother? Jill-of-all-trades? If he meant job-wise, why should it be relevant? I decided to go back to the beginning: "Well, I trained as a teacher...." Why was I even mentioning it? In the sixteen years since I had obtained the qualification in England it had been used only as an avenue to other employment, primarily in publishing, and since the birth of the children, various part-time, casual jobs. "But I've never actually-"

"A teacher ... a teacher," he interrupted. "I didn't know you were a teacher." He was stroking his chin, staring at a spot on the floor. Something made me remain silent instead of correcting him. Nor did I tell him anything else about my chequered work-history.

Within less than three months, I would look back and wonder about the true extent of this man's powers. Was he capable of spontaneous precognition? Or was it an actual ability to shape events?

Walking over to the window, Bob stared out into the blackness of night. Silence lay between us for a long time; I had a sense of him being somehow very far away. In the reflection I saw his eyes were closed, his lips almost imperceptibly moving. Suddenly he turned round, folded his arms over his chest and stared straight at me.

"You will hear many things about me," he said abruptly. "Many people will tell you things. There are those who say that I take advantage of women. But we each make our own decisions. I cannot make anyone do anything they don't want to do. Nothing will happen that you do not wish. Each of us is free to make our own choice.... And to those people who say such things about me, I say: 'Your suspicions are of yourself!'

"You will hear other things. But I'm telling you this: I am not a medicine man. No matter what they say, I have never claimed to be a medicine man. I am simply a man on a spiritual journey." His voice softened. "My grandmother cried when they cut down the Old Ones, who know all the songs. The Song came before the words, came from the very deep ... The Song that is everywhere around us, that is given us by the wind in the trees.... Ska-ool. They speak to us.... Song sings through us. What will grandfather say now, to the child who asks where the songs come from? Without songs, where will we be?

"You must learn how to listen, how to truly hear. Your Sumix will help you on this path, when you can truly pay attention."

Spellbound, I could only stare back at him, the poetic, magical, enigmatic words an anchor in a storm of whirling emotions and spinning mind, silencing any residual doubt I might have had. Where this Native man led, I would follow. Where he pointed, I would go. What he said and did, I would remember and record.

The type of people of whom he was speaking might say I was totally taken in, but spirit knows which way to move, which form to take, to experience and fulfil its purpose in life. Maybe I was but one of many women who fell immediately and deeply in love with this man. Or perhaps not so much with Bob, as with Laughing Thunder: not the man, but the spirit that moved within the man. Despite my enthrallment I sensed something far deeper than physical attraction at work, something which I could not begin to put into words.

After a long silence, Bob got up and left the room. I heard him go upstairs and then the sound of the shower. Without thought, simply in my body, I sat there, feeling the pounding of my heart, the racing of blood in my veins, watching the paling sky. Then I went upstairs and into my bedroom and lay down, rigid with tension, trying to extract myself from the chaos of my feelings. Hearing him come out of the bathroom, I went to ask if he wanted breakfast.

We met at the top of the stairs and the next few moments, minutes, hours, dissolved into a blur.

Whether I touched him or he me, whether any word crossed his or my lips, I cannot remember, but suddenly my arms were around his slender body and he was pulling me close. Intoxicating, the honey-sweetness of his breath; his lips a feather-touch on mine, a gentle tasting, a tentative seeking, an unbearably tantalizing, unending intimate connection.... My legs, lower body grew hot and weak, melting. Dizzy, I felt I might swoon but could not stop, did not want to, ever....

The cold wetness of a freshly-washed braid against my fingers startled me. Like a drowning person, I gasped: "Wow ... I would never have guessed a red man could kiss like that!"

I could have curled up in embarrassment, in dismay at the clumsy joke, the implied racism ... the broken moment ... and pulled back.

To my amazement, Bob seemed to be aglow: his skin a burnished gold, his eyes filled with light, so for a long incredulous moment I saw into the warmth of their dark depths. His smile gentle, he brushed back the hair from my cheek and then it dawned on me that he was caught in the first rays of sunrise, reaching in through the window behind me. Before I could say another word, he turned away and went downstairs. After some blank seconds, I followed.

He was nowhere to be seen, not in the living-room nor the room where his son was still deeply asleep, nor the kitchen. Then I noticed the back door was ajar.

In the middle of the garden, barefoot on the dewy grass, full of grace, straight-backed, arms raised in the direction of the rising sun, stood Laughing Thunder. Man on a spiritual journey, whose eagle feather directed the smoke of the sacred fire.

I could not stop myself watching, admiring, then it struck me that, only a couple of weeks ago, in the same place he was now standing, I had done something not dissimilar.

Heavy, dark clouds had been noticeably gathering several miles away down the lake and, in a fey mood, I had danced and sung to the blossoming storm, calling it, using as an offering some old trade-beads gifted me by a friend, that had apparently once belonged to a Native American elder. Thinking of Laughing Thunder and how, if anyone knew storms, he must, I had closed my eyes and visualised myself flying down the lake, through the threatening storm, over the miles and miles of scrubby sage-brush desert landscape to where I imagined he might live, touching him on his shoulder – a feather-breath – then zooming back home. Feeling fulfilled and slightly foolish at the same time, I had gone back inside.

The majority of thunderstorms travelling up Okanagan Lake veer away up the north arm when they reach the division of the waters some two or three miles away. This time, I had just started washing dishes when the first great crack had rattled the windows.

This storm had chosen to break directly over the house.

At that moment Sivan had come rushing inside, yelling, "You did it, Mum! The storm's here!"

I had been unaware that she and a friend, playing outside, had spied on my strange ritual, but how she knew or what might be going on was far from my mind as I ran outside into the stinging, freezing downpour. Above me, the storm-centre swirled, convulsed. Feeling a wild exhilaration, I revelled in the awesome power of the elements, my dress clinging wetly like a second skin as I danced and yelled back at the rumbling peals of ... Laughing Thunder, I was sure ... as Mother Earth was cleansed.

Had he felt me then? I could not, would never ask.

Waking his son, Bob left without eating or any word as to what might happen next, carrying with him, I felt, a part of me. I felt cut adrift and lost again but knew this made little sense and closed my eyes, visualising a fine silver silken strand, a spider-web filament, spinning out between us as the geographical distance widened. I knew we were connected: part of an unbreakable thread of the intricate, invisible tapestry that ever trembles with cause and effect, beyond time and space. He had told me that all I had to do was truly listen, to pay attention.

But to what? The wind in the trees? And that other strange word in his language, something that would help me: Sumix. What had that meant?

RITES OF PASSAGE

After a stay out at High Farm on the west side of Okanagan Lake where one of my friends fell from her horse but was not hurt, the children and I return home.

The front door is ajar. Sure I had locked it, I try to go in but it won't open any further. Peeking through the gap, I see a jumble of shoes is blocking it, but by pushing forcefully I manage to get it open, just as an immense, shaggy grey dog silently bounds up and stops beside me.

It's an Irish wolfhound; powerful, wild-looking, its great whiskered head level with my chest, mouth a fanged, panting grin, eyes a tawny glow: a breed I like, but a twist of fear makes me hesitate. The hound determinedly pushes past me, lopes into the living-room and sits down, intelligent eyes gazing at me expectantly.

The front door has skewed open, is hanging off one hinge. I notice that the window-blinds are weirdly on the outside of the house. There must have been a break-in! Fear of the hound forgotten, I rush into the living-room.

Everything seems to be in place. But oh no ... empty shelves.... My stereo, my entire collection of albums and cassettes are gone! Ah, my beloved music! Anything, everything else, but not my music! In their place, a cheap radio. Yet I know I have to let go.

The children have followed me inside. I turn to tell them what has happened and glimpse a familiar red-green-blue logo from the kitchen window: a Tilden rent-a-truck, parked outside. Going into the kitchen to see it better, I am taken aback to see someone sitting – of all places – at the children's play-table. Arms folded, his legs stretched out, a gentle smile playing at his mouth, it is Bob.

I start to gasp out my dismay about the burglary but before I can say a word, he grins and says: "It had to be something to make you see."

And I see: my sound system and all my music are stacked in the back of the otherwise-empty truck.

"And I've been having all these dreams," he adds quietly.

Our eyes meet, link. Warmth envelops me. "Yes." Somehow I know those dreams, for: "I sent them."

He seems to accept this. My children and others I don't recognise come into the kitchen and crowd round us; one sits on his knee.

"The loneliness was too great," he says, putting his arm round the child's shoulders.

"For me too," I breathe softly, a powerful, scintillating burst of happiness flooding my body. This cannot be a dream. I pinch myself to make sure. Can feel the pinch – it is real! I check outside again. Yes! The truck is really there!

In no time at all, arrangements to vacate the house are completed and I am packing my possessions. Everything flows easily, smoothly; I have to keep stopping in my busy-ness to bask in the glow of this incredible, delightful reality, these exquisite feelings.... And again experience that penetrating, enveloping eye-contact, as his softly-spoken words permeate my being: "And although I will not be with you all the time, I will be the one in you, and for you, as a husband...."

Oh, dream come true!

But what's happening? It's becoming darker ... and darker.... Is night falling? How, in the middle of the day?

Eyes wide open to darkness, I found myself in bed and with a sinking feeling realised it had been only a dream after all. Even the pinch, so sharply painful, had been a fantasy; the pain of awakening was reality. I could have wept.

For weeks Bob had occupied most of my waking – and now dreaming – thoughts; all my yearnings seemed to have been encapsulated in this vivid dream, which had an immediacy and clarity like the drum-dream, three months behind me. Bob's closing dream-words resounded through my mind: beautiful sentiments ... but with a strangely-familiar ring.

I was sure they were like words attributed to the resurrected Christ. What were they doing in my dream? I wanted to be able to take them literally, to be living that dream; the feeling of disappointment stayed with me for days.

At the time, I knew that the most commonly-acknowledged function of dreams is the processing of immediate and past emotional issues; that images and strange symbolic events conjured up by the subconscious are recognised as aspects of the psyche. I would soon come to appreciate that in the timelessness of the dream-state, there can also lie the gift of precognition.

A long, slow month had dragged by since Bob's unforgettable visit; summer was over and a replacement transmission had been located and installed in my camper-van, thanks to my mother's generosity. Interpreting the wordless language of spirit as a directive, I decided on our second and last camping trip of the year: to visit "Bob's valley", as I called the Slocan Valley. While preparing, I reflected on how strange it was, the way things had unfolded: my plan for the summer had been a westwards trip to visit friends and relatives on the coast and the Gulf Islands. Which meant we would not have been at home for Bob's unexpected visit. In fact, I probably would not even have felt the need to "call".

Clear, sunny and bright; the weather matched my mood as we wound our pioneering way eastwards, with no plan other than to see "the Valley" and perhaps find the burial-grounds Bob had told me about – they had to be well-known locally. Perhaps, I mused, I would have help: special, otherworldly kind of help. A couple of days before, I had dropped a line to the post office box number in the States that Bob had given me, asking for guidance. I knew it would not reach him in time, but then part of me did not expect things to work that way.

Leaving orchards and farmlands behind at the little community of Cherryville, we threaded our way ever more steeply upwards through increasingly-thick forest cover into the hushed stillness of the Monashee Mountains. Having learned that Monashee is Gaelic for "secret place of the fairies", I was all the more aware of the mystical, haunted atmosphere pervading the dark forests, seemingly devoid of human habitation. Yet man's hand had been cruelly at work here: unsightly clearcuts marred my daydreaming.

Beyond the pass, forested mountainsides gentled into woods and meadows; a glimpse of a roof or a driveway signalled the return to so-called civilisation as we descended toward the Arrow Lakes, preceded by the long shadow of the van. Passing the turn-off to the village of

Edgewood, I remembered the plaque dedicated to Bob's "extinct" people; when we passed the gravel road leading to the site of the Rebirth of Mother Earth gathering my heart warmed and for the next few miles I thought back to the beginnings of this journey.

A final great swooping curve, and the highway suddenly and shockingly disappeared into a mighty body of water. The little yellow ferry cutting across the deceptively still Upper Arrow Lake looked like a child's toy, dwarfed by perfectly-mirrored, dramatic up-thrusting heaves of granite rock tenaciously coated by a ragged evergreen mantle: the Selkirks, which towered over the scattering of houses, restaurant and gas station comprising the tiny town of Fauquier on the far shore.

Passing over the drowned village of Needles – for which the ferry was named – I thought about its inhabitants being moved on when the Hugh Keenleyside Dam was built, flooding the valley. Beneath the vibrating deck I could imagine a shadowy darkness lanced with dim, flickering shafts of light; empty, collapsed shells of houses; the muffled toll of a submerged church-bell mourning yet another harnessing of the great Columbia River. Heavy, dull-grey smudges of cloud were gathering at the north end of the valley and the air was noticeably cooler as we docked, a reminder of what Bob had said about the effect of drastically altering an environment. Disembarking, we joined the little rush-hour of ferry-traffic, a chain of scurrying ants skirting the eastern shore of the lake at the oblivious feet of the mountains, and found a spot to camp just south of the little mill-town of Nakusp, unknowingly only a few hundred feet from another Arrow Lakes burial-ground, drowned along with the village of Needles.

The following morning I was woken by the drumming of rain on the roof and the whimpering of Nicolas. Earache, and not the first time; familiar with the routine, I drove straight to the emergency department of the tiny local hospital. By the time we emerged it was close to midday, and a uniform greyness awaited us: the lake hazed by drizzle, the mountains shrouded by low-hanging cloud. Cold and dispirited, worried by my son's malaise and frustrated by the change in weather I considered returning home.

But I had never believed in turning back.

After a simple brunch we headed east on a black, shining ribbon of highway fringed with crumpled, burnt-orange bracken. It narrowed as it climbed, snaking between a gauntlet of dark evergreens under an oppressively-low, grey shroud; the only bright note in the dreariness an occasional sudden lutescent fountain of birch.

Rosebery ... Hills ... New Denver ... Silverton. The little communities through which we passed were ghost towns in the mist; the Slocan Lake, invisible; on the far shore, the vast mountain range known as the Valhallas was truly the kingdom of the gods: unseen, unknown. The only break in the monotony was when, heart in mouth, we crept along a single-lane stretch of highway clinging to the sheer side of a mountain above the hidden lake. The drop-off hinted at a great height; to my relief we met no other vehicle for the long five minutes or so it took to get back to two lanes. Yet I appreciated the bottleneck: it had to limit the amount and type of traffic that accessed the valley from the north.

Neither Slocan City, at the foot of the lake, nor neighbouring Lemon Creek seemed to exist other than as a roadside sign. Much like Bob's people, I thought. Paying scant attention to places I would soon come to know intimately, I stopped in the tiny community of Winlaw to consult the map and buy some treats for the children. Since Bob's valley seemed reluctant to reveal itself, I decided to push on to the city of Nelson – an hour further – and look up a couple Bob had introduced me to at the gathering, who had been about to move there from Montreal and were seeking his input for a potential wilderness school.

The valley narrowed; a massive, sheer rock-face encroached on the left side of the road. Mentally ahead of myself, I peripherally noticed a break in the drizzling mist to the right of the long sickle-bend I was negotiating and a corresponding curve in the river below, where it was crossed by a narrow bridge. On the roadside, a hand-painted sign caught my eye: "Vallican Whole".

It was fortunate that no other vehicle was on that part of the road at that moment for, seemingly of their own volition, my hands wrenched at the steering-wheel to take the turn-off.

My stomach lurched: the angle was too acute. I came to a sudden stop with the front end of the van inches from a pine-tree clinging to the edge of the cliff and the back end sticking out across the road. Thankful there was no other vehicle in sight, I swiftly reversed, compensated and turned down the unpaved road, heart thudding in my chest. The attraction had been compulsive, irresistible; what was going on?

An old, single-lane Bailey bridge took us across wide, clear, fast-flowing waters. Reaching a T-junction on the other side, the same impulse took me left past a house with a collection of brightly-painted old farming implements in the front yard. The trees closed in briefly, then at the far side of a golden-grassed meadow I saw a handsome, two-storey log-house: someone's dream-home, sheltered by a small stand of fir and built from what I guessed from the warm honey-glow to be cedar. Again the trees closed in; the road wound on. It was like driving beneath an old grey blanket. Another side-road snaked away between the misted evergreens, but despite a feeling about it (had I exhausted the gentle voice of intuition?) I decided to stay on the main route, passing some more log buildings, one of which, due to its rambling construction and prominent location, I guessed must be a community building. The road began to climb, becoming narrower, increasingly rutted and pot-holed. Then the electricity poles came to an end.

Obviously I had reached the end of the line. What was I doing here?

An approaching pick-up pulled up to allow us passage. As we drew alongside, I asked the young couple what lay beyond.

"Coupla lakes, but without a four-by-four you probably won't get far.... We been up huntin' grouse." On a rack behind their heads were two rifles.

As they drove away I found myself thinking of the movie "Deliverance". What had possessed me to come this way, out in the sticks? Turning round with some difficulty, I drove back to the highway and on to Nelson.

Spread out on the lower slopes of a mountain hidden by pale banks of mist and clouds, west arm of Kootenay Lake at her feet, the "Queen City of British Columbia" put me in mind of a mini-San Francisco. The steeply-inclined streets were lined with colonial-style listed heritage buildings and there was a similar laid-back ambiance. Finding a health-food store, I asked if any wilderness school had started up in the area but was met with blank looks. It seemed like the whole area was closing me out.

Darkness was beginning to fall. Kokanee Creek, a large provincial campground, lay on the east side of the city but it was too early to camp; a soak at the hot-springs at Ainsworth, some twenty miles further on the shores of Kootenay Lake, seemed a good idea. The uniform-grey tedium of the winding, forty-minute drive was soon forgotten in the pleasure of the reviving warmth of the pools and the fun we had in the caves. By the time we set up camp, it was late and very cold.

Frost laced the windows of the camper when I woke next morning. Outside, chinks of bright, autumnal-blue sky peeked through a canopy of russet, copper and gold. It was a heart-warming sight; cosy under our duvets, we waited for the sun to take the edge off the chill then went to explore.

Preferring to camp off the beaten track, a designated campground normally would have been a last resort for me, but the time of year meant we had the place practically to ourselves. The children rode their bikes through crisping mounds of fallen leaves down to the sandy beach. The vista was awesome. Kootenay Lake extended a ruffled steely-blueness far into the distance, where a jagged row of massive, serrated teeth, the Purcell Mountain range, scraped against a patchwork of clouds. Above us towered the Selkirks, thickly, darkly coated with evergreen. Totally veiled the previous day, it was a majestic wilderness that took away my breath and made my heart soar. Following the children, exploring nature trails, enjoying late wildflowers and gradually building up an appetite, I felt renewed and glad I had not simply continued on round the loop beyond Ainsworth to Kaslo, over the pass to New Denver and so back home. Given the remarkable change in weather, Bob's valley would get another chance. A hot breakfast in Nelson seemed part of the equation but the city was deathly quiet early on a Sunday morning; nothing seemed open on Main Street and within minutes we found ourselves outside the sleepy little city.

No turning back.... The highway curved along a precipitous mountainside; below, unseen the day before, Kootenay River curled sleek and slow, hemmed in by a series of hydroelectric dams. Turning north at the junction into the Slocan Valley, I noticed a couple of cars parked in front of a sprawling log building with a colourful hand-painted sign: "Rose's Restaurant".

We ordered a full breakfast: eggs, bacon, pancakes, toast. As the teenaged waitress was putting the laden plates onto the table, I suddenly thought to ask if she had heard about an archaeological dig in the valley.

"Oh, you must mean Vallican," she said. "My dad owned land there but he had to give it up when some finds were made. It's about fifteen minutes north from here; there's a sign that says 'Vallican', I think. Follow the road to the left then turn into the subdivision. You could just drive in there and ask someone."

She was talking about the same road I had impulsively taken the day before, and the other one I had chosen to ignore. And of all the people I could have asked, I had picked the daughter of the man who had owned the site. Oblivious to my astonishment, she told me she was leaving to study at university in Alberta the next day.

Another day and I would have missed her. It was almost too much. Whose hands had been at the wheel? Was this what it was like, to receive guidance?

In all its mountainous splendour, the Slocan Valley now revealed itself: a forested, rocky grandeur, not overpowering but enclosing, protecting. From the south, the turn-off to "Vallican Whole" was easy to negotiate.

What did the sign mean? Vallican: a place to be made whole?

Again the log-house at the back of the meadow caught my eye then I turned a corner, and nothing was ever quite the same again. Directly in front of me, centred above the gravel road, a great up-thrusting peak stopped me in my tracks. Darkly-silhouetted against the clear blue of the sky, it stood apart from and towered above the surrounding ranges. A sense of awe swept through me; as I crept on down the road I was put in mind of the mountain in the movie "Close Encounters of the Third Kind", not only for its appearance but its magnetism.

Following the waitress's directions, I turned into the subdivision and soon realised that even if I had followed my intuition the day before, it was unlikely I would have found anything. A few driveways disappeared among the pines then the road came to an abrupt end. I was about to give up when I caught sight of a newly-built house tucked away among the trees, where a couple about my age were working on a garden with their two young boys. In a friendly manner, they directed me onto a narrow, sandy track, barely visible among the undergrowth.

The slender branches of young birch and cottonwood screeched along the sides of the van; I stayed in first gear until a right-angle bend brought me round to another unpaved road in the subdivision, which obviously headed back to where I had started. It seemed I was going in circles.

Why was Bob's village still proving so elusive? I stopped and turned off the engine. As far as I could tell, there had been no evidence of any site. Perhaps this was not meant to be. Then I heard the chock of an axe, coming from a secluded barn-shaped house almost totally hidden among the trees.

Should I ask again? Why were things not just falling into place? But I had come this far.... Thinking to give my interest in the site more authority by introducing myself as an ex-teacher, I related my quest to the wood-chopper.

Although I was at the time unaware of the concept, synchronicity was doing its magical work: the small and friendly, bearded man turned out to be the secretary of the local society that acted as steward of the "Vallican Archaeological Park," a designated heritage site. Enthusiastically he told me about its discovery and the unearthing of the nine-hundred-year-old skeleton of a young girl.

Barely able to contain my excitement, I let myself be directed back along the narrow track. As I drove away, I thought it strange that neither of us had made any mention of the Arrow Lakes people. Nor had I told him how I came to know about the place.

Back at the right-angle bend I finally caught sight of the signs, posted high on the trees at intervals on the other side of the track:

> *"This heritage site is protected by the Heritage*
> *Conservation Act of British Columbia. It is unlawful*
> *for any person to knowingly destroy, desecrate, deface,*
> *excavate, move or alter this site."*

Parking on a small, grassy area on the bend, I explained to the children where we were and they went off to explore, but I was in such a state I found myself unable to enter the site, dark and mysterious under the shadowy evergreens. It felt like a holy-place; and wrong to intrude upon it. For a long time, I sat meditatively on a tussock of grass beside the track, clearly part of a long, wide swathe of land cleared some years ago and since self-regenerated with cottonwood, birch, pine, fir. Wild strawberries, Oregon grape, service-berries and a myriad of delicate plants and seeding grasses carpeted the earth between the young trees. Sweetly-resinous, the air was soft and warm; the pale sky was streaked with wisps of cloud. All around, massive, hazy-blue, the mountains basked benevolently in the sun. In a far-distant cleft, my wandering gaze caught sight of two tiny specks, wheeling, spiralling.

A thrill ran through me. They could only be eagles. Recalling the striking, mysterious dance of the eagles above Vernon and what had followed, it seemed especially significant, a reminder that I had been guided. As if Bob were here with me.

As if I had walked into a dream.

Feeling utterly at peace, I lay back on the warm earth and closed my eyes. But for the drowsy hum of an occasional insect, it was absolutely quiet. Bob's valley; the village and burial-ground he had spoken of, found....

I must have dozed, for suddenly an hour had passed. Hearing the children among the trees, I climbed a narrow, stony path to the top of the next terrace, most of which seemed to have been cleared at about the same time as the swathe below, and took some photos.

As we were leaving, I had the sudden idea to stop at the wood-cutter's home again to give him my details and ask him to let me know about any kind of development at the site. He promised to mail some literature then went on to tell me about the Valley, as if it had a capital "V", just as Bob had said. It sounded like a remarkable place, having attracted musicians, writers, artists, environmentalists, ex-hippies, counter-culturalists, back-to-the-landers, conscientious objectors, a variety of religious groups. "... And many strong women," he added, raising his eyebrows and staring intently at me.

You won't get me that way.... The spontaneous thought that popped into my head surprised me.

There was a brief silence, then almost as an afterthought he added, "We've got an alternative school here, for which I'm treasurer. The Whole School. It's housed in a big wooden building further down the back-road, our community hall."

"Yes, I noticed it." The meaning behind the signpost "Vallican Whole" seemed a bit of a let-down: he explained that the building had been a hole in the ground for a long time, while the community fought to come to an agreement about the style of the building.

For two days after we got home my feet barely touched the ground. Then came the call. Not an otherwordly direction this time, however, but a male voice, through the wires: "You probably don't remember me: Laurie?"

"Oh, but I do!" My stomach lurched, filled with a butterfly-trembling. It was the bearded wood-cutter. Was something already happening at the site? "I just got back the photos I took there. In fact, they're in my hand right now."

On top was a view of the burial-ground, although I didn't know it at the time. I had just been showing the pictures to a visiting friend, the one in my Bob-dream who had fallen from the horse. A sense of inevitability began welling up in me.

Laurie laughed. "You must have a twenty-four-hour developing place in Vernon – there's not one in Nelson yet." He paused. "Well, you'll probably think this is weird, coming out of the blue, but ... you don't think you'd be interested in a part-time teaching position at the Whole School, our alternative school, here in Vallican?"

So this is what this is all about, I thought, as a "Yes" crossed my lips without hesitation.

"You see, on Friday the Steering Committee recognised the need for a part-time teacher and on Sunday you turned up on my doorstep...."

I was barely listening, remembering a Native man central to my life, musing: "A teacher ... I didn't know you were a teacher...." It was too weird to think about.

Job interview, acceptance and all the stressful details of a major move flowed so smoothly that I never doubted the wisdom of taking this opportunity, although I would have moved heaven and earth if I'd had to. For it was not only about a recent, magically-prophetic dream but the chance to realise another long-held dream. At the time of my educational training, Summerhill, the famous experimental alternative school in England, had been reaching its height; its radical philosophy seemed to mirror my personal theories about education but the thought of applying to teach there had been too intimidating. The philosophy of the Whole School was remarkably similar; and I felt I now had the capacity to fulfil a dream shelved for sixteen years.

Only six weeks after Laurie's call, I was teaching at the Whole School and living – of all places – in the log-house at the back of the meadow, with the grouse-hunting couple – of all people – acting as agents for the owners. Apparently it had been standing empty since sold months before; tracking down the new owners in Toronto turned out to be straightforward and they immediately agreed to rent it to me. It was as if the house had been waiting for me; later, my landlady would tell me my voice had sounded inexplicably familiar.

Yet throughout it all there was a sense that the teaching was but part of what was unfolding. As soon as we settled in, it became clear there was an "other" kind of life in and around the house. Never before had I been aware of such activity: sudden darting movements from corners across the room, along the walls or just outside the window; small, dark, unformed shapes, commonplace, yet unthreatening. Becoming familiar with the forty-acre property, I discovered its southern boundary met with the designated heritage site; learning to recognise the signs, I found features – groupings of hollows in the earth – indicating that other parts of Bob's Indian village were located on this property as well. The strange activity in the house began to make sense, and kept me constantly aware of the ancient Indian village just below us, which had a sort of presence, simultaneously magnetic and soothing, arousing feelings in me similar to those aroused by a cathedral. As I would soon find out, many other people felt the same way about this magical place, seemingly nothing more than a forested area and a scattering of hollows in the ground above a clear and winding river.

The distinctive peak that had stopped me in my tracks on first sight was now part of daily life. A previous owner had cleared a swathe of trees so that Frog Mountain was visible from the house, and each day on the way to school, all the way down the back-road it towered above me. Once the snows came, the reason behind the name was made all the more clear.

Our nearest neighbour was beyond sight and earshot; the back-road little-frequented. Each evening as the light faded, deer guardedly grazed the meadow on their way to the river; coyotes sang and danced, shadows in the twilight. I learned the rewards of caring for a woodstove and discovered the wonder of moonlit snowy walks in a silent, forested world overlaid with silver. Following meandering deer-trails along the riverbank, I became intimately familiar with the Indian village. The peace, quasi-solitude and closeness to the wild spoke deeply to a part of me I had neglected for many years.

The first friends I made were the couple who had initially directed me to the site: friends who would soon prove a tremendous support, for despite the extraordinary circumstances that had brought me here, things would not continue at all smoothly.

The signs were there from the outset, when to my consternation at the first parent-teacher steerage meeting I was given the responsibility of academic subjects – English and mathematics – for the older children. It was a majority wish; the school had been closed for a few years and I imagined people just had to find their confidence in an alternative system. I decided to do my best to make this happen. For a while, the Whole School became central to my life.

Twelve children, ranging in age from four to twelve, attended the school; the other teacher, there for a year already, was an art specialist. As directed, I began working with the older children, using materials I found in the basement and backrooms of the rambling building. I also came across sheaves of papers and mountains of books from the school's inception in 1973 and the following years, and set about researching the methods implemented and the materials used, swiftly learning that there did not appear to have been much of what I called progress in the academic field since that time, but that education had taken several steps backwards from a child-centred, creative, imaginative mode into one dominated and controlled by market forces, and fear.

One of the positive things about working as a teacher is immediate involvement in the community. Shortly before Christmas, at wood-cutter Laurie's seasonal "barn-that-turned-into-a-house" party, I finally met someone else connected to what I felt was the underlying reason for my coming to Vallican: the president of the Vallican Archaeological Park Society (VAPS). Enthusiastically I told him of my interest in the Indian village, sparked by two Arrow Lakes descendants.

Looking down his aquiline nose at me from a cold blue-eyed height, Rick was abrupt: "No. It belonged to the Kutenai."

These were the indigenous people for whom the area was named, although I had understood them to be a neighbouring Band situated on the east side of Kootenay Lake. Despite a tightening in my chest, something made me stay quiet; after all, I had only one man's word to back mine up and there was no way I could convey the integrity and authority of that man and his word. Turning away from what I saw as a closed mind, I found myself thinking this was going to be a long journey.

Wherever it came from, that thought would prove terribly accurate.

The encounter depressed me. Feeling quite distanced, I left the packed, boisterous room, intending to slip away unnoticed into the night, but as I was lacing-up in the boot-room, Laurie's wife came to see me out. As the door cracked open to darkness, Bridey whispered: "You know, he thinks you were 'sent'." She nodded, as if to indicate her agreement.

Thinking I knew them both by now, I was deeply and pleasantly surprised. I would never have expected Laurie to think this way, or his wife to express such a thing.

"I think that, too." Although not for the purpose that lay in their minds, I was sure, and could not say. Yet when would that purpose reveal itself? Or was I just fooling myself?

I had not long to wait for an answer. The day before school broke up for Christmas, very early in the morning, I woke to the sound of a vehicle approaching the house and got up to see a rusted white hatchback slithering along the icy rutted track. Somehow I was not surprised when it stopped and Bob got out.

I may have appeared calm but inside I was quivering. How had he known to come here? And was it my imagination or did he look different? Pale, he appeared tense, distracted, exhausted, but offered to help while I got the younger children ready for school and went with Sivan down to the basement to light the woodstove. Minutes later she came rushing back up, eyes wide. "Mum! I've never seen anything like it! He talked to the fire, and when it took hold he thanked it. He laid the wood in ever so gently, one piece at a time, right inside the stove. And he thanked each one. He put his whole arm into the flames, Mum, and didn't get burned!"

My heart glowed. Laughing Thunder was with us.

He did not want breakfast, nor was my stomach in any state to cope with food. When I asked how things were, he said difficult things had been happening on the Reservation. He did not elucidate and I felt unable to press him further. I wished desperately I could take the day off but we had to leave then. The rest of the day passed in a blur.

As promised, he returned in the early evening, seeming more relaxed. Over supper, I told him about the amazing series of events that had led us to live beside his ancestral village, but he only nodded absently, as if it was to be expected. But when I mentioned that the village was a designated heritage site, his dark eyes flashed and anger suddenly spilled over, controlled but intense, as he heatedly and at length denounced the marginalisation of the Native people. Devastated with empathy, I said, "It makes me feel so bad, all these things that have happened, are still happening. This is your land. In fact, I shouldn't even be here, I wasn't even born on this continent-"

"Oh no!" He said strongly, suddenly so calm that I was taken aback. "You've come home. And why I'm here is linked to you. We will keep in touch...."

Enigmatic but deeply reassuring, these final words before he left would become like a mantra during the following difficult months: I had come home; we were linked; we were in touch, on a subtle level. How else had he known where to find me, this amazing man? It seemed he was somehow with me all the time, just as he had promised in my dream.

SKY-WOLF

In despair, I knelt down and ground my fists into the powdery snow, the thin edge of my voice piercing the stillness: "Why am I here?! Why did I come to this place?! I can't stand it any more! Why on earth did I come here?! I need help.... Help me before I go out of my head!"

My cry was swallowed into blue-green shadows; silence swooped back like an owl's wing. Only the tall evergreens, their branches heavy with snow, responded: ghostly showers of fine white powder drifted noiselessly to the ground.

Falling forward, I plunged my face into the snow, welcoming its cold caress and the steely taste melting on my lips. Into the earth, I whispered: "Please help me. What am I doing here? Why did I choose this?"

Lying still in the flinty light, my misted breath the only movement, I looked up at the mountains. No longer inspiring, they seemed remote, impervious and unheeding sentinels. Leaden, the afternoon sky hung as a callous backdrop. The cold seeped through my clothes. I waited. Nothing happened.

It was madness, to come out and behave like this. Wondering what had possessed me, I got up and on legs stiff with cold trudged back home through the darkening woods, following a winding deer-trail stamped out by delicate cloven hooves. Below, the silver-backed river curved by in sleek silence.

The warm honey-glow of the log-house did nothing to cheer me; drained and chilled to the bone, I pushed open the back door. Nobody was home yet. I was glad of the chance to be alone.

Sivan was in Vancouver, spending Christmas vacation with her father; Natalie and Nicolas had been taken to see a movie in Nelson by their father, who had turned up unexpectedly a couple of days earlier to visit over Christmas. It was the first day Nick had been able to go out since he had fallen ill with shingles ten days earlier; we were both exhausted, but the brief respite from his care made little difference to me. Old, familiar, painful and unresolved issues between his father and me were beginning to erupt and I could see he would overstay the time-span to which I had reluctantly agreed. There was also of a sort of nervous tension affecting me, as I was realising I was not at all suited for the job which had brought me here. My philosophy, values and aims, although in line with the original tenets of the school, were not what the parents wanted. Compromise followed compromise; I felt I was fighting a losing battle for their confidence while failing the children, myself and my own children.

The extraordinary circumstances that had brought me here had been forgotten as I began to question the wisdom of leaving the security of the housing co-operative and a decent income working as a fitness instructor and free-lance proofreader in exchange for a tenuous rental and low-paying, stressful employment in a school disliked by my children. Sivan resented having been taken away from her friends in Vernon and I now had little time for all three kids. It seemed my decision had been based on a selfish flight of fancy: I had left Vernon on the wings of a dream, expecting a new, exciting and fulfilling life; the reality was the erosion of a dream, a host of new difficulties and the same old problems dogging me.

The Christmas break might have offered a chance to draw breath, rest and re-evaluate the situation, but on the first night – the night after Bob left – Nick had fallen ill. Chickenpox had been doing the rounds and he had developed shingles. Apparently there was no treatment for a four-year-old with this distressing illness; all I could do was support him, day after day, night after night, through recurring attacks of acute pain and increasing weakness. A third of his slight weight lost, he had just turned the corner when his father had turned up.

Reflecting in a detached manner on all these circumstances, I stoked the woodstove and settled into the birch-wood rocking chair, placed so I could look up to the westward cleft in the mountains where two eagles had majestically spiralled the thermals, only three months ago. How excited and optimistic I had been then, riding on the words of a charismatic Native American and the wonder of finding his ancestral village. Where was all the magic now?

Defined on one side by a forest-spined ridge which thrust upwards then fell away, on the other side of the cleft loomed a rocky, snow-draped, rounded peak I had dubbed "the Ringmaster", because in it I could see the curling moustache, bunched cheeks, amused black eyes and surprised brow of a jovial face. I looked to him now – he always made me smile – but could raise no emotion. My mind strangely empty, I stared vacantly into the eagle-cleft as the light faded.

It had been a windless day, grey and still, so the weird movement in the sky made no sense: the clouds, a strange, sickly yellow-grey, began to twist oddly, to swirl as if the eye of a storm hung there, and before my incredulous eyes a form began to take shape. As if a lens were being adjusted by some almighty hand, a face came into focus: an old, benevolent-looking Native American man, gazing into the distance. After a few moments it sort of dissolved and then another form began to manifest: facing away from me, the upper torso and head of a young Native man, the edge of his face just visible, a thick braid coiled over one naked shoulder. Then he too faded.

Gradually, tantalisingly, the clouds regrouped and a third image began to appear: two immense shining eyes ... luminous brow ... shaggy, pale smoky-yellow ruffs of hair ... shadows of pricked ears ... long pale streak of muzzle, dark smudge of nose....

It was a massive wolf's head, filling the sky, eyes and brow lit with an eerie, silvery brightness, intent on some otherwordly distance.

Transfixed, I stared at the fabulous luminescent image for a timeless span, no thought in my mind. Then it began to blur around the edges. I jumped up to get a pencil and a piece of paper from the table where the children had been drawing and just managed to sketch a semblance before the wolf's head merged back into the clouds.

I was trembling, my mind racing. Never before had I experienced anything so real and yet so ethereal. Was this what Native Americans called a vision? But I had not gone out into the mountains on a quest. I had not fasted or prayed, night after night. But I had cried out for help. Could a vision happen like this? What did it mean? Or had it been my imagination? Why had I not thought to get my camera? Looking at the all-too-real drawing, I recalled one of the more unusual questions asked at my job-interview: which animal I would most like to be, and why.

Wolf, I had immediately, unhesitatingly responded; for its beauty and grace, spirit and intelligence; for the family and clan life of the wolf-pack; for the ability to work in a team yet howl alone at the moon, lone-wolf-song that seemed to resonate in my blood, my bones....

Now a Sky-Wolf had been put before me. Feeling strangely exhilarated and renewed, I knew something of great significance had just occurred. From the depths of my being I had asked for help and I had been presented with a response – not a Native man on my doorstep this time but an incredible cloud-formed vision. I had never experienced anything like it; it sang to me, song without words. What could it mean? There was no-one I felt I could ask. Except maybe Bob. But when would I see him again?

Not understanding at the time, I had forgotten the deeper levels of which Bob had spoken during that long night in Vernon: the Sumix, the energy or force that lies at the foundation of the Native American spiritual way, also known as the totemic guide or guardian spirit that "walks" with a person – a symbolic representation of the person's subtle energy.

Nor had I any idea that I had thrown myself down and cried and beaten my fists directly upon the resting-place of Bob's ancestors. Some of whom, lost wanderers, were not at peace.

It seemed like my life was falling apart, but I was on the brink of an intense, arduous, magical part of my journey: a journey that would bring me to play a small part in the coming-home of the disinherited, fragmented Arrow Lakes descendants and those same people to play the central role in my own coming-home, to myself.

I may have thought I came to Vallican through choice, but would soon question the concept of freedom of the will and wonder about the power of the ancestral spirits, beyond space and time, spinning out the threads of the greater Plan.

WIND of CHANGE

During the cold season, the natural world appears dormant but secretly, in the darkness under the earth, the roots are active. That winter, a number of people from the Medicine Wheel gathering began to slot into my life, such as the couple from Montreal who had moved to Nelson a month after my move to the Valley and some of the core-group members, including the pipe-ceremony leader, Grey Wolf, who had also just relocated from Vernon to the tiny community of Appledale, fifteen minutes north of Vallican. I wondered whether this was the beginning of the new community Bob envisioned.

Esoterically-articulate, Grey Wolf also seemed to be bringing people together. Seeing him as wise elder, I told him about the dream of the drum and the vision of the Sky-Wolf; nodding sagely, he implied I had responsibilities to the Medicine Wheel gathering and that he had sent the vision and was "watching over me". Partly because of his name, I allowed myself to be taken under his wing (strangely, I kept miscalling him "Grey Owl"), even though I felt his interpretations smacked of manipulation. But I did not know who else to ask; I had not seen Bob since his brief visit out of the blue.

As well as local people, many people who had been at the Medicine Wheel gathering visited Grey Wolf and attended his weekly sweats, for which most would be "sky-clad", as the elder preferred. Finding this uncomfortable – the roughly-built sauna was dimly-lit, unlike a true sweat-lodge which was totally dark inside – I nevertheless forced myself to attend and thought I was learning a great deal.

By this time, my interest in the Native American way of life had become central to my being and organically spilled over into the teaching. It began one morning when the other teacher was absent; I found myself telling the children about Medicine Wheel earth astrology, as taught by Sun Bear, whose book I was reading. Perhaps it was my enthusiasm, or simply that most children, being fair-minded and close to nature, love Indians; the Wheel started rolling. Before long, one morning a week I was implementing the child-centred, holistic mode of education in which I had always believed, then after a couple of meetings with the Steering Committee the Whole School was back on its originally-conceived alternative track. I was elated, but it proved hard work because although I had a general plan, the key to holistic education is allowing for, following through on and integrating the unexpected. Drama was a key component; Grey Wolf not only gave his support but personally enthralled the children with legends to act out.

His role regarding the Medicine Wheel gathering was less clear. It seemed he was trying to put it on a new footing and wanted to involve me closely, but what he proposed made little sense to me since it did not include those whom I thought had more right to it than anyone else: the Arrow Lakes people. Then in the spring Laurie invited us both to attend the Annual General Meeting of the Vallican Archaeological Park Society.

Initially, I was not interested; the view of its president and the role of the society seemed far removed from what I held in my heart: this was not a designated heritage site but a living ancestral Arrow Lakes village. Yet I let myself to be persuaded.

As if to validate my feelings, even though re-elections were in order, only the Board of Directors was present. To my surprise, Laurie nominated Grey Wolf and me onto the Board. I could see there had been some complicity but it seemed churlish to refuse, so I went with the flow and was glad I did, for my nebulous discomfort with Grey Wolf was clarified within a couple of meetings, which were held every six weeks. Whenever I brought up the subject of the people whom I thought ought to have a say in what was happening, Grey Wolf curtly overrode me, saying the wool had been pulled over my eyes and the record showed that the land was shared by four tribes. I had not known there was any record, nor did any member of the Board. It emerged the canny old man had plans of his own for the Indian village site, none of which included the descendants of those buried there: a "New Nation", with himself as leader.

Given his name, his many exotic tales of his experiences among Native American tribes and his gift for story-telling, like many others I had assumed the elder was of Native American descent. To give him credit, Grey Wolf never claimed this birthright but also never corrected anyone who said this of him. When I later read about an Englishman who had successfully passed himself off as a Native American in the early part of the century, my "Grey Owl" [2] slip-of-the-lip made a strange kind of sense.

Spring, time of new growth above the earth, seemed turned on its head. Distancing myself from Grey Wolf meant I had also separated myself from plans for the Medicine Wheel gathering; no longer attending his sweats, I lost touch with those I imagined might be part of a new community. As for the school, it felt like a struggle upstream in a river that no longer called me. "Trust the children to learn, in spite of us!" My silent plea was lost in the fortnightly parental assessment of our "progress", which served only to reflect their insecurities about what was going on, which in turn was picked up by the children and reflected back.

My own children were affected; a budding understanding of a new and deeper view of reality convinced me that Nick's shingles had been a manifestation of my own unease. To resign seemed the only recourse, but the idea galled me; I believe in seeing things through and feared I was letting the children down. Natalie and Nick, however, were delighted with the possibility of being withdrawn from the school and returning to my original commitment to home-schooling, for despite being employed part-time I was at the school all day and often researching and planning lessons late into the night. The notion of tendering my resignation at the Easter break was made marginally easier because of the immediate availability of a keen and able member of the Steering Committee, a parent long involved with the school.

Unconvinced I was doing the right thing, on the first day of the Easter vacation I decided to walk the couple of miles down the back-road to Laurie's house and deliver my letter of resignation in person, imagining this would at least give me a last chance to talk it through – perhaps be talked out of it – by someone who seemed for the most part sympathetic. With a defiant spurt of gravel, the children sped off ahead of me on their bikes and were soon out of sight.

The afternoon was still and overcast; the only sound, the faint buzz of a chainsaw. Wracked by indecision, I barely noted the beloved, dramatic landscape until I turned down the last stretch to Laurie's house and was stopped by the sheer rock-face of Elephant Mountain, towering above

---

2 Since made into a film by the same name, starring Pierce Brosnan in the title role.

the end of the dirt-road like a wall, fire-swept ridges bristling with blackened tree-trunks. At its foot, the evergreens cloaking the ancient Indian settlement seemed to shimmer.

A mirage, like my reason for being here, I thought, unable to find pleasure in any of it. Furious at being so self-absorbed, I looked up and cried out: "What should I do? I don't know what to do! Should I go ahead with this?"

From somewhere down the valley came a strange rushing sound. Above me, the tops of the pine-trees stirred and began to sway then whip violently back and forth, caught in the mad sweep of a roaring, gusting wind. An eerie moaning, a creaking and a clacking filled the air. Then, like a train in a tunnel, rushing down the road behind me came a powerful gust and I was caught in a forceful, stinging whirl of twigs, pine-cones, sand and dust that made me close my eyes and propelled me stumbling forwards. Branches cracked and thumped to the earth, then as suddenly as it had started the roaring subsided. I opened gritty, irritated eyes to see the treetops had stopped their frenetic whipping about and were all bowing, bending in the same direction.

It was so obvious that I laughed aloud: I was being shoved in the very direction I had been holding back from, the soughing trees clicking and clacking and waving their branches, encouraging me impatiently: "Go on; that way! Just get on with it!"

Somehow freed, I briskly walked down to Laurie's house as the strange wind passed over. There was no-one home. I slipped the decisive letter under the door.

If only life were so straightforward. The next day I received notice to vacate the log-house, the owners having decided to move from Ontario a couple of years sooner than they had told me. It came as a shock; we had only been in the house six months. The children did not seem to mind, however, and Natalie helped put things in perspective: "It's so fun to move!"

On reflection, the timing was intriguing, somehow reassuring: receiving notice to relocate on the heels of handing in my resignation suggested a clearing-away of the old to make way for the new. The feeling that coming to Vallican was not really about teaching had always been with me; perhaps I had been given a taste of a long-held dream so I could put it to sleep once and for all. But I could not see the point of being involved with the Archaeological Society either; people talked and nothing happened. And (something I had pushed under as deep as possible because I couldn't bear thinking about it) where was Bob? There had been no word in all this time.

Or was he somehow here, "although not with" me? The odd wind pushing me so dramatically down the road could not have been chance. From where had that come? To cry for help in this place seemed to bring the most odd and powerful, elemental responses. Had it been another kind of guidance? There was nothing I could do but trust in the way things were unfolding. It was just that I needed some kind of reassurance besides so-called visions and winds that sprang up out of nowhere.

THUNDER SPEAKS

Valley house-vacancies were not listed in any newspaper; it was all word-of-mouth, connections, serendipity. I began a daily routine of combing the back-roads, asking anyone I saw if they knew of a place to rent.

It did not escape me that serendipity played a Native hand.

Having reached the south end of the Valley, one morning I was driving through the community of Crescent Valley when I saw a familiar figure standing outside his home on the side of the highway. Of Haida[3] lineage, good-looking in a dark, moody-teenager sort of way, skinny and intense with a shock of black hair, Jimmy was fostered by a local family. I had hired him to buck firewood for me the previous autumn and since then he occasionally dropped in to visit and play cards with my children. On probation at the time (I never bothered to find out what for), he seemed to skip school a lot and I was worried about how he seemed to be limiting his future options.

Thinking I would give him a ride to Mount Sentinel, the local high-school, so he would at least get there in time for lunch, I turned round and went back. But when I pulled up, he was nowhere in sight. Instead, sitting on the ramshackle steps of a little wooden house that desperately called for attention, scruffy and unshaven, bottles of beer in hand, were Jimmy's foster-father and another man. Apparently, neither had seen Jimmy since early morning.

"I'm not a truant officer," I offered, thinking they might be shielding him. They only shrugged. Suddenly it struck me that as locals, they would know the area well; did they know of any houses for rent?

Out of that puzzling episode came our next home: within two weeks we had moved into a massive pan-abode[4] hidden away in a private little valley adjacent to Crescent Valley. Something about the Lodge provoked a "yes" before I had even set foot inside.

Previously the engineers' house in the nearby mining-town of Salmo, it had been taken apart and rebuilt in its present location by the owner and, his wife later told me, consciously imbued with a sense of the spiritual. Rambling, musty and uninsulated, it promised to be a monster to heat but winter was three seasons away and I was sure the palatial proportions and peaceful seclusion would be worth it.

The lodge was now situated on a small bench of land at the foot of Mount Sentinel. Sweet-smelling cedar, pine, fir, spruce, birch and cottonwood crowded against the back of the house and swept up the slopes behind. To the front, the land gently dropped down several more benches to a swift-flowing creek, hidden among evergreens, then soared up into a tree-coated ridge. Half an hour by foot on an old trail up through the forest behind the house and over a ridge

---

3 Coastal Salish.

4 A log house built of factory-manufactured logs, common in California and definitely more suited to a southern climate.

brought us to a backwater of the Slocan River and a private hundred-foot sandy beach. It was an idyllic location for the children, who learned to confidently explore and play in the wild, our dog Muffy acting as a sort of nanny as they forged their vital connection to Mother Earth.

That spring, brown bears came down to snack on lush dandelions and raid the kitchen garden; shy creatures who bellowed in outraged fear when I chased them away. In late afternoon, high in the forest, coyotes yipped and sang. And once, not long after moving in, a movement at the edge of the forest caught my eye: a dark, silent shadow slipping through the twilight. It was the first time I had seen a wolf in the wild and although it immediately disappeared into the trees, it left me trembling, heart in throat.

I had been given a sign: I was definitely in the right place.

It was uncanny how many aspects of the Lodge reflected the "homework" the children and I had done before starting the house-search, when together we made a drawing of the kind of house and environment we wanted: lots of space, bedroom doors that locked (all the children), a chandelier (Natalie), a big kitchen, a safe place to play, ride bikes and swim, a creek, trees, mountains. It was the first time I had tried out this exercise, a focussing of consciousness I had recently learned about.

Not one detail on that drawing was unmet, but I would also appreciate how you get what you ask for. Taking it for granted, I had not thought to draw a sun in the sky. For four months of the year the house lay in the shadow of the trees and Mount Sentinel, untouched by the rays of the sun. On the other hand, I also had not drawn in any other house. Our nearest neighbour, the landlord's son, shared the hundred-fifty-acre property but lived tucked away at the end of the driveway, out of sight and hearing. Nor had I considered the landlord himself, so it was a gift to gradually find out I could not have asked for any better than the kindly, soft-spoken, insightful, open-minded and engaging elder who would prove less a landlord and more a surrogate father until his untimely death only two years later.

The other strange thing was that I had often driven past the entrance to the private little valley en route to the Organic Mechanic (my car-mechanic) and every time, my eyes had been drawn to the curve of the gravel track that disappeared into the trees.

Almost as if I had recognised it at some level.

It seemed the Whole School was a closed chapter. Vallican was twenty minutes' drive to the north, the city of Nelson equidistant the other way. It seemed strange to be living so far from the Indian village. Surely that was not also a closed chapter?

Soon I would appreciate having been removed from close proximity to an energy which was not only stirring but gathering itself into a force which would have a dynamic, irrevocable effect on more people than I could ever have imagined.

The seasons had turned full circle; only a month after settling into our new home, summer solstice was upon us. In a state of high anticipation, I returned to camp at this year's Rebirth of Mother Earth Medicine Wheel gathering. Six months had passed since I had seen Bob; I could not wait to tell him how my life had changed.

If he did not already know.

Although he had told me this was not the way he would do things, I spent most of the weekend looking out for a rusted little white hatchback. Nor was I the only one to be disappointed; rumours and gossip about Bob's non-appearance made the rounds. The gathering seemed lacklustre, without direction; I was not surprised when the question was raised about the point of continuing without the founder.

My detached state removed me from the immediacy of the debates, allowing me to perceive the way old Grey Wolf would sit in silence while people made their various points, then throw in a remark about protocol or tradition, get up and walk away. Within a few minutes heated arguments would blow up out of all proportion and everyone would storm off in different directions.

Out of the chaos he knowingly created, I suspected Grey Wolf was hoping to form a new order: his own. Nor had he given up on what he saw as my place in his "New Nation": the woman with whom he would "walk". No matter what I said, he would not be disillusioned; as for what he considered my illusions about Bob, he persuaded me to visit the "lodge of Princess". Out of curiosity, I agreed.

No-one could have missed this striking woman, also known as Skunk Woman for the two white streaks that ran the length of her long black hair. With her remote, regal beauty and slim height she could have been a model. Nor was finding her lodge difficult; her large tent was adorned with exotic drapes and rugs, luxurious jewel-coloured cushions and throws. Gracefully she received me, as if I were paying court, waving me to sit on a cushion outside her lodge as she seated herself on a director-style chair.

About what did I wish to know?

Despite an inclination to giggle and ask for my copy of the script, I briefly told her about who I felt should be running the gathering.

What followed was a series of cautionary tales: Princess's experiences among Native Americans, solely of the paranormal. They sounded like something out of "National Enquirer", several copies of which I could see lying half-hidden under the velvet cushions inside her tent. I was thinking I should have brought along a salt-shaker when her tone changed: " ... And stay away from the Colville Reservation." Her voice grew tight with anger. "I know all about what people like that Bob...." She paused, her dark eyes black with emotion. "Just stay away from there! They'll put handsome young men onto a woman like you.... Oh, they'll seem nice enough and they'll be offering to help you, but before you know it they'll have sucked dry all your energy! Beware of their offers. And never take your children there!"

Wrong person to play drama-queen with, I thought, guessing she must have fallen for Bob and been brushed off; a woman of her stature, beauty, arrogance would not take that kindly. If Grey Wolf had primed her to put me off, he did not know woman.

"It's time for the pipe-ceremony." She got up. I had been dismissed.

"What pipe-ceremony?" I asked

"To release Red Cloud's spirit. He needs to move on. Grey Wolf's going to conduct the re-naming ceremony for him."

It seemed bizarre to rename a dead man, although I knew that traditionally, Native people might change their name when something of import happened to them. Had this been something the elder had wanted? The memory of the great bear of a man who had hugged me so warmly, who had entered my dream and given me a drum was warm in my heart; he would always ride there as Red Cloud, but I had no sense of him still hanging around. Out of respect – and curiosity – I decided to attend the ceremony.

Only about eight people turned up; another rift had been opened up by arguments about whether the concept was traditional or even existed. I recognised a couple of core-group members and Princess and her partner, a tall and handsome, slim, young Native man, Do-do-nee-ha, who claimed an ancient shaman-warrior lineage and told us tales to match.

We did not sit at the sacred fire but at another small hearth. Like most of Grey Wolf's ceremonies, it was a slow, ponderous affair, interrupted by a touch of light relief when Do-do-nee-ha suddenly leapt up and raced across the meadow so swiftly and lightly I would have sworn his feet never touched the ground. The object of his silent chase was as shocked as I when I saw who it was: our dog, sneaking away from Princess's camp with a large joint of cooked meat held awkwardly in her mouth. She yelped as Do-do-nee-ha seemed to appear out of nowhere in front of her, dropped her prize and streaked away, tail between her legs, although he never so much as made a sound or touched her. I had never seen anything like it: silent and swift as an arrow, the flight of the young man, upon the dog before she was aware of him, before any of us knew what was going on. Once the general merriment had subsided, Grey Wolf, who was not at all amused, proceeded with his ceremony until, with a final flourish of his pipe, he decreed that Red Cloud's release as "Thunder Speaks" had been accomplished.

Something made me look up. A blue heron was flying directly over us, long raggedy wings steadily pulsing. Silently I pointed it out and we all watched as it flew under the arc of a double rainbow that had appeared in the southwest. A sudden shower sprinkled, light, cool and refreshing, so brief we were hardly dampened, and as it died away, a rumble of thunder, low and long like a chuckle, rolled across the sky.

Mouths fell open. Old Grey Wolf gave a satisfied smirk.

But it was Bob – Laughing Thunder – who was at the forefront of my mind.

An odd string of coincidences? I was sure it had been a series of messages. Nothing happens by accident, Bob had said, a universal truth I was beginning to appreciate.

Had it been the renamed and freed Thunder Speaks, rumbling his approval? Or the Thunder Beings, chuckling at our puny pretentiousness in the land of Laughing Thunder? What about the heron, flying into the setting sun? On the Medicine Wheel, West is the place of introspection and insight and is connected to the earth. Was it about Red Cloud being a sort of fisher of men, bringing together people who were to work together for the good of Mother Earth in some way, before he passed on? Coming out of nowhere, the sudden little shower might denote cleansing; the rainbow, a promise. And what about the dog episode? Why my dog – symbolically my energy? What about the meat – sustenance – stolen from the camp of a woman set to turn my mind, and rescued by her man in such a spectacular way?

That is the problem about symbols – they raise more questions than they answer. There was no-one I felt I could talk to about any of it. The only new contacts I made at the gathering that year were some people who were exploring Celtic, Arthurian and Knights Templar traditions, which despite my origins left me cold. It was the Native American way which stirred the depths of my soul.

Not once did I question why I should feel so strongly for and be so moved by a life-way that had nothing to do with me. Not in this life, at least.

WHITE EAGLE

The experience made me realise I needed something more truly Native American. The first opportunity seemed extraordinarily appropriate: less than a month later, the annual pow-wow at Sqwlax, near Chase, British Columbia, where four years earlier Red Cloud had held the first Rebirth of Mother Earth Medicine Wheel gathering. Apparently in those early days it had attracted figures such as the renowned shaman-healer, Rolling Thunder.

The site sprawled over several acres: campsites, rows of stalls, cars parked everywhere. As I had hoped, there were not very many white faces amid a throng of Native people. Knowing only that a pow-wow was a kind of Native gathering, there was a lot to take in. Central to the site was the dance-arena, a great circle of beaten earth hedged in by banks of bleachers, crammed with onlookers, between which the dancers waited their turn. Hanging tightly onto the children's hands, I found space to stand behind some young Native men wearing fancy, colourful shirts and pants with long, thick, rainbow-hued fringes of yarn attached to shoulders, chest and knees and colourful bandannas wound gypsy-like about their head. Most had short, modern haircuts; only one had long hair flowing free. Behind me, I heard a clinking noise: several Native girls in their late teens were walking by, chattering and giggling. They were wearing brightly-coloured, close-fitting, knee-length dresses made of a shiny material, to which were fastened rows of shining metal cones, and Apache-style boots.

I did not know what to think. When a few elderly men dressed in deerskin tunics and leggings decorated with complex beadwork walked across the arena, they seemed to fulfil something of what I had been expecting, except for the spectacles most seemed to be wearing. Decorated only with porcupine quills, one outfit looked something like I had been anticipating, but even it was compromised by the prominent display of a competition number.

A p.a. system crackled into life with an indecipherable announcement, then the sudden thud of a drum made me jump. A wailing chant began; I was looking for where it originated when a lone dancer leapt into the centre of the arena. Wearing fringed deerskin leggings and tunic, a fan of feathers haloed round his head, with outspread arms the dancer stepped in a strange circling, swooping motion. Belatedly I realised it was Eagle whose soaring flight was being honoured. The singers wailed and chanted, cutting through the hum of voices, drowning them out. With another thud, the dance ended and the crackling voice thanked the eagle-dancer and announced the first heat of "fancy dancers".

Another drum somewhere on the edge of the arena throbbed into life and the young men in front of me became part of a whirling, twirling, leaping swirl of colour spinning round the dusty earth. Even though the materials were definitely modern, I could feel the spirit of the past breaking through. Almost of their own volition, my feet shuffled to the fervent, compelling beat. The powerful group-singing was unlike anything I had heard musically; before long it began to feel overwhelming and I had to distance myself.

Away from the arena, pounding drum and wailing singers relegated to the background, the rows of stalls were distracting and relatively peaceful. We checked out the arts and crafts, quasi-artefacts, memorabilia, crystals, bead- and leather-work, popcorn and hamburgers, ethnic Native American food. Then I noticed a familiar figure, his back to me.

I hesitated. Probably he would not remember me, I thought. One of the core-group at the Medicine Wheel gathering, he had been a dynamic master of ceremonies both years but the two brief exchanges I had with him had not been particularly pleasant. Yet I had a sense that encountering someone from the Medicine Wheel gathering in this place had to be significant.

Bryan seemed pleased to connect with a face from the gathering; discovering we shared a similar concern for its future, we found a place to sit at the edge of the arena to discuss it further. A well-built man with considerable presence, long, thick steel-grey braids, a fleshy, hooked nose and strong features that could almost pass as Native American, he explained that he had recently split from his partner and as a craftsman in leather and precious metals was following the pow-wow circuit in British Columbia. The first I had heard of such a concept, apparently not only artisans but many Native dancers followed it nationally full-time, the dancers at best living from the prize-money.

As we talked against a background of drumming and singing, I began to realise there was more to this man than had been evident at the gathering. He had no Native American blood, but had been recognised by Native spiritual leaders, endowed with a ceremonial pipe and the name White Eagle, and made chairman of the Muquabeak Cultural Society, located on the coast. Muckle-beak, I immediately – and privately – dubbed him, for the generous proportion of his nose.

When I learned he was versed in astrology and had trained for almost a decade under the master adept of a Western mystery school, I was deeply affected, for his life-views seemed to strongly resonate with my own, even those about the nature of reality that had seemed too wild to share. When I told him about the drum-dream (no-one but Grey Wolf knew about it, not even Bob, strangely enough) and how I came to the Slocan Valley, I suddenly had his full attention. It was then I learned of the strange circumstances of Red Cloud's death: the way the elder-visionary had given away all his treasured personal items and retired to his tipi to die, just after the two Arrow Lakes descendants had appeared. Bryan was convinced of a powerful link, the purpose of which was in its nascence, and in which he also wanted to play a part. Before long I could physically feel the heady effect the power of his personality and force of his intellect were having upon me.

A small voice within whispered caution. Last year, it reminded me, you were not so enamoured of him. Remember what happened the last night of the gathering? How he acted towards you; how you felt? Mouse-whisperings of intuition, they were swamped by the overpowering intensity of the man's energy, his wide-ranging esoteric knowledge and obvious keen intelligence.

Despite my on-going, deep-running feelings for Bob and the lingering, treasured memory of our brief but exquisite physical connection, which I irrationally felt that I was somehow betraying, to the background of Native American drumming and chanting which continued throughout the night, I embarked upon an intimate relationship with the man I thought of as White Eagle. A seemingly-fitting counterpart to Sky-Wolf. And eagles gathering.

INTERWEAVING WAYS

A tricky business, hindsight. Because it did not work out in a conventional or expected way, to look back and regret or condemn an action or decision is pointless, especially when the lessons it brings are powerful, if painful (as good lessons often are). At the time, force of personality, seductiveness of intelligence and a sense of soul-matedness made joining with this man seem fated, inevitable. He accompanied me back to the Valley, a place he knew well and where he had several long-standing friends. Asked to go with him to Sooke on Vancouver Island, where he had been invited by a Native American pipe-carrier to consecrate a new sweat-lodge, I was thrilled. Not only did I love the Island (with a capital "I", like the Valley) but my life seemed to be taking the direction I was longing for.

A trance medium, esoterically-trained, and a practitioner of Wicca as well as a pipe-carrier, Lynne immediately took me under her wide and generous wing and a new part of my education took off. Both she and her husband James, small, soft-spoken and bearded like a Druid, a hypnotherapist, would prove to be a vital enlightening and earthing support during the turmoil yet to come.

Apparently the Native people local to the area had lost touch with their ritual and ceremony; the Native woman who had asked Lynne for help met us at the edge of a small wood and joined the sage-scented purification and pipe-sharing meditation Bryan conducted in the willow-framed, canvas-covered sweat-lodge. The ceremony was powerful in its simplicity; I could see why Lynne had selected White Eagle.

When we returned to the Valley, Bryan decided we should visit Bob's ranch on the Colville Reservation to find out his intention for future Medicine Wheel gatherings, brushing aside like dead leaves the words I repeated about Bob's lack of interest. I did not protest (nor consider the implication of my words being considered irrelevant); the idea of seeing Bob's ranch – perhaps Laughing Thunder himself – sparked old, familiar feelings which Bryan must have sensed yet was willing to accommodate.

Following the designated scenic route – the Crow's Nest Highway – the journey passed as in a dream. The mountainous landscape seemed lit with a new, ethereal beauty. But then I was in a state of high, trembling anticipation, like the first few heady days of falling in love, magnified to an almost unbearable degree. Bob would have followed this route ... as well as his ancestors before him.... Perhaps, I imagined, they had camped at Christina Lake, now a small resort, which felt somehow as special as the Little Medicine Waters (as I called the glacial pool Bob had said was sacred to his people); although they would not have crossed the delicate bridge, which, spider-like, straddled a great ravine at the bottom of which gleamed another miracle of modern man's engineering skills: a silvery thread of railway line.

Curving down steeply between mountain slopes scarred with derelict, blocked-up mine-shafts and tumbles of scree and tailings, the highway suddenly levelled out on the open grasslands of the Kettle Valley. At the mill-town of Grand Forks, I remembered Bob telling me about his relatives who had lived there and wondered if that had been before the creation of the Forty-ninth Parallel, to the south of the valley. Punctuated by an occasional stark, rocky ridge, the landscape curved and folded soft as a woman's body; among the scattering of ranches, farms and small-holdings stood the distinctive square dwellings of the Doukhobor people, of whom Bob had so warmly spoken. In the small town of Midway we came across a poignant monument: two pine trees spliced together, growing as one, and a plaque commemorating the establishment of the International Boundary, when "one of the original people, now residing on the Colville Reservation" had bound the trees to remember that "although divided, we are still one". I had my answer. Deeply moved, I wished something could be done to rectify the injustice.

Gradually the land rose again, becoming increasingly arid. At the final pass before the dramatic descent into Osoyoos at the south end of the Okanagan Valley, the spectacular view made us pause. A patchwork of lush greens – the vineyards, and peach, apricot and cherry orchards – and scrubby, bleached-out land stretched hazily across the valley to the purple-blue foothills of the coastal mountain range; buzzing with recreational activity, Osoyoos Lake sparkled turquoise-blue. Strung along the highway, heavily influenced by Spanish tastes, the hacienda-style white buildings and red-tiled roofs did not seem out of place in the glaring sunlight. A garish gauntlet of motels and hotels along the main route through the town proclaimed the area's other main resource.

Leaving Osoyoos, we turned south to the main border crossing near Oroville, Washington, busy with Canadians passing back and forth for cheaper petrol and cigarettes. As soon as we were through, I felt the difference, nebulous, indefinable; it seemed ridiculous, it was a man-made division but I always had a sense of entering another country: one less safe, more on a knife-edge.

The Okanagan had become the Okanogan: hot, sere and dusty; a scorched-sagebrush, desert valley contained within stark, towering, burnt-ochre ridge-walls peppered with sparse stands of lodge-pole pine. Without stopping, we passed through the small, sleepy township of Tonasket. On reaching Omak, where I remembered Bob saying his mother lived, we headed east to begin another climb through extensive ranch-lands.

The border of the Colville Confederated Reservation was denoted by a large wooden sign. Again I had a sense of passing through an invisible wall into another kingdom. Or dimension. Not on a knife-edge any more.... Or maybe it was just my imagination.

Our journey was nearing its goal. I was so tense I could hardly bear it. How would it be to see Bob again? Part of me wanted to jettison Bryan there and then but another part whispered it was better this way.

Grasslands gave way to trees, which thickened into forest as we climbed; a sign near the summit proclaimed Disautel, where Bob had said he lived. There was no evidence of a community, not even a house. No power lines, no telegraph poles. We stopped by the side of the highway to let the engine cool and work out what to do next. The only traffic we had met had been loaded logging trucks heading down to the mill at Omak. In a state of high excitement, I half-expected the ranch, complete with pit-bulls, to magically reveal itself. But nothing happened. Resignedly we continued on down to Nespelem, address of Bob's post office box.

There was no hint of how familiar the desolate little Reservation township would soon become to me. My first impression was of a ghost-town. Many of the little houses were derelict, paint peeling off, windows boarded up, doors smashed off hinges. Most of the yards were filled with rusting hulks of cars and appliances, old tyres and assorted piles of junk. Lying in the middle of a dusty street, a couple of flea-bitten dogs panted despondently in the heat. Not one person was to be seen.

There did not appear to be any shops or post office; the only public place we could find was a bar, "The Warbonnet", a flickering neon sign indicating it was open. Intending to ask for directions, we were getting out of the van when a battered, hospital-green pick-up screeched to a halt in a cloud of dust only a few feet away. Two small, wiry Native men, dressed in faded denim jeans, T-shirts, cowboy hats and boots jumped out, glanced narrow-eyed at us as they made their way into the bar and slammed the door, leaving a sneering comment hanging on a swirl of dust-laden air: "Huh! White folk!"

With his distinctive nose and impressive braids, I had thought Bryan might pass as a Native American; there was no possible ambiguity about my blonde, blue-eyed self. I guessed by the way he hesitated that Bryan felt intimidated but I was sure I had detected an amused undertone and followed the two men into the bar, curiously unafraid.

After the searing brightness outside, it took a few moments for my eyes to adjust. Softly-lit, the bar was spacious, the many functional tables and chairs empty, the linoleum floor scuffed but clean. A row of flashing gaming machines stuttered a tinny, tuneless, electronic tinkle at the back of the room. Drinks already in hand, the two Native men were hunched silently at the bar; behind it, the barkeeper was studiously wiping a glass. I walked toward them but before I could say anything Bryan poked his head in the door and blurted out Bob's name: "Who knows where he lives?"

Without turning round, one of the seated men snarled: "An' who wants to know?"

Annoyed by Bryan's rudeness, I quickly said: "I'm from Canada. Bob came into my life a year ago and turned it upside down and inside out. I've been put on a whole new road ... a spiritual path. I'll always be grateful to him. He walks with the Creator." Although heart-felt, the flowery pretentiousness of my words made me cringe mentally, but something about the atmosphere changed.

"We-ell, that's alright then. Just wanna be sure," chuckled the same man. "But what about him over there?" With a flick of his thumb he indicated Bryan, who had slipped into a corner seat as far away as possible.

"I'm ... with her!" Bryan said quickly.

If there had been any sense of threat, it had evaporated. The two men not only gave us detailed directions to within inches of Bob's house but offered to escort us: " ... Not that he'll be home. Cousin of his jest died; he'll be busy with arrangements. I'm one of the pall-bearers – funeral's tomorrow."

"We're brothers," the other said, "Tom and Gary. Our claim to fame bein' our skill in the suicide race."

My puzzled expression sparked jibes about my not having lived yet and I was told to look out for the race at the annual rodeo in Omak. One of the brothers indicated his obviously-prized, elaborate belt-buckle: a rider astride a bucking bronco. It was like Bob's. I wondered if he, too, were a "suicide rider". They continued to joke and flirt, trying to get me to drink with them; we left to teasing offers of their service as scouts, should we get lost again.

Just before reaching Disautel, I turned down a trail marked "Summit Lake" that I had noticed earlier. Somehow I could not just go to Bob's ranch, excited, hot and sweaty, without some sort of ritual cleansing. The waters of the tranquil, sheltered lake were dark and cooling, holding me in a soothing embrace as I floated on my back, listening to the gentle whispers of the breeze sighing among the pines and absorbing the steadfastness of the rocky cliffs around the lake until I regained an inner equilibrium.

With clear directions, the narrow, tightly-angled gravel track leading to Bob's ranch was easy to find. The two-storey house looked as if it were still under construction; only one car was parked there and not the one I was anticipating. Kicking up cones and pine-needles, half-a-dozen little brown hens pecked lazily in the dusty yard; a stream cut between the trees by the house, disappearing into a muddy drinking-hole in a meadow where two Appaloosas grazed. I recalled Bob telling me that he bred these unusual, tough, lean horses, developed by the Nez Perce Indians and ideal for outlaw activity, the solid-coloured front and spotted white rump of the breed blending easily among the trees.

A tall, thin, mournful-looking man with a ponytail answered the door and suggested we wait for Bob, who was at his late cousin's house. He introduced himself as Dan, a friend from Seattle, where he lectured at the university. Carmen, his attractive and vivacious South-American wife, came to sit outside with us and told us that when Dan had become seriously ill some years ago, Bob stayed by his side until he had nursed him back to health. Since then, they and their little boy spent most of their spare time with the man to whom her husband felt he owed his life and in whom he deeply believed.

I could not help thinking that this was only our second encounter on the Reservation and we were hearing only regard and respect for the man who had so deeply affected my own life.

Before long, a familiar white hatchback appeared, followed by a couple of other cars. My stomach lurched and filled with butterflies. Bob got out, then Manny, Bob's sidekick from the gathering. Among the others I recognised Virgil, inches taller and rangier than the year before, now a handsome young man.

"Hey! It's really good to see you guys!" Looking care-worn, Bob hugged us both briefly but warmly and invited us into his home. Trying to still the familiar trembling in my solar plexus and with a terrible sense that I had been untrue to my deepest feelings, I followed him inside.

Open-plan, the living, eating and cooking space took up almost the entire ground floor. A large bathroom lay off to one side; open-fronted sleeping areas overlooked the living-space. Although there was still work to be done, it was liveable, spacious, light and airy. Carmen made coffee while Bryan and I offered our condolences and we all sat down.

Suddenly Manny, who had been hovering like a thunderhead in the background, fidgeting and frowning, blurted out: "What're you folks doin' here?! What d'you want with Bob?! What d'you want, comin' round here?!" Fists clenched, he stepped forward. A cold rush of fear coursed through my body, adding to my inner turmoil. I looked to Bob but he only folded his arms and leaned back on the couch, his eyes half-closed.

Was it some kind of test?

To my relief Bryan responded, calmly talking about the Medicine Wheel gathering and linking it to the need for white people to learn from Native American teachings and wisdom, and for people in general to overcome their differences and work together for the future. An articulate, effusive speaker, he was still talking when Manny fixed me with his obsidian glower and broke in: "An' you, what d'you want here?"

Perhaps, I had thought, he might overlook me – woman sitting quietly on the floor. The few words I had been mentally rehearsing flew out the window and several moments passed before I realised no-one was going to stick up for me. I indicated Bob. "He's the reason I'm here. You can ask him. Beyond that, I don't know a thing."

Manny turned away, tense as a tightly-coiled spring. As if nothing had happened, Bob said: "Been a difficult year. One night, I was called to help a friend incapable of driving himself home, an' I obliged by driving the man's car for him. We was stopped by the police, held at gunpoint while the car was searched. They found a small cache of heroin, I was arrested an' confined to the Reservation until the trial, with the details splashed all over the front pages of the Spokane newspapers.... I was eventually cleared, although the papers don't rush to retract their headlines, or proclaim a man's innocence. My freedom was taken, for almost two seasons...." Then he added, so quietly that, sitting near his feet, I may have been the only one who heard: "In the spring, I suffered a mild heart-attack."

A sudden memory seared through me. I made a mental note to ask him more about it when I had the chance.

"Another couple from the gathering turned up here a coupla days ago," Bob added with a chuckle. It was irrational, but I cringed at being thought of as a couple and almost missed what came next: "Do-do-nee-ha and Princess showed up here at my home, an' without any preliminaries accused me of neglectin' my duties and foregoin' my responsibilities by not being at the gathering in my ancestral lands...." Bob shook his head, amusement playing at the corners of his eyes. "That Princess ... a space cadet. Too much acid in the sixties!" But his eyes flashed darkly as he added: "That young guy, if he's tryin' to walk a spiritual path, he should know better."

The following autumn, we heard that while fire-fighting in the vicinity of Seattle, Do-do-nee-ha narrowly escaped with his life, suffering a broken arm. The man beside him was killed. With his years of tutelage in the esoteric, Bryan was sure this was the backlash of challenging a spiritual man in his own land.

Again Bob made it clear he had no direct interest in the future of the Medicine Wheel gathering. It was time to leave. At the last minute I managed to draw him aside and ask the question burning in me: when had his heart-attack occurred?

As he cast his mind back, a sort of inner sense gelled into certainty; by the time he zeroed in on the date, I knew what it would be and told him about the morning I had been woken by an unearthly, piercing, drawn-out scream which I recorded in my dream-notebook and eventually rationalised as the screech of a dying animal. I had searched the land around the Lodge for whatever it might have been but found nothing. It had been a terrible sound, unforgettable.

His eyes fixed on a spot beyond my shoulder as he listened, Bob nodded: "As I said, our paths are connected."

It was exactly what I needed to hear. Everything else – emotions, regrets – fell away and I was again filled with a calm, inner certainty about the way things were going.

"I'm plannin' to bring my Ma up to the village soon," Bob said as Bryan and I prepared to drive away. "You should come meet her."

A window to our next meeting, to me it was a life-line. And I appreciated how Bryan left me alone to my long, tearful, introspective silence as we returned to the Valley.

WHITE WOLF

Within a couple of weeks, we heard that some Native people were camped at the Archaeological Park at Vallican. My heart soared; I had been worrying how I would know without visiting the site every day, which seemed obsessive, and to make things worse, Bryan had seemed annoyingly laid-back. Yet the significance of what was unfolding obviously affected him as deeply as me, for he wanted to drive there immediately.

Sultry and warm, no cloud in the sky, it felt like a day out of time. Parking at the same spot as I had that first time, less than a year ago, I told Bryan to go ahead with his gift – two bolts of cotton cloth, red and blue, which Bob had told me were the colours of the Arrow Lakes people. I wanted to linger, savour the precious, dreamlike moments.

It seemed deeply significant that it was the time of the new moon: time of beginnings, of new growth. Thinking in Tarot imagery, I saw Bob's mother as the Empress, returning home to her lands after years in exile; her son the High Priest at her side. The image of the Fool popped into my mind's eye: eyes to the heavens, dog at his side, tripping lightly over the cliff.... So who was the Fool? Old Grey Wolf? Never. The Fool is the wisest of all; sees with the eye of the Seer, knows all is one. With his negative feelings about "the Colville people", as he summarily dismissed them, Grey Wolf had separated himself from those who embodied the spirit of the land. As for the Medicine Wheel gathering, it was becoming a spaceship for an old show-man's ego-trip.

Making my way as slowly as I could up the overgrown track and along the edge of the trees to the first camp of an exiled people come home at last, my fantasies shifted into Biblical terms: Exodus; Eva, First Woman. The sight of three tipis, gleaming ivory-fresh against a dark backdrop of forest and mountainside, intensified my feelings, although I noted in passing that they had been erected upon what I had recently learned from research into the archaeological record to be part of the ancestral burial-ground, and wondered if they knew. But then people like Bob knew things on levels other than the mundane.

The chock of an axe caught my attention. Bob was among the trees with Manny and Dan, cutting lodge-poles. All three were shirtless in the heat; Bob raised a hand briefly in acknowledgement and I nodded back casually, trying to calm the fluttering in my stomach.

A local woman whom I vaguely recognised was busy near one of the tipis, together with the same woman who had led the first sweat I took part in at the Medicine Wheel gathering, and Carmen was just going into a tipi, bowl in hand. None of them seemed to notice me, which was fortunate, since I couldn't have entered into everyday chat with anyone at that moment. Bryan was nowhere to be seen. Or maybe I just did not want to see him.

In a trancelike state I walked up to the tipi closest to the edge of the cliff, and there found the Grand Dame herself, sitting in the shade of young silver birch overlooking a great silver-green curve of the Slocan River. She was wearing a sky-blue scarf over her grey-white hair, a blue-and-white checked blouse, blue slacks and strong glasses; her round, lined, brown face was calm in repose.

My voice a croak, I introduced myself and offered my red-and-blue gifts – baskets of plump raspberries and blueberries – and a framed copy of the photograph I had taken of her son and grandson just before they had left Vernon. She smiled and nodded: "Visit with me."

Feeling honoured, I sat on the grass near her feet, river at my back. The elder pointed out the magnificent painting of a stylised buffalo-head on the tipi behind her and spoke of how peaceful she felt, how good it was to be here. I was happy to listen and plunged all the more into thrall when Bob joined us, sitting slightly behind his mother. She continued chatting and I tried not to look at his lightly-muscled chest, the enormous eagle with outspread wings tattooed across it.

Above their heads I could see the eagle-cleft in the mountains. Eagle flies high, sees all, I remembered, flies close to the sun, to the Creator; represents the direction of the east, enlightenment. Eagle had so often been part of my experience since all this began. Goosebumps ran down my back. My hands were trembling. Because of Bob's close proximity? Or the nervous tension of the past few weeks, catching up on me? I could not see his eyes, hidden behind dark sunglasses.

Despite the warm day, I shivered and suddenly felt foolish, imagining I was sitting with an Empress, a High Priest. Better pay attention.

"Well, I sure am impressed with the clean water and air I've found here," Eva was saying. "I remember being brought up to the area by horse when I was a child. My father and my grandfather always talked about it. They was always talkin' 'bout comin' up here: what they saw, what they done ... I never forgot the places they told me of. It's exactly like they said an' like I remembered."

She recalled various incidents and details. I thought about the fifty or sixty years that had passed since the land had known its own. Then Bob said: "Ma, you wanted a walkin'-stick. Why not go with her and find one? She knows her way round here."

Grateful for his trust, I determined to use the opportunity to show Eva another place to which I had often been drawn while living at the log-house. Stopping occasionally while she told me about plants and dyes and I looked among the undergrowth for a suitable stick, I unobtrusively guided her to the edge of a thickly-forested area further along the cliff-top where there was a series of different-sized hollows in the ground and took her to the edge of the largest one. I said nothing; for quite some time we stood together in silence on a carpet of pine-needles on the lip of a large, deep, oval-shaped depression, looking at the remains of an earth-lodge that I had yet to learn was over two thousand years old.

"I get a feeling it had something to do with women," I offered tentatively. "It's also one of only two places in the village which affords a clear view of Frog Mountain." I pointed out the impressive peak, just visible between the trunks of the trees.

"In the old days," she said, "the village would've been cared for and the land kept clear so's it would've been possible to see the mountain from most places in the village.

"Swar'ah'ahin-shw'il-shw'al. Frog Mountain in our language."

Frog Mountain it still was.... Thrilled and determined never to forget them, I whispered the ancient, new words over and over under my breath as we made our way back to the tipis and almost bumped into the elder when, walking in front of me, she suddenly stopped. With bated breath, I waited. I had forgotten the extraordinary nature of this spot; the only other place from which Frog Mountain could be seen, it had a strange sense of an invisible barrier being traversed, a momentary shimmering of the lush greenery around us. Knowing nothing yet of the existence of the grid of ley lines encompassing the planet, I called it a "spatial wrinkle". Eva clearly sensed something but said nothing.

Coming to meet us, Bob did not seem to notice the lack of a walking-stick. Back at the camp, Eva indicated she wanted to go for a rest and one of the women escorted her into her tipi. Bob was curious to know what his mother and I had talked about; I told him of plants she had identified and their uses, of the upper part of the Indian village I had shown her and how on the way back she had been affected by a place that seemed special to me for reasons I could barely explain. "Oh, and I learned a new word," I added, bravely trying it out on him.

The lack of any kind of response made me think I must have got it totally wrong. I was about to ask when he said in his smooth, quiet way: "The mountain is sacred to my people. It has a spirit-name."

A prickle of anticipation blossomed between my shoulder-blades.

"Heha-aykin."

Like misted breath on a cold day, the alien word hung in the air. As in a dream, I heard my voice asking what it translated to.

"White Wolf."

Like a blanket of snow, a profound silence covered the whole area. Goosebumps crawled up my arms, down my body, into my legs, over the top of my head. I had never told Bob how I had pounded on the graves of his ancestors the previous winter, on the same spot where his mother's tipi now stood, nor of what had been revealed to me in the clouds afterwards. Nor could I tell him now. I needed to be alone, savour this shining jewel of experience.

Perhaps Bob sensed something of what I was feeling; smiling gently, he turned and walked away. I looked up to the eagle-cleft, the same place where the massive, luminescent, cloud-formed wolf-head had hung, gazing, I knew now, at the sacred mountain that carried its spirit-name.

Of course it had not been about old Grey Wolf. That bright head, the response to a heartfelt plea ... White Wolf.... My purpose here was intimately linked to this sacred mountain, its disinherited people. Which I had known at some level, all along. This was my destiny, I knew it. My heart thudded, full to bursting; my thoughts whirled away into blankness. In a state close to ecstasy, I stumbled mindlessly back along the track to my van.

Manny blocked my way. "I was outta line back there, down at Bob's place," he said gruffly, holding out his hand. "He told me who you was, after. I shouldn't have let fire like that."

For the first time, his dark eyes met mine. Too out of myself to feel surprise at this sudden peace-offering, I nodded, accepting his firm, warm handshake. Having read about the traditional Native American teaching to never correct or reprimand a person in front of another, in order to preserve that person's dignity – true as much for child as adult – I understood why Bob had not spoken up at the time of Manny's diatribe and had almost forgotten it.

Bob had told him who I was. Wondering what he had said, part of me registered and discounted a residual shadow of tension beneath the man's gesture. Because of the extraordinary nature of the circumstances that had brought me this far, I took it for granted that trust and acceptance would follow.

PLACE OF THE FOUR WARRIORS

The next day, Bryan left for the Stein Valley Gathering, a prominent annual event supporting the preservation of one of the few remaining first-growth watersheds in northern British Columbia. Wrapped up in the magic of what was unfolding in Vallican and not wanting to miss anything, I turned down the opportunity to go with him but to my surprise found I missed him intensely.

Maybe it was because of his intelligence – my erogenous zone – and his understanding of the subtle levels; I felt as if my reality-checkpoint had been removed. Independent woman as I believed myself to be, it was another intangible to add to the amorphous, churning mass of feelings. At a loss with myself, for the next twenty-four hours I lived in a kind of suspended state, barely able to complete simple daily tasks. I wanted to go back up to the Indian village and camp there with the returned tribe but it did not seem appropriate. Perhaps, I thought, I could capture something of what I was feeling on paper.

Spacious and open-plan, the living, dining and kitchen areas of the Lodge were central to its construction. I sat at the large table in the dining-area which we used mainly for art and craft projects; closing my eyes to draw from deep within myself, my hands trembled with the effort of bringing the words together. For whom or for what the poem spilled out will probably never be clear but as I stabbed the paper with the last dot of punctuation, I was brought back into myself by a sudden roar as the front door (which we never used and I thought was locked) crashed open and a powerful gust of wind banged open the hallway door and burst into the dining-area, whipped behind me and blasted open the door to the next hallway, lifted high a Mexican wall-hanging, pushed open the side-hall door and left as the front door slammed violently closed. Behind me, a gentle breeze wafted in through the open kitchen door, delicately tinkling the red glass heart chimes suspended in the window, and played around my ankles, a soft, warm breath, a fairy-touch.

Every hair on my body was standing to attention. It had all happened so fast I barely had time to catch my breath. A spirit-wind had just come calling. Bryan had explained the concept when I told him about the strange wind that played with the birch-trees after Bob's eulogy for Red Cloud and the one that had roughly chivvied me to my resignation from the Whole School. Even the touch of humour was part of the signature: having the good manners to close the front door as it left; the final playful stroke.

Was it an indication of the power of what was going on at Vallican? That was what I wanted to believe. Yet I had been thinking of Bryan. Was there more to our relationship than I appreciated?

Or was I being toyed with by forces I could not comprehend?

Where had that thought come from?

When Eva and Bob came for supper at the Lodge a couple of nights later, I was in a such a state, my mind dipping in and out of realms of romantic fantasy about dining with the Empress and the Hierophant, that I forgot the incident.

Eva loved the Lodge, saying she had never seen a place like it. While we ate, she told me how the elders still went out seasonally to gather roots and berries at the traditional places and where they were, and about plant medicines. I learned that her grandfather had been a full-blood Arrow Lakes descendant, and that even he had carried the name of Wolf.

As the evening drew to an end, part of me wanted to invite her to stay – she would be more comfortable in a house and a proper bed – but I knew my motivation was clouded and even though the whole area was traditional Arrow Lakes territory, the village was where she had come to be. It was a moonless light, the house had no external lights and the ground was uneven, so I escorted them out to Bob's car. As she was getting in, Eva mentioned her concern at what was happening in their ancestral lands, at the Medicine Wheel gathering.

"They're doin' fine with it, doin' what can be done." Bob's tone was reassuring as he bent to gently close the car door. He had said very little the whole evening and I had been careful not to look at him much. Straightening up, he turned and faced me. In the soft light falling from the open door of the Lodge I could just make out the fine features of a face as familiar to me in my dreams as in reality. "You see, when I do it, it will be truly in our tradition, with full preparation and purification. An' whole families.

"I feel sorry," he added, his voice firmer, more authoritative, "an' I can only say this from the strength of my own roots: I feel sorry for all them New Agers. Well, they are searchin', seekin', but they grasp at all the nice an' easy parts of the different ways an' mix 'em up, and when the crunch comes, they'll have no real foundation – the ground'll be swept from under them; they'll be blown away like leaves before a storm."

My mind ran with his words. What "crunch"? Did he mean a personal challenge? "Blown away, like leaves before a storm." No, he had to be speaking of the prophesised Earth Changes, which, coincidentally, my daughter Sivan called the "Grand Crunch".

My whole body was sort of tingly-buzzing; I could not find it in myself to speak and watched the car purr off into the darkness, headlights dipping and flicking as it made its way along the lower track between the trees. Nor could I move; rooted to the spot under a bright canopy of stars, I could still hear his words, echoing through my mind. He had to be talking about the apparently-imminent global changes.[5]

Nor was that the only thing within me that was jangling, seeking my attention. My own roots lay in a land thousands of miles away; my years of spiritual searching had included New Age modalities. Nor was it the first time this nerve had been touched. "Discover your origins, give life to your roots, and you can still be a beacon before civilisation." Paraphrased from a 1982 speech of Pope John Paul II, although I did not understand how to go about it, these words of the head of a branch of the religion I had been born to in this life had remained with me.

A global citizen was how I liked to think of myself; my roots not in any specific geographical location but in Mother Earth. Standing there starry-eyed under the starlight, the combined words of a holy-man and a spiritual journeyer resonating powerfully through both my mind and being, I wondered if I might one day need to return to the place of my origins to fulfil whatever it was I had come to do on the planet.

It made little sense. I was on the brink of involvement with a race with whom I had felt a

5 A representative of the Hopi spiritual leaders had recently passed through the Valley, carrying the prophetic message that in the very near future, the road of life would fork and the people wearing two hats – two-hearted, duplicitous people – would choose one fork while those wearing one hat would choose the other.

deep empathy since childhood; this had to be my destiny, it was more powerful than anything I could imagine back in England. Never in all my journeyings had I felt as much at home as I did in this part of British Columbia. Except, for a while, in Jerusalem. As for Christianity, I had searched there: dry, dogmatic, institutionalised, how could it ever be a spiritual walk to which I could give life? Or Judaism, to which I had converted after three years' study, but which my Israeli ex-husband had found wanting, as had I, eventually.

A nebulous sense of something else lurked just beyond the edge of my comprehension. Irritated, I pushed it all to the back of my mind.

The next day I was walking along to the Arrow Lakes camp at about noon when I met Bob's car slowly making its way along the overgrown, rutted track. His mother was with him; I remembered he was taking her home today and waved a farewell. As soon as she saw me, however, Eva impatiently motioned her son to stop and rolled down the window.

"I got to tell her my dream!" she admonished. " ... Last night...." She paused, turning her round face up to me. The light reflected off her glasses, then she turned away and stared straight ahead. "I dreamed I woke up an' went outside the lodge [tipi]. Sittin' on the tree-stump in the moonlight, facin' me, was a pretty young woman with long braids, wearin' a beautiful white buckskin dress.

"Her story was a sad one: she died at sixteen of a lung disease. She hadn't been allowed to marry, so's her weakness wouldn't be passed on. But she greeted me, an' told me how happy they were to see the people come back. They'd been lonely a long time, no-one come to visit them....

"She said good luck'll follow all them that come to this place with respect. Any bones found should be left to rest where they are, an' it's the priority that the bones that was taken away be brought back an' given a proper burial." She paused briefly then forcefully added: "She said no matter what, the four warriors' burial-place must remain undisturbed."

At my puzzled look, she pointed back over Bob's shoulder. "You r'member that place we stopped, when we was comin' back from that place you showed me."

The "spatial wrinkle".... Was the odd sensation there about their spirit-presence? Why four of them, together? An image of crossed spears, of shields painted with symbols came into my head. Bob's chuckle brought me back. "Hey ... how come no-one told us we was camped right on our ancestors' restin'-places?"

Any other tone and I would have felt mortified. "I thought you knew, and that that's what you wanted!"

As we all laughed, I told him about the clearing on the lower terrace where the archaeologists had camped in 1981. Part of me wished I had told them about it right away. But if they had set up camp there, I would probably not have taken Eva up as far as the four warriors' resting-place. And would the young woman in white buckskin have visited the elder's dream-state, given her these messages, if they had not been camped on the burial-ground? And why had she felt it necessary to tell it to me?

LITTLE WOLF

Arriving a couple of days later at the newly-relocated camp to find it empty of people, I spread my blanket on the ground, laid down the camera, notebook and cassette recorder I always carried with me and lay back in the cool shade of the pines to relax and contemplate the wonder of what was going on.

The two tipis at the periphery of the small clearing were an amazing, compelling presence. How often I had sat in this very place and imagined a scene like this; how incredible that it was now reality. After a while, my mind quietened; something about the place always served to slow my breathing, even the beat of my heart.

Whether I closed my eyes, dozed, I am not sure, but suddenly Manny was standing before me. Moccasins had aided his soundless approach; thin-lipped, frowning, like a snake about to strike, he silently stared down at me, thick, raven-black tendrils of hair curling over his naked, muscled chest, his hands clenching the thick leather belt of his shorts. A curl of fear uncoiled in my gut. Since shaking hands several days ago, we had not spoken; reminded of his volatile nature, I froze.

"Turn that thing off when I'm around!" he barked, indicating the recorder. "An' don't be takin' no pictures of me, neither!"

"It's not on," I said, calmly as I could. "I'm not much good at remembering to use it. And I would never do anything like that without asking your permission first."

"Why d'you go round with them machines anyway?" His strong, stubby forefinger admonished me. "What're you up to?"

Like that other time he had confronted me, I stumbled mentally: "Um ... I feel that ... what's happening here is really important ... and there should be some kind of record of it all."

He seemed to relax a little then and sat down cross-legged on the blanket directly in front of me. "A recorder, huh?" His tone was still brusque. "You got them in your religion, don't you?"

I frowned in puzzlement.

"A recordin' angel," he said impatiently. "Don't you know your own religion?"

Where was he going with this?

Suddenly he leaned forward, startling me. His face inches from mine, his tone still gruff, he lowered his voice: "You know about the Indians that wear the one eagle feather, don't you?"

A tingly rush of excitement coursed through my back, down my arms. I shook my head.

"What do you know then?" he said in a faintly-disgusted tone. Before I could respond – not that I could – he continued: "It was long ago. Them with the one eagle feather, they travelled up the east side of the Rockies and down the west." His hand mapped an imaginary trail. " ... They carried the sacred teachin's. Where people wished to learn, they'd stay an' pass 'em on, then they'd move on. If the people wouldn't listen, they'd leave 'em to their ignorance." He paused. "They were the Initiators."

Deep within, I felt a trembling thrill. Then, so quietly I had to lean forward to catch his words, he said: "You know, the Eagle Clan ... I guess you might call 'em ... angels." Suddenly, and a bit painfully, he poked two stubby fingers at the mother-of-pearl eagle I was wearing on a gold chain at my throat. "You see what you're wearin'. Nothin' happens by chance."

His two fingers poised like a ritual blessing, he leaned even closer, so our faces were a hand's breadth apart. The blackness of his eyes locked into mine; the sweet, crushed-blueberry scent of his breath mingled with my own. He frowned a little, his eyes sort of sparking as he breathed: "Who are you?"

Absolute stillness covered the forest around us. The tipis seemed to fade away; around us, the greenery shimmered as if underwater. Everything but the deep, dark pools of his eyes receded in a blur. It was as if the whole world were holding its breath; even I forgot to breathe. Then he touched my forearm with a gentle finger. "Hey," his tone reflected wonder: "you're shakin'."

Looking down from some unreal height, I observed hands and arms that belonged to me, and were trembling; savoured the scintillating life-force that seemed about to burst from my veins. "No, I'm resonating...." Even my voice did not sound real. " ... And if ever I was going to levitate, that would have been the moment." Managing a shaky grin, I noted that the world around us had slid back to near-normal. Except I was unable to move, was rooted there, still oddly distant, a humming in my ears.

"We never had no religion," Manny said. "Not like you guys invented. We don't set rules 'n' regulations, live by what another man says or believes. We each got our own way, inside. Creator's in everythin', all around everywhere. You just have to look, an' you can see. Everythin' has spirit, not just us two-leggeds, but the animals, plants, them trees...." A sweep of his arm took in the Tall Ones around us. "An' the rocks, the river. The two-leggeds were the last one to be created, we're at the bottom."

"Like Coyote." Suddenly I understood something I could not articulate.

"There you go.... We learn to walk in balance by watchin' what's happenin' round us. The lessons are there. The spirits of all these things can guide us, help us. If we let 'em ... Like I said, plants, animals, them trees, the rocks."

"I've heard people speak of devas," I offered.

He looked directly at me again and shrugged. "'S long as you know which spirits're helpin' an' which're up to mischief!" He laughed then, his weathered face creasing into a myriad lines, like an ancient manuscript. It was the first time I had seen him laugh: he looked elfin.

"Do you know?" I asked. There was a few moments' silence.

"The ancestors are always at work," he said, serious again. "Miracles are happenin' all round us, even as I speak. Walkin' the Red Road's about walkin' in balance with all things. If you know that everythin' you do's a spiritual act, your intuition'll tell you how to be 'n' act."

I could hardly believe what was happening: Manny was opening up to me in the most profound way. And there was something about him: something extremely deep and special.

"My intuition is that I'll get a photo of you sooner or later," I joked.

"Machines again," he almost snarled. "What's wrong with your memory?"

Knowing he was right, I still tried to defend myself: "Only what my society's method of education has done to me. We lost our oral tradition long ago.... But I know what you mean about the helpers. For me, the main one, I think it's Wolf, and has been as long as I can remember, only I only just realised." I couldn't bring myself to tell him about the Sky-Wolf, however, nor of learning the spirit name of Frog Mountain.

A grin lit up his lined, expressive face. "Guess you don't know my Indian name?"

I shook my head.

"Little Wolf."

A PLACE in HISTORY

A black-and-white border collie by my side, I walk in an unfamiliar landscape of softly-rounded, rolling hills dotted with sparse clusters of evergreens. A warm, gentle wind plays across the seeding long grass, a strange grey-green in colour, making it ripple like water. The cloudless sky is so pale it is barely blue.

Slowly I make my way down the side of a hill and into a small town. The streets are unpaved and dusty; the buildings made of old wood, clapboard. It might be a frontier town. Or a movie set.

Coming to a restaurant, I go inside and pass through the eating area, almost deserted, and into a long, narrow room at the back of the building. Sunlight streams in through the many windows; the people seated in small cliques around a long wooden table that almost fills the room look somehow diminutive, maybe because of the high ceiling.

Suddenly I know where I am: the scheduled meeting between the Board of Directors of the Vallican Archaeological Park Society and the manager of the Heritage Trust of British Columbia, a vital meeting being held to decide the future of the Arrow Lakes ancestral village and burial-grounds that comprise the Vallican heritage site.

But what is being discussed by the various groups is beyond me; it seems to have no relevance to the purpose of the meeting. Nearest to me, some old women are simply knitting, gossiping. As if waiting for the knife to fall....

I don't recognise a soul and don't seem able to make any impression; it's as if I am invisible. A deep frustration wells up in me. I know I have called the Arrow Lakes people to this meeting but not one Native person is present. Where are they? There seems little point in remaining. I leave through a back door and follow a narrow grassy pathway up the hill behind the building.

On the crest of the hill appears a wonderful sight: silhouetted against the sun, a prancing horse, its rider wearing a feathered headdress. The restless animal dances sidewise and rears, forelegs stroking the sky.

A strange shift of light: it is a white horse with a spotted rump; the rider's buckskin clothing is the colour of old ivory, decorated with red and blue beaded designs outlined with porcupine-quill sunbursts. A magnificent, full eagle-feather headdress trails down over the straining flanks of the horse; the shield on the rider's arm is painted with the vivid slash of a red thunderbolt.

The horse plunges, the rider cleaving to his back, a willow-supple curve. At one with each other....

Sunglasses! The ubiquitous sunglasses, the wide smile. It is Bob ... Laughing Thunder....

A tsunami of relief floods through me. Raising an arm in greeting, Bob beckons, turns his horse and disappears over the hill. In a dream-like, floating state, I follow, up and over....

Snatching away my breath, dream-come-true is stretched out below, among the pines: Bob's people, setting up camp along the edge of a small creek. Several tipis are already erect; smudges of smoke drift above newly-lit campfires. Some children and adults are dancing with linked hands in a circle. It doesn't seem odd that some people are wearing traditional Native American dress and others are in modern attire.

My heart explodes with light and joy. They have arrived! At last they have arrived! It didn't need a meeting!

Three attractive young Native women wearing blue jeans, white blouses and high-heeled shoes are coming up the hill; they ask me where the nearest washrooms are. I point them into the town and start to walk down into the camp.

Halfway down, three women elders, traditionally dressed in long, plain, tanned buckskin dresses, their grey hair immaculately braided, their wrinkled faces solemn and stern, silently acknowledge me. In respect, I incline my head. They gesture me into a large, unusually long lodge, covered in birch-bark, off to my left, which I hadn't noticed before. Somehow I know Bob and other elders are inside.

Trembling with elation and anticipation, I enter the deep darkness. Inside, a faint glow of red embers is all I can make out, so I stretch my eyes open as wide as I can to see better into the depths....

I woke up, eyes wide, not in a birch-bark lodge, but home, in bed. The sense of loss, sharp as an umbilical cut, brought tears to my eyes. All I wanted was to go back into the dream-reality. Closing my eyes, I revisited the figure on the horse, the scene, the elation, the sense of completion. What an honour, those three women elders.... What would have happened next, in the council-lodge? And why oh why had it been snatched away?

At least the first part of the dream had been true to life: the pivotal meeting about the future of the Vallican Archaeological Park, for which I had been psyching myself up for over three weeks, was tonight. But the rest of it had to be more than a processing.

The Australian aborigines call what we perceive as waking reality, the Dreamtime. Since the Native people had come into my life, it had taken on a dream-like quality, yet I felt like at last I was really living. Life had become so much richer; sometimes it seemed like I had stumbled into a great river and was being carried along through an amazing landscape; all I had to do was remember how to swim.

It was autumn; over a year had passed since we had moved to the Valley. Jobs were hard to come by in the area; sometimes I wondered about the wisdom of leaving the Whole School but I taught fitness classes and took on some landscaping at the Lodge in exchange for rent, and began to take my role on the Archaeological Park's Board of Directors more seriously. Held at the Vallican Whole, the meetings had primarily been about the potential of the site; it seemed that the Valley was plagued by people determined to set up alternative communities and it had made me uneasy that Grey Wolf's ideas were being given increasing consideration even though they did not in any way include the input of the people I felt ought to be "running the show". Whenever I suggested there was protocol to be met, my raising of the subject of the Arrow Lakes people was met with blank stares and an argument that reflected only confusion as to the ethnic affiliation of the people who had originally lived at Vallican. While the majority of the Board had eventually conceded there should be Native input, no-one could agree about whom to contact or how to go about it, even though Rick, re-elected president, and Laurie had been approached by Bob for permission to bring his mother and set up a temporary camp there the previous summer. Recalling Rick's reaction when I had first mentioned the Arrow Lakes people to him, I obtained copies of the archaeological reports.

It was soon evident that no-one on the Board had read them, for there it was, in black-and-white: a directive that the Arrow Lakes people on the Colville Reservation be notified of the discovery of their ancestral site. Somehow, it had been overlooked and a Native person from the neighbouring Kutenai people had been invited to oversee the dig. Familiarising myself thoroughly with the contents was made all the more easy by my intense personal interest and intimate knowledge of the site.

Despite the toll taken by logging and mining – the forest is mainly second-growth, the prime growth having been consumed by a great fire that raged for miles along the slopes on the west side of the river in the days of silver-mining (rumoured to have been set by prospectors) – the Slocan Valley is considered one of the most pristine habitable areas in British Columbia. Located at the confluence of two rivers, the Slocan and the Little Slocan, enclosed and protected by a ring of steep, forest-cloaked, granite-faced mountains, Vallican is known for its micro-climate, being one of the milder, drier, more sheltered areas in the Valley. Deer and coyote abound; bear and mountain lion stalk the higher levels; on the lower terraces, shy, industrious beaver scar the trees and litter the earth with their labour. The flora is rich and surprisingly diverse given such a small area: sun-loving Oregon grape thrives yards from cool, moist, secret mossy glades; shallow-rooted lodge-pole pine, at home in dry, sandy soil, grow mere yards from deep-rooted cedar, who prefer wet feet. Few of the Old Ones remain, standing tall among the many immense fungus-ridden, rotting stumps, some over eight hundred years old, cut by early loggers. As the trees came down, roads cut through the area and houses sprang up. Two hundred years of European activity have made a drastic, lasting impression; the indigenous people passed this way for over ten thousand years and all that remains are some hollows in the ground, no more than might have been left by trees blown over in a storm.

Although not the oldest in the area, the Indian village at Vallican, a permanent winter settlement, is the largest and most diverse known to still exist in British Columbia, the majority having been lost to development or inundation. First noted in 1959 as a chance discovery by a local Q.C., who lobbied successfully to have it officially recognized in 1969, the site was practically forgotten until 1980 when bulldozers turned up human remains while attempting to push a road through that part of the subdivision. It was realised that the site was far more extensive than previously thought, but only due to the efforts of several concerned individuals was construction halted and archaeological investigation commissioned. Evidence of almost three thousand years of occupation and a wide variety of type of dwelling resulted in pressure to have the land set aside as a heritage site: the Vallican Archaeological Park. Even so, the government was more or less embarrassed into purchasing the site, following as it did on the heels of setting aside in 1983 the vast expanse of the Valhalla Provincial Park, which borders the Slocan Valley. In 1984, a group of interested local people voluntarily set up the Vallican Archaeological Park Society, their mandate being the protection and preservation of the site, but all that could happen until the land was purchased were meetings, a little fund-raising and a lot of speculation.

Reluctant to comply with a purchase order, the owner of the property, a real estate agent (the father of the young waitress I had met on my first visit to the Valley), insisted he would only sell "over his dead body". I learned that at about the time I relocated to Vallican he was confronted with imminent bankruptcy, which forced him to release the land.

How careful we must be with our words: bankruptcy could be interpreted as death of the financial body.

Some four months after I had become a member of the Board of Directors, British Columbia Heritage Trust, a branch of the Ministry of Housing, Recreation and Culture, had notified the Board that it had finally completed acquisition of the site, to be "held in trust for the people of British Columbia", and scheduled an autumn meeting to discuss a management and development plan.

Despite the general excitement and enthusiasm about this great step forward, the Board had still not been able to agree about which Native people to contact, so at the last minute I took things into my own hands and phoned Bob's mother. To my surprise, Eva seemed disinterested; she said she had no idea where her son was but would see what she could do. Hearing nothing more, by the night before the meeting I had worked myself up into a frantic state. Not knowing if any Arrow Lakes descendant would turn up, I gathered together every piece of documentation I could lay my hands on with the aim of representing with at least some scientific credibility the people I thought ought to have first say in any plan for their ancestral site.

Having already having proved itself a thorn in the side of government, the Arrow Lakes Indian village would soon begin to live up to the Sinixt word for the Valley: Slo'heen – "pierced in the head". The West Kootenays may have been painfully devoid of a living Native presence, but I was becoming aware there was a presence, unseen and powerful. Nor was it only my experience, and while I felt a profound peace at the site, others more sensitive than I found otherwise.

There had been the physiotherapist, of French origins, whom I had met at Andre and Marilyn's, the couple who were starting up the wilderness school. Seeking land in the area with the intention of beginning a communal venture, he had been intrigued by my description of Vallican and insisted on coming to lunch then setting off to explore, explicitly on his own, heading down the riverside towards the Indian village. In less than twenty minutes he was back, white-faced and agitated: "Zere is a great, a powerful presence in zere! I cannot stand it! It is not good, nor is it evil ... but it is too strong for me!" He left immediately and never came back.

On a separate occasion, a psychic came back from walking through the site, pale and talking of "the many presences among the trees" and maintaining she could never live near there. "Your soul knows things your mind will never know," she said as she left.

Enigmatic words. Perhaps, I had thought, I was more closely connected to the site, which was why I was not negatively affected.

Fools rush in....

VOICE OF THE ELDERS

The last part of the powerful dream – the three woman elders, the council lodge – haunted me through what was turning into one of the longest days of my life. So wound up was I that just before Bryan and I left to attend the meeting, I rowed fiercely with him. He was sure everything would work out as it was meant to, which seemed to me dangerously complacent. We had to make it happen, if need be. Part of me did not even want him to come, perhaps because I did not know how much of a fool I might make of myself.

By the time we arrived at the Sandman Inn in Castlegar, where the meeting was to be held, I was a bundle of nerves. As soon as we had parked, I raced ahead of my so-called partner and burst into the hotel, a dramatic entrance sort of like a Hollywood gun-slinger; only I was armed with files and folders, my head loaded with facts and figures.

The first person I saw was Bob, and if my customary inner reaction was sparked, I was already in such a state I could not have separated it from the rest of my raw emotionality. He was sitting on a couch opposite the entrance, arms folded across his chest, talking with a man in a suit beside him whom I assumed to be the B.C. Heritage Trust's manager. Overwhelmed with relief, I took in the red shirt Bob was wearing, and the blue-and-red baseball cap. Arrow Lakes' colours. Next to the two men sat the executive member of the Heritage Trust who had carried the news of this meeting to the Society, a history lecturer at Selkirk College in Castlegar. On another couch sat Manny, wearing a pale shirt and denims, darkly-glowering as ever.

The two dark-skinned men, their long, sleek black hair bound in neat braids, looked decidedly out-of-place in the bland, contemporary setting. Both got up as I approached; only in hindsight did I appreciate their gentlemanly behaviour. Bob shook my hand and to my surprise gave me a brief hug. I caught a faint, deliciously-evocative scent of wood-smoke. "Hey there!" he smiled. "Good to see you!"

A huge weight had been lifted from my shoulders; I felt light-headed. "Oh, it is so good to see you here!" Turning to Manny, I added: "I'm so glad you came." Feeling like I could hug everyone in the lobby, the hotel, the world, I hugged him for the first time. He seemed to relax a little and grimaced something like a smile.

Watching the faces of the rest of the Board members as they arrived, I could not help feeling glee at some of the surprised expressions. When everyone was present, the Trust manager led the way through the hotel to the meeting-room. Small and featureless, it was dominated by a long, narrow table; with a rattling and scraping of chairs, we squeezed in. Night of the long table, I thought, noting we were twelve in number. Only later did I realise how uncannily similar it had been to the room and table in my dream.

Sitting next to each other at the head of the table, Bob and Manny beside them, the two Trust representatives introduced themselves. Then Bob got up and, speaking briefly but eloquently, introduced himself and Manny, related his lineage and claimed the Arrow Lakes' ancestral relationship with the heritage site at Vallican. He produced two envelopes. "I'm present only as a voice for the elders, who've sent letters to be delivered by hand. One's from my mother, Eva; the other's from John, Arrow Lakes elder and hereditary chief." He read them out; both missives stated that the priority was the location and reburial of the ancestors' remains, and requested input into any plans for their ancestral village.

Bob put the letters down on the table in front of the Trust manager; neither he nor the executive said anything or made a move to pick them up. I was appalled. At least they could have the manners to acknowledge their receipt; these were historically significant papers, of profound relevance. I had never imagined the Arrow Lakes people might still have a hereditary chief.

An embarrassing silence followed, dragging on until several of the Board hesitantly began to mutter conjectures as to the whereabouts of the ancestral remains. From the opposite end of the table I studied the Trust manager's thin-lipped silence. Why was he saying nothing? In his position he must know; his silence was insulting.

A major lesson about provincial government decision-making was waiting for me in the wings. The provincial seat of B.C. government lies in Victoria on Vancouver Island, hundreds of miles from the Kootenay region, and decisions are often made on paper by people who have never seen the area. It would not be the first nor the last time that planning-at-a-distance would blow up in many faces.

Rick suddenly spoke up: "It was the Kutenai and Shushwap Nations who were originally invited to oversee the archaeological dig, because we did not know who to contact."

Irritated by the politicising, I said: "The archaeologist Gordon Mohs, who conducted the archaeological sampling in 1981, knew who to contact. His report states quite unequivocally that the people indigenous to the area are the Arrow Lakes people and that they are not extinct, but number approximately two hundred and fifty, most of whom are living on the Colville Reservation in Washington State." I let this information – almost a direct quote – sink in for several seconds, then added: "I visited the Museum of Anthropology at the University of British Columbia in Vancouver in the summer, thinking I would get on the track of the ancestral remains, but there was no record of any from Vallican."

After a sidewise glance at the Trust manager, Rick said, "The archaeologist should be contacted for this information."

Not one person there, with the possible exception of the Heritage Trust manager, had any idea of the sensitive, complicated nature of what we were getting involved in: the politics of bones.

After a short silence, the Trust manager backtracked, suggesting that the rest of us introduce ourselves and state our reasons for being there. At the time, I interpreted this as politeness; later I would wonder whether it was because he wanted to size us all up. What followed made me realise how little I knew about my fellow Board-members.

First to speak was Nellie, a lively, white-haired, likeable grandmother with sparkling clear blue eyes and round apple-rosy cheeks: "I wanted to come here and sing a song tonight, but I just can't do it now." (Her people, the Doukhobors so highly spoken of by Bob, are renowned for their angel-voiced choirs and heart-rending spiritual songs.) "But you know," she added proudly, "we found some hollows on our property in Vallican and they were designated as ancient food-caches. They're still intact.... I've loved the Indians since childhood, you know." Smiling shyly, she leaned over the table and pinched Bob. "Just to make sure you're real!" she giggled.

Bob smiled his gentle smile. Forgetting how I had once nearly done the same thing, I thought it might have been more polite if she had made the reality-check on herself.

A proud note in his voice, Rick announced: "I've been the first and only president of the Society since its inception in 1984. And I was personally involved with the dig in 1981.... The site must be preserved. There's a lot of work ahead, especially as it is a spiritual place."

It was the first time I had heard him express such a sentiment.

"It's been purchased by the Province for the people of this province," he continued. "There have been no precedents[6] for anything like this."

"I'm acting secretary of the Society," said Laurie. "And I'm interested as a neighbour of the site."

It had come round the table to my turn. All I could think to say was what lay in my heart: "The most important thing is the wishes of the Arrow Lakes people."

Sitting beside me, Bryan followed with an echo of another time not so long ago: "I'm with her." I thought that was it but then he opened up. An articulate speaker, he gave the table a lecture about Native rights. Neither the place nor the time, I thought, uselessly trying to distance myself from him; this would only put the wind up certain people.

Another Board member, Ross, said: "I'm here to see what happens."

I could not understand how he could be so nonchalant.

George, a retired local, liberal-minded, and with a keen interest in history (one of few on the Board for whom I had a lot of respect), said: "I am for preservation. Whatever that means. And personal interest."

Finally Paul, another neighbour of the site and perhaps the only Board member besides myself sensitive to the Native side of the story said some words, but spoke so quietly I was unable to hear him.

Then to my surprise, the usually-taciturn Manny stood up and began to recount his lineage – half Arrow Lakes and half Flathead – and speak of his background, but since Rick and Laurie started talking to each other at the same time, I could barely hear what he was saying except something about a Pendosy family, the wax museum in Kelowna, the museum in Summerland in the Okanagan and the name Joe Adolf. "I was raised back in the mountains. Not used to talkin'," he ended. "The elders don't talk much either."

The subtlety was lost on the two men who were still muttering, heads together. Their bad manners disgusted me.

As impersonal and remote as the institution he represented, the Trust manager leaned forward and addressed the table: "What Victoria wants is for a local group to take initiative and responsibilities."

Victoria? He sounded as if the historical queen herself had given him a directive; the voice of his elder. Nor was he saying anything we did not know. Society meetings had produced a few ideas and no real direction. Talk revolved for some time around the issue of funding and the relationship between the Society and the Trust.

"Let's move slowly," said Laurie. "This is a major responsibility. We need a conceptualisation. We've a range of visions: there's a four-fold plan we've discussed, with heritage, archaeology, education, ecology...."

---

6 Precedent-setting president!

These were some of Grey Wolf's suggestions. It struck me that the old man was strangely absent; I knew he was disgruntled by my pairing-up with Bryan and my continual emphasis on the input of the Arrow Lakes people, but he certainly could not have known the "Colville people" would be here. The more I thought about it, the more weird was his absence.

Paul spoke up: "Most important of all, is to bring in the Native people!"

Surprised by his outspokenness and grateful to hear another voice like my own (I had been feeling they were being rudely marginalised; no-one had addressed the elders' request for input), I looked at him anew. Not a tall man, he was soft-spoken, kindly, but the strength of his features hinted at hidden reserves. About my age, his hair was prematurely silver-grey and flowed thickly down to his shoulders. An intriguing mix of hippy and patriarch.

Almost immediately, Rick rejoined: "It's an opportunity to redress some wrongs."

We all fell silent at the implication, and I began to wonder if I should revise my previous assessment of the man.

The government representative sat stony-faced as the silence lengthened, then Bob's soft drawl rolled clearly through the room: "We're here to follow the ways of the elders; it's foolish to follow our own simple ideas. I'm here only as a voice of the elders; if they was here, I'd be sittin'" (he pointed at the corner behind him) "over there somewheres in the background. And they can't be here, because three elders died and the funeral is tomorrow."

A cold finger traced down my spine. The three Native women elders in my dream ... was there a connection?

"But I have letters, as I told you," Bob continued. "Maybe you should file 'em." He picked them up again and held them out to the Trust manager, who ignored him. He then offered them to the Trust executive, who took them and, without looking at them, slid them across the table to Laurie. It was like a game of "hot potato".

"As for the ceremony, for reburial," Bob resumed. "In the spring, we reckon. You have our agreement: bring your cameras, your tape-recorders. We're aware of the need for retention of culture. You'll be witnessing a twenty-five-hundred-year-old heritage, the miracle of what the Native people have to offer...."

Although no-one blinked an eyelid, I knew that the idea of a reburial ceremony on the site was new to most of the people there.

"I'm not a medicine man," he was continuing. "I'm a man on a spiritual journey." (I recalled a night in Vernon, fourteen months ago.) "I'm not tryin' to teach," he added. "But if you want to, watch, listen an' learn. My mother has praised the government for savin' the site. You did find somethin' sacred, so you are part human!" Laughing aloud, he winked directly at me. A warm feeling flooded my body.

Nellie squeezed his arm. "I have to feel whether you're a ghost or real. Good Indians need a chance to come out."

The patronising remark made me squirm but no-one else seemed bothered, not even Bob.

"We finally got some education," he said with a shrug. "Be good maybe to have part of the village rebuilt. Be educational to rebuild it the old way, over a long period, say twenty years, so the benefit is spread over an' shared by many. Volunteer, do it by hand, like children learnin' the old ways. When work becomes play, then you're livin', not just survivin'." He paused and chuckled. "We're not out here to scalp you. We'll work with you. We have our language, our culture. We're human beings."

"My grandfather was a trapper through the mountains and valleys of the Slocan area," said Nellie. "He cured my grandma of pertussis with Native medicine. Everyone has to participate with respect; there should be no desecration."

"Perhaps small groups could be taken on interpretive tours through the village for educational purposes," said the Trust executive.

"But what about funding?" asked Laurie.

The Heritage Trust manager had been conspicuously silent throughout. He seemed restless, anxious to draw the meeting to an end. "There are a lot of issues: education, an interpretation centre, a brochure or information package, the involvement of the business community.... The role of the Society will be to oversee day-to-day management of the site. Funds will be provided by the Trust. I propose a second meeting, in midwinter. I'll be hiring a consultant to work over the winter."

Brusque and impersonal, he seemed to have totally ignored the input of the two Native men and most of what had been said. An interpretation centre? Brochures? Involvement of the business community? I was staggered. Perhaps he realised how he had come across; at the last moment he conceded the possibility of a reburial in the spring.

Looking back, I doubt he would have said as much if he had any idea of what that might mean in the grander scheme.

Loudly scraping back his chair, the Trust manager stood up, shook hands with Bob and Manny and suggested they become honorary, constitutional, active paid members of the Society, forking out the ten dollars to accomplish this. It seemed a bizarre offer and it was clear, as they turned it down, that the two Native men couldn't have cared less. In fact, Bob was adamant he would not become a member.

As we made our way back to the lobby, I hung back, hoping to get some idea of what would happen next from Bob. At the door, he took me aside and shook my hand. "If it wasn't for you, I wouldn't be here."

"If it wasn't for you, I wouldn't be here, either!" I laughed. I had a feeling he was trying to shield my role in his and Manny's presence but I really didn't care who knew.

Strangely enough, the question of how the Lakes people had come to know about the meeting was later raised at a Society meeting, despite my having often spoken of my connection to them and meeting them at the Sandman with such obvious familiarity. It was not the first or the last time that what I had to say would go unheeded, exacerbating what was already a potentially explosive situation. Was it simply because I am a woman? A previous Board-member had apparently regarded me as an "English upstart who thought she could just walk in and take over", although I felt I had kept a low profile and it certainly never seemed that my words had much sway.

"Wonderful, the way the Creator works." Bob smiled and turned away.

At the last moment, as we stood on the steps of the building, I remembered. Bob was talking with Bryan; Manny stood nearby. "Those three elders," I asked him, "the ones whose funeral is tomorrow, were they women?"

"Well, yeah ... they were. All women...." He looked at me suspiciously.

Hardly able to breathe, I shook my head. "I had a dream...." I could not go on; his expression was impassive, like a wall, and I could not confide my amazing dream in the face of such seeming distrust.

But for me, the connection was made, was real. What had they known, those three women elders, in life, in death? From the place of spirit, had they spoken to my dream-time spirit? In their timelessness, clothed in their tradition, had they touched upon my dream-state?

Only in hindsight did I perceive that being beckoned to enter into the council-lodge implied my impending direct participation in the affairs of their people.

EAGLE FLIES HIGH; FLIES ALONE

Breaking into the peace of early morning, the phone rang, shrill and insistent. Barely had I picked up the receiver when Grey Wolf's voice blasted out: "Celia, there is something I simply have to say to you. I just can't keep it in. You have to see what is happening....

"You are being used. You are being used as a buffer, as a middle-person, as ... as a go-between. You're being used by that bunch from Colville, that wild bunch of hopheads! I laughed about them being part of the Free Trade deal,[7] but it's not amusing. There were four cultures here and it does not belong to them, or anyone else. That land does not belong to anyone."

Having just heard about his resignation from the Board and unaware of all the vested interests in the area, I mentally dismissed his words as prejudiced, narrow-minded rubbish. Before I could respond, however, he ploughed on: "And they bring bad things onto the land. They bring bad things into this country with them. They bring that dope. And peyote...."

Bob had told me he was a minister of the Native American Church.[8] It made no difference to me; much like him, I believe each person should have the freedom to choose his or her Path.

"And when I asked permission," Grey Wolf ranted on, "when I asked at that meeting if we could have the Fall Gathering at the Vallican site, they shrug their shoulders and hum and haw and worry about beer-bottles, when they know that no drugs or alcohol.... But oh yes, when that bunch of, of dope-smugglers from Colville show up, they're greeted with smiles, and with open arms.... Well, I only hope that when they are there, the Mounties will be there too, and I hope they are busted and the whole Board of Directors of that Vallican Park Society are busted with them!"

His voice had grown increasingly hoarse throughout his diatribe (probably the only tribe he would ever belong to, I thought, remembering Princess and her tirade: his dire-tribe) and rasped to a climax: "You could have had Nirvana, but you've chosen reincarnation!"

As he no doubt intended, the grand finale intrigued me. A sly and manipulative old fellow, he knew my weaknesses. In a perfectly normal voice, he added: "We are still friends, are we not, Celia? I just had to speak out."

I felt sorry for him. He had failed to take over the Medicine Wheel gathering and now the chance of his "New Nation" happening at Vallican was slipping away.

"To each his own," I responded, a shrug evident in my tone.

Soon after, he moved to a small community near Nelson called Blewett. The self-styled old show-man had indeed "blown it", I thought when I heard. If only he had not been so set against Bob and the Arrow Lakes people; I could think of nothing more important, more vital, more of a privilege, than to be involved in the return of a Nation of the Old Order. Even my relationship with Bryan played second string to this miracle.

---

7 North American Free Trade Agreement. At the time, 1988, in the works; implemented in 1994.

8 In 1989, the courts in Salem, Oregon, upheld the ceremonial use of peyote by the Native American Church, a right protected by the U.S. constitution.

That a powerful if volatile connection existed between Bryan and me was beyond doubt; the intensity of it cleaved me to White Eagle, despite inner whisperings of caution, despite my deep-running feelings for Laughing Thunder. Bryan had set up his workshop on the bench of land below the Lodge, certain that the ambiance of the place and the equation of our relationship was an indication of the role we would take on as a couple. And it was flattering to learn I would be involved in conducting ceremonies to honour the turning of the seasons, and eventually, as he had been instructed by his Master when he found the right partner, setting up the next Order of the esoteric school with him.

Against my better judgement – feeling that those who were meant to find it, would – I agreed that the discrete entrance to the property should be marked. Remembering a dream, a rider on a rearing horse, I suggested a red thunderbolt-sign. Bryan painted it, and as a supportive gesture I walked the quarter-mile from the Lodge to the road with him and waited while he ritually placed and dedicated the distinctive sign. "Now watch what happens," he said.

Half-expecting people to come streaming along the driveway like children called by the Pied Piper, on the way back I glanced over my shoulder a couple of times but the track remained empty, the forest silent. Back at the Lodge, busy in the kitchen, I forgot his words.

Somehow I missed the gradual darkening; a sudden simultaneous loud crack and flash of searing light and dramatic roll of thunder that made the floor tremble almost took me out of my skin. Long-time lover of storms, I dropped what I was doing and ran outside, and stood on the grass in my bare feet, my body tingling. The next blinding flash and crashing, growling rumble almost overwhelmed me. Above, an eerie milky-yellow-greyness swirled and uncurled. Not even the storm I "called" at Vernon had exposed itself to me so dramatically, so nakedly.

For long, breathless moments, that was all there was in the world: the weird dance of clouds like the unfolding of a deranged lotus-flower. There was no more lightning, or thunder. Then with a mighty sweep of wind that whipped the treetops, the clouds infolded and there fell a deluge of great, heavy, cold drops which soaked me immediately. The weird movement ceased; relieved of its burden, the storm-cloud stilled into a mere smudge. The rain eased, and stopped. It was all over, in minutes. I found I was shivering violently, energy depleted, exhilaration gone.

I looked for Bryan, but he was nowhere to be found. By the time he reappeared, the strange sense of unease I was feeling was not eased by his shrug, the triumphant little smile playing at his lips, when I sardonically complimented the "happening".

Had he done something to draw a storm, create one? Had I been part of whatever he had done, albeit unknowingly? Part of me did not want to know. If there had been some kind of uncanny manipulation of energy, I did not want any part of it. Strangely enough, I did not feel that way about Bob's psychic abilities. If that was what this was about.

But I was involved in something bigger than my own wishes and imaginings, something that would not go away just because I refused to think about it. And I was willing enough to fall under the spell of the glamour of all the "nice" parts, of which Bob had once warned.

As if to reassure me, in a small but touching ceremony, Bryan endowed me with an eagle feather. This I knew to be a great honour: eagle medicine symbolises connection to the Creator and implies the ability to live in the realms of spirit while remaining connected to the earth. Used by medicine men for hundreds of years as a sacred healing tool, an eagle feather is normally only bestowed on a person who, through hard work and self-discipline, has come to trust in the workings of the Great Spirit and realised their personal power.

I could live with that, I thought. It did not matter to me that the long, narrow flight feather was a little tattered or that the bird had been found dead by the roadside, for the original wing had been given Bryan by a highly-respected coastal Native elder-advisor who had been awarded an OBE by Canadian ex-premier Pierre Trudeau for her work on cultural preservation. I felt as if I had been recognised, or invested with a certain power.

The river I was caught up in was growing stronger, swifter, carrying me along in a powerful, irresistible grip.

Soon after, in the autumn, Bryan took me to meet Grandmother Dorothy at her home in Surrey, near Vancouver. A heavy-set woman in her eighties, almost blind, the formidable elder barely acknowledged me and immediately ordered Bryan to drive her to a meeting of the Muquabeak Cultural Society. Despite being honorary chairman, nomadic Bryan had not mentioned any meeting; when I asked him if the Grandmother had "called" him, I only got one of his little shrugs and enigmatic smiles. Once there, I felt awkward – the only other non-Native – and sat at the back while some eight or nine Native people discussed the direction their organisation should take.

Most of the session was taken up by a stunning, charismatic Native woman who made a detailed presentation of her research into alcoholism among Native Americans and then dramatically announced her resignation; her life was taking a major change in direction. Placed beside her at dinner, where as a vegetarian I learned that taking just one mouthful of the deer-meat offered by a Native American host is simple good manners, I fell into conversation with Pinishi and told her about what was happening at the Arrow Lakes ancestral village. She asked how I had become involved and I found myself confiding the vision of Sky-Wolf and how I learned the spirit-name of Frog Mountain. Bryan was the only other person who knew of this private, precious connection; even as I related it, I wondered why I was telling her.

Pinishi's eyes never left mine throughout my little tale. Then she suddenly stood up and without a word, left the table and the room. I wondered if I had offended her or come across a little flaky. She was gone so long I thought she must have left, but about fifteen minutes later she came back, carrying a bulky brown envelope which she thrust into my hands. "This is all my research. And my ideas. You might have need of this."

"Why are you doing this?" I asked, simultaneously thrilled and mystified. There was a short silence.

Then she whispered: "My Indian name, it is White Wolf." She sighed. "It is not often that something like this happens."

I shivered. It was an amazing thread of connection. Had our paths magically crossed to share purpose? This profound giveaway, did it mean she "saw" that I had a part to play in the healing of the Native people? Was that what Vallican was about, at least in part?

I was so thrilled, I could not speak. No-one seemed to have noticed our brief, intense interchange and I was relieved that I was left to digest it. Bob had spoken of helping people recover from addictions at a place like he envisioned at Vallican. Was I being provided with the material to be a part of this vision? I could not imagine anything finer to do with my life; after years – a lifetime – of searching, I was on the threshold of my true destiny: the reason I had come to earth in a white skin, this time round.

As if that were not enough, Pinishi, who worked as a presenter on the Native co-op radio station that broadcasts from Gastown in Vancouver, then got on the phone, pulled some strings and booked me into an evening slot to speak about the Arrow Lakes Band's ancestral site and make a plea for help from concerned parties. Carried by the floodtide of her energy, the entire group crammed into a couple of cars, and even though she had difficulty in getting about, Grandmother Dorothy came too.

It was a live broadcast; no script, no prompting. I was beyond nerves. Sitting alone in a little booth with earphones clamped over my head and a microphone in front of my face seemed unreal, yet inevitable. From deep within me spilled a surprising torrent of words, none of which I could later recall. Reeling from the pace of events and the thought that this might be how things would be from now on – Bob had intimated that there would be a great deal of interest in what would unfold at Vallican – when it was over I dazedly followed the others outside.

Grandmother Dorothy, sitting in the passenger-seat of one of the cars, called me over. Giving me a painful poke in the arm, she brusquely said: "And you, you get on and write that book!"

Her parting shot, and all she ever said to me; I never saw her again. The idea of there ever being a book had not occurred to me; in fact, it would be over six years before I would begin to write it down but even now, I can feel that sharp prod and imagine a grimace of acknowledgement on her stern face.

At that moment, did she sow in me a seed-idea? What did she see, down the line? It took me long enough to begin to follow the elder's instruction, even though Bob had already made it clear that when an elder tells you to do something, you do it without question, and immediately.

The season turned; my experience deepened. Bryan opened up to me the world of theosophy, and the power of affirmation, right thought and action; ten years of esoteric training were poured into me over six months and like a sponge, I soaked it up. As with Bob, it was not like learning so much as "re-collecting". Then, in midwinter, a pivotal point was reached.

While intimately joined and in meditation with Bryan, I found myself sort of clinging to him and in my mind's eye looking down over his shoulder. Below us, the planet was receding, a deep blue and swirling-white globe. Feeling neither fear nor surprise, only a vague sense of wonder, I let it happen, then the thought "Too high!" entered my detached mind and I found I had the conscious control to bring us back down and below the cloud-cover. We "floated" in above the Americas.

The continent was barely recognisable. North America was a strange, skinny shape: the west coast seemed to have shrunk back to the Rockies and the Atlantic bulged into the mid-West, while the rest of the east coast was an unfamiliar contour. South America was slender: most of Brazil was gone, along with Argentina and Chile. The two land-masses were not even connected.

Fascinated, I mentally directed our strange little two-as-one spaceship over the Atlantic to "take a look" at what was happening in Europe, and indeed sped across a blurry, steely-grey, serrated mass to find Spain almost totally gone, along with part of Morocco. The mouth of the Mediterranean gaped wide; somehow I knew it had been cleansed with a mighty sweep of the greater waters.

There was no sense of time past or future; only a feeling of deep peace and contentment, filling my being: at last, Mother Earth had been cleansed. A sudden curiosity directed my attention towards northern Europe but at that moment Bryan moved and I was reeled back in fast as a bungy-jumper – a painful, ripping sort of experience – and lost it all.

I had no idea what had happened, but felt simultaneously awed, cheated and bruised. "You shouldn't have moved!" I accused, barely knowing what I was talking about. Some minutes passed before I felt able to tell Bryan of my experience.

He gasped. "But it was me who was supposed to have it!"

When I asked what on earth he was talking about, he explained "it" was the astral journey he had been attempting to attain, through the level of Tantric congress we were apparently able to reach together, the sum of the equation of his abilities and my receptiveness. Having only recently learned about the concept and unaware he had been practising with me, I felt upset and somehow used.

It did not spoil the experience, however, which still haunts me. Was this how things had once looked? Or had I been enabled a glimpse of the planet on the other side of the prophesised Earth Changes? Such massive changes could only come about in the wake of tremendous destruction, a disturbing thought but for the enormous sense of well-being accompanying the vision. Or was it a potential rather than an actual future? My understanding was that nothing prophesised is written in stone; that such visions point to the likely outcome if things continue as they are. Why had I been granted this Sight? To somehow act in mitigation of such drastic changes? Did that not seem totally arrogant?

Although for the most part our belief-systems meshed well, once I got over my awe of White Eagle and mundane expectations raised their predictable heads, our personalities began to clash. Once after he became particularly angry, I tried to calm him and placed my hand on his arm. He admitted to what he called the dragon in his belly and did quieten, fairly swiftly, while I gradually became colder until my teeth were chattering and I had to lie down wrapped in blankets and cuddling two hot-water bottles. Still I shivered, and for the rest of the day felt peculiarly emptied and weak. Something was deeply wrong in our relationship, I began to admit to myself; it seemed somehow out of balance.

Later, Lynne told me that she felt Bryan was not fully aware of the extent of his psychic strength and that his draining of my energy had been an unconscious act. It sounded like something out of the Dennis Wheatley books that had fascinated me during my teenage years; I had never imagined such things might happen to me. Woken to a certain aspect of myself, over the following years I would become increasingly aware of my sensitivity to the interplay of subtle energies between people, whether close or strangers. A wonderful tool to aid understanding of human dynamics, I am still learning how to cope with it.

There seemed to be no indication that Bryan and I would overcome what he termed our polarised stance; not long after, our relationship flared out of control, searing itself beyond repair. He returned to the coast.

Although I still felt deeply for him, a sense of lightness filled the space left by his departure. No doubt he felt the same as he drove away from an area that seemed to invite confrontation – something to do with the narrow valley, the high mountains, energies bouncing back and forth.

And to be completely honest, there was still a part of me that felt I had accepted second-best. White Wolf may have joined with White Eagle, but it was the memory of a graphic, tattooed eagle with widespread wings that beat at my doorway to my heart; a chuckling roll of thunder that echoed through my mind.

KEEPERS OF THE ORDER OF LIFE

The end of winter heralded new growth on levels political as well as personal. Barely had Bryan left when the VAPS Board of Directors received a letter from the archaeologist who had overseen the dig in 1981. Aware from the record that six burials had been exhumed: three adults, two infants and a foetus, we learned that erosion had exposed two of the burials, which had been further disturbed by relic-hunters. Scientific analysis had demonstrated that these people had subsisted mainly on salmon. Once catalogued, the remains had been shipped to the B.C. Provincial Museum in Victoria, where they were stored in a basement, "awaiting further investigation".

In his letter, Gordon Mohs stressed that the exhumation had prevented a highway going through the site and led to the concept of a park to protect the area. Apparently "international jurisdiction" had prevented contact with the people of the Colville Reservation, but the archaeologist felt their present involvement would not be a problem. Almost as a postscript, he mentioned that the issue of reburial had been raised that same year – 1981 – and agreed to by heritage representatives at the time, but no-one had come forward.

While informative, in my opinion the letter exposed a lack of true consideration by those heritage representatives, and I wondered how the Lakes people would feel when they found out that fragments of sacred remains had been destroyed to prove that the Salmon People ate salmon. As for the 1981 reburial possibility, only the descendants would care what happened to ancestral remains. The Lakes people had never been informed; that the Kutenai who oversaw the dig had not truly cared seemed to me proof positive that they were not directly connected to the area.

Unaware of all the vested political interests, to me it all seemed straightforward.

Since convening with the Heritage Trust representatives, the Board had decided to hold meetings in the Vallican Heritage Hall, the original one-roomed community schoolhouse. Built of red-painted shakes and now a listed heritage building, it was used for a variety of community functions. As it happened, the next meeting was scheduled to take place during days of heavy snowfall, and I worried whether Bob, or any Lakes person, might simply not bother to attend, given their disinterest in belonging to the Society and the terrible weather conditions. In typical laid-back Slocan style, the locals drifted in and caught up for a while before sitting around the table. Opening procedures were gone through; reading of minutes; discussion of old business.... We were at business at hand and I was on the edge of my chair, when I heard the outer doors open. Accompanied by a blast of icy wind, brushing snow from their shoulders, Bob and Manny walked into the hall to an enthusiastic welcome from everyone there except myself, who was too overcome for words.

Repeatedly throughout that winter, Bob and Manny would turn up for meetings with the same uncanny sense of timing: they knew the scheduled starting-time yet consistently turned up the moment "business at hand" was reached. Despite occasional disparaging remarks by those who did not appreciate it, it was a demonstration of the instinctive nature of "Indian time": being in the right place at the right time.

From these experiences I began to appreciate the uselessness, indeed danger, of being "in a hurry". Seeming hold-ups, even simple things such as a farm vehicle on the road creating a snail's pace when I need to be in a certain place at a certain time, or being unable to get hold of a certain individual when I think I should, are signs that a situation or idea still needs time to come to fruition. To appreciate the natural flow of energy and learn to move with it, rather than push it, brings not only inner peace but allows for the best, the truest outcome.

Much of those early meetings passed in a blur. It seemed to me that Laughing Thunder, red bandanna around his Taurean throat, radiated an inner glow; wherever the two Native men sat became the centre-point. Something about their calm presence seemed to affect everyone in the room, which itself seemed filled with a soft, otherwordly light.

Word about the Native involvement spread swiftly and more local people began to take an active interest. We seemed to be gradually forging a working bond between the two cultures, sharing the vision of what was possible at the site and how to go about it.

"The elders' primary concern is the reburial, an' we have to keep their thoughts in our minds," Bob told us one snowy night. We were all wrapped up warmly; the little hall could barely cope with below-freezing temperatures. "We're workin' for the sake of the children. It's necessary to forge ahead an' work on a variety of things at once, so there will be somethin' to look at, no laggin' behind. That's the function of this Society, an' it must fulfil its responsibilities.

"As for the name of the place, that could change with the final proposal. Any name is alright, so long as it's in keepin' with the purpose; we can change it as we decide what we'll do. This is an experimental model. It can an' should be educational; if that's the way it will benefit more people, then we'll go that way.... The ultimate goal is to find an' fence off all the local burial-grounds. In this way, the Society could grow. It will oversee all of this. We must leave the whole thing open. It could lead to many good things."

As I made note of the concepts – experimental, experiential, educational – I was thinking about what Bob had told me of his personal life-journey and his quest for his grandfather's resting-place, the place his own bones would eventually be laid to rest, and suddenly realised the implications: it wasn't only about his grandfather, himself, the return of his people to their ancestral lands. It would involve engendering respect: for different peoples; for the land; for the sacredness of life. Something far, far greater than met our limited understanding was unfolding here.

Manny interjected: "'S difficult to know how to go about workin' with the Society in Canada. Must respect the law, even if to an Indian there really are no borders."

"Native Americans from the States have no rights in Canada," I explained from newly-acquired knowledge. "Set up in 1794, the Jay Treaty operates as a one-way street: a Canadian Native person has the right to live and work in the States, but not vice versa."

A chorus of women's voices offered to marry both men at that moment, to give them rights in Canada. I could not join in the laughter; not knowing Bob's exact present marital status, it hit too close to the bone. Various people expressed their desire to meet with the Arrow Lakes elders.

Bob shrugged. "It's hard to get them all together. Usually the only reason's for a funeral, which is what this burial is. If you take care of the burial, good things will follow. If you do something good, then something good will return.... There'll be the sunrise reburial ceremony, the women'll have the food prepared, then after an hour or two, they'll eat, an' exchange gifts.

"One of the main families that survived is the Marchands. In this family alone there's over fifty members. When the time comes closer, I'll put something in the papers; it'll be an intertribal event. All the old folks'll come, an' half their children'll follow to see what's goin' on!"

"I saw the name Marchand on art-work from the Okanagan Reserve," I said.

"There's three Marchand families, not related," Bob explained. "Some're truly of French descent."

The possibility of the next Victoria Day weekend (late May) as being suitable for the ceremony was raised. Some people were concerned that it might compete with other events, but Bob pointed out that this would not necessarily happen: "A certain type of person will not respond to a spiritual event, an' the pow-wow people're in a different space. Everyone is always welcome at a burial. This meal's representative of the last meal with these people, an' the people who bring food in the spirit of givin', their prayers'll be answered. An' the spirits'll be happy that all is being taken care of.

"Everythin' is fine if it's done in the right spirit."

Silence fell as we reflected on the implicit teachings. It is to their credit that all the directors listened carefully to the proposals of the Arrow Lakes representatives and fully intended to comply with their wishes.

"The beginnings of all this lie in talks with elders Charlie and John," Bob continued. "I'll talk with Charlie to ensure all's done correctly. He's Lakes, an elder who's done this before. They must be buried sittin' up, facin' the sun, the east, all separate, an' as close to the original spot as possible. It must be ensured that there'll be no reoccurrence of erosion.

"The young people'll participate an' help. Anyone who wishes can participate. There'll be further discussion with the elders. Everything'll be prepared on the Friday; the actual ceremony, at sunrise, will not take long. After an hour or two, we can share the main meal; it may be at about ten in the mornin'. Some of the people may not wish to camp, but maybe stay in homes."

A chorus of voices immediately offered invitations; we were prepared to do everything we could to facilitate what we all saw as the most vital action, before anything else could proceed.

Nellie's husband, Nick, taking his wife's place because of her poor health, said gravely: "My Doukhobor ancestors came to this area in 1895. Would it be appropriate to make some representation of our spiritual ways at the event?" Long-faced, hollow-cheeked, craggy, his distinguished features and thinning white hair put me in mind of a Biblical patriarch. I remembered that the meaning of Doukhobor is "spirit-wrestler".

"Yeah, it'd be very suitable," Bob replied warmly. "My family owned land in Grand Forks an' would trade with the Doukhobors. My grandfather, he died twenty-three years ago. I've spent all that time in prayer for him. Finally his spirit will be laid to rest.... We all pray to the same Creator, an' there's great power in prayer. If you pray with us, if we put our energy together, we are creatin' together for the happiness of souls. It can be any prayer in any language; this is what the Creator wanted." When he talked like this, he seemed to glow; to me, it was Laughing Thunder we were hearing.

"Yeah, an' we was taught that the Doukhobors was pushed around same's the Indian people," said Manny gruffly.

"Yes, well, our histories do parallel," said Nick.

"In terms of religion an' persecution an' standin' by your people, an' for what you believe," added Bob.

"The Tibetan monks, too," stated Nick.

Incredibly, less than two years later, representatives of all these peoples would pray together for world peace at the Indian village.

Laughing Thunder's words about the power of joining with others in prayer made me think of the teaching of the great Master of my birth religion: "Where two or more are gathered together...." I had only recently become aware of the concept of the power of consciousness, especially when joined in purpose.

Discussing how we might proceed after the reburial, Manny mentioned an ancient site in California over which controversy had arisen about the building of a road (later, I would wonder if this were some kind of prescience). "There was a small Band of Indians nearby," he added, "so elders was put on the Board as spiritual guides, so's the place wouldn't be torn apart."

"Yeah," said Bob. "It'd be good to have an elder as a consultant. That's why Manny 'n' me, we're not interested in bein' members. It's a conflict of interest, 'specially if staff are needed. The goal is to have all such places put aside; this is the foothold. I already have a lawyer arranged to take care of any consultation if necessary. This Society will gradually oversee all these sites. The Board is makin' history, makin' history right here 'n' now."

While I totally agreed about the making of history, the reference to a lawyer shook me; what did Bob know? The idea of a foothold would also prove to be uncomfortably accurate.

"The elders will come up," Bob continued, "an' they'll step forward. I'm here to speak, not to make decisions for the people. I carry information back to 'em, give my viewpoint, an' the decision is theirs. Spiritual people will join later. Well, not join, they don't go round joinin' everythin'. One of us will be here all the time. An' my mother will be happy."

"The Okanagan people are closely related to the Lakes people, their ways, their language," Manny informed us. "My mother married on the Penticton Reserve, so I have Okanagan relations from my mother's side. Now, I been studyin'; I been studyin' the sacred paintings.... I'm just a beginner, y'know, a beginner on this road. I'm just startin', learnin'.... An' the more I learn, the less I know!"

We all chuckled.

"An' y'know that moccasin telegraph is as fast as it need be," commented Bob.

Mention was made of contacting an Okanagan spiritual leader from the Penticton Reserve, who regularly attended the Stein Valley gatherings.

Sighing deeply, Manny said: "Well, I been learnin' many things, but there's a universal truth about ourselves, a one truth. He says he's a medicine man. Well, the medicine men, they don't go round sayin' they are medicine men.... But what do I know? I've heard it said like this: what I know, you could put in a notebook about this big," he patted his shirt-pocket. "All the rest is hearsay! But the elders know who they'll hear."

The meeting wound to an end. Afterwards, as we all stood around to socialise I took the opportunity to show Bob a book I had recently obtained, "People of the Falls", a sensitively-written account of the prehistoric and historic activities at the now-inundated Kettle Falls, near Colville in Washington State, just across the border. According to the record, this was the southernmost area of the Arrow Lakes ancestral territory.

Pointing out fishing-sites he recognised from the old photos in the book, Bob named the families that had frequented them. He was especially interested in the photo of the Salmon Chief from the 1860s. "Not a chief in a sense of leadership," he murmured, "but the one who held the Sumix. Just like there was a Root chief, a Berry chief. Might just as easily be a woman."

My understanding of the Sinixt word was growing: not only a totemic guide, but something to do with the power of the knowledge of the animal or plant.

"I read something in the book which I found really intriguing," I said. "There's evidence of massive flooding that occurred around 2000 BC. And there's some strange, inexplicable, tennis-court-sized rectangular patches burned three or four inches down into the earth, dating back to about 1400 AD. But what affected me most of all is that there's a subtle implication that your people's spiritual influence extended far beyond the ancestral lands."

"Yeah, my people're a peaceful people," he said thoughtfully, his eyes taking on a far-away look. "We were the arbitrators for the whole area, from the north down to California. Issues that couldn't be settled was brought to our elders."

For some reason, this information did not surprise me. Then there occurred one of those exquisite events that serve as a reminder of the deeper levels, hidden from the everyday surface reality, powerfully flowing beneath this process.

"Because we are the Mother Tribe...." The words came slow and ponderous. Bob's eyes met mine. "We are the Keepers of the Order of Life."

The hall seemed to blur; the buzz of voices faded away as his gaze held mine. His eyes, like dark, swirling pools, pulled me in; every atom of my being thrilled as he seemed to lock into the centre of my being.

Slowly, emphatically he repeated: "Remember.... The Keepers of the Order of Life."

Then he was gone.

Motionless I stood there, stunned, trembling. What did this mean? Some deep, hidden part of me seemed to Know, and I fished at the connection between the fragmentation of his people and the chaos in the world, but was a long way from articulating this Knowledge, which, yet again, felt like re-collection.... Feeling light and unsubstantial, I left the hall and went outside into the cold air and snow, and breathed deeply, wondering at this man's ability to seemingly lift me out of myself.

After a few minutes, Paul joined me, and, demonstrating the kind of sensitivity that I would learn is characteristic of many Native people, said nothing. Together we looked up at the hard, brilliant dusting of stars overhead. Suddenly a meteor creased the heavens.

"Did you see that? The shooting star?" Paul whispered.

"Oh yes." My heartfelt, breathless reply carried something of the profound experience I had just undergone.

Paul's voice was soft as he asked: "What does it mean? Is it good?"

"Yes, a promise," I murmured, off the top of my head. It was what I wanted it to mean: I wanted the star to be the promise of fulfilment of those wonderful, magical words, "The Keepers of the Order of Life", even though I could not say what that might mean. Or incur.

"You know, I always know the second those two Native men walk in," Paul said gently, "because you light up like a star."

AN ISLAND IN TIME

The muted grumble of a motorbike woke me. It was barely seven; I thought someone must have lost their way, so I got up. A misty early-spring morning light diffused over the little valley, still deep in shadow. From among the evergreens below the house flashed a gleam of silver, then with a roar, the motorbike sped up to the front and sputtered into silence.

A visitor so early in the "slow-as-you-can" Valley was unusual enough, but this was extraordinary: it was Cliff, not known for early rising. An artist with an intense creative energy and a deep appreciation for the Native American way of life, he had recently started coming to the Vallican Archaeological Park Society meetings, having just moved to the area. When I learned he was renting the little log cabin beside the house we had lived in at Vallican, I had a sense that he would be affected by the energies of the Indian village. Maybe he had been drawn there, too.

Bounding up the steps in his familiar springy way, Cliff had no time for a greeting. "It must be you! You're the one!" Barely in the hallway, he was bursting with revelation: "I had this dream, and soon's I woke up I had to come straight down and tell you! It couldn't wait! You've got to put yourself forward at the meeting tonight!" Unable to contain himself, he paced back and forth. "You're the only one that can do it! You know the site, you know the history, you've read the reports, but most of all, you know the people! You're the one for the job! You can see that, can't you?"

As soon as he laid it out like that, see it I could. Believing it was another thing. A dream, I thought, you have to watch out for dreams.

Almost five months had passed since the meeting with the Heritage Trust manager; despite the regular meetings and further correspondence from the Trust, the Vallican Archaeological Park Society was adrift on a sea of words. Any real progress seemed to be taking place after the meetings, when I would go with Bob and Manny to where they usually stayed, the house of Elizabeth and her partner Mickey.

Elizabeth I had met when she had helped out at the Indian village when Bob and his mother first camped there. A gentle-spoken, attractive local woman with long, dark, curling hair, she embodied the hospitality Bob had once told me about, while Mickey, a Doukhobor with strong features, grey, curling beard and shoulder-length hair put me in mind of another Biblical personality: not a stern, Old Testament patriarch this time, but the loving-kindness of the great Teacher of the New.

It seemed the magic of moccasin telegraph would spread word of the Native men's presence in the Valley, and a diverse group of local people was gradually being drawn together into a loose circle of friends connected by a belief in a shared future. Long into the night this growing group, each with their own history, ideas, opinion, paths in life, would come together in a Oneness I had never before encountered. Central to these impromptu gatherings was Bob, who shared stories about his life and tradition, tales filled with dry humour and a deep wisdom.

All I recall of those scintillating nights is a darkened room lit by candles, figures on chairs, on the floor, and the soft, hazy, golden-white light, laced with sparkles, that seemed to cocoon Bob – Laughing Thunder – as he was deep in the telling. Tales of the supernatural, the paranormal; words which would sink not so much into my mind as my being, as I somehow fell away and lost myself in a state beyond the physical. It was beyond the first incandescent feelings of falling in love, when the body feels more alive than ever before, when everything in the world is touched by an ethereal beauty and there is a sense of absolute Oneness with everyone and everything; it was more refined. They were a kind of heaven for me, these gatherings; for days after I would be charged with a high energy, the greater part of me living in another dimension yet still able to carry out the everyday tasks of caring for home and children.

When neither Bob or Manny had attended the most recent Society meeting, however, I lost patience with all the talk. Only the day before, I had confided to Cliff that I would resign from the Board at the meeting scheduled for this evening.

Now a dream had moved him so powerfully, that he had to come rushing down at this unlikely hour.

"No way!" Yet even as I reacted, I recalled another dream: a drum refused. Before me, bursting with conviction, was a message-carrier, a sensitive who lived on the fringes of the Indian village, as I once had.

Within half an hour I had persuaded myself that I could at least attempt what he was suggesting: act as a liaison or facilitator between the parties involved, and prepare a formulation for the village that honoured the Arrow Lakes people's wishes.

So it was, almost at the eleventh hour, that I offered my services as co-ordinator for a management plan on behalf of the Society, and was more than a little taken aback by how readily and unanimously my application was accepted by the executive. It was pointed out that a source of remuneration (something to which I had not given a thought) would have to be found. Laurie knew of a new Provincial employment initiative related to tourism, a grant which would also enable the hiring of an assistant, a local woman called Jacquie who had recently started coming to the meetings, and Cliff as artist for promotional material for fund-raising as well as caretaker resident on-site, since pot-hunters were still a threat.

Only later did I appreciate the significance of Bob and Manny arriving just in time to witness my appointment. The last item of business over, Bob announced that the Arrow Lakes Band had begun to hold regular meetings on the Colville Reservation to keep descendants informed of what was happening in their ancestral lands. "Her presence," he waved a casual hand in my direction, "would be appreciated to give detailed reports. Next one's in a couple weeks."

Amazed at the way all the pieces had slotted into place, I was so thrilled I could barely speak. Now my Walk with the Native American people would truly begin.

Doing things to the best of my ability is a deeply-ingrained part of my make-up but in this case it was no effort: my heart was totally in it. My energy levels soared; I began to appreciate what it meant, to have a true vocation. None of what I did in the following months seemed like a "job" or work; I took a deep and abiding pleasure in my multi-faceted position, which came to so totally consume me that there would have been no room for a man in my life, had Bryan still been around. These were the conceiving moments of nine months of the most intense activity in my life; even my children would become peripheral.

In many ways I was my own boss: although answerable to the Board, I was left to get on with it, even down to my job-description. My private standing joke would come to be that I was employed by the Society, paid by the government, and worked for the Native people. Fully absorbed and deliriously happy, I had no idea of the delicate tightrope I was walking.

Collecting together all the material about the Vallican site and the Arrow Lakes Band to set up a library, I contacted the relevant archaeologists and ethnographers, as much to inform them of recent developments as obtain information. The most useful document to come into my hands at this time was the unpublished report by Bouchard and Kennedy, the "Lakes Indian Ethnography and History", prepared for the B.C. Heritage Conservation Branch in 1985 to be utilised specifically in the interpretation of the site at Vallican.

There emerged a tragic tale of cultural genocide. All Bob had told me during our long night together in Vernon almost eighteen months ago was there, and more: a people decimated by disease and further fragmented by the encroachment of white settlers and government policies, their traditional lands bisected by the creation of the International Boundary, the survivors either dispersed onto Reserves throughout British Columbia or assimilated with twelve other tribes onto the non-treaty Colville Confederated Reservation in Washington State. Despite considering themselves "good King George men" (British subjects), the Arrow Lakes people were disallowed from crossing the border back into their traditional lands.

I was intrigued to learn that two Arrow Lakes Reserves had been posted and surveyed. A small one at Brilliant, near Castlegar, at the mouth of the Kootenay river, had "slipped through the cracks"; despite a twenty-year plea by a Lakes descendant for the protection of a burial-ground there, the government twice doubled back on its word and sold land it did not own to new arrivals to the area, the Doukhobor people. The irony did not escape me.

The other Reserve, at Oatscott on the west side of the Upper Arrow Lake, almost directly across from Burton, was originally posted at 640 acres and finally signed in 1902 at a scant 255 acres. The "last, recogni[s]ed" member of the Arrow Lakes Band who lived there was recorded as Annie Joseph, who died in 1954. She had willed the Reserve to the Okanagan Band, but after her death, an official declaration of extinction was laid on the Arrow Lakes Indian Band; following the reversionary interest clause of an Order-In-Council passed by the Privy Council in Ottawa in 1956, in an unprecedented move, the Reserve reverted to the Province.

Several years later, a U.S. Bureau of Indian Affairs publication noted that 257 members of the Colville Confederated Tribes were considered to be Lakes. According to unofficial sources, present-day Arrow Lakes descendants number between 2300 and 10000, including a Member of the Legislative Assembly in Ottawa.

In the 1970s, the Arrow Lakes elder Charlie, of whom Bob had spoken, had set the ball rolling again by asking a question that no-one could satisfactorily answer: what happened to the Arrow Lakes Reserves?

When I contacted the ethnographer, Bouchard told me that one of the main sources of information had been Charlie, who was one of the few remaining fluent speakers of the Sinixt language. Speaking highly of him, Bouchard thought he would appreciate knowing about the developments concerning his ancestral lands and gave me his telephone number.

The friendly voice that responded effusively through the wires spoke highly of Bouchard, not the least because the ethnographer had apparently managed to wrap his tongue and memory around the Sinixt language. Immediately insisting I call him Uncle Charlie, the elder proceeded to tell me about Kettle Falls, traditional centre of the prime salmon fishery on the Columbia River.

Almost fifty years had passed since the construction of the Grand Coulee Dam cut off the salmon's migratory route and created the Franklin D. Roosevelt Lake, inundating the falls. But the memory remained strong. Long before Hudson's Bay Company established the trading-post known as Fort Colville, he told me, seven tribes had gathered at the great falls each year for the abundance of fish that lay at the centre of their subsistence. The Kalispel, the Sanpoil, the Spokan, the Pend d'Oreilles, the Flatheads, the Bitterroot mountain tribes of Montana; each had their traditional place on the banks while the Lakes people commanded Hayes Island – apparently the best site – in the centre.

The river would transform for days into a silvery shimmer of glistening, gleaming, leaping bodies. Countless thousands of great-hearted fish battled their way up to the spawning-beds, to die, begin again.... It had been a time of hard work and great joy and celebration: the intense labour of catching, cleaning and preserving balanced by the knowledge that the hard winter months would be well-provided for. The tribes would mingle; there would be news to catch up on, gossip and stories to share, maybe a hand or two to exchange in marriage.

As the elder talked, Bob – and the promise of the laughing thunder – was strong in my mind.

"The traditional Salmon chief was Lakes," Uncle Charlie continued. "He oversaw the fishery, ensured the water upstream was not fouled, but kept pure and clean so the migration'd be successful. Fishing began only when he gave permission, which was when he was certain by the number of fish comin' through that there'd be enough for the next year, the year followin', the year beyond that. He said how many traps could be laid, and where. Distribution of the salmon was overseen by women of different families of the tribes."

The Salmon People, I thought; they had had a technology for centuries.

"There's a salmon-feast this comin' weekend. You should come down. They're openin' the new historical centre at Kettle Falls. Be good to get in touch with the committee that runs it.... And there's a pow-wow, on Hayes Island. A 'Callin' Back the Salmon' pow-wow. First time since, that the draw-down's been sufficient to expose the island. It'd be a good time for you to meet some important Lakes people. Call me soon's you get down."

Calling back the salmon? I imagined a Native medicine-man, long black hair flowing free, precariously poised on a rock above the mighty falls, beating a drum, his mouth open in a chant which was drowned out by the crashing of waters. And what did "draw-down" mean? The timing was extraordinary; things were moving fast. I had not yet even been to a meeting of the Lakes Band, and could scarcely believe I was on my way to meet one of the elders.

Following the eastern shore of Columbia River down to Kettle Falls, I fantasised about the journey that the indigenous people would have made. Canoes on the smoother parts of the river, portage bypassing the rougher. It was exciting to think that the contours of the mountains must have looked the same to those who had gone before.

The children and Cliff were with me. St. Paul's Mission, where the salmon feast was supposed to be taking place, was easy to find but it was deserted and the door to the new-looking, large, windowless building locked. Uncle Charlie had mentioned it would be possible to access Hayes Island, so I followed his directions across the metal bridge spanning Roosevelt Lake.

Far below stretched an immense, steely expanse of water, broken only by the ragged outline of an incongruously small mud-bank. Long gone were the immense, torrential cascades of water, stretching across the ravine, broken by great upthrusts of rock to which trees and vegetation were stubbornly clinging; now there was just a humpbacked sliver of mud and rock, long dead to any plant-life, its desolation all the more poignant for the small circle of tipis on the higher terrace. It was so far from the picture in my mind, fed by images of Kettle Falls painted by Paul Kane in the 1840s, that for a moment I lost track of where I was, what I was doing there.

Nor did I seem to have the knack of Indian time. From the dearth of activity on the island it was apparent that the ceremony was over. Annoyed that I must have got the date wrong – which was not like me at all – I turned off the highway, followed a dirt track over some railway lines and pulled up on a rough parking area on the cliff-top beside a camper, where a young Native man was playing with two small, dark-haired children. He told me there had been four days of sweats, prayers, drumming and dancing on the island; it was all over. Deeply disappointed, I looked down over to the island and could just make out a tiny hump that had to be the sweat-lodge, almost indistinguishable against the sandy mud.

"I'll take you over there if you want." It was as if the young man, whose name was Gary, had read my mind. We scrambled down the cliff to be loaded into a shallow motor-boat beached on the shore below.

It was a formidable, unforgettable crossing, serving to remind me that this wide and seemingly peaceful lake was the bloated remains of the once-free and wild, mighty Columbia River. As we puttered away from the shore, I looked back at the scars of erosion: great, sandy-white gashes in the cliffs, caused by swiftly-rising waters. The day was still, overcast; initially we slid smoothly enough across the water but about half-way, gusts of wind began to snatch at the boat and we were told to sit quite still. The river was not quite dead: sudden strange eddies, swirling whirlpools and a sleek oily movement hinted at the churning depths and power of a trapped, frustrated river writhing beneath the deceptive calm. In a wry tone, our Native guide told us of some scary moments when they had been crossing to the island carrying tipi canvas, poles and supplies. It may have been for dramatic effect but it had the desired result: we sat still as statues.

As soon as we beached, the others jumped out and headed up toward the tipis. Filled with a sense of the extraordinary, I stayed in the boat for a few moments. To be stepping for the first time onto ground that had just hosted a spiritual ceremony of its traditional people for the first time in half a century would be one of the most profound experiences of my life. I took off my shoes and the moment the soles of my bare feet connected with the sand, raised my camera to capture the moment.

The developed photograph would show a desolate heave of mud and rock crested by tipis, faded streamers forlornly waving from the tips of the poles, and a lowering, grey sky. My initial reaction was that it was a sorry representation of what I had felt when I took it, until Natalie, then eight, asked: "What's that coming out of the tipis?"

My disappointment had clouded my sight: a great, ghostly head of a creature with shadowy, pricked ears and hollow eyes emanated like a wraith from the centre of the circle of tipis, pale against the heavy grey clouds.

It filled me with awe. Had some kind of supernatural energy been generated during the ceremony that could imprint itself upon a photograph? Was it Wolf, rearing his head again? A friend of Coyote, Wolf often falls into trouble because of his friend, who then saves him. Symbolising teacher, pathfinder, one who runs ahead with new ideas which he then takes back to the pack, I had also learned that in some Native American cultures, Wolf is represented by the Dog-star, Sirius, considered the home of the gods by the ancient Egyptians and the contemporary tribe of the Dogon of Africa. As I let the image settle in my perception, however, I saw it was thinner and sharper than a wolf's face. Was it Coyote himself?

Whoever it was, it was an amazing photograph. I commissioned a framed enlargement, and the owner of the studio, whom I had always thought of as a down-to-earth guy, asked if he might hang it for a time on display in his store in Nelson. Later, he told me that customers commented on it regularly. "There's something about it," he said. "You can see something in it, can't you?"

I chose to play the enigmatic, and only smiled. Actually, I didn't want to lay my interpretation of what I could see on anyone else. Hung in place of honour in my living-room, the photo challenged many people, but when Bob eventually saw it, there was no hesitation. "Ol' Man Coyote, hangin' round where he oughta be!" he chuckled. Another Lakes elder I would meet saw an angel; another, an eagle. Interpretation of a symbolic image is a deeply personal territory.

Putting away my camera, I walked slowly up the shallow terraces, savouring each step. The ground underfoot was sandy, peppered with stones and a few rotting, blackened tree-stumps. The island had been logged off prior to inundation. Reaching the circle of tipis, which were being dismantled by some Native people who had not been visible before, I was met by one of them, a man with short grey hair and a round, friendly, nut-brown, lined face.

Introducing myself, I explained why I was there. He beamed a wide smile. "I'm Pierre – an' you missed the whole show!" he laughed. "Four days! We even had a television crew here for the dancin'. They all just left. All in all, quite a crowd."

"So how do you think the salmon will actually return?" I asked ingenuously. "A few sticks of dynamite would take care of the obstruction-"

"Never like that!" he interrupted, frowning. "We pray to get the help we need.... We've asked the people, we've been on television. We want to have some ladders built into the Chief Jo Dam an' the Grand Coulee, so's we can have the salmon up here again some day. Maybe I won't see it, but my children, my grandchildren will see it. Somewhere on television ... somewhere, someplace ... somebody with a li'l more education than we have will see what we're tryin' to do, an' maybe they'll help us get our fish back. So this gatherin', me 'n' my brother put it together with the Parks Service. The people have really helped us get our tipis an' our wood out on the island. It was a lotta work, but we got here."

Although I had not yet seen the immense feat of engineering that is the Grand Coulee Dam, I was aware of the scale of its construction; the run would have to be many miles long. Pierre said he would speak to me again at the salmon feast that was taking place at the new historical centre the next day.

Glad to learn I had that much right, I recalled that Indian time worked in its own way: there was a reason why I had not been here for the ceremonial part. But for the life of me I could not work out what that reason might be, especially when that was the part that interested me the most.

OF ELDERS AND ROOTS

The Board of the Kettle Falls Historical Society had invited us to dinner that evening, and amongst other things we discussed the possibility of a liaison between the heritage site at Vallican and their new centre, which focussed on local history and prehistory. Enthusiastic about the involvement of the Lakes people and the future, they were a friendly bunch of people but I found it hard to come back down to a historical, white-man earth and was glad when my kids evidenced sleepiness and we could go to our motel.

Early next morning, I was awoken by a knock on the door. A woman's voice told me someone was waiting for me in the coffee shop and stumbled over a name that had me out of bed, showered and dressed and on my way over in minutes, excitedly wondering how Uncle Charlie had known we were staying there, how I would recognise him and what we would talk about. But as soon as I stepped into the steamy warmth, the only Native American in the crowded diner immediately stood up and waved me over. Smiling broadly, he shook my hand – a warm, firm grip – and loudly said: "H'woy!" Almost everyone looked up.

Tall and slim, wearing a brown-checked shirt, he had a presence that made him seem robust. I guessed he was in his early eighties; his hair was silvery, thick and short, and his weathered, lined face spoke of a long, outdoor life. His glasses were strong; his eyes faded with age and crinkled and creased around the edges. "Lakes' informal greeting," he said, indicating I should sit down opposite him. "Better learn it now."

I need not have worried about topics of conversation, for Uncle Charlie had plenty to say, his false teeth clicking an accompanying staccato. His manner was engaging, his chuckles infectious; he was clearly a man who enjoyed the company of ladies, as much, I am sure, as I enjoyed his.

"Kin-sin Sinixt," he told me: "I am Sinixt. Ah-sq'eest ... I am called." We introduced ourselves to each other in Sinixt, although his Indian name completely passed me by and I didn't like to ask him to repeat it.

Acknowledging Bob's efforts to further the situation of the Lakes people, Uncle Charlie told me how in the 1930s, the ethnographer Verne Ray had gone through the area with Lakes Chief James Bernard and had made a record of many of the original places-names. Qepi'tles, the settlement at the mouth of Kootenay River near where Castlegar now stands, seemed particularly close to Uncle Charlie's heart. When I made reference to ethnographer Bouchard's account of the Lakes family called Christian who had tried to protect the ancestral burial-ground there, Uncle Charlie said he knew the living descendants. He did not tell me its meaning (it did not seem right to ask), or the meaning of the name for Vallican, Nkweio'ten, although I later saw it tentatively translated as "shallows" (the river runs relatively shallow and fast there). "Slocan," he told me, "was derived from Slo'heen, which means 'pierce, or strike on the head'. Maybe somethin' to do with how the fish were caught there. Most probably in weirs, then speared."

"Well, it's a knock-out place," I grinned. "Have you been there?"

He shrugged. "Salmon were plentiful throughout that whole district, 'cept on the Kootenay, which they could only access far's Bonnington Falls. That's where S'ink'leep, Coyote, made a barrier for the salmon when the people there wouldn't give him their wives," he chuckled.

The distinctive grey pillar of rock that juts out of the water just below the falls is still known as Coyote Rock, although the dams must have vastly changed the appearance of the area, which has the strange, mystical feeling I have since come to associate with power-points in the landscape.

"That place, up the north end of the Slocan Valley," he continued, his eyes twinkling. "Nakusp." He pronounced it with a swallowed "a": N'kusp. "The books – they say it's named for a meetin'-place, but I'll tell you how it really is....

"When the white folk came, of course they wanted the best places for themselves. The Indian had to move; they went up to Kuskanux Creek. Then the white folk wanted to call what they took from the Indian, something in our language." His tone took on a shade of mocking disbelief: "Said they wanted to name it for an Indian princess. 'Tell us the name of one of your princesses,' they said." He shook his head. "We never had no princesses, we had nothing like that. An' I guess my ancestors were more'n a little bit sore. So they told them...." The elder paused, grinning widely. He looked outside at the traffic swishing by on the wet highway. "It's not a word I'd repeat in the presence of a lady ... but it's the part of a deer you see when it's walkin' away from you!" Watching my dawning understanding, he laughed heartily. [9]

In the afternoon, the official opening of the Historical Centre took place. Less like a warehouse once the great double front-doors were open, the building was light and airy. Prehistoric and historic artefacts, historical documents and photographs were on display, and the walls had been painted with extensive wall-murals depicting traditional Native American scenes, commissioned of a Lakes artist. The place was crowded, mostly with non-Native people. As he had promised, Uncle Charlie escorted me round, first introducing me to the grandson of Baptiste Christian. Joe told me he had never known his grandfather, who had passed away before he was born, but his grandmother had told him how they eventually had to give up their long, heart-breaking plea for the preservation of the burial-ground at Qepi'tles and come south to live at Marcus Flats in Washington State. But she had never forgotten where they used to hunt and fish, "clear up the Arrow Lakes".

After warning me about the old man's sharp sense of humour, Uncle Charlie then steered me in the direction of another Arrow Lakes elder, Martin, father of Pierre, whom I had met on Hayes Island the day before. A tiny, frail-seeming man in his eighties, something about the way the elder stared at me – like a small, hunched, white-capped bird of prey with piercing blue eyes – made me nervous as a rabbit. He seemed to pay little attention to my mumbled introductory words about the Arrow Lakes settlement at Vallican, geographically the heart of their ancestral lands.

"This place, this was the centre," he said abruptly. "We had game of all kinds, berries, roots, camas, all kinds of fish. We had the food from all the four directions. That's been our Indian culture – tradition; tradin' that fish for buffalo robes, buckskin, bows 'n' arrows, moccasins, whatever.... But now I'm gettin' tired of all this control. Same way with my Council, my own people: 'We – us – in control.' I don't like that. I don't like it one bit. I want to find out, where did the

---

9 Local history books relate an appropriately-ambiguous account of the origins of "Nakusp": a Native man illustrated its meaning by holding open his little tobacco-pouch then drawing together the ties to close it. Interpreted as "the place where people gathered", it looks fatefully like the action of the anal sphincter muscle.

government get the land to give us a Reservation? It was already mine, nobody had to give it me. An' it's still mine. As long as our two feet's under the sun on the ground, it's still mine. I don't like to hear that word 'control'.

"An' another thing: I been asking that question – I asked in Washington, in San Francisco, in Victoria. I asked that one question and never got no answer yet. When somebody, for instance you or these men, or as far as that goes, a-ny-bo-dy," he emphasised each syllable of the word, "goes to sell somebody else's property.... That's what the government done, sold my property to his own people.

"You're white. Alright, you don't exactly own everythin' you got. You gotta pay for it every year, what's called tax. But I'd like to know, what's that word called, when you sell somebody else's property? But the main office couldn't tell me that.... You didn't know I was fightin' for that." He cocked his head to one side. "I got lawyers in San Francisco. And in Victoria."

It was beginning to dawn on me that I was listening to a powerful man, whom I would learn was an elder-advisor and religious leader who had not only fought long and hard for Native rights and instigated the revival of the Arrow Lakes people's traditions on the Reservation, but was a prime source of cultural information for the academics who were forever trawling through the Reservation. And it was clear I was there to listen.

"I'm not sayin' you don't have the same rights I have. 'S long as your two feet's on the ground and ... to an Indian, the sun is the Creator ... as long as that sun is on top of your head, you've got the same rights, the same title, as I have. Now that water over there...." Martin indicated Lake Roosevelt, which was just visible, a silver sliver beyond the pines. "That water controls all life. If it hadn't been for that water, you'd be just like that stone." He pointed to a small rock lying nearby. "They took my fish, they took my land, my diggin' grounds an' everything, an' what did I get? You know what I got? I recently found out that what I got is polluted water and polluted air. Very interestin'....

"They're puttin' all this on...." Raising one skinny arm, hand like a claw, the elder encompassed the centre. "But they're not puttin' it on with a smile. There's tears in our eyes. What we used to have, what do we get for that? Ever since Columbus landed, we've been dominated.... But they got that fence, so damn high an' so damn mighty. We can't even get behind that fence they call the Law.... April seventeenth I'll be at Chenie University. From there, I go to UBC."

The University of British Columbia, in Vancouver. I realised he had to have considerable authority. "I'm not sure if you've heard about what's happening with the Arrow Lakes settlement in the Slocan Valley, in B.C.," I said tentatively. "It's to be hoped something can be preserved there-"

"There you go again – 'preserve'," he said sharply. "What did that goddam Forestry do when they 'preserved' the country? They reamed it.... I was up here at one of our old huntin' grounds a while back. I got one of my boys to take me up, an' the scrub timber is so thick that even a chipmunk couldn't run through it. The leaves an' the pine-needles, about that thick." With his thumb and index finger he indicated a space of about four inches. "That's what the forestry done. Never burned it off. They never cultivate the land. Forestry Service ... who'd they serve, I'd like to know!" His voice twisted in disdain. "I wasn't scared! I told 'em in Spokane. I'm not afraid. They can throw me in jail or shoot me; I don't give a goddam. I'm gettin' old an' sick.... An' some of my own people're doin' it too. They got that word: 'control'. 'We – us – in control'."

Turning away, he dismissed me with an abrupt wave of his hand. No sooner had he gone than Uncle Charlie appeared again and introduced me to his nephew, who taught history at the local Indian school. Jim called his uncle "grandfather", which confused me until I learned that this happened when a relationship was particularly close. In his early thirties, Jim was apparently the only man of his generation who could speak Sinixt. With his short, light brown hair, hazel eyes and rugged good looks, he looked more like the epitome of an all-American football star than a Native American. When I mentioned this to Uncle Charlie, he told me that many of their people had traditionally been light-skinned and light-haired.

Jim heard my little speech about Vallican through but was more interested in my roots because he was trying to trace the English branch of his family. The places he mentioned were all in the south of England, most of the names unfamiliar to me.

We were interrupted by an announcement that the feast was about to begin. Uncle Charlie went up to the microphone and in Sinixt recited a short prayer and a blessing on the food. The resonance of the unfamiliar sounds thrilled me; absorbing the half-swallowed glottal stops, the rounded vowels, I wished there were some easy way of learning the language.

A feast of barbecued salmon, bread, salad and dessert had been laid out, with the traditional foods, bitterroot and camas (a bulb which flowers in the spring, looking like a lily). Highly nutritious, they tasted strong and so bitter I could not imagine eating them out of choice.

Finding Bob's mother eating alone, I asked if I might join her. For a while we chatted about the centre then I asked when she might be coming back up to Vallican.

She shrugged. "I don't think.... Well, maybe only Bob. But none of the other family. I've had seven children; they're all here in the States. They can never imagine themselves in Canada. They're all educated people, they all have good jobs and they all have this 'n' that. They have a good living. But Bob is not like them, he's the only one that could.... Well, they said they'd never go up there. They won't ever say that their heritage is not from up there, it always has been. That country from there, down this far and toward Inch'lium, them are all Lake Indians, an' then back out toward Curlew, all Lakes."

The way she pronounced Inchelium, a small township on the Colville Reservation, was the same way as Uncle Charlie: as if there were no "e". It tickled me to think of Bob as a sort of black sheep of the family, and I made a mental note to check out the place-names.

"But most of 'em are gone now," she continued sadly, "an' the young ones don't care. They don't care. You talk to them 'bout it, an' they always look at you as if you're out of your mind, you know. They don't care where their ancestors are from. But we do. We always have. We were brought up that way. My Dad, he never let us forget. Never. He spoke about it all the time. He spoke to us about where we were from, an' when Bob 'n' I were drivin' through there, I recognised the places my Dad was talkin' about." Her voice softened: "We was so happy.... We didn't have a camera, but if we go up there again we'll take some pictures of the places he talked about."

Making another mental note to send her copies of the photos I had taken, I thought about the terrible tragedy of the people of the earth, torn from their roots. That Jim, an Arrow Lakes descendant, should be searching for English relatives, disturbed me; part of me did not want to hear about what seemed to me like contamination of the blood.

"The elders," Eva was continuing, "they know their people are from up there. They know a lot of incidents an' things that happened up there. Same's I do, but they know diff'rent things. The ones camping on this side came from Cusik, an' from Montana...."

I realised she was talking about the tribes who had traditionally gathered at this central salmon-fishery.

" ... An' on the other side, they're the ones from Nespelem an' all camped there. The ones from Spokane camped there ..." a wave of her hand " ... then right in the middle, that's where the Lakes were, on the island.... They didn't associate with other people," she giggled mischieviously as a child. "That's what my Dad told me."

After the feast, a demonstration of Native dancing took place behind the building. There was one big drum with several drummers; with a characteristic thump and wail, they launched into a traditional song, and from among the pines, two Native men in buckskin, one carrying the American flag, the other an eagle-staff, dance-stepped their way into the small dusty arena, followed by several others. It seemed this might be as close to tradition as I might get: no gaudy outfits, no prominently-displayed numbers; each man dancing in an individual style to the succession of songs that followed. These were war-dances, I learned; one of the leaders, his head crowned with a shock of thick white hair, his painted face passive, unemotional, carried a shield and a wicked-looking war-axe. I had noticed this man earlier, inside the centre; one of those rare individuals who stand out in any crowd in an indefinable way, I thought he had to be a person of some authority but he appeared too formidable to approach.

After the dancing, this same man climbed up on the podium to address the onlookers; when he introduced himself, I realised he must be another son of the spirited elder, Martin.

"My great-grandfather used to trade over here in Fort Colville," Tom began, "an' then my grandfather traded with the white man also. They learned how to get along. They learned how to share, to share their hard times an' their good times. An' that's where it brought us today – to this gathering. An' we're still struggling, tryin' to get along with the white man. Somewhere between my grandfather an' my generation, somewhere in the gap, we lost it. Not only my side lost the hope, but also the white side. We quit learnin' how to share. We quit learnin' how to care.... It was all dog-eat-dog; we all turned our backs on one another an' we all put a face-value on that almighty dollar. An' therefore we don't have the closeness, the bond that my grandfather and my great-grandfather had with the white man up here, for he used to trade his goods an' he used to get along, an' they used to be glad to see one another. Regardless if he was white."

I was fascinated; never had I had expected to hear something positive about the past from a Native American viewpoint.

"Met a man out on the island," he was continuing. "I don't know him from Adam, but he became a great friend of ours. For he understood where we come from, an' we try to share. A lotta you people round here pro'bly know him ... I don't know if he changed his name, but I learned it was Fiddlin' Red, something like that! But he's a great man, an' to us who was on the island, he was chief. We elected him chief. 'Cause this man's ninety-nine percent more Indian than our own Indians are.... He believes in what he does. He believes in the culture, an' I hope, in gatherings like this – not only on the Indian side, but on the white man's side too."

To me, his words were powerful, but I wondered if any of the Native people there might find some of what he was saying offensive.

"Maybe we won't benefit from this," he added strongly, "but maybe our offspring will, maybe our young will. Maybe they'll learn how to get along once again. Learn about the carin' an' the sharin' an' the love for each other. The world is gettin' so bad; the almighty dollar has taken over, an' the drugs 'n' alcohol.

"We've all took our old people out from the centre of the ring – our teachers, our guides – an' we've set them all in the background, our children in the middle. I for one have nothing to offer them, because all the teachers, all the old people are put back here. Not only of my culture, but of white cultures also. Wherever I travelled, I met a lot of old white people an' they have a lot of wisdom, a lot of knowledge of what's goin' on around 'em. An' if we could ... isolate 'em, an' put our kids back on the outside an' the elders back in the middle, we could all learn something. We could all benefit. An' then maybe we could deal with the drugs 'n' alcohol, an' get along with one another, white and red.... Thank you."

He stepped down to a smattering of applause, but I found I could not join in; it seemed a weak response. If only more people could hear what this man had to say, I thought; and act on it.

Before leaving, I went to say goodbye to Pierre.

"The pow-wows are not enough," he said. "What we're lookin' for is culture an' tradition now. Have a big four-day feast or whatever, an' then invite all the people an' enjoy each other.... If I can help you, call. I don't know how I even got into something like this, but I like to do it, I like to put things on. Get things started, then some younger guys follow in an' get doin', an' I just back out, an' it goes on.... Like to do things like this, gatherin' the people."

"Maybe your people's village in Vallican could be a suitable place for healing in the way you're talking about," I said, hoping I was watering a seed-idea.

"I tried to do that down here, you know," Pierre said thoughtfully. "Wanted to put in a traditional treatment centre an' sweat-lodge, an' just couldn't get no-one to help me. I can do it, but I have to have a little help from my Tribal people, but nobody wanted me to do it."

It was difficult to believe that people should not want to recover their heritage. I wanted to say I felt this would change, and soon, but he was continuing: "But in my heart, one day I'm gonna do it. Whether they're gonna help me or not. I have an AA [Alcoholics Anonymous] encampment – this year's the twelfth annual. An' I have people from as far as New England State an' New York.... People come here. I'm not doin' this all by myself. This is my twelfth year of sobriety. We get a lotta teenagers, an' a lotta kids. I like 'em.... It's not right in the town – Inch'lium – it's out in the trees, right along the river. We have two sweat-lodges an' our arbour where we have meetings. The chairs are log. There's nothin' fancy about it. An' if there's any way I can help you, just call." He shook my hand and left to help with the clearing-up.

Things seemed to have turned out well after all; there appeared to be interest in what might happen at Vallican and I was sure Pierre would come through. I looked for Uncle Charlie to thank him and say goodbye.

Uncle Charlie. I felt somehow accepted, already accorded the familiarity of a title which is a normal manner of address among the Native people. Older people were called "grandmother", "grandfather", "uncle" or "auntie", depending on degree of closeness (Jim had been "adopted" by Uncle Charlie); the word for "cousin" was the same as for "brother" or "sister". As I drove back up to Canada, I remembered how, at the Society meetings, I had thought it presumptuous to imagine the Arrow Lakes elders being interested in us. To me, Bob's role as go-between was good enough; more than enough, in fact. Yet I now had a Native American uncle.

Missing the ceremony had not mattered after all. Indian time had its way of working things out. I promised myself to not get agitated when things were not going the way I thought they should.

SWEAT-LODGE

Bob's suggestion of reconstructing the Indian village at Vallican in a traditional way seemed to mesh with Pierre's views on rehabilitation. Looking to network, I contacted the Round Lake Drug and Alcohol Treatment Centre, located between Vernon and Kamloops, B.C. They informed me that nothing like that had been attempted before but there was sure to be interest, and invited me to attend their annual spring gathering.

Again, the timing seemed more than chance. As I drove along the hauntingly-familiar north Okanagan highway, I wondered whether interest would come from political or traditional people, or a mixture of both. The sign indicating the turn-off to the Centre, which disappeared almost immediately among the trees, had always intrigued me. When we were living in Vernon, an opportunity to teach aerobics at the Centre had come up but the distance and cost of childcare made it unviable. Instead, my employer Sandy, who was also a close friend, took the position and in time, brought back a weird tale about a "sweat-lodge". Having no idea what it was, I had been mystified by her story of heat and smoke and being joined by an eagle in what I had imagined was a log building, poorly-ventilated and stuffy, with a smoky hearth.

A lot of water had been splashed over the rocks since then.

The narrow gravel road wound through meadows and small stands of pine and fir. There was no sign of any lake. Eventually I came to a cluster of buildings and a parking-lot filled with cars. Starting in the main building, I began making my pitch at the administrative level but was met with little interest. Outside, where crowds of Native people were mixing and mingling, I didn't feel brave enough to approach any of the spiritual leaders but made a connection at the grass-roots level of counsellors. Invited to eat supper with them, I explained what was going on in Vallican. It was a relief to find people who could see the potential, and they encouraged me to keep in touch. As we left the restaurant, Lucy, a counsellor, said: "We're having a woman's sweat tomorrow morning, the last day of the gathering. I'd like to invite you. Down by the lake, at six-thirty."

Having made contact with the people who would probably be the most important, I had already decided not to come back the next day. "Thanks," I prevaricated, "but I'm staying at a friend's in Vernon. I don't know if I could be here in time."

The truth was, the thought of attending another sweat made me break out in a cold sweat. It hadn't been that long since Grey Wolf's sweats, where something always came up. I knew that was how it was supposed to be, but I had invariably failed to understand what was going on and would be left with uncomfortable feelings for days. Another part of me felt I shouldn't miss the opportunity, however. Since I hadn't brought an alarm-clock with me and my friend Anne was away, I decided it was up to the Creator: I would go if I woke early enough.

A perverse part of me kept me reading till two in the morning.

Three and a half hours later, Bob came galloping into my dream-state on a white horse, waking me with the thundering of hooves. Woken reality was an early freight-train rumbling along the tracks a couple of blocks away, but I was on my way to Round Lake within ten minutes.

Despite the compelling beauty of the landscape, shrouded in early-morning mist, the forty-five-minute journey was more than enough for butterflies to have established a frantic fluttering in my stomach by the time I turned off the highway. What was I letting myself in for? I didn't know where the lake was, or exactly where the sweat was taking place. Something directed me to take a barely-discernable trail, which turned out to be so rough and rutted I was sure it was a side-track. Then I saw the lakeshore and through the trees, a bunch of people. It had to be the sweat; who else would be up and out so early?

Thanking who- or whatever it was that had directed me, with more than a little apprehension I joined what turned out to be a small, silent group of Native women. They were dressed in simple shifts or t-shirts and leggings and standing near a massive, blazing fire, which was being tended by a Native man. As I approached, he threw on another log, sending up a great fountain of gold-red sparks.

"Hi! So glad you could make it!" Lucy's enthusiastic welcome did little to warm me. I was shivering, but whether because of the chilly dawn breeze scudding across the lake, or the realisation I was the only non-Native there, or a sudden, terrible awareness of the sweat-lodge, squatting below us, by the lake, was hard to tell. Made of a framework of willow branches and covered with old blankets and quilts, the inverted-basket shape was familiar enough, but somehow ominous: ready to swallow up the unwary. What had possessed me to come?

But now I was here, I could not run away.

Feeling conspicuous with my white skin and blonde hair, and distinctly out-of-place, I joined the cluster of women round the fire. Unable to look at my sweat-companions, I stared into its great, glowing heart where I could just make out the shapes of the Old Ones, as the lava-rocks were called, who lay there, remembering, preparing.... Lucy appeared beside me, her round, kind face beaming a warm smile, and for a long while there was only the crackle and cackle of flames, fiercely consuming wood.

"Don't break the path of the Old Ones." Thin-faced and frowning, Sophie, the other sweat-leader, indicated the route from the fire-pit to the sweat-lodge. "We show the rocks respect – they're our oldest living relatives. They're the facilitators concerning what happens in there. All we do is serve them, an' conduct the proceedings.... There'll be four rounds, based on four related themes. Between each round, those who wish can rinse off in the lake. I like to make the heat inside the lodge fairly intense, but it's not a test of stamina an' if anyone wants out, she just has to say the closing words, 'All my Relations', an' the flaps'll be opened an' she can leave.

"And remember, revealing personal details of what other people pray or say in there is like breaking the confidentiality of the Catholic confessional."

The intense fire gradually subsided into a heap of brightly-glowing embers, revealing the dull-orange gleam of the pitted lava-rocks, which could take extremes of heat without fragmenting or exploding.

The Old Ones have proven themselves in the fire many times, I reflected, still feeling nervous. Now they'll put us through it, to be tempered and refined.

"She'll be serving the Old Ones, the Grandmothers," said Sophie. Looking up, I noticed that the man tending the fire had gone, his place taken by a woman.

"That means she'll be the one passin' the rocks inside," Lucy explained to me. "That's the work of an apprentice leader. It's a great privilege."

It was the first time I had heard of "serving the Grandmothers" – Grey Wolf's sweats had seemed to come ready-served – and wondered if they were "Grandmothers" because this was an all-women sweat.

Sophie pointed out a small mound of packed earth near the entrance of the lodge. "Leave your jewellery on the altar there, and any items you want blessed."

One by one, the women entered the sweat-lodge. I noticed some were crawling in backwards.

"So as to be in balance with how we emerge," Lucy explained.

On my turn, I did the same, taking the next narrow space in the closely-packed circle of women sitting around the central fire-pit, knees bent. The bare earth was covered with cedar-boughs; crushed by our passage, they released a sweet scent into the confines of the lodge. Sophie and Lucy entered last, sitting either side of the entrance, and a bucket of water was placed beside Sophie. Then Lucy beckoned me to sit beside her. Feeling like the new kid in class, I awkwardly scrambled over the other women's legs to do as she requested.

The first Grandmother appeared, seeming to magically float inside the lodge, but actually riding on the tines of a garden-fork. Using two sets of deer antlers, Sophie manipulated the red-hot rock into the fire-pit. When seven Grandmothers had crunched heavily into place, the entrance flaps were closed, plunging us into complete and utter darkness. A wash of fear coursed its prickly, nauseous way up through my stomach and chest, but I was prepared for it, having felt this claustrophobic reaction before and knowing it would pass. Breathing deeply, slowly, I watched as the baleful red glow of the Grandmothers came into focus.

Lucy murmured a brief prayer of gratitude and respect, and I felt her arm move. Orange and yellow sparks crackled and danced across the Old Ones, and the pungent, evocative scent of sage swooped around the lodge, causing some brief coughing.

The preliminary cleansing.

There was a loud sizzling and spitting sound; Sophie had splashed water over the rocks. She did this again, three times, and the steam furled and uncurled over and around me, a warming, welcome cocoon: breath of the Creator, primal earth-breath. This part of the ritual would release the ancient earth-records that the Grandmothers carried. I began to relax.

"I can't stand this! Let me out! Oh please, let me o-u-t!" The sudden, panic-stricken wail cut through the velvety darkness like a serrated knife-edge, startling me out of my new-found equanimity. Beside me, Lucy's voice was soft and calm: "Sister, don't be afraid. You can leave if you wish. Are you sure?"

"Yes! Let me out!"

I wanted to tell the woman that the fear would pass, that she had our support, that the circle should remain unbroken, but it was not my place. Or my experience.

Lucy ordered the flaps open. Light flooded the lodge; gasping a hurried "All my Relations", a young woman of about eighteen scrabbled over our feet like a crab and hurried to the fire, where she wrapped herself in a towel and stood, pale and shivering, hugging herself.

"Will you be okay?" Lucy asked.

The girl nodded vehemently.

"The rock-server will look after you. And you're welcome to rejoin us at any time. Just let her know."

Telling the rock-server to keep an eye on her, Lucy asked for the flaps to be closed again. Darkness again descended, but I felt unsettled: I could sense the space where the young woman had been, sort of like a missing tooth.

A short, eloquent prayer by Sophie dedicated the first round to Mother Earth, and the circle began to turn in a clockwise direction, each woman offering a prayer. Except for the two leaders, who were counsellors, they were all undergoing treatment at the Centre, and I listened to these recovering women pray for Mother Earth with an awareness and intensity I had never before experienced, each prayer ending with the reminder that we are all part of the web of life: "All my Relations!"

On my turn, last, I felt anything I might have to say had already been well-spoken. I muttered "All my Relations", and the round ended with the same words cried out by Lucy. The flaps were thrown open.

Blinking like owls in the sudden light, one by one we emerged, moving stiffly on cramped limbs coated with twigs and crumbs of earth, and made our way down to the sandy edge of the lake where we dabbled in the shallows, rinsing off our legs. Occasional eye-contact and a shy smile made me feel more like part of the group. The young woman who had fled the lodge was still sitting by the fire, seemingly calm now, but unwilling to rejoin the sweat.

Seven more red-hot Grandmothers joined us for the second round. Already warm, the lodge re-heated swiftly. In the darkness, amid a cloud of sage-pungent steam, Sophie dedicated this round to the "Sisters".

Woman as a microcosm of Mother Earth, as Bob had once related. But as I listened to what had happened – and was still happening – to these women, to their mothers, sisters, daughters, friends: pain and grief that made my own life seem sheltered, privileged and uncomplicated, I was appalled and humbled. After each emotive outburst, Sophie flung another splash of water onto the Grandmothers; the heat became ever more intense and it was a relief when it came to my turn and I only had to gasp out "All my Relations" and be followed by Lucy, and the flaps were again flung open.

Not one woman played at the edge of the lake this time; we all plunged in, grateful for the cooling waters.

As seven more Grandmothers entered for the third round, the third tumbled heavily off the fork. Using the deer-antlers, Lucy carefully manoeuvred her back onto the tines, and she was withdrawn and another entered in her place. I was fascinated. Obviously, that Grandmother had not wanted to be part of this sweat, and that had been respected.

Dedicated to the "Brothers", the round became increasingly intense as intertwined anger, grief, love and forgiveness poured out, choking up the cramped space. My own losses and failed relationships paled into insignificance beside the catalogue of pain, loss and abuse experienced by every single one of the women in the lodge. Like tiny fireworks, the sage sparked and shrouded us in pungent smoke, made all the more powerful by the water spattering and steaming during and after each prayer. Sometimes we too would be showered with lukewarm droplets, for which I was deeply grateful: the lodge was becoming unbearably hot.

Eventually it came to my turn. I thought of my older brother, whom I had idolised and who had died of leukaemia when we were still children; of my father, who had passed over at the same hour that Natalie, my middle child, had come into the world, eight years ago, before I had made my peace with him; of the failed marriage with the father of my first-born; the failed relationship with the father of my two younger children. Even though it was a shadow of what these Native women had undergone, it was still a herstory of abandonment, of failure.

What a mess I had made of my life. Even though I had all kinds of advantages, I still had failed. I had to pray, and I would begin with my brother.

But nothing would come out. It was as if the passageway to my voice-box had closed down. I tried to force a sound past the constriction, spluttered, choked, and to my horror, my stomach convulsed and I began to retch. Lucy put her arm across my shoulders and leaned me forwards. "Give it to the rocks, sister," she said softly. "The Grandmothers are here to accept."

Having eaten nothing since the previous evening, there was little but mucus. When my body finally gave up heaving, I curled up, exhausted, on the earth and whispered the magic words.

"All my Relations!" Lucy's strong cry signalled the opening of the flaps, and daylight flooded in.

Given my position, I should have followed Lucy out but I was immobilised by a strange weakness. Unable to move, I lay on the earth, breathing in the sweet aroma of crushed cedar boughs and feeling intensely embarrassed as the other women carefully picked their way around me.

Eventually, with Lucy's encouragement I managed to drag myself outside. Dizzy and trembling, unable to find the strength to get to my feet, I crawled down to the lake and flopped into the water. The cold shock helped me pull myself together, and after a while I found I could get to my feet. Two of the women, their faces expressing amusement, gently encouraged and supported me back to the sweat-lodge. Nearly all of them had somehow connected with me since I had left the lodge; it felt as if something had changed, as if I had somehow been accepted. I had never stopped to look through their eyes, to consider what they might think about a white woman being there – I had been too involved with my own view of myself, feeling like an impostor, vicariously observing the suffering of others.

Now I was revealed to be carrying my own load of baggage.

Lucy gave me a hug, and took my hand. "Ah, sister," her soft voice was filled with compassion, "you have much pain buried in there. There is unresolved business with the Brothers. Find the place. Acknowledge it, release it and clear yourself."

Shivering uncontrollably, I felt comforted by her caring words. I had no idea how to go about what she was advising, however, even though it was not the first time I had been told something like this.

At the previous year's Rebirth of Mother Earth Medicine Wheel gathering, disappointed by Bob's non-appearance, to help fill the time I had looked in on a workshop on emotional healing that was taking place in the big tipi. Only to watch. Or so I thought.

There had been about thirty people sitting inside. In a sort of reverie I watched the Cree facilitator seemingly picking out people at random, and within seconds magically finding his way to the core of their inner pain, reducing them to tears, yet supporting them, clarifying what was going on.

After witnessing three or four people being affected in this way, I was losing interest. Then I felt his eyes on me. Sure I was mistaken, I looked behind me but I was standing at the back, beside the entrance. Or exit. But I could not leave now. Feeling like a kid called out to be tested on homework she hadn't bothered to do, I had found myself carefully stepping over a myriad of legs, going to him, even though he had done nothing other than make a slight movement with his hand.

When I reached him, his wife appeared at my other side.

Nothing much wrong with my emotions, I was thinking, acutely aware of the sea of faces turned our way. He's made a mistake.

Taking my hand in his warm, dry one, Frank had simply looked at me; looked me in the eye, with those amazing dark and deep pools that some Native people seem to have.

You've picked the wrong person, I was thinking, staring right back.

"Tell me," he said quietly, his eyes softening, warming. "Tell me...."

For a few moments I had scoffed, mentally. Then I became aware of a strange feeling. It was like something within my body slipping, sliding, melting.... My eyes grew hot, and prickled. Cowed and embarrassed, I found the tears were welling up so powerfully that I could not control them. It was impossible; the floodgates had been opened. It was like an Ice-Age, ended.

When I had finally been able to speak again, a disjointed, gasping confession of a deep loneliness (of which I had not been consciously aware) and a supposed strength and stoicism which was only a steeling, a coat of armour against the world, tumbled out.

Four times, he had made me cry out my pain, then said: "You must find your way into that troubled area that houses all the hurt and pain: the place where the abandoned child weeps. Then you can release the gift of your sensitivity again."

Then, as now, I had mostly felt an intense embarrassment at being so out of control of myself. I had thought I had my act together and although his words had touched some deep part of me, I had little idea of what it meant or what to do about it. And here it was again. Vaguely aware that in steeling myself against any further pain, I may have dulled some finer, more subtle senses, I realised that it was a sort of self-abuse not dissimilar to excessive alcohol consumption or drugs misuse, which can also cloak acute sensitivity and dull inner pain.

Entering the sweat-lodge for the final round, I felt different, somehow lighter. When everyone was in place, a woman who had not been present earlier joined us. Excusing herself, she clambered over the others' legs and sat opposite the entrance, in the position of honour.

Slim and graceful, her long, straight hair falling jet-black over her shoulders, she was a strikingly-beautiful woman of regal bearing, exuding an inner peace. Introducing herself as Standing Eagle, she said she had asked that the flaps be left open while she spoke to us.

It was the problems facing Native people today that she had come to address, and she seemed to glow with intensity in the subdued light of the lodge as she eloquently stressed the power of the language, of tradition and spirituality, all of which are essential to healing.

It was just as important for my own race to hear this, I thought.

The final seven Grandmothers were brought inside, and the flaps closed. Sophie announced this would be a silent meditation dedicated to the self and to the Creator.

Sage fizzed and sparked; both leaders repeatedly flicked water onto the rocks. Steam enveloped us, and it swiftly became excruciatingly hot. Unable to meditate, barely able to breathe, I curled myself up into a mushroom, pressing my cheek against the coolness of the earth and concentrating on sucking in gasps of searing, dank-smelling air. The skin on my shoulders and back felt like it was frying; my scalp like it was frizzling. Just when I thought I could not stand it a moment longer and would have to give in, Sophie cried out: "All my Relations!"

It was soon obvious I was not the only one to feel an enormous sense of relief and elation as the flaps were flung back and a swirl of cool, fresh air swept inside. With whoops and cries, we hastily scrambled outside into the golden light of a rising sun that had just cleared the hills, and rushed into the lake, where we splashed and giggled like little children.

I was feeling an incredible sense of accomplishment and lightness of being: emptied, light as a feather, my feet barely skimming the ground. Never before had a sweat made me feel this way. But then I had never been to an all-Native, all-women sweat; it had been so intense, on so many levels.... I was further amazed to find out that over three hours had passed since we had first entered the lodge.

The great fire had collapsed into an ash-grey mound that still breathed and stirred, its heat tangible. We wrapped ourselves in towels, and went to recover our things from the altar. I left a pouch of tobacco there.

"Thank you so much for inviting me." My gratitude to Lucy was heartfelt. "It's not the first time I've sweat, but I've never experienced anything anywhere near as powerful as this. In fact, I feel like I haven't really experienced a sweat truly, until today. So whatever comes out of what happened here, I thank you."

Lucy gently grasped my arm and took me aside. "I don't know where you sweat, but take care if you do this again. It's important that the leader's traditionally trained. There's powerful energies in there, they have to be handled right. A good leader'll stay in control an' protect people. You see, things come up and they have to be dealt with right, else people'll end up getting hurt, or their lives affected by what's landed on 'em, what they take home with them.

"Stay away from mixed sweats. That's not traditional. When you get men and women packed close together, some of them near naked, well, not everyone can contain themselves. Packed together in a little space, their sexuality gets charged up and like any energy, flies round and it can land on the vulnerable or open ones, who leave the sweat thinkin' an' feelin' all kinds of things they never did before, an' wonder what's wrong with them." She frowned slightly. "D'you understand?"

My expression must have given me away; not only was I remembering what Bob had said but some of my own experience.

"Thoughts are powerful," she continued. "People don't realise how much power a thought has. And in the sweat-lodge a thought gains power, great power. You see, a man with a strong sex-drive who can't keep his thoughts under control, because his desire's focussed on the woman pressed up against him – his sexual desire flies round in that little space, and a quiet, shy sort of woman who's in there, well, she leaves with his sexual desire attached to her. She doesn't know where it came from, this feeling, and she wonders what's wrong with her, to feel like that from what's supposed to be a spiritual experience. It goes the other way too. If a strong woman lets those kinds of thoughts go, a vulnerable or weak man can leave all twisted up with her desire. Doesn't matter even if it wasn't him she was thinking of....

"And another thing: a traditional person'll never take their clothes off in the sweat-lodge, even though they're all women. Or all men. None of the old folk would ever show themselves; they believe in modesty." Giving me a warm hug, she added: "You're always welcome to visit and sweat with us, any time."

Unable to speak, I nodded. She had given me so much to think about. As for another sweat, I couldn't imagine going through something like this again. This had been a crowning experience; looking back, perhaps the only genuine one. As I drove home, a number of puzzling episodes were beginning to click into place. Lucy could have been talking directly to my own experience: mixed sweats, unclothed participants. Although unreserved about my body, I had never felt comfortable with the idea of going into a sweat "sky-clad". And both during and after some of Grey Wolf's sweats, I had experienced powerful sexual feelings which had made me wonder what was wrong with me.

Driving back to the Valley, I thought about Sandy's tale of her experience in the sweat-lodge. It must have been in the same place. And we, too, had been joined by an eagle, albeit a human one: Standing Eagle. What a stunning woman: so calm, composed, wise, articulate and beautiful.

Yet again nothing had turned out as I anticipated. I had intended to raise interest in the concept of a cultural encampment that would facilitate healing; instead, I had been drawn into a situation where personal issues had come up and it was I who was being helped with healing. Had Lucy seen something in me, which was why she had invited me to the sweat? In a similar way, had the Cree healer, Frank, also been able to see into the depths of my being? I thought about Bob, and what he had said about being able to see what was lying inside a man, what drove him. It was a kind of sensitivity I had not come up against before; one I had fantasised about being part of the Native people's birthright. Something which my own race seemed to have lost.

Just as I still felt lost, in a way. How on earth was I meant to deal with what had come up? I was sure that just being aware of it would make little difference, but maybe that was the first step in healing. How was I supposed to go about finding the next step?

THE HEALING OF THE NATION

Parked on the hill-side above the community long-house at Inchelium, the easternmost township on the Colville Reservation, my children playing outside, I waited for the Lakes people to arrive. Nervous about my new, official capacity, I had left home purposefully early, as much to get an impression of the place and a feel for the land as to be sure I would be on time. From this vantage-point, I looked down over sweeps of golden grasslands, fringed by evergreens which crept up the gentle slopes of the foothills. Situated in the middle of a meadow, the long-house seemed a long way from the rest of the town. In the distance, a stretch of Roosevelt Lake, cobalt-blue, was just visible.

Reflecting on the vivid relevance of my dreams, the strangely-coincidental nature of everything that had conspired to bring me here, it felt as if my life-purpose, a vital sense of destiny related to something that had moved within me as long as I could remember, was at last coming to fruition.

Televised in England in the early 1950s, "The Lone Ranger" had inspired me with my first childhood hero: the enigmatic Tonto. To me, the "masked man" was a pale, babbling, cardboard character overshadowed by the handsome, noble Indian, whose sparsely-worded eloquence was poetry to my young mind and provided me with my role in childhood games of cowboys and Indians. The only girl in the neighbourhood, I would refuse cook or squaw and insisted on being Indian scout to the cowboys (my older brother and his friends), loving to race ahead (a scar on my left eyebrow to show for it), galloping my imaginary pinto pony to the end of our street and into our favourite playground, an overgrown graveyard.

Old, lichen-covered sarcophagi became rocky outcroppings, ideal look-out points. Faintly-inscribed tombstones, awry and tumbled among the undergrowth, were perfect ambush hide-outs. Shadowy yew stands were a great forest; the bare ground beneath, our camps. The long, lush grass was the prairie, and deadly rattlesnakes lurked among the dense nettle patches.

Now, some fifty years later, when I return to the churchyard where my father's ashes lie and look upon the managed trees, manicured grass, tidied graves, almost all sense of that childhood wilderness is gone. Yet faint echoes of little pounding feet, whoops and gasps of the chase, cries and laughter, sound in my ears. We played knowingly among the dead; that was part of the thrill. And when the others moved on to new games I continued my love-affair with Tonto, roping in my mother as playmate. Her part was to sit in the deck-chair in our large garden while I galloped around, scouting and hunting in my own little world, occasionally reporting back to "kemo sabe". A solitary child by nature, I preferred this kind of play, which gave total licence to my imagination.

The illusionary lens of Hollywood had its influence, but no matter how represented, I would always root for the Indian. An avid bookworm, I trawled our small local library and at age ten or twelve came across Will Henry's historical novel, "From Where the Sun Now Stands", which relates the tragic story of the dispersion of the Nez Perce Nation in the late 1800s. Learning about their courageous leader, the outstanding statesman Chief Joseph, I found my first non-fictional hero. The final words from one of his last speeches, from which the book's title had been taken, have never left me: "From where the sun now stands, I will fight no more forever." Although the story wracked me, I was drawn back to it again and again.

Growing up in a small English market-town, with open access to the private parklands of the Duke of Northumberland's estates where I played in secret, mossy, faery-glens and by hidden streams I would populate with imaginary tribes; being taken on picnics, heathered moors stretching mile after unpopulated mile under an immense, open sky; and thriving on seemingly-endless summer holidays spent free as a little bird on the vast, lonely sweeps of a wild, castle-crowned coastline once raided by Vikings, I was blessed by a landscape that answered a need in me and moulded me in ways I now deeply appreciate. Perhaps, in a way, it prepared me for the greater wilderness of North America.

Looking back, I wondered at the intensity of that young English schoolgirl, growing up on a small, highly-populated island, and deeply yearning for a vast land thousands of miles away and a way of life that thrived hundreds of years before her limited experience. And although Bob had told me about life on the "Rez", his words had so far done little to dispel fantasies spun over many years by a vivid imagination: a romantic illusion that the Native peoples of North America continued to live a natural, free and harmonious way of life, albeit on a smaller scale, on the land allotted to them.

Aware of the way some people feel deeply attracted to a specific culture or era, or fascinated by a particular historical figure, I have often wondered whether it is from more than simple interest. At about fourteen, I voluntarily researched a couple of personal historical projects, on the Vikings, then on Roman charioteers – outside of the curriculum, which did not make me any more popular with my peers. Can it be that such intense interest stems from the memory of a life lived before?

Not pinto ponies, but cars were pulling up at the building below. When Bob's white hatchback arrived, the thought of seeing him again added to the jangle of my emotions. I drove down to join them, feeling terribly conspicuous, but several Native children immediately appeared and persuaded my children to go off and play with them, while Bob's warm greeting and insistence I sit beside him helped make me feel less of an odd-white-woman-out. Of the twenty or so others in the hall, a large space set up with a crescent of chairs and a table, Manny and Eva were the only ones I recognised. I had been looking forward to seeing Uncle Charlie again, and maybe Pierre, but neither was there.

Barely had the meeting been opened when Bob introduced me in such glowing terms that my toes curled with embarrassment. Relating how I had become involved with their ancestral site, describing it and the latest developments, helped me regain my equilibrium. I brought out a gift for the elders, entrusted me by a friend in Crescent Valley. A query flew round the hall: "Who should accept it?"

"Aunt Tootie," was the consensus.

A white-haired elder with a warm smile came forward and opened the package, and a Canadian flag tumbled into her hands, smooth and silken. As she unfolded it, I said, as requested: "'My sister presents this flag as a gift, a reminder of the Canadian soil which has called you. So long I have dreamed, so long my prayers have been lonely. And it has been written: "And the leaves of the tree shall be for the healing of the Nations; and the fruit shall be for meat and the leaf for medicine." Jessica, Kenna-Tay Ranch.'"

Tears pricked at my eyes. Nor was I the only one moved, as Auntie Tootie held up the flag to display the red maple-leaf. A lump in my throat, I sat down as Bob stood up.

In his usual eloquent way, he told of other ancestral sites he had located and how he was travelling across British Columbia tracking down far-flung Arrow Lakes descendants, and as the meeting progressed, the full significance of what was happening began to really sink in. It may seem strange, but it was only in the presence of this group of people, some of whom might have been, for the first times in their lives, attempting to find a sense of who they really were, that I realised the miracle I was witnessing: the beginning of a drawing-together of a fragmented people; the rebirth of a First Nation.[10] Nor was it simply a matter of returning home like some prodigal son; it was not like they had chosen to leave in the first place.

The rest of the business revolved round practicalities; at the end, it was decided that future meetings would be held in a more traditional way, beginning with the sharing of food. About to leave for the long drive back home, I found myself surrounded by Native women who insisted I stay overnight.

Their hospitality turned out to be just as Bob had described during that long night in Vernon. Taken back to the home of a Lakes woman whose home would became ours whenever we were in Inchelium, where the children vied with each other as to who would give up their room for us, we were plied with plates of food and cups of drink. Jackie's younger brother, a kindly, gentle man nicknamed "Babe", was so polite to and considerate of me that I hardly knew what to say.

That night was another long night, as five women – four red and one white – sat and dreamed together of what would come next, and what would eventually be. It was on cloud nine that I returned the next day to British Columbia.

---

10 Like Bob, I had a strong sense of "history in the making" and taped each meeting, giving the cassettes to a member of the Band executive at the end.

SPIRIT-GUIDE

A flickering, orange-yellow; fire-warmth; shifting shadows. A soft sound, like the one that woke me.

Awed, I watch shadow-caster: glowing sheen of naked, dark-skinned shoulder and chest, cascade of silver-grey tendrils; head tipped back, eyes closed, beak of a nose triumphantly jutting skyward. Sinewy arms, long-fingered hands grasping; groin pressing, sinuous and fluid, against round, gleaming-umber buttocks. She, hidden among folds of rough-haired hide....

I woke suddenly, a profound feeling of awe flooding my being, a memory-smell of wood-smoke somewhere in the back of my nose. The images had been so clear; accompanied by such strong feelings, I was sure it couldn't have just been a dream, but some kind of a past-life memory. Perhaps, as a small Native American child, I thought excitedly, I had been woken from my hearthside sleep by the lovemaking of elders. The rest of the morning, the image stayed strong in my mind and eventually I felt compelled to try and put it down on paper.

As usual, the dining-table was strewn with art materials; I found some paper and a pencil, and hesitated. The human figure had always been difficult for me to reproduce. About to try anyway, I noticed a little smudge of dirt on the otherwise pristine sheet of paper, just in front of the pencil-point.

I put down the pencil and got an eraser, but the mark was gone. About to start again, I noticed it was strangely back. Not a mark, after all, but a faint shadow. Except the light from the window was not related to its position, and when I moved the pencil, the smudge moved too, seeming to lead the way.

I followed.

Wordlessly, incredulously, I trailed the weird little shadow and realised it was an arm that was appearing, then a shoulder. Around the contour of a head, tipped back, I went; not a beaked nose, but a rounded one; and I could "see" where the eyes should be, closed; the hair, a sleek blackness. The emerging figure was sort of like the skinny, grey-haired elder in my dream, but only in pose; this Native man was heavily-muscled, in his prime; his hair was black, a heavy waterfall. Following whatever was leading, I found myself tracing a halo-like fan of feathers above his head, then over another shoulder and down another arm, which faded at the wrist into an implication of mist, cloud. Nor was it a woman at his groin that emerged, but Mother Earth. And it was done.

Starting to breathe again, I sat back in wonderment. This fine figure had nothing to do with my ability, and little to do with the man in my dream. I had simply followed a shadow.... What had happened? Where had this come from? And who was he? The first person who came into my head was Lynne. I rushed to the phone.

"Automatic drawing," she said, as if it were the most natural thing in the world. "Like automatic writing: a message from the Other Side. This man is your guide as you work through this part of your life. He was your husband in a previous life but you agreed you'd work better in this life with him helping you from the Other Side."

Not for a moment did I doubt the concept, but everything inside me rebelled: "Who thought that up! I'd far rather have him here with me for real! Whose idea was this, anyway? No wonder I keep choosing the wrong kind of guy, if the right one isn't even on the planet this time round! And no wonder I'm so attracted to Native Americans."

While it was exciting to think I might have a Native American spirit-guide (a current New Age fad), I could not get rid of a feeling that this was not quite what the experience had been about. Like many western women raised on fairy-tales, I had always had a sense that somewhere in the world was the one – and only – man who was right for me, and he would be in this world, not some other.

And despite my father's view that marriage was difficult enough without adding such spice to the pie and despite my failure with an Israeli husband, I was still sure that it would be a man of another race and culture, and that we would be an example of how love overcomes all differences.

So although I could not quite take aboard Lynne's interpretation of the figure, from time to time I would look at the drawing and yearn for that being in some other reality and the time out of time when we might be together. Never dreaming that my desire might manifest, but in a way I would never have imagined.

A WINDOW ON THE RESERVATION

Startling me out of a dreamless sleep, the short burst of frantic rapping was urgently repeated. After a few disoriented moments, I remembered where I was: Auntie Vi's, in Nespelem.

It seemed no-one else was stirring. I switched on the bedside lamp to see it was just after one in the morning. Auntie Vi had not been well the previous day; I thought it better not to wake her, got up and pulled on some pants and a sweater.

Switching on the hallway light, I spoke softly through the back door: "Who is it? What do you want?"

A male voice responded: "Vi! Let us in, quick! The cops're after us; we'll be in big trouble if they ketch us this time!"

"This isn't Vi," I said. "I'm a friend of hers, visiting. Who are you?"

"Mike 'n' George. Quick, open the door. They're just down the road!"

I hesitated. I did not know the voices or the names, but then the whole Reservation was an unknown. "Just a minute, I'll get Vi."

Knocking gently on her bedroom door, I went in and knelt by the slight, huddled figure, faintly-illuminated by the indirect hall light. Auntie Vi's husband, Junior, was a motionless mound on the far side of the bed, having come home late from bingo.

"Auntie Vi," I whispered, laying my hand feather-light on the sleeping woman's shoulder. She moved slightly. "There's two guys at the door, Mike and George. They said the police are after them."

A faint snort emanated from the heap of blankets. "Them two drunks again! Just give them a couple of blankets an' let them go pass out on the living-room floor."

Closing her bedroom door, I scooted back down the hall, unlocked and opened the door. Two dark, powerfully-built men were standing there, blinking in the sudden brightness; a powerful reek of alcohol belched inwards with the cold air. I took an involuntary step backwards. "Vi says to come in."

They stumbled inside, filling up the narrow kitchen. One had long, black braids that trailed over his broad chest and disappeared inside his battered "LA Raiders" jacket; the other had short black hair and black-rimmed glasses and was wearing a stone-coloured jacket. Car headlights swept in a sudden arc past the end of the driveway. I closed the door and locked it.

"Please go in there." I indicated the living-room and went to get some blankets from the airing cupboard in the hallway. Breathing heavily, they were still standing in the same place when I returned.

"Who're you?" the one with the glasses slurred.

I thrust the blankets at them. "A friend of Vi's. She said you're to camp out in here."

Taking the blankets, they followed me like two large, scary but acquiescent hounds, jostling each other and sniggering. Without another word, they lay down on the carpet, rolled themselves up in the blankets and were snoring before I got back to bed. My room was adjacent to the living-room; the sky was turning pale before I managed to shut out the racket enough to get some sleep.

The mouth-watering smell of frying bacon woke me; Auntie Vi had a full "Reservation breakfast" on the go by the time I joined her in the kitchen. Wrapped up like mummies, the two men were still laid out on the living-room floor when I went to set the table, but were up and sitting at it, faces shiny-clean and hair tidy, by the time the food was ready. They stared at me in silence as I carried in the serving-plates, piled high with eggs, bacon, hash-browns, pancakes, toast, sausage and chunks of deer-meat.

"Better get to eating before it's cold," Auntie Vi admonished, bringing a pitcher of orange juice to the table. Silently we obeyed her.

Barely a mouthful swallowed, the man with the short hair and glasses said: "Christ, Vi! Thought I was dreamin' last night, when an angel answered the door! I mean," his eyes twinkled, "I know you got Jesus, jest didn't know you'd have an angel to breakfast, too!"

I had to smile.

"Sun just come out, or was that a flashback?" he laughed. "Thanks for lettin' us stay, Vi. We was in real trouble last night, cops would've locked us up for sure. Then we come to your door, Vi, an' there's an angel opened it! Boy, I'll never forget it!"

"Oh, you just quit your teasin', Mike," laughed Auntie Vi, who seemed much brighter and her usual vivacious self again this morning. "This here's my little friend Celia, from all the way up in Canada."

"Canada, eh?" the other man asked, in a mockery of the Canadian byword. "You married then?" he added with a grin.

"Now George, you just leave her alone." Auntie Vi frowned in mock severity. "She's helpin' us Lakes Indians with our business about our land up in Canada. She's been comin' to the meetings and keepin' us informed. Lookit all this information she just brought us." She indicated a sheaf of papers on the dresser beside the table, photocopies of archival documents from the turn of the century that I had brought to the previous day's Band meeting.

"You one of them 'pologists?" asked Mike. "This is somethin' else: a blonde angel that's got brains!"

Wishing I could match the easy, teasing way of the Native people and wanting to make a joke about being neither an anthropologist nor an apologist, but not knowing how it might go down, I shook my head. "I'm just an ordinary person who happened to get involved with the Arrow Lakes' rights." Just saying it made a warm feeling bubble up inside my chest. "And no, I'm not married. But I do have three children." Enough to put most men off, I knew.

"God, she even talks like an angel!" Mike exclaimed, grinning at his friend. An English accent often seemed to make an impression in North America, for better or for worse. "Three kids," he mused in mock thoughtfulness, "three kids. Good start. Get good welfare with three! You ready to get together an' make some more?" He poked his friend in the arm and both of them tipped back their heads and roared with laughter.

Never having had an offer like it, I had to smile. I had read that according to some Native traditions, a woman with children who became available for remarriage was highly prized, because her fertility was evident. Perhaps this was the twentieth-century version.

"You just quit now! Don't be embarrassing her! 'Bout time you went and found yourselves somethin' useful to do. Leave my little Celia be."

Seeing the slight, spirited woman taking two hulking bears of men to task was worth any embarrassment. Auntie Vi's husband, Junior, his smooth, round, friendly face creased in a smile, joined us, soon followed by a yawning and stretching Carly, their pretty little granddaughter. I remembered Bob telling me how, traditionally, grandparents took care of grandchildren. A tradition which was still alive in this home.

There was a knock on the door: more arrivals to share food and company. I was learning that the door to Auntie Vi's home in Nespelem was always open and how rare it was to find this diminutive power-pack of a lady alone or have her to yourself for long, for her warm heart, sharing nature and nuggets of wisdom were like a beacon, attracting a steady stream of visitors from many different walks in life. My new circle of relations was growing.

Auntie Vi was one of the Lakes women who had sat through that long night in Inchelium. At the close of the previous night's meeting, held in Nespelem, when she insisted I come back to her home for the night, Bob had taken me aside and quietly said: "You're in now; you're in with the people.... An' these are the best people. You have to be at all the meetings."

I hadn't really understood what he meant, but his words implied an acceptance and a future that was almost beyond belief. I had never felt so happy or fulfilled. It wasn't until Uncle Charlie told me that the elders who were becoming my aunties and uncles were part of a group called the "Kelly Hill bunch", that I realised there was still a loose sort of clan arrangement within the fragmented Band.

Situated on the west bank of the Columbia River, north of Kettle Falls, an area of steep-sided hills coated with grassy meadows and stands of aromatic pine and fir, Kelly Hill comprises the south-west of traditional Arrow Lakes territory. Each year toward the end of summer, the Kelly Hill branch of Lakes descendants spend a weekend at the cemetery there, tending the graves of their forebears, who include the last two chiefs of the Arrow Lakes Band: Andre Aurapahkin, who died in 1910, and James Bernard, also known as the "Prayer Chief", who died in 1935.

Although educated in mission schools, these elders had retained their language. It was deeply affecting to hear them talking "Indian" together, and how much they laughed when they did; Auntie Vi often said she wished she could share a subtle joke, an untranslatable play on words. This made me think about how much I missed "Brit-wit", the subtle, dry sense of humour and the clever punning of my rootland. It was apparently also a characteristic of Ancient Egyptian, and in my opinion, reflects a sophisticated intelligence.

Similar to the Jewish ghettos in Eastern Europe, the confinement of the Reservation has enabled Native people to stand by each other and keep racial memory, language and tradition alive, even when forbidden by law. The extended family is still a vigorous entity: largely taken over in the dominant society by the impersonal cogs of governmental departments, a vital exchange and support system continues to exist on the Reservation in the form of "visiting", doing things together and generally sharing lives. Yet this confinement sets them apart from the outside world. Although some Native people have successfully chosen to make their lives off-Reservation, for others it can act like a cocoon or be a refuge to run to when the going gets tough; there is always room at an uncle's, a cousin's.

As for the dilapidated state of many of the homes on the Reservation, their yards cluttered with useless junk and rusting wrecks of cars and appliances, I realised it to be a literally up-front, dramatic political statement about the conditions under which Native American people have to live: a Third-World existence in one of the wealthiest countries in the world. The truth about the relatively high standard of living I had been enjoying in Canada for over a decade was beginning to sink home: not only was it riding on the back of the rape of the land but also on-going, quietly-systematic genocide.[11] My romantic illusions about what it was to be a Native American in the twentieth century were swiftly being dispelled, yet at the same time I could appreciate that, despite the terrible conditions, the Native American spirit lives on. In Bob, I had seen evidence of an on-going shamanic tradition, and the wisdom of the teachings he had shared with me were all I had imagined. The way the Lakes elders accepted me, treating me with a natural generosity and kindly consideration, with sensitivity and compassion; these were qualities I had fantasised about all my life as being of the essence of the Native American, and they were real.

More than ever, I felt I had come home; only to a race, and not their place.

Finally signed in 1872 at some 1.3 million acres, the Colville Confederated Reservation had originally been signed as almost three million acres, reaching to the Canadian border, but the northern half was soon signed away in yet another paper-shuffling breach of trust. After some sixty years of marginal existence, in the 1930s the thirteen, non-treaty tribes who had been confined there were next deprived of their main, traditional source of dietary protein by the construction of the Grand Coulee Dam. Nor did they gain any benefit from the immense revenues generated by the dam: it was built just outside the designated boundary of the Reservation. Political and social accounts write of well-intentioned policy-makers, but this claim is belied by an examination of the history of any Indian Reservation.

Spawn of the Grand Coulee, the Franklin D. Roosevelt Lake marks the southern and eastern boundary of the Colville Reservation. Coming from the west, I had noticed how the boundary falls short of the town of Omak, where the pulp mill primarily fed with Reservation trees is located, and to the north, skirts the Sherman National Forest and any potential revenue from logging. Originally all the tribes were segregated; perhaps as part of a more subtle programme of genocide, the Reservation has become something of a melting-pot.

Named for the original settlement of N'chaliam ("hits the water" – a creek flowed into the river at that point) which along with the traditional herb- and root-gathering places lies drowned beneath the waters of the man-made lake, Inchelium is a quiet sprawl of trailers and uniform, cheaply-built American HUD (Housing Urban Development) housing a few minutes' drive up from the Gifford ferry-landing. The town hosts a community centre, a post office, a gas station, a fast-food and video outlet, a couple of churches and on the outskirts, a large supermarket. The local high-school is renowned for its basketball team, and there is a small restaurant which doubles as a youth centre, intriguingly named: Steem'as Spa'uss, Sinixt for "What's in your heart?"

Above Inchelium, the brooding volcanic cone of Moses Mountain, place of vision- and prayer-quest, watches over the community. Climbing westwards, the highway snakes through Twin Lakes, a sudden, small string of houses and location of a lakeside resort; from the pass,

---

11 The appalling cycle of degradation that began with the prohibition of identity and heritage continues; severe addictive and other self-destructive behaviours are common on the Reservation. The Native American teenage suicide rate is six times the national average. Centred on subsidised government commodities, the average diet is reminiscent of the 1950s: white flour, sugar, salt and processed foods dominate.

looking out over miles of a wild and uninhabited mountainous terrain, the attempts of the Reservation to sustain itself economically are painfully obvious: naked shanks of mountains lie exposed in every direction.

Descending into the next valley, the landscape dramatically changes. Carved out by the incredible masses of water that rushed through the area when the ice dams broke at the end of the last Ice Age, craggy, fortress-like cliffs crowd the banks of the Sanpoil River. In a way, it was my favourite area, in that it is sparsely-inhabited and for the classic, distinctly Native American profiles etched into the contours of the cliffs.

In my perception, images such as these seem to characterise the mythology of the land. In the English landscape, I make out Arthurian-type profiles and mediaeval figures; in the Middle East, hawk-nosed, Biblical profiles; in Asia, rounded Oriental features; in rocks by the sea, fabulous sea-creatures. Long debated by investigators and generally dismissed as a quirk of nature or the tendency of the human mind to create order out of chaos, the incidence of simulacra is in my opinion connected to the power of consciousness and the unconscious, to create what we call reality.

Redolent with the scent of pine, the tiny, sleepy Reservation township of Keller is the southernmost community in the peaceful Sanpoil valley; the highway winds on until swallowed by the great expanse of lake-waters, where the thread is taken up by a small, grumbling ferry.

Before Keller, however, and unmarked on most maps and at the time lacking a sign-post, lies a T-junction, one arm of which follows a forested route that climbs again westwards. After passing over a ridge, the road gentles downwards into sweeping open grasslands dotted with ranches and small-holdings, some thriving, some neglected or deserted. An occasional dirt side-road points the way to other ranches, hidden among the hills; on the verges, small white crosses and colourful posies of flowers poignantly mark the site of fatal accidents.

The dramatic snake-bend that begins the steep descent into Nespelem is unforgettable. The small Reservation township is rendered insignificant by an awesome vista: a sere, dusty-brown moonscape retreating mile after untold mile into a hazy, purple-blue distance. Sweltering in summer, freezing in winter, the Interior Plateau has an undeniable, wild and mystical beauty: table-top mountains, gashed by gullies and studded with crater-like depressions; creeks tumbling into hidden lakes teeming with fish; eagles and hawks riding the thermals; deer, coyote, jackrabbit frequenting the valleys and high places. A magnificent, desolated wilderness, a place of solitude, a place to be reminded of the great gift that is life, to be ridden high and free as the wild creatures that soar above and run through this unforgettable landscape.

A landscape for the dreamer.

Patchwork of polarities, Nespelem seems to have almost as many abandoned houses, their boarded-up windows blank as blind eyes, and decaying trailers, with grass growing in gaping doorways and tumbleweed trapped under rotting floorboards, as immaculate homes with well-tended gardens and smart cars parked outside. To the south of the town, across from the pow-wow grounds and a large, modern community centre, lies a hypermarket, the Trading Post ("cash only"), next to a sprawl of buildings not unlike an army base: the bureaucratic centre of the Reservation, the Colville Tribal Agency.

Less than twenty minutes' drive further south, lies the Grand Coulee Dam. It straddles the valley, spawning a mass of power lines which string across the scrubby landscape like a nightmare manuscript. The immensity of the great body of water trapped behind the massive, featureless concrete wall, and the mere trickle of the Columbia River far below on the lower side, squeezing through the rip-rap – a concrete and rock barrier that channels the great river like a canal – is a strangely disquieting sight. The first time I saw it I recalled Bob's words about man's fear of nature and saw the Coulee Dam as a most potent symbol of man's need to control and overcome nature in return for short-term, debatable benefits: a breathtakingly-monstrous marvel of engineering that inundated the most fertile land in the area and destroyed an entire people's way of life.

To me, it stood as a metaphor of what had been done to the Native spirit. The day would come, I imagined, when the dam would go, whether by design, deterioration or natural forces, and the mighty Columbia, mother-river of the north-west, would be dramatically liberated.

And what might that do for the Native spirit?

FROM WHERE THE SUN NOW STANDS

When Bob had given me his post office box address at the Medicine Wheel gathering, almost two years ago, I hadn't heard of Nespelem. Nor, when Bryan and I had briefly visited the township, searching for Bob's ranch, had I noticed the signs.

Shortly after returning home from the second Band meeting, I came across the book "Touch the Earth", a self-portrait of Indian existence, and found in it one of the last addresses of Chief Joseph, and learned that after spending his latter years campaigning to be allowed to return to his Wallowah homeland, he had died in exile of a broken heart. A small caption gave the date and place of his death: September 21, 1904, on the Colville Reservation at Nespelim [sic], Washington. Filled with the oddest of feelings, I thought about coincidences which seemed too many and too profound to be labelled chance: it felt like a number of threads were being drawn together, although what the final picture might be was impossible to guess. For the next few weeks I went about my work and family affairs in a half-daze.

The next Band meeting, held at Keller, attracted even more Lakes people. Part of my contribution was an emotive speech about the injustices perpetrated upon their ancestors and themselves, but halfway through I became so choked-up that I could not continue. Indicating someone should take up the next item on the agenda, I pulled a tissue from the box one of the women put in front of me. Then she took one. Ours were far from the only snuffles in the following long silence.

To my dismay, I realised they were waiting – and would wait – until I was able to pick up my thread, tie it off. Heartened by such consideration, I managed to falter to a tearful end, deeply embarrassed by my display of emotionality. Yet they had not seemed to mind and I felt strangely emptied but full: what lay in my innermost heart had been laid out on the table. Then an elder I barely knew came over and gave me the most enormous hug and I had another new relation: Uncle Archie.

It became a standing joke at Lakes Band meetings: "Here comes Celia. Who's got the Kleenex?!"

That night, I went back to stay at Auntie Vi's again. Surprised by my ignorance of Nespelem's claim to fame, she told me she had previously lived directly across from the little cemetery where Chief Joseph was buried: "You should've seen the state it was in. I'd've been ashamed to let an ancestor's place go like that. Who was supposed to be tending it, I'd like to know.... So I took it on myself. Even though there was no love lost between us Lakes and the Nez Perce."

None of this was chance, I was sure. Perhaps the spirit of that great man was reaching through time and space, knitting certain people together.

The next morning, too excited to eat breakfast, I was glad that neither of my children or anyone visiting at Auntie Vi's was interested in visiting the cemetery. Heading down the back lane, I stopped to gather some wildflowers. Everything I did or looked at had an unreal quality; there was a sense of an unknown past catching up to meld with the present, which would never be the same.

Barking fiercely, a couple of flea-bitten mongrels suddenly appeared from a backyard and ran at me, starting up a chorus as several more appeared. Within seconds I was surrounded by a small pack of mangy dogs of various sizes and dusty hues, some of which were barking and yapping; others more worryingly silent, staring, lip curled. Heart in mouth, I said aloud: "Well, what d'you want of me?"

As one, the fearsome creatures melted into a bunch of tail-wagging, grinning mutts, jostling for a stroke and a kind word; a strong, unwashed-dog smell clung to my hand until I could wash it again. My first experience of Reservation dogs, it was a powerful message about appearances. After following me for a few yards, the little pack lost interest and drifted away. Barely had they disappeared when I came across something gleaming ivory-white, half-buried in the dust, and fished out a large, curved dog-tooth.

I was sure it was no accident that this had been put in my path: I was about to visit the resting-place of a great man who had passed into the next world but seemed to be reaching out into this one; it had to be a sign. Embodying unconditional love, loyalty and protective energy, Dog medicine is related to a sense of service to others, and to guardianship, an aspect evident in many traditions. Anubis opens the way to the next world in Ancient Egypt; Cerberus guards the gateway to the underworld. Putting the tooth into my little medicine pouch,[12] I continued on my pilgrimage. In no time at all, the gateway lay before me.

Sun-bleached and parched, the cemetery was a waste-ground of desiccated weeds and baked, cracked earth: the rows of unmarked, un-named mounds, faint paths meandering between them, seemed terribly sad, yet another part of me appreciated the anonymity granted the dead. As I progressed, I saw that some of the more recent graves had small white memorial tablets or little wooden crosses, and bright posies. Despite the overall appearance of neglect, some of the dead were remembered.

As Auntie Vi had directed, I made my way toward the only tree in the cemetery, a macabre skeleton at the foot of the only grave with a tombstone. Obelisk-like, its top broken off, it was bone-white, stained and scuffed. On one side, I noticed the all-too-familiar etched likeness, which made me stop in awe, and I saw Chief Joseph's grave was covered with tributes, as was the bare earth round it: tobacco, coins, crystals, photographs, written prayer-requests, fresh bouquets of flowers.

It was deathly quiet, the air so hot and still, it was like being in an oven. I placed my simple tokens of esteem – wildflowers, a small pouch of tobacco, the dog-tooth – among the offerings and stood back and closed my eyes. So overwhelmed by being there that I couldn't pray, or even think, I became aware of a ringing in my ears and a tightening sensation in my chest, making it difficult to breathe. Beneath my feet I could feel something like the faintest of vibrations, which gradually intensified. The ringing in my ears heightened to a thundering; the ground under me felt as if it was about to crack open. All of a sudden, my chest blazed with a searing pain; I wanted to wail, but, peripherally aware of the houses nearby, managed to suppress it into a moan. My body shuddered and shook; great, silent, gasping sobs burst out of me. Then the tears came, my legs turned to jelly and I sank to the ground and wept helplessly.

---

12 A small pouch worn round the neck and usually resting against the heart chakra, that contains medicine items – things that come to a person in a significant way and carry special meaning and therefore power, which is what "medicine" means. The items themselves hold no real power, but are symbolic foci for the power of consciousness.

How long I sat there in that state, I have no idea. And long after the stormy buffeting subsided, I remained on the earth by the great man's burial-place, weak, stunned and bewildered by the power of whatever it was I had experienced. I had never reacted so powerfully to anything in my life.

Something of my experience must have been evident back at Auntie Vi's; she did not ask how it went or what I thought, or anything at all. As I drove home, I realised that talking about it would have somehow taken away from the experience, dispelled the magic.

My childhood hero, realised in adulthood. Why had I been drawn here? What was the connection? Was it really something to do with a past life?[13] Or the spirit of a powerful man, able to reach across time and dimension, and influence living people who were for some reason, some purpose, attuned to him? There was definitely something licking at the edge of my understanding, which I felt was not just about the Lakes people, but myself.

Perhaps it was not an earth-tremor I felt by Chief Joseph's grave, but an encased heart cracking open.

Or more darkly, perhaps another soul, coming into its own realisation.

---

13 About a year later, an Anishinabe (Ojibway) poetess gave a poetry-reading in Nelson, B.C. After, I asked Marie Annharte Baker to autograph my copy of her anthology, and mentioned in passing my involvement with the Arrow Lakes people and how deeply the traditional life-way affected me. I noticed her eyes sort of glaze over and thought I must be boring her, but she placed a gentle hand on my arm and I was surprised to see her dark eyes were brimming with tears. My own filled, for some unknown reason. What she then said, she encapsulated in her dedication in the book: "Thinking of Chief Joseph and Looking Glass: their spirits help us in our work ... and especially one woman who rode into the camp in Canada with a bullet in her shoulder and a baby on her back...."

I was staggered. I had made no mention of the great man but somehow he had come forward in her consciousness while I had been talking. Did she mean I was that woman? Was the "work" about the Lakes people? Or Native people in general? As ever, I was unable to ask any of the questions clamouring in my head.

ILLEGAL EAGLE

Intending to give thanks, I drove directly back up to the Indian village. A heritage convention, where I had made a presentation about developments at the site, had taken me away from the area for several days before the Lakes Band meeting, so I had not been there for some days. The profound experience at Chief Joseph's grave still resonating within me, I drove past the log-house that had once been our home with barely a second glance and my world came crashing back to earth.

A hundred-foot-wide swathe of newly-scraped bare earth, banked with mounds of splintered young trees and crushed shrubs, marked the labour of bulldozers all the way down to and alongside the boundary of the site. My stomach churned. Eight years' healing growth from the previous attempt at a road had been drastically undone: the delicate young birch and cottonwood, child-sized fir and pine, clusters of Oregon grape and service-berries, the carpet of wild strawberries and myriad types of wild grasses, the moss, the fungi and mushrooms, all were but a memory. The devastation of the land ripped into my soul; I could have wailed in anguish.

The Indian village was a holy-place to me. It was the place I went to meditate, to pray; where I found wonder, mystery, peace. I knew more about it than any other place in my life. To build a road here was the greatest travesty I could imagine.

Unable to even enter the site, I rushed home, an agenda already forming in my fraught mind. Informed by the local branch of the Ministry of Transportation and Highways that the "long-delayed access road" was finally underway – the representative seemed to expect me to express my appreciation – I insisted on speaking to the project manager. In response to my query about an unannounced, unpublicised commencement of construction interfering with recent plans for the heritage site, the manager was complacent, giving me the impression he did not even know it existed.

Appalled, I was sure there had been some dreadful failure of communication. An emergency meeting of the Board of the Archaeological Society was convened; as one, they joined voice with most of the people living along the route of the proposed new highway and others in the area to protest.

Traditionally active and vociferous participants in planning processes that affect their environment, several Slocan Valley residents informed me that when the original route had been shelved due to discovery of Native American burial-grounds, a public enquiry had been pledged before any final decision would be made about a new route. The Slocan Valley Development Guidelines, a policy document for responsible land-use painstakingly prepared by Valley representatives and local government, was dusted down from the shelves of the Regional District of Central Kootenay (RDCK). Meanwhile, trawling the regulations, I discovered a government policy directing archaeological assessment of the route before any road is built next to a designated heritage site.

It turned out that since it was named the "Little Slocan Bridge Project", a linkage of the two back-road communities of Vallican and Passmore via the Little Slocan River, the crucial word "Vallican" had been delegated to small print. To give them their due, when the existence of the site was officially made known to them, Highways immediately stopped construction and brought in an archaeologist familiar with the area.

The Society had been planning to retain this same archaeologist for his innovative ideas and empathy with the Native American way of life. At the time working with the Kutenai, Wayne had walked the site with me less than a month before and explained its features in more relevant detail than any commissioned report, information I was using to enhance the interpretive tours. Much as I respected him as a professional who had openly told me how sensitive the entire area was, I knew any report he now made would be subject to vested interests.

Local feelings swiftly divided and escalated. Many residents were furious that two quiet, dead-end back-roads were about to become a through-road; others were anxious to have the old bridge and challenging turn-off to Vallican replaced (the same one that had almost sent me over the edge eighteen months earlier).

There was only one party who would be deeply concerned about the potential disturbance to more burials and an ancestral site that was being compromised before most of them had even set eyes on it. They would be united on the issue, I was sure.

Auntie Vi had told me she expected the next Band meeting to be the largest yet. Hurrying to Nespelem, my mind on what I saw as a devastating development, for once I neglected to carry out a small ritual, a sort of protective affirmation: the visualisation of great white wings beating before and beside the van – angels, eagles, it did not matter – and "Hanta Yo!"[14]

The officers at the small border checkpoints south of Christina Lake and Midway were already familiar with my van, my face and the purpose of my visits to the States, and invariably waved me through. This time, finding myself at the main border checkpoint south of Grand Forks, I wondered what had made me come this way. The customary perfunctory questions were trotted out: "Purpose of visit?"

"A meeting with Native people in Nespelem."

There was a short silence, then the balding, overweight, sweaty, red-faced U.S. customs officer suspiciously muttered: "Some kinda religious ceremony?"

Unaware of recent controversy about local meetings of the Native American Church in the area, I shook my head. He seemed about to wave me on, then suddenly poked his face in through the open window of the van. His unwholesome breath smacked me in the face as he snapped: "That an eagle feather you got hangin' there?" A pudgy forefinger indicated the two feathers suspended from my rear-view mirror.

Inspired by what I had seen on the Reservation and appreciating the symbology, I had attached my eagle feather and an owl feather Natalie had found to the rear-view mirror of my van. The combination of day- and night-hunter had seemed a nice touch. I had a lot to learn. Many Native American traditions regard Owl as such powerful medicine, it should not be combined with any other. It is not to be used lightly; some Native people will not even touch an owl feather. Also known as Night-Eagle and associated as much with witchcraft and death as

14   Part of the war-cry of the famous Plains tribal leader, Crazy Horse: "Clear the Way!"

wisdom and paradox, Owl is a feminine energy, which sees where others cannot.

I was about to be shown up as lacking in both vision and wisdom; the customs officer had fixed on me as his latest prey. Ingenuously, I nodded.

"You an Indian?"

My blonde hair, blue eyes, English accent and the presence of two small, fair-haired children in the back of my van seemed answer enough. Puzzled at this line, I shook my head.

"You got an Indian card?"[15]

Again I shook my head.

His next question was unbearably smug: "Didja know it's a federal offence to carry an eagle feather 'less you're an Indian? Protected species."

A fluttering filled my stomach. "No. But I was given it." I could not believe he might think I would be so stupid as to so flagrantly flout the law.

"Better come with me," he flatly ordered, "an' bring the feather with you." As he turned away, he tossed back over his shoulder: "Five hundred dollar fine...."

Numbed by this turn of events, I parked the van. A plaintive little voice behind me piped up: "Are we being arrested?"

"Maybe I'll just have to wash dishes for U.S. Customs and Excise for a while," I joked in an attempt to reassure the kids, only six and eight at the time. Maybe a long while, I grimly thought, unless they're willing to listen to the full facts.

But there was no "they", only this one man, determined to carry out his little coup. How I came by the feather and the spiritual meaning it held for me – a symbol much like a cross to a Catholic – had no more bearing on the situation than my ignorance of the law.

The officer picked up a phone; I heard him asking to be put through to the Fish and Wildlife Bureau. Guessing he needed someone to confirm the identity of the species, I held my breath until he impatiently hung up; the line had been engaged.

Outside, a car pulled up; as duty-officer, he had to deal with it and several more that followed in a string. Two other officials were in the back office but they seemed to be either unaware of or ignoring the little drama being played out under their nose.

Each time there was a gap in the traffic, the officer tried unsuccessfully to get through to the Bureau, a situation which dragged on for three-quarters of an hour, increasingly unbearable and laughable at the same time. As a diversion, I opened a box of cookies meant as a contribution to the Band meeting meal, and encouraged the crumbly mess the children made in the pristine waiting-area as a form of protest.

Then, out of the blue, the officer leaned across the counter: "You can leave." No preamble; no caution. I was too relieved to press my luck and ask why. " ... But I'm keepin' this!" He waved my eagle feather at me. I did not dare protest.

We arrived at the Band meeting over an hour late, missing the sharing of food. The meeting-hall in the little Catholic Church was packed out; there were many faces I did not recognise. Apologising for my lateness, I recounted my misadventure, which had upset me more than I realised at the time, but inspiration struck me as I neared the end: "The strange thing is, apparently the feather came from an ailing eagle. Perhaps it really was an ill-eagle feather...."

15   A white woman who marries a Native man gains the full rights accorded a Native American, one of which is the right to carry an eagle feather. An Indian card would have been proof of this, or of official adoption into a tribe.

Although chuckles rippled round the crowded room, almost everyone was appalled. Bob promised to try and get the feather back for me.

The largest meeting yet, it lasted hours longer than usual and saw an important political development: the supportive attendance of leading Native figures from the Penticton Reserve in the South Okanagan of British Columbia. The long history of injustices and betrayals was revisited and many relevant issues were brought up. When my input was requested, I briefly and rather emotionally recounted what had transpired in Vallican since the last Band meeting. Since it had been officially admitted that the full extent of the site was not known and adjacent terraces had the same features as the burial area, the immediate concern was that more burials might be disturbed by any new construction. The scant interest in a recent invitation to the next Annual General Meeting of the Vallican Archaeological Park Society, taking place in a couple of weeks, was replaced by a powerful vote to attend.

Arrangements were quickly organised: I offered to put up as many people as could fit into the generous confines of the Lodge and promised a list of other local people I knew would be willing to offer accommodation. As we were leaving, Jenny, a Lakes woman of about my age, pressed a beautifully-worked silver and turquoise Zuni bracelet into my hand: "It's not the same as an eagle feather, but perhaps it'll make up a little. I feel so bad about what happened."

Crossing back into Canada the next day, I asked the Canadian customs officer what happened to such confiscated items. To my surprise, she knew about what had happened: "So that was you, was it? That was so disgusting. Don't let him get away with it." She gave me an address in Washington, D.C. to contact but I never received so much as an acknowledgement of the two enquiries I wrote.

Although the Zuni bracelet and the Canadian officer's attitude helped, some of the amazing buoyancy on which I had been riding for months seemed to have deserted me. Perhaps it was from the shock of the devastation to a piece of land I knew intimately, and the way Eagle medicine had been stripped from me. I also had a feeling that when the Lakes people came home to Vallican, my role as go-between reporter would be over. While on one level I knew that was exactly how it should be, on another I felt bereft. Never in my life had I been so filled with energy or felt such purpose as during these heady few months; it would be difficult to let go. But the friendships forged on the Reservation existed outside of the Lakes Band meetings, and they would not end. And my contract with the Archaeological Society was in place until the end of the year.

For the present, what could be more thrilling than the knowledge that, whatever the immediate reason, the Arrow Lakes people were at last coming home?

Never will I forget the guiding sense of destiny, the bright optimism of that time: not only was I witness to a Native American people coming back into their heritage but I was involved in a ground-breaking project that called for the cooperation of two races, red and white.

Yet just as this metaphorical bridge was being forged, the construction of a physical bridge was about to tear it asunder.

CALL OF THE DRUM

Arriving home, I saw a thin blue plume of smoke coming from the chimney of the Lodge. Like many people in the area, I never locked doors (only a spirit-wind used the front one) and was not too concerned; when a lively yapping greeted our arrival I recognised Max, Lynne's bright-eyed little dachshund, rushing out to guard his beloved mistress. The pipe-carrier and her husband James, whom I had met on Vancouver Island through Bryan the previous summer and with whom I had kept in touch, had arrived the day before and in true Valley and Island style, made themselves at home.

It was wonderful to see them again. Her black hair tied back in immaculate braids, Lynne was dressed in a long, colourful ethnic skirt and a loose blouse, her little medicine pouch nestled among the strings of multi-coloured beads on her breast. Cheerfully she enfolded me in a warm hug. Like many sensitives, she was a heavy woman, her thyroid having been damaged by a childhood illness she miraculously survived (I have often wondered if on another level, the excess weight could be a physical manifestation of a need for protection in an insensitive world, just as some psychics and mediums shroud themselves in clouds of tobacco-smoke), but her spirit always shone through: positive, considerate, nurturing.

One of the few men I knew with whom I felt completely safe, James' hug was only slightly less all-enveloping.

I was bursting to tell them about what had been happening, for they had become mentors as well as friends, their wide-ranging gifts, experience and knowledge of tradition helping me understand the more subtle levels of what was unfolding with the Lakes people and follow the correct protocol, but neither of them said much. A sense of expectation hung in the air. I noticed a brown-paper package on the couch and my heart thudded. Silently, Lynne unwrapped it and handed me a red cloth bag, smiling warmly: "We decided to deliver it by hand."

I knew what it was, and slowly pulled out the drum.

Bryan hovered at the edge of my mind. This drum had been meant for him, but had arrived rather tardily; he had been gone for five months. And the design was not the white eagle I had commissioned but a bright geometric design.

Why had it come now? Why had they seen fit to bring it all this way themselves? What was going on?

The previous summer, when Bryan had first come to live at the Lodge, an acquaintance of his had started up a Native American teaching-drum in her secluded mountainside home. A long-time Slocan Valley resident, Daystar was a gifted and accomplished singer, musician and composer and leader of the local Dances of Universal Peace. I often thought that, in another time, this independent, strong-minded and feisty woman might have been the local wise-woman.

Knowing of my interest and wishing to improve his own skills, Bryan had suggested we join her sessions. It had been an intimidating experience for me. Sitting at the drum, her long, thick, grey hair wild and loose around her determined, strong-featured face, her eyes closed, Daystar's powerful voice confidently led the way and Bryan readily joined in, but although the rhythm was relatively simple, the subtleties of the chants eluded me. Trained in another mode, my ear seemed unable to attune to the patterning. Self-consciousness made me give up, but Bryan continued; by autumn, his progress and commitment inspired me to get him a hand-drum of his own. A drum had once been offered me in a dream and I had not accepted it, but I now had a partner who understood these things, who drummed and chanted as if it were second nature.

Then Lynne had "happened" to call. At the time, she and James were working with traditional Native elders and pipe-carriers on the West Coast; among other things, she mentioned that a friend of hers wished to sell his hand-made Ojibway drum to help finance his return back east to his people. New to the power of medicine items, I thought this was obviously a meant-to-be and without hesitation told Lynne I would buy it. When I told her who it was for, she suggested having a symbol painted on it and I commissioned a white eagle in honour of Bryan's endowed Native name. She promised to have it sent over by Greyhound in time for Thanksgiving.

Wanting it as a surprise, I had said nothing to Bryan. October drew to an end on the note of the extraordinary meeting with the Heritage Trust representatives, the Arrow Lakes descendants and the Board of the Vallican Archaeological Park Society; Thanksgiving came and went. There was no sign, nor word, of the drum. November turned over. When I called to find out what was happening, Lynne promised it in time for the winter solstice.

Despite escalating personal difficulties, that solstice Bryan and I hosted a twenty-four-hour prayer vigil for world peace at the Lodge with a group of twelve friends. He conducted a superb pipe ceremony; we shared prayers, stories and teachings throughout the long night, ending with a grand giveaway.

No drum had arrived for me to give away, however.

My impatience with the process tempered by an increasing appreciation of "Indian time", I had planned it as a New Year gift but it still didn't happen, and that month our relationship came to its abrupt, if unsurprising, end. Bryan returned to the coast. I put the drum out of my mind.

Toward the end of winter, a new teaching-drum had opened up in the Valley, led by a couple who had recently moved from the west side of Okanagan Lake to rent the same house where I had spent such long afternoons the previous winter, talking with old Grey Wolf. Only Cliff's (the dream-carrier) persistence persuaded me to give it a try: one of those small steps that turns out to have far-reaching consequences.

Versed in the esoteric and with wide-ranging experience in the religious and political arenas, the drum-leader was not of Native blood but had a profound empathy with the Native American life-way. He and his partner were well-acquainted with spiritual elders and pipe-carriers throughout British Columbia and received many Native visitors in their home. Small and lean, strong in body, great in spirit and intense in energy – perhaps because of having six planets in Scorpio – Yellow Bear's dark, penetrating eyes, hooded by bushy eyebrows, had put me in mind of a bird of prey when I first met him. And like Eagle, he easily sees beyond the illusions with which we surround ourselves. Strong features, deeply-etched character-lines and a tumble of waist-length, thick, black hair streaked with grey, usually tied back into a ponytail or thick braid, added up to a striking-looking individual with undoubted charisma.

A healer, his partner Linda's quiet, gentle nature provided a pleasing complement to the intensity of her partner, her long vibrantly-red hair and clear blue eyes an attractive counterpoint.

The atmosphere at their drum was friendly, laid-back; with other beginners I had been able to laugh at our ragged, faltering attempts to learn this strange new way of singing. The couple's patience and willingness to serve others gradually paid off as our small group slowly began to assimilate, understand and manage a sort of diluted version of one of the most powerful ways of communicating with the Great Spirit.

Heart in mouth, I held the drum Lynne had given me gingerly, like a new-born, and studied the design. In the centre was painted a small, solid red circle from which emanated four red arrows, quartering the drum-skin; then a circle of tiny yellow triangles with four yellow rays bisecting the red quarters; a thick, green circle with four little green peaks painted over each of the four yellow rays; finally, a thin blue circle just inside the outer circumference, running under the red arrowheads. The frame was wooden, a dodecahedron painted yellow, and the tightly-stretched drum-skin was secured by a woven lattice of sinew to which were attached four small, spotted, downy feathers. I knew they were eagle feathers.

The diameter of the drum was exactly the length from my elbow to my fingertips; my fingers slotted naturally into place between the strands of sinew. Lynne handed me a long, thin wooden drumstick. It had a soft leather wristband decorated with wine-red glass beads; the leather head was the size of the ball of my thumb. I had never seen a drumstick like it: small, dainty; surely not meant for a man's hand?

"James made the stick," Lynne said softly. "And yes, they are eagle feathers. To carry the song to the Creator."

I tapped the drum for the first time quite lightly. It spoke back with a deep yet gentle resonance. Suddenly dizzy, I took a long, shuddering breath.

"We smudged it when we got here." Lynne was referring to the simple but powerful ritual of purifying an article in the smoke of sage, the strongest cleansing herb. Primarily used as protection and to drive away negative energies or evil spirits, it is also associated with wisdom. (Even in English, a wise person is known as a sage.)

"You know it's your drum, don't you?" Lynne's tone was compelling. "I knew it was a woman's drum from the moment I first set eyes on it." With an amused lilt, she continued: "But you had your heart set on where it was going, and you wouldn't have heard me! I was wondering what it would take for it to go where it belonged; I didn't guess he would have to be taken out of the way!

"But that's the way it is with Native medicine: things go where they need to, happen as they're supposed. We don't often get to know the reason, but we don't need to. Just learn to trust in the unfolding. Everything happens at the time that's ripe; everything is as it's supposed to be. Takes faith, I know, but we all need to practice that. And patience....

"Sometimes we might get a glimpse of the reason, like when we eventually realise that it's good that we didn't get, say, this job, or that house, because a more suitable one was just round the corner. It's when we can't accept the unfolding and begin to push, that things go wrong. And it can be hard, because we've gotten used to quick returns: fast foods; fast cars; fast entertainment."

I nodded, thinking how the concept of Indian time was facilitating a calmer, more philosophical acceptance of the seeming unpredictabilities of life and vagaries of human nature, enabling an immensely liberating overview.

"The drum had to wait for you to clear some of your 'stuff'," Lynne continued. "Bryan was part of that ... at least, a symbol of it. There's no doubt you were soul-mates, but that doesn't mean you have to spend your lives together. Or even sleep together. You meet many soul-mates in a lifetime; usually you have an important lesson to teach one another and then you're on your way again. It's great if you can do it amicably, but we have our social conditioning and personal patternings and expectations to deal with.

"Make your peace with him; he doesn't have to be here for that, you know, but you must consciously make the separation in forgiveness. There's a big difference between soul-mates and twin flames. I told you about that profound connection between two people, often telepathic. It might not be an intimate relationship; could be sister and brother, or in the context of a deep, platonic friendship."

I said nothing but thought of their obvious devotion, their harmonious relationship which shone like a beacon. They had to be twin flames. All my life I had dreamed of finding such a deep and powerful connection with a man, but my experience so far suggested it only existed in fairytales. Yet on what are fairytales based? Perhaps within them is secreted an arcane truth. Some say that the "Other" lies within, but perhaps the point of duality is that when the "other-ness" within is understood, accepted and loved, it can manifest on the outer.

"But you must know the story of your drum," Lynne resumed. "Remember you wanted an eagle painted on it? I took it to a Native artist I know, the daughter of a traditional Nanaimo Band man.[16] We prayed on it together, and I left her to get on with it. It took a long time before she came up with a design, then she showed me the sketch.... Next time I spoke to her, she'd been having trouble getting the right kind of paint: the store she liked to buy from was out of stock. And when she finally got started, the image just wouldn't go as she wanted. Then she knocked one of the pots over. You can see this little bit here, that's discoloured." She pointed out a faint smudge. "She got really upset, said she'd have to put it aside, so she did and we prayed on it some more. That was when this design came into her head. 'Go ahead,' I told her."

We all laughed.

"Finally, when she was done, that was when you called to tell us that Bryan had gone back to Vancouver." A small smile played at her lips as she gently shook her head. "It's a wonderful tale." Picking up the drum, she continued: "It's like the Medicine Wheel, you see. This red circle is the heart centre, the place of balance, the place to live from. These four arrows are the four directions. This yellow circle symbolises the sun, the principle of creative energy. It made me think of a thistle; maybe that's your Scottish heritage showing up.... And the green circle, that's Mother Earth ... looks like there's little mountains on it, only little ones mind, like you've got in your native England!" She chuckled. "This blue circle is the water, the carrier of life, surrounding it all. And you crossed the ocean to come here.

"I see your heritage held in this drum, and you've got some work to do with it. And once you start to use it, never put it away. It's what keeps you connected, as you make your Walk, following the lessons of the Wheel, moving ever closer to the centre. Drumbeat is the heartbeat

---

16 An abundance of resources from sea, shore and land enabled the Coastal Salish to develop a rich tradition of vibrant art and craft. Renowned in British Columbia, their style is so prevalent that most of the population of and visitors to the province assume that these are the only indigenous people in the entire province. Lynne had told me of their efforts to recover stolen artefacts, sacred items such as masks, some of which can be found on display in museums in Vancouver and Victoria but most of which were spirited away into collections throughout the United States and the rest of the world.

of the Mother, calling to her people."

Not only were my hands trembling but my entire being felt like it was being shaken to the core. Images from a dream close to two years old flooded my mind. Breathlessly, I told them for the first time about the Medicine Wheel gathering and the uncanny, warm reception of the red-jacketed elder-founder, Red Cloud; the dream and his admonishment to "take the drum, call the people"; the elder's sudden death following the appearance of the two Arrow Lakes descendants. "A Medicine Wheel gathering," I babbled, "and that's reflected in this design ... and that came of its own accord...."

It was difficult to take it all in. Even if my last dreaming-waking thought had been to refuse the drum, some part of me had willingly taken up a role in an incredible drama, in which the people had been called. Now this drum had arrived, bringing four eagle feathers, just after one feather had been taken away.... And in just a few days' time, the Arrow Lakes people would be arriving in the Valley to take care of their ancestors' resting-places, returning to their ancestral lands, to their heritage.

Home, at last.

The visionary-elder, Red Cloud, must have at some level known about all this; his role had been pivotal. But how had he known? What was it he had seen in me? What was it that had reached through into my dream-state?

And why had this real drum been directed to me now, after the people had been called?

VOICE OF THE ANCESTORS

My life had never been filled with so much purpose, meaning and excitement; I was not about to take a step back. To witness, actually play a small part in the renascence of a fragmented First Nation was an incredible privilege, while the strange coincidences and powerful dreams made me feel more alive, more appreciative of the mystery and beauty of life. Every aspect of my broad (self-penned) job-description was a pleasure: research; setting up a comprehensive library; synthesising ideas for an experiential traditional Native American site and exploring avenues to bring it into manifestation; contacting related organisations; representing the Society at heritage conventions; keeping a detailed record of events; facilitating interpretive tours of the site; and most vital of all, acting as liaison until such time the Arrow Lakes descendants took charge of their site, And then, who knew? Under – or over – it all, a bright promise on the horizon, beckoned Bob's vision.

In hindsight, the removal of the eagle feather may have been a warning that I was losing the overview, forgetting to keep the bigger picture in mind. At the very least, it might have been a good time to slow down and re-assess.

Did news of the road-development by the Lakes ancestral village precipitate an action that should have happened in its own time? Certainly, it seemed that from then on, events took on a life of their own, rushing off in a totally unforeseen direction; for a while, even the issue of the removed ancestral remains was put on hold. Yet perhaps this catalyst was a necessary part of the greater Plan; the Native American way is that everything happens as it must.

As for myself, I would like to think I was acting out of altruism and a sort of calling, but sometimes it seemed as if the reins of my life were no longer in my hands. Later, I would be told how my body language and the way I expressed myself had gradually begun to change, and my mother would tell me she did not recognise the person who was writing my letters. Looking back, I remember this time as becoming increasingly unreal, as if I were acting out a part, responding to prompts, while another part of me looked on, amazed and occasionally aghast.

Locally, the issue of the new road swiftly spread over the newspapers and public hearings were begun. Strong feelings were expressed about the way hard work, voluntarily undertaken to put reasonable planning procedures into place, was being shunted aside. Rumours circulated about hidden agendas, mainly that the impending expansion of the pulp mill at Castlegar would mean heavier logging-traffic and if a reasonable secondary road existed on the other side of the river, local residents couldn't complain about an increase in industrial traffic on the main highway. Taken a step further, the idea of two roads in such a narrow valley fuelled fear that plans were in place to invade the mountains west of the Valley for logging, which would be facilitated by the new road and bridge.

The Society's AGM promised to offer an open forum. A meeting which had attracted scant local attention for the past five years would now take on unexpected proportions, and become a memorable event.

After a week of clear, balmy June weather, on the morning of the meeting the sky was overcast. Gentle rumbles of thunder began muttering to the south and west of the Valley, over which a strange tension seemed to lie. To my fertile imagination, it was nothing to do with a change in weather but as if something unseen but powerful were waiting, with bated breath. Were the Lakes ancestors, restless spirits on the move, anticipating the return of their descendants?

The "little invasion", as the Lakes people laughingly called it, was spearheaded by Auntie Vi, her husband Junior and their niece Viv, who arrived at the Lodge early and unloaded coolers stuffed with food, and boxes and tins of commodities (generic foodstuffs supplied to the Reservation by the U.S. government). It was a consideration typical of the Native people; when the fifteen or so guests departed, my house was stocked with more food than they consumed and cleaner than they found it. Native American hospitality works both ways, as Bob had told me.

"It's so beautiful here. No wonder they moved us down onto the dry ol' Rez!" Auntie Vi observed without bitterness.

I showed them photos of the area and gave them a framed print of Frog Mountain. There was a few moments' silence.

"Junior, his Indian name...." said Auntie Vi softly. "So he was named for that mountain. We had no idea why he was called that."

It seemed an auspicious beginning. This was going to be the most exciting and revealing voyage of discovery, I was sure.

Auntie Vi held out a package. "We brought this for you."

A bundle of sand-coloured material and silken, golden-yellow tassels tumbled out. It was an Indian shawl, like the ones women dancers wore. I was stunned: did this mean I might dance with them some day? Auntie Vi took it from me, deftly folded it into a triangle and then I saw the kind of shawl it was: a superb bald eagle was embroidered on it, white head gleaming, fierce eyes smouldering, yellow beak agape, black-tipped wings swept back and talons agape as if about to grasp an unseen prey.

Numbly, I let the two women drape the shawl over my shoulders. They showed me how to tuck in the corners and put my hands on my hips so my elbows stuck out in the way of the dancer, displaying the eagle in all its magnificence. Acutely aware of the splendid creature riding my back, the spread of wings – like angel's wings – I dance-stepped, causing the long, silken fringes to sway like grass in the wind.

Eagle had come back, in a new way; could travel with me anywhere without problem. I hardly knew what to say.

"Just look how it matches her blonde hair," said Viv.

Auntie Vi smiled. "Knew it was just perfect for her."

Profoundly affected in ways I could not put into words, I span round in a liquid gold swirl.

"Now we just have to get you the rest of your dancin' outfit!" Auntie Vi laughed, a sparkle in her eyes. "I'll make your moccasins next."

Her words lifted me even higher. Although I would never have asked, I had been longing for a pair of personalised, hand-crafted moccasins. Who better to make them than Auntie Vi, who was fast becoming a close friend?

As soon as the rest of the Lakes people who would stay at the Lodge had arrived, I gave them directions and we set out, a caravan of five cars, for their ancestral village. Although

Auntie Vi was riding with me, I felt it was not my place to arrive with them, and stopped for petrol at the little community of Slocan Park, south of Passmore. We were chatting as the attendant filled the tank, when a voice yelled: "There she is!"

A local man was walking agitatedly towards my van, shaking an accusing finger. "There she is! There's the woman that's bringing all these Indians up here to cause trouble!"

"But they're ahead of me!"

He stormed off, unappreciative of my little double-entendre.

Auntie Vi was furious. "What a rude man!"

But I was riding high; oblivious. "Don't worry. Gives me a kick to think he believes I'm so powerful I could rally an entire people."

By the time we caught up, the others were waiting for us in the clearing where Bob and Manny had set up their second camp the year before. Most of the women were in tears. We joined hands to form a prayer-circle; Aunt Tootie prayed and then we sang a hymn I hadn't heard before. The melody and words were simple: "This is holy ground; we are standing on holy ground...."

Nothing could have been more appropriate. Tears in my eyes, I felt more than ever like I had come home: this was where I belonged, in this place, with these people. Nor did I want to leave, but that afternoon I was scheduled for an interview on CBC (Canadian Broadcasting Corporation) radio. Yet as I drove away, I understood why I was being removed. Whatever my feelings about the place and what was happening, I was an outsider. It had been enough of a privilege to be included in their first prayer and song.

The rest of the day was fully occupied with finalising arrangements for the evening meeting, but I was constantly aware of what was going on at the Indian village, for the Thunder Beings never ceased in their growling and grumbling.

Not until evening did the storm break, however, literally and metaphorically.

Advised by a sympathetic and supportive local civil servant of the complicated political implications of the various levels of interest in the proposed road, information I had passed on to the Society's Board of Directors, as they arrived, I could see from the disconcerted look on some of their faces that yet again my words had gone unheeded. By the time the president and secretary arrived together in typical laid-back Valley style, some twenty minutes late, obviously expecting a customary small meeting, they found a hall crammed with about one hundred people and an expectant, charged atmosphere, and were obliged to run a gauntlet of sarcastic comments as they made their way through the middle of a crowd impatiently waiting for their presence to begin.

Conspicuously silent, over thirty Arrow Lakes descendants from the Colville Reservation were seated on one side of the hall. Local people filled the rest and more were standing crowded at the back, with late-comers on the grass outside, crushed up against the door, straining to hear what was going on. Local government officials and representatives of the Ministry of Highways were also present, as well as six members of the media, who had gotten wind of the increasingly volatile nature of the situation. Readied by the helpful civil servant, I had prepared press packages as well as information pamphlets.

Despite having found common ground with some local people, it soon became clear that the Native people would be allowed no more voice in what happened to their ancestral land, than they had in the preceding four hundred years. Those anxious to hear the voice of the elders were about to witness them being interrupted and ignored.

Initial conventional Society business was swiftly dealt with as a loud, concerted demand arose that the road issue be addressed immediately. Briefly, the Society's objections to the road were delineated: a twentieth-century feature built directly adjacent to a proposed experiential Native American heritage site would destroy its ambiance; access to the site would be facilitated before any management plan had been put in place; the full extent of the site was not known. Procedures were still fairly under control at this point, and the Lakes people were invited to speak.

Uncle Charlie stood up and turned to address the crowded hall. Introducing himself as primary spokesperson, he stressed that the repatriation of the ancestral remains was their foremost concern. I was glad of this reminder, and of his calm demeanour. "We're no strangers to reburial," he stated, and described a reburial he had conducted in Kettle Falls in 1939. He went on to clarify the status of the Arrow Lakes Band as a non-treaty Nation whose aboriginal title had never been extinguished, which unfortunately were not words which made some of the people there feel any more at ease.

"We had freedom," he told his audience, some of whom had begun a loud muttering among themselves. "You could leave your huntin'-ground, and come back, and it would still be there. We had a living system. Europeans thought once a place was deserted, it was abandoned. We didn't abandon anything-"

"The road's the only issue to be dealt with!" The interruption was backed up by a loud, aggressive chorus, and it soon became evident that this vociferous minority feared a land-claim. The meeting degenerated into a melee amid cries of: "Go back home!" "You're Americans, this is none of your business!"

"Let the Highways representatives speak," appealed a director of the Board.

A face I did not recognise, apparently the Highways regional manager, curtly stated: "I'm not here to negotiate."

"Then why are you here?" "For shame!" Amid the ensuing uproar, Bob stood up from where he was sitting in the midst of his people and turned to face the hall.

Something about him and his quietly-spoken words swiftly calmed the crowd. Eloquently, he recounted the terrible history of the Lakes people and what the land meant to them, a speech later reported by the media as impassioned. Yet he spoke evenly and calmly; what went unreported was the way the climax of his address was dramatically punctuated by the thunderstorm, which finally and violently unleashed itself directly over our heads.

" ... It is history in the makin'." Almost drowning out the last word, the first great flash-crash cracked overhead – a whip of the gods – causing the little Heritage Hall building to shake, and rattling the windows. People ducked, jumped, and looked about in shock.

Everyone except Bob, who remained absolutely still. "Spiritually, we're taught to follow our ancestors." Another great flash and boom rocked the foundations of the building.

Bob folded his arms across his chest and smiled. "We're not here to cause trouble; we're here to ask for the protection of our ancestors."

The final "s" was drowned in a great rending crack and simultaneous blinding flash and long, reverberating crash of thunder, followed immediately by the roar of a torrential downpour as the thunderheads discharged onto the roof. It was wonderful, exciting and terrifying; I could see I was not the only one who wondered whether the old building could withstand such an onslaught.

"We're a tribal people who've passed back and forth here for over nine thousand years...."

The driving force of the torrential rain whipped the tree branches, which scrabbled against the windows like skeletal hands seeking entry.

Thrilled by the violence of the elements, the timing, I could not take my eyes off Laughing Thunder. Slight and slim, wearing a dark blue shirt, two neat braids coiled over his chest, a small, enigmatic smile playing at his lips, he stood impassive, calm and still as the eye of the storm.

Laughing Thunder, who could send smoke of the sacred fire to the four directions; who could hear a call on another level than physical; who could see into the soul of a man.... His mother spoke of him as special; I had heard his stories of events and experiences that were nothing less than pure magic, and he seemed exquisitely aware of the perfect timing for maximum dramatic effect in orchestration with the storm exploding directly over our heads. As he sat down again, a last grumble of thunder growled overhead and faded into a mutter, the wild wind dropped and the rain decreased to a steady drumming.

Had he called it? Did he have the power to manipulate the elements? I found myself thinking about Chief Joseph, Hin-Maton-Yalat-Kit, "Thunder Rolling in the Mountains", and wondered if his spirit was somehow involved. Or was this an impressive gesture of the Thunder Beings, in elemental support of those ancestors for whom, or maybe of whom, Laughing Thunder was asking protection? Or the restless spirits themselves; had they called up a storm? One of the group of reporters taken through the Indian village by Bob in the late afternoon later told me of the strange preternatural haze hanging over the burial-ground area, causing it to shimmer and shift.

It was close to midnight by the time the meeting was drawn to an end. What was accomplished was nebulous: officials and bureaucrats had stood silent and unmoved throughout, as if their power and policies were engraved in stone; several new directors, including Arrow Lakes representatives, had been nominated onto the Board; a division in the community had blatantly come to light and overflowed outside in ongoing, heated arguments. Exhausted and bewildered, I was glad of the distraction of clearing up the hall, which gave me time to think.

How could so many people be so blind to the truth of the incredible unfolding of which they had unwittingly become part? As Bob had said, it was history in the making. Yet ideals which I had taken for granted would come into play once the full story was known were desperately lacking. How could I have been so naïve as to think that they would all understand, be supportive, once they heard the whole story? It was clear that those violently opposed to the return of the Native people were full of fear. Was it fear of otherness: racial fear? Or was it about something Bob had once said to me, in another place, another context: "Their suspicions are of themselves"? Were they afraid of what a people returning to their stolen homeland might mean to them personally; that, despite reassurances and the law, the Native people would act as they themselves might (and as some of their forebears probably had) and try to reclaim the entire land?

Racism; territorialism. Such basic instincts: fear-based behaviour. How on earth could these people be moved beyond their fear? What would it take to enable them to see through the eyes of those they thought of as somehow "other"; to open them up to compassion?

GREEN BLANKET

It was another of those times I did not want to end, but after a slow start – we had talked long into the night – my Lakes guests were leaving. As I was wishing them a good journey, Auntie Vi grabbed my hand. "I know who you are!"

Her intensity took me aback. Waiting for her to continue, I found myself thinking of Manny and a moment out of time when he had told me about the Initiators, and asked who I was. Since coming into contact with the Native people, aspects of myself I never knew existed were bubbling to the surface; any help in understanding myself would be deeply appreciated.

Her hand was still gripping mine, she continued: "In the old times, there used to be raids 'tween the tribes, back and forth. Though us Lakes were mostly a peaceful people.... The Blackfoot'd come over from the east, to steal horses. Sometimes they'd even steal women. Us Arrow Lakes women were always known for our beauty, you know!" she chuckled.

I nodded. Auntie Vi had clearly been beautiful in her youth, and her illness-ravaged features were still lit by her spirit.

"One time, they stole away a young girl – she'd be about twelve. Took her 'way over the mountains to Montana. She was very unhappy, wanting to go back home. Was always waiting for a chance to escape. An' that's what she did, soon's the chance came. She ran off. Six months it took her to get back to her people, over the mountains all the way from Montana, through the cold seasons. Her people were amazed when she walked back into her village – it was in the Keller area. Her feet were wrapped in the last rags of the green blanket she'd used up, strip by strip, to protect them.

"They couldn't believe she'd crossed over those mountains in the winter on her own like that, but when they asked how she did it, she said, 'I have a story to tell, 'bout Coyote....' But I'll tell you that part of the story another time." She glanced at the others sitting waiting in their cars. "I don't like making people wait for me.... But you see, her people'd been falling off their spiritual path an' what she did was such a miracle, she led them back onto their spiritual path again. Now you come along, and the Lakes are coming back together. Coming home...." Squeezing my hand tightly, she smiled. "It puts me in mind of that old story. Maybe if I believed that people come back round again – and I'm not saying as I don't – maybe that Green Blanket is workin' through you."

For a moment, the world span away. She was speaking of reincarnation, of spirit reaching through time and space. Knowing her to be strongly Christ-oriented in her beliefs, I wondered how this fit in. And there was something else....

I remembered a green blanket, almost two years ago, right at the beginning of all this.

On the last evening of my first Medicine Wheel gathering, after the encounter with the handsome Native speaker, I had decided to attend the core-group meeting laying down plans for the following year. It had been dark and the meeting already underway when I arrived with my two younger children: a small circle of people were sitting round a fire in front of a tipi, listening to a well-built man talking animatedly about protocol. Flickering flames illuminated his strong features; he had officiated a number of times over the weekend but despite the red bandanna tied round his head, his generous nose and long, steel-grey braids, his sentiments on the state of the planet and the value of Native American teachings, his articulate manner of speaking was more a lecture than the poetic eloquence of the Native American whose words had so enthralled me.

Little did I know how both these men would soon come to have a powerful, lasting effect on my life.

When a gap had finally appeared in the speaker's lengthy monologue, I tentatively offered: "I was at a multicultural Mother Earth Day last month in Toronto. It was really inspiring. Has anything multicultural been considered?"

"I hate it when people turn up late and ask questions about stuff that's already been dealt with! Last thing we need here is a bunch of pot-smoking Rastas!"

I had been mortified. It was not just his impatience and rudeness but something about the force of his abrupt dismissal; I would not forget it, although I also would not let it serve as a caution when I later took up with this man (Bryan). Chilled, I hugged my children close, my enthusiasm draining away in discomfiture. At that moment I felt the rough caress of a woollen blanket being laid over my shoulders. It was the Native American with whom I had spent such unforgettable moments only that afternoon. His smile gleamed in the firelight as he tucked the blanket round the children and sat down beside us.

One moment, I was embarrassed and dispirited; the next, trembling and glowing with fiery pride and an upsurge of emotion. Aware that the eyes of the entire circle were looking our way, I noted the sudden deference in the speaker's voice: "Bob! Good of you to join us! D'you want to take over?"

"No thanks," came the amiable response. "You just go ahead. You seem to be doin' ju-u-st fine." Raising a sardonic eyebrow, he winked at me.

The firelight played over the warm tones of his skin, bringing his high cheekbones into sharp definition. My heart was thudding loudly and heavily in my chest. Acutely aware of his presence, the Native man whose name I had only now learned (such a terribly ordinary name), I did not dare look at him again and sat staring ahead in a numb, unseeing state. As the speaker resumed, Bob began talking quietly to Natalie. He seemed to be paying no attention to the proceedings; I could hear only the thundering in my ears.

At the end, Bob was directly addressed: "We'd be honoured to have you lead the gathering next year."

"I can't make no commitment to anythin' right now. I just hope I can come back next year," he responded.

Silently, I resolved to return the following year. As people began to disperse, I got up, folded the blanket and held it out to Bob. "Thanks for your consideration."

He shook his head and smiled: "You keep the blanket." Turning to my children, he added: "You little 'uns, now you take good care of your Mom. I'll come visit your camp in the mornin' 'fore we leave." He melted away into the darkness, leaving me hanging onto his parting words like a lifeline.

The next morning it had seemed like a dream, but the rough texture of the olive-green blanket in which I had wrapped myself all night was real enough. For a long time before the sun hit the clearing, I lay with my cheek against the precious memento and breathed in the musky aroma of wood-smoke.

Black hair wetly shining, neatly braided and tied with deer-hide thongs, Bob appeared as I was preparing breakfast. "I gotta good instinct for fresh coffee," he grinned, then peered into the camper and greeted the children, who were just waking up. "Neat set-up. I like that. You sure look cosy in here." He turned back to me and accepted a coffee. "Come walk with me," he said.

Thrilled that we would spend more time together and inordinately proud to walk by his side, I had happily agreed.

Every single person to whom Bob introduced me during the following half-hour would reappear in my life over the next few years, almost all of us feeling the same sense of interconnectedness, like members of some distantly-related tribe. For a long while, I would believe that the "people of the heart" were finally coming together.

When we got back to the van, Bob had asked me for a pen and paper and wrote down an address and a phone number: "This here's my post box, an' my ma's number. There isn't a phone where I live, but know that if you ever need help, I'm only a few hours away."

Nespelem, I noted; so many places in North America had Native names. While unable to imagine ever calling his mother for help or needing help that was hours away, I found his words reassuring. And even though I had wanted to stay wrapped in it forever, I offered him back his green blanket.

He seemed reluctant to take it.

"Others might have more need of it than me," I found myself saying. It was really strange: part of me wanted to keep the blanket, while another part scoffed at what seemed like inverted snobbery, and yet another part seemed anxious to be rid of the thing. In an attempt to lighten an increasingly heavy moment, I picked out a couple of cassettes from my glove compartment. "Here. Another Bob: Bob Marley. Music to ease your travels."

He smiled, accepted the blanket and the cassettes. "I like Marley."

Not knowing if Native people cared for reggae, I was relieved and the sense of confusion retreated.

Blanket over one arm, he produced a twenty-dollar bill and pressed it into my hand. "It's not easy, bein' a Mom on her own." He smiled at my silent, round-eyed children: "You make sure you all get a hot breakfast now!"

I had not wanted to accept money from him either, but it seemed rude to refuse him twice. In any case, his appreciation of my situation had touched me deeply. As he walked away, my eyes rested on his slim, graceful, retreating figure; dry-eyed, I could have wailed for him to stay. Afterwards, I had walked round in a daze; but for the crisp, green note in my hand, it might have been a dream.

Telling her about it now, I said nothing of my romantic longings but Auntie Vi read me a lot better than I could read myself.

"That man!" Her amused tone reminded me she was his cousin. "You know, it's tantamount to an insult to refuse a gift from an Indian." She laughed at the horrified expression on my face. "Although maybe that's not always the case. Guess you don't know that, traditionally, when an

Indian presents a blanket to a woman, he's making a proposal of marriage!"

A smile pasted itself onto my face, belying the sick feeling in my gut. How could I have known? What had I missed out on? And what was I thinking of?

By now I knew he was married to his third wife. And all his words to me in Vernon about his reputation had since come forward in one way or another: it seemed that almost every woman with whom he came into contact was intensely drawn to him. I had heard one disappointed woman venomously lashing out about his "string of women"; another whose long-term relationship foundered because of her unrequited obsession with him; yet another who had to go on a vision-quest on a mountain to save her own marriage from what was essentially an illusion. He had told me about coming home on several occasions to find a woman waiting on the doorstep of his ranch, wanting to bear his child. And who was he to refuse? "Us Indians are in short supply...." Rumours circulated of another five or six children besides the seventeen from his marriages, scattered about the land.

My own feelings were the most powerful I had ever experienced: simple anticipation of seeing him reduced my insides to a quivering ferment so that Band and Society meetings, and any other encounter, were shrouded in a haze of exquisite, heightened sensitivity. I could sympathise with those women who wanted a child by him. Yet I managed for the most part to keep my feelings concealed – even from myself – in clouds of fantasy and romantic imaginings about the magic of the bigger picture. At some level, I was also increasingly aware that it was not so much the man himself, but what moved within him, that was so powerfully attractive.

Not Bob, but Laughing Thunder.

An understanding of the power of spiritual attraction is sadly lacking in modern, secular western society. Interpreted at the sexual level, instead of being raised from the sacral chakra and refined into creative, spiritual expression, it is invariably discharged as base, sexual energy. I was lucky to recognise Bob's charisma for what it was, before it overwhelmed me physically.

What it was Bob had recognised in me, however, I had little idea. And while part of me wondered if anything might have been different if I had accepted the blanket, I had not forgotten the strong compulsion to return it.

No matter how I might wish things were otherwise, it seemed clear that it was not on the physical plane that our connection lay, but on the spiritual.

SNAKE MEDICINE

In an attempt to enlighten the RDCK members and the Highwaymen, as we had taken to calling them, I offered an exclusive interpretive tour and for almost three hours walked and talked them through the Indian village. The project manager was surprisingly sympathetic, raising our hopes; at the last minute, an appeal was made to the RDCK to implement the Conflict Resolution Procedure outlined in the Valley Guidelines. Only two voices out of twelve present called for further consultation, however; it was clear that the sensitivity of heritage had little sway once that most powerful of ministries, Transportation and Highways, was on the move. Their current promotional slogan, "Freedom to Move", rang loud with irony in my ears.

Bryan had once said that through dialogue, dedication and determination, the political arena would be the place where we could put spiritual principles into practice; despite my own misgivings, I had wanted this to be true but it seemed this would not be the time or place. Dispirited by the lack of local governmental support and absence of vision, I returned to Vallican to prepare myself for the next Lakes Band meeting, scheduled in Inchelium the next day.

Several people were at the Indian village, including a prominent local environmentalist. At the Earth Summit conference in Rio de Janeiro that year, Colleen had courageously represented British Columbia as the "Brazil of the North". She had taken time out from her intense schedule to personally encourage support of the Native people, and helped me come up with some new ideas of whom to turn to for advice. I made a couple of phone-calls and immediately left for the East Kootenays and Cranbrook, B.C., to meet with the Queen's Counsel who had been the original discoverer and protector of the Vallican heritage site.

Then in his eighties, Leo was still the VAPS' main benefactor. Delighted to hear of the involvement of the Arrow Lakes Band, he drew upon his years of experience in the legal system and over cups of tea, advised that it would probably only be the Lakes people themselves who might be able to stop the road going ahead until a thorough assessment had been made of the route, but they would need expert counsel.

Next on my agenda was the archaeologist, who lived at the south end of the valley. As I drove, I could not help noting evidence of Native presence, so lacking in the West Kootenays, in the form of several small Native arts-and-crafts outlets dotted along the southbound highway. To the east, the horizon was dominated by the immense foothills of the Rockies; more than once I saw eagles soaring, tiny specks against the clear blue of the sky. Near Moyie Lake, I caught sight of a moose, grazing knee-deep in a marshy area. I had never seen one in the wild before; it was huge, and totally oblivious to the nearby highway. Several minutes later, a coyote trotted nonchalantly across the road mere yards in front of my van, giving me a cursory, sidelong glance. Around the next curve, a hawk hovered, quivering intent above the verge.

Had I been less single-mindedly wrapped up in my quest, it might have dawned on me to pay attention to the messages: Eagle, urging me to keep in mind the overview; Moose, representing self-esteem, telling me that I had reason to feel good about what I was managing to accomplish, even if I felt powerless and fraught; Coyote, warning not to let ego trip me up; and finally Hawk, reminding me to be aware of messages.... But the intrusion of a road had become the driving force; frustrated by the lack of vision, I was stooping to politics.

When we arrived at the small community of Yahk, Wayne was not at home. Exploring the land behind his log cabin, Nick and I found a little creek running through a secluded stand of cottonwood and birch, and a sweat-lodge, covered with colourful layers of old blankets, mostly red. It was a side of Wayne I had not anticipated; I knew he had worked with Native people for many years and respected their beliefs, but he had seemed estranged from any idea of spirituality.

The site was enchanting. While Nick played by the creek, I sat down on the grass by the lodge. There was something about the light in this place: it shimmered, flickered, and gradually sort of enveloped me, making me relax for the first time in days. Lying back, I watched a fairy-dance of sunlight through the filter of delicate greenery. Then I heard the voices, singing.... Only they were not exactly voices, but a sort of distant, ethereal, wordless, heavenly choir, coming not from any direction but all round me; as if the light itself were humming, toning the sparkles. All my agitation and tension began to fade.

I recalled the only other time I had been to the East Kootenays: invited by Grey Wolf, barely a year earlier, on a trip to set up the camp for Dancing Mountain, the wilderness school that was the brainchild of the couple from Montreal. Although he had said I was welcome to bring the children, I had almost turned it down; the plan to have Bob and Manny as advisors had evaporated and I was to be cook for the three men involved, which brought back childhood memories of refusing to be squaw: I was scout. But the idea of camping in a pristine area inaccessible by road and travelling there in a twelve-man canoe had been too tempting.

Setting out from Kaslo, for almost two hours the graceful craft had swept northwards between steep, forested mountains where there was no sign of any human habitation and little of any activity. With only an occasional small clearcut and no other boat to mar my day-dreaming about a more natural way of living, I remembered Auntie Vi telling me how the Arrow Lakes people had had very little to do with the Kutenai, upon whose land I would soon be setting foot. The vague sense of unease that had been with me from the outset intensified.

We beached several miles south of Johnson's Landing, but barely was I out of the canoe when I began to sneeze. Not the usual two or three times, but a series that continued without respite until my eyes and nose were streaming. Never had I know anything like it: like water, mucus poured from my nose. Deeply embarrassed, I had to leave the men to unload the tipis, poles and equipment and supplies, and then something even more unexpected happened. Barely had I taken ten steps when I felt my moon-flow begin. It was ten days premature. And of course I was not prepared for this either.

I had been devastated: it was too much to expect to be taken back to Kaslo; it would take hours, there was a schedule, and in any case, I had left my van at home and ridden there with Grey Wolf.

Yet within minutes I perceived the advantages of the situation, and the humour in it: not only was my sudden cold unhygienic, but the birth of a camp modelled on Native tradition had better follow protocol: I should not cook for them, touch their things; my outward creative flow would overpower them. I announced that I would retire to my moon-lodge.

Typical men, they had grumbled, unable to appreciate I would be dripping all over the place in one way or another.

Despite the initial inconvenience, it had been a vast relief not to have to do the cooking; as for my children, they were used to simple fare when camping. And the weather was clear and warm; I did not need to build a shelter. I found a beautiful little mossy glade about a half-mile away, next to a little creek. With nothing to fall back on, I recalled how Native women had traditionally coped, apparently using moss. Not quite able to bring myself to do that, I had been quite content to sit next to the water, using it to wash myself when I needed.

The rest of that first day of forced "confinement" had brought me a moon-time peace I had never before known and, as the outward show of my creative power flowed down to join with the lake, a deep sense of connectedness with the steep, forested Purcell mountains at my back, the calm, steel-blue body of water before me, and the Selkirks soaring into the heights on the far shore. Like never before, I tuned into the energy of my creative cycle. And that night, instead of having to sleep among snoring men in a tipi, I laid out our sleeping bags out under the stars and as Lynne had taught me, asked for a clarifying dream.

Through a tunnel, entering as if from stage left into a dull-red-ochre, parched, Negev-desert landscape. Underfoot, sharp bone-white rust-dusted stones; overhead, searing bright-blue sky-sun-shimmer.

Many people are walking past me, in silent expectation, up and over the gentle slope. Men, women and children, wearing simple, belted shifts or tunics of a sackcloth-like material, dusty and stained, in beige, olive-green, ivory. Barefoot, or wearing rough sandals thick with dust.

Acutely aware of my twentieth-century garb, I have a distinct feeling of being a time-traveller. And somehow I know what this is, where I am....

A small, stooped, skinny man wearing a knee-length, coarse, dirty-brown tunic, torn and frayed at the edges, is trudging slowly past me. His feet are bare on the unforgiving stones; a pudding-bowl hack, his black hair is greasy and matted. His wrinkled face is nut-brown, his beard sparse and scraggy. A woven basket is looped over one shoulder.

Even though I know the answer, I ask: "Where are you going?" I speak in English, which I somehow know he will understand.

"To hear the Master teach." He walks on, steadily trudging upwards, carrying a precious load. Are there fishes in his basket?

Shrugging, I turn back. "Of course," I think. "And I know what the Master said, so I don't need to be there."

Waking, I had deeply regretted leaving the dream-scene so lightly and, to the awake-me, prematurely. The dream had been so vivid, it belonged to the exceptional dreams involving Native people, but on what seemed like an entirely different track, and had left me wondering about the symbolic processing of my inner world.

Lying dreamily on the earth next to Wayne's sweat-lodge, I wondered why this memory had come back now. Had the dream been a message from some deeper part of myself, reminding me of the spiritual way I was born to in this life? Or had it been a dip into a past life? Hearing

Wayne's pick-up, I put the whole experience to the back of my mind. I did not know the archaeologist well enough to share any of this, a sense which was borne out when I learned that he used the sweat-lodge solely as a sauna.

A tradition not confined to North America but used throughout the ancient world, by Celts and Arabs, in northern Europe, Scandinavia and Russia, in Africa, Japan and Greece, most of these cultures viewed spiritual and physical cleansing as intimately connected. Before I knew what I was saying, I asked if I might consecrate his sweat-lodge, and was surprised by his ready agreement.

It was a strange experience. As if I had split myself, a self-conscious part of me watched the person playing this role: laying out all my medicine items on a blanket before the sweat-lodge; smudging them, the fire-pit, the Old Ones, the lodge, ourselves. While Wayne heated the rocks, I sang and drummed, calling in the spirits.

Whom I was sure had been there long before either of us or this sweat-lodge. Had I not heard them sing? Only they had not seemed Native American, those voices....

Drawing on my experience but feeling self-conscious, I conducted four rounds on the themes of the elements, taking a cooling rinse from the little creek between each round. All the while I felt I was not fully involved but acting something out, while having little real idea of what I was doing.

Playing with fire, had I been more aware. I knew that the leader of a sweat-lodge ceremony is traditionally called to it by a vision, and receives years of training, including a long stint of "serving the Grandmothers and Grandfathers". Responsible for both the physical and spiritual well-being of the participants, he or she must not only be aware of the subtle energies at play, but be able to control and direct them. As with most training in the mysteries, the length of time spent as an apprentice is not so much about what to do in the ceremony, as how to handle what comes with it. A little knowledge is a dangerous thing: not for the first and far from the last time, my guardian angel must have been working flat out.

The next morning Nick and I went back to the site to collect my medicine things, which I had left outside the newly-consecrated lodge to be cleansed by moonlight and dew. After a few minutes, Wayne joined us. Good-looking in a tall and rangy sort of way, a knowledgeable and articulate speaker and a fount of creative ideas for the betterment of humankind (epitomising his sun-sign, Aquarius), he took up our conversation of the night before.

Only partially listening, my attention was on the ethereal toning I could again hear all round us in the sparkling light. It had not been there in the darkness, and I was thinking that it might be something to do with the light when Nick, who was playing by the water, cried out: "Look at that!"

He was pointing at the creek, at a place in the shade where it ran wide and shallow beneath overhanging vegetation. There, in the middle of the water, a moss-green snake was drifting down slowly with the current, squirming, twisting back upon itself. It seemed in extreme discomfort; from its wide-gaping jaw protruded the silvery tail of a small fish, on which it seemed to be choking. Coming level with where we were standing, a single shaft of sunlight caught it. It began to writhe madly, then convulsed and regurgitated the entire fish, which, veiled with translucent shreds of skin like some weird bride, drifted down to the sandy creek-bed. Curving its way effortlessly through the water to the bank, the snake slid ashore and up to my feet – which were rooted to the spot – where it coiled into a spiral and seemed to rest for some moments before swiftly gliding off into the undergrowth.

Throughout it all, the three of us had been mesmerised, our eyes and mouths wide.

"What does it mean?" Wayne's usually-confident voice quavered.

Strangely unsettled, all I knew was that I had to leave immediately; the meeting at Inchelium that evening seemed to beckon like a safe haven.

A couple of days later, intrigued by what had happened, Wayne called to tell me that when Nick had called to us, he had felt something like a seismic shock, a literal thump from under the earth. Until then, I had not let myself think about the unusual nature of the incident; when he repeated his question, off the top of my head, I let myself ramble on about symbolism: snake, symbol of ancient wisdom: fish, symbol of Christianity; bridal veils, the Church. Wisdom almost choking on the dead teachings of the Church? The end of the Age of Pisces, during the latter part of which the Church has almost wiped out the ancient, esoteric teachings? Snake, dragon-symbol, one of the effigies of the sign of Aquarius, shedding itself of dead Piscean energy? Snake in a spiral at my feet: the spiral-ascent to wisdom, enlightenment?

According to Native American tradition, snake medicine is very rare, and represents transmutation. Initiates experience snake bites and learn to survive them by transmuting the poison (fire). Later, I would wonder whether the message may have been one about transmuting a thought or action that was being driven by passion.

FINDING A WAY HOME

Leaving snake-fish East Kootenay discomfort behind in a cloud of dust, I drove down to the border, thinking about what I would have to say at the Lakes Band meeting at Inchelium. They had already retained a competent legal advisor; nothing I had found out would be of any help to them, but, relieved to be out of the area and on my way to the Reservation, it didn't seem to matter. I looked forward to seeing Auntie Vi and being again among the people with whom I felt so "right".

On a route new to me, I realised I was facing a long loop to the north or a long drive south before doubling back to the Reservation. Then, just south of the checkpoint, I noticed what seemed like a short-cut: a gravel road, crudely signposted "Waneta". It was not marked on the map but I remembered that there was a dam near there; true to my Sumix, I decided to take this new, unexplored route.

For several miles, the road wound through forest with no sign of any human habitation. Then the trees opened out onto a huge body of water and the road gradually degenerated into little more than a track, which became increasingly stony, dusty and rutted. Frequent signs began to appear, warning of the rising waters of a new dam and the instability of the route, which in places hung over the lake below, raw, freshly-exposed earth marking a recent slide. On the far shore, steep, crumbling cliffs and trees toppled like matchsticks were more evidence than I cared to see. Long, jagged cracks latticed the track. It was my worst nightmare, and didn't take much imagination to see my vehicle being the last straw and a whole chunk of unstable earth slipping down into the deep waters, taking us with it. No-one would ever know, until we were spat up again, months later, pale, bloated and unrecognisable, at some remote point. Increasingly anxious, especially since we had met no other vehicle, I crawled on, hugging the side of the road furthest from the edge, except where the ditch was several feet deep, which I was sure could only exacerbate matters.

At the pace I was going, no time was being saved. But turning back was not in my make-up. The journey dragged on; my sense of direction was becoming confused. I had little idea if we were heading in the right direction or simply wandering in the wilderness, and despite being in the kind of landscape that I loved most of all, fear blinded me to it. Things were not helped when the track forked suddenly and I had to guess which route to follow.

After about two hours of snail-paced tension, I crawled around a hairpin bend and found myself on a highway. Jet-black with freshly-laid asphalt, the road was totally void of any other vehicles and seemed quite incongruous, but a surface smooth as silk was a welcome relief. Ahead lay the new dam; beyond, gleaming gun-metal silver in the watery sun, lay the wide reaches of the Columbia. I had to laugh: I knew exactly where I was.

Only in hindsight did I understand the metaphor.

The familiarity of Inchelium, my warm reception and the sharing of food which always preceded an Arrow Lakes Band meeting helped me normalise, although my usual reaction on seeing Bob again was a mere shadow of what it had once been; probably because of what I had just gone through, I thought.

Once the meeting began, I hated being in the position of having to report that the last possible local effort to resolve the conflict about the road had been to no avail. To try and balance it out, I also tried to tell them what a privilege it had been to be with the Lakes people at their village, and join with their prayers. Which reduced me to tears. There was a long silence; a dispirited mood seemed to creep into the hall. Then Lou, appointed chairman of the Band meetings, suggested: "Maybe some of those who attended the AGM of the Society in our ancestral lands might want to share their impressions?"

The testimony and tribute to the importance of ancestral roots and cultural identity that followed was so poignant and powerful that I never understood why no-one would accept the tapes I made of the accounts related at that meeting. Although all the others I made are in the hands of the Band, for some reason, these ones stayed with me. That day, I heard perhaps the most profound statements about the power of the land that I would ever hear, and feel they should be made known, for the sake of those who have lost touch.

After a short, pregnant silence, Jenny, who had given me the silver and turquoise bracelet, was first to speak. "Elders first?" she murmured.

She was waved to continue.

"What she just said...." Indicating me, Jenny paused and gently shook her head. Her thoughtful expression softened. "Really touched me too. It was a great feeling to be able to go back and put your feet.... As my Mom says, it is holy ground, and I felt like it was holy ground.

"It was just a real touching experience to go back and see where your ancestors started from, and where they travelled, and where they lived. To see the river, going by so fast. And some of us sat there, on the bank, looking out, and that was real special.

"The next morning, before we went out to the site.... I stayed at Celia's, and slept on her floor in the living-room. There's a great big plate-glass window, and I don't dream very often, but that night I dreamt, and it was a real peaceful dream, and I dreamt that I could see this huge ocean of water. The next morning, we were all standing outside, and somebody mentioned about dreaming – if anybody dreamt – and I said, 'Well, I did', and I didn't know to what it was worth. And Celia goes, 'Oh gosh, it just gives me goosebumps', and she told me why: that years and years ago there was once a body of water.... They say the original coastline of North America, thousands of years ago, ran along there. Some seismologists came from California and found there's a fault-line, deeper than the San Andreas, maybe seventy miles deep, that runs under there...."

"A long way for roots to go," I could not resist murmuring. Bob, sitting beside me, chuckled. I wondered whether Jenny was dreaming of past or future: in the oral tradition of the neighbouring Okanagan Nation, Okanagan Lake was once salt-water and according to prophecy will again become salt-water.

"So I saw this body of water," continued Jenny, "and I had a real sense of our ancestors being there; it was a moving experience. And to be there...." She looked at me again. "She said, 'My home is always open to you. It's not my place, it's really your place.' I find it...." Her dark eyes sparkled with brimming tears and she shook her head, unable to continue. During the ensuing pause, many muffled sniffs and snuffles could be heard.

I reached for the box of tissues. "I've learned to carry my own tissues whenever I'm around you people!" Many of them laughed as I blew my nose.

Jenny's mother, Aunt Tootie, spoke then, so softly that absolute silence attended her words: "Ever since we started these meetings, I looked forward with anticipation to going up there. It was everything I thought it would be, and more. Usually when I make a trip like that, I worry 'bout different things at home, but it seemed the closer I got to arriving up there, it seemed like all my worries went, and I felt so peaceful. I truly felt like I was coming home." There was a long, emotive silence. "And as I stood there at the Vallican site, I felt ... like my heart breakin'." Heaving a deep sigh, she continued: "We're told they could no longer go back up there. And I thought of the good times they must've had together, of hunting and fishing, and raising their families, and just having a real free way of life. And then the Europeans came. And then it was totally different for them.... I cried too. I could feel what they had felt. And I was proud to be of that ancestry. I thanked God for Bob 'n' Manny going up there, and finding all this out.

"And if I knew, from what my Dad had told me, that we were from the Arrow Lakes and that someday the Arrow Lakes would go back.... I really didn't realise what he was telling me at the time, until I was up there. And then I knew, what he was tryin' to tell me. And it even felt that I could feel my grandparents, and my Dad's grave up there.... It was truly a feeling of coming home, after you've been away for a long time.

"I just can't describe how I really felt, but I'm happy I made the trip, and I plan on going back, many, many more times. I haven't made the decision yet, whether I'd want to live there, though. It's a mixture of feelings; it's like two different worlds. So it remains to be seen.... But I really do appreciate what all the people have done up there to help." She smiled at me so warmly that I felt tears pricking at my eyes again.

After a long pause, another elder, a small, grey-haired lady in her seventies, began: "There's a mountain there, that has dominated our every move, every part of the day that we were there. It's called Frog Mountain, and we'd look to it everywhere we went. It represents something to all of us, when we were there, and there's a couple of legends about it.

"But as you stand on the hallowed ground of that site, you are in the midst of these mountains that just seem to be protective. And as we each would feel the ground beneath us, so we also would see the power of and the beauty of the mountains around us, as if trying to direct our very steps.

"And even during the meeting, and during the time we were there, visiting the site, the elements were just bouncing off those mountains, all the time we were there. Lightning was going ev'ry which way; the thunder was talking to us ev'ry minute of the day. We laughed, Tootie and I, because we were walking quite slow to the site, and the thunder was bouncing back and forth, as if it were saying, 'Hurry up, you two old ladies! Get on the move, 'cause we aren't gonna wait!'" Everyone started to chuckle. "And soon's we got to the car, the heavens opened up and just drenched us about four steps before we got to the car!

"But there was just a feeling.... All of these inner feelings were there, but all these other environmental activities were going on just to emphasise our visit. It was just a tremendous experience."

In the following silence, which quivered with shared memories and deep feelings, I remembered the rumbles of thunder that had hovered over the Valley all that day, culminating in the violent storm during Bob's speech. "The Thunder Beings...." I found myself murmuring aloud and was grateful that it seemed only Bob, from the small smile that graced his handsome face, had heard.

Marie, a Lakes descendant about Jenny's age who had come up from Seattle, where she lived and worked, to join with her people in this effort, spoke out next. A dynamic, articulate and attractive woman, she had made her presence known at the Society meeting. "While we were actually at the site, an' we were holding hands," she said huskily, "an' doing the prayers an' the songs before we started out, it was such a moment of reverence. An' we walked all through the site area.... It became no doubt in any of our minds, the importance of pursuing this, of bringing people back home. The sense, the urgency of realigning ourselves there, it gave us a feeling that we were doing the right thing, an' that we should be here, whatever it takes, or however many trips we must make. It was like a responsibility....

"Some of us talked about it. You just were overwhelmed with the sense of responsibility that we have here, to do what we know must be done, to reunite the Band with the ancestors."

Bob's warm drawl broke in: "I believe it's kinda like the ancestors are reuniting the Band, you know. If it wasn't for the treatment of those ancestors, this would pro'bly blew over our heads an' nobody would've paid any attention. The only ones could protect 'em was the living, an' so I think that might've been the way that our ancestors prayed also.

"I don't think anybody can really know what was goin' on in those people's minds when that smallpox hit them people; they had no idea what it was, an' so it was really devastating. Whole families ran away to the hills to get away from it, an' they died in them hills an' never received any burial at all. The hills are full of people that tried to run away, an' just a few, y'know, the remnants – we're the remnants of what really happened there. The people that survived, our gran'folks, an' then there's us. There's a large majority of them that left....

"It's strange, because from the spiritual aspect of looking at it – we're all spiritual to a certain extent, I'm sure," he grinned mischievously. "The real thing about our ancestors is, they all left together. A lot of people, a lot of spirits, all left at one time together, to another place. Where we're sitting here now, we lose one person, then usually three'll die or somethin', in smaller groups. But right there, a whole bunch of ancestors left all at one time....

"There's a lotta comfort in that. Seems like if the Creator came an' called all of us in here; if you guys were goin', I wouldn't feel too bad – I'll go with you!"

His chuckle rolled among laughter which it seemed to me he had artfully sparked to lighten the atmosphere. I found myself grinning widely: I would go right along with them, if I had any say in it.

"But you understand what I'm sayin', if that's any consolation," Bob ended quietly.

"The first I heard," began a woman I had not seen before, "I heard about this a week ago, but nobody seemed to know. We thought it was a hoax!"

There were several chuckles.

"Because I remember, you know, bein' told I was Lakes when I was small," she continued, "but you know, nobody ever explains things to children. An' I thought, 'Lakes? Well, Lakes?' 'Cause there weren't any around here!"

Laughter again ran around the room; the spirit in the hall was warm again.

"It was confusin', and I feel good, now I know where I came from. An' to know that there's people you don't even know, that care...." She lapsed into a tearful silence.

It struck me that bearing witness to this incredible renascence was almost as powerful as giving birth; a labour of love, but less painful. Or so it seemed at the time.

Bob's mother, Eva, took up the thread: "I am prob'ly the oldest Lake here, an' when I first understood, I was talkin' Indian. I didn't talk English. I was raised by the old ones, an' that's all they ever taught me: that I was a Sinixt." She said it with pride and an inflection I could never reproduce. "I was a Sinixt all the time. That's what they called the Indians up there, all through there: Sinixt. An' they told me about those people all the time, that's all I ever heard. They told me stories about things that happened there, an' why they left, an' all that.

"When they died, when they all passed away, all them old ones, then my father started tellin' me things. My father was educated. He went to school, to Pennsylvania, and he graduated there. He was in the Business Council on the Colville Reservation for seventeen years. He died, when he was still in.... But that's all he ever talked about. He'd go back there, now 'n' then, to visit. Him 'n' his brother would go back there to some of the places that they knew. Ev'ry now 'n' then, they'd hire a driver an' go back. Sometimes they would be gone three, four days; sometimes they'd be gone ten days. We didn't know what they did up there. When they'd get back, we'd ask 'em, they'd say, 'Oh, we were just visitin'. We were just visitin' the places that our old ones knew and were at.' That's what they'd say. An' he visited the place up there 'bout five years before he died. An' they've told me a lotta things that happened up there."

I wondered what it must have been like to see everything so swiftly and irrevocably changed. Or had they simply hunted and fished the way their fathers had before them? Had their feet trod the valleys lightly, unnoticed by the new, self-occupied occupiers?

Eva continued: "An' not only in one family; in diff'rent fam'lies – I practically know all the Lakes, because it was told to me, an' I went through it with Charlie," she indicated Uncle Charlie, sitting beside her, "an' one of them that had the rolls. I could tell who belonged to this party, that party. Charlie an' I went all through it, an' we know all the fam'lies. An' there is a lot of them. All the ones on the north half, an' Inch'lium, they're all Lakes. An' some of 'em, when they first came down, there's some of 'em on that side of the river, an' they went out t'ward Kettle Falls, an' out t'ward Colville. Them were Lakes. They call them the Valley Indians, but they're not Valley Indians, they're Lakes. Because on both sides they came down, some on that side, some on this. They weren't all one. That's the way they were. So that's what I know 'bout my people there."

Bob had mentioned the many Lakes descendants living scattered around the area; only a small representation had shown up at the meetings so far. I wondered if the clan arrangement still existed.

"I went back with Bob last year, an' we stayed up there one week," Eva resumed. "An' I'm real happy to see all the interest of all these young people, concernin' their ancestors." Her eyes swept round the meeting of over forty people, and she nodded. "That's very good. An' you're not the only ones. There's a lot in Omak I know, that belong there, an' there's a lot of them ev'ry place else. It's a good thing that you let them people know, so they can make their own minds up what they wanna do. Maybe there's some of them that want to go back there, but maybe there's some that won't. But they can't say you didn't tell them. So that part I'm glad to hear about. Because I have children, I have grandchildren. My mother an' Dad were both Lake, an' those children get their Lake blood from me. There's a lot of 'em wouldn't even think of goin' up there, they're in different places."

I found it difficult to believe that they would not want to know the place of their roots and live there if possible. Thousands of miles from my own roots, the plank in my own eye was greater than the splinter I imagined in those people's.

"They know who they are," Eva was continuing, "but they don't go there. Even my own family. An' I think a lot of the diff'rent fam'lies'll be the same. But there's a lot of 'em that will. I have a grandson, and he said that he was goin' up there." She chuckled, as if she couldn't quite believe it. "It's just diff'rent, an' I haven't talked to the others, they just might.... But I went up there, an' I've seen the country...." She stopped and gave a little shiver, as if she had just remembered something: "I went up there years ago, on horseback with my great-grandmother, ridin' all the way there. But I was too young to realise."

Images crowded into my mind's eye, embellished by photographs I had seen from the early part of the century. It would have been before paved highways, before dams; the way I loved to imagine.

"When we went in there, though," she was saying, "I went to Nelson. Then I began to pick places up, last summer. Just like I know the country, because it was told to me so many times when I was little, growing up. That was always told to me: what I was, who I was. I was always told that I was a Lake Indian; nothin' else. I'm happy that all you young ones wanna know; it's a good thing. An' I thank you. That's all I have to say."

Her words were enthusiastically applauded, then, as some people got up to stretch their legs, she added, "An' I talk Indian fluently, too. But you know, my own language up there is not the same as it was when the old ones was there. The way I talk now, it's all mixed up. Guess they can understand me, but it's not the same," she emphasised. "It's touched up here 'n' there, that the real Lakes – I've heard it, the real Lakes – they have a diff'rent way of talkin'. An' that's a shame, it's not the same.... Now you can talk to others as old as I am – I'll be seventy-eight in August, so I think I know a li'l bit of what I'm talkin' about."

Bob grinned suddenly, remembering someone far older than his mother, and baldly exclaimed: "We camped in the graveyard there!"

Several indrawn breaths, "Eh's?" and extensive laughter greeted this.

"Shows how brave she is!" laughed Auntie Vi.

"Almost a week, we camped in the graveyard," Eva said, an amused lilt in her voice. "Bob an' I had our tipi right over one of 'em!"

By now, the hall was pealing with laughter. Remonstrations of "Bo-ob!" rang out.

"I was teasin' her." Bob's voice was coloured by his own amusement. "The way that happened: I was just teasin' her. When we put our tipi up, I looked, an' there was some li'l round stones there an' I says, 'We got a graveyard right here; I think I'll use this for a pillow.' I was just teasin' her, 'cause I never really thought I was there...."

Everyone was still chuckling.

"Then all of a sudden Cecile" (as I was often called by the Lakes people) "an' them guys came up, an' I noticed they looked at us kinda funny, you know.... They didn't say nothin', an' later on Mom told me, 'You know, I had some dreams; there is a grave right there, I think.' I says, 'Why?' She says, 'There was a girl sittin' there, talkin' to me in Indian.'"

I remembered the details of Eva's dream – the lonely young girl, welcoming her people home at long last.

"See, that's what she was dreamin' that night," continued Bob, "an' I said, 'Oh, that's fine.' An' the next day I was askin' Cecile, 'Are we really on a graveyard?' An' she says, 'Yep!' An' I says, 'Is there really a graveyard right here?' An' she says, 'Yes!'"

Everyone roared with laughter.

"An' here I was, thinkin' I was teasin' her! An' I looked at Manny, an' said, 'Manny! Why didn't you tell us?!' An' Manny says, 'Well I didn't know!'"

"So we camped in a graveyard! All the spirits didn't have to go find us!" He was chuckling. "We were right there!"

When the subsequent merriment finally subsided, another woman elder took her turn: "Some of us go through life, mixed up, wonderin' who we are, because no-one ever told us. I knew I was a Lake Indian, but my mother died at a young age – she was fifty-eight when she died. And we have a lot of relatives in Canada, but I was never fortunate enough to meet any of them. My grandfather died when I was about four or five years old; I can't remember. Archie...." She smiled at the Lakes elder. "He'd probably remember more about that than me.

"But he was teachin' me how to speak the language, and all our Indian traditions, an' kinda sneakin' around about it, because at that time we was not supposed to learn our language, so my mother didn't teach me. But I always felt cheated, an' probably lost, not being able to be the person that the Creator meant me to be."

Her words affected me profoundly. Hearing it put that way, the state of being "lost", disconnected from cultural identity, was made graphically clear: she was saying it meant disconnection from spirit, from the Creator. Perhaps, I realised, this was why so many people sought solace in the chemically-induced altered states of alcohol and drugs, where they might forget their cheated, separated, lost self. And not just the Native American.

"But I'm so thankful for all the interest, and all the hard work," she was continuing. "An' I do know that this is meant to be, because as I sit here tonight with the different people that speak, I could just feel the spirits, an' I feel it was the spirit of our great Creator an' our ancestors speaking through him," she indicated Bob, "to let us know, 'You're finding your way home'.

"So continue with the path and do whatever you can to help. I don't know what I can do, but whatever I can do to help support the group, maybe financially in a small way, or maybe with some fund-raisers or whatever; I'll be more'n glad to do that. An' I'm so happy.... I was so sad when I was hearin' about, you know," her voice quavered and became rough with feeling, "that grader, you know, just diggin' up...." She breathed a deep sigh before continuing: "Seems like they're always diggin' up us Indians; they don't even care. I don't know if they do that to other people or not, but it's so sad when people don't even care an' appreciate those that are gone on before us, an' they become so cruel to do that.

"I'm so thankful that this was found out, put a stop to it. This li'l beautiful lady here – may God bless her always for doin' all the hard work she's doin', because that paperwork to me is nothin' but a big headache. In the first place I don't know how to do that; it's not one of my gifts, but I sure thank God for her. An' thank you, Bob for all your hard work."

Being placed alongside Bob like this was a thrill. He shrugged, laughing it off as applause rippled round the hall, but I was embarrassed. I wanted to say I was grateful: grateful to be able to put heart and soul into something that meant more to me than I could say; grateful to play a tiny part in this monumental unfolding and simultaneously experience a sense of destiny. In fact, it was like I was not even myself any more, but some quiver of light and de-light, which I could hardly bear.

WHEELS THAT GRIND

After a few moments of silence, Lou indicated that another Lakes Band member, a striking-looking woman with long, curling, prematurely grey hair, should speak.

"I was able to go up there June eighth," she began, "and I'm really glad that I did, for a lot of reasons. I'm still tryin' to sort it all out in my head, but most of all, it's like a puzzle bein' put together. A lot of the things that came to me in my dreams, that are just now being realised, an' for a long time they made me just so curious. 'Why did I dream that? Now what made me dream that?' You know? An' so this is just part of that. It's not finished by far yet, there's a lot of work to be done, an' I'm really proud an' honoured to be part of it."

She could have been speaking for me: the puzzle; the dreams; the sense of privilege.

"What I didn't know before I went up there," she continued, "was that this was the Annual General Meeting of the Vallican Archaeological Park Society; that they were going to elect officers an' the whole bit. An' I don't know the first thing about archaeology – I've always had a problem with studyin' things. You know, I didn't ever want to question anything of the Creator; just accept it, an' revere it, an' hold it."

It was a viewpoint I appreciated, for I felt that my race was always analysing, taking things apart that we didn't know how to put back together. Like a child.

She breathed out a short laugh and tossed her hair. "But they nominated me, an' I became a member of the Board of Directors, along with Lou and Marie, an' ... who?"

"I don't really remember," said Lou. "There was a fourth person.... No, Bob was nominated – he turned it down. There was three."

"Well, I felt a real conflict there at that meeting," the woman continued, "an' I was warned – I mean forewarned – and I had a chance to decline, but I didn't. There was a point in there, I was glad I was there. Certain people in that meeting sort of revealed themselves to me, an' where they were comin' from, an' I thought two things: Celia testified at that meeting that there was evidence that there were artefacts right in that roadway. An' there was another man there, the caretaker, testified that he was there when an expert also saw evidence."

I recalled how Cliff, dream-carrier, artist and site-caretaker, Jacquie and I had assisted Wayne on his allotted day of archaeological investigation, commissioned by the Ministry of Highways. A scant six hours on a quarter-mile of highway had allowed examination of only a couple of small areas; even so, Wayne had come across features – fire-pits and tool-carving areas – on the right-of-way that he considered of cultural value.

"That's why I felt a conflict," the woman was saying. "They're wrong then in puttin' that road there, because this is established. And I, as a descendant of the Arrow Lakes, should have a say-so; like you said before, Celia, if there's any archaeology going on, we should have a say in the matter. On the one hand I felt like I wanted to say, 'Hey, stop, guys, you're all wrong!' an' then on the other hand I wanted to participate in the slow action of making motions an' doin' all the other stuff. Most of all, I'm glad I got to witness there, an' I guess that's why I was there in the first place – 'cause I have to see an' know ev'rything! An' hear ev'rything, you know, so I can share it with people.

"As far as the land.... Well, it's as Manny told me, it's like paradise. I didn't really believe it till I was there. Soon's I got there, like Tootie, I felt at home. We got lost. As it turned out, we didn't feel lost, because we were home! I mean, nobody was worried. We circled a mountain before we even went to the meeting; we had plenty of time. An' the pureness, the purity of the land.... I was told one time that 'Canada' means clean, an' I don't know what language it was derived from, but Europeans came an' asked the Natives, 'What do you call this place?' An' they said, 'Well, clean.' An' that's what it is. An' we should applaud the people who kept it that way, the government, the people. The spirits, I guess. Or the ancestors."

Bob quietly explained to me that this Lakes woman, Yvonne, had from the beginning played a major role in organising the Band meetings. I thought about how her response to the pristine beauty of the Kootenay region was typical of most people who come there for the first time, including myself.

Yet it was changing, even in the short span of time I had been there. That year, a spate of house-building had erupted throughout the Valley and flashy little sports cars were becoming commonplace as people cashed in on the soaring price of houses in the city and moved to the country, some able to semi-retire on the proceeds. But city-dwellers tend to bring the city with them; once the novelty of going "back to the land" wears off and boredom sets in, they want faster roads for easier access into the nearest city. With little idea of what the area was like before the first-growth forests were logged off and the silver mines reamed the land, and because they have come from the city or other places with little natural beauty, for the most part these newcomers tend not to stand up in strong defence when the Valley's pristine nature comes under threat. Some only see natural beauty as an extractable resource with market value. In the six years I lived there, despite huffings about sustainability and the knowledge that resource extraction was coming to a non-renewable end, there was a distressing increase in clearcuts, not only on Crown land (held by the government "for the people") but also privately-owned land and, more worryingly, in the watersheds; and a three-fold increase in logging and chip-truck traffic.

The cost of progress? Many of the locals agreed it was not progress at all. One of the special things about the Valley had been its leisurely, neighbourly pace: often the back-road would be blocked by a couple of battered old workhorse vehicles, engines switched off while their drivers "shot the breeze". Nor had there ever been any accident on the disputed (admittedly drastic – I would never forget my own frightening experience the first time I used it) turn-off into Vallican; in fact, in many opinions, the way it forced everyone to slow down added to the unique quality of laid-back Valley life-style.

The year the Lakes people came home also saw the blowing-up of half a mountain, when the bottle-neck above Slocan Lake, along which I had crawled heart in mouth many times since that first experience and which I saw as another desirable feature of the Valley in that it restricted the flow of heavy traffic, was blasted away to make way for a three-lane highway. Industrial traffic now had "Freedom to Move" through the entire Valley.

"An' one other thing," Yvonne was continuing, "to help you people in deciding whether you wanna go up there or not, is that some of the prophecies are telling us that things are gonna get worse. Man has meddled with Nature and a lot of the elements are changing. And Earth is changing. And in that time, we'll be told what to do, I'm sure. But for ev'ry Indian Nation, there's a place they can go, to survive, if they're listening. An' one of the clues is to go north, you know, where the pure air is.

"I just felt like sharing that with you people, and I really am privileged and honoured to participate in this, to help in any way I can. Um, that's all."

A burst of applause rippled through the hall. All I could think about was her reference to the prophecies and Earth Changes. What did she mean by "a place they can go to"? An inner sense told me the ancestral site at Vallican was one; the Medicine Wheel gathering-grounds another. Reminded of the previous winter, when the group of people brought together by Bob and Manny had sat and talked and dreamed together, long into the night, I recalled our diverse backgrounds and our shining thread of belief – held in common – in the role of indigenous people in the changing times of which Yvonne was now speaking; our dream of co-founding a new cooperative community. At the time, I had wondered if anyone besides Bob appreciated that to manifest such a dream would require more effort and substance than shared ideology and innovative thinking. Yet the dream has to be dreamed, before all else.

Manny spoke then, bringing me back: "You know, I was thinkin', the people were dwelling there for over two thousand years. Surely there's a lot more. Like you say, there's a lot of generations passed through there. There's an upper bench there; maybe that whole area, right up into the mountains'll show us the people had roots there."

"It'd probably be difficult to ascertain where any of these sensitive areas might lie," said Lou.

"The archaeologist told me that evidence of human presence had been found near the peaks," I said, "suggesting that people had passed through there during the Ice Ages, when only the tops of the mountains were visible. We felt the less said about them the better, for fear of renewed scientific and academic interest."

"That's one of the reasons, when they asked me...." said Bob, a slight frown on his face. "You know, that's why I had to decline before, when they wanted me to become a member, because of the same thing. Because the site, important as it is, what it is – it's a stepping-stone. There's so many of them sites that are up there, an' my overall concern is about all of 'em, not just this one site. There's a lot of 'em out there we have to go out an' protect, just like the Europeans take care of their graveyards. They have to be protected, an' this one particular site, it's important, but so are all the rest of 'em. The rest of the sites is – in my mind – what I'm goin' after. I wanna ensure that ev'ry one of them sites'll be protected. An' I'm sure litigation'll achieve that. I don't know as to how the government's plannin' on doin' that, but it'll be up to them to determine that."

Litigation? My blood ran cold. Unaware that the Supreme Court of Canada had already ruled on the right of the aboriginal people to determine the future of their land, and that the government continued to ignore this ruling, I realised I had been living in a dream; being realistic, there would have to be a political-legal dance, especially as this was a potentially precedent-setting issue.

"As far as the graveyards are concerned," Bob was saying, "them graveyards belong to the dead. An' the dead they belong to, well, that was our ancestors. So we're gonna have to do the talkin' for 'em. We're gonna have to make sure they're taken care of. An' accordin' to our lawyer, well, the wordin' will probably have to be changed round. But that Heritage Trust manager, he keeps sayin' they own that site, but our lawyer says he doesn't own it, that we own it. An' when the dust all settles, he's gonna prove that man doesn't have anything to say about the site. An' whatever happens after that will be determined by you people. When the dust's settled, all them sites up there will be owned and controlled by the Arrow Lakes Band."

In hindsight, I wonder whether Bob had any inkling of how great a cloud of dust would be kicked up.

"So," he continued, "with that in mind, I couldn't get involved in no Board of Directors, when I see this all unfolding. You know, we'll play it by ear, take it step by step. An' eventually all them sites we got in them reports an' books – I'd like for you all to see 'em."

At this point, a man I had not seen before, who had come in after the meeting was underway, began to speak. Bob whispered that he was the son of a highly-regarded Arrow Lakes elder, Aunt Mary, and a member of the Colville Business Council. Barely had he begun, when a sudden shriek drowned out his words, followed by a second scream as two of the women simultaneously jumped to their feet, their chairs clattering to the floor behind them. Then they both started giggling.

"I'm so-o-o sorry!" one of them laughed, as other people began to chuckle.

"My goodness!" said Auntie Vi.

I saw it then: a bright-eyed field-mouse, sitting in the middle of the crescent of people, its only movement the twitch of whiskers. Suddenly it zipped out through the open door and into the freedom of the fields beyond.

"Guess you haven't touched the books much lately!" Lou joked.

Only later did I appreciate the timely appearance of Mouse, telling us to examine things closely, see what was right before our eyes and be aware of everything around us but not chew every little thing to pieces.

Butch began again after the merriment had subsided: "The Native concern an' objective right now is to stop the road from goin' through the burial-grounds. Just take a moment here, to get some kind of relationship about what is sacred to the Indian people. When it comes to the land, there's a kind of a feeling that you have, or it's instilled into you, from the time that you're born, in the Indian tradition, by the things you experience, the tradition, by the things people do. This is how we're taught to respect the land. An' sometimes we don't even know we have it, until somethin' comes up, an' this is how we feel.

"When it comes to graveyards, I've got a grandmother an' a grandfather, some ancestors up on Kelly Hill. I've always considered this sacred ground. It's where Chief James Bernard is, an' Aurapahkin, an' many other relatives. When I go up there, I get a special feeling. An' we go up there every year, on Memorial Day. You get the experience, that people have some kinda thing goin' with the land."

An irrational feeling of irritation, or something I could not put my finger on, began to make me feel restless.

"I just buried a daughter," he was continuing, "last year, in the Inchelium graveyard. An' I've got a brother there. I know that if the Department of Highways considered putting a highway through Kelly Hill graveyard, or Inchelium graveyard, there could be no end to the battle. Today we just buried an Indian leader, an' if they tried to put a highway through that graveyard, governments would move! 'Specially the Colville Indian Nation, they would move."

Perhaps it was because people had been sitting still and listening for so long, that a lot of comings-and-goings and whispered conversations had started up. The speaker was quite difficult to hear, sitting way back in the hall behind the others; people had to crane over their shoulders if they wanted to look at him, a tall, round-faced man with short, darkly-greying hair. Undaunted by the shuffling and the whispers – perhaps used to it as a council-member, I thought, a little unfairly – he continued: "I wanna tell you a little story 'bout the place where I worked, down at Portland. They put in the third powerhouse down at Bonneville, they had to move the town. The Department of Highways has to get their marchin' orders from somebody. An' when you go against the Department of Highways, their first policy is to tell you that ev'rything is settled. You know, they got their marchin' orders, all the papers signed, all the t's are crossed an' the i's are dotted, an' there's no turnin' back. That's their standard policy."

If he understood bureaucratic workings, this man might be of help. I tried to re-focus.

"Down in Bonneville," he continued, "they was gonna move the whole town. Give people a pocketful of money an' say, 'Okay, move!' But they had a lawyer that was educated from back east. He moved to Washington for a slower pace, happened to settle down in Bonneville. He became mayor. An' it was through him that they got the courts to provide 'em a new townsite. Totally rebuilt like a subdivision, where they could relocate to.

"Another thing: I was a surveyor an' I helped build this highway, do some of the staking. An' there was a train right-of-way that went through this area, in a straight line, until it came to a graveyard. A European graveyard. An' that's where it took a turn, an' it missed the graveyard. It didn't go through it, an' they didn't remove it.

"You look at civilization; you look at somethin' like National Geographic, an' the archaeological things an' the great studies an' the great lengths that they go to, to discover about man. They are interested in it. An' the thing about the Department of Highways is that pressure can be brought to bear, through the chain of command. Someplace you can bring pressure. The train had to miss the graveyard. The town had to be relocated at the government's expense. Because people got together an' said, 'You can't do this!'

"An' the only way we're gonna achieve success right now, is applying the pressure at a different level. An' you keep goin' up on those levels, till you reach those points, where pressure can be applied. You might have to do it through the Press; you gotta get the governments involved. I think right here, at this point in time, the Colville Tribal government's gotta be involved. At least we can get pressure to bear.

"An' there's also a thing called the DIA, the Department of Indian Affairs, up there that should be contacted. An' we have to move pretty fast an' I think one of the places to start would be letters an' an ambassador of good-will, or whatever you want to call him, outta the Council. An' letters of support. Try to get the inter-tribal government here to apply pressure."

He was obviously unaware that Bob had been appointed ambassador of the Band. What he was saying sounded reasonable enough, but then I was ignorant of Reservation politics, although I guessed from the noncommittal shrugs, shuffling feet, and eyes gazing out the window, that not many people cared for what he was saying.

"Try to get other Bands up there together," he continued. "To do one thing: to stop that road. Ev'rything else can follow, but our immediate concern is to stop that road. Maybe the burial-ground belongs to the dead, but the responsibility belongs to us."

No-one could disagree with that. I thought he was finished, but he went on: "Those are our people. Just as much as that graveyard in Inchelium. That's my responsibility, because my daughter's in there. An' Kelly Hill – my grandmother's there, an' my ancestors. How close those ancestors are to me, because they're three thousand years gone before me, makes a li'l bit hard to kinda bridge that spiritual gap, to make it important. But if you can relate it to: 'These are our people, my grandmothers, my grandfathers, your grandmothers, your grandfathers', this is our responsibility. This is the way we Indians have lived: to respect the land, to respect our ancestors, to respect the traditions.

"An' this is why, when the Europeans came, all of North America was intact. The rivers weren't polluted, the air wasn't polluted; didn't have all the concrete an' the buildings. An' all the wildlife, there was plenty of game, plenty of fish."

There were several soft cries of "Yes!"

"There was a way of life. If one of them old ladies broke off a branch, of a dead tree, she gave it thanks. This is some of the things that we learn, kinda after the fact. Some of us get kinda removed because we're a product of the 50's, 60's, 70's an' 80's, an' we wear blue jeans an' Jordache stuff."

There were several chuckles.

"An' we eat hamburgers an' grew up on John Wayne movies. We got a li'l problem ourselves, tryin' to find the thing that's instilled in us. By our own people, our grandmothers, our grandfathers, an' the things that we did, an' we experienced. Nevertheless, they were there. An' we heard the language, an' we saw what these people did, an' how they buried each other.

"Point number one is: the Department of Highways. There is a place where you can bring pressure to bear; they receive their marchin' orders from somebody. An' things like this are as important to the Canadian society, as to the United States government. The Smithsonian Institute, they can bring pressure to bear on a lot of places. Washington University students can do a lot. Things like that. Publicity, get the papers up there, do somethin'. Get the governments involved. Thank you."

As people applauded, I appreciated how his spontaneous speech had turned full circle and rounded off. Perhaps my initial negative judgement of him as a representative of institutional authority was unfair; I did not know him personally and was ignorant of how the Colville Business Council operated. I wondered whether they knew of other vested interests. Some months before this meeting, after having made a presentation about the Vallican site and the Arrow Lakes Band's involvement at a heritage conference in the Okanagan, I had been bluntly informed by a representative of the Shuswap people (to the north) that the Lakes' land had been a "common area" used by four different peoples, just as old Grey Wolf had claimed. According to the archaeologist, however, the Lakes people would have only left their ancestral lands if all the resources had failed and it was unlikely that other peoples would have done much more than make the occasional foray.

Ethnographical and archaeological evidence supported the Lakes' presence, but to my mind the proof lay in the fact that they were the only ones concerned about the repatriation of the ancestral remains: their ancestors, their land. I was quite unaware that it was already under three overlapping land-claims, of the Okanagan, the Kutenai and the Shuswap Nations. When I later spoke to Okanagan and Kutenai leaders, they told me things had been put in place this way in order to ensure that the land was under a claim, and willingly conceded it was the Arrow Lakes territory. Would that things could be so simple.

When the applause faded, another diminutive, grey-haired woman elder indicated her wish to speak. Her information would shock many people there, perhaps myself most of all. Turning to face Butch, she began quietly: "I'd like to talk to you 'bout the Councilmen. They were notified here, a long time ago, about this, an' they didn't seem to want to do anything about it. That's the reason that we haven't asked them for help or anything. It's a political thing, as you well know; you've been in there.

"And the reason is, that they have something going up there and they don't wanna get the government upset up there, for these other reasons. Political, of course. So that's the reason we haven't gone to try to get them to help us or expected any help from them, even if they would wanna give it. They have the research; they sent the people up there to do research, an' they won't let us have it. They won't let us see it. So it's hard to try to get the Councilmen to do anything for us."

Bob spoke up then, in a tone that had lost all trace of lightness: "I'd like to respond to that. All of us Lake Indians, we're like a block, you might say, a voting block, an' a lotta people are interested in the voting block. I myself ran for Council a couple of times, an' knew this was a pretty good push, you know, in influencin' a lotta people. An' so I know how you can get in there, an' it all fits out to you.

"One thing we wanna kinda refrain: you know this here's the Arrow Lakes Band. An' so far, we've accomplished an awful lot. Them Councilmen had people hired to go up there to Canada an' do a lot of research, I guess, an' they came back empty-handed. An' that was it. Didn't want to get involved in international law, either. So it was left up to the Arrow Lakes Band as an individual. An' we're Arrow Lakes as individuals; we also have rights. Just because we don't have a whole Band backin' us up, don't mean that we don't have rights. Each individual has rights, an' when you get a lotta other people backin' you up on the same issue, you have more power. Right now, we have a lawyer that's workin' on this. All our Tribal Government, well, the ones they pay an' play with down here doesn't have any say-so at all in Canada. They don't carry any weight in Canada.

"Right now, we have one thing in common: we're all Arrow Lake Indians. That land up there is our ancestral land. We have our lawyer workin' for us. We'll be up there to meet with Highways; we'll give 'em one more chance, we'll let 'em know these letters have been written. Next thing, they'll have an injunction put against 'em. This is what our lawyer is gonna do, if they don't wanna listen to reason.

"So it isn't like somethin' hasn't been done. Somethin' definitely is bein' done. The injunction will definitely stop it, an' it'll stop a lot more, too. Then the government has to deal with us. It isn't just the highway goin' through the place, it'll be the whole area'll be in question then. This whole thing is building up; it'll be a land-claim. The Arrow Lakes' land-claim against the Canadian government, and it's already being handled by Canadian lawyers that're familiar with the system and have been successful in the past, in dealin' an' winnin' their share of litigations, when it pertains to Indian rights.

"An' so we've come an awful long ways. This is just the fourth meetin'. The first meetings were just to let people know what they were doin' up there. An' since that very first time right up until now, a lotta things have happened and we're continually goin' further. I figure that things are really goin' faster as a matter of fact, than most of the people can keep up with. If you miss a meetin', then you come back an' realise how much you really missed, because a lotta things have been happenin', an' happenin' fast. So the lawyer will be at the next meetin' down here, after all that, an' you can speak to him an' listen to what he has to say.

"The Society could only take it so far, writing letters an' such; the only one that could really do anything an' put an injunction against 'em was us. So we had already planned that, an' it's been put in motion. But a lotta people didn't know that."

Including myself. But it was what the Q.C. had advised. It struck me that this impetus would compel an entirely unknowable direction; the mighty, impersonal wheels and cogs of the legal and governmental systems tended to grind dreams into the earth. I found myself wondering how many people would fall off unnoticed by the wayside, be choked by the dust, be crushed. Or – a faint ray of hope – choose to work outside the system.

Things were turning out to be a far more complicated than I had ever imagined, although from my experience in Israel in the early seventies – living for almost four years among Jews and Arabs and witnessing the '73 Yom Kippur War – I knew well enough the fraught situation of dispossessed peoples. The Lakes ancestral village at Vallican might be the foothold (Bob's words would prove prophetic), but it seemed like my own footing was slipping. Not a bridge between cultures lay ahead but a crossroad, and I could foresee only dangerous divisions of opinion regarding choice of direction.

A SPIRITUAL GIANT

That night, I went back to Nespelem to stay with Auntie Vi, and in the morning she told me something of the nature of Reservation politics and the operation of the Tribal Council. There seemed to have been a lot of difficulties and friction over the years, reminding me of what Bob had said about the way the Reservation was run.

Despite the fact that she had not been well recently, as ever, her immaculately-kept home was buzzing with grandchildren and visitors. I could see the many hours spent "visiting" were often as not a form of counselling, and was told that Auntie Vi was a "prayer warrior", renowned for her gift of healing suicide desire. During the late-night sessions after the meetings, the Lakes women had mentioned the prayer efforts for what was unfolding, and I had taken it for granted this would be something like the way Bob had used the eagle feather, and his dawn prayers to the rising sun (the expression "prayer warrior" served to strengthen this illusion). After everyone had left, however, Auntie Vi mentioned, almost in passing, that the power of her prayers lay in her "direct line" to Jesus.

It may seem strange, but I was staggered: the people by whom Bob had seemed so pleased to see me being accepted were Christian. Yet as Auntie Vi explained her belief-system, I understood that it was not Christianity as I knew it; no institutionalised dogma, or Bible-thumping, evangelical drive, but a Way I have come to believe might be closest to what the Master intended, with an added power that might be something to do with the Native American soul.

"Not the Bible, not what some old men wrote down. If those priests could hear me now!" Auntie Vi giggled, a little like a wayward child. "It's what Jesus said and taught, what we were all given, that matters. I don't need no priest coming along to tell me what to think an' do, thinking he has the right to do that for me! He's coming between me and Jesus.

"Jesus never said we were to follow someone, that we needed an intermediary. 'Wherever two or more are gathered....' He didn't say one of 'em had to be some ol' priest! An' He would never have wanted us to worship Him, or look at Him stuck up on the cross like that, so we're made to look at Him suffering, remember Him that way. That's how they want us to remember Him, but that's not about His power the way I understand it.

"The lessons He brought were about love and forgiveness, and about our own power. He healed the sick, He rose from the dead, and He said that whatever He could do, we could do, and more. You can read that for yourself....

"It's like He's with me all the time, by my side, like a good friend, or a brother. I can feel Him. All I have to do is turn to Him, an' ask Him."

That day, the local Catholic priest stopped by to visit. I sat in silence with another couple of visitors, drinking coffee, as he debated the scriptures with her. Auntie Vi's knowledge of the Bible was formidably accurate, she had strong opinions, was relentless and showed no mercy, yet she clearly enjoyed the exchange as much as the priest.

Before he left, the Father privately told me how much he loved to debate with her, even though she usually got the better of him. It was clear he respected her highly, and he also told me how he appreciated the vital contribution she made to the community and that for him, visiting with her was one of the best things about working on the Reservation.

When everyone had left and with the children playing outside, we cleaned up. Then Auntie Vi put her feet up and took out a magazine of crossword puzzles, her consuming passion. "Sometimes I wish I could just be rid of this old body and be at peace with Jesus," she confided with a deep sigh. "Twenty-five years I've been battlin' cancer. Had a Heinz variety of operations – about fifty-seven in all! – and my insides're all glued up by the radiation and all those other treatments they gave me. The medical specialists say they've got no idea what's keepin' me alive – they say with my insides like that, they don't know how I get any nourishment from the food I eat. Guess you've noticed I eat for about six!"

Small and frail-looking, she had seemed to eat a great deal but I had just put that down to her tremendous energy, busy-ness and warmth. Horrified to hear about her long-term illness and concerned about the effects of the radiation, given at a time when dosage was less understood, I had often noticed that her face looked pale and crumpled.

"It's the pain-killers," she said. "Sometimes I think they'll do me in before the cancer. A powerful cocktail, but the side effects, they really take it out of me.... Once, Junior took me on a pilgrimage, to Lourdes." Her dark eyes became misty with memory as she told me about the trip. " ... I'd sure like to go back there again some day. Seems after that was the longest time there was no pain, no weakness."

Seeing the long confrontation with the disease etched into a face lined more by years of illness and pain, than by the half-century she had walked the earth, I did not know what to say.

"And lookit my hair!" She pushed her hands angrily into what I noticed was a wiry frizz, not the usual mass of soft, dark curls. "It sure annoys me when it gets this way! Can't do a thing with it. Guess He won't take me, lookin' like this!" She giggled, covering her mouth as she laughed, a habit I had noticed before which added to the appealing child-like quality that played hide-and-seek in her personality.

I asked about her childhood years.

Able to speak Sinixt, she did not have one unkind word for the nuns who had educated her so strictly in the mission school, but perceived it as a necessary and valuable education to help her fit into a changing world. "One of them, I've been in correspondence with all my life. She wants to be buried beside me at Kelly Hill."

There was something about this that seemed terribly appealing. Spending time with Auntie Vi was like sitting next to a hearth; despite adversity and tragedy, the warmth and openness of her heart was uncompromised; her sense of humour, dry and playful; her will, of iron. I often wondered what it was in me she had taken to so strongly, and for a while thought it might be that she wanted to "save" me. But she never spoke of her spiritual walk unless asked; never proselytised.

Perhaps because it was not being thrust upon me and she was not trying to convince me of the truth of it, I began to re-think. It had been the organised nature of the Church that had put me off, but the idea of a direct connection to Jesus was appealing. Not that it was new: a couple of times, inspired by the father of my two younger children, I had prayed in that way when I had really been desperate and had my prayers answered in a very short time. Perhaps this was an opportunity to come to terms with the spiritual walk to which I had been born in this life.

But could I do this alone? It would be much easier if I lived closer to Auntie Vi.

FANCY FOOTWORK

A few days later, Auntie Vi phoned to invite us to the Independence Day pow-wow at Nespelem, a weekend intertribal event. "I'm encouraged by the return to cultural ways," she told me. "There's more 'n' more Indians choosing the 'pow-wow highway', even as a way of life. It's just that the motivation leaves much to be desired: the dancing's competitive, with grand money prizes.... An' don't think I forgot your moccasins. I began beading the design. It's a secret, though," she added.

The promised moccasins danced in my heart with as much significance as a covenant. Unable to ask, I was pleased she mentioned them: I had not heard a word about them since the day she had given me the eagle-shawl, when she had traced the outline of my feet on paper to ensure a customised fit.

Feeling herself again, Auntie Vi went with us to the opening night. As we approached the pow-wow grounds, a few miles south of Nespelem, my excitement grew. Long before the turn-off, I could see a mass of parked cars, windscreens glinting in the oblique sunlight, and, mushroom-like in the centre, the great, circular canopy of parachute-silk which shaded the dancing arena. Against the arid, scrubby, desolate beauty of the Interior Plateau landscape, it was a romantic, paradoxical scene: a host of tipis towering nobly over rows of campers and motor-homes; parked cars stretched out in every direction. Edging the dance arena were avenues of stands selling Native arts and crafts and foods, and popcorn, hamburgers and hot-dogs.

Auntie Vi had timed our arrival for the Grand Entry, the procession which officially opens the proceedings, but took the time to point out one of her relatives, who was operating what she assured me was the finest food-stall. Barely had we found a space on the bleachers when a heavy, slow beat began. Three elders wearing traditional attire entered the arena, carrying an eagle staff and two flags, American and Canadian. Sedately they stepped in unison to the beat of the traditional Grand Entry song, making their way anti-clockwise round the arena.

Other dancers followed, first those in traditional dress, men and boys, then women and girls; then the other categories of dancers until, after several circuits, a great, milling mass of colour, nodding feathers and quills and clamour of jingling bells filled the area. It was a breathtaking spectacle, all the more impressive when, on some unseen signal, they all magically stilled into silence. A prayer and blessings were recited over the proceedings.

The evening consisted of non-competitive intertribal dances which anyone was welcome to join. I had brought my eagle-shawl, but could not find the courage to be one of the few white faces among them. We watched until Auntie Vi grew tired; as we left, a stream of vehicles was still making its way into the grounds. Contestants and visitors, some from hundreds of miles away, she told me, would continue to arrive throughout the night.

The next morning dawned clear, promising another sweltering summer day. Limited by her state of health, Auntie Vi sent us out after breakfast to watch the qualifying heats.

Closest to my heart were the traditional dancers. The women were wearing long buckskin dresses, tan or bone-white, decorated with shells and painstakingly beaded, as were the bags some of them carried, and their feather fans. Their moccasined feet glided over the ground so smoothly they seemed to be floating, a dignified elegance accentuated by the liquid flick of fringe on shawl and dress: a clear expression of their grace and beauty as women. Some wore hats made of tightly-woven tule, a marsh grass, woven into a conical or angular shape; their sleek hair was meticulously braided, which apparently symbolises earth-connectedness. Most of the younger women had left their hair loose, which I was told denotes a free spirit.

The tan buckskin tunics and leggings of the male dancers were also fabulously beaded, or decorated with shells and porcupine quills. Symbolic of the qualities of a totemic ally, the head-dresses were elaborately feathered or horned, or made of animal-skin. One eagle-dancer had painted his face half-black and half-yellow, and carried a power-staff embellished with a cruel clutch of taloned foot. It struck me that the fan of his magnificent eagle-feather headdress looked like an aura or a halo; when he danced, more expressively than most, his magnificent bustle – a double circle of long flight feathers attached to his lower back – took on an ethereal quality, like a Catherine Wheel. Or a spinning chakra. It seemed to me that many subtle levels were represented in these fabulous outfits.

The traditional men dancers made a deep impression on me. Their bearing noble and stately, their movement fluid and graceful, some looked so proud and fierce that it was weird to pass by a group of them outside the arena and overhear them discussing car loans.

In contrast, the fancy dancers were dressed in flamboyant, brightly-coloured outfits of a striking combination of synthetic materials: pants and shirt of shiny polyester, heavily trimmed with long, thick fringes of coloured yarn; on their head a bandanna looped with strands of beads, or a fan of porcupine quills which blurred into a fuzzy bright-tipped halo as they danced. And dance they certainly did: the vivid spectacle of the athletic young men and their wild and graceful, leaping, whirling dance was enthralling.

Almost all the men dancers were wearing bells tied round their ankles, some also around their knees: large harness bells, small brass ones, a whole range between, jangling and tinkling, clinking and jingling. I guessed they were worn to indicate how accurately the dancer synchronises with the beat of the drum and ends on the final stroke. Later, I would learn that before European contact, a shaman might tie pebbles around his ankles; the clacking noise would dispel negative energies or, in the wake of a spirit-journey, direct his spirit back into his earth-bound body.

Another twentieth-century innovation was one I had noticed at Sqwlax: the jingle-dress dance, a category exclusively of young women wearing knee-length dresses of colourful, shiny material, to which rows of rolled-up tops of cans have been attached. Holding an eagle-feather fan in one hand, the other on their hip, their posture perfectly erect, these young women danced a nimble, skipping step, accompanied by the tinkling clash of metal: a treble to the bass of the drum.

Nor were children excluded; some were less than two years old and they were all heart-wrenchingly sweet in their elaborate outfits, their little faces frowning in concentration as they danced with natural agility and grace. I found myself wishing they did not also have to wear numbers which covered almost half of their little bodies.

There seemed to be about seven drum-groups; often "family drums", bringing traditional and modern songs and chants to pow-wows from all points of the compass. No-one seemed able to tell me if one big drum was traditional or whether hand-drums had been used. Hollywood constructs may have a lot to answer for.

Several Lakes people came to sit with me and visit; in the early afternoon, I found Auntie Vi's relative and ate a delicious lunch of "Indian taco": bannock, or Indian fry-bread, heaped with a steaming mass of chilli and salad. Barely had I finished when Uncle Charlie appeared. He took me for a walk round the area and told me anecdotes about his work with the ethnographer Bouchard, then went to join other elders. Returning to the dance-arena, I found a space high on the bleachers from where I could easily see all the action. Barely had I sat down, however, when I caught sight of Bob's mother on the second row about a quarter-way further round.

Thinking to visit with Eva, I made my way round the back of the bleachers but when I reached the spot where she had been sitting, it was empty. Nor was she anywhere to be seen, even though I had kept an eye on her blue headscarf almost the entire time it took to get there. I sat down in her place, just as a song designated for the over-fifty traditional male dancers was announced. Perplexed at how the elder had seemingly vanished into thin air, I was paying scant attention, however.

The ululating cry that opened the song came as a shock. Situated almost directly in front of me, the drum pounded into action, and the impressively-costumed, proud figures, many grey-haired, began their sedate dance round the arena. Despite this being my favourite category, I was still trying to locate Eva when something, a kind of subtle shift in energy, brought my attention back.

Seven men were sitting at the drum, pounding it with a singular intensity. I could feel the beat through the soles of my feet, leeching up through my body; their song cut the air, drowning out the wisps of conversation, drone of car engines and whoops of playing children in the background. Closing my eyes, I began to nod my head and let my body sway in time to the beat, which increasingly seemed to become part of me, taking over the thump of my heart, the rhythmic rush of my blood. A thrill of ecstasy ran up my body, making me shiver.

A familiar smell tickled at my nostrils, a faint tang of wood-smoke ... mixed with something else: the smell of dusty earth. Not the smell of the pow-wow area, but somehow other....

Barely had I registered this when into my mind's eye flashed an image: swirling clouds of dust; galloping horses, bodies dull with grime; on their backs, half-naked riders pale with sweat and congealed dust, long black hair whipping. Briefly visible beyond the fallout of their frantic passage, the pale, conical upward thrusts of several tipis; in the background, arid, treeless hills overhung by an insipid, grey-white sky. A feeling of urgency; desperation.

The drum-beat seemed to intensify, drummers' hands and voices in perfect oneness, outside and dizzyingly inside my head. A quivering in my solar plexus and heart area spread throughout my body like the blossoming of a lush, red flower, and suddenly a tear sprang from my right eye and ran, hot and swift, down my cheek. Unable to bear it – although what it was I was unable to bear, I had no idea – I opened my eyes.

About ten dancers were no longer moving round the arena but had gathered in a ragged crescent that opened in front of the drum. Shuffling steps and swaying and nodding in time to the beat, they were waving or twirling their dancing-sticks high in the air, or pointing them down into the drum at the centre of the hunched, wailing drummers, whose eyes were closed.

Suddenly one of the dancers leapt nimbly forward directly in front of the drum. Twisting and slashing his eagle-claw stick, he danced an intricate, twining dance; beautiful, breath-taking; a soaring and swooping display of power and grace, inspired and carried by the pervasive heart-thud of the drum-beat and the yips and whoops of the other dancers.

An elderly dancer was raising his fingers one by one in an obscure count of the actions of the dancer, who leapt back after some long minutes I wanted to never end. Then another span and whirled in his place; his style quite different, his light-footedness and agility like that of a much younger man. As the other dancers whooped and shook their sticks in approval, he moved faster and faster, feathers and fringes a blur.

When his time was done, an elder who must have been in his late eighties moved sedately forward into place, nodding his crown of hawk feathers in time to the beat as he alternately raised an intricately-woven, webbed dancing stick to the sky, then pointed it into the centre of the drum. The beat intensified even more, sticks thudding ever more powerfully. The dancer moved increasingly lightly and energetically, carried by an energy, a power I could feel like an electrical tingling.

When he moved gently back into the crescent, a younger, heavy-set man with long black braids, his face painted black one side, white the other, leapt lightly into the centre. Long buckskin fringes swirling, eagle feathers a blur, he danced like one beyond himself. Gripped between his tightly-pressed lips was a small, slim bone, attached to a thong about his neck. Suddenly there flew forth a high, piercing whistle. I had never heard a sound like it; it seemed to tear through the firmament, cut through my breast. Again and again the dancer blew his bone-whistle; the wailing singers' voices a keening wind, the perpetual thud of the drum like thunder.

It was becoming increasingly and intensely unbearable. I had to close my eyes.

Again, the scent caught in my nostrils: a smoky, dry, dusty earth-scent.... A strange feeling, a sort of yawning emptiness, stretched nauseatingly in the region of my solar plexus, and tears began to run down my cheeks. It was like the greatest loss, the deepest homesickness a person might feel; as if I were being torn in two, turned inside out. My head spinning, I thought I was going to faint. Then with one great final thud, the drum and voices stopped, leaving me poised on the brink of a great, black, swirling emptiness.

A profound, throbbing silence stretched and stretched.

The master of ceremonies, a loud, talkative type who had often annoyingly chatted mid-song (but had, I later realised, been silent throughout this one), cleared his throat and spoke softly into the p.a. system: "Well, now.... I'd like to remind you all where we are.... An' them that have the eagle-bone whistle, I'd like them to remember what it's used for."

Jacquie, my co-worker for the Society, who had also come south for the pow-wow, came rushing round to find me a few moments later, eyes wide. "What was that? What happened there?"

Dizzy, shaken and drained, I shrugged my shoulders in bewilderment.

When I told her about the experience, Auntie Vi thought the song probably came from the tradition of the annual great spiritual ceremony of the Plains tribes, the Sun Dance, and that drummers and dancers had been transported by its energy, while unsuspecting watchers like myself had been taken along for the ride.

Through time and space, I thought.

As for the eerie whistling, she told me the eagle-bone whistle is used to call in the spirits of the ancestors. It carries an awesome responsibility, and each time he blows upon it, the user gives away a year of his life.

The Sun Dance ceremony was not one with which she was familiar. She explained that the Plains peoples had a patriarchal tradition, while the Lakes' was matriarchal, and the Plains tribes held their annual spiritual ceremony in the summer while the Lakes held theirs in the depths of winter. She felt that the Arrow Lakes ancestral territory marked the cross-over point between the patriarchal-based Plains tribes and the matriarchal tribes further to the west.

This was intriguing information, but in the light of what I had experienced I had to put it aside for the time being. The extremes of emotion; the strange scent; the feeling of being taken out of myself – carried on the energy of a group of Native people who had apparently temporarily forgotten themselves; the envisaged place, of which I had no conscious knowledge; all of it had been too powerful, too vivid to have been just imagination.

How come Eva had been in that particular place, drawing me to it then disappearing so strangely? I could not have been closer to the heart of whatever it was that had been about to happen. It was definitely more than simple chance. And if it had been the exciting of some supernatural power, it seemed to have served as a sort of catalyst. Perhaps, I thought, the experience had stirred and transported me back to the memory of another time and place, another life....

Intrigued by this powerful, unforgettable experience to which I often went back in my imagination, I never guessed that there might be an actual force or energy, bubbling up through the layers of my consciousness, which would take ever-greater control of the reins of my life-direction.

THE CALL OF THE ANCESTORS

The non-reciprocal nature of the Jay Treaty not only disallows Native Americans free passage from the U.S. into Canada; they are also afforded no status in Canada. No status equals no voice, except through Canadian legal counsel. By a strange coincidence, the solicitor retained by the Lakes people was the son of a close friend of my landlord and his wife. Of Métis lineage and instrumental in obtaining recognition of the Métis as a distinct people, he was now working with a law-firm out of Nanaimo, B.C. and put in his first appearance at the next Lakes Band meeting in Inchelium.

The turn-out was by far the greatest yet; at the back of the crowded hall I noticed Tom, the speaker from the opening day at Kettle Falls Historical Centre. Having learned he was not only a son of Lakes elder Martin but also a pipe-carrier, I was sure the strength of the Band could only grow.

After the customary meal, the meeting was brought to order. The solicitor advised that one of the first things that had to be in place was an established criterion for Arrow Lakes Band membership. According to Mary-Kay, an attractive, light-haired Lakes descendant, a membership committee was already hard at work; she explained that they had begun organising the Band Roll, interviewing people and combing the archives for proof of identity and status, but that the Tribal Agency had proven uncooperative about allowing access to the Tribal Rolls and further warned them that by uniting as a Band with a view to a claim on their lands in Canada, they risked being struck from the Rolls on the Colville Reservation. Cries of outrage sounded throughout the hall; the threat of disenfranchisement was immediately denounced as a political ploy to force them to accept the Agency's representation on their behalf.

Fears were brought up that the "extinct" status of the Arrow Lakes Band would prove the greatest hurdle, but the solicitor lightly dismissed them, convinced they could prove a breach of trust by the Canadian government.

The terms "land claim" and "compensation" were becoming common tender. Things had moved a long way from the initial vision of a place in their ancestral lands where the elders could camp, hunt and fish with their grandchildren; where traditions could be revisited. With all my heart I wished that the injustices could be righted through a gentle, harmonious unfolding, with consideration and respect, and not through the harsh, confrontational gauntlet of legality and politics.

Meanwhile, in the Slocan Valley, quiescent divisions in the community had cracked wide open. It was clear that those opposed to the return of the Lakes people saw the road issue simply as a veneer for a land-claim, and feared for private property. Not long after the meeting in Inchelium, I attended a public meeting called to air the issues at the community hall in Passmore, south of Vallican. The local joke about how it was possible to tell when Lakes people were coming into the Valley held true: grumbles of thunder heralded the arrival of their representatives.

Chaired by the RDCK chairman and attended by almost a hundred people, the meeting began quietly enough. After introductions, the Lakes' counsel was asked to clarify the situation. He was swift to point out that all owners of private property were fee-simple title owners, and, as such, immune to any possible land-claim.

Elected Lakes Band chairman Lou had barely begun to ask for consideration of the Lakes people's heritage, when a vociferous exchange between several Valley residents at the back of the hall drowned out his words and he was forced to concede to those who wanted to voice their feelings and opinions.

The words "land-claim", taken out of context, had fired certain people up and it took most of the rest of the time to manage some clarification. Eventually drawing the meeting to an end, Sue, the local businesswoman who had organised it, summed up by saying it had served its purpose: rumours were cleared up and "now everyone knows what people think".

In my opinion, few of the local thoughts I heard loudly articulated that day were anything to be proud of.

Within a week, tenders were being called for the construction of the Little Slocan Bridge. The archaeologist's impact assessment report had not yet been made public, nor was I able to get hold of him.

The following Lakes Band meeting, again held in Inchelium, seemed dispirited even before I reported that tenders had been put out to contract and construction was about to start on the right-of-way. Bob stood up as I sat down, and I soon understood why he had been detached and withdrawn when I arrived.

His hand shaking, he was holding a letter. "This come, just this mornin'. The request for the repatriation of the ancestral remains has been refused."

The silence was one of the heaviest I have known. Bob and a couple of other Lakes representatives had visited the B.C. Provincial Museum in person the previous month to see whether any special arrangements would be necessary, and officials had told him that it was a straightforward matter and everything would be ready at about this time. In a shocking turn-around, the Lakes people were briefly apprised that a policy for this kind of request needed to be drawn up, as a precedent was about to be set in Canada. There was no mention of any intent to include or consult with Native Americans in the preparation of the policy.

"We got to see the head guy." Bob quietly remembered the visit to the museum. "Another curator said, 'It's the first time in history that anyone has gone back for their ancestral remains to be buried.' I could see it kinda took 'em back a little bit. The guy was kinda embarrassed; he wasn't satisfied with the condition the bones was left in. So we didn't ask him to bring us down into the basement and see the condition, because we figured we would leave him with that much embarrassment anyway." With a twist of dark humour he added, "It's a moot point as to whose ancestral remains might end up in the ground at Vallican.... An' we won't need no truck, neither," he laughed grimly. "There's not too much of 'em left."

Later, I would learn from an insider that conditions in the museum basement were frightful: unlabelled bones lying haphazardly on shelves; bones falling out of half-open boxes; boxes used as footstools.

"Not only that," said another Band member. "They've started watching at the line. Harassing us. Some of us've been turned back for the flimsiest of reasons."

I was horrified. This was politics: the lack of morality and ethics more apparent with every twist and turn. How could spiritual practices ever be implemented in such a void?

"Word's been put about that members of AIM're involved," she added. People looked around in shocked disbelief.

Lou whispered in my ear: "The American Indian Movement. The radicals."

It was hardly surprising: given all of this, some feelings were bound to become increasingly militant. I wondered if they were connected to a faction of the Lakes people whom I had been told were suspicious of my involvement from the outset, sure I was a government agent, or at the least yet another white person meddling in their culture, aiming to capitalise from it, or, as was once said to my face, "intending to steal one of our men". ("Tempted, but that's all," was what I could not respond.)

I could not blame them. At least I had the support and friendship of those whom Bob had called "the best people". I liked to think that my motivation was altruistic, although no doubt there was at the very least a touch of that old temptation, glamour, involved. Yet it was also a fact that the force driving me to be part of this unfolding was relentless, and seemed irresistible.

The day before the road-building project was due to begin, a Band meeting was scheduled in Nespelem. Poorly-attended, overshadowed by listlessness, it was brief and unproductive. After it ended, I was returning to my van when I was approached by one of the Band members usually wary of me and asked who in the Valley might be supportive of direct Native action, the very next day, before the bulldozers turned up. Hardly able to believe my ears and almost overwhelmed with relief that at least some kind of action was being taken, I came up with a couple of contacts. Filled with new heart and purpose, I was about to drive away when Uncle Charlie knocked on the window of my van and beckoned. I turned off the engine and got out again.

"Come over here a moment." He took me over to Lou and told me that he and the Band chairman were about to leave to represent the Arrow Lakes' situation at a meeting of the British Columbia Union of Indian Chiefs at Kamloops, B.C. Distracted, I nodded politely and was about to take my leave when Uncle Charlie added, quite firmly, "I think it would be a good idea if you were there."

My heart sank. My mind was full of things to do when I got back; if direct action was their intention, the Lakes people would need all the support they could get. Part of me knew it was not something I could bring up with Uncle Charlie, however, and besides, I knew only too well that when an elder tells you to do something, you do it and you do it now, without question.

It was about four hours' drive in my old van to Kamloops, where I camped out for the night, met up with Uncle Charlie and Lou at their motel the next morning and rode with them to the Secwepemc Cultural Centre. Imagining what might be going on at Vallican, I was unable to pay much attention and felt increasingly frustrated and agitated as the meeting and the day wore on. Finally it was Uncle Charlie's turn to speak. He represented the Lakes' case succinctly and as he ended, for the hundredth time I wondered why he had insisted I be there, and wished I had not agreed to ride with them to the centre in their car; I still had to wait for leave-taking and other protocol. Although I would never have left without Uncle Charlie's approval.

It was late afternoon before we went our separate ways; midnight before I arrived home, feeling weirdly split, as if some part of me had flown ahead.

The scene that awaited me at Vallican when I got there the next morning will stay etched in my memory always: two huge, driverless, earth-moving machines standing idle outside the proposed route; no bulldozers and graders tearing up the earth, spewing out foul fumes, but three tipis, spaced out along the cleared route, blue wisps of smoke emanating from the fan of tipi poles: no roaring and revving engines, only stillness and silence. Not a person to be seen, anywhere. Direct action had succeeded where everything else had failed.

Hearing voices, I went to the closest tipi. A couple of local and Native families were sitting inside, and they enthusiastically related how, early the previous morning, the approaching flotilla of machinery had been stopped in its tracks by the courageous action of a small group of primarily women and children, both Lakes and local, who had strung themselves out across its path. Concerned about the human rights issues represented, many local people (far more than I had anticipated) had apparently rallied to support the front-line warriors, directly and indirectly.

"Where were you?" It was almost an accusation, but then I learned how fortunate it was that I had not been there, for my name had flown around on the wings of rumour and blame. Most of the names of these people – some of them close friends – now appeared on a warrant. Suddenly it hit me: mine would have been among them. I had never thought about the possibility of being arrested.

Stunned at the implications, my thoughts flew back to Uncle Charlie. He had known nothing about the plan for direct action. In fact, I knew he would have disapproved: elders act according to protocol. What had been behind his insistence that I come to the Chiefs' meeting? It was not as though I had made any contribution; I had simply been present. And therefore not at Vallican, at the crucial time. Had I not been spirited away, I would now have a criminal record.

Intuitively, I knew I had been protected, but by what or whom, I had no idea. What was it that had impelled Uncle Charlie to direct me hundreds of miles north at this crucial time?

Then I realised that someone else whom I thought would be vital to this effort was also not there. Immediately after the meeting at Nespelem, I was told, Bob had left for the coast of British Columbia, following up the trail of some far-flung Arrow Lakes descendants.

He too was obviously under protection; neither of us was meant to be a front-line warrior.

AN ANCESTOR SPEAKS

Within a few days, tipis and a kitchen area were set up in the clearing where Bob and Manny had camped less than a year before, turning it into a busy little village-centre. Three more tipis were erected on the right-of-way, making six altogether, and the matter went before the Supreme Court. A legal wrangle about rights was grinding into action, but as far as I was concerned, those who had the right to this land were here. At last one of my dreams was manifesting: the Arrow Lakes descendants were setting up a camp and beginning to put down roots in their ancestral land again.

The interpretive tours, which I had used to not only explain the diverse features of a unique site but relate the tragic tale of the Arrow Lakes people and tell of a valid and valuable way of life that had almost been lost, were now over. Part of me would miss them; I believed I had come to know the site intimately and had enjoyed creating an atmosphere, a sense of something beyond the natural. Not difficult, given the ambiance of the place.

During the initial stalemate between the road-builders and the Native people, I was surprised and flattered to be approached by a Lakes descendant who wanted to know everything about the site, including the archaeological record, and walk through it with me. This was unusual in that he was the only one of this first wave of occupants to express interest in the scientific study.

The lower terraces of the village, the ones closest to the river, hold the most recent evidence of occupation; recent evidence can also be found all the way up to the higher terraces of earlier occupation, because the people who came later could use the earlier levels, but not vice versa, obviously. The burial-ground is situated on the uppermost terrace of the designated site. Two of the disinterred burials had been carbon-dated as recent as 200 BPE (before present era), while another was dated at approximately 2000 BPE, with the others lying between, so the area must have been used as a burial-ground throughout.

Many different kinds of lodges throughout the site had been demarked. Known variously as pit-houses, kekuli, or kickwillies, winter-lodges were partially subterranean. The floor was dug out and a ledge retained round the wall for storing goods away from the damp, and perhaps also for sleeping. A framework of four central poles supported a roof of slim cross-poles laid close together, over which was laid a sod cover that swiftly took on a greening life of its own. Accessed from the inside by a long pole with notched steps, an opening in the centre of the roof served as exit and entrance, and smoke-hole. The design also meant no animal could get inside. A well-built lodge would be returned to winter after winter, and might have been in use for as many years as a woman's reproductive cycle lasted. A mere hump in the ground, barely noticeable, it would eventually return to nature, leaving but a slight hollow in the ground.

The archaeological report addresses only one dimension of archaeology, however: it relates to the pit-houses, but not to the landforms or the sediments. Since people do not only do things inside their houses, rather than simply looking at the artefacts, I had often thought it would probably be of great value to examine the evidence of human behaviour in response to their environment.

Just as a whole forest holds out together: if the big trees are taken out, the little trees that depend on the big ones to break the wind will fall over. In a similar way, this settlement had been a specialised one: there was a technology for getting the fish, processing and storing it, which meant people could live in houses and survive there through the winter. It was a lot of eggs to have in one basket, however; if the salmon failed, the people would have had to look to other resources. And fail it did sometimes, as in times of great floods when the river would have been too silted up to allow the salmon egress.

All the activities would have been scheduled. For example, camas, a super-nutritious lily, grows in rich soil that is not well-drained and is available at the same time as the salmon. Since Vallican was on the fringe of the salmon area, different groups would probably have had responsibility for obtaining each resource from each area. Thus, despite appearances, it might not necessarily have been a bustling village, but a residence of about six months centred on wintertime.

Quietly-spoken and friendly, Pat had introduced himself to me for the first time at the previous Band meeting, and had been among the spearhead of occupation, purely out of interest in the ancestral site. Of the traditional fairness Uncle Charlie had described – ash-blond hair, blue-grey-green eyes – he reminded me of stories I had read about the Pale One, a prophet with "eyes of earth and sky and sea" who had once walked among Native Americans. His wife Lucy, classically-beautiful and of a sweet, kind nature, decided not to accompany us; heavily-pregnant, she stayed with the rest of the small group of Lakes people gathered round the campfire in the kitchen area, for although it was now well into summer, the weather had turned cool and closed in.

There was not a breath of wind. Low banks of clouds veiled the mountains and a grey, damp shroud hung among the evergreens, snagged on branches draped with dank, dripping tufts of wolf-hair, a black tree-lichen. Fine drifts of moisture rolled between the trees as we began to follow the path delineated at the time of the survey. Behind us, the voices murmuring at the campfire were swiftly swallowed up by the enveloping damp and the barrier of undergrowth and greenery; the smell of wood-smoke was replaced by the pungent scent of crushed pine needles, which littered a carpet of emerald-sparkling mosses. Diamond-drops splashed heavily from the branches; underfoot, the earth was soft and yielding. We paused to interpret the symbols on the map and relate them to what lay round us, but within minutes the paper was soggy and our planned route and the symbols melded into an indecipherable ink-blot, rendering the map useless.

Laced with sage-green and startling yellow-orange lichens, the clusters of rounded, shining-wet stones that lay everywhere seemed to stand out more than usual. I remembered Bob joking about using one as a pillow when they camped on the burial-ground; Eva telling me about the traditional burial: matriarchal, under the ground, the body in a seated position facing east with grave goods – favoured or valued items – to accompany them on their journey, and a cairn built over. "Like an ice-cream cone," she had said. Could these little heaps of stones, especially those lying in the hollowed-out areas, be remnants of burial-cairns?

Musing aloud, Pat eerily reflected my thoughts: "But what of them that Bob spoke of, that died of the new sicknesses?"

"Bob said that so many died," I remembered, "and so fast, that there wasn't enough time to bury them. Whole families at a time. He thought that they might simply have been left where they lay in their lodges."

Had anyone carried out whatever were their last rites? I guessed not. Chilled, I realised that not just the ancestors whose remains had been removed, but other Arrow Lakes ancestors might lie, dust under our feet, all over the village, their spirits trapped and restless. Something our rather unorthodox archaeologist had said came back to me, and I repeated his words aloud: "There ought to be a branch of archaeology which pursues psychic investigation."

I had no idea how close such thoughts were to a deeply personal psychic realisation.

Passing several small circular depressions in the ground, which according to the scientific interpretation might have been storage-places, we stopped on the edge of a large, oval-shaped hollow which Pat thought might have been a one- or two-family dwelling-place. Deeper in the woods, at the foot of the next terrace, we came to a hollow I knew to be the largest and deepest on this level. Pat surmised it could have been a council-lodge, as I had long thought. Then he indicated the faint indent leading into it from a small hollow. "Passageway from the sweat-lodge," he murmured thoughtfully. "They'd have purified themselves and prayed, before making any decisions." Then he pointed out an even smaller depression nearby. "An' that's the fire-pit where the rocks were heated."

I was speechless. I had not noticed either feature before, nor were they marked on the survey. The tables were turned: it was a living Arrow Lakes guide who was bringing the site's features to life.

For a long time, we stood together in silence in the centre of the great council-lodge. Closing my eyes, I visualised shadowy confines, a shaft of pale light lancing down through the murk; pale, curling drifts of smoke; the flicker of flames playing across weather-darkened, lined features; hide and fur; feather, claw, bone, horn, shell. A circle, to show all were of equal importance. I imagined murmured inflections of the Sinixt language, the cadence of the ancient tongue of the land, as they discussed and debated....

What had it been like, to live in a society that operated by consensus; where all the information was available to everyone? Where days might be spent in discussion and deliberation, with interest, courtesy, fairness of thinking, until all were in agreement? The traditional Native American council was a collective process which gave Benjamin Franklin and Thomas Jefferson the inspiration for the American Bill of Rights.

Peace covered me in that place like a warm, soft blanket.

Gently, Pat said: "I gotta tell you 'bout my old aunt.... When I was young, she used to order me round, always telling me to do for her. If I had a question, she'd never answer directly, but tell me some story I never did get. If I asked her about things, she'd yell at me to do it myself an' grumble 'bout how she had always had to do everything for herself, an' how young people today wanted everything handed to them on a plate.

"She told me about a stick ... well, a power-staff. When I was in my teens, I asked her how I could get one, but all she did was scold me: 'I'm an old woman. As if I should be wastin' my time and energy on such a lazy boy. Why, I would never've been so forward as to ask'. I'd had enough. She frustrated me, so I gave up on her. Haven't seen her or thought of her for years.

"Then a couple of days after comin' here, this place where my ancestors walked, I found a stick. Had to pick it up, an' suddenly it sort of spoke of how it needed to be shaped. So I carved it, an' when I was carving, I was humming, an' that song ... that song came from somewheres, but I never heard it before." He ducked slightly and looked around.

Spellbound, I found I was holding my breath.

"Wish I'd paid more attention to the old lady," he continued, almost to himself. "She knew 'bout the plants, the medicine plants, for healin'. An' there were other things. But I was young and stupid; it was boring. My green young mind wanted excitement, magic, power, in my hands, right there and then." He shook his head slightly. "Being in this place has changed that. I never saw so many different plants growing in so small a space.... You know, now I understand she was tryin' to teach me, in the old way."

"Is she still alive, your aunt?"

"Oh yeah. An' it's time for me to go back to her."

Warmth blossomed in my chest. I had never expected to hear anything like this; the land was working its magic already. But perhaps it was not only the land.

We left the old council-lodge and climbed up to the next terrace, moving backwards in village-time over a thousand years. Leading the way, Pat said he wanted to take me to a place he had found on his first walk through the village site. We turned off the path into the undergrowth.

Feeling constrained out of a kind of respect to walk only the defined pathways, I had never been through this part of the site before. Without experiencing the powerfully-sacrosanct feeling that pervades the area, it is probably difficult to understand that it was only through the invitation of a Lakes descendant that I felt able to tread elsewhere.

Clambering over more small piles of round, grey, shiny-wet stones laced with curlicues of lichen like coded messages and brushing through wet shrubbery, our legs were soon soaked. Then we reached what was approximately the centre of the site. Pat gestured; we both stood still.

Broken only by the faint splat of dripping trees, the heavy silence pressed in; the faint, misting drizzle emphasised a feeling of disconnection from the rest of the world. Wordlessly, Pat indicated a dark, conical mound, chest-high and covered with black and bottle-green mosses. It looked like it had just risen from the forest-floor, a humpbacked sylvan fungoid that at any moment might raise twiggy arms and a faceless, hooded head, and lurch towards us.

An old midden, I recalled from the map, bringing myself back to earth with a shiver: a place where the shells of river-clams had been discarded. A waste-place; an archaeologist's treasure-trove. Not for the first time, I thought about the way we study a people from the things they had lost or discarded: their broken or useless, unwanted rubbish. What would archaeologists of the future have to say about us?

Like a promise of hidden treasure, a mother-of-pearl gleam caught my eye; simultaneously, Pat reached forward to pick something up from the earth or out of the midden (I could not see which) and held out his hand. Cradled in his palm was a small, dull-sandy-brown, stick-like object. Strangely, it was not a piece of shell; it was thin and long, and rounded at the ends.

As one, we gasped: "It's a bone."

It had a slightly greenish tinge, and to my inexperienced eye, looked like a finger-bone. "A finger-bone?" I breathed. My right index finger twinged in some weird kind of empathy.

Holding it delicately between his thumb and forefinger, Pat examined it closely. "Very old," he murmured.

I nodded, feeling no desire, indeed a strange reluctance, to touch it. My mind was racing. The Lakes people had been advised that any find, especially of remains, should be kept and recorded, as it might provide additional evidence to support their claim.

But the young Native woman in Eva's dream had instructed that all the remains should stay where they lay.

We debated our way through this contraindication, eventually coming to an agreement that we must have been directed to find it in order to help the Lakes' claim. Before we took it back, however, Pat decided to pray on it and said he would take it up to the altar, which lay on the edge of the burial-ground on top of the next terrace, and ask for guidance.

It was still strange to think of the altar, the large, flat stone put in place by some Lakes people around the time of the storm-rent meeting, on the east-facing cliff above a salmon-backed curve of the Slocan River, close to where Bob and his party had first camped. For it had been situated exactly where I used to sit and meditate and pray, and, as I would learn, where many others had been attracted to pray, conduct a pipe ceremony or commune in their own way with the spiritual realm. Many offerings lay there now; like at Chief Joseph's grave, simple things like sage, sweetgrass, flower petals, tobacco, shells, stones, coins, and crystals. Coloured ties adorned the branches of the young spruce that grew beside it, mere feet from the spot where I had pounded out my desperation upon the snowy ground two winters before.

I followed Pat for two or three steps, then something told me he should do this alone. Almost halfway up the terrace, he paused, then came back down to where I was standing and began to tell me about another childhood memory. The soft, wet earth, layered with pine-needles and dark, crumbly leaf-mould, began to yield under my feet and I shifted position to find a more secure footing. At that moment, I sensed, rather than saw, a movement off to my left along the terrace, level with us. A moment later, from the corner of my eye, I caught a flicker of movement at the same spot, and an impression of colour: bright red.

Pat was still talking but I was unable to listen; my eyes were on him but my attention was on the odd movement. It could not have been a bird; it had been too low, too bright. Then I saw Pat's eyes slide off in the same direction.

"What is it?" I wasn't sure why I was whispering.

"There's someone there," he breathed.

The quality of the silence seemed to alter, becoming heavily ominous. Even the dripping seemed to have ceased.

"It's a man," he whispered. "He's been here a little whiles. That's why I stopped and came back down. I keep glimpsin' him out the corner of my eye, but when I look, I can't see him."

I shivered. "Me, too.... It's the bone!" The words were out before I thought.

"It feels okay," Jim whispered hesitantly, then exclaimed: "I see colour!"

At the same moment, out the corner of my eye I saw a startling, definite flash of red. It had seemed to spring from a small shrub that stood next to a young birch, whose trunk was no thicker than my forearm. No person could have been hidden there; there was nothing that could screen anything larger than a squirrel.

"Red.... I'm gonna pray on this." Decisively, Pat turned and started to head up the slope. I was just realising I had said nothing about the colour I had seen when he gasped: "Holy smokes!"

"What is it now?" I asked, hardly daring to breathe. This was becoming unbearable.

Wide-eyed, he stared at me. "The bone – it just broke in two, right in my palm! I was barely touchin' it!"

I asked to see it. He extended his open hand and I gingerly picked up the smaller of the two pieces and delicately laid it on my left palm. It seemed extremely fragile and brittle-looking. All of a sudden, it started to crumble away at one end, like some eerie morphic special effect. A cold rush of fright coursed through my entire body, and I held my hand out to Pat. "Take it back! Go and put it back!"

Rooted to the earth, chilled to my bones, I stayed where I was as, without another word, he took both pieces and swiftly returned down to the midden, where he stood for a while, fist closed and pressed against his chest. I could see his lips moving. Then he stooped, reached down, straightened up and looked around. Taking a branch from a wild rosebush, he used it like a brush over the area.

A sudden crackle of thunder ripped over our heads, softened to a muttering and faded away. Our eyes met, and although neither of us found anything to say, something had changed.

We were finished here. Or I was, at least.

"The rose branch?" I queried, closing my mind to the idea.

"For protection. Uncle Charlie taught me."

When we emerged from the woods in the failing afternoon light, the half-dozen Lakes people huddled round the warmth of the campfire turned as one and stared at us. "What happened in there?" Almost accusingly, the question came.

By this time, I should have been used to the acute sensitivity of Native people. I was too shaken to respond. In any case, it was for Pat to tell. And although the Valley remained overcast for the remainder of the day, no storm broke; the skies remained a uniform dull, heavy grey, but there was no more thunder at all.

Only three weeks later, I would accompany an Arrow Lakes delegate to a World Archeological Congress, "Archeological Ethics and the Treatment of the Dead" at the University of South Dakota (1989). As representatives of indigenous peoples worldwide came together to demand respect for their beliefs and practices, and the repatriation of the millions of ancestral remains on display and languishing in the basements of museums and private collections throughout the world, I learned of the global proportions of a fundamental, emotionally-charged issue.

It became clear to me that the lack of respect accorded indigenous ancestral remains has the power to unite indigenous peoples in a way that little else can. Subsequent publicity heightened general public awareness and sympathy, and 1989 saw many changes in U.S. government policy towards the treatment of Native American burials, culminating when the Smithsonian Institute released eighteen thousand unidentified skeletal remains.

Whether it is the living uniting to take care of their dead or as Bob had once said, the dead bringing the living together again, is a matter for private contemplation, but as I listened to speakers from all over the world, my thoughts flew back to the little bone Pat found at Vallican. Through which an ancestor had spoken.

THE POWER OF THE DRUM

The wait for the court's decision seemed interminable; angry confrontations flared up almost daily at the site, peaking when a tipi at the periphery of the new encampment was torched. The sight and scorched smell of the blackened, tattered remnants sickened me; it felt like a personal violation and filled me with a cold anger, the strength of which shocked me. The Lakes people spoke in terms of the death of an elder, an ancestor. Some good came of the sacrifice, however, for both the local police and the RCMP revealed themselves to be not only sympathetic but supportive; they were the first to officially point out that the Native people were within their rights.

On behalf of the VAP Society, I organised a local public meeting at the Vallican Heritage Hall to emphasise the cultural, historical and public significance of the site, again clarify the legal processes and answer any questions about the intent of the blockade, for the issues had openly mushroomed from protection of a burial site and travelling, hunting and fishing rights to a comprehensive land-claim and financial compensation.

Sometimes I felt bewildered by what it really was that I had become so caught up in: a "chance" meeting with a charismatic Native American had somehow drawn me into something that had initially seemed to be about human remains being brought back to their rightful resting-place and the founding of a cooperative community, but it was turning into some kind of vortex, increasingly wider and bigger, taking on a life of its own. Much as I believed in the Arrow Lakes people's right to decide what happened on their ancestral land, as a romantic, a dreamer, I had been slow to understand it could only happen through political and legal avenues. Increasingly, I felt out of my depth.

Despite the short notice, over seventy local residents attended to hear Yvonne, the Arrow Lakes Band coordinator, make an impassioned plea for understanding: "I came up here to attend a funeral, to rebury bodies taken from here, to put back what was. I'm proud to be one of those who fulfils a prophecy."

I knew she was referring to her grandmother, who had told her that one day the Arrow Lakes people would come back home to Canada. But had that elder seen this as the route?

Again their solicitor reminded us that the Lakes people had been run out of their land. Apparently the first seven treaties negotiated by the Canadian federal government in 1871-77 had been supplemented by only four (as land under title to Native occupiers became valuable), and after the date of the last treaty, 1921, vast tracts of land still remained unsurrendered. In 1973, after initiating court action, the Native people of British Columbia had won the recognition of the Supreme Court of Canada as a group whose aboriginal title had not been extinguished by treaty, but although the Supreme Court has continued to act decisively on Native rights, the courts have proven bolder than the government.

To the obvious dismay of those entrenched in fear, the solicitor joked that in effect, the whole of British Columbia was under a land-claim.

In turn, the archaeologist stressed the importance of preserving culture and heritage, and the particular value and sensitivity of the Vallican site. Wayne's brief but vital contribution was lost to those who, the solicitor's words ringing in their ears, were muttering among themselves.

Three speakers had been my intention, but the Native American way is four. About to announce a question period, I was surprised when an unassuming Native man dressed casually in a grey, hooded sweatshirt and jeans stood up and asked if he might make a contribution.

In a quiet voice, he introduced himself as a hereditary chief of the Gitksan-Wet'suwet'en Nation, who had long been engaged in a court battle with the government of British Columbia for recognition of their land claim. With a graceful hand, Ralph indicated the Lakes representatives: "Their struggle is mine." Something about this small, ordinary-looking individual had made the whole hall fall silent. "In my own land, I'm fighting for freedom and respect. The hereditary chiefs will set policies that will reflect good ecological use of the resources. Nobody's going to lose. People here have a chance to do something good." As he continued, his eloquent sincerity underlined by an obvious humility, I could not help thinking I knew whom I would prefer as my landlord.

Later, I would learn that not only the Gitksan had been monitoring events at Vallican; many Native Bands were watching, poised to rally in support of a precedent-setting effort. However, at about this time, a fatal decision appears to have been made, possibly because of the unfamiliarity – as American Native people – of the Lakes representatives with the overall Native situation in Canada.

At first it seemed like there was a good chance of success in stopping construction of the road, but within a week of the blockade, a local RCMP inspector negotiated a truce between the Highways contractor and the Lakes representatives and obtained the Lakes' agreement for work to proceed south of the designated site without confrontation until the courts granted an injunction on behalf of one side or the other.

It was apparently a decision taken without consultation with the Lakes' legal representative, nor was it made known to the local supporters, who arrived at the site one morning to find clanking, revving, fume-spewing machinery going about its destructive task. It especially pained me to see the remaining young trees simply pushed over and bulldozed into piles of slash to be burned, as the ground was ruthlessly cleared and levelled in the area south of the site, toward the Little Slocan River. Ignorant of the agreement and not understanding how this could go ahead when the courts were still reviewing the case, we could only watch as the sandy riverside beach that locals and their children had enjoyed for decades was obliterated in a single afternoon.

A great, silent witness, Frog Mountain towered impassively above the devastation.

Unable to stay away, on the following day, feeling helpless and numb with sadness yet hoping and praying that some miracle would stop it all, I was watching the machines from an upper level of the cleared route when Melanie, an Arrow Lakes elder from the Colville Reservation, appeared by my side. I barely knew her but was glad of her company. After some silent minutes watching with me, she indicated Frog Mountain. "Gives me the shivers just to look at it."

"There's a legend I heard about it," I told her. "'Frog stole the Fire from the people. When Frog falls, Fire will return to the people.' In my opinion, 'Fire' means our creative energy or power, but I don't know who or what is meant by 'Frog'.... Maybe some kind of people we don't know about yet, like fairies, only big and bad." I was talking off the top of my head, trying to make her smile, not realising how close I might be to the truth, as is often the case with top-of-head (crown chakra) talk. "I haven't been to see it for myself, but I've been told by locals that the far side of the mountain has already begun to crumble."

Melanie said nothing, just kept on staring at the peak, her long, tanned, narrow face serious, her brow furrowed.

To fill the rather heavy silence, I found myself adding: "Bob told me some things about that mountain. I guess you know it has a spirit-name...." It was something I had not told anyone but Bryan, but she was Arrow Lakes. Still she said nothing, so I made an attempt to enunciate its spirit-name in Sinixt, adding: "White Wolf."

Melanie was so still I thought I might have overstepped myself. Auntie Vi had warned me about saying too much about what I knew: that some people might not like it. Several tense moments passed, then Melanie drew in a deep breath and whispered in a faltering tone: "That name ... the spirit-name of the mountain. It's the same as my Indian name. The one I was given. I never knew...." Shaking her head gently, so that her thick and curling dark-brown hair slid over her narrow shoulders, she continued: "I was always told to stay well away from anything to do with Indian spirituality. I was raised by my uncle an' aunt, an' as long as I can remember, they all filled me full of fear of nature, even animals small as squirrels. They said that li'l critters might speak to me, an' tell me things it was dangerous to know. They made me so scared, I stayed away from the forests and the mountains....

"But I understand now my relatives was only tryin' to protect me. It was the mission-school education filled 'em with a superstitious fear of the old ways." She paused. "Who knows? Perhaps they even sensed in me my true calling. Which I'm just now realisin' is probably tied up in this area." She stared at the mountain for which she was named. "I been feelin' a profound connection to it ever since I had arrived. I know now I've got a real responsibility here."

Amazed as much by the incredible coincidence as the fact she should reveal such intimate information, I looked from her to the peak, which seemed to soar to even more significant heights. A faint trembling began in my stomach. Bulldozers and scrapers forgotten, my mind raced with the implications.

This elder had been intimately connected to the mountain sacred to the Arrow Lakes people since birth. Yet she had never known, not consciously, at least. What had been in the minds of those who had given her this name? Had they been here; had they known legends, prophecies? Or had White Wolf spoken to them, across time and space, reminding them of their origins, calling them home? Had some specific role been seen for this woman? Would she become medicine woman, within the sight and influence of the sacred mountain for which she had been named? It almost made up for the devastation in front of me.

From then on, every day, Melanie prayed, sang and drummed her little hand-drum, grounding herself in her ancestral home, and within a short time was telling tales of strange things that happened: odd flashes of movement and colour (like I had experienced with Pat) among the still, silent trees, that were definitely not animals or birds; being woken up by things crashing off shelves or returning to camp to find things rearranged, when no-one else (human, at least) was there; items going missing and suddenly turning up again, in or out of place. Sometimes she would hear a faint ripple of laughter when she came across a missing item, and in turn she laughed at how the "li'l folk" would have their fun; she was never afraid of or angered by their activities.

It reminded me how Cliff had been inspired in his artistic work while living as caretaker in the village. His work had blossomed, taking on a distinctly Native American flavour, and he too had spoken of odd things happening and "messages" being given him. I would never forget the time I went looking for him and he came bounding out of the site, declaring triumphantly: "It just came to me: the dead can take care of themselves – it's the living we must care about!"

In my opinion, such supranormal activity was an indication that the dead were also taking care of the living, which was part of the original intent of situating the burial-place in such close proximity to the place of the living.

As the court hearings ground their slow, irrevocable path to resolution, men and machinery prepared to put the new bridge into place. The archaeologist had informed us that because of its wide clear waters and shallow gravel beds, the Little Slocan would have been an ideal river for spawning salmon, and this place in particular a likely area for fishing. Having been made of organic materials, however, any traps and weirs probably would have long ago decomposed.

On the same day as the thrice-edited redraft of Wayne's commissioned study finally surfaced, belatedly warning of "significant indirect adverse impacts" if the road went ahead as planned, and confirming all the concerns raised by the Society, the first vehicles ploughed their way across the river, obliterating any possible remaining evidence. The river bled a dusky-brown.

Cut to the quick by this stage of the proceedings and knowing that Melanie would be spending the day drumming, singing and praying at the burial-grounds, I thought I would join her. Drum in hand, I positioned myself on the same terrace, only outside the site about a quarter-mile up from the river. I had not forgotten the power of what had happened at the pow-wow in Nespelem the previous month, and chose the chant Melanie had taught me (which, strangely enough, I could only sing when near her. Native American chants have a way of coming and going, as I would learn).

There are two basic patterns to the drum-beat of North American chants: an even, staccato beat, or a syncopated rhythm like the beat of the heart. Most songs begin in the higher ranges and curl and spiral down to finish on a lower note; they vary from simple and repetitive to highly complex forms, such as the Butterfly Song of the Kutenai Nation, which meanders through a steady beat like a butterfly flitting from flower to flower, alighting briefly, basking in the sun, lifted by the breeze. Despite the patient teaching of a Kutenai elder, I never managed to grasp it.

As through practice I grew more familiar with the form, I began to understand some of its subtleties and innate power: the voice, resonated breath, sacred gift of the Creator, reaching to the sky, drawing down energy from the heavens and earthing it through the channel of the body. Yellow Bear had explained how energy is gathered in the solar plexus, from where it is "punched" out or through, rather than projected from the throat. It took a lot of practice to find the place from where this power came; he would tease us to leave school choirs behind, and I realised I was beginning to access it when my diaphragm would feel tender and bruised after a session at Grandmother Drum.

Strong in me was the memory of a peaceful place, filled with green growth and a sense of magical expectancy. Looking down on raw, exposed subsoil, churned and rutted by bulldozers, scrapers and graders; on cremation piles of uprooted, splintered trees and heaps of discarded top-soil, it was difficult to keep my voice steady. Strung out along the naked earth, pearl-grey and ghostly in the slowly-dissipating morning mist, stood the tipis, elegantly beautiful amid the despoliation.

If only some miracle would spirit away all this ugliness and restore the beauty and the vision, was my inner plea. I drummed with tears in my eyes, Melanie's song staying with me, going round and round so many times it seemed part of me, as another part of myself was lost as the morning progressed and the sun burned off the mists to reveal the terrible labour. I was glad to be out of sight of the work on the bridge, but the grumble of machinery ate at my soul.

Suddenly, shockingly, silence fell. I stopped singing, let the drumbeat fall away. It seemed like everything was holding its breath. Then I heard shouting, and two engineers' pick-ups parked on the terrace below raced down the right-of-way and around the curve to the bridge-site. Silence descended again.

Except for the thudding of my heart. What was going on? Had an injunction forbidding work on the road arrived? My heart leapt; it seemed the logical explanation. Or had the workmen been suddenly stricken with a conscience? Or a sort of "road to Damascus" experience?

The silence dragged on. Looking as excited and bewildered as I felt, Melanie appeared by my side, just as another pick-up came racing up the right-of-way. It was the archaeologist, commissioned to be on hand should any bones or other "sensitive" material manifest ("after they've munched it up", as he had earlier cynically observed). Leaving his vehicle, Wayne strode up the terrace towards us.

Apparently a temporary metal ramp had been put in place across the Little Slocan. A pick-up had used it to cross the river and then the first gravel truck began to trundle across. Wayne had been standing on the river-bank with the project foreman, watching its progress, when there had been a great creaking sound of tearing metal and, in a sort of slow-motion, the vehicle had dramatically keeled over and capsized off the collapsing ramp into the river. Unhurt, the driver had clambered out, leaving his truck on its side in the water like a beached, wounded whale, its life-blood, diesel oil, leaking a rainbow stream down the swift, shallow current. Members of the press, anticipating such a scoop, had leapt to capture the drama.

Superstitious fears were swiftly proven to still exist in a modern, technologically-dominated, materialistic world as construction workers had started yelling: "Hex!" "It's voodoo!" Apparently, an outcry arose that something be done about "the old witch who drummed a curse down on us".

For her part, Melanie was amused and even a little gratified by the notion that all these white people should think she was so powerful. How they had known that Melanie had been drumming and praying, I had no idea, but I wished with all my heart it would be enough to make them walk away from the job. My faith that something would turn up to permanently stop construction had been renewed.

OF ANGELS AND EAGLES

Impersonal and relentless, governmental right and might was not to be dammed; after a flurry of injunctions and counter-injunctions, the final ruling was made: the road would go ahead. The obstructing tipis were ordered to be taken down, and it was agreed that they would be ceremonially dismantled, one by one, at sunset over the following six days.

The decision should not have come as a surprise to anyone. Highways had been so sure of their ultimate victory that work on the right-of-way alongside the site had been on-going for days before the final ruling; massive, roaring machinery heaving their bulk around the tipis as the ground was cleared and flattened, barely skirting the pale, silent sentinels of the route, which still housed several stalwart protesters.

During this difficult period, a number of people, Native and non-Native, confided to me their dreams, the common theme of which was that it was vital that the tipis remain, or it would be the "beginning of the end".

The end of what? Unspoken was a sense that it was not about the end of an effort to prevent a road cutting through such a sensitive area, nor the end of an attempt by two races to work in cooperation, but something greater: this was the time when South Amerindian tribes were warning that lack of respect for the sacredness of the earth would lead to mankind's undoing; when Hopi spiritual leaders were releasing their final prophecies; when environmentalists were claiming that an ecological point of no return had been reached.

For me personally, the removal of the tipis represented the end of an era. For months I had been living out something like a dream-come-true, but nothing was turning out like I had imagined. It was as if the dream was running away like sand trickling out of an hourglass and there was nothing I could do about it. Even what it had been about had become cluttered; so much had happened since those long, heady, late-night meetings in the Valley with Bob and Manny, when we had all dreamed together. Bob had said that what we were about to do together would attract a lot of interest, but surely he had not meant in this way? Something had to turn up to rescue the situation.

For five days I stayed away from the Indian village, at each setting of the sun feeling the pain of another tipi being taken down. Nothing intervened. On the sixth day, I could stay away no longer. I had to make my own farewell to whatever it was that those tipis represented.

The only non-Native present, I kept a respectful distance from the small group of Lakes men, women and children, and from there joined in the drumming and chanting as the canvas of the tipi was slowly and reverentially folded back, wrapped and put aside. Gathered in an eloquent point, their energy channelled toward the heavens, the exposed tipi-poles stood as a final tribute to the efforts of a people trying to conserve the integrity of one of their last remaining intact ancestral sites. Skeletal, they symbolised dashed hopes for a shared vision and joint effort.

Trembling like a reed, my voice had little strength. Running tearful eyes up the stripped right-of-way to the mountain I had named Ringmaster, I recalled the mystical appearance of the great Sky-Wolf, that difficult winter almost two years ago.

Where was the guardian now? Where were the ancestors? Had we not done all we could to protect the village? What had been left undone? Why were we not getting the help we needed? Not the first time in this mountain-rimmed, challenging Valley, I found myself thinking: "I shall lift up mine eyes unto the hills, from whence cometh my help...."

It was a still, cloudless evening. The sun had just passed from sight; the deep lapis of the sky was contained like a jewel within the girdle of mountains, and a golden light suffused the higher forest. Beyond the crest of the mountains to the north, I saw a slight wisp of cloud, and watched as it swiftly and majestically sailed into full view, immense sweeps of feathery white streaks trailing behind as it sped down over the Valley.

It was the most eerie sight, because there was no wind.

Transfixed, I watched it approach. It seemed to regroup, taking the form of an elongated, robed being, both arms extended, long hair flowing, two great sweeps of flexed wings: an ethereal angel-figure, painted by immense brush-strokes of the gods.

My throat and chest tightened, making it difficult to breathe. I glanced at the Native people, who were still singing, drumming, doing their ceremonial work.

Memory of another sky-vision strong in my mind, I broke away and ran back to my van to get my camera. No-one seemed to have noticed or looked up, and I managed four swift shots of the cloud-form hovering over our heads before it began to unravel, lose form; moving away in an unexpected direction – toward the south-west – just as the ceremony was coming to an end.

Once the last note of the chant had faded, I burst out: "Did anyone see that? Did anyone see that, in the sky?" Although it was on the tip of my tongue, I didn't say "angel". This was a Native American ceremony.

Faces turned up to look at the jellyfish-tendrils of a dissipating cloud, and heads were starting to shake when one of the men said, just as excitedly, "Yeah, there was an eagle. Flew right over as we was finishin'!"

Everyone else became excited then. I stayed quiet, not the least because I had seen no eagle, nor had the cloud looked like one to me. In any case, angels, eagles – they were almost anagrams but for the "n" (the unknown factor?). I remembered Manny making the connection when he told me about the Initiators, and thought about how the cloud had come from the north – place of wisdom on the Medicine Wheel; and how it had veered strangely off to the south-west – between the places of trust and introspection.

The message was clear enough to me. Knowing that a number of people who were unable to be present at this final ceremony had been praying in support, and that linking in this way (synchronised prayer-effort, chant and heart-thud of the drum) carries immense power, I was sure that this conscious melding of different belief-systems and effort had manifested two congruent symbols of faith in a greater unfolding.

This was the miracle: to receive reassurance that there was some greater Plan at work here than my own limited vision could perceive. For when my film was developed, in the last shot, the eagle showed up as a dark winged form, flying through the heart of the angel.

BEGINNING OF AN END

Community spirit seemed rekindled when a Thanksgiving dinner was organised at the Vallican Whole for "our new friends and neighbours, the Arrow Lakes Band". Over two hundred local and Native people shared food and good spirits, but I thought Bob, whom I had not seen for a couple of months, looked weary. His face was deeply lined and threads of silver glinted in his hair; his opening address seemed strained. And although his presence still evoked a response deep within me, it was a mere whisper, and it struck me that the spirit that had once so powerfully moved within him seemed to be draining away. I wondered whether the recent twists and turns of his journey had taken their toll.

Reminded of the original intent, I realised how clouded the vision had become; it seemed no-one was talking about the ancestral remains any more. But I felt unable to approach him; there was a sense of distance made more acute by several Native people who seemed to place themselves protectively around him.

Now that the true stewards of the Indian village were living there, it was clear to me that the role of the Vallican Archaeological Park Society was redundant, taking my official role along with it. So when I got word that a meeting had been called between the Board of Directors and the resident Lakes people, I was expecting an announcement to that effect.

As we waited outside the Indian village – which was where meetings were now held – for it to begin, I was pointing this out to Yellow Bear, who had recently been elected onto the Board: "Show's over for us...."

Rick, yet again re-elected president of the Society, came striding purposefully toward us. "Don't you talk to anyone any more," he blurted out at me. I knew he was referring to the many interviews, on radio and in the local papers, where I'd been able to say what I believed to be in the best interests of the site and the people to whom I felt it belonged. "You're not the mouthpiece of the Society! You've said more than enough! I'm the spokesperson from now on. You don't need to be at this meeting – you're not on the Board, you're just an employee of the Society. You don't need to be at any more meetings."

He stared at me belligerently, as if waiting for me to argue, but I had nothing to say. Fleetingly, I wondered what he might think his function now was, never mind mine; mostly, I felt relief at being able to step back from the intense level of energy output that I knew I could not sustain much longer, and also that I would not have to interact with a certain faction of the Lakes people now spearheading their cause, some of whom were making it increasingly clear that they did not want me around.

Not that it bothered me, either. So much had happened: the sharing of a dream, a vision; the incredible renascence of the Arrow Lakes Band I had been privileged to witness; the friendship of people from a way of life I had always felt drawn to; the many other dynamic people who had come into my life; the fabulous, evocative landscape I had come to know; the swift lessons in human rights, politics and law; the number of times my unedited opinions had been reported in the newspapers and on radio (I'd been lucky to say as much as I had). As for the many magical, scintillating, unforgettable dreams and experiences....

I glanced at Yellow Bear, who was maintaining a neutral expression, and thought I detected a sardonic glint in his dark, expressive eyes. The silence stretched, everything poised in stillness.

A slight movement caught my eye.

Like a sycamore key, a downy, white feather came twirling down between the evergreens, descending into the centre of our threesome. I held out my hand, and it easily and naturally settled on my palm. Looking up into the clear blue sky, I saw no sign of any bird, and closed my fingers over the fragile gift, intuitively knowing it carried a message. It made me smile, a smile I turned towards Rick. He gave an exasperated sigh, turned and walked away. I looked at Yellow Bear, who broke into one of his handsome grins.

"But it's not over, Celia," he chuckled, indicating my closed fist. "It's not the end. It's just that you're done here."

The timely appearance of a white feather is one of the ways we are reminded to have faith in the unfolding. A message that would occur at other times of uncertainty or doubt in the future, I imagine it being shed from the downy under-wing of an attending Angel, sweeping over. Or from Eagle, who flies closest to Creator-energy. Or from Hawk, messenger from the Heavens....

But "done here"? Much as I respected Yellow Bear and knew he had Sight beyond the mundane, there was no way I could agree. The Indian village had been part of my life too intensely and for too long for me to let go that easily. And when, shortly after, I was given the opportunity to say what was truly in my heart directly to the one man I felt needed to hear it, it seemed to me proof of my on-going involvement, no matter what Rick or anyone else thought.

Rick himself was probably annoyed that when the Heritage Trust manager arranged his first visit to the Lakes ancestral village, he specifically asked that I should introduce him to the Lakes elders. Guessing that he wanted to assess the occupation of "his" site, I accompanied him into the little encampment, having sent word of his request ahead.

Not knowing quite what to expect, I was gratified to find Uncle Charlie and hereditary chief John waiting for us at the periphery of the trees. These Lakes elders had never made me feel other than warmly accepted. As we approached them, I suddenly appreciated this was a one-off chance to say what I had wanted to say to the Trust manager from the beginning, only now I could do so in front of the elders to whom this little parcel of land meant so much.

Banging the final nail into my own coffin as Society coordinator, I made a simple introduction then dramatically added: "It is my privilege to introduce you to these Lakes elders, the real owners of this land!"

Uncle Charlie broke into a deep chuckle and the serious but kindly face of the hereditary chief beamed at me as I turned to leave – exit, stage left – trembling, but glowing within.

Red Cloud, Cree visionary
and founder of the
Rebirth of Mother Earth
Medicine Wheel Gathering.

Rebirth of Mother Earth Medicine Wheel Gathering,
Edgewood, B.C. Summer solstice 1987.

Laughing Thunder
(Bob), social historian
and visionary member
of the Sinixt/Arrow
Lakes Band,
with his son, Virgil.
Vernon, B.C. 1987.

THIS PROTOHISTORIC POLE DEPICTS THE
LIFE HABITS OF THE LAKE TRIBE OF INDIANS
(SENATCHEGGS) WHO MADE THE ARROW LAKES
THEIR HOME.

THE SENATCHEGGS, NOW EXTINCT, WERE WATER
TRAVELLERS, HUNTERS, FISHERMEN AND
BASKET WEAVERS WHO BELIEVED IN A MYTHICAL
GOD, THE COYOTE.

THEIR PIT HOUSES AND PICTOGRAPHS ARE NOW
COVERED BY THE WATERS OF ARROW RESERVOIR.

DESIGNED BY DOROTHY CRABBE-CARVED BY JIM WILKINSON

Plaque dedicated to the memory of the Arrow Lakes/Sinixt tribe, Edgewood, B.C., c.1968,
exposing the whiteman's limited perception.

Uncle Charlie, Arrow Lakes elder, with the author.
Independence Day pow-wow, Nespelem, Colville Confederated Reservation, Washington, 1989.

Aunti Vi, Arrow Lakes elder,
much-loved, indefatigable
mentor and friend of the author.
Sacred Heart Medical Centre,
Spokane, Washington.

Frog Mountain, Vallican, B.C.; sacred to the Arrow Lakes people.
Photo with permission of Cliff Woffenden.

Calling Back the Salmon ceremony, on reclaimed Hayes Island,
the central Arrow Lakes' fishery, Roosevelt Lake, Kettle Falls, Washington, 1991.

Ed, Spokane spiritual leader,
ferrying the author across
Roosevelt Lake to
Hayes Island, 1991.

Grave of Chief Joseph
of the Nez Percé,
Nespelem, Colville
Confederated Reservation,
Washington.

Tipis line the disputed
right-of-way through the
Arrow Lakes ancestral
village site,
Vallican, B.C. June 1989.

Laughing Thunder (Bob), Lou (chairman), the author and Uncle Archie (behind Bob) at an
Arrow Lakes Band meeting, community long-house, Keller, Colville Confederated
Reservation, Washington, 1989.

The author (in black) with Northern Lights drum group at the Inchelium camp-out, Colville Confederated Reservation, Washington. Members of Spokane Little Falls drum group behind and standing.

Little Wolf (Manny), wearing a great kilt, with the traditional Scotsman, Arrow Lakes Indian Village, Vallican, B.C.

Patches of Snow (Tom),
Arrow Lakes pipe-carrier,
dancing with his
granddaughter at the
Inchelium camp-out,
Colville Confederated
Reservation, Washington.

Whitestone, a sacred gathering place, Roosevelt Lake, Washington.

A LONG WAY to go FOR ROOTS

In November, the Court of Appeals passed down the final judgement: almost complete, the road project would be allowed to stand. Strangely enough, the fact that this part was over came as a sort of relief. It had taken a lot of energy and almost blinded me to the real miracle that had been happening all along: a fragmented people, a nation deemed extinct for decades, had reunited, had been recognised as an entity by the courts of law, and were committed to a permanent occupation of their ancestral village. The focus of the Arrow Lakes Band turned back onto the original, fundamental issue: the repatriation of the ancestral remains.

My position was winding down to its official end. Collating the information brought together over the previous nine months, including some newly-uncovered historical documents from private collections throughout the area, many of which had lain out of sight for decades, I wondered what would happen next. The most important thing to me – the Lakes people returning to take care of their ancestral remains and their ancestral village – was in place. Logically, my part was over, but emotionally, I was unable to separate or remove myself.

Convinced that my role would now metamorphose into the next stage, I was thrilled when Auntie Vi produced the first of my moccasins, the right-foot one, at the Remembrance Day dinner at her home. The beaded design was a yellow rose, its petals edged with red and set against a powder-blue background. "The yellow rose of peace and friendship," she explained, her eyes gentle and warm.

The worked hide was soft and supple, sensuous against my skin, faintly aromatic. Thinking how this was the beginning of a whole new dance, I began to pull it on. But it would not go over the top of my foot. No matter how I wiggled my toes and gently tugged, it made no difference. Frustrated and strangely shame-faced, I measured it against the sole of my foot. The lovely creation was the right length, but simply too narrow. My "earth-mother" feet, a problem again.

The usual crowd of friends and relatives was there and expressed their disbelief; Auntie Vi was known for her adept craftwork.

"Just have to tear it all apart an' start over again when I get another piece of hide," she laughed it off. "There's not enough of that piece left to make two new ones.... Good thing my old aunt isn't here to see this. She'd be tannin' my hide for sure!"

It had taken almost nine months for my drum to reach me. I had been employed by the Archaeological Society for nine months. Maybe not only medicine things, but anything to do with Native people had to go through a gestation period. I resigned myself to more waiting; counting ahead, it would be Spring by the time I would be able to be a part of the dance, wearing yellow-rose moccasins, the eagle shawl and the hand-made, flowing, black-and-white tunic and pants Jackie had gifted me.

The only problem was that a secret part of me did not want to dance that way at all: not a seamless glide over the earth; no expression of grace and beauty as a woman. I had never told a soul that the dance that stirred my heart, my blood, my bones, was a swirling, leaping, blur of colour.

Focussed on disappointment and the vagaries of Indian time, I never considered any possible underlying symbology: an adept craftsperson, a prayer warrior; an incorrect fitting.... Within a couple of days of returning home, the first indications of the next major shift in my life were already presenting themselves.

At the time, it seemed an impulsive decision, the outcome of a short telephone call informing me of my stepfather's sudden, unexpected death. Yet in hindsight, what transpired during that emotive call was extraordinary: my spontaneous response to my mother: "I should be with you at this time."

"Then come."

"It should be for a few months, maybe six." Even as my mouth uttered them, I wondered where the words were coming from.

"Of course."

As if to prevent any possibility of acting out second thoughts (which flooded in almost immediately: what had possessed me, how could I leave now, or ever?), my landlord paid a visit the following day. This was not uncommon; more a friend than a landlord, Ken loved the Lodge and often stopped by. But this time was not a social occasion. With a tone of genuine regret, he told me that his son and daughter-in-law were returning from Saudi Arabia some four years earlier than anticipated, and would want to live in the Lodge. He immediately added that he would not expect me to leave until I had found another suitable place, and even offered to arrange alternative accommodation on his land.

Numbly, I explained what had transpired, whereupon he offered to store our possessions and have the alternative ready for our return. Something in me had gone stone-cold, however. I could not commit myself to his condition, which saw me living there for at least another three or four years.

How could I make decisions about so far ahead, when my present life was being ripped out from under my feet?

Not once did I make the connection to another time when things had clicked into place, only two years earlier, carrying me where I needed to be. Instead, I rationalised how it was only the power of blood-connection that could tear me away from the forces that held me in the Valley; how right it was for a daughter to be with her mother in her time of grief; how it would be an opportunity for a grandmother to get to know her grandchildren.

Only in hindsight did I appreciate the intuitive and synchronous processes strong enough to be heard and acted upon, shaping lives in ways we would never imagine, guiding us on to the next spoke of the Wheel, to the next twist in our tale. The voice within, which, if allowed, pays no heed to our Coyote-side that mirrors human weakness – over-inflated ego, fears and petty desires – but pilots us to our greater potential: that which we came to Earth to fulfil.

The day before we were to leave the Valley, Melanie came to wish me a good journey. She had taken up full-time residence in the village and become its heart, always ready to visit and listen to anyone's problems. I personally remember her as the "Winter Warrior", for she endured the privations of autumn and winter that year without running water or electricity, first living in a tipi and then in a small trailer. As we visited, I mentioned the difficulty I had recalling the song she had taught me.

Without a word she began to sing it. I joined with her, our hands drumming the coffee-table. After four rounds, she turned her dark eyes on me and with warmth and authority stated: "Celia, I give you my song!"

During the flight to England, out of a dark, velvety sky that seemed to accompany us most of the way, her song came back to me. And over the following months, it was never far away, providing me with comfort and support. For although it seemed like I was doing the right thing, my body was swift to inform me that my emotions were not in agreement: the day before we left Canada, I fell ill, as did my two younger children, and it took a full month in England to regain my strength and some equilibrium.

But in a way I did not really recover. That sojourn in the land of my roots marked the pivotal point of a painful inner journey that was taking me down into the depths of myself; to the place of shadows, the cave within. Without conscious awareness, I had reached mid-life and was deep in an intense – and of necessity, difficult – period of self-examination.

On the one hand I embraced the opportunity to renew my relationship with my mother and younger sister and the time to fully be with my children again; but like an open wound, my yearning for the great open spaces and wild grandeur of the North American landscape, the intensity of my involvement with the Native people and the sense of destiny that had made me feel alive in a way I had never experienced before, almost tore me apart.

After an absence of almost twenty years, I had lost contact with all my English friends and had a weird sense of being an alien in my own land, which visits to my favourite childhood haunts did little to allay. Alone at night in my bedroom, enveloped in pungent clouds of sage-smoke, often in tears, and with a yawning emptiness in my heart, I would drum and chant, mentally flying back to the Valley. Often I found myself wondering what I was doing so far from home. Then I would ask, what was home? What was I looking for? What indeed was I? A woman awake ... or dreaming? Even my name seemed the name of a stranger.

The little library in my home-town became a place to which to retreat; as in my younger years, I scoured the shelves, looking for I knew not what. Then in the spring, the first clue: a book called "Quicksilver Heritage."

Reflecting not only one of the issues – heritage – that had been so much part of my awareness recently, but also a mercurial element – the energy of Coyote – the intriguing title caught my eye and for the first time, I learned about the concept of ley lines and the existence of a planetary network or grid of subtle energies. Reminded of the strange sense of an invisible wall at the place of the Four Warriors at the Indian village, I wondered if this was part of the reason I had come to England: to be directed to a deeper understanding of what it was about places like Vallican and the site of the Medicine Wheel gathering, and others which had a rather strange and distinctly special sort of atmosphere.

There was no other book on the subject in the little library, however; it was the deep purple of a little leaflet that next caught my eye.

Eileen loved to relate the story of how I had found her; never having had a response from anyone in my home-town, she had almost given up leaving Northumbria Seekers' leaflets (she had chosen the colour) in the library. Indeed, the one I had come across had been the only one on the stand, but the idea of an organisation dedicated to spiritual education and exploration intrigued me.

After a couple of lengthy phone conversations, we met at a local café. As soon as I walked into the crowded room, I spotted her, partly because of the jewel-like purples and greens she favoured but mostly because of the way she sort of glowed, this slight but strong-minded, grey-haired lady in her eighties, whose eyes were of the clearest blue. Formerly principal of a teacher-training college, she was also a trained Jungian psychotherapist and chairman of the Northumbria Seekers, which was linked to the Wrekin Trust, whose founder, Sir George Trevelyan, was one of the greatest New Age spiritual figures in England.

Our meetings and conversations blossomed, energising us both. Certain we were of the same "soul family", Eileen invited me to join the guided group meditations she was then leading. The first time I had experienced anything like this, each meditation brought a profound experience couched in symbology, which she was able to competently decode. She then persuaded me to take part in "The Way of the Mystic", a six-week seminar she was teaching.

All these new experiences were taking place in the city of Newcastle, and she happily picked me up and brought me back to my mother's house, even though it meant going out of her way.

Then came what I will always look back on as her master-stroke, the most catalytic piece of networking I would ever experience. A couple of weeks before we were due to return to Canada, she insisted I meet a couple affiliated to the Gatekeeper Trust, a charitable organisation that conducted sacred landscape pilgrimages, and become part of their spiritual journey into the heart of Northumbria.

The teaching was still strong in me: when an elder tells you to do something....

For the first time, I consciously acknowledged the forces that helped shape me, the wild landscape that had nurtured my love of nature and nourished the romantic flame in my heart: vast, desolate stretches of purple heath and rocky-ridged moor, populated by hardy, black-faced sheep; soft-breasted hills bearing faint traces of the terraces built by my Neolithic forebears, whom I imagined must have been attuned to earth and stars much like the Native Americans; secret valleys laced with cold, clear-running streams tumbling over stony places and meandering through marshes: tiny, stone-built mediaeval churches with the spiritual presence of a cathedral, their graveyards dense with undergrowth and over-shadowed with yew, symbol of eternity; great, sweeping, golden crescents of a lonely coastline, punctuated with the ruins of abbeys and Norman castles standing tall on hunched cliff-shoulders, overlooking grey fingers of rock that reached out into the lead-grey North Sea.

The North Sea had lapped at my soul as I grew, and I loved it with all my being. And although their invasion had been the beginning of the end of the golden age of Northumbria, once a kingdom in its own right and home to great saints and scholars, the Sea-Wolves struck some chord of recognition deep within me: the Vikings, who had crossed not only this sea, but the oceans beyond.

A small group of pilgrims we were, only three men and three women, but closely-attuned from the outset, as if we had specifically been drawn together to share a seven-day of dream, meditation and simple ritual; ideas, information and experience; and to dance, sing and, blessed by unbroken, unseasonably good weather, to walk for miles on beach and heath under the great Northumbrian sky, a sky which somehow seems bigger than any other, anywhere.

Through the knowledge and understanding of the couple who had organised the pilgrimage, Earth Mysteries – the magical energies of earth and stone – began to make themselves known to me: great and small stone circles, Medicine Wheels for the most part overlooked; lone standing-stones, pointing to some forgotten knowledge; cryptically-marked stones, their use and purpose unknown; the stone-built solidity of mediaeval churches, not simply places of weekly dogma but charged with atmosphere, full of carvings and stained-glass rife with unnoticed, overlooked or misunderstood symbology. All around, as Anthony, the leader, explained, were cryptic messages, hinting at arcane knowledge far in advance of our own, their meaning hidden in the mists of time but whispering of star-lore.

Among these holy places – ancient sacred groves, patternings of stone – I discovered that which I had sensed at the Indian village in Vallican and the Medicine Wheel gathering grounds at Edgewood: a raw and powerful yet subtle energy that spoke deeply to me. Shocking and thrilling, the secret, sacred heart of Northumbria was opening itself up to me. Called for the folk-song "The Fair Flower of Northumberland", the pilgrimage was a profound experience which served to forge my spiritual connection with the land from which I had sprung in this life.

And once, significantly, when being driven through the soft-breasted, undulating, heathered hills of the sparsely-populated Border area, the unbidden thought entered my head: "I could live here." With something close to dismay, I tucked away the idea, unable to imagine why I should even want to. I loved Canada; my home was there now; my children were Canadian.

In the course of the last century, our relationship to our place in the world has been radically transformed. Many people no longer live in the place where they were born, but move throughout their life a number of times to different areas of their county, country, the world. The geographical sense of roots, of belonging, has largely been lost, which is probably why many people are turning to their genetic history to compensate and provide a sense of their origins.

My experience with the Arrow Lakes people had taught me how important it is to "pay attention to the root, or wither at the branch". I was beginning to understand how knowledge of and connection to my roots was vital to the sense of who I am and why I am here, my unique identity. Until then, I had liked to think of myself as a global citizen, but now I understood this did not address the inner need for a more specific sense of belonging.

I also discovered that I could carry places I loved, whether the wild and lonely coastal places of my childhood or the mountainous wilderness of my adult life, within me, as part of me, instead of yearning for them as something separate or missing. Instead of being caught between two worlds, the one of my roots and the other of my heart, I could learn to contain both. This was immensely liberating; instead of feeling "homesick", looking back with regret or worrying about what happened next, I was learning to live in the here and now.

Nevertheless, my children and I were relieved when the time of our return tickets came due. Canada was the home of my children, after all, and the place I had chosen to make my life now.

Reaffirmed in my roots, I was sure that was why I had come back; despite the occasional flash of thought as how at home I eventually did feel and how comfortable I felt with the group of pilgrims with whom I had shared so much, not the least a sense of humour and congruent belief-systems, nothing turned up that made me want to stay. In fact, I was sure I would never need to return to England again.

The universe had other plans, however.

STICK INDIAN

Now, almost fifteen years older and debatably a little wiser, I ask myself who or what I thought this all-powerful "universe" might be. Explaining away the unforeseen, the unplanned, the unexpected in life by pointing a nebulous finger at some mighty unseen force is the easy way out. Laying blame, wallowing in self-pity and staying stuck in the mud – where one firmly puts oneself in the first place – involves much less effort than trying to understand and live by the great teachings about personal power. Victimhood is a deceptive mantle, a form of avoidance or laziness that comes at the greatest price of all: personal disempowerment. Forgetting who we truly are, we choose to give away our power.

Filled with anticipation and a sense of relief as the cloud-shrouded peaks of the coastal mountains came into view, even on the plane I was wondering how my new-found knowledge about Earth Mysteries would relate to North America. Landing in Seattle, as arranged we were met by the younger children's father, with whom they would stay for a couple of weeks, and Bryan, who took Sivan and me back to Vancouver.

Out on the highway, my excitement ebbed. Everything seemed sickeningly too big. Six months among narrow country roads, small, hedge-bound fields, and compact villages and towns had imprinted; these wide roads, over-sized, languorously-moving cars and the sprawl of buildings seemed out of proportion. Worse, against the sense of permanence engendered by stone-built England, which seems like it has been and will be there forever, the wooden buildings seemed like a movie set: here today, gone tomorrow. My gut-reaction was that I wanted to go home.

Home? My home was here.

Leaving Sivan to spend some time with her father, I collected my van from storage and set out for the West Kootenays. Expecting the vague feelings of unease to fade as I drove through British Columbia, I stopped several times to appreciate the beauty of the province and familiar stopping-off places where my children had often played and gone swimming. Yet something felt different. Reaching the southern end of the Slocan Valley and the evocatively-familiar landmark of Rose's Restaurant, I was even more troubled. Basking in soft spring sunlight, the beloved landscape I had revisited in my mind and heart time and again over the past half-year was leaving me strangely untouched. It was as if the mountains were giving me the cold shoulder.

It wasn't the first time I'd left a place I loved and returned to find that nothing was as it once seemed, as if the time and experience that lay between had changed things irrevocably. Sometimes it seemed like I was forever looking for "home". But had not Bob said – here, in this very Valley – that I had come home? So much had happened since to confirm his words. Never had I felt such purpose as here, and I was not ready to give that up.

Another heart-rending, soul-bending, ultimately liberating lesson of non-attachment was underway.

Most of my friends greeted me warmly enough, yet from the outset I had an odd sense of being an outsider, which wasn't helped when my once-close co-worker Jacquie commented that I seemed somehow different. Even more strangely, I didn't feel able to visit the Indian village, where Arrow Lakes descendants were still in residence, continuing their efforts to recover the ancestral remains. Dismissing it all as a combination of jet-lag and concern about the immediate future, I busied myself with finding a job and a house to rent. Both proved elusive, however, and I began to regret not having taken up my ex-landlord's offer. Sadly, Ken had passed over the month before and any possibility of returning to his land had passed with him.

After a fruitless month or so, the sun reached its heights; at the solstitial full moon, I put the search on hold and returned, loyal child, to camp at the Rebirth of Mother Earth Medicine Wheel gathering. At some level, I was hoping it might prove some kind of turning-point. Despite the unseasonably cold, wet weather, more people than ever attended, reflecting a growing desire for spiritual connection, but even there, where so much had begun, I felt strangely peripheral. Nor could I rustle up any enthusiasm for workshops. The only place I found I wanted to be was the moon-lodge, even though I wasn't in my moon-time.

Similar in structure to the sweat-lodge, a frame of willow branches bent and tied together so the shape resembles an overturned basket or bee-hive, the moon-lodge was draped with light canvas, so that instead of pitch-darkness inside, the light was soft and forgiving. In place of a pit filled with red-hot Grandmothers, a small central hearth served as residence of a tiny fire fed with splinters of kindling: not much more than a flame, lovingly tended. With room for only four or five "sisters" to quietly rest and share, it was here I felt at peace. Paradoxically, listening to the outpourings – words and tears – of the women who passed through the lodge, needing to share some of the issues that tend to come bubbling up at this time of the month, much like during a sweat, was relaxing; the odd feeling of distance enabled me to empathise without becoming emotionally involved.

It seemed that an entirely different vein of Native people had taken over the gathering, none of whom I knew. Only after the final ceremony did an indication of a possible opening door arise, when I was invited to take part in a ceremony of the Native American Church. It was to be held the following weekend, however, when I was supposed to be visiting Auntie Vi. I knew she would understand, but something in me did not feel comfortable with the thought of changing our arrangement. Auntie Vi had been a life-line for the past six months, her letters communicating her love as much as any news, and this would be our first visit since I was back. Reluctantly, I turned down the opportunity.

Auntie Vi was delighted to have us "back home" again and I began to feel better. Her frustration with my moccasins had continued, however; this time, she had cut the new piece of hide against the grain.

"Maybe we should just forget about them. It's not like it really matters." I felt I had to say it, even though I wanted those moccasins with all my heart.

To my relief Auntie Vi vehemently shook her head. "No. It matters. I'll start again. I said I'd do it, and I will."

You don't argue with an elder. And I knew well enough that medicine items came at their own speed – if something as innocuous as footwear could be called medicine.

Again enveloped in the warmth of this dear friend's caring nature, I began to appreciate how I felt more at home with her than anywhere else. I could tell her anything: of the ceremony of the Native American Church I had turned down (the dismissive expression on her face told me what she thought of that) and of an odd errand entrusted me only the day before.

Old Grey Wolf had often and admiringly spoken of Celina, a Native woman he wished I could meet, who had lived in the Valley a number of years earlier. Shortly before the historic AGM of the Archaeological Society, I heard she had returned, bringing her small grandson, Tam.[17] Hearing his name, I had wondered if we would become linked; and when she was pointed out to me at the meeting, I had been in awe. Of Cree ancestry, a fine-looking woman in the classical tradition, she carried herself in reflection of her Native name, Strong Standing Woman: her demeanour proud and severe; her brow deeply creased; her finely-chiselled lips down-turned; and like the old portraits of traditional tribal leaders, she seemed aloof, disapproving of the world in which she now found herself.

Coming to know each other over Grandmother Drum, where she had become "whip", overseeing and interpreting Native American protocol and teachings, we had discovered much common ground; given our diverse backgrounds, our world-views were surprisingly similar, and she had studied Western esotericism. We had become friends, and I had learned that marriage to a white man had come at a great price: her rights on her Reserve in Alberta.[18] When the marriage had ended, she had felt cut off; her roots shaken loose and her connection to her people broken, she led a nomadic life-style, feeling she belonged nowhere. Yet she too was aware of the powerful magnetism of the Valley. Part of me was sure she'd come home; that she was another of the Eagles, gathering.

Celina had also been a regular correspondent while I had been in England. When I had mentioned to her I was going to the Reservation to visit Auntie Vi, she had given me a cantaloupe. "Go up into the mountains," she'd instructed, "and leave it as a treat for Bigfoot. Cantaloupe's their favourite fruit. You can call them with a whistle. They'll hear you, though they might not let you see them."

Also known as Sasquatch, this legendary, large, shy and retiring creature is believed to be a possible throw-back to the Stone Age that still inhabits mountainous places in North America. Other sources conceive of an undiscovered, underground race. Popularised as the Abominable Snowman, it is also known as the Yeti in Asia, while other cultures have their own version. Blurred, indistinct photographs and casts of large, ape-like footprints provide the only hard evidence of the creature's existence but folk-tales and eye-witness accounts abound, as I was about to discover.

It had seemed a strange thing to ask of me, but flattering to be so trusted. I had been wondering if I should even mention it to Auntie Vi after not seeing her for so long, but found it spilling out anyway. Far from being dismissive, she laughed: "Now there's a thing!" Rummaging through the pile of crossword-puzzle magazines on the coffee-table, she pulled out the latest edition of the Reservation newspaper, the Tribal Tribune. Coincidentally, the front page was devoted to encounters with the "Stick Indians" – how Bigfoot is known on the Rez – by people who included elders and members of the Tribal Council. And there was more inside.

Most of the accounts were first-hand; many were childhood memories: descriptions of tall,

---

17 Soul-name of the Wolf-clan leader in Wendy and Richard Pini's excellent comic-book series, *Elfquest*.

18 By law, upon marriage to a non-Native, a Native woman was divested of her status and rights, which did not revert upon divorce. Ironically, this law did not work in reverse: the non-Native wife of a Native man gained full status, including rights to the land. This policy was contended as a subtle route towards total assimilation and extinction of rights. Only in the past few years was Bill C-31 passed in Canada, which allows Native women to re-enfranchise back into their Band and regain Native status.

swift, silent, usually red-haired creatures, their presence accompanied by whistles; tales of endless pranks, such as tools being taken and later returned. Apparently strange whistling noises were often heard in the mountains. The synchronicity of the article astounded me as much as the ready acceptance of what most people assume to be a myth.

Auntie Vi remembered incidents from her own childhood: whistling, things going astray, but the most memorable was much more immediate. "It was winter," she recalled. "One of my uncles, he went up on a lone week-end fishing trip, up to Summit Lake, by Disautel. But when he was gone three, four days without a word, his family got worried. They all got so concerned as to his welfare that the whole community came out to search for him.

"They found his pick-up, parked on the side of the highway near the pass, but there was no sign of him, not anywhere. They combed the trails up over the mountain, but they found nothing. Not a trace, not even a track in the snow. And they hollered, they were all hollerin' but all they heard was the echoes of their own voices. In the end, they gave him up for lost." She shrugged her narrow shoulders. "Then, 'bout ten or so days later, he burst into his house. He was hopping mad. Before anyone could say anything, 'What's goin' on?' he yells. 'I come back down, an' my truck's gone! I had to walk all the way back! Who's the sorry so-and-so who took my truck? When I find out, I'll show him a thing or two!'"

A small smile on her face, Auntie Vi shook her head. "It was a real strange thing. He thought he'd been gone a couple days, an' didn't believe when they told him it was near two weeks. And he had no idea what had happened to him, that whole time. Two weeks. And he was healthy and well-fed, and he only had a couple days' stubble on his chin. So someone'd looked after him that whole time, somehow. But who that was...."[19] Again she shrugged and shook her head.

"So it was the Stick Indians who had taken him?" I remembered how I had swum in the lake, alone.

"I heard tell they know how to tamper with your memory. And they sure make useful bogeymen!" She laughed. "But I'm not teasin'. That's a true story." Suddenly serious, she added: "And if you're taking the kids to Omak and you plan to go up there after, I want you to take my car."

"There's plenty of room in my van," I remonstrated.

"No. You take my car."

It was the usual Saturday afternoon outing for my kids and Carly and James, Auntie Vi's grand-children, but this was the first time she had insisted I take her big, burgundy-red Buick. Admittedly, purring smoothly over the pass and down to Omak and eventually back, and up a randomly-chosen dirt-road near Disautel (not the one to Summit Lake) as far as it went was a comfortable ride.

Telling the children I would only take a few minutes and they should stay near the car, I left them with their new toys and treats, and, cantaloupe in hand, feeling a little foolish but also slightly exhilarated, followed a faint trail leading up the steep slope. When it petered out, I continued climbing, winding between the pines and the great outcroppings of rock, taking deep breaths of the clean, sweet-scented air, my mind empty, until confronted by a sheer cliff of bare rock.

A massive slab of grey-speckled granite, niched with natural shelf-like protrusions, lay nearby; placing the fruit on it, I stood back and whistled.

Cutting through the air, the only sound I had heard for some time, it made me aware of the silence: heavy, eerie. Not even a whisper of a breeze stirred the stiff-brush pines. Again I whistled,

---

19 In today's conspiracy-theory climate of opinion, such an inexplicable time-loss might be considered evidence of alien abduction. Interestingly, Bigfoot has recently been linked to alien activity.

my piping more tremulous this time.

The silence pressed in. Then a movement whisked among the scrub.

Flicking up desiccated pine-needles, a grey squirrel darted across the sandy earth and scampered effortlessly up the rough trunk of a lodge-pole pine, chattering angrily at my intrusive presence. Satisfied that its scolding had frozen me into place, it darted off, and perfect silence again descended.

Sometimes, under certain conditions, it is as if we can step outside of ourselves. The stillness covered me; I was not even conscious of breathing. After a timeless time, I became aware that the trees and rocks seemed more sharply defined, the colours stronger; the quartz in the great rock sparkled, catching my eye. Everything looked strangely different, as if I were seeing with another's eyes....

A cold shiver coursed up my spine, bringing me crashingly back into myself. I found I was trembling, and nervously realised it was almost dark. If I didn't hurry back, I might get lost. The walk back down didn't seem at all familiar, and I was flooded with relief when I finally caught sight of the dull-red and chrome of Auntie Vi's car through the trees.

Waiting for me were not the boisterous, clamorous child-spirits who had just been shopping in Omak, loudly full of energy, stimulated with pocket-money pleasures and a surfeit of fast-food. All four were subdued, three of them in the confines of the car. Winding down the window, a tumble of dark curls framing her pretty little face, Carly's brown eyes were wide. "You took so long...." she said plaintively. "Did you see one? Did you then?" Without waiting for a reply, she waved to her brother, the only one brave enough venture out, and then only as far as the rear fender. Bouncing up and down in agitation, she urged: "Hurry up, James. Come on. Let's get outta here!"

Now I knew why they had refused to walk up the trail with me. They had been listening, earlier. The Stick Indians were real to them.

And somehow, a couple of hours had disappeared.

It was completely dark by the time we got back, and the relief on Auntie Vi's face was almost tangible. "That's why I loaned you my car. Don't want your old van breaking down up there. Someone might get 'lost'." She looked at me meaningfully.

I did not tell her how lost I had been to myself, or for how long, since I was not sure what had actually gone on up there in the mountains.

This experience was not one I would forget, especially since, in hindsight, it seemed to have been another symbolic hint of what was to come. The strange feelings of dislocation and disconnection; the inability to find a place to call home or a job to pin me down; a pair of moccasins that fought against manifestation: all these were indications of a process already underway on the inner planes. Neither of us could have been consciously aware how close I was to both "breaking down" and being "lost". At the time, I thought that a mid-life crisis happened only to married men who ran off with their secretary: sad, middle-aged men who, out of the blue, bought black leather outfits, motorbikes, sports-cars. Unaware of the deeper meaning of the process and that I was at my own point of mid-life, I was oblivious to the fact that a deeper part of me, fragmented as the Arrow Lakes Band, was goading me to make sense of what I thought my life was about. Before long, I would be wishing that the Stick Indians had spirited me away, to return me, clean and nourished, when my personal winter was over.

INDIAN SUMMER

Despite the uncertain circumstances, I was not too concerned. It was summer; the camper-van served as home; Sivan was still in Vancouver and my younger children were happy with what seemed like an extended holiday. I told myself that what I was supposed to do next – something to do with Native people, of course – would soon materialise.

How swiftly and easily I forgot what I had been learning about personal responsibility in making things happen. Like thistledown, I began to drift where the winds of seeming chance took me, often ending up at the Indian village, my only point of reference.

Without a fixed address, getting a job was problematical; as time passed, I grew uneasy. Why was nothing turning up? I could not – perhaps would not – summon up the energy to find an answer. Taking it a day at a time, living in a sort of detached, numb state, I could remain oblivious to the strained nature of my relationship with the small faction of more radical Lakes descendants who had taken up residence at the Indian village. Bob and his mother turned up one day, and a familiar, trembling, inner response which I had thought was behind me rallied me enough to ask how things were progressing, but he seemed more distant than ever and I could not find it in myself to touch upon the issue that lay in my heart. At some level I must have been aware it would have been too devastating to my precarious state to find out that the bright optimism of a shared vision had dissipated like morning dew burned off by the rising sun.

Bob had mentioned that the ancestral remains were still under dispute. Inspiration struck me: my state of limbo had to somehow be linked to theirs. The political shenanigans had been a long and terrible distraction, a side-track that had made me lose sight of the most important issue. How could I have forgotten the initial impetus, seen by the elders as the priority?

It was an analogy onto which I latched like a drowning woman: as long the ancestors were not at rest, I could not settle. Once the remains were repatriated, I too would be at peace and my "real" life would begin. A life which would involve continuing to work with Native Americans, of course; there could be no other way forward. Hooking myself onto the words of Yellow Bear I wanted to hear: "not the end", I chose to block out his perception that I was "done here". I chose to forget that in the dream-state, the visionary Red Cloud may have admonished me to "call the people" but had said nothing about "walking" with them. And there was another element, about which I knew nothing as yet, not consciously at least: exactly which ancestor was not at rest and how that might relate to me personally.

Circling blindly in a holding pattern, unable to take off for new fields or come down to earth, I was unknowingly creating my own Charybdis; slowly but steadily stirring up an emotional vortex that was sucking me deep into my shadow-side.

One morning, I visited the Indian village and found everyone gone but for Bob, Eva, Manny and another Lakes descendant called Kous and his partner Marianne, the non-Native woman who had attended on Eva at the first encampment. The small, familiar group reminded me of a time of dreamlike beginnings, so I set up camp there too. The following day, two spiritual Doukhobor leaders visited and invited Bob to address their community at Krestova, in Crescent Valley. Knowing both men personally from my time working for the Archaeological Society, and remembering Bob's admiration for the spirit and self-sufficiency of their people, I saw it as an opportunity to rekindle the vision of a self-sustaining community.

Invited with the others to dine with the elders on the day, I was so excited I could barely listen to the dinner-table conversation. Even when one of them was showing us round his immense garden and small-holding, which had supplied all the food for our meal, my mind carried me forward, imagining what sort of things we might learn from this community and apply to a new one.

After the meal, we drove over to the community meeting-hall, an unassuming, long, grey building situated on a grassy hill above the little valley. It seemed we had arrived early, for there were no other vehicles parked outside and no sign of life, so it was a shock to enter the silent hall and be confronted with what appeared to be the entire local adult Doukhobor population, seated in tiered rows facing each other, men one side, women the other. All the men were wearing crisply-pressed white shirts and dark trousers; the women, white blouses, long, dark skirts and white headscarves.

Not one head turned as we entered. As if carved from stone, about a hundred people sat looking straight ahead, their faces composed, backs erect. Nor was one word uttered as we were ushered to our place, and as soon as we were seated, as one they all stood, starched clothes rustling like dry leaves lifted by the wind.

On some unseen signal, they broke into a soaring harmony which filled the hall: a traditional hymn in the rich, exotic intonations of the Russian language. There was no instrumental accompaniment, only their voices, their God-given breath, given back in praise. I had never heard anything like it. My eyes misted over; plain-looking farming folk had been usurped by a choir of angels. All my hopes and imaginings fled; my heart felt like it would break for the fullness of such a yearning, joy-filled, harmonious expression of love and praise.

As suddenly as it was begun, it ended. The ensuing silence resonated with a fine, clear vibration, as if on all levels the atmosphere had been cleansed. As the elder introduced Bob, it struck me that it would be a hard act to follow.

Drawing parallels between the history and beliefs of the two peoples, Doukhobor and Native American, Bob explained in political and spiritual terms what the return of the Arrow Lakes people to their ancestral lands meant to their new neighbours as much as to themselves. Yet something was missing. Just like at the Thanksgiving dinner in Vallican eight months before, when it seemed to me that his words had lost their power and clarity, it felt as if he were speaking by rote. Even worse, I could sense that his audience was not impressed, either. A wave of loss and hopelessness swept through me.

With the ending of the school-year, most of the Lakes people directly involved with the Indian village had to stay home on the Reservation to take care of family affairs; only Manny, Kous and Marianne remained. Sympathetic to my situation, Kous set me up in one of the larger tipis.

Another dream-come-true, it felt like a sort of coming-home. Not that I learned much about the rigours of traditional life in a tipi, for this one had rugs, beds, wooden chairs and side-tables, oil-lamps and, in the centre, where the hearth should be, a little pot-bellied stove. The stove-pipe protruded through a hole in the canvas and looked decidedly odd from the outside, but as the nights drew in I was grateful to be snug and warm. Kous showed me how to train rivulets of raindrops down the inside of the poles instead of dripping all over inside, and to raise the bottom of the canvas to regulate the temperature.

On another level, however, I entered the experience fully. To live in such grace of form – a constant, subtle reminder of our connection to the heavens – close to nature and the rhythms of the day and the season served to lift my spirits and quieten my inner turmoil. I soon got into a routine of rising before the sun cleared the mountains, firing up the woodstove in the communal kitchen area and, following tradition, going down to the river to bathe.

The Native American chants I had learned became a natural part of the early-morning ritual, helping ease a warm, sleepy body into the cold rush of water. All my inner tension was washed away as I communed with a great, sensual force that seemed like it could barely contain itself and might at any moment snatch my fingers from their precarious anchor among the round, slippery stones of the river-bed and tumble me over and sweep me away, like one of the half-submerged pieces of deadfall that sometimes sailed smoothly by. Powerful, invigorating currents playfully tugged at my body, filling my mind's-eye with river-images: steep, craggy mountains where it was birthed; a plunging, tumble-down, gurgling, babbling stony-passage; a slow, sensuous twining among tree-roots; the wild creatures whose lives depended on it. Rational mind stilled, doubts dissipated, I emerged vitalised, moved to spontaneously chant my appreciation of and gratitude to the spirit of the place, which seemed to have entered me, become part of me. It was more than an experience of the aesthetic. Opening my senses to the full, I embraced the nature of the river, bathing in puris naturalibus, in the essence of Creation. Like never before, I felt I was connected to everything, part of the Circle of Life.

Throughout the day, people, mostly local, would visit and for a while the Indian village became a sort of drop-in centre where troubles, worries, happiness and laughter were shared. Perhaps one of the greatest sources of entertainment was the stick-game, especially when Kous decided to teach me this art. Or more realistically, how I would never learn such artfulness.

A Native American gambling-game, it seems childishly simple: in his hands behind his back, one player hides two small sticks, one of which is somehow marked or coloured. Then he holds out two closed fists. The opponent has to guess which fist holds the marked stick.

If we had been playing for stakes anything like at the pow-wows, where, accompanied by fast, feverish drumming and chants and intensely watched by scores of spectators and team-participants, one player shuffles the sticks behind his back as hundreds of dollar-notes in double-figure denominations pile up in a crisp, green heap on the blanket between the two sides, I would have swiftly been made a pauper. Instead, I became a laughing-stock: even when I repeated to myself in my mind, over and over, that the key stick was in the other hand, Kous guessed right, every single time. The thick lenses of his spectacles made no difference: "You're that open, I can read you like a book!"

On my turn, I never guessed right, not once. Eventually Kous took pity on my frustration: "It's not so much 'bout winnin' the money. It's 'bout learning to read people, an' bein' willing to stake everythin' you own on your faith in your ability to do just that." Tall, rangy and grey-haired, Kous looked like he had come through many tough lessons in life. "Man might lose everything he got, right down to the shirt off'n his back, but he'll work hard to get it all together again so's he can come back again 'n' play that same man again. And again. 'Til he learns to read him.... You wanna play for shirts, then?" His eyes twinkled suggestively, making me laugh; I wasn't ready to play (and lose) strip-stick-game with him.

As the days slid by, Manny's reticence gradually ebbed and his curt manner softened. Eventually he told me he had only recently emerged from almost forty years of alcoholism. Knowing about the terrible Reservation statistics, it did not come as a complete surprise; his addictive tendencies were still evident in his daily use of marijuana. Adamant he would never have succeeded without it, he called the herb "the sacred pathway out of alcoholism". I could see how it tempered the rawness of his racial anger and bitterness, and occasionally allowed chinks in his armour, but while some shamanic traditions made use of marijuana in a sacred manner to assist in allowing access to the inner planes, Lynne had told me how the spirit of its use had long been lost and its misuse tears holes in the aura and binds a person in a state of spiritual and mental stagnation. Inner planes can be accessed without any chemical "helpers", through meditation and other practices of self-discipline.

It had already become evident to me that, apart from Bob, not many people on the Rez appeared to have much time for Manny. But when he left the Reservation, he left behind his history; in the Indian village, with local people who knew him for the first time, he could be himself in a whole new way. I knew this was healing: he would clear himself of "smoke" when he was ready. In the meantime, his sense of humour increasingly shone through.

One afternoon, he appeared from among the trees by the camp kitchen. His long, black hair was soaking wet, sending rivulets of water coursing over his broad, smooth, tanned chest, and his shorts were dripping. I had never seen such a big grin as the one now splitting his face; his eyes were so crinkled with amusement they were barely visible. It was so rare to even see him smile that we all stopped what we were doing to stare at him. Instead of ducking away, as he once might have, he burst out with a laugh: "I was washin' myself, in that place where the reeds grow thick, when I heard voices. I was nekkid, so I crouched low so's no-one could see me." He squatted down. "You know, an' get offended.... Then round a bend in the river come some guys on them inner tubes."

This was a popular local recreational activity; sometimes from as far north as Lemon Creek all the way down to Crescent Valley, which might take up an entire summer's day.

"One of 'em was readin' a newspaper; other had a book in one hand and a pipe in th'other." Manny mimicked how they looked. "Well, I couldn't re-sist.... I waited till they was level with me, then I leaped up high's I could with an almighty whoop!" Straightening up quickly, he waved his arms. "You shoulda seen it! Book flyin' one way, pipe 'nother, newspapers ev'ry which way! I hid myself again, quick." He crouched down again as we fell about with laughter, then stood up and smoothed back his hair, wryly adding: "Wonder what they made of it.... Prob'ly set round the barbecue tonight an' talk about the primitive throwbacks at Vallican!"

As darkness fell in the Indian village, we would gather round the campfire and share stories, experiences and dreams, and gradually the true light of Little Wolf would shine through. At these magical times, it seemed as if spirits were talking through Manny; not only was he capable of great insight and wisdom, but a hush would fall over the area that made my skin crawl.

"That Manny!" Auntie Vi smiled, shaking her head when I paid her a visit and told her about this side of him. Becoming thoughtful, she added: "But he was born with the veil over his face."

Puzzled, I imagined Manny covered in bridal lace. Seeing the expression on my face, she explained: "He's got something great laid on him, to do for his people. But I sure wish he'd give up foolin' round and get on with it, or else it'll kill him!"

Shortly after, I found out that the monks of Tibet have a similar belief about a person born in the amniotic sac.

It seemed to me that over the weeks we were camped at the Indian village, Manny was "getting on with it". He knew many of the old ways, and legends and stories. I also knew he was regularly using the sweat-lodge, which was bound to have a powerful effect.

Perhaps he sensed my implicit support of and belief in him. He began spending more time with my children and me, which seemed to culminate when he invited the three of us to join him for a sweat, proposing it as a good experience for the kids. Never having expected anything like this, especially the inclusion of my children, I was touched. Perhaps this would be a turning-point; perhaps something would at last be revealed about my reason for being at the village, and what would come next.

Five seasons had turned since the women's sweat at Round Lake and all the sound teaching that came with it, yet even though I was aware that since its inception the sweat-lodge at the Indian village at Vallican had been a focus of dispute among some powerful people, all I could think about was that by reconnecting to the power of Native American spiritual practice, I might root out the feelings of separateness and loss that had been haunting me since returning from England.

What was actually rooted out – or took root – during that sweat with Manny is debatable. Already in a highly vulnerable state, I unknowingly set in motion the next stage of the process that would take me yet further into myself.

Or a part of myself.

Or possibly, a fragment of the Oneness.

MESSAGE OUT OF THE BLUE

Manny prepared the sweat, and acted as server and leader; I felt proud of Nick and Natalie, then seven and nine, for their calm acceptance of the enveloping inky-darkness, the eerie glow of the Old Ones, the pungent sage-smoke and the swirling steam as Manny ritually doused the rocks with palmfuls of river-water. Beginning with East, he dedicated the first round to its symbolic attributes, and to the beauty and sacredness of nature and our relationship with and responsibility to all of life. His prayers were simple and direct, ending with the Lakota, "Mitakuye Oyasin!" I appreciated that he did not generate as much heat as he normally might, for the children's sake, and although they had nothing to say when invited on their turn to pray, I would never forget the gift of the experience.

At the end of the third round, dedicated to the West, both children decided they had enough. Later, I would wonder if they had been guided by an intuition which I might have been wise to heed, but when Manny suggested I return after taking them back up to the camp and finish the fourth round with him, I agreed.

After he served the rocks, closed the flaps and dedicated the round, Manny explained the lay-out of the lodge, which reflected the Arrow Lakes people's way of the sweat, with the fire-pit to the side instead of in the centre, leaving a crescent of space for participants. "It's like a spiritual hospital. A place where people take their troubles to be cured of them."

"All hung up ... and getting smoked, like kippers?" The words were out before I thought. I was grateful it was too dark to see Manny's face.

Several silent moments slid by. Then he said in a neutral tone: "In the Old Order, a medicine man might take a couple who're having marital difficulties into the lodge, encourage 'em to expose their differences-"

"How literally?" I giggled. Appalled at myself, I could have curled up in embarrassment. It was totally unlike me to be so irreverent, especially in a holy-place. I could feel my face burning.

"An' the medicine man'd help clarify the issues," Manny resumed as if I had not spoken. "Eventually he'd leave 'em alone in the lodge to work it through together."

This time I managed to button my lips, but the image of what the couple might get up to in the dark warmth was vivid in my imagination. What had got into me?

I tried to concentrate on Manny's prayers, which eloquently and powerfully related to the fourth direction, North, and the element of fire, but he was making the round extremely hot and protracted and it took all my focus to be able to cope. Keeping my eyes closed, I curled up on the earth and let his words flow over me. As his prayer ended, he must have shifted position; I felt his foot brush against mine and a rush of tingling electricity coursed up my leg. Barely able to think, shocked and embarrassed, I pulled my leg away.

For a long while, there was only silence and the close heat of the lodge. Sweating heavily, I knew we were supposed to be meditating but I could not clear my mind; snatches of his beautiful prayers chased themselves round the inside of my head and I found myself battling an increasingly powerful urge to reach out in the darkness and touch him. It was a huge relief when he deemed the round over and we emerged into the soft light of early evening.

Bathing alone in the river, I rationalised that, like those medicine men of old, Manny was helping me resolve my inner turmoil, and my aimless wandering would soon be over. Certainly, his way of conducting a sweat had impressed me deeply and something seemed to have changed in a fundamental way. What happened next, however, came as much as a surprise to me as everyone else: irresistibly drawn into an intimate relationship with Manny – which I sensed would be a disastrous liaison – I attended to neither intuition nor reason.

In hindsight, I would wonder about that last round in the sweat, dedicated to fire, the connection between fire and desire, and why I let myself forget everything I had learned about the energies in the sweat-lodge.

No sooner had I linked myself with Manny, than two visitors arrived at the Indian village. One I knew slightly through Celina: an esoteric astrologer sensitive to earth energies and able to perceive elementals. The sort of person that stands out in an indefinable way, he was strongly-built, with startling blue eyes, a salt-and-pepper beard and thin, straggling, ash-blonde hair, and like many Vietnam veterans invariably wore army fatigues. What I was not aware of at the time was that Sam had long been involved with Red Cloud, and with Bob and Manny.

The newcomer he had brought with him immediately became the centre of attention. In his late twenties, tall and lean, with striking marmalade hair curling in long, soft tendrils over his shoulders, he was wearing, of all things, a great-kilt, battered, dusty leather sandals and a ginger bearskin cloak, and carried a small pack, a stout wooden staff and a bodhran.

A traditional man from the land of my paternal ancestral lineage could not have been a stranger apparition in the Indian village and it gave me an extraordinary thrill to witness two traditional men from life-ways an ocean apart shake hands. Manny's normal reticence and suspicions about another "white" were strangely absent as Alan, in a thick Glaswegian accent, explained how he had been directed by his people – "the traditional people, the blue people" – to communicate with traditional Native Americans through Celtic folk music, and partake in a Sun Dance. In passing, he mentioned that he had not been allowed to participate this year, but was invited to return the following year to take part in the great spiritual ceremony of the Plains tribes. Obviously he had been not only readily accepted, but something about him recognised, to be so greatly honoured.

And loathe though I was to admit it to myself, hearing the strong Glaswegian accent made me deeply nostalgic.

Nimble and light-footed, he demonstrated the use of his staff as a weapon; much like the parry and thrust of a swordsman. Then he took up his bodhran and began to drum, the double-headed stick thrumming so fast it was a blur. I had never heard this kind of drumming before, yet it was achingly familiar, stirring me deep within my blood, my bones.

Amused to discover that Manny's last name was Scottish, Alan brought out his change of clothing: another great-kilt, in a different tartan, which he laid out flat on the ground in a massive rectangle, some twelve by six feet. Explaining how, according to the old ways, two warriors would blood-bond, help each other dress for battle, watch each other's back and take responsibility for each other's life, he gradually but deftly folded one-half of the length of great-kilt into immaculate pleats, rather like the modern-day kilts I remembered seeing in shops in Edinburgh.

"This is no' how they do it in the factories!" he laughed, slipping a wide leather belt underneath the middle part where the pleats ended. Then he asked Manny, who was wearing shorts, to lie down on the material, brought the pleated part round him and secured it with the belt. When Manny stood up, he was wearing a traditional kilt, the rest of the material being looped over one shoulder and tucked into the belt, so an arm, the sword-arm, was left free.

Despite part of my own heritage being Scottish, I had not known such a thing as a great-kilt existed. It not only served as clothing, but as a cloak against the harsher elements, as a sleeping-bag, as a towel. That I could understand, but the time-consuming, impractical tradition of the pleating?

"It's like a meditation."

I was even more confused. Surely meditation was about becoming peaceful, not being a warrior or going into battle?

"Ye've no heard of the peaceful warrior, then? My people, the blue people, they sent me here, in peace, for peace...."

I had no idea what he was talking about, but hearing about the "blue people" fascinated me. People of the woad, I guessed, although I thought they had disappeared with the Druids. I told him my last name, a clan-name which came through my father and I had liked enough to return to, after my marriage ended.

He seemed taken aback. "Ye'll know your people's history then?"

A raised fist clutching a sword was the clan insignia; "aut pax aut bellum", the motto. "Either peace or war." It had seemed straightforward and was not something I had cared for. Feeling ashamed at how little I knew – not even my grandfather's name – I muttered: "It's connected to the Norwegian 'gunnr', I think, which apparently means 'warrior' ... although I guess I'm one of those peaceful ones."

He shook his head, his handsome mane sliding silken over his shoulders. "There's new research. If you peel back the place-names, the old names.... When Arthur died and Guinevere, who was from the north, tried to rule in his place and failed, and she went to the nunnery, her followers had to flee, they went back to the north.... The followers of Guinevere, the people of Guin. That's your people: People of the White Light...."

His story excited me so much I grew dizzy.

"The story of the Gunn clan's one of the saddest of the Clearances," he continued thoughtfully. "They were a peaceful people, and they were treated the worst. You need to know who your people are...." His startling green-blue eyes seemed to look deep into my soul. Not for a moment did I doubt what he was saying. Root-bonded to me, this stranger seemed more real than the man with whom I had just begun to share my life. The strong Scottish accent was music to my ears, and the sense of connectedness to all the Scotsman represented made me feel weird, sort of excited, unsettled, and torn. It was not that I was physically attracted to him, but there was such a basic commonality that my budding relationship with Manny seemed disturbingly fantasy-based.

Quashing the thought, I told myself not to be such a romantic. Here I was, now, and I had made my choice. The extraordinary nature of the meeting was enough; why try and give it deeper significance?

It was amazing to watch the two men, dressed in tartan great-kilts, sparring and feinting with staffs, joking like old friends; one pale, tall and thin, with long, curling hair of flame and narrow facial features; the other stocky, brown-skinned, hair silky-black, features pure aboriginal.

Apparently there is an X-gene that Native Americans have in common with ancient Europeans which is not present in Asian peoples, a recent finding which has thrown the Bering Strait migration theory into disarray. Despite their obvious dissimilarity, these two men had meshed well. Was genetics part of the reason? Yet the material realm is the grossest level; there had been a powerful spirit-connection.

And perhaps I was aware of the more subtle level because I felt it, too, but I did not delve deeper into why someone who triggered such powerful root-feelings in me should appear just at this time: someone who reminded me of where I come from in this life, who brought me crucial information about my blood-line. I was sure I had not lost sight of who I was, and in any case, the Native American way was opening up for me at last.

GETTING IT RIGHT

With the departure of Sam and the Scotsman and the return of several of the Lakes people to the Indian village, the idyll ended. Neither my relationship with Manny or friendship with Kous made any difference; nothing was overtly said or done, but I knew I had to move on. The only available places to rent I'd seen over the previous couple of months had either been too dilapidated or too small, but as it happened a temporary house-sitting opportunity had just arisen in Slocan Park, a small community south of Passmore. I had been hoping for something more permanent, but, situated on a quiet back-road on the west bank of the Slocan River, the quaint little log-house was a sort of vacation hideaway. In any case, I hadn't any option. Perhaps, I thought, what came next was still "in preparation"; two months was not long to wait.

Unaware of the way outer circumstances reflect the inner state, I stuffed my unease under my figurative carpet, lumping it together with the vague sense of dislocation and purposelessness that still dogged me.

Having taken it for granted that Manny would rather stay at the Indian village with his own people, than with a non-Native woman and her three children in a rather cramped situation, I was surprised when he showed up at the door the day after we moved in. Against my instincts, I let him stay.

Before long, I decided I still had a lot to learn about gut-feelings. Manny took us to visit his friends throughout the Kootenays, a friendly, fascinating bunch of individuals from many walks in life, quietly living a life slightly apart from the mainstream. We visited areas new to me, and he guided our journeys to take in other sites with traces of Native habitation. As our lives intertwined, I learned he had been traditionally raised by his grandparents in the mountains of northern Washington State, and had avoided involvement with the dominant culture longer than most. He carried a lot of traditional knowledge.

After an entire day at a remote site above Slocan Lake, studying cliff-faces daubed with ancient, red-stained rock-paintings – for which Manny had some intriguing, novel interpretations – he told me of his greatest and most private dream: to journey through Washington, Oregon and California and record the stories and songs of the spiritual Native people he had met on his travels over the years.

The thrill I felt was indescribable. This had to be what I had been waiting for, and it exceeded anything I had imagined. Barely able to contain my excitement, I told him his dream was about to be realised. I could barely believe it myself. Everything clicked into place: the short-term house-sitting; my camper-van being exactly what we would need for the journey; the combination of his knowledge and experience and my ability to record, by tape, camera, notebook. When he said that my two younger children should come along, it was the icing on the cake: this would be a remarkable educational experience, fitting right in with home-schooling. All that remained was to make an arrangement for Sivan to stay with a friend so she could continue at school for the several months we would be on the road, which, given the friendships we had made in the Valley, would be straightforward. We would head south for the winter, like migratory birds, and gradually work our way back north; both the journey and the experience would make a marvellous book, vital as the cultural record. Planning for the enterprise became our main topic of conversation.

When all three children went for a fortnight's holiday with their respective fathers, Manny suggested we spend the time travelling through Washington State visiting other friends of his, beginning with Bob at his ranch. A feeling I could not identify made me hesitate. While it was sensible to make a sort of trial run, I did not want to visit Manny's closest friend. It felt as if I had betrayed ... what?

My irrational feelings?

But how could I refuse?

Always something of a Bohemian, with a streak that relishes challenging convention, I thought how we were doing our bit for race-relations: dark, aboriginal Native American and fair-haired, blue-eyed Englishwoman, clearly a couple. Barely had we crossed the border, however, when a demonstration of the blatant kind of prejudice that might lie in wait for us sobered my carefree attitude.

Leaving British Columbia, Manny insisted we cross the border by way of a small checkpoint on a very minor road south of Penticton, B.C., where his face was known. Having witnessed the harassment suffered by Native people at the main border-crossings, I was agreeable. Passing through presented no problem; it was on the other side that things turned sour.

At the wheel, Manny was just pulling away from the checkpoint when a couple of burly American rednecks wearing grubby shirts and jeans appeared in front of the van, blocking our way and forcing him to brake.

"You got any smokes?" one of them yelled.

Thinking they meant cigarettes, I wound down my window, shook my head and pointed to the small grocery store close by.

"Don't speak to 'em!" Manny hissed, hunched protectively over the steering-wheel and trying to manoeuvre past them. They stood their ground; one reached through the open window on my side and grabbed my arm, frowning and slurring words to the effect of: "Yuh oughta be with your own kind...." The fruity-sour stink of his alcoholic breath was like a slap in the face. His hair was dirty-blonde, greasy and tangled; the skin of his face red-veined and pock-marked; his horribly unpleasant leer made me feel nauseous. Over his shoulder, in the back of a pick-up parked a few feet away, where a couple of what appeared to be his buddies were standing watching and grinning, I glimpsed rifles, hung on a rack.

My kind? Stinking, ugly, rude, racist, violent....

"We've got no smokes." Sharply, I disengaged my arm as Manny revved the engine. The man recoiled and we scooted out of there fast as my old van could manage.

"They was lookin' for marijuana," Manny said as soon as it was clear we weren't being followed. "You know, incidents like this ain't uncommon. Guess this is a whole new education for you."

Still shaking, I nodded silently, feeling deflated and stupidly ignorant.

Reaching Bob's ranch to find him at home (of course – Manny's timing), I again felt an illogical awkwardness; the familiar, lilting cadences of his speech still caught at some inner part of me. Oddly distant, I helped the two long-time friends work through a pot of coffee as they reminisced over their "war-dancing" days. Bob's regalia had apparently been stolen from his car at a pow-wow, which was when he had quit dancing. Then Manny mentioned he was intending to dance again. My scattered thoughts came together in a rush.

If he danced again, if he took part in something so fundamental to a traditional way of life, it would surely have far-reaching effects on his healing. I privately determined I would help make it happen. When Manny mentioned to Bob that he and my son Nick, whom he liked a lot and who had expressed an interest in Native dancing, might eventually team-dance together in the father-son category, the whole issue was sealed.

Leaving Bob's, we made a detour through the remote, mountainous part of the region where Manny had been raised: back to where it all began for him. Was this trip symbolic of new beginnings? For many miles, he brooded in silence, his lips pursed in what seemed like disapproval or pain, and I began to worry that the memories triggered by his childhood landscape had opened the raw wound within. All of a sudden he chuckled. "Up this area's where I learned to make a bow 'n' arrows. My grandfather, he taught me.... An' I gradually improved my skills till I shot a squirrel out of a tree." His face creasing, he grinned widely. "At which point my grandfather produces the smallest fry-pan you ever did see an' says, 'What you kill, you eat!'

"Never seen such a little fry-pan!" He laughed, making a circle with strong, short forefingers and thumbs. "An' it was just a little squirrel, lotta work to skin an' not much meat!"

At my suggestion, we called in at the annual sobriety camp-out in Inchelium, but he became morose and jumpy. After a couple of hours, we left and headed back across the Reservation to look up some good friends of his who would help him with "something he needed to do". He offered no explanation, but I did not need to ask.

Reaching the arid, burned-ochre, scrubby Okanogan valley, we turned off the main highway and drove into the remote hills above Tonasket. Soft-flanked, they stretched for mile after uninhabited mile, peopled only by an occasional lodge-pole pine, imposingly tall and lonely among the spiky grey-green-gold grasses. In what seemed like the middle of nowhere, we turned off onto a dusty, rutted, winding, roller-coaster track. The incredible vistas that stretched for miles compensated only partially for my concern that my aging vehicle might not cope with this new stress and we would break down miles from anywhere and anybody. Curving and dipping, the track suddenly disappeared into a stand of trees and to a chorus of frenzied barking, we pulled up by a small log cabin, the first of a number we visited over the next few days. Built by chainsaw and hand in a variety of styles, most of these places had no electricity, telephone, or even running water.

Apparently the area had been over-grazed and the resulting low land-value had attracted those seeking a simpler life, an alternative to the relentless, repetitive round of contemporary life, where so much personal energy needs to be spent on things like the public utilities most of these people lived without. Warmly welcomed wherever he went in this area, Manny was clearly highly regarded, even loved. From each place, he came away with something he had stored there, some of which he had been given, others which he had crafted while following his nomadic life-style, inadvertently earning himself the nick-name "Manny Rotting-Hides", because rarely was he in one place long enough to complete the lengthy task of curing hides.

Chased by clouds of swirling dust, we travelled deeper into the arid hinterland. The track grew increasingly rough, some parts steep as a switchback; I worried that the engine would choke up. Sweeping around a sharp curve onto the crown of one of the highest areas yet, with magnificent views for miles on every side, ahead of us lay an incongruous sight: a yellow school-bus and, under the shade of a small huddle of pine trees, a canvas tent. Several tanned, blonde-haired children of varying age were throwing pine-cones beside the bus; they stopped and stared until we were close enough for them to recognise Manny, then, whooping and shouting his name, they ran to meet him.

A huge grin on his face, Manny hugged each one. From behind the trees appeared a slim and extremely handsome man wearing buckskin leggings and moccasins, his upper body naked but for a red bandanna around his neck. Long, silken and sun-bleached, his hair flowed over his shoulders and down his smooth, hairless, deeply-tanned chest. Gracefully he walked, lightly, his face composed in the serene, proud manner of the classic Native American.

The essence of a Hollywood romantic ideal, Cheyenne wasn't Native after all, but the way he followed seemed as close to traditional as I had yet seen: making his own weapons, he hunted and fished for his family, and gleaned a small income from tanning hides, selling or trading them for staples, and crafting buckskin clothes and moccasins. Strongly-built, his dark-haired wife coped efficiently and cheerfully with a life-style that had to be about the most minimal I had ever come across and six barefoot children between the ages of four and twelve, who were lean and fit, inquisitive and intelligent, polite and quietly self-assured. She told me that leaving the city – only some two years earlier – had been the best decision they had ever made. Much as I admired her, I did not envy her.

Stored in a compartment in the side of the bus were some of Cheyenne's tools and wares. Manny pushed them aside to recover a large container which looked like an over-sized hat-box. "Came to get this." He drummed a roll across the lid. "See, I got the urge to dance again. Maybe at Omak. This's the last item."

Cheyenne's face lit up. "You really gonna do it, man? You got your stuff all together, then?"

Thrilled that he had at last said it – and to one of his closest friends – I was positive this would literally be the first steps in clearing the way for the purpose Manny was born to.

Manny opened the box and took out the crowning glory of his outfit. The chief of the four-leggeds and of the winged ones were both represented in his head-dress: horns affixed to a multi-coloured beaded headband of stars, haloed with immaculate white, black-tipped feathers. Buffalo and Eagle, the two most powerful allies: Buffalo symbolising the power of prayer and reconnection to the meaning of life; Eagle, a reminder that nothing is achieved without the help of the Creator. Yet although it was magnificently appropriate, something about it made me uneasy.

"Took me a lo-ong, lo-ong time to make this...." Eliding his vowels like Bob did, Manny lovingly held his head-dress up in both hands and with a laugh, placed it on my head. It was very heavy, and made my scalp prickle.

"Gotta see this for yourself." Cheyenne held out his hand for my camera.

Feeling uncomfortable, I stretched a grin across my face. It was not just the weight of the thing; there was a lot of medicine wrapped up in it, all of it Manny's. And if it was at the very least symbolic of his aura, why should he want to cover mine with his? To overpower me? Hastily I took the thing off, wondering about the places my imagination sometimes took me.

"He's been wanting to do this for years," Cheyenne said quietly, handing me back my camera and seemingly unaware of my discomfort. Manny was surrounded by children clamouring for stories. "An' this's the first time he's drawn all his stuff together at one time. You help him with this, if you can."

Still feeling a little strange, I shivered, despite the heat. "In my mind, there's nothing more important in the world right now than that Manny should dance again. I'll make sure it happens. I know how important it is. I understand what it means."

And if he quits the smoke, the spirits will be able to come through as intended and he'll fulfil that to which he was born, was what I did not add.

The next morning, to a chorus of plaintive goodbyes, we left the high, lonely place and amazing little family, and drove back down to the highway and south to Omak. Visible long before we arrived as a haze of dust, the rodeo site was being fed by a long, slow snake of vehicles. Revving engines drowned out an amplified voice making announcements over the Tannoy; what looked like hundreds of people were milling about.

"D'you wanna go down to the rodeo?" Manny asked.

I shook my head. I had never liked crowds, and had little interest in seeing animals being man-handled; even less in mixing with cowboys and cowgirls.

"Used to be a bull-rider," he added quietly. "Was one for years."

Thinking about the hundreds of red-necks that were bound to be there, I wasn't sure I'd heard him correctly. "What? But why on earth would you want to do a thing like that?"

He chuckled. "No better way of appreciatin' bein' alive! There ain't nothin' like those last few moments 'fore they throw open the gate. Settin' astride that great back, you can feel the muscles a-quiverin'; all that power contained between your legs for a few seconds before all hell breaks loose. An' there ain't no goin' back. You're sittin' waitin' for the gate to open, scared shit-less, starin' death right in the face.... Now that strengthens the character."

I nodded, unable to imagine ever wanting to be put through such a grindstone.

"Pretty rough on a body though." He grimaced, twisting in his seat. "Did my back in. An' some ribs, they never did heal prop'ly."

Steering us out of the long line-up, Manny drove away from the immense rodeo parking-lot to the small area reserved for the pow-wow. Auntie Vi had told me that the original owner of the site had willed it to the Native people as pow-wow grounds, with a small area set aside for the rodeo, but that the rodeo had gradually spread out, encroaching on and taking over the pow-wow grounds until the Native American celebration had been pushed to a small corner, abutting a busy highway.

History keeps turning the same circle....

Finding a campsite among the Native people, I could not help reflecting on how much more comfortable I felt here, than among my "own kind". Yet I was curious. Leaving Manny to pull his outfit together (I sort of felt like the groom who shouldn't see the bride until she is ready), I decided to take a look at the rodeo after all.

As I had imagined, wearing a light dress and sandals instead of the uniform of checked shirt or blouse, tight jeans, Stetson and cowboy boots made me stick out like a sore thumb. Trying to get near the main arena proved too daunting a prospect; noticing a small crowd gathered along the edge of the river, I went to see what was happening and was told they were waiting for the climax of the suicide race.

Remembering two Native brothers in a bar in Nespelem, laughing at my ignorance of this event, was like remembering another life. I had always wondered what it was like; it seemed no accident I had arrived at this place, at this time.

"How do they get here?" I asked.

"They'll show up over the top there, any moment." The friendly, if gruff and heavy-bellied, cowboy pointed across the river and I gazed in awe at the impossible: not only were the cliffs on the far side terribly high, but almost sheer, right down to the water. Barely had I taken this in, when the crowd gave an anticipatory roar and a line of horses and riders appeared, silhouetted along the cliff-top. For one awesome, breathless moment they hesitated, then, almost as one, leapt over the edge.

Down they plunged, riders yelling and hollering and waving their arms, glued to their straining, stiff-legged mounts, whose haunches coiled and bulged like great springs as they heaved, loped and slid downwards, their flanks white with lather, their legs sinking deeply into the sandy loam, which shifted and slid around them like quicksand. How they did not all tumble down in a terrifying tangle of man and beast but arrived at the foot unscathed, to gallop in great sprays of water across the dark green waters of the river as the audience cheered wildly was beyond me. It was one of the most incredible scenes I had ever witnessed and I found my breath again only after it was all over.

There were too many people crowding forward for me to see what happened next, but it did not matter. Walking back to the van, images imprinted on my mind's eye, again and again I saw the silhouettes on the cliff-top; lived through the electrifying pause; the vertical descent. A death-defying challenge, like bull-riding. Strengthening the character, Manny had said. Was this what the rodeo was really about? But I could not reconcile that with the treatment of the animals.

That evening, Manny and I watched the Grand Entry and the opening dances, but I could barely pay attention. Would he dance tonight? In time, on time. After a few songs, he said, "Let's go watch the gamblin'."

Unsure whether he was procrastinating or backing out, I was glad of the distraction: perhaps I could learn something of the knack of the stick-game. The fervent pounding of hand-drums welled up as we drew close, drowning out the pow-wow drum, and a strange, wailing chant sliced through the air. Under awnings strung with lights, several teams were competing. The atmosphere was intense, fervid, and hundreds of dollars were swiftly changing hands in a way I could barely understand.

At the nearby craft-stalls, we encountered some men who Manny quietly told me were his drinking buddies from the past. Their speech slurred, they enthusiastically greeted Manny. I was a little nervous, having thought that reformed drinkers would avoid old associations, but their warmth was mutual and genuine, and unlike the red-neck drinker at the border, they were incredibly polite to me. Nor did they stink of the toxins ruining their bodies, their lives.

Not for the first time, I reflected on the natural etiquette of Native people, and how I had never met one who suffered from bad breath or body-odour. Aware that my own sense of smell is much more acute than the norm – a curse as much as a blessing – I could not help wondering what the indigenous peoples must have thought on first contact with the great unwashed who had made their unsavoury way to the New World.

That night, camped by the pow-wow grounds, it was all I could do not to press Manny about the dancing. After breakfast, remembering the piercing in his ears, I gave him two of my favourite earrings: a weasel tail, winter-white, black-tipped, set in a brass bullet-casing, and a sky-blue stud with a yellow star. "I'd be honoured if you'd wear them as part of your regalia," I said, as if taking it for granted that today was the day.

Without looking at me and without a word, Manny took them and disappeared inside the van. Half an hour later, he emerged, and my heart skipped a beat.

A carmine-red breech-clout, cut from a trading blanket and held in place by wide leather belt, was his only item of clothing. His moccasins were plain, his ankle-ties of long-haired white fleece. Braided rawhide thongs were tied around his lightly-muscled biceps and he was holding a hand-drum, decorated with a five-pointed blue star painted on a red background. In his other hand was a bone-white gourd rattle adorned with long strands of coarse, black horse-hair. Sheared across the top of his head in the flat, spiky cut that had given half his bloodline their name,[20] his long, jet-black hair hung loose and shining over his smooth, tanned, well-defined back and shoulders, one immaculate braid nestling among its thickness.

I was utterly thrilled. Before me stood a figure that hearkened back to another era; the time before.... No fancy dancer or pow-wow "traditional", but a figure that had long lived in my imagination.

Then I noticed, on a sinew thong round his neck, the eagle-bone whistle. The man born with a veil over his face; but of course.

Self-consciously, Manny shook back his hair. The two earrings caught my eye. He grinned. "Well, what d'you think?"

That it was English coming out of his mouth seemed all wrong. Rubbing away the tears that pricked at my eyes, I whispered: "Perfection."

He looked down at his drum, caressed it lovingly. "This here's my 'dog-days' drum. Made it from the hide of my favourite dog, when he died."

Any other occasion, I would have found the thought repulsive.

Picking up his head-dress, Manny led the way over to the arbour where the competitive dancers had already begun to go through their rounds, and found a space to sit among the onlookers. Pulling out a knife from his breech-clout, he absorbed himself in what I guessed were finishing touches to the eagle-bone whistle. Filled with awe, I had to keep stealing looks at him. Something seemed to have changed: an aura I had not sensed before encompassed him.

There was no cue. Suddenly he was up and gone.

He had chosen an intertribal chant, non-competitive. I hurried to position myself where I could unobtrusively use my camera.

Carrying his magnificent head-dress, Manny joined the slow-moving dancers casually shuffling in time to the beat. Immediately I realised from his preliminary lightness of step that the head-dress would be too heavy, too cumbersome to wear and after a few moments, it became clear that he was not getting into the dance. Heart in mouth, I watched him leave the circle. Had we come this far, only for him to give up?

He went back to our blanket and lay down the head-dress, gently, carefully, as if it were a sleeping child, then returned to the arbour and leapt lightly back in among the dancers, a flash of tan and red. I was immediately put in mind of a time among the still, misted trees at the Indian village at Vallican: an ancient bone; a flash of red....

---

20 The Flatheads. According to some portraits, a style very similar to that of Chief Joseph.

There was no time to dwell on it; Manny had entered the arena beside a small group of male elders in traditional regalia sedately stepping in time to the beat and chatting with each other. Next to their elaborate, colourful regalia and prominent numbers, Manny's near-nakedness and simple outfit marked him apart. In perfect time to the thud of the drum, his feet skimming the ground, he swooped, crouched, twisted, turned and leapt with a smooth, sinuous, sensual movement that held me in a state of suspension. Only in my imagination had I seen such dancing; he brought a vitality to the crowded arena, and a clear and vivid sense of the animal spirit for whom he was named: Little Wolf, poised and watchful, racing, twisting and turning, leaping, gyrating; in hunt, in chase, in play.

For several suspended moments, it was as if the other figures faded into a blur and there was only Little Wolf, dancing. The great image I had seen in the sky at Vallican pricked at the edge of my memory, and the Initiators whispered in my inner ear. It felt so powerful and so right: my destiny had to lie with this extraordinary man....

Returning to the moment, I saw that the traditional dancers had cleared a large space around Manny, which they maintained while continuing their shuffle-step, nodding in time with the beat and watching his wildly exotic movements. All too soon the song ended on a heavy thud, but another drum began almost immediately. Manny danced on, his special space reserved for him.

When he finally returned, grinning proudly, sweat gleaming on his smooth brown skin, his hard, muscled chest heaving with exertion, I could not stop the absurdly proud grin stretching my mouth; could not find the words I really wanted to say. "Incredible. You're amazingly good. I've never seen dancing like that.... Did you see those old traditional guys, how they cleared the way for you? Now that's respect."

He shook his head. "Didn't see nothin'. Was lost in the dance...." He held himself a little straighter. "But what's it all about, anyway?" he laughed breathlessly. "What do women want? They like to see a little bit of skin; an' I like to give 'em what they want.... What do people really want more'n anything in this life? What did we come here for, if not to get it right between man 'n' woman? What's more important in life than that?"

On the heels of such a fabulous experience – sensual, sexual, spiritual – the unexpected sentiments wrapped up in a short, breathless speech from such a solitary wanderer stopped me in my tracks.

That was what we had come here for? We had come into incarnation to "get it right between man and woman"? Resonating through me clear as a bell, it made a beautiful, wonderful, ultimate sense: if that could happen, it would take care of everything else, because there would be balance, harmony. It was so obvious, it was ridiculous. How come I had not understood this before?

At the same time, my heart sank. The fact was that despite all the grand plans, despite the miracle happening here today – what I saw as a turning-point for Manny – I could sense our "honeymoon period" was over, and although with all my heart I wanted to fulfil the vision of travelling and recording, I was becoming aware it was only a pipe-dream, a smoke-dream. At least until he cleared himself of his mistress, Mary Jane, Manny would remain a dreamer, not a doer; and the potential of making his dream a reality had been the glue of our relationship. I had already been harbouring a secret notion that it would probably be best for me, with my record with men, to remain single and find fulfilment through service to others.

Yet I knew that in order to grow as a human being, we need the reflective nature of a long-term, intimate relationship. To "get it right between man and woman" was what I wanted, with all my heart. And here I was, contemplating yet another failing relationship. How on earth could right relationship ever come about, when something fundamental was so obviously awry? And although in the past I tended to blame the man, I had come to understand that, after all, I had chosen him and it was not the man, any man, at all, but something in me.

What to do about this was another issue entirely. I put it out of my mind; the most important thing was that Manny had come back to the dance, and this was sure to have reverberations on many levels. As I remembered his deceptively simple regalia, his amazing, captivating dance and the respect accorded him by those other Native elders, I felt a sudden, deep sadness. Some part of me had been hanging onto the idea that the Old Order still existed somewhere "out there", and these last vestiges of a romantic and totally unrealistic illusion were being painfully, irrevocably swept away. For the rest of the day I felt increasingly bereft, as if part of me were dying, and by evening was on the verge of tears.

As we drove away from the pow-wow grounds, Manny spoke softly, wonderingly: "You really do care, don't you? I don't get it, but you really do care."

I had said nothing for a long while, yet in his usual way, he had intuited what I was going through. The tears flowed then; not only for a way of life that was irrevocably gone, but because despite all they had undergone, Native Americans were still capable of the most profound empathy. Despite my inner anguish, I felt comforted. Perhaps we could work together after all; perhaps this relationship had a chance.

CONFRONTATION

It's one thing to have a dream, a vision; to bring it into manifestation calls for total commitment and a lot of hard work. Manny's primary commitment was to marijuana; everything, including myself, would always play second-fiddle to the first woman in his life – Mary Jane – and it would not be long before his need for her took him back on the road again, full-time and alone.

The signs had been clear but I still felt hurt by Manny's abrupt disappearance, without a word, the day before the house-sitting contract ended. Having committed myself to a fantasy, I was again homeless and still without a job. Yet even as I wallowed in self-pity, another part of me slid eel-like and uneasy beneath the surface. Instead of faulting the man, an inner voice urged, look within. But it was like looking over the edge of a precipice into a darkening whirlpool.

Only one place seemed to have any relevance to me, but when I went to visit the Indian village, I felt like an intruder. I was turning to leave when Bob came out of a tipi. He raised a hand in friendly welcome. "Hey, how are you?"

For the first time, even his familiar drawl raised no reaction in me. I shrugged, unable to look at him, feeling his cordiality masked the widening gap between us. "Fine, I guess. How's things going?"

Planting himself in front of me, he crossed his arms. "We been talkin' 'bout going over to the museum. You know, in Victoria. If the mountain don't come to Mohammed...." He chuckled. "Maybe them guys need a push to get things moving."

Something changed: it was like the sun returning after a dark winter. This was the Bob I had known and shared so much with, seasons ago. Something flipped in my chest and my mind stepped outside of its petty concerns. "You're going to get the ancestors yourselves? But how?" Images thronged my mind: raids on horseback, hostages carried off....

Bob read me, as usual. He shook his head and grinned. "Nothing wild. We're gonna go over there in a caravan, three or four cars filled with Indians, an' just hang out there till they're embarrassed into giving 'em back to us. You'll see. An' so will a lot of other people."

He told me the date they planned to make the journey, gave one firm nod of his handsome head, smiled, raised his hand again and turned away. A whiff of wood-smoke tantalised my nostrils; as I watched his familiar straight back and light-stepped walk, my eyes suddenly filled with tears. My mind racing, I hurried back to the van.

They were planning direct action. While on the one hand I was glad to hear something was happening, I was not sure this was the right way to go about such a delicate matter. And why tell me about it? If I were a government agent, as I had heard some of these Lakes people suspected, surely I would be the last person to be told. But then Bob knew me, knew what was in my heart. Maybe it was because he wanted me to be there, perhaps as a kind of witness? Why else let me know? He had even said, "You'll see."

Confused, I put it to the back of my mind and again began to drift on feelings nebulous as the unseen winds that carried me from one place to the next, seeking some indication of which direction to take my life, some purpose to ground myself.

In fact, I was losing touch with myself. All I could manage was one day at a time; it took all my energy to attend to my little family's immediate needs. Fortunately, arrangements fell into place for Sivan to stay with friends as she started her new year at school. When she was settled, I took the other two with me to visit Auntie Vi, who had somehow become aware of the attitude of the Lakes representatives at the Indian village. "Don't pay them no attention. They're a small, if out-spoken, minority. We here all know what you've done."

"It doesn't matter," I said, embarrassed. "It honestly doesn't bother me. I barely know them, and it's my friendship with you that matters. That's what's real. And there's Uncle Charlie and Uncle Gilbert-"

"And that Manny!" she interrupted. "I don't like the way he treated you! But what goes around comes around, I always say, and I'll tell him that straight next time I see him!"

I was doubly embarrassed. Moccasin telegraph was terribly efficient. And it seemed everyone except me was aware of Manny's pattern of "a woman for the summer", although even if I had known, I doubt I would have acted any differently. We all think we're the one who can make the difference; sort of like Natalie when she was little, believing that if only she loved her teddy bears enough, they would come alive.

From Auntie Vi's, I went to Inchelium to visit Tom, the Arrow Lakes pipe-carrier and speaker who had impressed me so deeply at the first "Calling Back the Salmon" pow-wow at Kettle Falls. It had been a surprise to come back from England and find him sitting at Grandmother Drum as mentor of our little group; I learned Yellow Bear and Linda had met him at the pow-wow that had taken place while I had been away, and he had since been regularly coming north to the Slocan Valley – his first time in this part of his ancestral lands – to share his songs and traditional knowledge.

This was a fairly unusual situation. For several generations, traditional Native American spiritual practice had been suppressed as much as the language; what survived had gone underground, a closely-guarded secret. The restrictions had since been lifted, but for many Native people, sharing with the race that had crippled their heritage was unthinkable.

Not so Tom. The speech I had heard him make at Kettle Falls implied otherwise, and his friendship with and support of our group proved it.

A pipe-carrier has a sacred responsibility to all of life. Called to the position by a vision, he or she earns the privilege of carrying the pipe through years of instruction, and initiation. Only the pure of heart may use this highly symbolic tool, which acts as the bridge between the worlds of matter and spirit. I had become aware, however, that as part of a New Age upsurge of interest in sacred indigenous traditions, non-Native pipe-carriers seemed to be popping up all over the place, flourishing "endowed" pipes and leading ceremonies. And I witnessed the cost: before long, the personal lives of these hastily-elevated "instant priests" would begin to fall apart, as energies with which they were unequipped to work overwhelmed their ego and its trip, through sickness, the break-up of relationships, financial collapse.

In his mid-fifties, a medium-built, striking-looking man with a shock of thick white hair and a smooth, tanned face, Tom had a subtly-powerful presence. Only in the hunch of his shoulders were the passage of years and the tragedies that marked his life evident. As for the demeanour I had once found so formidable, it turned out to be all in my imagination, for he evinced only care, compassion, generosity, hospitality and a gentle humour.

Often I wondered what must it have been like for him, perhaps the closest to a full-blood Sinixt I might personally come to know well, journeying to his ancestral lands after a gap of two or more generations and, on the invitation of a couple new to the area, sitting with a group of mainly non-Native people attempting to emulate his race's way of drumming and singing. Some might have found it laughable, pathetic or insulting. Yet like a true human being, Tom accepted and encouraged us, singing with us, sharing traditional knowledge and songs, some newly come to him in the lands of his ancestors, given him "by the waters and the wind". It made me remember Bob's words about the wind in the trees: the concept of Ska-ool, come alive.

The pipe-carrier also took part in the gatherings Yellow Bear organised for the turning of the seasons and other special occasions; and his home, a double-wide mobile situated under the pines on the shores of the Lake Roosevelt below Inchelium, had been made open to us all.

It was Tom's partner Louella who opened the door to my knock, late in the afternoon. "He's takin' a nap, but you're welcome to visit with me in the meantime."

I hesitated. A short, rounded woman in her early fifties, her eyes the palest of blue, ice-cold and penetrating, Louella's direct gaze unsettled me now as much as it had all that time ago. Seeing that Tom was asleep on the couch in the living-room, I felt marginally better: he was sure to wake up soon.

Telling me to help myself to coffee, Louella busied herself tidying up, then came and sat down. I began to tell her of the past few days, but as usual, moccasin telegraph was ahead of me.

"I heard 'bout Manny, an' as for them people at the site up there...." She gave a dismissive little toss of her short, greying curls. Then she looked straight at me. "So what's all this need to be savin' others?!" Shaking her head, she added: "I meet up with it so damn' much!"

I frowned, unsure what she meant.

Her voice a little softer, she resumed: "You've been at the low end of the totem pole yourself. You know what it's like at the bottom, so you're sympathetic to others who're there an' you set out to help them. But it's your own need that drives you!"

My need? Where was she coming from? Although it was true about knowing what it was like at the bottom: I had been a shy and solitary, withdrawn child, overweight for a time and often hurtfully teased by other children.

"Thing is, these people you think you're savin'," she stressed the last word, "they won't ever thank you. No-one likes to admit they have need. An' just as soon's they feel better 'bout themself, they'll climb over you, trample you, use you as a stepping-stone. So you're underneath an' they're higher up; they're on top, lookin' down on you....

"It's like this: you see the victim an' you feel their need an' you set out to rescue them, because you think you understand. But it's a reflection of the need in you. Then the tables are turned, you become the victim. I seen it all over – my people, your people.... Nobody wants to be saved, an' they won't thank you for tryin', neither. Nobody really wants to change, an' even if they did, no-one else can do it for them. Or tell 'em how. You can only do it for yourself.

"You got to move out of victim mentality, victim behaviour. Or maybe...." Her eyebrows arched in questioning irony. "Maybe you enjoy the pain you created for yourself – it's what you're familiar with! Maybe it's all you know.... All these skeletons in the closet, we all got 'em. You should check out some of them people you think so much of...."

Skeletons in the closet? What was she talking about? Which people? I was no victim. Unable to think of anything to say, I remained silent, feeling my anger hooked and rising. She stared at me a while longer, then laughed, a short bark. "An' the only reason you're so quiet is 'cause I've pushed all your buttons!" With a triumphant grin, Louella got up and left the room, leaving me stunned and seething.

Tom woke up soon afterwards and we all had supper together, but I couldn't eat much or concentrate on anything we talked about. After the children had gone to sleep, I lay awake in the little guest-room, reflecting long into the night. Perhaps I slept a few hours, because suddenly it was light and things were becoming clearer.

The pattern was revealing itself: at the age of thirteen, my first crush, on actor Richard Burton, an emotionally-complicated man who drank himself to death; then Scott Walker (of the pop group the Walker Brothers), an enigmatic solitary who had attempted suicide. My early boyfriends had more in common than a certain level of intelligence: almost all had been cool, emotionally-distant. In fact, I realised, I had never lasted long in a relationship where I was warmly treated. There had been an Israeli millionaire: kind, patient and loving, and boring; an American with a great sense of humour who had treated me like a goddess, devastated when I ended our budding relationship, because, as I tried to explain, barely understanding it myself, he was "already so nice, he didn't need me".

My "great love" for my Israeli husband had faded away after only three years of marriage as the parity I had dreamed of failed to materialise; as for the father of Natalie and Nick, a tall, dark, handsome sportsman, remote and enigmatic (which I tragically found appealing in those days) – that had been a passionate on-off affair that lasted a painful three years until I realised I preferred the "off" parts. Looking back, he seemed the most severely wounded of all, yet had been the most compelling. Complicated by the presence of three children, subsequent relation-ships had been brief, floundering affairs, but the thread was there, too.

I liked to think of myself as balanced and accommodating, but was I just another of those women whom men accuse of wanting to change them? Why did the decent sort of man not attract me? Why fall only for ones with an unpredictable "edge"? And where had all this started? Travelling back down the years, I returned to my first male relationship, the one psychology books claim sets the tone for all subsequent ones, and remembered my father, who had died almost ten years earlier: intelligent, upright, honest and conscientious, and emotionally distant; from whom I had distanced myself, first emotionally, then geographically. There had been another primary male relationship: my older brother, whom I had loved madly and deeply and who had scant patience with a doting little sister. He had died of leukaemia at the age of nine, when I was almost seven. These were my foundation male relationships: twice-loved, twice-lost.

As first light brought the guest-room at Tom and Louella's home into definition, the root of my emotional patterning came clear: wounded female child-within, whose experience has shown her that to love means to lose, to be abandoned. Subconsciously attracted to and attracting a wounded mate whom she can try to heal (an impossibility), so can never fully commit and sooner or later ends the relationship, each time vilified in her subconscious belief that eventually, in one way or another, all men leave. The reason I was unable to find a "spark" with an uncomplicated, emotionally-balanced, receptive, loving type of man was because he did not serve as the mirror I needed.

It was like a great floodlight casting light into the murkiest corners of my psyche. This was what Frank had meant, when he had broken down my ice-walls in the tipi at the gathering; what Lucy had been talking about, after the powerful sweat at Round Lake. If I felt an instant, unaccountable attraction to a man, instead of diving into a relationship with him, all my alarm bells should go off: here it is again – the frying-pan you've created for yourself. Want to get burned again? And again? What would it take to free myself from this hellish round? Yet despite my failures, I still believed with all my bruised heart in the old fairy-tale: out there somewhere was The One. I kept thinking I had met him, innumerable times already, but it was "the man with a thousand faces": my emotionally-distorted patterning. How on earth would I recognise him with such a powerful subconscious notion, acting like an insurmountable barrier? How did one break through to the subconscious? Was there was a Prince Charming out there, who could fight his way through the briars and kiss the sleeping princess awake after her hundred years' sleep? What did I have to do to change, to heal the deep scar that ruled my perception?

Another jarring thought struck me: was it this neediness that had triggered my involvement with the Arrow Lakes people?

It did not bear thinking about. In a state of high, vibrating energy, I got up, wanting to talk further with this harshly-insightful woman who had cracked me open to expose a shadowy, writhing mass of twisted emotional perceptions, but Louella was busy in the kitchen and left early to be about her daily affairs. Feeling unable to visit with Tom, I continued on my way.

Feeling a deep reluctance to return to the Valley, which sat in my mind as a dark and vaguely oppressive presence, I headed west to Vancouver Island, where the funeral of the mother of a close friend was taking place. I was so outside of myself, however, that I mistimed the ferry crossing and missed the ceremony. Appalled at letting Hetty down and uncomfortable among the bustle of her large, extended family at the wake, I left and drove south, harbouring a vague idea that a visit with Lynne and James might help me orient myself.

Their warm, unconditional welcome and the energised, yet peaceful atmosphere of their home and burgeoning garden wrapped round me like a cocoon. Several golden days of an extended Indian summer slid by as, more exhausted than I had realised, I slept late, took the children to the beach then spent the rest of the day helping harvest fruit and vegetables and put them up for the winter: simple, earthing tasks. In the narrow confines of their cosy little kitchen, enveloped in the aroma of sweet autumnal ripeness, we peeled and sliced and bottled and in her gentle, quiet way, Lynne spoke of things of the spirit: "A man needs to sweat. But it's not the same with a woman. A man needs to go into the sweat-lodge regularly, he needs the womb-energy in order to purify himself, to keep in touch with his feminine side and be renewed. But a woman doesn't. She has her moon-cycle, a monthly purification. The four days in the moon-lodge are a period of rest and regeneration."

We were in the midst of washing piles of little cucumbers, and packing them into jars for pickling. "That's the end of the sweat-lodge for me, then," I laughed. "And I keep saying we should bring back that moon-lodge tradition. My moon, it's like being put through the fire alright. And those four days when we're supposed to rest? It always seems to work out that it's my busiest time."

"The ways in which we sabotage ourselves.... But you might want to consider this: in some cultures, a woman uses a grounding-pit. It's a sort of a shallow trench," she explained in response to my querying look, "lined with cedar-boughs. You lie down in it, long as you wish."

My hands busy, my mind was free to go to where cedars grew near the Lodge and in my imagination, I was there, bathing in cold, silver moonlight, receptive to moon-lore; above me, a diamond-dusted velvet night sky framed by the arrow-tips of the cedars who had given of their limbs and their cleansing energy; the pungent scent of crushed boughs, the scratchy give of them under my back; the soft night-air-breath on my skin, and my body-warmth exchanging with the coolness of exposed earth; Mother Earth absorbing all my troubles. A lone, silent earth-moon-star connection; it sounded like heaven.

One day, we took a break from preserving to visit nearby Chemainus. Small and picturesque, this coastal, Island town is famous for the immense murals of historical scenes artfully painted on the facades of its heritage buildings. Even on a Sunday afternoon in late September and despite the fact that most of the gift shops and arts and crafts outlets were closed, visitors were thronging the streets. The museum also turned out to be closed, so Lynne decided we should visit a friend of hers who worked out of a Native American woodcarving workshop situated on the edge of the town.

In poor repair, the building looked more like an autobody shop than a studio, but inside was a different world: light and airy, cedar-scented, a sense of expectancy. Images of bear, eagle, raven, orca, blue heron and salmon, carved from sweet-smelling red cedar or engraved into silver: on large and small totem poles (a Coastal Salishan tradition relating to clan and nothing to do with Hollywood fabrications), boxes, bowls, letter-openers, spoons, jewellery, T-shirts. A slim, handsome Native artist in his forties, Lynne's friend Lloyd warmly greeted her and showed us the area dedicated to his unique, free-flowing style of painting. A couple of other Native men were carving at the back of the store, and another was in a workshop beyond. While the two friends visited, I made my way round the display. In some ways, it was like being in a museum.

"You know," said Lynne when I said as much to her, "what we might term 'art' isn't really a suitable label for what Indians create. These are spiritual symbols, reflecting an understanding of the harmony of life."

With this new understanding, I went to take another look at everything and on a low shelf, came across a small bowl carved from cedar which I had overlooked before, and which on close examination revealed itself to be in the image of a wolf. I suddenly realised that in the fifteen years I had lived in British Columbia, never before had I seen Wolf represented in Coastal Salishan art. It made no sense: an inexplicable absence that hit me all the harder because of its particularly personal nature. How could Wolf have been left out? What did it mean?

Picking up the little wolf-bowl, I approached a middle-aged Native man sitting bent over a canoe-sized length of cedar, skilfully unfurling curls of wood with a mallet and chisel, and waited until he paused in his work. "Excuse me. I just wondered...." Feeling awkward, I held out the bowl. "This is the first time I've seen Wolf depicted in your people's ... in Salishan art. Would you happen to know why this is?"

Heavy-set, his sleek black hair pulled back into a pony-tail which snaked down the middle of his back, the woodcarver did not acknowledge having heard, or even look up.

I stumbled on: "It wasn't till I saw this that I realised. I've got this ... kin-feeling with Wolf, you see."

Turning his chisel over and over in his thick, short fingers, he frowned and sighed. The silence lengthened. Feeling exposed, I wondered if I had spoiled his concentration. Or had it been too eccentric a question?

"Well, you see...." His voice was soft; I had to bend close to hear him. Without raising his eyes from the nascent form he was creating, he ran a dark, broad hand over his head. "The Wolf Clan, they were first to go out and meet the Europeans. That was one of their responsibilities: to welcome and assist newcomers. So they bore the brunt of what followed: the diseases, the aggression. They were almost totally wiped out. So that's why you don't see it."

"So what does that mean? What was their place in the order of things?" I burst out, perhaps unconsciously looking for confirmation of what I thought I already knew: "I mean, what does Wolf symbolise?"

Although I had read that Wolf symbolises pathfinder and teacher, and that in the Great Star Nation, Wolf is represented by the star Sirius, which according to many global myths is the home of the teachers of the human race in ancient times,[21] for some reason I needed to hear it directly from a Native American.

"Family. Structure and stability of the family." He pushed back a lock of shiny black hair that had escaped its tight confines and, straightening up, looked me in the eye for the first time. Something about his look, the way his eyes glinted, catching the light, stopped my thoughts, held me. "But they're comin' back!" He smiled; it was like sunlight breaking through clouds. "You watch. You'll see a lot more of 'em soon enough. They're comin' back...." Bowing his head, he returned to his carving.

I watched without seeing, my whole body tingling, buzzing with something I could not name.

Family. This was new, unexpected; not as glamorous as pathfinder and teacher or romantic like lone wolf howling at the moon, yet obvious, thinking of the wolf-pack, a clan-like arrangement. Mingling the two interpretations offered the best of both worlds: a cohesive part of society, but still able to embody individual desires and dreams.

A solitary person by nature, I was beginning to realise that a sense of belonging was something I had been seeking and battling with for years. In my final year at college, there had been a brief involvement with a commune until personalities and belief-systems clashed; a kibbutz in Israel had followed, but reality fell far short of my idealistic notions. Marriage into an extended Israeli Sephardic family had made me aware how much I needed personal space – a painful lesson, for I had long thought that the nuclear family in which I had grown up had been somehow lacking.

Not a modern phenomenon but one seeded at the time of the Industrial Revolution, when rural families were forced into the city to be swallowed up by the factory, the splintering of the extended into the nuclear family was completed by subsequent mass geographical relocations to go where the work was. It had seemed to me that without the subtle sense of continuity that elders provide their grandchildren, a vast chasm lay between what went before and what came next, in which the present was losing itself. Yet, given the opportunity, I had not been able to cope with living with an extended family.

Learning this new interpretation of Wolf-energy made me wonder whether the break-up of family was somehow symbolically connected to the near-annihilation of wolves in Europe and

---

21 Jamie Sams and David Carsons, *Medicine Cards*.

North America. It made sense, if one considered how everything was supposed to be interconnected: the Oneness of all. Would this now begin to be turned round? Despite immense and on-going controversy, wolves were being reintroduced into Yellowstone National Park, and impetus was building for wolves to be brought back to the highlands of Scotland. Did this mean the concept of family would begin to heal?

Not once during these restful, enlightening days, however, did I forget that time was creeping by, pointing like an arrowhead to the confrontation at the Provincial Museum (perhaps what had subconsciously drawn me to the Island in the first place); when the day came the pull was irresistible. Despite the insistence of my two friends that I should let the matter rest, and the advice of a Coastal Salishan elder and spiritual leader, a friend of Lynne's who had periodically corresponded with me on matters of spiritual protocol, I had to be there. I promised to keep at a distance.

Arriving just as the museum opened, my children and I were the first visitors. There was no sign of any Lakes people. We spent an hour in the Natural Science section and then went to view the collection of Coastal Salishan exhibits: massive, weathered cedar canoes; carved masks of eagle and raven, painted in red and black, their beaks prominent, menacing; rattles and drums; a complete reconstruction of the interior of a lodge with recorded low-key drumming and chanting that gave it an eerie, haunted atmosphere which the children did not like at all. Having been made aware by Lynne of the sacred nature of the masks and other ritual artefacts on public display, I felt uneasy, my thoughts never far from the other sacred items, stored somewhere below my feet, restless to go home.

There was no sense that anything was disrupting the increasing stream of visitors and I began to wonder whether I had the date wrong. It was close to eleven; two hours in the museum had been long enough for the children, so I decided to go back to Lynne's. Pushing open the heavy glass exterior doors, I saw no sign of any Native people and with conflicting feelings – disappointment and relief – went outside.

Assembled about a hundred feet away, to one side of the forecourt, was a rough crescent of Lakes representatives: Bob, Kous, Yvonne and others who had been at the Indian village at Vallican when I left. Not parading in a circle as I had anticipated, but motionless; their voice, placards denouncing the museum's heartless policies. Most passers-by barely afforded them a glance.

Feeling suddenly and inexplicably exposed and uncomfortable, I took my children by the hand and walked swiftly to the other side of the immense forecourt and from what I thought was an unobtrusive position watched as two dark-suited museum officials came out of the building and went over to the Native people. After some discussion, Bob and one or two of the others accompanied them back inside.

Had the museum been embarrassed into giving in, as Bob had anticipated? It would be a complete turnaround in policy, as well as an admission that these were the people whose ancestors had been taken from the Slocan Valley – an immense step forward in their reinstatement as a viable, recognised entity with a claim to the land. I began to tremble; if Bob came out carrying a bundle or a box I was not sure if I could hang back. Not for the first time, I wavered over my misgivings about direct action.

Nor had I been unobserved. Watching the museum doors in a state of suspension, trying to imagine what was being said and done inside, I did not notice my one-time co-worker, Jacquie, who had continued to be closely involved with the Lakes people at the Indian village, and Marilyn, another actively-supportive Valley woman, until they were directly in front of me.

"Celia, we just want to warn you," said Marilyn without preamble. "You'd better keep away. For your own safety."

Shocked at her words, her grim expression, I looked at Jacquie standing beside her, silent and nodding, her arms folded across her chest. The tension was thick and heavy as molasses, and I felt a wave of nausea.

I have as much if not more right as you to be here, I wanted to say; I was deep in this before you had any idea. But it was the first time anything like this had been said up front, and I had never expected to hear it from non-Native people whom I had considered my friends. It was easy to understand the suspicion and resentment that came from the small faction of Lakes people: walking the delicate line of attempting to ensure they had control over what happened at their ancestral site, without alienating the other parties – local and governmental – involved, I had followed my own, natural style: not front-line warrior, but diplomat, peacemaker. To some of the Lakes representatives now gathered outside the museum, I must have been a kind of go-between between the institutions and people they most distrusted, all of whom they saw as having too much of a proprietary interest in their ancestral site: ethnographers and archaeologists who exploited their culture; the Heritage Branch, an arm of the government; the Vallican Archaeological Park Society, a group of "arrogant white folk"; and the Colville Business Council (the Reservation governing body). Elected tribal councils had long been regarded as the fifth arm of colonisation.

What stymied me was how, even if these two women did not know the exact circumstances of how I had become involved, they could have shut me out like this. For months we had shared our feelings and thoughts, hopes and dreams, which had seemed the same, and I had never criticised in any way the action any Native person took.

Nor had I shown anyone the unsolicited letters I had received since returning from England, addressed to me as coordinator of the Vallican Archaeological Park Society and written by Arrow Lakes descendants from the Colville Reservation and the Reserve at Osoyoos, B.C., who had been unaware that my position was ended. The common thread of these letters had been that the actions of the few did not represent the wishes or intent of the many, a theme echoed by people like Auntie Vi and other Lakes elders who felt that matters were being forced too swiftly.

Staring at the two women in disbelief, a little voice in me urged confrontation but before I could pull myself together to speak, something changed. There was a definite shift in energy; suddenly the two women were not looking at me but over my shoulder. I turned. Lynne and James were standing behind me, dressed in black and wearing black armbands. In respect they had come, to the strangest wake I had ever known.

Big sister and brother come to the rescue just in time, I thought, as without a smile but with a few choice insights, Lynne turned the two women away. Then she and James shepherded the children and me to the empty courtyard behind the museum, where they sat me down on a bench between them.

"Celia," said Lynne gently. "When will you realise your part in this is over? It's time to move on. The Valley is a stepping-stone. It's time to move on."

It was not the first time she had said this and she no doubt read the silently-screaming denial behind my eyes. Grateful but still confused and defiant, I said: "Look, it was the ancestral remains that moved me to get involved in the first place. All I really wanted was for them to be taken care of and that's what's happening. Maybe I don't need to be here, but I deserve to be. Anyway, it was too powerful an attraction. And now you're here too...." I tailed off, remembering that they had said they definitely would not come.

"Concern for your safety was the only thing that brought us here," said Lynne. James nodded in agreement. "Direct action and confrontation is not our way, no more than it is yours. This will not restore the bones to them. Or if the museum hands them over, which I doubt, well, if things are done without the elders, forced before their time, there'll be a price to pay. So even if they get their bones back, it'll backfire somehow. There'll be a price to pay."

INTO THE SHADOWS

In a subdued, confused state, I returned to the mainland. Standing on the upper deck of the ferry, wind in my hair, watching the golden light of a setting sun streaming hazily over the retreating Island mountains, it struck me – coastal woman – how much I missed the coast I had grown up beside, and that my closest friends lived on the Island.

"If we should move here, give me a sign," I cried aloud to the foaming wake of the ship, to the softly-serrated clouds in a deepening-blue sky. A great "X" hung there, where two planes had coincidentally left their mark.

"X does not mark the spot!" The immediate inner response came as a relief: despite everything, the Valley – or whatever it represented – held me even more powerfully than the "talons of gold" I had felt in Jerusalem. Plus it made logical sense: Sivan could continue at the same school, and seemed to be coping with being an itinerant in the home of her friends for the present. In any case, what other possibility was there?

My decision seemed ratified and my confidence in Lynne's clairvoyant ability was shaken, when I heard that an agreement to return the ancestral remains had been forged the same day as the protest. Then I learned that not until Bob and whoever had accompanied him into the museum had success lying before them like a bright doorway, was the formal condition for the release of the ancestral remains made known: the documentation had to be signed by them as "representatives of the Okanagan Nation". However they felt at only being allowed to proceed if they identified themselves as a separate, recognised group, their protests came to no avail, and at this stage it must have been unthinkable to walk away empty-handed. The cost of direct action turned out to be a lost opportunity for official governmental recognition of the existence of the Sinixt First Nation. Lynne had seen clearly, after all.

For a couple of weeks, the two younger children and I camped out on friends' land in the Valley. Then autumn truly arrived; the cold, wet weather drove us to stay with my friend Hetty in Nakusp. She had just lost her other parent, her husband Kori had fallen seriously ill again and Natalie and Nick's father had also suffered a relapse; imagining we would be able to support each other, I began a house-search in the area which almost immediately came to an end as a new pressure hit me: tension headaches. Never having suffered anything like it, I guessed it might be something to do with sensitivity to the karma of a mill-town; whatever it was, I could not stay. With Uncle Charlie's tale about the anal origin of the word "Nakusp" ringing in my ears, I returned south to Crescent Valley on the invitation of a Pentecostal Christian friend (the same one who sent the Canadian flag to the Lakes Band meeting, eighteen months earlier), to stay with her until I found my feet again.

As with the museum protest, the imminence of the reburial ceremony probably played no small part in this decision. Presided over by Frances, a hereditary Arrow Lakes chief, the long-awaited ceremony finally took place in mid-October, beginning with an open, all-night wake and culminating the following day with reburial in an undisclosed location on the Indian village site. Plans for a ritual tribal ceremony open to all had been abandoned in favour of a simple ceremony, which was attended by many of the descendants, a small number of locals and a couple of reporters.

Not that I saw any of it. Veiled threats against "that government agent" had been whispered in various ears. Apparently my non-presence when the initial road blockade took place had sparked off deep suspicion – few people were aware that Uncle Charlie had spirited me away to a meeting in Kamloops. Warned by moccasin telegraph to stay away, I spent the corresponding time alone downriver, meditating on an after-death journey which included nine years in museum storage and wondering how it came to be that I should be excluded from the very thing that had gripped me so powerfully in the beginning.

The Slocan river silently slid by, smooth and clear. Above me, gently stirred by a soft wind, sighed pine, birch, cottonwood. Maybe it didn't matter where I was, geographically. Would there be some sign when the ancestors were again at peace? An animal; a bird? Would the ancestors ever be at peace, given the situation of their descendants? So much still needed to be put right.

Nothing happened. It was like there was no living creature anywhere around; like I wasn't even there. The natural world barely touched me, cocooned in a strange numbness.

Looking back on this fraught, difficult time, I must have been reaching perhaps the lowest emotional ebb in my life: at the same time as the Lakes' ancestral remains were being interred, emotionally I was "down to the bone". The purpose that had defined much of my life over the previous three years had been fulfilled; homeless and jobless, I had no idea what should happen next.

As the light began to fade, I knew the reburial ceremony would be over and reluctantly went back to where we were staying. My whole situation had never seemed so hopeless: the headaches had returned, the house felt oppressive, my children hated being there, and accepting a fundamentalist brand of Christian hospitality had come at the price of an intense, proselytising barrage of religious beliefs. I could barely think for myself any more.

A car pulled up soon after I got in. Recognising Washington licence plates, I felt marginally better when Auntie Vi and five other Lakes women climbed out of the vehicle.

Irritated by her inability to do anything about my having to stay away from the reburial, Auntie Vi vented her feelings until I pointed out that if I were some government agent, my cover – single mother, homeless and broke – was pretty convincing, even to myself, which made them all laugh. Then Auntie Vi was suddenly serious: "Celia, we've got to do a prayer circle for you. Jackie...." She turned to the Lakes woman. "Don't you think we should do a prayer circle for her?"

Jackie nodded decisively.

I didn't know what to say, what this meant. But I trusted Auntie Vi and knew I needed help, feeling cut adrift on the ocean of life: a schooner whose pilot has lost his navigational skills, his compass, his star-lore; no land in sight and the Wheel kept turning....

With an ease that spoke of familiarity with the process, the six Native women arranged themselves around me with Auntie Vi in front and Jackie behind. Auntie Vi gently placed her hands on the crown of my head and I felt Jackie's on the back of my shoulders. Uncertain at this loss of control over the spiritual goings-on in her home, Jessica hovered anxiously in the background.

"Close your eyes." Auntie Vi's voice was as soft as wind in dry grass. "Trust in Jesus." She began to pray in a soft murmur and Jackie took up her words, echoing and amplifying them behind me.

A great blast of heat swept up through my body. I felt my face flush and beads of sweat break out under my arms and breasts and begin to trickle down my ribs. Filled with an incredible, dizzying warmth, as if some kind a furnace had been set alight in my body, I wondered if I should contribute. Inspired by Auntie Vi's faith in Jesus, I visualised a shining, white-robed being of Light, unseeable face suffused with brightness, palms benevolently held open toward me....

A huge, black spider scuttled up my inner vision, startling me and blocking out the image, and was gone. My scalp pricked and crawled, and I tried to bring the robed Light-being back into my mind's eye. Instead, a fuzzy, Cyclopean eye gradually came into focus, resolving into a graphic representation, thickly outlined in black. Feeling vague surprise, I recognised it as an ancient Egyptian symbol. It made little sense: ancient Egypt and its confusing pantheon of gods had never caught my interest. Runnels of sweat prickled their way down my skin and the sensation of heat gradually faded, but the great Eye held steady and bold in my inner vision. Out of nowhere came the words: "The Eye of God ever watches over you." They echoed through the caverns of my mind and an immense peace began to fill me.

"Was it one of the old men from down there?! Was it one of them that did this – put a devil in you?!" Jessica's shrill voice startled me. She threw out a couple of names.

Bewildered by her odd line of thought, I shook my head and opened my eyes. The room seemed hazy, the women ephemeral, my voice ugly and grating: "How can you say that? Those elders are some of the finest people I have ever known-"

"You shouldn't interrupt!" Auntie Vi turned on Jessica. "What do you know?! You don't know even one of those old souls! How can you say such things about people you don't know?!"

A dark frown on her face, Jessica turned and left the room. Auntie Vi shook her head, then turned to me and gently asked: "How are you feeling?"

The sweat was cooling on my brow. Apart from light-headedness and some confusion, I felt incredibly calm and at peace.

"Maybe she's got the devil inside her!" Auntie Vi cocked her head in the direction Jessica had disappeared. Her smile was grim, her tone unamused. "No, I didn't really mean that. But I don't know about this house. Sure feels weird to me in here."

We all nodded in agreement. A couple of the women sighed deeply and got up to stretch. Behind me, rubbing her arm, Jackie thoughtfully said: "Well, I don't know what was going on exactly, but when you were about half-way through, Vi, something shot out of her back, went up my arm and out my elbow."

Her words made me shiver. I told them everything that had gone on in my inner sight, hoping they would not think I was crazy.

"Spider medicine," one of them said. "Heard 'bout some of them ... the old lady, things like that, you know, at ... that's why I don't go...."

The others were nodding, reading between the spaces. I had no idea what she was talking about.

"One thing I do know, Celia: you need to get away from this house," Auntie Vi said firmly, her hand sweeping an arc that took in most of the room.

"Or else some little ol' devil'll be jumpin' back inside of you!" Jackie added with a laugh, but I could tell she meant it and looked around, almost ready to see some shadowy, hunched, displaced little entity lurking in a corner, watching us balefully.

The women would not consider staying for coffee, which was extremely unusual. At supper, Jessica said nothing about the experience; in fact we barely spoke at all. I knew Auntie Vi was right: I had to leave. But I had no idea where to go.

"The Eye of God ever watches over you." The following day, Linda rang. In a whirlwind of activity, she and Yellow Bear were preparing to move into the new home they were building and were hardly at their rented house any more; I would be welcome to stay there until they were fully moved out, when a new tenant would take over. It was the reprieve I needed. We were moved in by evening, leaving behind a furious Jessica. Only in hindsight did I understand the "saviour" dynamic: a subtle form of control that easily held sway over me at an extremely vulnerable time, and almost sucked me into her evangelical church.

My feeling of release blossomed at being back in the familiar little old house in Appledale where Grey Wolf had lived, in the occasional company of two hospitable, caring, like-minded friends. After a couple of days, Auntie Vi rang, having tracked me down as usual. She seemed unsurprised that things had changed so quickly and got right into what she wanted to tell me: "Remember Lisa? She got sick soon's we drove away from that house. She was ill a couple days, laid up in bed."

"Oh, I am sorry," I said, wondering why this should be so important.

"She was the youngest, see?"

"What d'you mean?"

"Usually it's the youngest gets hit. Have to be real careful in that kind of situation."

I realised she was talking about psychic sickness, something I thought existed only in fiction.

"I had this notion...." I hesitated. But I could tell Auntie Vi anything. Feeling embarrassed, I laughed uncomfortably. "Well, I had this sort of fantasy: you know that sweat I had with Manny at Vallican? Well, I had this idea that the spirit of a mischievous little old woman must've entered my body during that sweat. Because sometimes my actions felt driven; it was not like me, it was as if myself was somehow under and I was acting out...." Thinking it sounded like something out of the Dennis Wheatley books I had devoured as a teenager, I added: "Mind you, if she just wanted to have some fun, that little old lady sure must've been confused by some aspects of twentieth-century reality!"

Auntie Vi did not laugh. "I've heard of stranger things. You have to be careful, in those sweats, in those old places. Who knows what's hangin' about a place like that, just waitin' for a chance to get up to some mischief? Y'know, I sure had a funny feeling 'bout you, all summer. And then I got this powerful urge to do a prayer-circle for you; there was something about you.... And then that house...."

I hardly knew what to make of it all. When I told them about it, Linda and Yellow Bear were sceptical; on issues such as the spirit-world and possession, we turned out to be not so like-minded after all. We discussed the power of the mind, and the nature of evil; they were of the opinion that such a thing as possession did not exist and that there was no such thing as evil.

Aware that blaming negative behaviour on an outside force can be a way of eschewing personal responsibility, I was concerned it might seem as if I was using the concept of possession, or an attached negative entity, as an excuse for the Manny-episode and my inability to pull my life together, but I could not get away from an inner conviction that something outside of me had been at work. So much pointed towards it: Auntie Vi's sensibilities; Jackie's sense of something leaving me through her arm; Lisa's sickness; the unprompted vision of a black spider. Many parts to this equation did not add up to a purely psychological process, including the great Eye.

Having become aware that the Indian village had been long recognised as a sacred site, where people came to pray from as far afield as the coast, Alberta and the States, and that the return of the descendants had seemed to stir up the long-dormant energies of a powerful place, I wondered whether the raw and powerful negative emotions that had eventually flooded the site might not have attracted, on a subtle level, a certain type of entity. Had my sense of a "little old lady" been an encounter with a soul held in an obsessive trance between dimensions, perhaps a disturbed ancestor, attracted by my openness, or the "gaps" in my vulnerable self during this dark, difficult period? Or had something been "thrown" at me? Had Jessica's interruptive intuition hit closer to the mark than anyone realised? Not many people knew that she had once been a sensitive, a psychic who had fiercely turned her back on her Tarot and astrology practice and dumped it all into a Christian fundamentalist devil-bin.

Unsatisfied, I knew I would have to find out more. For the present, I decided to distance myself from ritualistic practice and psychic and mediumistic processes. Whatever may – or may not – have happened, my life was my responsibility: I had given myself over to the energy dynamics in the sweat-lodge with Manny without first checking whether they were connected to and motivated by open-heartedness, selflessness and love.

As for the nature of evil, that will probably be a life-long study.

It also struck me how my children had rarely been with me at the Indian village during these turbulent times. Remembering the way they had wanted to leave the sweat, and aware that neither innocence nor youth are protection against psychic or astral forces – indeed, they can act like an invitation, rendering children the most susceptible – I was grateful for whom- or whatever had protected them. Difficult as it was, I decided to stay away from the Indian village in Vallican and never again enter a sweat-lodge.

No-one had anything to say about the strange great Eye that had appeared during the session, but I did not – could not – forget it. Not until some six years later, when for several years ancient Egypt would unexpectedly become a central part of my spiritual exploration and gathering of knowledge, did I learn that this symbol, the Utchat, represents the Eye of Re and symbolises the balance of nature and physical laws. It was believed that when the Eye was lost, a great disturbance would occur in the natural order of the planet; when the Eye returns, order will be restored.

Looking back, I have often wondered whether it was a precognitive vision, somehow connected to the role of the Sinixt people, as Bob had told me one wintry night in Vallican, as "Keepers of the Order of Life"; and to the tale of Coyote.

I'm not sure why I didn't tell anyone that Lynne had felt my prolonged trip to England was about being "removed" because of being "over-involved and under-protected". Perhaps it was because I was still unable to detach myself from something like an addiction: an obsessive journey that was taking me on a gradual downward spiral into the depths of myself, into my shadow-side. And despite whatever it was that had happened in the prayer-circle, I still had a sense of something within, something other than or beyond "me".

What it was that shot out of my back and up Jackie's arm, I shall probably never know. However, this was not the end of it: whatever or whoever was moving me, or moving within me, holding me in a kind of thrall, would apparently not allow itself to be simply put aside by the action of a group of prayer-warriors or a decision based on the rationale of my conscious mind.

SPIDER MEDICINE

"You must give away the shawl!" The female voice, brusque, commanding, startles me. An elderly woman is standing on the other side of the room. Wearing a pale blue-grey, tailored suit and white blouse, her greying hair pulled back into an immaculate bun, arms folded across her narrow chest, she looks like a top-ranking executive, a tough woman who has made it in a man's world. Or a grammar-school headmistress.

Voice quivering with dismay, I cry: "No! Not the eagle shawl!"

Light glances off her rimless spectacles, thankfully masking the icy stare of her pale eyes. A frown creases her brow; her lips tighten into a thin line. Implacable, she silently stares at me, waiting for me to do as I am told. And despite my resentment of her arrogant, authoritative tone, deep within me I sense inevitability.

Reluctantly, like a petulant child: "But if I must give it away, then ... to whom should I give it?"

"Tipi Doug!"

The immediate, assured response takes me aback: the last person I would have thought of. In fact, I was sort of expecting her to say it was obvious and I would have to work it out myself: a sort of test. " ... Tipi Doug?"

It was pitch dark; I had spoken the words out loud and woken myself. Only a dream, I thought, relieved, and turned over in an unfamiliar bed. Remembering I was at Auntie Vi's, I saw it was just past four in the morning and tried to go back to sleep, but the dream-memory was too vivid. How could I have imagined I might give away something so precious, so close to my heart? A gift from Auntie Vi, it commemorated one of the most exciting periods in my life, had danced with me at pow-wows, and wrapped me in its energy at gatherings and when I smudged and prayed; in Canada, the States, England....

And what a time to have such a dream: Thanksgiving, a celebration of the welcome extended to the Pilgrim Fathers by the Native Americans; of the foods they had shared – turkey, cranberry, potato, sweetcorn and pumpkin – and of how the Native people had taught the newcomers to fend for themselves.

Just as they had been taught by the Animal People, long ago.

Thanksgiving: time of the giveaway.

As for the deemed recipient, never in a hundred years would I have thought of Tipi Doug, or any man for that matter; a shawl was a woman's thing. How on earth had he come into this?

I had known Tipi Doug for about three years. He had earned the nickname by living for a while in a tipi by the Slocan River in Winlaw, ten minutes' drive north of Vallican. Now caretaker of Winlaw Trout Farm, which provided him with an abode and a meagre wage, he made a precarious living crafting porcupine-quill earrings, bone and claw chokers, and hand-drums.

Often seen walking along the highway on some mysterious mission, a slight figure in battered old leather boots and, hanging loose on his lean frame, faded denims and a red-checked jacket, an old canvas backpack slung over one shoulder and a skinny, hand-rolled cigarette nipped between his nicotine-stained fingers, his lined and weathered face barely visible under a bush of deep-brown frizzy hair and beard, he looked for all the world like a mountain man. Emulated at local Hallowe'en no-booze boogies, he was practically a landmark of the little community.

The traditional life-way of the Lakota people was his inspiration, and as a fellow founder-member of Yellow Bear's teaching drum, he never missed a practice session, his deep, resonant voice serving as an anchor: root-voice, earth-connector, grounding our efforts.

Inside each of us there is a higher connection with the Divine; and the dream-state is one of the gateways. Since the vivid dream of Red Cloud and the drum, I had been recording my dreams as soon as I woke, even if only fragments remained. In them, there was a certain directness and immediacy which implied a sort of guidance; it seemed that if I followed their general direction, certain events transpired that seemed destined, making me feel more alive, more passionate about life, and strengthening my faith that I was on a path I was meant to be travelling.

Of course, free will remains the name of the game, and I was as powerfully attached to the shawl as I was wrapped up in myself: "Ate too much last night ... sleeping in an unfamiliar bed ... only had it a year ... a shawl's a woman's thing." And of course: "It was only a dream."

Yellow Bear and Linda were moving into their new house; I had not found a rental but fortunately a vacancy at the Duck Stop motel in Winlaw came up, available on a monthly basis. There was no phone in the self-contained little suite, but that suited me, for despite the confines, I was not only grateful to be independent and housed, but I did not feel like talking to anyone or going anywhere. The small city of Nelson had become weirdly claustrophobic and shopping in a supermarket impossible: even as I approached the bright flickering of the fluorescent lights and the rows upon rows of choice I would break out in a cold sweat and have to turn away. Being among people I did not know had a similar effect.

My strange state of numbness kept me unaware of these anomalies until they were pointed out, and eventually a state of hypertension was diagnosed. The doctor told me it would pass; I accepted this in the same, detached way that I managed to get through each day, one at a time.

Auntie Vi seemed to understand something of what I was going through and kept in close contact through a payphone across the road, inviting us shortly after Thanksgiving to the Remembrance Day pow-wow, a non-competitive celebration of Native cultural heritage which pays tribute to veterans of the two World Wars and Korea, Cambodia and Vietnam.

An indoor event, held in the gymnasium of the community centre at Nespelem – tradition in the confines of a modern building – it had at times an unreality, as if at any time one of the extremes would melt away to the time-space where it really belonged.

Taking me with it, I would find myself wishing.

The bleachers were already crowded when we arrived; I followed Auntie Vi, squeezing past a sea of familiar and unfamiliar faces until she found a space halfway down one side of the hall. Barely had we sat down when a powerful, keening voice broke out into a wailing chant which was picked up by the rest of the drum-group, and to the slow funereal beat of an old, traditional song, the pow-wow opened with the Grand Entry. Auntie Vi always knew the perfect moment to arrive.

Sedately stepping in time to the beat, two elders entered the gym, wearing jeans, cowboy boots, and a ribbon-shirt. One was carrying an American flag, the other, a rotund bear of a man with long, thick, grey braids, an eagle staff. For several suspended moments my attention fixed on this individual, whose presence seemed to eclipse all else.

Behind them followed a stream of Native men, stepping in time to the beat. Two were in wheelchairs and some walked with the aid of a staff; a few seemed incredibly old. Every single one was dressed in contemporary clothing, in jeans, jackets, shirts, t-shirts, cowboy boots. Several of the younger ones were wearing army fatigues and combat boots, and two were wearing sunglasses.

Again I had that strange sense of displacement: the Old Order – the drum, the chant, the light and graceful step, the dark faces and black, flowing hair – mixed together with the modern in this way was somehow disquieting. A glint of metal caught my eye, settling my attention: amongst the many medals I recognised several Purple Hearts.

War-stories of the heroism of Native Americans are many and outstanding; their contribution for the most part unrecognised and unacknowledged. During the emotive silence for the remembered dead, I felt a yawning ache for the lost men and for the veterans, who had given their energy, their health and their lives in distant lands for a doubtful cause and in support of a government which had warred on them, which had taken away their lives, their land, their children, their language, and destroyed their heritage. The ravages were inscribed on every single face, but they held themselves with pride and a grace that made my heart twist painfully in my chest.

The younger men wearing fatigues, their long, black hair flowing free, were Vietnam veterans, I guessed. They looked like they were still fighting a war: a war for their basic rights, to preserve what little was left of their traditional way of life.

As the various categories of dancers went through their paces, my eyes were repeatedly pulled in the direction of the eagle-staff carrier, although he and his small, fragile-looking, white-haired wife did no more than sit at the end of the gym, motionless and unsmiling, watching the dancing. Eventually I asked Auntie Vi if she knew them.

"That's Chuck 'n' Aggie. He's an Indian doctor. [22] They're some of my closest friends – I've known Aggie for years." The way she made the last word slide made it sound like millennia. "They're good people. You'll get to meet them after. Said they'd come visit."

My stomach flipped. Auntie Vi had told me stories about the last great Indian doctor on the Reservation; I had not felt comfortable asking if any were still alive. Thinking about the way this man had somehow stood out, I wondered if at some level I had sensed his power. After that, it was hard to pay attention; my imagination flew on wings of anticipation. On the way home, Auntie Vi enthused further about her friends, then added: "Chuck doesn't have much truck with white folk, though."

My elation nose-dived. Was this some kind of caution? I could not ask, and she said nothing more. As we pulled into her yard, I wondered if I should keep out of the way or go straight to bed, but it was too late: an unfamiliar car was parked by the back door.

"Oh my, they're here already." Auntie Vi hurried inside. Knowing she was annoyed at not

---

22   The fundamental difference between a shaman and a medicine man (Indian doctor) is that the latter does not manipulate energies but communicates with the spirit-world in general and solely for the benefit of the people.

being there to welcome them and unsure whether I should show my all-too-white face, I took my time. I could hear enthusiastic greetings then Auntie Vi's voice drifted back through the kitchen: "And this here's my little friend Celia, from up in Canada. Now, where is that girl?"

Steaming cups of coffee in hand, her two friends were in the sitting-room with her husband, Junior. Three grins were directed my way.

"At last we get to meet you." The Indian doctor stood up, held out a broad, meaty hand and wrapped mine in its warmth. His dark eyes twinkled. "Started thinking Vi's been makin' you up."

A well-built man about my height, he seemed to tower over me, envelop me. Yet there was only warmth and friendliness in his face, his smile, his touch; and over the next half-hour, my earlier sense of a formidable appearance was proven yet again to be in my imagination. Uncle Chuck and Aunt Aggie were some of the most genial people I had met, and had a grand sense of humour.

All too soon, they were leaving. Uncle Chuck's bear-hug took away most of my breath.

"You come visit with us 'fore you go back," Aunt Aggie said.

As we waved goodbye, Auntie Vi squeezed my arm: "You know, it's not often they invite white folk to their home. In fact, I never knew a time when they did. Never known Chuck to touch a white person, either."

That night, I could barely sleep. Being invited to the home of an Indian doctor had been beyond my wildest imaginings.

In the morning, Auntie Vi gave me detailed directions. I made a swift trip to the Trading Post to fill a bag with groceries, then followed a back-road that swiftly deteriorated into a rutted track, winding upwards through the arid hills above Nespelem. I thought how treacherous it would be in the winter, or in times of heavy rain, and remembered Lynne telling me that true medicine people lived anonymously and simply way out in the hills, so that a person seeking their help had to effectively make a pilgrimage to reach them. The power and phone lines gave out long before I reached their home, a weathered old mobile with a few outbuildings scattered round it.

Aunt Aggie came out to greet me and for a few moments we looked down over the far-reaching hazed moonscape of Interior Plateau country, melding mistily blue-violet into the distant skyline. The whole world seemed spread out at our feet: this was a place where the presence of the Creator was a constant.

"I'm a Colville," Aunt Aggie told me as she made coffee and set out chocolate-chip cookies. The Anglicised name was familiar, covering the area and a tribe, but I felt I did not know her well enough to ask the name in her own language or to which tribe Uncle Chuck was affiliated; it was not my place to ask them anything at all. I sipped my coffee and munched on a cookie.

For a while we chatted, then Uncle Chuck came in. Joining us at the table, he said: "We still follow traditional ways. Each turn of the season, we sweat, back to back." Seeing the expression on my face, he laughed. "By that I mean dawn 'n' dusk sweats, for twenty-one days."

Thrilled to be given such information and to know that I was at last close to what had been in my imaginings for most of my life, I tried to imagine what that must be like. One sweat – a real sweat, like the one I had experienced at Round Lake – had left me limp and exhausted for days. Twice a day for three weeks at a time, four times a year; how did these two elders endure the rigour? Not only the sweat, but all the preparation; it must have taken a ton of firewood and the area was practically devoid of trees. Aunt Aggie seemed terribly frail, and Uncle Chuck walked with a slight limp.

Medicine people, I remembered. They hold the Order of Life; they have the strength of thousands of years of tradition behind them.

"Sweat-lodge's down at the bottom of our land, near the creek," he added. "It's not the first lodge I built. That one's abandoned."

Aunt Aggie got up, gathered up our coffee-cups and went over to the sink. I had a sense like storm-clouds gathering; Uncle Chuck shifted his chair so he was sitting directly across the table from me, his broad, tanned face serious. Deep creases running from nose to jaw pulled his mouth downwards; his dark eyes did not seem so warm now. The hairs on the back of my neck prickled. "That year, snow was thick on the ground. I was preparin' the sweat, buildin' an' tendin' the fire, and heatin' the rocks. It all has to be done right, you can't hurry a thing like that. But then when your mind's in the right place, the cold don't matter. People complain 'bout cold. Cold just is.

"When it was ready, for some reason, 'stead of waitin' for Aggie like I always do, I went inside. I was barely sat down, when I saw a spider run across the entrance." Something in his eyes changed: he was back there again, in his mind's eye. Softly he continued: "It was freezin' out there, and this wasn't no ordinary spider. It was a black widow."

Imagining it, black and skeletal against gleaming-white snow-crystals, made prickles run up the back of my neck and over my scalp. I remembered a great black spider, scuttling up the front of my vision.

"She was totally out of place, and time." The Indian doctor shook his great head slowly. "I knew this was serious medicine. Someone was out to do us harm; maybe Aggie, maybe me, maybe both of us. But I got my own ways of protection.... Still, I had to abandon the lodge. It was contaminated."

Utterly fascinated as to why he should be telling me about this dark experience, I fleetingly wondered if Auntie Vi told him about the prayer-circle, and my experience.

"We had a good idea of who was behind it," he added. "But we don't believe in retaliation. That just feeds the energy, brings it right round back again."

What goes round, comes round: Auntie Vi's creed, too.

"The problem is, I like spiders," I found myself saying, wondering why I was talking as if he had told the story for my enlightenment. "When I was a kid, there was one made her web in the porch window and I fed her with flies I swatted." I took a deep breath. "Surely Spider medicine can't be all bad?"

Uncle Chuck smiled, shaking his head, his eyes twinkling again. "Her medicine's extremely powerful. How medicine is used, that's down to free will. But whether it's for negative or positive, Spider medicine's powerful."

My mind was racing. Had he told me this story because of my experience, by way of illustration, as is the Native way?

According to many world mythologies, Spider medicine is the power of creation: millions of years ago, Spider wove the dream of the physical world now manifest. I had also read that, on another level, as Spider weaves a web which decides the fate of those who become Her meal, She serves as a reminder that humans can get tangled in a web of illusion, become caught up in the polarity of good or bad without realising their own power to change things at any time.

What I still had to perceive, however, is that it is we who are the weavers: we are infinite beings who weave the patterns of life and living.

Perhaps, I thought once back home, Uncle Chuck had been teaching me about negative medicine at work in my life, which had been cleared by the power of Auntie Vi's prayer-circle. This seemed apt, since things in my life seemed to be moving forward: I found a large farmhouse to rent just in time for Christmas, and a job opportunity swiftly followed.

Viewed from the clear heights of hindsight, however, and although I can never be certain as to how much he could actually "see" in me, it seems just as possible that Uncle Chuck's story was telling me that my inability to let go and move on was consuming me.

A CAUSE FOR REFLECTION

When the job opportunity evaporated in the logistics of a daily commute into Nelson – over an hour's drive each way in winter, on sometimes snowbound roads – and the prohibitive cost of childcare, I was not too concerned; becoming manager of a new recycling initiative was not what I believed I was destined for. Towards the end of winter, Auntie Vi phoned to invite us to a children's pow-wow at Nespelem and mentioned that a couple of teaching vacancies at the Reservation school were coming up.

I had never thought about making my place among the Native people this way but now it had been suggested, it seemed obvious, especially coming on the wings of a children's pow-wow. I knew Auntie Vi wanted me to move down close to her, and would do everything in her power to help. All I had to do was jump through the necessary hoops. By the time I left for Nespelem, I had pulled together most of the paperwork and, wanting to see how the place where I imagined I would soon be living looked in winter, chose the route that crossed the Rez from east to west.

It was a big mistake. Normally a drive that might take about forty minutes, it turned out to be a torturous three hours' slithering and crawling along unploughed, un-sanded roads across two mountain passes, heart nauseatingly pulsing in throat. I arrived at Auntie Vi's house utterly exhausted. Although she had been anxious, she had to laugh: not under the jurisdiction of the State Department of Highways, this was apparently the normal condition of Rez roads at that time of year.

Nothing happens by accident. But I still only partially accepted this universal truth and missed the symbolic message of the experience.

The community centre in Nespelem was by now a familiar place. After inspecting the craft and food stalls, we took our places high up on the bleachers in the gym. Looking round the mostly unfamiliar faces, not for the first time I found myself wondering why I so much wanted to be here, when I stuck out like a sore thumb. Then the pounding drums thudded through my bones and the chants sliced into my heart, drowning all thought.

Watching children dance into the future of their race's dwindling life-way was deeply moving and poignant. The categories were the same as for the big pow-wows, the competitors ranging between six to twelve years. It was the little ones who made the greatest impression on me: two or three years old, dressed in animal-skin, fur, quills, feathers, their faces painted and brows furrowed in fierce concentration as they stomped their little moccasined feet, joining any category whenever they felt like it, encouraged by their families.

During the semi-finals for the traditional young male dancers, I had just noticed something lying on the scuffed wooden floor when, in the middle of the song, the drum-beat broke off with a loud thud, the singers fell silent and the boys came to a ragged, bewildered stop. The aborted song echoed inside my head; the atmosphere seemed suddenly oppressive. Eyes downcast, the boys shuffled their feet as one of the judges, magnificently attired in a fringed buckskin tunic and leggings, beaded moccasins and a full eagle-feather head-dress, strode smoothly across the gym towards them.

Tall and well-built, he towered over the young dancers, one fringed arm elegantly indicating the object on the floor. At the same moment, a curt, amplified announcement broke the pregnant silence: "An eagle feather has fallen."

The import was clear. A ten-year-old had already given himself away, his face and ears glowing red, knuckles rubbing at his eyes. There was a brief conference among the judges then four of them – older men in traditional regalia – came forward and positioned themselves at the four quarters around the forlorn-looking little feather. One of the drums commenced a slow, pounding beat and a wailing song pierced the taut atmosphere. The four men began a dignified circle-dance around the eagle feather.

Approaching it one at a time, again and again, the men swooped forward and drew back as the song keened. It was breath-taking: the solemnity, the grace, all for one small feather on the ground.

Which suddenly was not there, as the chant cut off on a drum-roll. Transfixed by a ceremonial dance new to me, I had been watching intently yet had not seen it picked up; it was gone, as if by magic. The drum-group had to have been watching like hawks.

A woman appeared beside the boy, whose shoulders were now heaving. After a muffled consultation with the judges, she handed them something and the eagle feather was restored to the red-faced boy.

"They sure get out of things the easy way these days!" Auntie Vi scathingly remarked. "That young man, he should be startin' all over again!"

"What d'you mean?" I asked.

"In the old days, that boy would've had to give away his whole outfit, ev'ry bit of it, and begun to work toward a new one again. From scratch." She nodded in disapproval.

"But why?"

"Letting an eagle feather fall. He didn't check his outfit properly, didn't take care to make sure everything was secure, in place. It's not the right way – he doesn't really appreciate where he's at, and my way of thinking, instant cash payment doesn't provide any true or lasting teaching or recompense."

"It's our society," I commented, not really understanding. "Fast-foods; fast entertainment. People've grown to expect instant return. Most people think money solves everything."

"No-one does things properly no more. What'll they do when money doesn't work?" Auntie Vi mused.

It was the first time I had heard anything like this from her. Was she saying she believed there would be an economic collapse? Apparently the breakdown of institutions – a Piscean-age construct – would be part of the prophesised Earth Changes. I found I couldn't broach that subject with her, however.

Before heading back up to Canada, I went up into the hills to visit with Uncle Chuck and Aunt Aggie. Uncle Chuck wasn't in; as Aunt Aggie and I shared coffee and gossip, I found myself telling her about some of my concerns: "I know I have work to do with Native people. It's not about what's happening up in Vallican any more. In fact," I added, as if this were a relevant feather in my headdress: "I've stayed away for two seasons now."

At some level I was aware that I was under a kind of spell; of whose making was another matter.

After a long silence, Aunt Aggie said: "The mirror. Look in the mirror."

"Look in the mirror?" Alice – anagram of Celia – climbing through the looking-glass popped into my head.

"Yes, the mirror. All the answers you seek lie there."

What did this mean? Play at being Snow White's stepmother? Look where a mirror got both her and Alice. "Bathroom or bedroom?" I joked.

"It's hard to fool yourself when you're looking into your own eyes," Aunt Aggie said softly, speaking a thought that had just occurred to me. "But know that the world round you, it's a mirror too. All of it: every person, ev'ry bird, animal, ev'ry situation.... Ev'rything round you, you draw to yourself; tells you something 'bout yourself."

Everything? How could that be? The world didn't revolve round me. Sometimes, things just happened. But you don't challenge an elder.

"I had a dream...." I surprised myself by telling her about the shawl-dream. "Funny thing is, since then I've been feeling reluctant to wear it. And I can't really ask Auntie Vi what to do with the gift she gave me. I might appear ungrateful, or she mightn't like the idea of who I'm supposed to give it to. In fact, I haven't even told her about it." I was just realising how strange this was; she never gave me a hard time about anything. I remembered something else: "And it's interesting that she's never asked to borrow it since, either, and she hasn't said anything about me not wearing it."

"Who is this Tipi Doug to you?" Aunt Aggie asked with a small frown.

"A friend. I've known him a couple of years. He's a quiet, okay sort of guy, a craftsman. Empathic to Native ways. And he drums at the same drum I'm learning at-"

"He's a white man, isn't he?" she said sharply. "And what has he ever done for you? Ever given you anything? Done something for you, or your kids?"

I shook my head. Similar questions had popped into my mind but I had a feeling they were irrelevant.

"This woman who orders you round in this dream, she's a white woman?" Aunt Aggie asked. At my nod, she continued: "Then ignore it. This is about Indian things. What's a white woman doing, telling you what to do with Indian things?"

Offering back-up to something that had also struck me, her words made a kind of sense. Yet nothing changed; I still found myself unable to use the eagle shawl and the memory of the dream continued to haunt me, like scar-tissue tightening.

WHERE EAGLES FLY

Lesson of the fallen eagle feather foremost in our mind, we had Nicolas' regalia almost completed. It had been almost two years since my son had first asked for a dance-outfit; not adept with needle and thread, I had half-expected it would somehow just materialise, Indian time, until Tom, the Lakes pipe-carrier, knowing of Nick's desire, admonished me: "You wait too long, that young man's gonna lose interest. You don't want to let something like that pass him by." Producing a battered old hide pouch, he had given it to Nick. His words, and the look on the boy's face as he shook out an antique set of brass bells, acted as the catalyst.

Painstakingly fashioned from a handsome piece of white moose-hide picked up at a pow-wow on the Spokane Reservation the previous autumn, Nick's fringed kilt and leggings were barely finished when other items began to "happen": a fringed buckskin vest from Linda and Yellow Bear; fleecy white anklets from one Valley friend and braided rawhide armbands and wristlets from another; a belt from Louella; a buffalo-bone and badger-claw necklet Nick picked out at a pow-wow; a dancing-stick, forked like a two-year-old deer-antler, which he painted red and yellow then added tiny bells and two white goose feathers, the tips of which he painted black. (The lesson about who had the right to carry an eagle feather was strong in our memory.)

The moccasins had needed the most thought and effort. Regarding them as fundamental (I was still waiting for mine), I commissioned them from Tom's sister-in-law. Peggy took Nick's foot measurements just as Auntie Vi had taken mine; within what seemed like no time at all they were ready. Beaded with a dynamic design in red, black and yellow which Nick had come up with, they had been made from the last piece of the first hide Tom had cured in a traditional manner, which seemed somehow deeply meaningful. His head-dress was proving elusive, however. Made from animal hair, a roach simply did not seem right, and the complicated ones made from porcupine-quills were too expensive to purchase. In any case, Nick was aspiring to the traditional style and his totem animal or bird had not come clear. I knew he had a partiality for the mischievous, trickster nature of Coyote, but had no idea how to represent it.

Tom suggested we just let things unfold. Elaborating on what Auntie Vi had told me, he explained that the attention paid to assembling and caring for the outfit is a direct reflection of the respect held for the creature that had given of its body and its life for it, and that the meticulous donning of the regalia is a kind of meditation. I remembered a man with hair of flame; and a great-kilt.

As soon as the moccasins were ready we picked them up on our way to Nick's first opportunity to dance. Typical of the way these things work, it was a very special occasion: Tom had invited our Slocan drum to participate in a small celebratory pow-wow in Inchelium. For some of us, the idea of drumming among Native Americans had been beyond our wildest imaginings; acutely aware of the honour and afraid we would let Tom down, yet strengthened by his teachings and the name with which he had endowed our drum – Northern Lights – we took our turn alongside four other Native drum-groups. And even though I thought we sounded weak, reedy, without much substance, the Native people danced to our drum as readily as any other.

When Nick finally got up the courage to dance (as sedately as the traditional dancers and not at all like the flamboyant and surprisingly-adept fancy-dancer I had watched practising alone at home) alongside his friend Victor, a Lakes boy of the same age, I thought I had never felt so proud. Inch by inch, we were creeping closer to what I believed was my destiny.

It is well-documented that parents can unwittingly burden their children with the fulfilment of their own unrealised hopes and dreams. Was something deeply personal at work within the boy? Or was it my own dream that my son was acting out on my behalf? Or, as I would later wonder, something within me that was beyond a dream? For he was not the only one with an uncanny ability for fancy-dancing. The previous year, after the closing of the big annual pow-wow on the Spokane Reservation, I had been walking across the empty dance-arena as one of the drum-groups was enthusiastically practising, and a powerful, irresistible energy had welled up within me, transporting me, leaping, swooping and whirling, for several yards until I came back to earth, abashed and glad no-one had noticed, and wondering from where this wild spirit – totally unsuitable for a woman – had originated.

It would not be long before a possible source would reveal itself. Or himself.

Towards the end of the intimate, non-competitive little pow-wow, the male dancers were on the floor when the drum suddenly thudded to a stop as the song broke off.

"What's going on?" whispered my Canadian friends, seated round our drum.

In disbelief that it had happened again and so soon, I indicated the eagle feather lying on the floor: "Eagle feather's fallen." Then I noticed Tom, who had been dancing in full regalia, walking off the floor, white-haired head bowed, eyes cast down.

"Oh gosh," I said softly, feeling mortified for the pipe-carrier. "It's Tom's." Of all people, I would never have thought this could happen to him. Not after all his support and encouragement, his generosity.

The ritual recovery of the feather commenced, much as at Nespelem. Tom stood watching the four dancers from the edge of the hall, his face pale, mouth set in a grim, downward-turned line. By the time the feather was recovered, he had already begun the giveaway. His vicious-looking dancing-stick; hand-crafted shield; porcupine-quill armbands; starburst porcupine-quill head-dress; chunky silver ring; all were randomly handed out to onlookers. When he was down to his leggings, he gruffly said: "I won't embarrass you all by completin' this now," and left. Even at a time like this he made people smile. When he returned, wearing jeans, shirt and trainers, he proceeded to give away the remaining items.

At Northern Lights drum, feeling weird that I had only just learned about this tradition, I whispered an explanation of what was going on. Tom was fulfilling it exactly as Auntie Vi had told: he had given away his entire regalia and would have to start assembling a new one all over again.

Getting Nick's together had not been easy; even though it would be easier for Tom, he had my sympathy. But what was it all about? The pipe-carrier had more respect for and understanding of the natural world than almost anyone I knew. On the one hand, Nick's initiatory dance and the debut of Northern Lights (thanks to Tom) seemed to mark a beginning; on the other, some kind of ending seemed to have been reached by the pipe-carrier.

At the end of the day, after my friends had left for Canada I went to visit Tom at his trailer and found him sitting alone at the kitchen table, subdued and reflective.

"What're the things that give life to a culture?" he mused, wistfully shaking his head. I had never seen him so downcast. "Little things. Parts of birds, of animals. Claws, feathers, bones, hide; sticks, stones, shells...." He grimaced a smile. "All of these simple things're a part of creation. They're of the spirit. An' ev'ry one of them carries a message."

When he talked in this way, every vein in my body became like a bare, live wire. Since coming into contact with the Native Americans, my perception and experience of the differing levels and interconnectedness of the other dimensions in the world around us was deepening, and I was becoming increasingly aware of how we are constantly being offered messages through the world around us: through birds, animals, insects, plants; the behaviour of the wind, of water; and not only through the natural world but seemingly inanimate things like our vehicles.

Just before the gathering where I had met Bob, I had been gifted a knot of wood shaped like a raven's head, which I later understood from Native American teachings indicated that something special was in the air, that I was about to undergo a change in consciousness. On the eve of one of the greatest transformative opportunities in my life, my van's transmission had broken down: a fore-warning that my "gearing mechanism" was about to be replaced. Owl feathers and once an owl's wing had been given me at times when I needed to look deeper into a situation or into the ulterior motives of other people. The gift of a buffalo tooth had served as a message to use my energy in prayer, since nothing is achieved without the aid of the Divine Will. On many occasions, a single white feather had come spiralling down from the sky, communicating to my agitated state that all was unfolding as it should and to reconnect to the beauty of creation. Eagle feathers, symbolic of the freedom of the skies and overview, had come my way, carrying the message of seeing both shadow and light and the beauty in both, and of flying high in the joy of following the heart's desire. A hank of bear hair I had come across at a time of great stress had carried a message to seek the answers within, intuitively, in meditation and in dreamtime.

"I've showed disrespect to my totemic guardian," Tom quietly continued, never raising his eyes from the pale, scratched formica of the table. "That was the message I was given: to pay closer attention to my spiritual walk. There's somethin' I'm neglectin'." He sighed deeply. "It's not.... This's the second time I've gave away my war-dance outfit. First was at the death of one of my daughters. The giveaway's part of the cleansing, the whole thing's an opportunity for renewal. I have to be meticulous and attentive to the task, creatin' a new war-dance outfit. The area I need to put to rights will be revealed while I'm about it."

Inspired by his words, I said: "Tom, I got a sort of message too, from Eagle, but I don't understand it." Rummaging in my bag, I produced a pouch of tobacco (you soon learn never to be without tobacco around Native Americans). "Can you help me with it?" I hadn't thought about asking him till now: the dream of the eagle shawl tumbled from my lips. "Should I take any notice of what a white woman says about something that's Indian?"

Tom lit a cigarette, inhaled deeply and leaned back in the chair, stretching his long legs under the table. "A shawl, that's a woman's thing." He blew out a stream of smoke towards the ceiling. I had to smile: my eagle-shawl's swan-song. "But I can tell you this story 'bout a shawl.... Back when I was startin' out, didn't have much medicine stuff yet, a woman come see me. A medicine-woman friend of hers had fell sick, an' she wanted me to pray for her. So I did, best I knew how.

"That year, I was at the Winter Dance. They had just put up the pole an' it come to me I had to go up there an' sing my song. I was out of order, it hadn't been opened yet, but I knew that I just had to sing my song. People was starin', but I didn't care, I had to sing it. When I was done, I went back to my place.

"I'd barely sat down when I saw a woman makin' a bee-line straight for me. It was the medicine woman that I'd prayed for. And boy, was she mad!" Shifting his position, he grinned at the memory. "She was carryin' a package, an' thrusts it at me. 'I had a dream,' she says, 'that I had to give this to the first person that sang at the pole this year!' Was she riled! 'A whole year I worked on it,' she says. 'It was supposed to be for the woman that helped me when I was sick, an' then last night I had a dream to give it to the first singer at the pole. An' it turns out to be a man!'

"I didn't want it, tried to tell her but she dropped the package on my lap an' stomped off, lookin' like she'd just chewed on some bitterroot. After I got back home, I opened the parcel up to take a look." His mouth quirked and his eyes softened. "It was a shawl. A black one, beautifully worked, with little white feathers embroidered on it, an' a black fringe. I could see a lotta work gone into it.

"Well, I'm a man. What was I to do with a woman's shawl? I hung it up on a wall at home, but that didn't seem right, draped it over a chair, that wasn't right either, so I folded it up an' put it in a cupboard. But I couldn't seem to get it outta my mind. In the end, I bundled it in my medicine bag." He took a deep drag on his cigarette. "Awhile later, I got called to help a little girl who'd fell sick. I went to her house, sat by her bed, sang my song an' prayed over her. Then I remembered I had some roots to make a tea that'd help her, so I opened my medicine bag to get 'em, an' there was the shawl. I'd clean forgot it was there. I made the tea and give it her. Then when she fell asleep I took out the shawl an' covered her with it, an' sat there and prayed, all through the night.

"At first light, I sort of came back to myself, an' looked over to where she was layin', to see how she was....

"The shawl was white, with black feathers."

Images of white and black feathers danced through the shadows of my mind. What did this mean? Something had been reversed?

"She woke up soon after, right as rain, got up, laughed, ate, an' went off to play." Tom shrugged. "Like I said, I don't know what a man has to do with a shawl. I left it with that little girl."

It wasn't only the magical story that had compelled my attention, but an eerie green glow, laced with pink, which seemed to cover Tom's shoulders and form a corona around his head as he was in the telling. If I looked directly at it, it wasn't there; only with peripheral or unfocused vision was it visible.

Only once before had I seen anything like this, about a year earlier at a performance of Tibetan sacred music and sacred dance. Transfixed by the deep resonance of their amazing, magnificent, massive horns, I had suddenly, dizzyingly, seen each robed monk engulfed in a carapace of strong, deep purple, topped with an opaque, golden-yellow, glowing oval. So solid were what I had immediately guessed had to be their auras, that it was like they were sitting behind a shield.

With Tom, the colour was ethereal, but I had no doubt I had been gifted a glimpse of the etheric field of the pipe-carrier's healing abilities, and the love he held for people.

Tom stubbed out his cigarette and his dark eyes caught mine. Quietly and slowly he said: "Creator tells us what we need to know in whatever way makes us sit up an' take notice. An' one thing I do know...." He smiled. "There ain't no such thing as colour to the Creator."

I smiled back: an authoritative headmistress would be one of the better ways to make my subconscious pay attention. The relief and clear certainty I was feeling informed me that Tom's story had cleared the way. "Thanks, Tom. I know now what I have to do."

"I'd never tell anyone what they should do," he said. "But whatever you decide, feel free to share this story I just told you, with whoever you want."

The shawl had already left; part of me knew that. I just hadn't been able to let go. Not only had Tom reached me in the traditional way – only when asked and using a relevant experience to cast light onto a dilemma; direct advice is rarely, if ever, given – he was enabling an opportunity to giveaway in turn.

Gradually, the lesson was sinking home that on a material or symbolic level, the appearance or departure of "simple things" in a person's life is a coincidence of the highest order: a "gentle guide". While aware of this fundamental Native American teaching, because of an inner imbalance, a play of ego, I had been unable to respond appropriately. On some level, I was fully aware the dream was directing me to leave behind this intricate eagle-dance, but letting go of the Native American connection was something I could not countenance. It would take almost another year – until the following Thanksgiving – for me to be ready to give Tipi Doug the eagle-shawl at a drum practice, where I would also share Tom's story. But what eagle represented had left me already. And nature abhors a vacuum.

WINTER DANCE

Originally a matriarchal group, the Sinixt had traditionally held one annual ceremony, which took place in the depths of winter and celebrated a renewal of faith in the rhythms and cycles of nature. After a hiatus of forty-seven years and following the American Indian Religious Freedom Act of 1978, Arrow Lakes elder Martin, Tom's father, reintroduced the Winter Dance onto the Colville Confederated Reservation in 1981,[23] and over the following years, a growing number of different families began to host their own version of the ceremony.

Tom had extended the Slocan drum-group an open invitation to these spiritual events, which seemed to me to promise something of an Old Order that was still in my heart to find. However, each time I got word about one it had been too late for me to alter some personal commitment and I had to be satisfied with hearing of my friends' intriguing experience: the gloomy, smoky hall; the potent central pole; the powerful old chants; and Yellow Bear's vivid tales of how the ritual would progress through levels of intensity and ultimately reach a high, vibrant point, when green-glowing lights would appear and shoot around the hall, spitting and crackling. Apparently the appearance of these balls of energy was evidence that the purpose of the ceremony had been attained; what they actually were, however, was never broached.

I could barely wait to witness this for myself. Knowing of my interest, while talking on the phone one day, Auntie Vi said: "How's about I go with you? Seems that way you'll be sure to go."

Her offer took me aback; I knew she had little interest in revived traditions and she had expressed deep reservations about the ceremony. Despite feeling uncomfortable, however, I thought it would seem odd if I turned her down. Yet as it happened, the next two opportunities proved inconvenient for both of us.

Even at the time I had a sense that this was more than simply chance.

Finally we managed to synchronise a date, but as the day approached I felt an increasing unease. The evening before I was due to drive down to the Reservation, I called Auntie Vi to finalise arrangements, which was unusual in that when I was doing anything with Native people, flowing with Indian time was second nature by now. "Um, you know, I don't need to go if you don't want to, Auntie Vi," I found myself saying. "I mean, are you sure you really want to?" I could feel my face burning.

There was a short silence. "Well, I said I would go with you. I thought you really wanted to."

"I thought I did, too. But to be quite honest I'm not so sure now."

"Well, I wouldn't have said anything if you hadn't of said that, but there's some strange little ol' ladies at some of those dances. They get it into their heads to do bad things. And one of them that goes there, she doesn't like me. Prob'ly like you even less. Got no love for no-one, 'specially

---

23 1981 was also the year when archaeological investigation removed the ancestral remains from the Arrow Lakes Indian village at Vallican. Is it possible that these two events are somehow related: that reconnection to the ancestral spirits through the newly-revived ceremony of the Winter Dance set in motion a train of events which would lead to the renascence of the Arrow Lakes Band?

not white people. You can never tell what people like that might get up to."

Uncle Chuck's tale of the abandoned sweat-lodge came to mind. Untangled from a web of my own making, I chuckled. "Just goes to show what friends'll do to each other. Here's me trying to drag you off somewhere I just realised I don't want to go, and I know you never really wanted to in the first place!"

A few days later I stopped at the Duck Stop in Winlaw just as Nadine pulled up in her car. Of Doukhobor descent, beautiful, blonde and fragile-looking with enormous hazel-green eyes that spoke of an inner melancholy, she had become part of Northern Lights while I had been in England, her strong and resonant singing voice adding a powerful dimension to the drum-group. Tom had immediately perceived her sensitivity and considerable psychic abilities, and endowed her with a healing-stick. Later, when his relationship with Louella foundered, Nadine had entered into an intimate relationship with the pipe-carrier and was often down on the Reservation.

Far from her usual vibrant self, she looked pale and exhausted.

"How's things?" I asked, as we sat down with our coffee, unwilling to say she looked like Death warmed over. "How's Tom? Coming to the drum this week?"

"Dunno. Just got back." She sat hunched over her mug, staring into its depths, her small, slim hands cupping its warmth.

"Back?"

"Went to a Winter Dance with Tom, in Inchelium." She heaved a sigh. "And I'm totally drained.... To be honest, this's not the first time, Celia. That I'm like this, I mean. What goes on there...." The golden streaks in her tawny mane of hair shimmered. Not only were her hands trembling, her whole body was shivering. Yet it was warm in the little restaurant. "The things that ... there's people there who...." She shook her head. "You don't want to know."

She had been at the ceremony to which Auntie Vi and I had intended to go. "Yes I do. Tell me."

Nadine's eyes unhooded; large, intense, like murky ponds with strange creatures lurking in the depths, they stared at me. "They, they throw things. During the ceremony, I mean. I guess it isn't going down too well there, me being with Tom.... Maybe you could ask your friend ... Auntie Vi, isn't it? If she knows what I should do?"

Aghast, I stared at her. "Gosh Nadine, that's terrible. But Auntie Vi's not into that stuff. I told you she's with Jesus. She'd only say to stay away. Although if I ask her she'll pray for you."

"Yeah. Need all the help I can get." She shrugged. "This's happened each time. Last time I was sick for three days."

I was thinking about directing her to Uncle Chuck and Aunt Aggie, then realised: "But what about Tom? What does he say?"

She shrugged and I felt unable to press for what that meant. Hadn't she told him? Surely he would have seen what was going on. But I couldn't ask her. Perhaps it was my fantasies that stood in the way: when the two of them had got together, I had been thrilled, seeing them as a manifestation of something I deeply believed in: representatives of two races working together to help restore harmony. It was a bubble I did not want to see burst.

After she wearily left to go home and to bed, I went down to the river. Watching the slick, dark flow of water, I found myself thinking of Aunt Aggie. Was there a message for me here, a reflection? Nadine's predicament had hit close to home.

Having only recently perceived a pattern, I had never told anyone – and barely admitted to myself – that whenever I stayed on the Reservation more than twenty-four hours, a pressure would begin in my head and intensify by the day. Worst of all was at a pow-wow in an enclosed space: within a couple of hours, a vice-like grip would press in on my head, and I was only able to bear it because the chants, the drumming and the dancing held me in such thrall. I could not call it a headache, it had an entirely different quality, and within forty minutes or so after leaving the Reservation, usually as soon as I got back into Canada, the strange pressure would be gone.

I had assumed it was some unconscious tension of my own. But suppose there were people who resented my white presence and were "throwing things" at me? I remembered why I had promised myself no more sweats. Was a pow-wow in the same sort of league? Perhaps, as I had suspected all along, whatever had stopped me attending the Winter Dance, the most powerful ceremony, held indoors, by and among people about whom I knew nothing, had been some sort of protection. It seemed as if something was conspiring to keep me away from Native American ritual. But who, or what? And why?

Blossoming perception was not enough to keep me away from the pow-wows, of course, but shortly after I received a sort of indirect confirmation during another pow-wow at the community centre in Nespelem.

Watching the dancing in a sort of reverie, I felt a light tap on my shoulder. There was only one person who could have been responsible: a small, grey-haired, Arrow Lakes elder whom I knew by sight but not by name, sitting behind me. I raised my eyebrows in query.

"Pay attention to what I say." In the traditional way, not once did the elder look at me, but gazed over my shoulder down into the melee of dancers, his lined, brown face neutral, his voice so quiet I had to strain to catch his words. "Watch out who you talk to, who you tell your secrets to. Watch out who you take into your confidence. Once they know things 'bout you, they got power over you. An' there's women here that it's better you don't trust."

I guessed he had me confused with Nadine. She was more involved, stayed for weeks at a time. Almost the only women with whom I had dealings now were Auntie Vi, her relatives and close friends. Perhaps to Native elders, I thought, all blonde white women look alike. "You must mean my friend? With Tom?"

"Well," he said, shrugging and still not looking at me, "you just tell your little friend to be real careful where she goes, who she mixes with, an' who she tells what. Because it can all be used, an' in ways you'd never know about."

Goosebumps lifted the hair on my arms. Such a small, frail-looking man, such a dire warning: he was talking about supernatural powers being manipulated by a human agent. What had Nadine gotten herself into? Yet it was I who had been given the message.

Nothing happens by accident. Was it meant for me after all? Was it meant as a caution to stay away from Native American ceremonies altogether? But why? It was not something I believed I could do; given the right opportunity, I would jump at the chance to attend one.

YINIPI

"Well, I didn't forget your interest. Since we didn't make the Winter Dance, Chuck and Aggie've invited you to go with them to a yinipi."

Despite having no idea what this was, I was thrilled. Any misgivings about attending a Native American spiritual event were dispelled; under the aegis of two spiritual elders who were also friends, I would be looked after. "What happens at a yinipi?" I asked Auntie Vi excitedly.

A familiar snort sounded through the wires. "I know as much as you. It's a kind of prayer-gathering. Aggie says you're to come down the day before; there's preparing to do."

This had to be the experience of a lifetime. As for prayer-requests, after twelve years in remission, Natalie and Nicolas' father had relapsed and a recent round of chemotherapy had weakened his immune system and compromised his circulatory system and kidneys; like Auntie Vi, his continuing existence was something of a miracle. My other concern was all too familiar: the farmhouse had been sold. Only three months, and we had to be on the move again.

All Uncle Chuck would tell me was that yinipi was the Lakota word for sweat-lodge and that it now took the form of a ceremony "carried" from reservation to reservation by medicine men of the Plains Nations, as part of a larger movement to reconnect to heritage. Not knowing what to expect, I sat in the back of their rumbling old gas-guzzler and watched the sere grasslands round Nespelem give way to forest as we climbed westwards through a landscape as familiar and loved as the Valley. At Disautel, I looked out for Bob's ranch through the pines and briefly wondered what he was doing now. In silence we coasted down towards Omak; not far from the Paschal Sherman Indian School (where I was hoping to get an appointment), Uncle Chuck turned onto a sandy track which snaked along the edge of a narrow gully under a canopy of lodge-pole pines and came to an end in front of a small, single-storey ranch flanked by outbuildings. Several cars were parked in the yard; some thirty or so Native people were standing round in groups of four or five. Little children played in the dust and on tyre-swings; a couple of teenagers lounged in the shade of the trees.

I remembered what Bob had said about whole families taking part in traditional activities, and my thoughts flew back to my own children, staying at Auntie Vi's: I should have brought them. Then I recalled their lack of interest and my intuitive feeling to keep them away from ritualistic practice. Be in the now, I told myself; all is as it should be.

Telling me to follow, Uncle Chuck went inside. We passed through a large, carpeted front room empty of furniture and down a narrow hallway to the closed door of a room in the back.

"Medicine man's in here," he said. "I'm goin' in now to tell him my prayers an' give him the ties. You go in after me. Got yours ready?"

He disappeared inside and I recovered the ties from my shoulder-bag. The day before, Aunt Aggie had shown me how to make them from the things I had been instructed to bring; we had sat at Auntie Vi's kitchen table and cut a bunch of little squares out of the white cotton sheet, placed a pinch of tobacco in the centre of each one and tied it with thread to make a little pouch. Uncle Charlie's tale of N'kusp had been strong in my mind as I drew each one closed. When twenty-four were ready, they had to be tied together along a length of red embroidery thread. It was a slow, meditative task; not only are my fingers not particularly suited to thread and to tying, but each one had to be imbued with the prayer I wished it to carry.

Strung out along the thread, they looked like a row of dancing, raggedy little Caspers, the cartoon ghost; all I needed was a black pen to paint round eyes and a sad mouth on the sweet little heads. Mouth dry with anticipation, I waited. It seemed surreal to be standing in a hallway, linoleum under my feet, waiting to ask the assistance of a medicine man. I wondered what he looked like, how he would be dressed, where the ceremony would be held, and drifted off into a fantasy just as the door cracked open. Uncle Chuck came out, blocking from view what lay behind him, and motioned for me to go in. I took a deep breath, knocked and pushed open the door.

The drapes had been drawn, dimming the small room, which was hazy with the pungent, evocative scent of sage-smoke. A heavy-set Native man was sitting on a single bed; behind him, another was bent over the suitcases and bags that cluttered the little available floor-space. A plain room with a bed and normal bedroom furniture; but the atmosphere sort of hummed, as if electricity had been let loose.

His eyes inscrutable behind the thick lenses of his black-framed spectacles, the medicine man smiled gently and beckoned me closer. Part of me registered and silently lamented the contemporary blue jeans, the open-necked pale-blue shirt. He appeared to be in his fifties, his skin dark and pitted and deeply creased around the jaw. Heavy black braids coiled sleek over his shoulders.

With a strange, out-of-place feeling, I proffered the ties and briefly spoke my prayer requests. My voice sounded strained, distant. Peering at me with eyes distorted by his glasses, the medicine man nodded and took the ties, cupping them in the palm of his large hand as he softly spoke a few words, of which I understood not one. Then he turned his attention to the other man, who was closing a suitcase.

Leaving the room, I felt strangely empty. Had I asked in the right way? Had he understood? The strange humming was still with me, not in my ears or head, but under my skin, in my veins.

Returning to the living-room, I found it dim and packed with Native people. The drapes had been closed; a single overhead light-bulb shed a cold, wan light. It seemed bizarre that the ceremony would take place in such everyday surroundings. Nervously I scanned the crowd for Uncle Chuck and Aunt Aggie, my eyes falling on the front door just as Manny walked in.

My stomach lurched; I hadn't seen him since his flight at the end of the previous summer and never expected he might be here. He looked better than I remembered: his bearing upright and graceful, face smooth and relaxed, hair neatly cut into a brush on top and flowing long and shining down the front of the well-cut, black leather jacket he was wearing. Then he caught sight of me.

His face remained composed, but his eyes shifted and his shoulders hunched. My heart went out to him. Greeting him warmly, hugging him like the old and quite special friend I realised I felt he was, was easy: there was no point in being any other way. The soft leather of his jacket was like a caress under my hands; a faint aroma of wood-smoke brought back a flood of memories. Manny visibly relaxed, and we amiably chatted as people began to sit down around the edge of the room. He asked if I would like him to sit beside me.

The idea appealed, but I told him I was with Aunt Aggie and Uncle Chuck, who were indicating that I should sit on one end of the blanket they had brought. Uncle Chuck sat down beside me and Aunt Aggie sat on the other side of her husband, and as I followed their lead in taking off my shoes and socks and putting them behind me, Manny took the space on my other side.

It felt good, protective, to have the arms of two familiar, trusted people pressed against mine. I scanned the faces round the room, some of which I recognised from pow-wows and generally from the Reservation. I had just realised I was the only non-Native person there when the soft murmur of conversation fell away. Even the little children were silent.

The medicine man walked into the room. He was wearing the same jeans and shirt, without any traditional adornment I could see, but the atmosphere was suddenly charged. Two younger men, laden with bundles, appeared behind him.

Untying the first bundle, one of the men rolled a massive buffalo hide across the carpet, the breath of its unfurling musky, exotic. Sacred animal to the Plains Nations, symbol of prayer and abundance, Buffalo lay barely six inches from my bare feet; rough and shaggy, a dark, powerful presence. It was all I could do to stop myself from reaching out to touch it. At the head of the hide, the other man reverently placed a gleaming white buffalo skull, painted with red and yellow symbols. The empty eye-sockets glared ominously in the dimness. Several strands of tobacco ties were brought out and looped over the skull. I tried to locate mine, but they all looked the same.

Other medicine items were placed around the skull and on the edges of the hide; simple things, which Tom had reflected upon as the makings of a culture: antlers, horns, feathers, rocks, a crystal. Finally, four thick church-candles were placed at each of the four corners of the hide. Honouring the four directions, I guessed.

The candles were lit and the overhead light switched off. The wail of a small child spliced the taut atmosphere, making me shiver. Was the child a safety-valve, speaking what perhaps most were feeling? I found myself thinking about Melanie and the fear of the supernatural inculcated in her as a child. It seemed an age ago.

Eagle feather in one hand and a large, concave shell in the other, the medicine man stood by the skull-head of the mighty buffalo. Into the shell he put some herbs, which he lit and fanned with the eagle feather. The pungent smoke of smouldering sage filled the room as he purified the energy then addressed the six directions: the four cardinal points, and above and below. He was speaking Lakota, softly-intoned cadences like wind sifting through prairie grass. Eventually I recognised two words: the escape-route from the sweat-lodge, "Mitakuye Oyasin". Something was completed.

Picking up a hand-drum, the medicine man began a slow, ponderous beat and led the other two men in a chant. All three started to dance with light, graceful steps, drumming and singing a powerful song that spiralled from high reaches, down into a guttural belly-grunt. There was not much space to manoeuvre between Buffalo and the people, yet not one foot was misplaced.

When the song had worked its way through four rounds, the medicine man resumed speaking Lakota, what I guessed were prayers which he then spoke in English: for the healing of the people; for the return to unity with all peoples; for life in harmony with each other, with nature and the land. Then he talked for some time about the ravages of addiction to alcohol and drugs, and to a negative behaviour-pattern: jealousy. I recalled Auntie Vi passing comment that she felt this was one of the most destructive forces on the Reservation.

More songs and prayers in Lakota followed, sometimes to the heart-beat of the drum – fundamental rhythm of life – or the sudden, startling chatter of a rattle. Surrealistic, elongated shadows shifted and darted over the walls; the atmosphere was growing increasingly close and heavy.

Then something changed. It was as if a door had been opened and cooler air moved through the room. There was a few moments' silence.

"It's time for the prayers contained in the ties to be released." The medicine man's voice was gruff. "Don't be afraid of anything that might happen." The candles were extinguished.

A sceptical little inner voice sparked into life and began dismissing his words as theatrical suggestion and mocking this pseudo sweat-lodge where the only person sweating was the medicine man. It was not part of me I cared for.

A slow chant began, resonating hypnotically through the velvety darkness. Then a sudden rattling startled me. I sensed it came from the far side of the buffalo hide. Three more bursts of the rattle followed in swift succession, seeming to come from each of the other three corners. A softly-glowing light appeared; the colour and size of an apricot, it hovered above where I thought the buffalo skull lay, disappeared and immediately reappeared high in the centre of the room, close to the ceiling. There was another angry chatter of the rattle and the soft little light sped vertically downwards then shot six or eight feet to the side at about shoulder height, trailing faint phosphorescence. Then it returned to hover above the hide, where it began a sort of light-dance, weaving curving swoops, infinity-signs, arcs, circles and spirals before darting at high speed into a corner of the ceiling. It hung there for a fraction of a second, then blinked out.

Remorselessly, the chant and drum-beat continued.

If it had been some kind of flashlight, whoever was manipulating it was extraordinarily dextrous. And it was a miracle that no-one had been stepped on in the dark. Yet the three chanting voices sounded as if they were close together, physically.

Barely had these unwelcome thoughts zipped through my mind when two pale yellow-orange glows appeared, hugging the ceiling. Baleful, like wolf-eyes staring through the dark, they hung there; then the rattle chattered and suddenly they darted apart, looped and swooped around, back and forth; in synchrony, independently. It was as if they were playing with each other, dancing to the sound of the rattling.

If someone was working the little lights, he would have to have rubber-elastic arms. Then I realised two rattles were at work. One for each light? The chant wound on, sonorous, compelling.

Suddenly, one of the lights zoomed down from the far corner of the ceiling at high speed and passed directly in front of my face, leaving a bright streak imprinted on my after-vision. The irritating inner sceptic was silenced; there had been no movement of air, no sense of a human agent. I remembered Yellow Bear's tales of green glowing lights at the Winter Dance. The chant ended on the thud of an honour-beat and the glowing energies flicked out of existence.

There was a long, heavy silence, almost palpable in the pitch-darkness. I was glad of the warmth of the arms either side of me. Time dragged on. Nothing seemed to be happening; pins and needles prickled at my legs and I was just about to change position when a breath of soft, sweet air blew gently into my face.

Unable to stop myself, I extended one arm and tentatively swept it up and down and side to side, a little ashamed of my suspicion and more than a little apprehensive about what I would do if I did encounter a trouser leg or an arm, or a hand holding a feather.

There was nothing there, nothing physical at least; only empty space at my fingertips.

Again the soft, sweet breath of warmth puffed into my face, a little more strongly this time, lifting the fringe from my forehead in a playful way.

A cold rush ran up my body; every hair on my arms stood to attention. A sense I didn't know I had informed me that the something was slowly moving in a clockwise direction around the room. Others were perhaps being visited. If that was the right word for what was happening.

After some time, the voice of the medicine man broke the silence; speaking Lakota, what sounded like a long plea, heart-felt. When he finished, there was another long silence. Then he cried: "Mitakuye Oyasin!" and the overhead light was snapped on.

Like owls, we all sat blinking. I looked at the buffalo skull, a forcefully silent presence. The tobacco ties were gone.

"All the prayers were accepted," said the medicine man quietly. "I'm very pleased with how the whole ceremony went." He said a few words in Lakota; and it was over. Slowly the three men started to put away their things and people began to get up, stretch, massage their legs. Some went to speak to the spiritual leaders; others began to drift outside. An announcement was made about the date and location of the next yinipi.

Unable to move or speak, I felt rooted to the spot. Manny was equally still and silent; on my other side, Uncle Chuck stretched and grinned and silently showed me his watch: we had been sitting there for almost three hours. Aunt Aggie craned round him and with a little smile asked what I thought of it.

When I finally found a raspy voice, I hesitatingly told them of the magic of the little dancing lights and the weird little puffs of sweet, warm air.

"Eagle was here," said Uncle Chuck. "That was the brush of His wing you felt, when He took your prayers. I felt Him too."

Much as Uncle Chuck likes to tease, he does not stretch the truth or fantasise about things of spirit. Light-headed, thrilling in every atom, I closed my eyes. Something brushing against my foot made me start. It wasn't Eagle or Buffalo but Manny, pulling on his boots.

"Words don't do it justice, do they, Manny?" I said softly. For a moment, a deep connection between us was revisited. Looking me in the eye, he grinned, his dark eyes warm, crinkling at the corners. Then he touched the top of my head in an odd way and left.

Thinking about the ones who carry the eagle feather, I sat there for several more moments, feeling his departure as a loss. Then I remembered Louella's words and shrugged the feeling away. Concentrating on the mundane task of my own footwear brought me back into myself, and I felt I had to confess to Uncle Chuck: "You know, I was suspicious about that little puff of air in my face so I put out my hand, real surreptitious-like, and tested to see who was doing it. But there was nothing."

Uncle Chuck broke out into a peal of hearty laughter. "Same's me, when I first went to one of these ceremonies. An' I felt nothin', neither. Then when we went to leave, I couldn't find one of my socks, nowhere. I knew I'd put 'em in my shoes and I had the shoes right behind me the whole time, so nobody could've touched 'em. We even checked outside in case I dropped it. Aggie practic'ly took the car apart!

"When we got home an' Aggie shook out the blanket, well, there it was, folded up neatly inside. Inside," he emphasised, "there was the missin' sock. I had never opened up that blanket, not before nor after. So I guess those spirits were havin' the last laugh on me! They sure sneaked one over on me that time. We've been goin' to all of these ceremonies, ever since."

Even as I laughed, a strange chill ran through me. I realised I was afraid he would ask me to come to the next one with them, and I did not want to go through something like this again. Unsettled by my reaction, all the way back to Auntie Vi's I reflected on what it might mean. Grateful though I was to have experienced it – it had been fascinating and magical and protected by two friends, I had been free of the fear of "things" being thrown – I could not imagine going through a yinipi again. Or anything like it. Having finally seen for myself the lights, which may have been akin to the balls of energy of which Yellow Bear and Nadine had spoken, it did not seem to make any difference; I had believed in them anyway. But what were they? Where had they come from? What did they signify? Had they been manipulated? If so, how much control did the medicine man have over them?

Feeling increasingly uneasy, I remembered how I had promised myself not to enter into this kind of experience without personally knowing the motivation and people behind it. I could not understand how torn I felt, how pulled, this way and that. On the one hand, this great attraction to the Native American way of life, of which the spiritual ceremony was an integral part; on the other, it was as if it was being made clear to me that this kind of ritual was not for me. And as Auntie Vi pointed out, what did it mean, my prayers had been accepted by Eagle? What had I in fact accomplished? What remained? Why this emptiness, this yawning cavern within?

Uneasiness roiled deep in me, but I could not work out what was going on. I determined not to analyse it but to assist at least one of the prayer requests by putting all my energy into going for the teaching position.

REBIRTH

Swift the flight of Eagle: within less than a month, the children's dad was improving and I was contracted to coordinate the production of a local tourism directory (freelance, it would do in the meantime). I might have become a fully-fledged convert, except for one thing: the last tobacco-tie, containing a prayer for a new home – had it been dropped? With only five days left before I had to vacate the farmhouse and nothing found, imagining the new owners moving in and my belongings in a pile on the snow outside, I had no time for an unexpected visit by Bryan.

" ... And don't think you can stay here." That I could be forthright and not pussyfoot around like when we were a couple did not escape me. "I've got to keep driving the back-roads, speaking to people. I don't have time for you."

A friend would understand and go, even if he had driven all the way up from the coast. But no, he stood in the doorway, a smirk plastered across his face. Behind him, bright against the snow, stood a buttercup-yellow, fifties pick-up, newly restored. Wheeler-dealer, I thought; nothing changes.

"Why're you in such a panic?" he drawled languidly. "It'll all work out."

"Not by sitting round and jawing with you. I have to keep the energy moving. And I'm not in a panic."

"Calm down. It's gonna happen, you'll see."

The amused, supercilious look on his face irritated me. "A house'll fall out the sky? Sure. Go see Daystar. Yellow Bear. Tipi Doug. Any of them'd be pleased to visit with you."

"You're worrying needlessly."

"What do you know? Since when were you responsible for anyone besides yourself? Just leave." Somehow the anger didn't feel real, more like I was acting out an expected role. Coming as close as I ever had to rudeness, I began to close the door on him when something small and light swirled over the top of his head and into the house. Something which made me stop and hold out my hand, like on another memorable occasion. The little white feather settled on my palm, downy fronds trembling. There was no sign of a bird in the cloudless, cerulean sky. For several long seconds, neither of us moved.

Little Eagle-gift: a reminder to calmly accept the way things are unfolding.

"You see, you haven't got a thing to worry about; I don't know why you're making such a fuss!" Bryan chuckled.

"Easy for you to say!" I smarted, closing my fingers over the feather, appreciating that he had understood the message but still feeling I had to play the role through. A little more softly, I added: "Please just go now."

Watching his vehicle slither back down the hill through the melting snow, churning up great gobs of mud, I thought how the mess he was making of my pristine driveway was symbolic of the way he had of pushing my buttons and taking off, leaving me to sort out my mess. But that was how lessons were learned; there was no point in feeling angry. Even if we hadn't been able to manage a relationship, there was a strong karmic connection between us: extraordinary things had happened when we'd been together and I'd learned a great deal. Now a little white feather had manifested over the crown chakra of White Eagle. I decided to begin the day's search at the Duck Stop, with the faint hope that he might have gone there and I could treat him to a coffee by way of recompense. Only one customer was in the café, however, and no Bryan, but within twenty minutes, arrangements for our next home were in place.

Just south of Winlaw, where the highway begins a long, narrow, snaking passage between miles of steep rock-face and the Slocan River, a log building known as Robert's Restaurant had recently been up for sale. Some locals had tried to purchase it collectively as a community building, but a private buyer from Nelson had pre-empted them and was renting it out until he decided what to do with it. The lone customer in the Duck Stop was his tenant; knowing my predicament, the waitress suggested I talk to her and I learned she was vacating the place in three days' time. A little white feather was dancing in the forefront of my mind as I immediately phoned her landlord.

Moving a family into the ex-restaurant required some creative thinking. A skilled carpenter and joiner, within a couple of weeks the new owner had transformed the large restaurant kitchen into a bedroom and playroom, while I reinvented the bar as a kitchen and the original dining-room, a large, light, airy space punctuated by massive supporting logs the size of telegraph poles, as a spacious open-plan living-area. One corner I screened off with plants and stained-glass; overlooking a fabulous view of the river, this was my sleeping-area. An elevated platform (its original function impossible to fathom) served as a loft-bedroom, while the split-level undercroft, with its own entrance and view over the river, made a perfect teenager hang-out.

Built before the strictures of planning permission clamped down in the Valley in the eighties, the finest feature of Robert's (the name too ingrained in local psyche to change, even after the new owner would move in and alter the sign which advertised the previous function of the sprawling log building) was an enormous covered deck which ran the entire length of the building on the side facing the river. Screened at each end by birch and cottonwood, it looked out over the heart of the Valley; less than a hundred feet below, the river slid past like molten pewter, broad, shallow and fast, and curved away towards Cougar Rock. Cloaked as much in legend as springtime mists, massive, dark and foreboding, this local landmark squatted beneath forested slopes and rocky ridges, marking the beginning of the long climb to Frog Mountain, which could also be seen from the deck.

Foot in the mist, head in the clouds: White Wolf, great mystical barometer of prevailing moods in the Valley. Prodigal daughter, I had been brought back home.

Despite our many moves, the first night in the new location was unsettling. Early in the morning, a dragon thundered into my dreams, spitting bright amber. Jolted awake, I caught a glimpse of orange and yellow flashes as a massive articulated chip-truck thundered away into the darkness. My heart pounding, it seemed like I had barely fallen asleep again when a soulful, haunting shriek and leaden rumbling brought me back into the world. On the river-bank below, a freight-train trundled slow and heavy on its once-a-day journey from Slocan Forest Products – the saw-mill at Slocan City – to the pulp-mill at Castlegar.

Not only the name, but something of the historical function of the once-popular eatery lingered. En route for friends' errands up and down the Valley, again Robert's became busy as Grand Central Station and behind the buzz of conversation I sometimes imagined I could hear the ghostly clink and chink of cutlery and crockery. The accommodating deck became a place to sit and listen to the rustle of light-fingered birch-leaves, the prattle of a passing shower, while the great silvery sweep of water carried away worries, troubles, and pain.

Including my own. For this was where I began an active involvement in my journey of personal healing (a journey well underway, although I didn't appreciate it at the time), never guessing how deep this would take me, what – or whom – I would access and how drastically my life would change as a result. About three weeks after moving in, a recent arrival to the Valley phoned. Introducing herself as Ratna, a psychic and healer who had just returned from Australia after years spent studying with Barry Long, a spiritual leader and teacher, she told me she was interested in learning about the Native American life-way. Imagining what she was seeking was probably akin to my old romantic illusions, I agreed to meet her.

A statuesque Masai-warrior beauty was not what I anticipated, no more than she expected a blonde Celt. Yet we were immediately comfortable with each other, speaking a common language in terms of spirit and feeling a soul-mate connection. For her, I represented an avenue into personal contact with Native Americans; as a sanyasin and healer, she offered me the opportunity to go within and clear negative emotional patterning. Having come to understand that it was only myself holding me back from my true destiny with the Native people, I was certain that, arising when it did, this was exactly what should come next.

Sometimes I would wish I had let sleeping dogs (or Indians) lie, for once I accessed an intimation of the powerful influence underlying (perhaps motivating) my attraction to the Native American way of life, there was no turning back. Fired by emotional obsession, the next phase of my life would twist and turn through light and shadow, inner pain and turmoil, and the way that would eventually open up for me would turn out to be the last I expected.

Dynamic meditation; kundalini meditation … through Ratna, Osho's practice of vigorous body movement combined with toning became my daily morning and evening ritual; and whenever I felt tired or disenchanted, I would think of Uncle Chuck and Aunt Aggie and their seasonal back-to-back sweats. For over two weeks, twice a day I danced, jumped, toned and grunted, sweated and ached. Then one morning, close to the completion of a session, the distinct sensation of something hot, oily and black seeping out of me and down my thighs made me stop. I looked, but there was nothing to be seen. Nor could my fingers feel anything. Whatever it was, it had to be at a subtle level, which still felt horrible. I imagined it flowing down into the river, being carried away; Mother Earth taking care of whatever it was. After that experience, the meditations seemed to take less effort, as if I were somehow lighter, more energised.

A trained and accredited rebirthing practitioner, Ratna felt I was ready to experience this method of healing, which purports to take a person back to the "place of beginning", to uncover any hidden or sealed traumas that have given rise to negative or defensive behaviour-patterns – which prevent progress in the soul-journey – and release them, so a fresh start can be made.

The sessions took place at her cabin, in a darkened room made womb-like by heavy, deep-red velvet curtains. A few candles added to the atmosphere and incense-smoke curled into the shadows; inside a circle of clear and rose quartz crystals, luxurious cushions strewn on the floor acted as a therapeutic couch. In full lotus position, Ratna sat next to me, slim, dark and powerful, attuned herself to my frequency by holding her hands over my solar plexus and crown chakras, and launched the session.

Known as "chaotic breathing" – although nothing about the technique she used is chaotic; it is controlled, forced, rhythmic, repetitive, and extremely demanding – apparently a kind of hyperventilation, the method is supposed to facilitate a breakthrough into a state of altered consciousness where the necessary changes to or revisions in the subconscious can take place. As I soon experienced, however, one of the major obstacles is that such a state of near-oblivion requires a kind of mini-death of the ego, which of course fights like blazes for survival. Especially an unbalanced ego, which will resist any kind of change to the status quo.

All I had to do was match her breathing and keep it going, but the concentration required was immense; the will, the most powerful I could muster. Before long, I felt like I was going to be sick, then that I would die, a belief so powerful I had to stop. Nor could I start again. In fact, everything in me screamed never to try this again. If it had not been for curiosity, and the strength of my desire to find out what seemed to have me in its grip, keeping me from realising my hopes and dreams, I probably would have given up. But I forced myself to return, even though I dreaded the sessions. Ratna persisted with me; guiding, assisting, holding the energy.

Eventually I managed to stay with the breathing and pass through the dizziness and the nausea, and override the panicked death-clamour of the ego. It was as if a door closed behind me, and I accessed the depths – or heights – of a vibrant state of non-being, an incredible combination of disassociation, peace, sensitivity. Part of me realised it was finally happening; a far-distant part, awed and observing, as an incredible electric tingling replaced my hands and arms. Whatever they had become seemed to float up and over me; my fingers become laser-beams, pulsing rays of piercing white light. Wonderingly, I let them have their way and they turned on me, towards the place of my upper body, which I "saw" as a network of black filaments, in places throbbing livid lava-red: places, I sensed, needing attention of the white light. Sure enough, the intense beams exploded the redness: I could feel a heat and an aching that I somehow knew was a restoring and healing.

For a timeless while, the beams focussed and blasted, then swept, widespread laser-digits, lower down over my body electric, over heart and abdomen. There was a violent sort of convulsion-implosion, and an image began to take shape in my mind's eye.

A dark place; glowing embers. Briefly, a waft of a sour smell.

Peripheral vision: my right arm. But mine-not-mine: thin, sinewy, grimy, burnished copper, dark-freckled. A grey rope of filthy, matted hair, coarse as hemp, trailing down over....

In the further darkness, a difference: a break in the uniformity, like a sneer. Beyond, a prickle of stars....

From not-knowing-where within, I felt a welling; my jaw tensed and from me-not-me keened a wail, tearing at my hearing. Observer-I listened as heart-break began to out-pour: a strangely beautiful crying-chant that made my chest ache. In the vast space of my lower abdomen blossomed a burning sensation; not acid but fire, it spread downwards and to my horror, felt as if it were oozing from my vagina. More real and intense than anything I had experienced during the dynamic meditation, the part of me observing was convinced I was prematurely and heavily beginning to menstruate. Concerned for Ratna's fabulous cushions, I put my hands over my groin area to check.

The sensation fled, the images dissolved. There was nothing at my groin, I-me was simply lying on the floor, feeling exhausted, limp, sort of one-dimensional....

Not one to interpret the experience of another, Ratna left it for me to marvel at, to work through. The only possible explanation seemed to be that I had gone back further than my own birth (which was what I had sort of been anticipating), and visited another time, another self. Knowing my fertile imagination, however, I couldn't be sure whether it might not be simply a fantasy, some kind of day-dream. Yet the images had been so vivid and unusual, the feelings so powerful, and the strange fragment of chant totally unexpected.

Feeling like I was approaching the edge of a precipice, wanting to look over but too afraid, I found myself unable to countenance another rebirthing session. Little did I know that an irrevocable process was underway.

SPIRIT-WALKER

A few days later, I was woken by creaking noise. Someone was pushing open the heavy front door of our new home (the ex-restaurant had a double entrance, carved by hand from solid cedar, which pre-announced any visitor). Since it was still a time and a place of unlocked doors and I was expecting a friend for lunch, I was not concerned. Although eight in the morning was early for lunch.

"Anybody here?"

It was not the voice I was expecting, or one I recognised. "Just a minute," I called, hastily pulling on some clothes before going round to the lobby.

A youngish man, Native American, was uncertainly holding open the inner door. He looked vaguely familiar, and I assumed he must be one of the Arrow Lakes descendants I had met in passing at Band meetings. "Hi! Come on in; you're welcome.... My name's Celia," I added, to save him embarrassment if he had forgotten. "Come in, I'll put coffee on."

Frowning, he took a tentative step inside and rasped: "This a restaurant?"

It dawned on me that I had just invited a total stranger into my home. In his late twenties or early thirties, his round face weathered, he looked pale and tired, like his clothes: faded jeans thin at the knees; boots scuffed and worn; a thin sweater, crumpled and moth-eaten, wisps of dried grass clinging to it. Trailing over his shoulders, his shoulder-length, black hair was damp and matted, entangled with bits of grass. Whoever he was, he had been sleeping rough. And he was shivering. It was late spring; the nights were still cold and the mornings heavily-dewed, especially on the west-facing side of the valley. My nurturing instincts took over.

Or was it some deeper intuition, about the way Native Americans tended to appear in my life and profoundly affect it? It never crossed my mind to be afraid or even cautious.

"It used to be, but it's not anymore," I answered lightly, adding with a grin: "In fact, it's way better, because you get to eat and there's no bill! Come on in."

I never thought how bizarre I must have sounded. Clearly bewildered, he limped inside, arms wrapped round himself, and in a dull monotone told me how he had been walking up the highway, which is narrow and winding for some two miles south of Robert's, and the wing-mirror of a passing car had clipped his elbow. Pushing back a frayed cuff, he showed me the swollen, discoloured injury. Nothing seemed broken, but it looked painful.

"That's terrible. Didn't the guy stop?" I said, appalled. "Ice. I'll get ice. It'll reduce the pain and swelling."

"'S nothin'." Shuffling his feet, he uneasily shrugged away my concern, his eyes shifting like a trapped wild creature's, putting me in mind of the wolf, Two Socks, in the film "Dances with Wolves", which had recently come out on general release.

"Come; sit here." I showed him to the rocking chair which looked out over the stupendous view of the river, mountains and Cougar Rock, and went to get him a blanket (green, bought at a pow-wow after Auntie Vi told me the story of Green Blanket) and a hot-water bottle. As the kettle boiled for coffee, I noticed he was looking round the room and seemed to be relaxing, maybe because he was warming up, or because of what he was seeing.

The immense room was practically a gallery dedicated to the Native American. Hanging on one wall was a Biederlack blanket, earth-hued, depicting the head and upper body of a Native elder, two upright eagle feathers in his hair, his corrugated brow and lined, noble face reflecting suffering and wisdom. Behind him, a golden eagle gazed sternly into the distance; below was depicted a small tipi encampment. Next to the blanket were two antique portraits by A. Sherriff Scott: a Blackfoot chief and a Stoney warrior. Another wall was filled with fabulous sepia prints of Native American portraits, taken by Edward Sheriff Curtis at the turn of the century. There was also a framed enlargement of the mystical spirit-photo taken on Hayes Island; a painting of a grey wolf racing across a creek; a print of a bald eagle regally perched on the branch of a skeletal tree above a steel-blue lake, with snow-capped mountains beyond. On the window-ledges were stone-people, shells, feathers, crystals, interestingly-shaped pieces of wood.

"Slept in a barn last night. My name's Michael," he volunteered. "Come into this area at Castlegar. In three days of walkin', only one ride. The guy who dropped me off last night, south of here, he told me there was a restaurant up this way. Gave me a couple of bucks."

"That'd be the Duck Stop, it's about a mile further north." A thought struck me: "What kind of vehicle was the guy who dropped you off driving?"

From his description of a battered white Volkswagen van and a bearded driver, my intuition was borne out: Barry, Marilyn's quiet, sensitive husband. Our friendship may have collapsed but our hearts were basically in the same place.

"Saw the flag in your window, thought this must be the place," Michael continued, indicating the Stars and Stripes which covered the only window which faced the highway. It had an added touch: the design was painted over with a traditionally-dressed Native man holding a ceremonial pipe. I had hung it there as a personal, political statement about Native American rights, as much as a shield against fire-breathing chip-trucks. A Canadian flag, red maple leaf similarly overlaid by a Native American warrior on a pony, hung outside on the deck.

"You were more right than you knew." Warned that the flags might attract negative attention, I was gratified by this positive effect. "And right now, a Rez breakfast's coming up."

Although not a strict vegetarian, I rarely had bacon or even eggs in the house but sometimes Nick and I had cravings for a breakfast like the ones we often enjoyed at Auntie Vi's. As familiar, delicious smells began to waft through the room, Michael got up, put the hot-water bottle on the kitchen counter and helped himself to a refill of coffee, seeming increasingly at ease as he inspected the picture-gallery. When we sat down to eat, even though he was obviously ravenous, he did not wolf down the food but ate slowly, thoughtfully. Barely halfway through, he put down his fork and gazed out the window for several minutes, still and silent. I sipped my coffee, waiting.

"Been three days in this valley," he said slowly. "There was six eagles that circled the place where I entered." His hand gracefully indicated the south. "Six eagles.... They was there a long time, so I thought to stay awhile."

Every atom in my being was alert and thrilling. Six eagles. I had never seen more than a pair, except for that one unforgettable time: the gathering of eagles. A six-fold connection to the Great

Spirit. Who was this man? Why had he come here, now? Directed, guided by eagles; what did he have to do with this area?

Dreamily, Michael's dark eyes wandered across the beautiful landscape beyond the glass. "These mountains, this river; they speak to me." It was like he was in a trance. And I was joining him, his words touching the part of my soul that it seemed only the Native American tradition could reach. "I see here no cars. No houses. No roads. Some tipis maybe.... People livin' in harmony."

Every hair on my body was standing to attention. Had he plugged into a vision akin to the one Bob and I had once shared?

"Last night, down there, in the barn, I had a dream. There was a mountain, just like the one over there." He indicated the range beyond the salmon-back curve of the river. "This mountain, it was hollow. A hollow, empty mountain." Gently, sadly, he shook his head. "So I could only think, to take all the cars an' fill the mountain up with all those cars.... I don't know. What would you fill a mountain with?"

I shrugged. Once I had been filled with the heady excitement of working toward fulfilling a vision, and now I felt as empty as that mountain. What was this about?

After a silent while, Michael resumed eating. When his plate was clean, he said in a normal tone of voice: "I like this area, this river, this land. Think I'd like to stick around a day or two."

Finding my tongue again, I told him about the Arrow Lakes descendants returning to take up residence in their ancestral village in Vallican, ten minutes' drive to the south. "Maybe it's the kind of place you meant. Some of the people there have good ideas," I said tentatively. "We could go visit."

I could have kicked myself. What was I doing? My reception would be doubtful and probably contaminate anyone I brought. But I had a strong sense that Michael must be some kind of key: a new player who would affect things in an as-yet unknown way. Surely he had not shown up at my home in this unusual way by chance, to simply move on again?

Of course not; he had been directed by six eagles.

It was as if he had heard not a word of what I said, which in a way was a relief. He indicated a picture on the wall. "One of my people, there. I'm a Stoney. From the Hobema Reserve. You heard of it?"

The portrait was one of a pair I had brought from Rose (of Rose's Restaurant): the beginning of the collection. I shook my head, taking in anew the strong profile, the hooked nose, determined mouth, the lock of hair tied in the middle of the warrior's forehead.

"Alberta," he explained. "My family's still there, but my ma's in Edmonton now. I like to travel, move round a lot. Work where I can, to get by." He got up, walked to the wall and spent several minutes looking closely at each of the pictures. Then he sat down again and ate a second helping. Too excited to eat, I told him a little about my background. When he had finished eating, he pulled a battered wallet out of his back pocket, from which he extracted several pieces of tightly-folded paper which he carefully opened out, smoothed flat and handed to me.

Spidery, tentative scrawls, faded at the folds: a set of poems. One was about breaking up with the love of his life; sensitive and passionate, it moved me deeply. Reading it over a second time, however, I realised there was more to it than a lost love: it was a metaphor for loss of heritage, loss of connection to Mother Earth. Another poem walked a road and spoke of the landscape through which the feet were travelling, seen with the eyes of an old man who remembered when there had been no road there at all. The quality of writing was superb.

"It's the poets who get it right," I said softly, feeling privileged to be sharing such an intimate part of the inner workings of this relative stranger. We had come a long way since he had walked, hunched and shivering, into my home; I was sure there had to be some connection with the Lakes people, with the Indian village. "These people at the Indian village I told you about," I tried again, "they're mostly from the Colville Reservation. D'you know anyone from there?"

"Yeah. I feel a strong connection to south of the line, to the Colvilles."

Now we seemed to be getting somewhere. Was he saying he had relatives there, or was it something more subtle?

"It's my dream," he added slowly. (This is it, I thought; here it comes: what's really going on.) "...To travel, write, be a photographer.... All them beautiful Indians out there.... With my girl. She's called Joanna."

"Not the one in the poem, then?" I managed to keep my disappointment under wraps. It was not that he had a girlfriend, but the revisiting of an old fantasy: Manny's dream.

Shaking his head with a gentle smile, Michael continued to talk about his plans and his woman, but I could not listen, bound up with a cynical voice in my head commenting on disappearing Indians and evaporated dreams. When he finished talking, I managed to keep my voice neutral: "I hope you do it. Travel, I mean, and write about your people and photograph them. Don't get sidetracked. Commit to it. Realise your dream."

There was no point in saying anything else. I was beginning to sense that despite my concern about how the traditional wisdom was being lost (I still had a lot to learn on that score), I was being gently told that this intimate task was for the Native people themselves.

Michael (I never thought to ask his Indian name) went out onto the deck. Feeling he wanted to be alone out there, I cleared up the dishes. When he came back in, he said in a new tone of voice, friendly, teasing: "I'm gonna send you some wolf-ties when I get back home."

I had only recently decided to grow my hair long. Tugging at my layered locks, I said: "What makes you think I need any?"

"You're the type goes out an' gets things done. Wolf-spirit." His eyes, dark, shining berries, met mine briefly and several of those strange out-of-time moments followed, then my mind kicked in: he had been out on the deck, looking down the Valley. But I had not said a word about the spirit-name of Frog Mountain, or about Sky-Wolf. "Woman like you, on her own, you oughta have a wolf-dog to protect you." He chuckled, and things slotted back to near-normal. "Maybe get you one of them, too."

Unable to tell him that I already felt wolf-guided, wolf-protected, I busied myself wiping down counter-tops. I was just beginning to grasp the understanding that Wolf represented a part of myself, an aspect of consciousness with which I needed to get in touch. How could he have become aware of that? While Michael took a shower, I made up my mind to invite him to stay a couple of days. The timing lent itself: not only was my job freelance, but the younger children were spending a few days with their father. Even if we didn't go to the Indian village, there were other sites I could show him.

I was about to suggest this, when the front doors crashed open and in walked the friend I had been expecting for lunch. More than a little irritated to find our arrangement forgotten and that I was engrossed in an unkempt Native American stranger, Andre was not interested in joining our conversation and went off for a walk while I prepared lunch. What I allowed to happen when he returned will always haunt me.

Before I understood what was happening, Andre had given his classy, thick wool sweater to Michael, put a couple of sandwiches into his hand and was escorting him firmly to the door. "I'll give you a ride a few miles up the Valley, to help you on your way."

Surprised that Michael wanted to move on already, I guessed I must have missed something. Andre seemed in a hurry; as he was shepherded out, Michael looked back at me. "I'll call you." He cocked his head in the direction of Andre and wryly added: "He even looks like a father!"

Mind blank, I was left in the kitchen, frozen into place as Andre's car revved up and sped away, and Michael's parting words sank in. The white t-shirt peeking from the neck of Andre's sweater had looked like a dog-collar, and he did have something of a priestly demeanour in the round shape of his pale face, his thinning, combed-back hair and dark-framed glasses. And priests had a proven history of pushing Native people around. Or, on another level, Andre had dispensed of my Native visitor in the controlling manner of a disapproving parent.

How could I have let it happen? I felt nauseous, as if something had been ripped out from inside me, as if something vital had been snatched away. Berating myself for my slow reaction, by the time Andre returned, I was deeply, almost unspeakably angry, feelings which he dismissed as a big fuss about nothing. The thought entered my head to go out and drive after Michael and bring him back, but I felt enervated, like I was moving through quicksand, and stayed in a kind of limbo as the rest of the day slid by.

Gradually, I realised that once again I had allowed my feelings to be dismissed: a giving-away of power that was not only part of my negative emotional patterning but also threatened the essential feminine part of myself in a fundamental way. My discomfort cracked open the fault-lines of a friendship brought about through Bob. Andre's long-standing ambition had been to create a wilderness school and he claimed to value the teachings of the Native American way of life, but that day it dawned on me that respect for the Native people themselves seemed sadly lacking. In turn, as a budding psychologist, he claimed my way of thinking was obsessive, romantic, idealistic nonsense: "You put Native people on a pedestal."

What I came to look upon as an impulsive, selfish action, camouflaged by the seemingly-generous giveaway of the sweater and a ride up the Valley, sounded a death-knell to our friendship. Nevertheless, his observation would prove uncomfortably close to the mark.

Over the following days, I thought often of Michael. Not only was it a long stretch from the West Kootenays to Edmonton but further north up the Valley lived and worked people who were not at all tolerant of Native Americans, some of whom had violently exhibited their prejudice both during and since the Vallican confrontation. He had left his mother's Edmonton address and taken down my phone number, saying he would get in touch sometime. After a couple of weeks, I thought I would drop him a line at his mother's to make sure he had made it safely and apologise for what had happened.

It was a warm, sunny afternoon. I was out on the deck and had barely started writing the letter, when I was interrupted by a knocking on the door. Two Arrow Lakes visitors from the Indian village was the last thing I expected. One of them I knew fairly well, as he was a friend of Mickey and Elizabeth: Francis, the Arrow Lakes' hereditary chief who had presided over the reburial of the ancestral remains.

"We never had no chiefs; more a referee. Decisions were made all together, like a family discussion," Auntie Vi had told me. Disdainful of a title which she held to be the white man's fabrication, she was more inclined to align with John, the hereditary chief who, in tandem with Bob's mother, had originally requested the return of the ancestral remains. Despite her concerns about Francis' colourful past, however, the quietly-spoken elder had often acted as an able diplomat when local feathers were ruffled. A small, slim, dapper man, with silvering hair combed sleekly back and something of a South American look, he was charming and effusive, probably had been something of a rogue and was still a bit of a ladies' man.

With him was a relatively recent arrival at the Indian village, who was swiftly proving himself active and dedicated, and showing signs of leadership. Robert had always seemed to keep his distance, however, clamming up whenever I was around. In his thirties, tall and lean, fairly good-looking with dark skin and long, thick, black braids, he seemed uneasy in my home and I wondered why Francis had brought him.

Thinking of the simple life at the village, I offered them the use of the shower as I prepared coffee. Somewhere in the watershed above, I had guessed there were hot-springs, as the tap-water reeked of sulphur. This usually elicited a series of amused comments but Robert said not one word. Cool and distant, his gaze skidded over me as if I was not there, not even when we were sitting out on the deck with the awesome view of river and mountains laid out before us. Frances chatted and joked; he was clearly trying to build bridges. I was grateful when the shrill insistence of the phone called me inside.

The voice was female, impersonal: "I have a collect call for ... ermm, Cecile? From a ... Michael. Will you accept the charges?"

It was Archangel Michael who flashed into my mind: a sweep of mighty feathered wings and slash of a great, glowing blue sword. Then I recollected: Michael.

"Woman!" he broke in on my acceptance. "Quit your worryin'! You're heavy on my spirit. You knew I would call. I said it."

Heavy on his spirit: what an amazing concept. How wonderful, how incredible he should have been sensing my concern. But to be heavy was the last thing I wanted. "It's just that I know what people can be like round here.... But the worst thing was how I let you be driven off."

"It's all fine. I walked two, three days an' many miles. Bears walked behind me, they warned me 'bout the cars. I knew the Great Spirit was puttin' strength at my back."

I closed my eyes, thrilling to the poetry of his words. Bear represented the power of going within: intuitive energy.

"Took me near a week to get to Calgary," he continued. "There was no trouble. But now I'm here, I got work to do. I'm goin' to care for some sisters in Edmonton that're bein' taught to sell themselves by white women."

"That's terrible…"

"Listen. Listen to the thunder."

At that exact moment, thunder crackled and rumbled above the house. Goosebumps ran rampant down my arms, my body. "I hear it," I whispered, looking out the window. Fluffy, dove-grey clouds; patches of soft-spring-blue sky. The thunder had no source I could see.

"In that thunder, I hear the pain of my people." His voice was dark, deeply pained.

As if suspended on the edge of some other reality, my mind empty, I looked into the sky and for a long while, silence lay between us.

"Fly up there, up above the eagles." It was as if he were seeing through my eyes. Softly, compelling: "Your mind is powerful. You can be above the eagles if you really put your mind to it."

Slowly, queasily, clouds began to swirl and churn, and before my incredulous eyes, an image formed: a great buffalo head, horned and bearded. It melted away, and was slowly replaced by a dark, prancing horse. Then the dignified, powerful profile of a Native American elder ... and another, and another. The atmosphere was pregnant, heavily poised, as if other dimensions were pressing against unseen portals.

"D'you know what a spirit-walker is?"

Thrilling, somehow I knew exactly what it was, from some ancient Knowing, deep within. I heard my voice speak: "Tell me."

His voice seemed to float through the wires, confirming that deep Knowing: "My spirit never sleeps. When my body sleeps, my spirit goes out. Know that I'll watch over you always.... I don't tell my dreams to many people."

He was gone. Hanging blindly onto the white plastic message-carrier, I stood at the window, a thundering like stampeding buffalo in my ears, barely on the ground at all.

Whose dream was I in? What was going on? How come the thunder had happened just as he told me to listen? Had he done that? What did it mean: "be above the eagles"? And the cloud-images, where had they come from? Created by a spirit-walker? Thunder Beings? Several long minutes passed before I was able to pull myself together and return to my two guests, who seemed to sense something and simply waited in silence. It was a while before I could bring myself to speak and when I did, the whole story of Michael came tumbling out. At the end, I indicated the sheet of paper lying on the little table. "In fact, I was just dropping the guy a line when you arrived.... Isn't it weird? I never realised that what you might be thinking about someone might actually affect them." Embarrassed at babbling like a brook, I went back inside to make fresh coffee.

To my surprise, Robert followed me in and sat down on a kitchen stool as I busied myself in the kitchen. "I'm from Washington State originally," he said, tossing back the heavy, wet weight of his single, long black braid. "Married a Kutenai woman. Well, that didn't really work out...." He chuckled, then began to tell me of some of the places he'd lived and things he'd done, circling deeper into his cultural knowledge and experience. After his coolness, it was weird to have him sitting there telling me all this; added to the buzzing in my ears and Michael on my mind, it was hard to pay attention.

" ... Prophecy about the comin' of the white people was fulfilled." Hearing these words, I was reeled back in. "My great-aunt, she told me: 'D'you think our forefathers didn't know what was happenin' two thousand years ago? When the skies turned dark over there, they turned dark over the whole world.' The whole world," he stressed. "'They knew they was slippin' off the Way,' she told me, 'an' they knew they had to wait for the White Brother to bring the new teachin's.' Only," he chuckled, "by the time they got here, it'd become Christianity.... Better to call it Crosstianity!" We both laughed.

When they finally left, a meal and many coffees later, the older man was beaming. On the way out, Robert shook my hand and said that as far as he was concerned, anytime I wanted to visit or bring anyone to the village, I would be welcome.

There was no more thunder that day. Nor did the weather change. Through one out-of-the-blue phone call, everything had changed. It was like Archangel Michael's great sword had cut through all the dross. And a spirit-walker was watching over me; one whose spirit I had to be careful not to weigh down.... Had what I said about the effect of the power of thought touched something in Robert? The synchronicity of Michael's phone-call had accomplished more than I could have imagined. Was this what the whole episode had really been about? Including his being driven away? Was the Indian village about to become part of my life again?

Why did the thought not excite me at all?

BROTHERS IN SPIRIT

Like the ghost-memory of a missing limb, the Indian village haunted the edges of my mind but despite Robert's reassurance, I couldn't bring myself to go there. I couldn't understand myself; even though it was now in the hands and under the feet of its own people, which had been the whole point, I still felt I needed to go there, yet couldn't, even though given the all-clear. Why should I still feel as if it were calling me?

For as long as anyone could remember, spiritual people had been visiting the Indian village. I'd heard how they mostly came and slipped away unseen, and had eventually encountered a group in the early days of working for the Society. After spending a day studying the site using the archaeologist's map, I had been returning to my van when two battered, rusting old gas-guzzlers rolled up and parked on the roadside. Protective of the site, which was still subject to visits by the occasional souvenir-seeker, I noted Albertan licence-plates and watched as six or seven Native men climbed out, some of them carrying small bundles. Heart in mouth, using my new official position, I asked if they needed any help. They stopped and looked at me, not threateningly, but in an amusedly-tolerant way.

"We been comin' to pray in this sacred place for many years," offered a small, bow-legged, heavy-bellied, wizened-faced elder with long, straggling grey hair. "You can join the pipe-ceremony, if you want."

Moved by the ready invitation, I'd followed the little group through the trees to, of all places, the burial-ground terrace I had just left, the area where I liked to pray and meditate. Carefully and in silence, on the same spot where the altar would later be consecrated, they set out their medicine items: feathers, stones, small pouches. Reverentially unwrapping a hide-bound bundle, the elder began to lay out certain items and I belatedly realised he was a pipe-carrier. He fitted the red-clay bowl of the pipe onto a slender wooden stem, and, holding it in his left hand, took a pinch of herb, blessed it and packed it into the bowl. When it was lit, he offered it to seven directions: North, East, South, West, Mother Earth, Father Sky and Spirit Within. Not that I understood what he was saying; the language that rolled off his tongue, smooth and rich-toned, was unknown to me. Turning the bowl round once clockwise, he passed it to the person on his left; by the time it came round to me, I knew I had to hold the bowl in my left hand (closest to the heart) and the stem in my right, inhale the smoke and pass the pipe on in the same, circular motion. When it had turned full circle, more prayers were spoken. But for the soft murmur of an ancient language, there was no sound; below, the river silently rushed by, glassy-green; behind us, the burial-ground area seemed to shimmer, a softly-breathing presence....

Heading back to the vehicles, I'd mentioned that Bob had recently camped there with his mother and that the Arrow Lakes descendants were at last coming home. The pipe-carrier's eyes twinkled at me from under the turquoise bandanna wrapped around his forehead: "What d'you think we bin prayin' for, all these years?"

Dumbfounded, I had watched as they piled into their cars and roared off. The site had been a spiritual focus for a long time. I wondered how many other people were anonymously contributing to righting an old wrong, and on what levels.

The Indian village had an obvious spiritual magnetism. Not long after Frances and Robert's visit, I heard from a meditation group in Nelson that, as part of a 1991 World Tour, a high-ranking Tibetan Rimpoche and his entourage had requested an audience with the Lakes descendants on their ancestral land, and wished to join with them in praying for world peace. I remembered Bob at a crucial meeting a seeming aeon ago, saying the Creator intended people to come together to pray, whatever their faith; how combining energies of positive spiritual intent is the most powerful form of action. The attraction of such a potent equation as Tibetan and Native American spirituality was irresistible.

It reminded me of the sacred Tibetan ceremony I had seen televised in England the previous year. For the first time in history, a Belgian film-crew had been invited into the mountains of Tibet to record this rite, the key part of which enacted the slaying of a despotic ruler by a priest, the karma of this murderous act balanced by the fact that an entire people were freed from tyranny. Fascinated that the Dance of Shiva had been opened up to the world at this time, I wondered how many in the west had seen the elaborately-costumed, masked dancers, the intricate steps, the electrifying act, normally witnessed only by local villagers.[24] According to prophecy, at the time of Earth Changes, all secret, sacred tradition would be opened up to the world; by broadcasting this ceremony, awareness of the energy of Shiva, creator and destroyer (Judgement Day god?), had been released into global consciousness.

On the day scheduled for the gathering, concerned about the attitude of the more militant Lakes people who would no doubt be there and that I might be turned away, or worse, I drifted up the Valley in my van, waiting for some universal wind to direct me. Reaching the Duck Stop, I noticed Tom's van parked outside. The Lakes pipe-carrier was inside, with Yellow Bear. "You goin' then?" Tom asked.

I was privately wondering why he was: as far as I knew he had had nothing to do with the ancestral site in Vallican, a lack of involvement which perplexed me. "I don't know. I'd like to, but I don't know if certain people there'd-"

"Celia...." Yellow Bear interrupted, shaking his head.

With a gentle smile, Tom said, "It's time to put the past behind you. Though if your spirit isn't up to it...."

He knew me well enough to know what fired me. But by the time I came to a decision, they had gone on ahead.

The disputed road by the Indian village had long been in use, but I had avoided using it out of some misplaced sense of loyalty to a cause long gone. Fortunately, Coyote did not arrange for my van to get stuck in a rut on this virgin passage, to metaphorically point out my foolishness. Unpaved, little more than a dirt-road, it seemed ugly, intrusive. A billowing cloud of dust followed my slow progress; the promised natural barriers to protect the site from noise and dust-pollution

---

24 Struck by the similarity of facial features between Tibetan and some Native American peoples, I was reminded of Bob stressing that his people had originally come from the south, overturning the academic theory that access had been via the land-bridge which once existed at the Bering Straits. I also was privy to elders speaking of habitation of the North American Continent in terms of time-scales in excess of five hundred thousand years.

were unsurprisingly nowhere to be seen. Ghostly conical shapes were just visible among the shadowy trees. I counted five tipis. The Indian village had grown.

Parking on the roadside, I walked along the sandy track that led to the encampment, an achingly-familiar trail between the pines. As I approached the lone tipi that acted as a sort of sentinel, a dozen children erupted out of its shadowy interior and clustered around me, chattering and giggling. I knew them all, local and Lakes. A ten-year-old Lakes girl grasped my hand excitedly and clung to it, as the others exuberantly bubbled over with questions. Knowing they had to be picking up the energy of the impending event, on impulse I reached in my shoulder bag and pulled out a gnarled piece of root.

The children fell silent. Most of them were familiar with bitter-tasting rat-root, regularly gifted Northern Lights by a pipe-carrier from Alberta. A recognised blood-purifier, rat-root had become part of the opening ritual of the drum: tiny pieces were chewed to clear the throat and strengthen the voice. Producing my Native-crafted knife, which always caught children's attention since the haft is made from the mandible of a fox, complete with teeth, I sliced off chips of root. "I ask your permission to enter this sacred place," I said solemnly, making the offering to the children.

It was a spontaneous gesture, probably based on one of the many things I had learned about sacred landscape pilgrimage the previous year in England: the approach to a sacred site has three gateways. These might take the form of actual gates – one site we visited had three farm gates to negotiate – or something natural, such as two trees "coincidentally" growing in three successive locations either side of an approach pathway. In Northumbria, gateway trees were consistently rowan and ash, which symbolise male and female energies. Sometimes there was a more subtle, mixed-bag sense of passage, such as a stile to climb over, a stream to cross, a boggy marsh to negotiate. Offering something personal like a few strands of hair, or some cheese, apparently a favourite of the fairies (what they made of a pinch of tobacco, I shall never know, but little people are little people everywhere), permission to pass would be respectfully requested.

These little gatekeepers solemnly accepted my offering, and, screwing up their faces at the dry bitterness of the root, clamoured approval of my entry. Taking my hands, they escorted me as far as the fence-posts that demarcated the entrance to the encampment and skipped happily away.

There was no-one nearby and I was intimately familiar with the area, but I hesitated. Before me was the shadowy clearing that had become the heart of the camp, three years ago. A lot of water had flowed under the new bridge over the Little Slocan since then. Melanie's little trailer was in the same place; like dignified royalty, not five but six tipis marked time among the pines. As for the little camp-kitchen, it had mushroomed into a huge area with tables and chairs, roofed over with immense canvas awnings.

Three turns round the sun, since I had sat here with Manny and almost lost myself; two turns since the emotional prayer circle of Arrow Lakes women on their first visit to their ancestral village; one turn since I had lived here myself, in one of these very tipis, and felt at peace for a while.

It was two turns round the sun since I had recognised and marvelled at the pale azure drift of camas flowers among the sparse grass in the clearing, one of only three beds I knew of in the Valley. Another was part of the burial-grounds and the third was near the local schools in Crescent Valley, once site of another Lakes settlement. But this one, where I had walked barefoot out of respect, was now bereft of any natural life, the earth naked and packed solid by the passage of vehicles and many pairs of shod feet. Sadness and something not far from anger filled me.

Fully aware I had no right to lay my feelings or judgement over what was happening here, I allowed myself to be comforted by the knowledge that those little bulbs would lie dormant and again reveal their beauty when the heavy, thoughtless, human feet had passed on. Lost in contemplation, I didn't notice Bob approaching.

Unexpectedly confronted with a warm greeting from the man who had so powerfully affected my life, I felt betrayed by the strength of the familiar reaction in my solar plexus, as powerful as the early days. Time had not purged it from me after all. I managed to keep my hand steady as he shook it, although the smooth warmth of his skin spoke to mine in a way I would rather not have experienced. We talked for a while, lightly, and it was almost like back in the beginning, except a new latticework of lines was evident on his still-handsome face and many were the silvery glints in his black hair. I wondered if I should resurrect the only vision that had any lasting relevance to me – a place where people might live communally, in harmony – but before I could broach the subject, his mother called him away with some pressing concern about the impending visitors. He excused himself and was gone.

For several moments I kicked my romantic self, but at least I knew I had arrived before the Tibetans. I hesitated about what to do next, then it struck me that Bob's unanticipated, warm welcome served as a second gateway.

I had only taken a few steps when a small cavalcade of cars slowly rolled in. The lead car pulled up beside me, driven by Terry, an English member of the Nelson-based meditation group. Recognising me, he wound down his window to ask if this was a good place to park.

Within seconds, the area was full of small, tanned men with smooth-shaven heads, their robes of saffron and dusky red-orange a bright statement in the green gloom, their dark, almond-shaped eyes sparkling as they looked around, smiling and chattering. One of the monks began speaking to me at an incredible speed in an utterly foreign tongue, bowing and smiling widely. Instinctively I bowed in response, and it dawned on me that he was introducing the older, bespectacled man beside him, the venerable teacher, the Rimpoche himself. Smiling, we extended hands simultaneously and I bowed again, thrilled to the core to be first to welcome these venerated spiritual guests to this most sacred place. As the group began to make their way towards the kitchen area, leaving me behind in a sort of suspended state, it struck me I had just experienced the third gateway. Feeling a genuine sense of release, I followed.

Catching up with the holy-men, who had stopped to warmly greet the children and hand out candies and lollipops extracted from within the depths of their robes, I saw the large group of adults, Native and non-Native, who were waiting for them at the central campfire. The monks took their time; some of them knew the names of the children and I learned that these monks had been here the year before. They had not forgotten one name. Several adults left the main group and came over to shepherd them away from the little people. I could not help thinking that the monks seemed happiest with the children, which to me reflected a high level of consciousness.

Guessing that introductions were to be made at the central fire area, where I could see Bob and his mother and other Lakes elders, I held back. I had never been comfortable in crowds and imagined the rest of the happenings would be lost in the melee. In this way, I unwittingly placed myself in a unique situation to witness what happened next.

Some eight or nine people, Native and non-Native, were escorting the Rimpoche toward the campfire. Off to one side, over a hundred feet away and well apart from the main group, stood Tom and Yellow Bear. After being led for a few steps, the venerable old Tibetan master was suddenly free of guiding hands and independently veering away. Unerringly, he zeroed in on the Lakes pipe-carrier. As if pulled by a magnet, the others followed in a stream. Cameras clicked and flashed as the two men shook hands, smiling and nodding at each other. Left behind by this sudden diversion, the interpreter came rushing up and pushed his way through.

As he made the introductions, I knew I had just witnessed a powerful recognition of like to like, but had no time to dwell on it. I was just realising that the two spiritual leaders were somehow clearly visible, above everyone else.

It had to be a mirage. The Tibetans are not a tall people; the Rimpoche was smaller than I and Tom about five feet nine. Some of other people who crowded around them I knew to be taller. Yet somehow the Rimpoche and Tom were visible above the others. As if they were levitating. It looked so odd I could hardly believe what I was seeing. Yet although I had my camera with me and this was a moment truly worth recording, I found myself unable to use it, feeling constrained out of a kind of awed respect for what was happening not to intrude with technology. I was still staring when Tom signalled me to join him and to my embarrassment, introduced both Yellow Bear and myself personally to the Rimpoche as good friends concerned with the preservation of Native culture. The Rimpoche nodded and smiled again. I noted how, physically, he was smaller than everyone except the interpreter.

Melding in a normal fashion with the others, the two men moved away towards the central fire. Left alone, rooted in place, I studied the ground where they had met. There was no rise, not even a hump. Yet these two spiritual leaders had stood head and shoulders above the rest.

In a strange state of suspension, I withdrew. There seemed no reason to be there any longer; nothing could follow this. Had I, as had been said was my tendency, put the two men on a pedestal? Or had I been fortunate enough to bear witness to the meeting of two spiritual giants? Had the energies of this mystical place something to do with it? My ears were ringing; the trees around me seemed fuzzy, a smudge of deep emerald green. The place was magical. This was where boundaries faded, where reality bent. How could I have stayed away so long?

AL'T'AS STEEM'AS SPA'USS[25]

Nothing changed; it was as if the psychic shield I once imagined setting up to protect the Indian village was in place, working against me. I put it to the back of my mind, and concentrated on finalising the paperwork for the upcoming teaching position at the Paschal Sherman Indian School. Auntie Vi offered to act as a character reference and began looking for a house I could rent, but things were significantly held up when the U.S. education authorities insisted on up-to-date documentation from the English side. I was impressed to find out that, over twenty years later and with a change in function, the records of the college I had attended were still intact. To avoid any possible mailing problem and missing the closing date, I drove down to deliver it all by hand to the Department of Education in Spokane, Washington.

Whenever the hold-ups and waiting began to get to me, the phone would ring and there Auntie Vi would be, ready to visit through the wires or with an invitation to stay. She seemed to have a direct line to my mental state, much as she had one to Jesus. From my reading, I was beginning to understand that her faith amounted to a kind of Gnosticism: no Church, no priest or other intermediary, no Bible-reading, no prayer-book, no service by rote, no ritual; simply a prayer from the heart.[26] Besides her healing work, she was inspired to help people reconnect with spirit without imposing any belief-system, apart from an occasional reminder that what Jesus taught and did is within the reach and capability of each and every one of us.

Despite the tragedies that had befallen her family and her dire state of health, her faith never faltered. Earlier that year, as we were going into a children's pow-wow at the Indian School, she had suffered one of the side-effects of her prescription drugs, keeling over in a faint before anyone could catch her and badly bruising her neck and shoulders. Even then, she could still joke that the painkillers would do her in before the disease. From time to time, the side-effects – consuming thirst, nausea, increasing general debility – would make her cold-turkey off the drug-cocktail, contrary to medical advice. Helped by a local traditional Native medicine, she would get stronger and regain her energy. For a while. The infusion was terribly bitter; she would "forget" to drink it and the descent into pain and enervation would resume. Back on the prescription drugs, she would improve; then the side-effects would kick in again. A Catch-22 situation, it seemed to promise only one resolution.

Accounts of the medical attention she received on the Reservation were invariably disparaging. In her opinion, most of the doctors were young and inexperienced, and anxious to leave this "apprentice" spell for a more lucrative practice.[27] Prejudice was common, and there was deep suspicion that Native people like herself were being used as guinea pigs for new prescription drugs. On the other hand, the doctor who treated her at the Sacred Heart Hospital in Spokane whenever

---

25 Sinixt: "Don't bullshit your heart". (Manny)
26 The Celtic Church had a similar way until the Roman Church took over and instituted church, priest and order.
27 In the U.S., medical student loans are forgiven, on completion of two years' service in the military or on a Reservation.

she fell seriously ill (at least once a year) received nothing but the highest praise. His competence and sensitivity instilled her with confidence; most importantly, he acknowledged the power that brought her back from the brink time after time.

"One time at the Sacred Heart," she told me, "I woke an' found two people standing at the foot of my bed. I was so embarrassed: how long had they been there and I didn't even notice? I felt worse when I saw one of them was my grandfather. Although that was strange – I was sure he'd passed over, years ago. And the other one, dressed in white, I thought he must be a doctor, but the light was so bright I couldn't make him out properly.

"My grandfather stepped forward and says, 'Vi, you been sleeping long enough. An' what're all them bottles for? All them things in your arm?'

"Well, I looked down, and he was right. There were all these plastic tubes feeding into me. Didn't know what they were there for, either, so I just shook my head.

"'You don't need 'em,' says my grandfather. 'Get rid of 'em!'

"Well, like I said, I did wonder if the other man was a doctor. But he just stood there, not saying a word, an' I couldn't see him so well.... In any case, my grandfather was not the sort of person you ever said 'no' to." Auntie Vi chuckled, shaking her head. "I sat up and ripped the tubes out my arms, an' felt better right away. Then a nurse come into the room and starts hollerin': 'What're you doin'? Why d'you pull out the tubes?'

"I didn't like her being so rude, in front of my visitors. 'Been told I don't need 'em,' I tell her but she's already gone out again. That's when I saw they were gone, my grandfather and the other man. I hadn't noticed 'em leave, and wished I'd had a chance to say goodbye. But in a way, it didn't matter. This feeling, so peaceful, was just spreading through my body....

"The nurse came back with the doctor, and he checked out the machines and took my vital signs. Then he says: 'Welcome back, Vi. I'm pleased you've come out of it so well.'

"'What're you talking about?' I say, confused again.

"'You've been in a coma for over three weeks,' he says.

"Boy, was I shocked! I had no idea. Then he says: 'But what made you pull out the tubes?'

"'My grandfather was here and Jesus was with him,' I told him straight, when I'd barely realised it for myself. 'And my grandfather told me to get rid of 'em,' I told him. 'You know, you get into trouble if you don't do what my grandfather says!'" Smiling, Auntie Vi shook her head. "Couldn't help talking 'bout him as if he was still alive. Then another sensation struck me. 'Boy!' I says, 'I sure am hungry!' The doctor, he just laughed. I went home the next day.

"It was a miracle, the way he accepted it. I don't know many as would. He told me he'd often felt a presence in my room an' he thought my recoveries were nothing short of a miracle."

Whenever Auntie Vi was taken to hospital, within a few hours a prayer-chain was activated and a battery of believers would be praying on her behalf. When she recovered, she felt it was because Jesus must still have work for her to do. Strength barely regained, her thin face and shadowy eyes alight with the joy of Divine purpose, she would organise a massive spiritual event – a weekend faith and healing gathering or gospel-fest – and throw herself into a host of fundraising activities to meet the expenses of the invited spiritual leaders and a weekend of catering for an entire congregation.

Reflecting their powerful surviving sense of community, the way Native Americans swiftly and successfully fundraise never ceased to impress me. When the hat was passed round for expenses at the early Arrow Lakes Band meetings, fifteen to twenty people would donate four or five hundred dollars on the spot. A hat passed round for the same reason at an environmental meeting in the Valley involving more than thirty local people raised a total of twenty-five dollars.

Like most perfectionists, Auntie Vi found it difficult to delegate. For days her house would be redolent of the smell of baked goods and she'd wear herself out preparing and selling home-cooked lunches to the employees of the Tribal Agency. A small woman with an immense will, even when she came home from hospital too weak to organise any fundraising, she could still make it happen. Totally against gambling in any form, she felt for this purpose the need was greater than the sin; after a "little talk" with Jesus, she accompanied Junior to the bingo-hall, played one game and won three thousand dollars. Another year, when her car broke down and needed a new engine she could not afford, she had another "chat" with Jesus about how she could not serve Him without a vehicle and went back to the bingo-hall. Her prize money covered the cost of a replacement engine, with a little left over to buy Junior a recliner. The key, she told me, was that her prayers were never for herself.

Before me shone the power of Auntie Vi's living faith; behind echoed Bob's words about New Age seekers, "without a foundation, blown away like leaves before a storm". It seemed to me I was one of those leaves. For as long as I could remember, I had felt there was more to life than what lay before my five senses. One of my earliest and strongest memories, not recalled until much later, is from when I was about six years old: sitting under a summer night-sky on the Northumbrian coast, looking up at the stars with a distinct feeling that I was ready to be "taken"; that the experiment was done. But no spaceship appeared.

Raised Church of England, by the age of ten, I had looked into the austerity of the Presbyterian and Baptist Churches, and found them lacking. As for Catholicism, religion of my maternal grandmother, the confessional made little sense, likewise the bewildering array of gilded images to which an appeal apparently could be made. Only hymn-singing seemed to touch some inner need, a sense of "Other", which in turn led me into reading global fairy-tales and mythologies, novels about the occult, and science-fiction and fantasy. During my years in higher education, like many others of my age, I skated through the teachings of Hinduism and Buddhism, tried agnosticism for size and dallied with atheism, socialism and communism. Interest in communal living, coupled with blood-ties through my maternal grandfather, led me to a kibbutz in Israel (not what I was seeking, either) and eventually Jerusalem. Something about the magical, mystical city met a need in me; my plans to travel to Afghanistan and eventually Morocco were put aside, and I found myself studying Judaism. This was not something I had planned but a sense of a thread I was following. Once a month for almost three years, the dayanim – Jewish religious judges – harangued me, testing my resolve as much as what I was learning from weekly lessons with a rabbi's wife. Increasingly a battle of wills, it ended when a senior Sephardic rabbi I had met by "chance" stepped in. I was accepted as a "ger tzeddek", a righteous convert, and given a Hebrew name.

In hindsight, had I known it existed, it may have been that what I truly sought were the inner mysteries of Judaism. The weird thing was that the teachings of the Kabbalah were literally at arm's length for at least two years, had I been aware. Following the 1973 Yom Kippur War in Israel, my partner's father, originally from Kurdistan, kindly, unassuming and supposedly poorly-educated, had pointed out to me codes in the scriptures that prophesied the war. He didn't speak English, however, and my knowledge of Hebrew was not deep enough. In time, on time.... Yet, out of Israel and into North America, for more than a decade I would be haunted by recurrent dreams that took me back to the Old City of Jerusalem, through narrow alleyways I knew intimately and into a small courtyard, where there would be a darkened, open doorway beyond which I knew lay something vital, but never attaining it. By the time of the cathartic Rebirth of Mother Earth Medicine Wheel gathering, I had studied Tarot and was beginning to explore other esoteric traditions.

Nothing, however, had affected me as powerfully as contact with a people and a way of life that had somehow been in me since childhood. Scent of wood-smoke, sage, sweetgrass; intoxication of drum and chant; intimate knowledge of four-legged and winged ones; whispers of tall standing brothers and sisters; the silent compassion of Grandmother rocks; the intensity of Thunder Beings: this was a world that sang to the essence of myself, was showing me my place on Mother Earth, green cathedral. For a while, I had felt like I had come home.

Yet deep within, uneasiness whispered: how could I, white of skin and fair of hair, sprung from across the Great Water, be home, so far from home? Sometimes it was as if I was acting out some kind of role: if I got it right, I could move on. Yet there was nothing I could imagine that could mean as much to me as being among the Native American people.

Coming to understand Auntie Vi's faith seemed to be bringing me back round, sort of full-circle. Investigating the spiritual path of my landlord at the Lodge, also a type of Gnosticism, had not caught me up. Nor had diving – literally, when I was re-baptised – into the Pentecostal church to which Jessica belonged, which had initially seemed dynamic but turned out to be a fundamentalist role which suited me even less. Auntie Vi's way seemed the closest to something I was looking for, so I decided to try and understand it better. Yet in the same way that the traditional Winter Dance had proved elusive, Auntie Vi's faith gatherings passed me by, as did a unique opportunity to attend a cursillo (a Catholic spiritual weekend) to which Aunt Tootie had invited me.

I couldn't work out whether it was a reflection of my own ambivalence, or if I was being shown that this was not the way for me. How come I could not find what was in my heart?

THE BREAKFAST CLUB

A sudden decline in the health of my kids' dad shook my faith in the power of the yinipi. Surely a ceremony should have a lasting effect? Perhaps it was wrong to dabble in other spiritual ways. Auntie Vi had been pressing me to attend her next faith and healing gathering, to be led by her favourite spiritual group, and this time, things came together. Dusan, the kids' dad, a charismatic Catholic, was prepared to come and, as if to dispel any lingering doubts, at the last moment the husband of my long-standing friend Hetty expressed a wish to join us. A blood transfusion in Montreal twenty years ago had infected Kori with hepatitis C; two-thirds of his liver had been destroyed and he was on the waiting-list for a new organ. We were wildly optimistic: maybe the power of prayer would heal his liver, at the very least bring about a successful transplant.

Like any true pilgrimage, it would prove challenging. Leaving home in the early hours, children half-asleep in the back of the van, I picked up Kori from Nakusp then collected Dusan from Vernon. He wanted to use the small border-crossing at Midway but, concerned that the circuitous, mountainous route might be too much for my aging vehicle and unwilling to be dictated to, I insisted on the main border-crossing south of Osoyoos, B.C. Intent on my own way, I had forgotten to stay alert to the way messages can come not only through four-leggeds, the wind or water, but even an irritating "ex".

Two middle-aged men, a woman and two small children in a white VW camper might seem innocuous, but seen through Stateside-eyes, this was a vehicle associated with hippies and drugs; one of the men was jaundice-yellow, belly distended like an eight-month pregnancy from prescription drugs; and the other pale and emaciated as a concentration-camp victim, tubes of a Brachman-Hickman line extruding from his chest. Both were equipped with boxes and vials of prescription medicine, pills and other medical paraphernalia, and to make matters worse, I forgot previous negative reactions to any kind of gatherings on the Reservation and gave the U.S. border official a straight answer about the purpose of our visit.

Ordered out of the vehicle and into the building, we were told to wait. The officer disappeared through a door then reappeared behind a glass partition, hunched over a computer screen. Eventually he called over another official. Over an hour slid by, Kori's sense of humour helping us ride out the inconvenience lightly. Less amusing was how, because of the number of employees who kept sauntering by with sidelong glances, we seemed to have become something of a peep-show.

Finally the officer returned, triumphantly waving a piece of paper: Dusan was denied entry. It emerged that in the mid-seventies, he had been obliquely implicated in the infamous "Czech Connection" heroin bust in Vancouver through an ex-girlfriend who had turned state's evidence. The smirking official added that an application could have been made at any time which would have wiped it from the record.

Disappointment rooted us to the spot; he had been to the States many times with no problem. I asked if we could make an application on the spot, but was cockily told it cost seventy dollars, would take three months and if I tried to re-enter with him before his record was cleared I would face prosecution.

Spirits thoroughly dampened, we returned to Penticton and made arrangements to meet up with Dusan's partner so she could take him back home. By the time that was accomplished, it was dark and the children had had enough of all this driving and waiting around, and decided to stay the weekend in Vernon with their father.

Back at the border, Kori and I were begrudgingly waved through; by the time we reached Nespelem, over fourteen hours had passed since I had left home. The arrangement had been to meet at Auntie Vi's and go with her to the local little Catholic Church where the gathering was being held, but as I had anticipated, her house was dark.

"Now we'll have to brave it alone!" Kori joked.

Never had I seen so many cars, row upon row, parked outside the church, nor such brightly-glowing windows. The singing was clearly audible. I could tell Kori was as nervous as I, so I forged ahead and pushed open the inner doors. Singing broke over us like a tidal wave; the promise of the parked cars was fulfilled: there was standing-room only. Scanning the back of a multitude of heads, I could see no-one I knew, but the entry of two lost-sheep late-comers had not gone unnoticed. A familiar figure came bearing down on us, grin almost as wide as his open arms: Father Jim, local Catholic priest and close friend of Auntie Vi. He escorted us to the annex by the kitchen, where our mutual friend and her helpers were clearing away the evening meal.

Auntie Vi always made me feel as if I were the most important person in her life. Hugging me and enthusiastically welcoming Kori, she told us how worried she had been. Exhaustion caught up with me; tears brimming, I poured out the whole tale. Auntie Vi didn't say a word, but led me to the edge of the podium, where two small, dark-haired men were standing and singing with the congregation.

When the hymn ended and the two men stepped back, Auntie Vi introduced me to the two leaders of the Breakfast Club. Solidly-built, with the aboriginal features and pudding-bowl haircuts of Amazonian Indians, "Ham and Bacon" was not some kind of joke after all, but their real names. When Auntie Vi finished her urgent whispering, Ham grasped my upper arm, softly but firmly. "You go on up 'n' tell the people out there what just happened." He steered me up to the lectern and microphone. "Tell 'em. An' pray for your friend. Ev'ryone can pray for him with you. Remember the power of prayer. Time 'n' space don't mean nothin' to Jesus."

Auntie Vi patted my arm encouragingly. "You can do it."

Put in front of the people like this, it would not only be cowardly but offensive to turn away. There was no time to be nervous; in any case, I was too removed from myself. Eyes blurred with tears and tiredness, my gaze took in the crowded pews, the men, women and children waiting in hushed expectancy, eyes on me. Vaguely aware of the Breakfast Club behind me and Auntie Vi and her helpers watching from the annex, I battled with two voices inside my head.

How wonderful, said one. So many minds and hearts, focussed in one-ness. What an opportunity.

How out-of-place you are, white fleck in an ocean of brown, said the other. Just who do you think you are?

An enormous tapestry at the back of the church caught and held my eye. Beautifully hand-worked in pastel embroidery-silks – eggshell-blue, dove-grey, white, lilac, violet, soft brown – Jesus gazed back at me above the dark forest of heads, flowing locks framing His infinitely compassionate visage, one elegant hand poised in the classic gesture of blessing.

A vagrant current of air caused the tapestry to shift and billow, and in my heightened emotional state, it seemed as if, ever so slightly, Jesus had nodded approval. Calm and measured, the words began to flow, carrying easily and clearly through the attentive quiet. As I neared the end of my little tale, my emotions caught up with me, rising like lava and sticking in my throat, making me dizzy. Again the great tapestry undulated gently: Jesus, gently nodding encouragement. Closing my hot and teary eyes, I flowed on into an impassioned plea-prayer for the absent, seriously-ill father of two of my children.

At the end, the power of the echoing "Amen" resonated through the little church like the tone of a great bell, and as it died away, I had a sense of total one-ness, as if all were breathing in perfect synchronicity. Reluctantly, I opened my eyes. Above the heads of the congregation, obscuring the inspirational tapestry, hung an ethereal sort of milky-opaque glow. Thinking tears had distorted my vision, I rubbed my eyes and blinked hard. The misty glow was still there, although fainter.

That night, crammed sardine-like with members of the Breakfast Club and several of Auntie Vi's relatives on mattresses on the floor of her living-room, I told them what I had seen.

"That's what we call 'being covered with the Light of Jesus'!" was the immediate consensus.

"It's a phenomenon that can appear above the heads of the faithful at times of profound spiritual experience," one of the guests explained.

Not knowing what to make of this, I said nothing more. It was just one of a number of experiences that night, apparently; with so much to share, no-one slept much and it seemed like in no time at all we were heading back to the church for breakfast and a full day of prayer, song and healing. My inclination had been to go home; I had done what I came to do and wanted to be alone and reflect, but Auntie Vi would not allow it: both Kori and I should have a "healing".

Kori was in no hurry to leave, either. His easy manner and sense of humour were going down well and although unsure about the "hands on" part, he was enjoying the spirit of the gathering. Rather like children who have neglected their homework and hope they will not be singled out in the lesson, we chose seats near the back of the church just as two familiar figures appeared. As soon as they saw me, Uncle Chuck and Aunt Aggie came and sat behind us.

"Surprised to see us here?" Uncle Chuck grinned.

"Kind of," I said carefully.

"Healin's healin'," he answered my unasked question. "It's not about any one way."

The church was filling swiftly. Two guitarists began to lead the songs of praise, which I always enjoyed. Ensconced near the back, I thought Auntie Vi would never find us but as the songs drew to an end and Ham and Bacon were taking their places on the podium, helpers either side, she suddenly appeared. Nor did she need to say much; it was as if a mighty hand propelled me out of the pew. Before I knew it, I was standing in front, first in the line-up.

Beckoned forward, I looked up into the darkly-weathered, kindly face and soft-brown eyes of the small, unassuming man. "Why are you here?" Ham asked gently, echoing the question that lay at the forefront of my own mind.

Focussing on the white buttons on his washed-out-blue shirt, I recited my little list of concerns about the children's father and waited for what came next. The quality of the silence sort of deepened and before I knew it, other more personal stuff began to spill out: my dismal failure to form a lasting relationship; my inability to provide stability for my children; my lack of direction. Aghast at my weakness, I buttoned my lips.

Ham said nothing. He laid both his hands on the crown of my head, closed his eyes and launched into prayer on my behalf, in a rapid, mumbling monotone, touching upon everything I had mentioned, omitting not one item.

Impressive, commented the cynical little inner voice, except for the increasing pressure on your head – he wants you to fall down, like they do on TV! Well, we won't oblige that sort of show.

My eyes fixed on the white buttons of his shirt, I braced my neck, tensed my shoulders and resisted.

Not very positive, when someone's intention is to be of help, said another inner voice. Work with him, not against him.

This was the voice I preferred. I closed my eyes and, as on another occasion, visualised the image of a benevolent, robed being of Light, hands open, palms towards me....

Suddenly I realised Ham wasn't praying any longer and I couldn't feel his hands on my head any more. I opened my eyes. He was gone; I had no idea where I was. Disoriented, I realised it was the rafters of the church I was looking at.

I was lying on my back, on the floor.

Auntie Vi's voice, filled with delight, was clear, if miles away: "She's gone down! Our Celia's down!"

I could have curled up in mortification. How on earth had I come to be in this position? I could not recall Ham's hands leaving my head, nor the last words he had said. I had no memory of anyone else touching me, no inkling of what had happened, could hardly believe I was here. To my relief, no-one seemed to be paying me any attention and the laying-on of hands was continuing. Nor did I really want to get up; beneath the embarrassment I felt quite relaxed and comfortable, even though the red carpet I was lying on was paper-thin.

Getting up was easier thought than done. Strangely weak, I rolled over, got onto my hands and knees, slowly stood up and began to make my wobbly way back towards Kori, who was coming forward to help me. Wanting to reassure him, I smiled. "Don't worry, I'm fine." I began to giggle, a rolling, gut-shaking giggle I could not control, and he had to help me back as it became increasingly hysterical. As soon as we sat down, my eyes filled with tears and I began to sob. Behind us, Uncle Chuck and Aunt Aggie were creased with laughter.

"Had to be first of the day, eh?" Uncle Chuck laughed as Aunt Aggie patted my shoulder sympathetically, making me smile, then start to giggle again. Gradually the emotional extremes faded, leaving me feeling cleansed and renewed, like a meadow battered but refreshed by a passing thunderstorm.

"When you go down like that, that's what Vi calls bein' 'slain in the spirit'. On the ground, you're 'restin' in the spirit'," Aunt Aggie explained.

"Don't think you've been singled out," Uncle Chuck said with a chuckle. "It don't mean you're all holy now."

"Except I'm high as a kite," I quivered.

"You should've seen my cousin Charlie, when he went down," said Auntie Vi when she joined us, smiling widely. "He thought it was all just hokum. Came to see me after his wife died, when he could finally face up to the fact that his life'd fallen apart. He begun to turn it round, then came the day when this disbeliever – he's a big man, over six feet tall – found himself tremblin' and shakin' on his back on the floor of the church. He went over like a felled tree; I almost yelled, 'Timber!' And him such a sceptic! It was so funny to see him lyin' on the ground like a great big li'l ol' baby!"

Kori went up to take his turn. Left to reflect on what had just happened, and feeling wonderfully light and clear, I began to hope that, despite what Uncle Chuck had said, what I had experienced might mean that I might begin to meld into this wonderful spiritual community. And as Dusan began to rally again, I became convinced it was only a matter of time before the door would open.[28]

28 About a year later, after two false starts, Kori underwent a liver transplant, a difficult, lengthy operation. Immediately, Auntie Vi activated a prayer-chain on his behalf. He spent about a week in recovery, in a light coma-like state, and eventually told me of strange goings-on in his room. Whenever he was left alone, a Native American in full traditional dress would step out of the cupboard, beating a hand-drum, and chant and dance around his bed. The first time, Kori thought he must be hallucinating, but it was a consistent event, no matter how he rubbed his eyes or shook his head. As soon as someone started to come into the room, the "chief" would slip back into the cupboard, but Kori could still hear a faint drum-beat.

A drug- or coma-induced fantasy? Imagination can be another way of seeing. Auntie Vi's prayer-chain would have involved other powerful prayer-warriors; I often wondered whether, even though they prayed through Jesus, the power might manifest through their racial spirit. Just as Uncle Chuck had said at the faith and healing gathering: all ways are one.

MEDICINE WHEEL

Time dragged by, snail-pace. The teaching positions at the Indian School were posted and filled. Finally the response from the U.S. educational authorities arrived: a more professional credential than a twenty-year-old English teaching certification was required. Auntie Vi's disappointment was almost as great as my own. Furious at the waste of time and fees I could little afford, I threw myself back into my tourism job, working overtime to catch up on areas I had neglected while chasing a dream.

But it was not a dream. My destiny was linked to the Native people; I could feel it. Knowing that in order to move on to the next phase, the next adventure in life, you have to let go, I wondered if my present job was somehow in the way. But I had a family to support. Night after night I lay awake, feeling I was living in limbo, waiting for my purpose to manifest.

The seasons turned. In the spring, for the third consecutive year the draw-down was sufficient to expose the Arrow Lakes' traditional fishery at Kettle Falls. For days I was torn between a subtle, whale-song call and a sense it was time to put anything connected to the Lakes people behind me. On what I knew to be the last day of the "Calling Back the Salmon" ceremony, I gave in and bundled the children into the van.

The heavy, early-April sky was shedding the last tatters of days of steady rain. Following the silky-leaden flow of the great Columbia, a journey I loved and knew in a way that seemed from a lifetime before this one, brought me an inner peace I hadn't known for some time. Like so many times before, I imagined travelling not by road but by canoe, mentally erasing Waneta and the Seven-Mile Dam, and traversing an imaginary landscape forested to the edge of a long-submerged canyon.

Nearing Kettle Falls, I strained for a glimpse of Hayes Island. The little hump was more prominent this year, but it was too far away to discern tipis. Thinking that the salmon feast was taking place at Kettle Falls Historical Centre that afternoon, I drove straight to St. Paul's Mission, but only a couple of cars were parked outside and not a soul was anywhere to be seen. Surely I had not got the timing wrong again? I had to laugh: all that was in my heart was to see Hayes Island, perhaps even set foot on it again; the feast did not matter (even if I had a notion that someone might have been there who would act as some kind of catalyst).

There was no sign of activity on the island. From the cliff-top, the same place I had stood two years ago, I could make out a tipi and two skeletal frames, and the sweat-lodge, beetle-back-camouflaged against the tawny-grey of the mud, on a lower terrace, one that had not been exposed last time I had been here.

Gunning its engine noisily, a pick-up sped up and stopped behind my vehicle. Two familiar faces grinned out from behind a dusty windshield.

Originally born to the Spokane Reservation but now living in Colville, Ed was a member of

Little Falls, a Spokane family drum who had befriended Northern Lights and at pow-wows invited us to sit with them and drum, a great privilege. One of their traditional chants had become known amongst ourselves as "Ed's song". In his late forties, well-built, dark-skinned and bespectacled, with a round, kindly face and long, thick, wispy braids, Ed had turned onto a spiritual path following his recovery from alcoholism, and now worked with troubled Native teenagers. With him was Gary, a tall, thin, painfully-shy Lakes descendant with tousled, lank, black hair. From the community of Twin Lakes, he was an uncle of Nick's friend, Victor, whose family we had met the previous year on a trip Tom had organised for local families on one of the new Tribal houseboats (a recent business enterprise purchase). Not only had Nick found a "war-dance" buddy, but a new family of uncles and aunties, friendly if reticent, although Victor's gregarious ebullience more than compensated.

"We've come to get the last canvas and anchor the tipi poles in place," said Ed. "Like last year, let the waters cleanse 'em when they rise again. And the sweat-lodge.... Salmon feast was yesterday," he chuckled. "Let's go."

Grateful that he took it for granted we would go over to the island with them, we scrambled down the cliff. After a needless reminder to keep absolutely still, he silently steered us across the waters. Ominous swirls tugged at the shallow-bottomed boat: over the drowned falls below, Kraken-like, writhed the Columbia. I could imagine the puttering little craft scraping the skin of the trapped monster, making it burst forth in a tsunami of frustrated energy.

"Three eagles...." Ed's soft, lilting voice dispersed my dark fantasy. "There was three eagles came durin' the ceremony, an' then three ravens an' after that three swallows. This year we was all men, but Woman was there in spirit. We all heard the voices that joined with ours when we sung the songs."

His words, soul-food, carried me further into a state of anticipatory otherworldliness. As we beached, I slipped off my shoes, took a deep breath and climbed out of the boat. The soles of my feet began to tingle, and not from the coolness of the wet sand.

"Over there," Ed pointed to the upper terrace, where, in a photo three years previously, a fabulous apparition had manifested over a circle of tipis, "was where we consecrated the Medicine Wheel last year."

Even before he spoke, I had felt drawn to the area. As I climbed up to it, however, I remembered the caution of the ethnographer Bouchard, at the beginning of this whole journey: "Beware the pan-Indians ... and resist any suggestion that the Medicine Wheel was a tradition of northern tribes."

Since my involvement with the Arrow Lakes people had begun at a Medicine Wheel gathering in their ancestral lands, the ethnographer's words had rankled. I felt that no-one had the right to judge the form a spiritual revival takes; it was bound to involve an organic sea-change. The rituals of the Ghost Dancers and the Native American Church are no less powerful because they developed and were adopted relatively recently, at times of great difficulty. Another of the ironies of the renascence of Native American tradition is that it is the institutions most criticised that have of necessity been turned to, since collections housed in museums, and academic investigations and records hold some of the only surviving clues to certain aspects of the culture. A further irony is that such shards of scientific information constitute the only "acceptable" evidence of Native American traditions, identity and rights; oral records, passed down through the millennia, have little weight or validity in a society that accepts only the written word as truth. An oral tradition, however, keeps the true essence of tradition alive and relevant in a way that something set down in writing cannot: it allows for change and adaptability. Facts can be passed on in the written word, but "knowing" is not.

Investigating what was written about the Medicine Wheel, I had found out that the best-known one lies in Wyoming, among the Big Horn range. Precisely aligned with the rising and setting sun of the summer solstice, Aldebaran in the constellation of Taurus, Rigel in Orion and Sirius in Canis Major, it appears to pre-date the tribes in the area, who have no reference to its creation or usage in oral memory apart from one story of a small race of men who came, built it and left. Anthropologists and archaeologists admit it is an anomaly; geometrically, it has more in common with ancient Egypt than anything in North America.

Now a new Medicine Wheel lay before me: the Columbia Wheel, a giant constellation of pale, speckled, water-rounded rocks, ceremonially gathered and positioned. Paths of stones representing the four directions rayed out from the centre, the heart-stone, contained in a small ring of pebbles, to the outer rim. Most of those involved in the Wheel's construction and consecration were known to me personally, and I had the highest regard for their spiritual beliefs and the integrity of their motivation. So what if the Wheel was not originally a tradition of this area? To me it was about energy, which cannot be destroyed, only transformed.

The concerted effort of the powerful spiritual leaders who had just spent four days here in ritual, sweating, drumming and praying, lingered. The sandy mud seemed to shimmer with more than reflected light; the tingling in my feet coursed like blood through my veins, making me think of the mighty currents of water that had crashed over the rocks for millenia, of the salmon that had once teemed up the falls. In my mind's eye, I recalled the ghostly spirit-presence of Coyote, captured by my camera.

No longer in the habit of carrying tobacco and sage, I had to do without these tools. Closing my eyes, I took several deep, cleansing breaths then offered respect to the Grandmothers and Grandfathers and spoke my gratitude for being in this place again. Mentally linking my energy and consciousness with those who had gone before, I prayed for harmony, visualising an enveloping pure white light laced with ribbons of pink, jade-green and violet blossoming outwards from the centre of the Wheel, the island, spreading throughout the waterways, the seas, the oceans, the waters within each and every living being, until the entire planet manifested as a great iridescent globe. With no sound to distract me, it felt as if every cell in my body were being ignited, as the tingling in my feet worked its hot and prickling way up my legs and body and down my arms. My scalp crawled and a sudden brightness made me open my eyes.

Lancing through a break in the clouds, a shaft of sunlight danced and sparkled on the water beyond the Wheel like shattering glass, almost blinding me. It struck me that if ever there was a time and place to clear my way forward, this was it. Aloud I cried: "Grandmothers, Grandfathers, look into my heart. My life is an instrument; help me heal so I can do what is mine to do, whatever it is, whatever it takes." I sang a round of "Harmony with Earth," an owl-dance song, to wing the prayer skyward, and for good measure and to cover all bases, sang another round at each compass-point, ending in the north where I placed the clear quartz crystal which had been the first item in my little medicine pouch. Almost invisible, it glinted, reflecting the liquid light pouring through a multitude of gaps in the overcast sky.

But I was not finished yet. Feeling for the crystal in the pouch, the first thing my fingers had touched was another treasure, a little gift from my mentor Eileen, the previous year in England. Knowing what this meant, I took it out, crouched down and buried the silver medallion of St. Christopher and St. Anthony in the grey, cracked, sandy mud.

Saint of children; saint of things lost. Thinking of the lost teaching opportunity, it seemed terribly appropriate.

That I might be attuning to a future purpose was nowhere in my conscious mind.

Both things were precious to me, but I knew I had to make some kind of giveaway. The Arrow Lakes ancestors were returned; their descendants were there to take care of them. More than any lengthy, tedious, doubtful negotiation with the government, it was a powerful, living statement of their rights. Even if it was like trying to prise a limpet off a rock, I had to let go. But that didn't mean it was the end of my connection with the Native people. What about the vision of the two races working together to build a better community? What about bringing to others the valuable teachings of the traditional Native American way of life? Where and what was my place in all this? Symbol of the turning of life, a metaphor for quintessential movement and change, at that moment, the Medicine Wheel seemed like a yawning black hole which threatened to suck me into oblivion. A sudden wave of feeling swept up my body. Before I knew what I was doing, with all my strength I cried: "Spirit of this place, this scrap of an island lodged deep in my heart, if anything remains for me to do with the Indians, show me what it is. And show me clearly, or I will focus my purpose elsewhere."

An ultimatum is not really a smart thing to offer the spirit-world, especially one that Coyote is known to frequent.

A heavy silence hung over the leaden waters, the desolate little island. There was not a bird in the sky, no whisper of wind or stirring of waters. What was I expecting? A Lady of the Lake, holding out the bright and shining sword of truth? Beyond emotion, I silently waited for the men to finish, thinking that I had to wean myself away from this obsession.

It was the first time I had admitted to myself that there might be something unhealthy about my desire to be among the Native American people.

Back on the cliff-top, I gazed down on the precious little mud-bank for a long while. The story of Lot's wife came to me, a reminder not to look back in bitterness. At that moment, Tom drove up.

The Lakes pipe-carrier chuckled to hear that I had not only missed the ceremony but the feast as well. "We set up a tipi on the island for our friends from the north, but none of you guys showed up this year. Funny, that."

"Oh, we were all with you in spirit," I said fervently.

"I guess. Sure was busy with spirits, this year." His dark, warm eyes creased at the corners.

Once all the equipment was loaded onto his pick-up, Tom asked if I had time for a few words. Curious as what kind of words, I nodded; when the others had driven away, I followed him over to a nearby roadside cafe.

"You 'member that giveaway, the last gatherin' in Inchelium?" he began once we had sat down with our coffees and the children were busy with their meal.

"Ed's...." I remembered the occasion but not the reason for it. In the customary way, a couple of large, colourful Indian blankets had been spread on the ground in the middle of the arbour and covered with the many items he intended to gift: pouches of tobacco, bolts of bright material, different kinds of feathers, packets of jellybeans and candies for the children and some beautifully hand-crafted items.

"You remember the drum?" asked Tom. I nodded, remembering the family drum at the centre of the display. "Well, when I seen that drum settin' there in the middle, I wondered who was gonna get that prize. An' I was not the only one. A lot of folk was lookin' at it."

"But he didn't give it away," I recalled.

He shrugged. "All them things was cleared off the blanket, 'cept the drum. Ed had no intention to give it away, it was there for show; he told me later. No-one'd say anything, of course, but everything that's put on a giveaway blanket's there to be given away." He lit a cigarette, and looked out the window. "The ceremony on the island was a more intimate event this year than last. But the spiritual focus was as strong. Ed brought that drum over, an' on the first evenin' we sat down round it together to open the ceremony. With a traditional song." He raised one arm in imitation of a drummer about to strike. "Brought down the drum-sticks, as one." His hand slapped down on the table, making me jump. "An' the hide split, all the way 'cross the middle." He laughed wryly. "It went real quiet for a while, we was so shook up. Real quiet. An' that split, well, after that, it wasn't somethin' that you felt you could repair. But it was all in order...

"That drum'd already left, back at the giveaway. Spirits were just waitin' for the right time, the right place to take it. An' they sure picked their moment. Powerful place, that little island."

Nodding, I imagined the spirits laughing with glee as they raced away with the freed drum-spirit over the silvery waters. But why bring me here to tell me this? I felt I should say something: "Tom, now that the whole business at Vallican is about over for me, I've been thinking about what I should do next. I had this idea recently" (this wasn't quite true unless "recently" was at that very moment: I was talking off the top of my head) "about developing something like an experiential Native Studies curriculum for non-Native schoolchildren. You know, so they can get a real idea about it, not some dry, academic interpretation that's all words...." I tailed off, wondering where this was coming from.

"Yeah, the real work's with the children." Tom went on to tell me about spiritual work he had done within the prison system, then fell silent again, his face falling into its now-familiar pensive severity. Suddenly he said: "Some very powerful an' positive things were said 'bout you by the Tribal Council."

I was nonplussed; I had met with the Council several months ago by invitation of Auntie Vi's cousin, Uncle Gilbert, to give my perspective of the overall situation in Vallican and Native issues in British Columbia in general. At the time, a couple of the Council members had been enthusiastic about my research and I had been hoping that with their support, I might obtain a cultural grant to continue working in a more official capacity, but nothing had come of it. I shrugged. "All that was about was-"

"You see, I had this vision.... For years, I been wantin' to create a comprehensive record of the traditional knowledge of the elders." He paused; and time seemed to stand still, holding its breath. "I been thinkin', to take the elders, small groups, two or three at a time, out onto the waters an' tributaries of the lake. We got these Tribal houseboats; this'd be a real good use for one of 'em. Take a couple of elders out, three or four days, beginnin' from the south by Coulee

Dam an' headin' north far's the boat can safely travel, an' make a recordin' of each journey, what they have to tell.... Could make it like a little vacation for 'em. Might be a couple of trips is necessary for each elder, dependin' on what they remember."

"Instead of down memory lane, up memory river." I murmured, feeling like I was in a dream, knowing what would come next.

"Get the elders to tell," he continued as if I hadn't spoken, "in the old tongue if they can, the names of all the landmarks 'n' the sacred places, an' the stories 'n' legends. An' any other memories that might be triggered. Me as interpreter; you to record, write it all up.... An' your kids'd be welcome to come along; there's plenty of room."

I could hardly believe my ears. Here it was again: Manny's dream, Michael's. But this was Tom, a pipe-carrier long involved in cultural work. In a state that was sort of outside myself, I fell headlong into his vision, and both of us became increasingly enthusiastic and vitalised as we discussed the practicalities, some of which were sorted out on the spot. Tom was certain that a Tribal grants writer would be able to garner financial backing.

Thrilled to the core, I knew this would not be a repeat of history. Tom was not only a visionary but had already brought into being a range of cultural activities. His voice was influential, heeded and respected, and he had a wide network of connections among Native and non-Native people. Suddenly it hit me: barely a half-hour had passed since leaving the Medicine Wheel and I had been given my answer. Breathlessly I told Tom about the prayer.

He chuckled. "Like I said, powerful place, that island. Guess I've finally shared my dream with the right person."

I was trembling, hardly able to believe what was unfolding. What he said next tipped me even further into unreality. "An' it's not my only dream. It's not just about the knowledge. My concern reaches deep into the loss of heritage an' identity, an' the separation of people from themselves, from each other, from spirit, an' from that greatest teacher and healer of all, the nat'ral world round us.... For a long time I've had this vision of settin' up a traditional encampment. A place where people of any age an' colour can participate in Native American cultural activities in a nat'ral settin'...."

"Which would help them not only rediscover their heritage and identity, and heal them, but also communicate the value system of the Native American way of life and a sense of the sanctity of the land." Rehearsed time and again at Vallican, the words tripped off my tongue.

This was it: the original vision for Vallican that seemed to have come to naught. I could hardly listen as he revisited territory I had envisioned in detail many times already: a cultural encampment, set in the mountains, away from the encroachment of twentieth-century life, where families – children, young people, adults and the old folk – could experience traditional teachings, learn the skills of hunting and fishing, weapon- and tool-making, the lore of plant medicines and food-plants; how to tan hides, make clothes and moccasins, weave with rushes, build an earth-lodge; discover the arts of tipi life; experience real story-telling. "This is true education," I gushed. "And I believe it's one of the keys to help turn our society aside from the wanton destruction of our environment and our headlong rush into extinction." Fired into a long discussion, we began marking out the trails we would have to blaze to manifest this vision.

After a couple of hours, we shook hands and parted company. I returned with the children to the Slocan Valley, light-headed with the realisation of this swift and seemingly-perfect answer to my prayer: working with elders to preserve what was left of the Native American way, and its relevance as a foundation for education and healing. I felt as if I had been resurrected. The synchronicity was astounding: I had missed the ceremony yet arrived prayerfully on time to meet up with Tom. Perhaps, I thought, this was the way Old Man Coyote worked: letting me think myself lost, deserted in a dark place then at the last possible moment, switching on the lights.

Strangely enough, Coyote had recently literally entered our life, in the form of a pelt from Tom which was now the crowning glory of Nick's dance regalia. While it seemed utterly appropriate, some people had wryly wondered whether I could handle the challenges that would accompany the presence of the mythical trickster-teacher.

If this was an example of how he worked, I was sure I could.

THE WHEEL TURNS

Over the next couple of months, Tom and I continued to plan the double-vision whenever he visited the Valley or I made a trip down to the Reservation, and I began to really get to know the pipe-carrier who had seemed so formidable at the first Salmon pow-wow, and who had since opened his heart and his home to our drum group from the Slocan Valley. Towards the end of spring, he dropped by to tell me to prepare a preliminary proposal and budget for the first project, which we called "When the River Ran Free",[29] to submit to the Tribal Council. "There are those who believe, an' we have their support: Dale, Jude, Doll, Mike. Those who care about tradition. But you should know...." His gaze, usually direct, wandered off to the view over the river. "There are those who'll talk. A liaison like this'll provoke gossip."

Words I had never forgotten sprang from my lips: "Their suspicions are of themselves."

The fact was, he was with Nadine, and there had never been the faintest hint of any physical attraction between us. Further, I was aware of the benefits of working closely with a man without the tensions inherent in an intimate relationship. Especially one that fulfilled a personal dream of bridging cultures: a Sinixt pipe-carrier who spoke the language, lived the traditions, knew the songs, the plant medicines, the stories, the land, what would be needed and who could help or teach, working alongside a blonde, blue-eyed Englishwoman whose skills lay in the "white" realm: organisation, translation of a vision into a written proposal and budget, and the record. Other words from a time that seemed like a lifetime ago echoed in my mind: "Remember, we thought it'd be of more use to have you in a white skin this time round."

With the help of mutual friends, we pushed ahead swiftly. Tom's elderly father had already served as an advisor and source of information for numerous non-Native academics; Tom felt it was time for "blood at the helm". We would begin with Martin, then take out at least three or four other elders while the weather still held up. With the final draft of the proposal for "When the River Ran Free" ready, en route to Auntie Vi's and the Independence Day pow-wow in Nespelem I called in at Tom's to go over it. He said we would meet with the Council sometime after the weekend.

This time, the pow-wow barely held my attention, but by Monday morning, I still had not heard back from Tom. Guessing he needed to present the proposal on his own, I was despondently packing up to go home when Louella pulled up in Auntie Vi's yard in a cloud of dust.

"You're supposed to be at the Council Chambers with Tom!" she cried the moment I opened the door. "He's been there since eight-thirty!" It was almost ten-thirty.

Aghast at how I could have misunderstood and appalled at the missed opportunity, I sped down to the Tribal Agency – fortunately only a ten-minute drive away – and rushed inside. Tom was sitting outside the Council Chambers. "Took it for granted you'd be here," he said by way

---

29 "When the river ran free, Salmon gave us life." Martin Louie, Arrow Lakes/Sinixt elder-shaman, Colville Confederated Reservation.

of explanation.

"You haven't been in yet?" I said in disbelief. At that moment, the door to the chambers opened and we were invited inside.

Getting up, Tom yawned and stretched, then poked me in the arm: "Now don't you go tellin' 'em you got a better handle on Indian time than me...."

For the second time, I sat in the large, airy room, far removed from my original fantasy about how a Tribal Council might meet: instead of a sacred fire and a ceremonial pipe, the twelve or so people were sitting round a large oval table, with glasses of water and sheaves of paper; wearing not buckskin but suits, shirts and ties. The Colville Tribal representatives had read our proposal with interest but certain reservations: the positions (such as mine) should be posted and bids for a contract sought, rather than an outright grant given.

"All these things'll take too long and they're unnecessary," said Tom sharply. "All I need to get goin' is to hand, apart from modest wages and some financial backin' for basics such as food an' videotapes."

It soon became clear that any go-ahead would not be immediately forthcoming, however. Silently berating my own unreasonable expectations, I followed Tom upstairs to another room for a hastily-convened meeting with the Cultural Committee. On the way, he quietly said to me: "You know, I was also asked, 'Why bring in outsiders?'"

Unsure what he meant, I raised my eyebrows.

He shrugged. "I told 'em: 'For four years I've been tryin' to get this off the ground. I've met with disinterest, resistance; ev'ryone fades away when it comes time for the leg-work. But I tell Celia 'bout it; she's enthusiastic, she's excited, she wants to do it an' she does it. That's how come we got these papers an' figures here to put to you. An' the ideas just keep on comin'. I don't turn helpers aside.'

"From now on, Celia," he added vehemently, "you've gotta be with me at ev'ry one of these meetings!"

Much as I appreciated what he was saying, I was taken aback. Of course I was seen as an outsider. No matter how strongly connected I felt, I was an outsider.

The next meeting with the Cultural Committee, a couple of weeks later, was headed by Aunt Mary, a Lakes elder I knew personally. In a more congenial atmosphere, it was mooted that two interpreters might be a wise idea and the names of several elders came up, to which Tom had no objection. The other positions would still have to be posted, however; in the meantime, three grants writers would be assigned to the project. Chilled, I tried not to worry. I had Tom's word.

As we left the Agency, we were joined by an Arrow Lakes Council-member actively involved in cultural enhancement. Expressing her full support of the project, Doll talked about it to Tom for a while then turned to me, her cheerful, pretty face beaming as she laughed: "As for you, you looked like you were in a trance! There's those of us that support you."

I took heart in the message. His usual calm self, Tom took me down to Coulee Dam for lunch but I couldn't eat for excitement. We talked of the future, and he had moved onto the second project by the time he was driving me back up to Auntie Vi's: "We gotta start lookin' now to find a place in the mountains for this camp. My grandfather, he told me: 'Go up to the mountain, that's where the answers are. The mountain has no price-tag. The greatest teachers are the trees an' the animal-spirits. Each animal, each plant has its own story....' I was raised by my mother, then given over to my grandparents soon's I could tie my moccasins. They taught me Indian." His eyes took on a faraway look. "I'd go to the water ev'ry day, even in winter, with my grandfather. Go to the sweat-house. Learn the medicines that thicken an' thin the blood. We was never sick a day.

"Then in time the Catholic priest turned up." He sighed, and his tone took on a tired resignation. "I gotta go to school. I didn't like it, but my grandfather said, 'In order to survive, you must learn these things. These are what you will need to live now.' So I was sent to school." He gave a brief laugh. "I also had to talk English in order to survive, even though my grandfather hardly spoke a word of it.... I was told I needed supplies for school. It was hard. It was a different concept for 'em. 'What do you need?' he says. I tell him, 'I need paper, a pencil, crayons.' 'Then go an' get these things.'

"Then I'd run out an' need more. 'What happened to the ones you had? You used 'em, gave 'em to the teacher? Why give these things away?'" Tom shook his head. "It was a different concept for them.... My grandfather made all the decisions, right or wrong, an' took all the responsibilities for his actions. It was all built around grandmother, she was the Queen Bee, the centre of the power. Woman is the foundation. When a man takes a mate, she leaves her home, her name, gives up ev'rything. He builds around the foundation. Without the life-giver, there is no foundation...."

Like Bob's words, they had the power to move me still.

"Had a buddy lived in Omak. A hard-livin' man, a drinker, a fighter, a logger. He turned hisself round when his wife died. When the foundation went. He got baptised at her burial. He's preachin' now." After a thoughtful silence, he continued: "When my grandfather died, I took over a little. But my grandmother, she sorta became as grandfather.

"It was always hard for her to get the concept of the dollar. We'd shop for groceries. Used to walk there 'n' back, miles on the dirt-road, packin' what we could carry. Never accepted a ride. Once my grandfather was gone, I'd see what was needed, go out an' spend twenty bucks. That was a lot then. Four gunny-sacks of supplies. Problem was how to carry 'em. Would take three, four journeys. So sometimes the police give me a ride home. My grandmother, she expected it'd always be this way. We ran low of some stuff again. I said I would take the dollars to school on the bus, get what was needed an' pack it home. This time it was only a couple of bucks of stuff, so I only took a couple of bucks, but she gave me a lickin', since: 'You stole the change! I know how much groceries cost!' No explanation would help – it was easier to take the beatin' than try to explain.

"So I was raised by my paternal grandparents, a full-blood Sinixt. My brother, Pierre, he was raised by our maternal grandparents; they was strong Catholics. So even though we'd have the occasional sweat an' pipe together, there's a big difference between us."

He was amused to hear of my early impression of him and how that had changed as I came to know him at our drum.

"You know," he mused, "part of the magnetism of Yellow Bear is that he's got those bushy eyebrows, like my grandfather. An' deep pain is an attraction to all of us."

It was like an echo of what Louella had said. What did it mean? Before I had a chance to ask, we were interrupted by the loud banging, and the car began to judder fiercely.

Tom was behind the wheel of a different vehicle almost every time I saw him; arriving at his home, I would invariably find him under the bonnet of yet another. Cars and vans came and went like I imagine horses and ponies might have, a century ago. This time we were in a big black old Buick whose windows opened when they chose, and usually stuck. On our way to lunch, a steadily increasing "dugga-dugga" noise had made him stop to change a tyre.

Like tattered remnants of a witch's dress, raggedy black chunks and strips of rubber were now flying past my window. It was surreal: they were flying forward faster than we were travelling. The car lurched sickeningly and the rest of the back tyre overtook us at speed before jouncing off into the ditch. Tom braked smoothly and with a horrible grinding sound brought the vehicle to a controlled stop on the verge.

I had to laugh. Tom chuckled, more with resignation with this lame old pony than any sense of relief.

Thankful that we were miraculously still in one piece, I never thought about a message being imparted. It was enough that we were stranded about four miles from Nespelem on a lonely stretch of road with no other vehicle in sight.

"Got any cash?" asked Tom. "Used mine up at the restaurant."

I looked in my purse. "Two American; twenty Canadian." Holding the notes out, I could not help wondering what use money would be in such a desolate place.

"Canadian's no use." He got out and walked across the road. Watching him in mystification, I noticed the long, battered, rusting, corrugated-iron roof, almost hidden from sight, he was heading for. Perched below the highway on a shelf of land on the edge of a cliff above the great rift carved by the once-mighty Columbia was a tumbledown garage. A sun-bleached sign barely exposed it as a tyre store. And of course, Tom knew the owner and struck some kind of a deal with him so that we were on our way again within twenty minutes on a couple of "new" bald tyres.

Tom's equanimity gave me new heart: I would practise patience, and trust. As we parted ways, he asked: "You comin' down for the camp-out this year? Northern Lights's invited."

"Of course. This'll be my third. Maybe it'll be a good time to network; there's always interesting things happening."

"More'n you might think," Tom said quietly, enigmatically.

COYOTE SWEAT

An annual summer celebration of sobriety begun in 1977, the camp-out was a weekend event traditionally organised by Tom's family and friends. Held on a twenty-acre site on the banks of Roosevelt Lake adjacent to the family property, a legacy still intact from the days of the former settlement of N'chaliam, it had annually increased in size. This year, the fourteenth, would see almost three thousand people come together in celebration, a testimony not only to the growing numbers of recovered alcoholics but also the healing role played by reconnection to heritage and to the land.

All land holds spiritual power, all land inspires, but some places are power-points, where lines of energy come together. Made sacred through ritual and ceremony, the memory of which is held by the Grandmother and Grandfather rocks, they act as a kind of storehouse of spiritual energy. Like the great henges in England and the Temple Mount in Jerusalem, the Arrow Lakes ancestral sites in Vallican and near Edgewood, the traditional fishery at Kettle Falls and the gathering-grounds at Inchelium are all places where for millennia human consciousness and energy has been focussed and directed. No great stone monuments mark ancient North American sacred sites, however; to the Native American, the Creator speaks through the natural world.

Approaching the encampment by ferry as the sun was setting was like entering another time-zone. Barely visible among the darkening trees, the tipis were ghostly shapes, hazed by smoke; on the shore squatted two sweat-lodges, separated by rough wooden palisades. But for the thrum of the engines, for a few, breath-taking minutes it could have been another, older age.

Parking my van on the periphery, near the water, I joined Northern Lights drum-group, one of many colourful conglomerations of tents mushrooming in random groups of families and friends. The air was sweetly redolent with the scent of crushed pine-needles, the earth soft and sandy, pricked with spikes of yellowed grass and littered with crisp pinecones and clumps of straggly Oregon grape.

Taking Grandmother Drum to the central arbour, a pressed-earth arena in the middle of which stood the sacred pole and over which, like a great wheel, was suspended an enormous, gently undulating, translucent parachute-silk, we were one of five drums given a space on the edge and invited to take our turn. Steady heart-beat, the drumming continued late into the night, accompanied by regular, mournful hoots of the Gifford ferry bringing load after load of new arrivals.

Expecting the next morning to begin in the usual leisurely way, visiting with friends and enjoying a Rez breakfast, I was surprised to be woken early by Nadine: "Get up and be ready to go."

"Go where?" Her intensity slid off my sleepiness like a lead weight.

"Tom said he wants to take Yellow Bear 'n' you 'n' me on a little trip. Something he wants to show us. 'A special place,' he said."

Intrigued, I was up and ready in a half-hour, including arrangements for my children, but

Indian time was operating. While waiting, I thought about offering to help out in the camp kitchen, where breakfast was being prepared. Over the weekend, two meals a day would be provided free of charge to anyone who wanted them, and since there was no entrance or camping fee, the camp-out depended entirely on voluntary effort – donations of food, service or money. Watching the formidable team of Native women preparing a mountain of food put me off; I'd only be underfoot. Knowing of their impatience with people who needed direction, it was simpler to make a financial contribution.

Just before noon, with no idea of where we were going and imagining we would be back within a couple of hours for the afternoon celebration, Nadine, Yellow Bear and I got into Tom's big sedan. It turned out to be an opportunity to really get to know Nadine, beside whom I was sitting, as we were taken over the pass to Keller, across Roosevelt Lake on the ferry and deeper into Washington State than I had ever gone before. Small towns flashed by; the only constant was the desert landscape of Interior Plateau country, shimmering in the heat: arid sweeps of a beauteous desolation, punctuated with massive black boulders, some of which were the size of a house. Pitted and scarred, scattered haphazardly across the landscape like game-pieces carelessly cast down by the gods, they were similar to the great boulders littering the land around Nespelem.

Whatever spat such massive boulders so far had to have been a monster. I wondered if it was connected to Crater Lake, in Oregon, where five years ago, I had cycled round the caldera's vast, thirty-three-mile rim, meeting not another soul, my breath taken away as much by awe as by the elevation. I recalled the archaeologist, Wayne, telling me of an ice-dam a mile high, situated at Missoula, Montana, which had given way at the end of the last ice-age, releasing a force of water that had carved out the dramatic landscape. And perhaps carried these great boulders for hundreds of miles.

With wide-open windows blasting furnace-heat through the taut atmosphere of an unvoiced question, four hours rolled by. Eventually, cruising down a long, straight, featureless stretch of highway seemingly no different from the miles we had already covered, Tom slowed the car and pulled up on the soft shoulder. Without a word, we all got out and stretched stiff, aching limbs.

Relentlessly the sun beat down on my head; my hair felt crisp as straw. Like the last round in a sweat-lodge, the stifling heat seemed bereft of oxygen. Short, shallow breaths were the only way to breathe. Wondering what on earth we were doing here, I scanned the sere, flat landscape, studded with scrubby clumps of sagebrush. Then I noticed Tom was already fifty feet away, with Yellow Bear and Nadine not far behind. Grabbing my drum, I scrambled across the ditch and followed them, crossing a slight ridge that had been indiscernible from the road. A few hundred feet away, on a flat, sandy area surrounded by scrub, were three massive, grey boulders which had not been visible from the road. By the time I caught up, the others were standing silently together by the largest. A weird fizzy, weighty sensation had begun in the area of my adenoids and a pressure was building in my temples.

Becoming aware of them for the first time while in England the previous year, I had come to connect such sensations to the presence of power-points in the landscape.

Starkly-blunt in the desert landscape as the black, Vulcan-tossed or meltwater-transported boulders we had passed earlier, the three hunchbacked great rocks, sharkskin-grey, seemed to shimmer, like a mirage.

" ... Old Man who made this," Tom was saying, his voice soft as a feather-stroke. "S'ink'leep."

Coyote.

Then I saw the opening. The largest grey boulder was a sweat-lodge, made from solid rock.

Tom was telling the legend of how it came to be there but my ears seemed to be stuffed with cotton wool and the stupefying, weakening feeling was intensifying. Closing my eyes, I was just thinking I should sit down before I fell over, when Tom's voice broke through the fug: " ... I know what Coyote done; I know what his purpose was here." He began a soft chant, took it through four rounds, then prayed, beginning in Sinixt and finishing in English. The last part was for protection. Without a word, as if she knew exactly what she was doing, Nadine crouched down and crawled in through the opening.

Like Jonah entering the maw of the whale. I shivered, despite the heat.

Motionless and silent, the two men and I waited. A smudge of smoke twisted out of a little aperture near the top of the dome; evocatively pungent, the aroma of sage drifted through the still, hot air. Nadine's powerful voice rang out: a Native American chant, spiralling from heaven to earth. Reflecting on how such a slight, seemingly frail young woman could sing with such force and depth, I was shocked by an anguished scream which ripped the chant asunder.

Wailing and screaming, every word clearly audible, Nadine tore the whole basis of her womanhood, her existence, apart. Warrior, I understood: in this life trapped in the form of woman. Eventually she fell silent, and emerged, dishevelled and pale. I found myself unable to offer comfort; unable even to look at her: raw, exposed, bleeding in the desert like a wounded fox, unapproachable.

Yellow Bear entered the lodge. There was a long silence then his familiar voice sounded, praying, chanting, but it was somehow hollow, dimensionless. When he came out, he turned away and faced the horizon without saying a word.

Female, male.... It had come round to my turn. A deep reluctance to enter the strange, massive Grandmother rock had by now filled me. Coyote, catalyst for painful challenges to an unbalanced ego, was working his magic and I was not sure I wanted any of it. But Tom had brought us here for a reason; I could not back down.

Scrambling awkwardly inside, I sat cross-legged facing the entrance, holding my drum to my chest, a shield of sorts. The inside of the rock was pale sandy-pink, smooth and curved, shell-like. I was inside the mouth of the Grandmother. Above my head were a couple of small, round apertures; before me, the entrance offered a hermit-crab view of the world.

By my feet, in a shallow depression among traces of charcoal were a couple of ripped-up lottery tickets. Dismay, then resignation prickled through me. Was no place sacred?

Tainted by my feelings, the silence pressed in. What was I doing here? It was hard to clear my mind. Then I thought about the lodge being of Coyote's making: where better to petition for aid in making the cultural projects manifest?

Brushing the scraps of paper to one side, I crumbled some sage into the little fire-pit, intending to burn the losing tickets and clear the space where someone must have unsuccessfully petitioned for another kind of aid. But the sage would not accept the flame, allowing only mere wisps of smoke. Feeling chastened that I could not even get such a simple thing as a smudge going, it came to me to sing the Grandmothers' song, a traditional song to which I had particularly taken (or which, perhaps, had taken to me). Yet despite the hot, dry air, my drum sounded dull and lifeless; my voice weak and wavering.

Enervated and bewildered by the disempowering equation of sun, rock and sand, I moaned a plea to Coyote that he knew our motivation and would give us the aid we needed, and crawled out again. Ashamed of my weakness and unable to face the others, I sat on the hot, gritty sand and tried to pull myself together.

Tom disappeared into the lodge with his medicine bundle. There was a long silence. Eventually smoke twisted out of the apertures, carrying a wordless chant. At least he sounded like himself.

The sun was lowering orange-red into the darkly-smudged horizon as we drove away. Several miles passed in a heavy silence, then Yellow Bear glanced sideways at Tom. "Did you burn that debris ... of gambling, Tom? Did you clear that imbalanced use of energy?"

The pipe-carrier nodded.

Despite the many questions hovering at the edge of my consciousness, I could not focus my mind to pull them together. Perhaps the others felt the same; the miles sped by in silence. Gazing dazedly at the passing landscape, I knew the exhaustion I felt was not just from the long, hot drive: sleep was impossible. As was trying to understand what it all had been about. It felt like one of those occasions jam-packed with symbolic significance, but elusive, unwilling to be pinned down. For some reason, Tom had been moved to bring us to this awesome place, Coyote Sweat. Four strong people, each remarkable in his or her own way: an Arrow Lakes pipe-carrier and healer; Yellow Bear, a natural leader, trained as a minister and graduated from establishment into personal, spiritual expression; Nadine, a Doukhobor (spirit-wrestler) descendant and a sensitive; myself, newly-aware of a sensitivity to earth-energies and individual and group dynamics, and an ability to perceive the more subtle levels.

Our arrival back at camp after dark was met by a multitude of complaints about our lengthy absence. I didn't know what to say to my kids, how to describe a day given over to a journey of almost four hundred miles in order to sit inside a hole in a rock in the desert and come out like a wet rag, return home in an exhausted state that reached into the following day.

None of us ever mentioned – not even to each other – the eerie place, Coyote Sweat. Yet after that day, our lives became for a while closely intertwined and mutually supportive; as if some invisible thread now connected us.

COYOTE DREAMS

Only a couple of days after returning home from the encampment, Tom turned up at my door, grinning widely. "The Tribal Council's agreed," he burst out, before he was even inside. "Since the Tribal Agency's cuttin' back, the River project's gonna be funded by a grant. It'll be in place by late summer."

My heart gave an enormous thud.

"But rather than kick our heels waitin'," he continued enthusiastically, "we should present the proposal for the cultural encampment. But we got no name for it yet."

"How about 'Coyote Dreams?'" I said excitedly. The name had popped into my mind just the previous night.

"'Coyote Dreams'.... Yeah, I like that."

"Do you get it? This," I waved my arm in an arc, "is all the Old Man's dream and it's time he woke up, because it's turning into a nightmare."

Tom grinned. "Yeah, I like that, too."

I thought of Coyote Sweat and wondered if whatever had happened there had inspired the idea. It did not feel like something I could ask Tom.

Within a week, Yellow Bear had facilitated a meeting with a couple who had recently set up a tipi encampment for young people at the north end of Kootenay Lake, an hour's drive and a ferry-ride away from Nelson. It had taken Peter and Jan almost six years to get the project going; Tom reckoned with their experience and advice and with the Tribal Agency's backing, we would swiftly wing our way through to opening day. By mid-August, the couple had prepared a detailed report for our use and agreed to accompany us to the next Tribal Council meeting.

Around the same time, a friend of Tom's passed on to me his personally-researched, twelve-page list of potential funding sources. An eccentric New Yorker, poet and lay member of the Order of Saint Teresa in Spokane, Al had been trying to start up a youth theatre group on the Reservation for several years without success. "Wishing you all the luck and more. Seems you might at last walk where no-one has managed to tread before." Something about the personal note he included made me uneasy. But how could I have doubts, on the brink of a long-held dream? My prayer had been answered; this was destiny at work.

Even the fact that my landlord had decided he wanted to live at Robert's and had given me notice to vacate didn't throw me; through a local friend who wanted to be involved with the River project, I found another house immediately on the quiet back-road not far from Winlaw. Not only did it have a private little beach on the Slocan River, it was cosy and would be easier to heat in winter. It was the perfect interim place, until my place on the Reservation was established.

Although convinced of the potential for success of Coyote Dreams, Tom and I knew we would have to persuade the Tribal Council in terms of financial return and opportunities for employment. Obviously, it would be a non-profit entity; part of the strategy involved specific times set aside for well-heeled foreign participants, enabling the project to be self-sustaining and the profits rolled over to subsidise the involvement of local families and follow-up cultural experiences for Native people undergoing rehabilitation treatment.

The location Tom had in mind was a long-abandoned campsite in the mountains at Twin Lakes. Although I was unimpressed by the access through a modern camping resort, the site had potential: clean, sweet mountain air; a wide, empty stretch of clear water; no sight or sound of anything to do with twentieth-century man but the presence of a couple of ramshackle cabins at the entry-point. Tom pointed out that they could be converted into an unobtrusive (obligatory) first-aid post and office, and would be well out of view of the encampment.

Throughout August, I worked on a comprehensive budget and made up a tri-fold leaflet, going as far as to obtain copyright permission from the University of Lethbridge, Alberta, for the illustrations. Everything was prepared together with a progress report in time for the crucial Tribal Council meeting at the end of the month.

First on the cultural representation agenda that day was Aunt Aggie, with a request that the teaching of Native language be given priority on the Reservation as the key to cultural continuation: "Without the language, the culture is without meaning."

"But which language?" one of the Council members asked. I remembered thirteen tribes had been thrown together.

"All of them!" she replied without hesitation, her voice strong. I wondered why she was doing this alone and made a mental note to talk to her later about Coyote Dreams, which I thought would be the perfect place to facilitate her ideas.

On our turn, after a short introduction by Tom, Peter gave a dynamic presentation about the instigation and success of the tipi encampment and Jan reiterated its validity as a cultural project. A new addition to our team, Leo, a Kutenai spiritual elder, told how he had recently become involved with the project through his friendship with Tom, and spoke of his experience working with Native youth and the need for direct involvement with culture. On my turn, I spoke of the importance of reaching out to children through elders and through nature.

It seemed a great impression had been made. Tom and Michael, another Lakes spiritual leader, were delegated to manage the project, a circle of thirteen tipis was agreed upon and it was decided that the Council would put up the seed money and supply the tipis. A grants writer was assigned. There was some reticence about using the site at Twin Lakes, however, and eighty acres at Bonner's Ferry was suggested. Catching my eye, Tom shrugged.

What seemed like mere detail didn't matter to me; I was ecstatic. It was happening: our dream, our vision was coming into being. At the last moment, as chairs were scraping and papers being shuffled together, the Arrow Lakes Council member who had – seeming aeons ago – spoken about politics at one of the Arrow Lakes Band meetings, said in a low voice, "There'll be a political run-around as regards this encampment ... as with anything else."

Looking round, it seemed no-one had heard Butch but me. I had no idea what he meant, and no inclination to ask anyone or press him for an explanation.

Later, I would wonder if it had been one of those messages meant for my ears only: a caution.

WHITESTONE

Tom reckoned the ideal starting date of the River project would be early September, so we could squeeze in several trips before the nights closed in. Since nothing more had been said about the posting of positions, we continued to fine-hone the preparations and trim the overheads while the rest of our little team prepared to make themselves available. Despite Tom's repeated enquiries, however, no response was forthcoming from the Council for over a month. We resigned ourselves to postponing the first trips until the following spring.

Then Tom phoned to tell me about an opportunity for a practice-run. Invited to pilot a Colville Tribal houseboat hired by the North Cascades Institute for a four-day seminar, "The Columbia: The Way It Was", hosted by anthropologist David Chance and historian Bill Layman, he had insisted he wanted me to videotape the lectures for the Tribal archives.

Coyote at work again, I was sure.

Staying true to the rhythm of the seasons, September drew to an end with a grand Indian summer finale. Under a clear cobalt sky, I drove down to Inchelium with Nick to meet Tom at his home. The arrangement was that we would pick up the houseboat from the landing above Coulee Dam the next morning, bring it back to Inchelium – a trip of about five hours – and the following morning, another two or three hours by water would bring us to rendezvous with the group at their starting-point at Kettle Falls.

It was still dark when Tom woke us, and bitingly-cold; under the glare of the car headlights, the rough grass outside his home had been transformed by frost into a carpet of sparkling opal-dusted spikes. By the time we reached the Sanpoil Valley, Snpakcin, the light for which Tom's father was named, illumined an oyster sky which seamlessly melded into the diaphanous veils of mist hooked on barbs of pine along the highway.

An icy, gusting wind snatched at the muffled, rounded, shadowy figure who waved us onto the ferry, and whipped frothy white horses out of the dull-grey waters of the lake. It was a short, Stygian crossing; we were the only passengers.

Reaching the dock of the Colville Tribal Houseboat Enterprise about an hour later, we found it deserted, the waste-ground of a car-park empty. Nick had fallen asleep. Tom got out for a smoke, looking lonely and lost against the seething pewter mass of water and sky split by a smudged pencil-line of distant shoreline. Slowly the rising sun burned off the mist, revealing a clear, blue sky.

Over an hour later, the staff arrived. No-one seemed aware that Tom had arranged to come early, and then we were confused with a booking to take out a party of elders on a pleasure-trip that morning, the irony of which only struck us after the paperwork was completed, for we left on the tail of the very people we wished to record.

"Should've taken advantage of the situation and eldernapped them," I said as we watched the sterns of two houseboats full of elders heading across the open water in front of us.

"Enough!" Tom cried, and opened the throttle. Irritated by the long, cold delay and poor communication, he exuberantly gave himself over to an illusion of freedom and adventure, cutting swiftly across the lake at an angle in order to overtake and leave the elders behind.

It does not serve to think you can be even one step ahead of the elders, especially in an area rife with the presence of Coyote.

We didn't consult the map displayed in the fore-cabin; all we had to do was head north. Nick and I went inside to explore the spacious, modern facilities of the brand-new, twelve-berth, fibreglass houseboat. Berths were curtained off for privacy; there was a compact bathroom and generous kitchen-dining area. Returning to Tom at the front of the boat, I excitedly told him how easy it would make our eventual purpose. So wrapped up were we in potential and the future, we did not notice the present-disaster towards which we were speeding.

Man-made, Roosevelt Lake pools one of the biggest river-systems in North America; looking back, the situation seems ludicrous, but suddenly I was aware that the banks of the lake (how could this be?) were barely a hundred feet away and narrowing at an alarmingly swift rate. Saying nothing to Tom, I ran up onto the top deck. Not far ahead, the water arrowed into a "V", too tight for a houseboat. A frightening sense of dislocation swept over me. "Tom!" I called as I ran back down. "Where are we? It's getting terribly narrow out here."

"Holy cow!" gasped Tom, who had been lost in reverie. He cut the engines, but momentum still carried us forward. We scrambled to examine the map and within seconds realised we had somehow overlooked the great eastern curve of the lake and in going directly north, had entered an estuary.

"We've come up the Sanpoil!" Concern coloured Tom's voice. "Hope I can git this thing turned round in time." Putting the engines on slow-ahead, he carefully pulled a U-turn which brought us round, but not without scraping against scaly, grey tree-roots, which snaked down the sandy banks into murky green depths.

When we were safely heading back toward the lake, I laughed in relief: "I always did want to check out the Sanpoil, but that was a bit close for comfort." Then, because I was coming to know Tom well enough: "Guess this isn't a story I should repeat. And I better make sure about the kind of Indian guide I get next trip!" For once it was not me on the receiving end of Native American humour.

"I'm never gonna live this one down!" he chuckled. "First thing I do is get us lost up the Sanpoil. What could've been easier than just headin' up-lake?" He shook his head. "Good thing there ain't no elders here with us. You got every right to ask what kind of scout I am."

Always ready to accommodate Coyote, Tom added the incident to his repertoire.

By the time we returned to the open waters of the lake, the elders were a long way ahead of us, chugging along close to the north shore. Thinking about the memories they might be sharing with each other, I chafed at the lost opportunity. Suddenly it struck me that we had just experienced a profound Salmon Story metaphor: fresh young 'uns, cocky, streaking away ahead, and first thing they do is follow the wrong channel and almost run themselves aground. By the time they cotton on, reorient, turn round and get on track again, the wise old ones are way upriver.

Way ahead; an indefatigable progress; Knowing the Way.

For a long while there was little to do but enjoy the leisurely pace and beautiful scenery, and watch out for the occasional half-submerged log. Cups of coffee in hand, we droned lazily along under an electric-blue autumn sky feathered with numinous streaks of high white cloud. The needle-sharp wind had given way to a soft, warm breeze which ruffled the wide waters, giving back the sky in a steely-blue reflection. In the lee of the shore, the massive, sheer rocky cliffs and sere hills were perfectly mirrored: ancient, exposed bones of the land. Small, secret coves, littered with tangles of skeletal, sun-bleached driftwood, tempted me to ask Tom to take a break. There seemed to be no sign that man had ever passed this way, until I saw the blunt, sawn-off ends of the logs that floated by and remembered: this massive body of water was the result of a major man-made interference. These eroded, crumbling cliffs and parched, scrubby, sand-coloured hills, sparsely dotted with clumps of pine trees, were the uppermost slopes of a once-deep canyon; far below the corrugated water lay the gathering- and hunting-grounds of a once-fertile valley. Age-old trails, settlements; all had been drowned. We were traversing an immense watery graveyard, an awesome monument to an entire way of life.

"This time of year," Tom mused, as if reading my mind, "the people would've moved up into the mountains for the hunting. The animals are movin'. Grizzly ready to go into his den as the tamaracks turn gold, before the first needles fall. That's how come we say in Indian: 'The needle has the strength to break the bear's back.' Bear is part of our winter ceremony.

"The deer are movin', they're easy to find. The bucks are about to rut, their necks thick with fat. Huntin', that's a test of skills, bravery, manhood. There's a lot of food, everywhere.... Then the people come back down for the fall salmon-run, for the chinook. The Sanpoil, Nez Perces, the Moses, they come from the south to Kettle Falls. The Lakes on the spit below where the bridge is now.... Berry-pickin' would be over. By now they'd have been crushed, dried, made into pemmican."

Dreamily I listened, picturing what had once been. After an hour or so, I became aware of an enormous outcropping of sheer cliffs ahead, that seemed to gleam brightly with a light that was not just about the sun. Almost white, they loomed vertically out of the water, like buttresses pushed up and hacked out by the hammers and chisels of the gods, a convoluted jumble of outcroppings, ledges, nooks and cracks. As we drew closer, I could make out images: stern, ancient Native profiles with high foreheads and strong features, frowning into the distance; exotic, alien-looking animals and birds, crowding the serrated surfaces. Just above the crest hung the pale shaving of an old, waning moon; a ghostly apparition.

But the feeling was not just about the look of the impressive cliffs. A heavy, ominous silence seemed to blanket them; an aura impregnated with the supernatural. A familiar fizz tingled in my adenoids and temples; not uncomfortable, but reminding me of a newly-discovered sensitivity to sacred sites. Filled with awe, I found myself whispering to Tom to take us closer. He smiled, inclining his head in some kind of acknowledgement that was more than agreement, and wordlessly steered us alongside the cliffs. Sheering straight down, they disappeared into darkly-greening depths. High above, great boulders perched on lips and ridges. Startled by flocks of rock doves that burst out of fissures and crevices, I had the sense of an imminent explosion of life, as if the sun-baked, wrinkled hide of an immense mythological monster were about to shiver and raise itself from a long, deep sleep.

"Whitestone." Respect breathed through Tom's gentle naming of the place. "Lots of stories about this place. Skunk got thrown off here."

"Could you cut the engines?" I asked. Tom obliged, and we were carried in a reverent silence under the awesome cliffs, the only sound a few clicks of my camera. Even that felt like an intrusion.

Clear of the area, Tom restarted the engines. "Imagine what they was like 'fore they flooded the valley...."

Unable to tear my eyes away from magnificent Whitestone, I stood transfixed until a bend in the waterway took it out of sight. Tom recounted tales of Skunk and Coyote's irreverent antics in the area, but I sensed there was more he was not telling me. I said nothing; it would happen if I needed to know. While Nick had a turn steering the boat, we talked of mundane things or stayed in quiet contemplation as we steadily made our way north, past the conjunction with the Spokane River and at length coming to the last stretch of water south of Inchelium where Tom took over again for a game of dodgems with the Gifford ferry. On waters smooth as glass we turned into a small sheltered cove on his land, and as we docked, a bald eagle swooped powerfully and silently out of the pines, gliding low over the water back the way we had come.

While I wished we could have avoided disturbing it, it seemed like a good omen. Tom said nothing, but from his slight smile, I guessed he thought the same.

COLUMBA-MA

"The Columbia does not flow, it is operated." [30]

The next morning, we faced a strong head-wind. It buffeted the houseboat, which suddenly seemed small and fragile. Choppy waves slapped and thumped at the prow and sprayed the windows; like a distressed creature, the craft shuddered and quivered. Both throttles had to be opened wide and even then we made slow headway. Calm as ever, Tom told us an earthy story about Coyote, Mouse and the Serviceberry Sisters that soon had us all in stitches. Then he pointed out a cone-shaped mountain, flanks stained a strange rust-red. "That's where my grandfather conducted part of my trainin'," he said reflectively. "When I was a small boy, I wanted my war-dance outfit real bad. Finally my grandfather says okay, but like anythin' else, I'd have to earn it. He says, 'I'll put a stick on the trail up the mountain an' the next mornin', you get it an' bring it back to me.'

"I was only six or seven but I was up at first light. I run up that mountain an' found the stick about half-ways an' brung it back like I was told. I was real proud. But next day I had to do the same thing again, only this time the stick was a little ways further up....

"It went on like this, day after day, till one day there was a moccasin with the stick, an' the next day, another. Just to give me a taste, I guess. But I was gettin' more'n a little sore, an' not just from all the runnin' up an' down.... But I'd've done anything for my outfit, an' you can be sure I never dared ask – I knew better'n to question my grandfather – but I was thinkin' to myself: 'What do I have to do all this runnin' up and down a mountain for? When'll I get my war-dance outfit?' Day after day, nearer 'n' nearer the top. But I was gettin' nearer 'n' nearer to blowin' my top....

"You gotta remember, my grandfather, he's up there afore me ev'ry day.

"Finally, he says it's time. That day I got up real early. I was determined to get up there before him an' laugh in his face when he come puffin' up with that goddam stick.... It was barely light enough to see my own feet when I started out, but I raced up there fast I could." He chuckled. "An' there's my grandfather, sittin' waitin' for me, laughin' at my red face. Me gaspin' my last, an' him not even breathin' heavy. An' beside him, spread out on a rock, was the most beautiful thing I ever did see: my war-dance outfit."

We both smiled, then Tom grew serious. "You know, my grandfather'd never ask no-one to do nothin' he couldn't. I know now he was teachin' me 'bout bein' willin' to work hard to get what you want, an' 'bout bein' patient. An' gettin' me into shape at the same time!"

The houseboat laboured on. A small island close to the shore, which had always intrigued me, came into sight.

---

30 Blaine Harden, *A River Lost.*

"Barnaby Island," said Tom. "It's one of the old burial-places. Boaters often have problems in its vicinity."

"The ancestors probably don't appreciate having their peace disturbed and polluted by twentieth-century technology," I commented. "Like Eagle yesterday."

Slowly we drew parallel with the grassy, tree-crowned knoll, the houseboat's engines straining in the powerful, gusting head-wind, roaring as the propellors lifted out of the prancing, white-capped waters. Then there was a stuttering; the engines puttered, and died. It was eerily quiet; like sad voices seeking entry, the wind moaned round us, slowing the boat. Rocking madly, it slewed sideways and began to drift south. Back the way we had come.

In the direction Eagle had flown, I found myself thinking. This was too weird for words.

Tom went out to the back and lifted the engine housing while I numbly watched our retreat from the little island.

Barely had Tom spoken of it, when it had happened. As if the ancestral spirits had been listening and thought they'd show us.... Had we disturbed them? Or was there some message? Whitestone; Eagle; ancestral spirits stopping our progress: it was like a bizarre dream, difficult to interpret.

Eventually Tom managed to get one of the engines going and we limped into the marina at Kettle Falls barely twenty minutes late. Neither of us said a word about what had happened; I hardly dared think about it. In any case, there were other things that called for my attention: people were still arriving, supplies and luggage had to be loaded and the houseboat's engines serviced. Despite our concern that it might have been forgotten, the Tribal video-recorder had been delivered but without an instruction-manual and only one three-hour video.

I wondered if this meant there would only be three hours worth recording. If so, out of two full days, which three should I choose? Probably Tom's contribution, I thought, as I taught myself how to use the machine.

Darkness was falling by the time everything was ready and an introductory meeting was called on the shore, under the pines. There were about fourteen participants, professional or retired, some pursuing university accreditation, others there out of personal interest. As they introduced themselves, I became aware of one incredible, revealing thread linking them all: the magnetism of the Columbia River. Each person felt like they were coming home.

These were not sentimental or New Age people; just ordinary, everyday folk. Thinking back to Bob, I wondered what was the memory; what scent of which source, had brought them to this great river; which lifetime....

Distracted, I was brought back to earth with a bump when I realised what had next come under consideration. While the participants were willing to accommodate the unanticipated presence of myself and an eight-year-old boy, it emerged that the long-distance arrangements had failed in one respect: they had been given to understand it was a non-smoking trip. It had been noticed that their pilot was a fairly heavy smoker.

As soon as the matter was openly raised, Tom said, quietly and politely, "I don't like the idea of havin' to sneak out whenever I want a smoke, leavin' someone else with my responsibilities. Nor am I willin' to compromise. I have my habits, I don't wish to offend no-one. I'll simply step down."

I was aghast. The two seminar leaders were not at all happy either, but had to accept the group's consensus.

Feeling terribly upset, as if everything was falling apart (was this the message: wasting time on the river with the wrong people? Go back to where you came from?), I broke in: "You're foregoing a treasure-trove; Tom's cultural knowledge will provide a vital depth and colour to your experience." What I did not have the courage to say was how history was being repeated: yet again, Native people were being marginalised. But nothing I could have said would have made any difference.

Tom had arranged to dock at the end of each day with a view to being picked up and returning to sleep in his own home ("why should I give up my comforts?") and rejoin the group the next morning. That evening, we returned with his arranged ride to Inchelium.

"That's it then," I said, unable to contain my deep disappointment. "What a shame."

"No." Tom's voice was firm. "You go ahead as we planned. I'll drive you back up in the morning."

"Not without you," I said adamantly. "No way. I'm not going 'less they take you. And I'm not going to put you out, either."

"Don't mind 'bout me. You have to go ahead. The experience'll be good for you, for what we have planned.... I'll pick you 'n' Nick up the end of the day and bring you back again."

It was no use protesting. I stared out into the darkness, down the ghostly tunnel formed by the headlights. "They were muttering like mutineers. Should make them walk the plank," I said tightly.

"Those folk," Tom said mildly, "they don't like my smokin'. I can understand that, that's why I simply removed myself – they don't like tobacco. But did you see how many cases of alcohol they were loadin' onto the boat? All the wine an' spirits? D'you think they won't indulge their own addictions? An' do that all the way down alongside the Reservation, on a Tribal house-boat.... D'you think they consider how offensive their own habits might be?"

The next morning, Tom drove us back up to Kettle Falls. I was sure the group would have seen the light but nothing was said and he left as soon as he had dropped us off. After some organisation, we all squeezed into four cars and were driven up to St. Paul's Mission, where the historian, a well-built, compact, ruddy-faced man with a jocular sense of humour, dated its founding back to the 1850s. Not knowing we were beginning here, I had not brought the video camera, but I was so irritated by Tom's exclusion that I didn't care: a smoke-blackened, rotting hulk of a decrepit, glorified log cabin did not seem to me like much of a monument.

"In 1805," Bill was saying, "the early explorers and mapmakers, Lewis and Clark, traversing the American West, discovered an immense, cold, swift-flowing river, the greatest salmon-river in the world, choked with the fall run of spawning salmon. It was the first time they used the word 'great' to describe a waterway. The salmon – coho, chinook and steelhead – were numerous and plentiful, and there for the taking, since unlike their Atlantic cousins, Pacific salmon die after spawning. The area was heavily populated with different tribes, whose annual catch didn't even make a dint in the incredible numbers. These mid-Columbian tribes were as yet unvisited by white explorers, unlike the Pacific coastal tribes who'd been so devastated by the arrival of white trappers around 1775.

"By the mid-1840s, diseases such as whooping cough, scarlet fever and measles, carried in by the missionaries and settlers, had wiped out close to ninety percent of the Native population of the entire Columbia Basin. It took only thirty years to cause an unprecedented scale of tragedy; the Native people had absolutely no resistance to these imported diseases. Of course, the mass deaths were interpreted and promoted as God's will and like everywhere else, the Indians' spiritual practices were denounced as the way of the devil. There were many conversions to Christianity. But the priests didn't always have an easy time with the Indians.

"At that time there was a priest here at St. Paul's Mission who was so swiftly and widely successful that he became quite famous. Noted by his superiors and full of himself...." He paused. "Of course, he only had this success since most Native beliefs had devolved, through attrition and disease, into superstition. Anyway, one of the chiefs at that time had something going with a young girl." His eyes twinkled. "This was of course roundly condemned by the priest, and the chief, who couldn't see anything wrong with his behaviour, was excommunicated. He subsequently got sick and died, whereupon everyone was informed that he had gone to hell.

"Soon after, a medicine man took ill, died and then came back, as medicine men are wont to do sometimes. He told the people what he had seen 'on the other side': Jesus riding on a horse, and on the right hand of Jesus, on an equally magnificent horse, the chief! They were riding together!

"This so greatly discredited the priest that all his converts fell away, and he was forced to retire and went to live in California."

We were led along a faint, sandy pathway, cushioned with pine-needles, weaving between the stately lodge-pole pines and scrubby shrubs behind the mission to the top of the cliff overlooking Roosevelt Lake. Undergoing its annual cleansing, Hayes Island was nowhere to be seen.

"This great stone...." Bill indicated an immense, grey granite boulder near the cliff-edge, crisscrossed with myriads of long scars, some deep as two finger-widths. "This was relocated up here from the area of the falls below, prior to inundation. It was used as a whetting-stone to sharpen the fishing spears of the tribes, for thousands of years."

Stroking one of the reams, I imagined the great falls, boiling over the rocks, misting the air; the thunderous roar, drowning out all other sound; the silver-gleam of leaping salmon, following an irresistible call; the hive of human activity; the spears flashing; the hundreds of racks of thousands of fish hung to dry. What tales this dislocated Grandmother rock might have to tell.

Having lost Tom, the two seminar leaders now had to act as pilot. Taking first turn, Bill headed diagonally northwards across the lake while David, portrait of the ethnographer – studious-looking, bespectacled, pipe-smoking, wearing corduroy and tweed – related the prehistory of the area. Absorbed in the mechanics of recording and still seething about the vital missing element, the living oral record, I could not at first pay attention.

" ... A river birthed in violence," he was saying when I at last settled into recording, "in great floods. About thirteen million years ago a great flood of molten lava carved out the basin. Then over a period of about four million years, wave after wave of basalt rock blanketed what is now eastern Washington until it was five thousand feet thick, forcing the river up into what is now Canada. In turn, the rise of the Columbia Plateau diverted the river round what has become known as the Big Bend, as it leaves Canada. Southwards, then east, and west...." His hands eloquently described the twists and turns of a great river carving its way through a raw landscape. "Even the eruption of the Cascades, about two million years ago, didn't hinder it from finding its way to the Pacific.

"But it was relatively recently that the greatest floods known to North America occurred, over a two-thousand-year period, fourteen to twelve thousand years ago.

"Imagine an ice dam, five times the height of the Grand Coulee. Situated in north-western Montana, it stood two thousand five hundred feet high, and behind it stretched a lake that was about half the volume of Lake Michigan.... Suddenly, the dam breaks; the lake bursts out with the force of over two hundred Hiroshimas. At speeds of over fifty miles an hour, it rips through the land, carving out ravines and canyons, cutting a massive gorge through the Cascades.... Events like this happened some forty times. It's these catastrophic events that are responsible for the dramatic landscape." He waved his arm, as if it were all still there, not blasted away and drowned.

A wave of sadness swept over me. Gone forever was the Columbia that had awed the explorer William Clark, almost two centuries earlier, into recording "the horrid appearance of this agitated gut swelling, boiling &[sic] whorling in every direction". Below the Grand Coulee dam, the rugged gorge's water-sculpted grandeur had been devastated with rip-rap, a facade of concrete slabs and rocks, to prevent erosion.

Slowly we approached Barnaby Island. Darkly-wooded, mirror-imaged, it seemed preternaturally still. Would the ancestral spirits slip unseen across the waters and give the narrow-minded among us a taste of the supernatural? My mood darkened as we cruised by without mishap during a coffee-break, and when Tom's training-mountain hove into view, I reflected how what might have been the most worthwhile and vital part of the Columbia "as it was" had gone up in smoke.

David took over as pilot as Bill continued the seminar, telling of the early pioneers and fur-traders. The voyageurs were clearly his personal favourite: "Five foot five or less and of a certain robust stature, they'd cheerfully carry a hundred-and-eighty-pound load and their canoes when necessary, for many hundreds of miles, singing their rousing songs, proud of their way of life and their passion for this new land."

Wearing tired jeans and a faded check shirt, his hair ruffled and jaw unshaven, his enthusiasm bright and contagious, he might have been a voyageur, in a previous incarnation.

"While the Mississippi is known as the longest river in North America, it falls only about a hundred feet over its seven-hundred-mile journey. The Columbia travels four hundred miles and drops over a thousand feet. That's the steepest drop per mile in the country.

"It's the last sixty years that have seen the massive changes in the Columbia river." A faint note I read as regret entered his narrative; I guessed it was the untouched wilderness that held his imagination, his heart. "The U.S. Army Corps of Engineers worked hard to tame it, attempting to make it navigable. They blasted their way upriver, smoothing out the rapids and the smaller waterfalls by blowing obstructions to smithereens. But it was the great falls at Kettle Falls that proved insurmountable. Only inundation could contain that force."

While the rest ate lunch, I retreated aft and watched the wide, calm reach of water behind us, cut by the wake of the boat. The only sound was the drone of the engine.

What must it have been like, hearing the sudden, awesome, incomprehensible thunder of dynamite; witnessing the shattering of the Grandmothers and Grandfathers, the mighty waters turning into a seething, muddied mass, clouded by dust rising mushroom-like into the air; changing overnight and forever that which had been there as long as memory held? Now it was a conquered, tamed river, slow and fat. But not completely. I recalled a family who had gone swimming in the waters near Edgewood a couple of years earlier, who had got into difficulties and almost been lost. The trapped, sullen waters swarmed with powerful, unpredictable currents and eddies.

The sun was lowering among the pines as we approached Inchelium. Two bald eagles launched themselves from the pines in Tom's little cove, coasting away through long, golden shafts of dust-moted light as a motorboat came sweeping out to meet us. Tom was at the helm.

"Good moorage at the sacred gatherin' grounds," he called to Bill as he steered alongside the houseboat. "Just follow me. An' tell your folk they're invited to experience the sweat-lodge if they want."

It was clearly the first time most of them had been on a Reservation: their uneasiness was apparent as they disembarked, seemingly taken aback by Tom's easy manner and ready generosity and the further welcome of a blazing campfire on the shore, where another Arrow Lakes spiritual leader was waiting, the same one who had been chosen to work with Tom on the cultural encampment project and who was also the Lakes artist who had been commissioned to paint the murals at the Kettle Falls Historical Centre. Michael greeted everyone warmly. "We got two sweat-lodges in preparation," he announced. "One for the men, the other for the women."

Perhaps because no-one but David and Bill knew what a sweat-lodge was, there was scant response. A sudden chill made me shiver: I was sure it was not just from the lengthening shadows reaching over us.

Fed by Michael's partner with pine and aromatic cedar, the camp-fire surged and crackled and did its age-old work: folding chairs were brought out of the houseboat and a circle formed around the flickering flames. Tom and Michael remained standing. The group was about to get a Native perspective after all.

PATCHES OF SNOW

Tom gazed into the crackling flames of the campfire. Belatedly I recognised his jacket: red-checked; party to an unforgettable embrace; figured in a drum-dream in what seemed another life. Left behind to be given away when Red Cloud took his final walk, it had sparked enormous controversy among the "executive" of the Rebirth of Mother Earth Medicine Wheel gathering when Tom had been chosen as the recipient.

"I met that young lady there," began Tom, indicating me, "as part of my journey into a deepenin', active involvement in the history of my people, the Sinixt."

Not surprisingly, neither the name nor its Anglicised form meant anything to any of the group apart from David and Bill; rare are the maps demarcating North American tribal groups that include the Lakes Indians.

"Now, I'm not interested in the better-known tribes such as the Sioux, Apache, Cree, Arapahoe or Nez Perce," he continued. "There's plenty of information about these peoples already written up in books, an' I don't read books. I only talk what I want; I don't go beyond my own grandfather. I listened to my grandfather an' he would say, 'This is what my father had said....' To me that would be hearsay. So I can only go back to my grandfather, because he is the one that raised me.

"As a very small child, just as soon's I could put my own moccasins on the right foot, get my pants on the right way they was suppos'd to go on, an' my shirt, I was given to my grandfather an' my grandmother to raise, for my teachin' an' schoolin' in the Native American way. My grandmother could not speak a word of English, not one whatsoever; my grandfather, he could speak very little. I was brought up with them till I was a young man."

Knowing Tom was about to open a window onto the two worlds of his upbringing, I felt a surge of protectiveness. Would these people appreciate what they were about to hear? If he went on to tell them his whole story, would they judge him?

"In the Native American way of life," he was saying, "there's only three stages that a man's born to. When you're small, you're a little boy. You need help, guidance. When you get to be eight or nine, ten, you leave that little boy, then you come to be a young man. After that, at sixteen, seventeen, eighteen years old, you're a grown man. You was already taught how to hunt an' fish, how to do all these things.

"I was brought up in this land right here. Down to Barnaby Creek, this whole area here was my teachin' ground. I could go on with incident after incident that my grandfather taught me. But at the beginning, I couldn't figure out why my grandfather hated me so much. I didn't know why he didn't like me."

I stopped caring what other people thought; I hadn't heard anything like this before.

"There's a canyon down here, they call Theodore Canyon," he continued in his quiet, melodious drawl. "An' in that canyon there's three trails. There's one at the head of it, one at the middle, one towards the bottom. An' when it was twenty, thirty below zero, four feet of snow, my grandfather said, 'Well, when I was out huntin' today, when I was down there lookin' for pheasants an' grouse,' he said, 'I shot this cayote [coyote]. I need this pelt of this cayote, I'm gonna do somethin' with it. But I laid it over this log at the first trail goin' down Theodore Canyon, I got to followin' the track of this deer an' I clean forgot about my cayote.'

"Well, I'd already had my moccasins off, I was ready to go to bed. But he wanted this cayote an' when the old people, my elders at that time, when they wanted somethin', they didn't want it yesterday, they didn't want it in five minutes, ten minutes from now, they want it now. So I put my moccasins back on, my leggin's, my snowshoes, an' went through the woods.

"Up on top, there's a big flat up there, could see all the way to Theodore Canyon. After dark, I got to the first trail at the canyon an' I walked down that trail an' I looked an' looked for that stupid log. The moon was out and bright an' I got down to the bottom of that canyon. No log.

"I thought, 'Well, the old man, he's gettin' old. Maybe he meant the second trail.' So I went to the second trail." Tom paused, shaking his head. "When I got home, it was about one o'clock in the afternoon the next day. I couldn't figure out why the old man would do things like that to me.

"But that was a very good lesson, a very good teachin' for me. Now I see kids an' grown men that can't sleep in their own house without havin' the light on." His voice softened, calling for full attention. "They can't walk out in the woods after dark. They're afraid of what's out there."

In the following emotive silence, I thought about Tom's ability to engage the listener emotionally, which is a reflection of the power of the oral tradition. To the Native American, knowledge can only be acquired through experience; "knowing" is a state and not an assimilation of facts. I was coming to recognise a fundamental truth that would profoundly effect my perception of the meaning of cultural preservation.

The pipe-carrier turned and indicated the mountain to the north. "You can see the mountain. That's called White Mountain, an' just off the left of White Mountain there's another called Buckhorn, then off of that one is Siddowns, that we call Sna-mut, then off of that is Grizzly. There's a winter creek comes down from Grizzly, and that's where my father was took when he was a little boy, and that's where I was took. I was up there about ten days, must've been seven, eight years old. And that was where I learned faith, where I learned understandin', the love that people have for one another.

"I seen a lotta Christians, a lotta people that go to churches, do a lotta things, but they don't have no faith. They just go like a record-player; you turn it on, an' it goes around an' around. That's what they do: they go to church ev'ry Sunday, they go through the motions. But they don't have faith."

"Yeah," a voice from the group interjected, "I heard it like you don't go into a church an' come out a Christian, no more'n you go into a garage an' come out a car!"

Tom chuckled along with everyone else, then gracefully raised one arm and pointed to the mountains. "When I was taken to the mountains up there, my grandfather had such faith, in the Great Spirit, the great power of Mother Earth, the power of the water that keeps ev'rythin' alive. Without these things none of us would survive.... An' I was took up there an' left. Built me a sweat-house, one that faced the east; built me a sweat-house on the other creek that faced the west. In the morning I would sweat in the one that faced the east, to greet the new day; sweat in the one that faced the west, that would take all my bad thoughts an' my sorrow, when the sun

went over. With the power of the Creator, I would know all the bad things wouldn't come back."
He shifted his feet, scuffed at the sandy earth, and continued in a quieter voice: "After I got older
I was given back to my parents, round about twelve, thirteen years old. When I got sent back to
my parents, I got sent back to a whole different life." His voice dipped and slowed: "I got sent
back to a life of alcohol, of violence."

At that moment, the ferry approaching the landing at Inchelium sounded its extended,
mournful horn, which echoed hauntingly across the valley. Exquisite timing, I thought.

"I was sent to school. I had a very hard time because I didn't know English very well an' I
was made fun of. It was just terrible growin' up, because on this Reservation here, there's half
'n' half. There's half Caucasian an' half Native American people. My whole family grew up
traditional. They had their ceremonies. There's a lotta people out here, what you call 'Apple
Indians': red on the outside an' white on the inside. An' they would condemn us, because we
were traditional. I was ashamed of my buckskin shirt, my buckskin coat, even though it had
beautiful quill-work on it. But I couldn't have a coat that was bought from J.C. Penney – didn't
have the money. I made it till I was fourteen, the doors were opened an' I was told that I was a
young man an' I was old enough to make it out there on my own. From that time on I grew up
very bitter. I grew up very angry. I was lucky enough at that age – I hit the loggin' camps an' I
logged all over Washington, Alaska, Idaho, California. Even logged back in Maine. An' that's
all I did, all my life.... Most of my life," he added after a pause. "There was six years of my life
that I spent in prison. Because I tried to live up to what the people put on me: that I was
nothin' but a dumb blanket-ass."

Tom had told me he had served time, but to me it was simply part of a dark and difficult
journey that had shaped the human being I had come to know. Named for the patches of snow
that lie on the ground at the time of his birth, Kay-pe-out was warm-natured, generous, honest
and reliable, often gently teasing like an old friend, and the spark of the company he kept; his
Aquarian vision and love of humanity evident in his heartfelt desire to bridge cultures. But
would these people appreciate this, or would they judge and dismiss him?

The air was cooling swiftly. A chickadee began chirruping, a sweet evensong
accompanying the harsh message of Tom's next, quietly-spoken words: "Nothin' but a no-good
Indian. The only good Indian was a dead Indian. An' it just about killed me, tryin' to live up to
all these expectations of me.

"Because I could go in a bar – I drank heavy, I worked hard an' I played hard – I could go
in a bar an' I'd see a bunch of people sittin' there an' I'd pick the biggest guy or the ugliest guy
or whatever, an' I'd attack him, right there on the spot. Because at that time I weighed
two-hundred-twenty pounds an' I was just as hard as any stone that you could see." His voice
took on a compelling rhythm: "I was a high-climber an' a hook-tender, an' I topped trees a
hundred-fifty feet up. I rigged 'em; I felled timber. An' it just about killed me, tryin' to live up
to these expectations that people'd put on me. Through that anger, through that bitterness, I
landed in prison. I spent six years in prison. Walla Walla...."

The high-pitched evensong of the tiny bird seemed to be reaching an unbearable intensity.

"Until a few years back, fifteen, sixteen years ago, I finally woke up." Tom shook his head
gently, as if sloughing off a bad dream. "Found out how sick I was. An' saw I couldn't go
through life being bitter, hatin' people. An' ever since that day I've worked so hard to keep a lid

on my hate. There's a lotta things happen, day after day after day, that upset me, but I still work hard and give thanks to the Great Spirit, the Great Creator, that I can keep a lid on it. An' I work today with the alcohol programs; I work with youth."

Part of Tom's work was attempting to instil a sense of cultural pride in young Native Americans. Like him, I often felt my own generation to be lost, caught in the middle of conflicting worldly value-systems. But as Tom put it, children have just come from spirit and elders are beginning to return to spirit; neither are fully of this world, so they are connected on subtle levels.

"I go to different ceremonies," he was continuing. "Medicine Wheel ceremonies, winter ceremonies, pow-wows. I war-dance. I do anything I can to show our people – not only the Native American people, but the European people, the black people, the yellow people. I don't care if you go to Safeway, you pull into a gas station – you walk anywhere, you rub elbows with these people. I figure it's up to me to step over that line, to try to make friends with all these people. To share my culture, to share my tradition an' share what I have. To let these people understand and know, that yes, the Native person still lives. An' he's still practisin' his Native ways.

"An' I also learn a lot from the European people. When I go to a ceremony, even right now today, and there's nothin' but Native people sittin' around, I've been so angry ev'ry time I hear these Native people talk about: 'Honky-this, honky-that. God, I hate that white man. White man has took all this away from us. He's took that; now he wants this, he wants that.'

"I took it as long as I could, an' I spoke. I spoke at a winter ceremony. A lot of my elders were sittin' around." His voice softened. "I got up an' told them people: 'If I hated the white man this much, I'll be damned if I was wearing this shirt I got from J.C. Penney. I'll be damned if I was wearing these Levis. An' I'll be damned if I'd walk outside and jump in that iron horse an' go – white man made that.... But without all that, it makes it pretty tough to survive!'

"An' I said: 'The worst of all, one of the worst creations that man made, you'll lie for it, you'll steal for it, you'll even kill for it. But we put that way up here,'" his hand reached into the air above his head, "'on the highest pedestal. And that's that almighty dollar. Worst evil that was ever created. We all value that. We value it so much that our loved ones are falling off by the wayside. We put a high price on money.'" He paused, stroked his chin then continued: "You know, I can only go back as far as World War Two. That's as far as I can remember. I can go back that far and remember that the United States had a war over there, with Germany, with Japan."

A deeper sound joined with the chickadee: a lonely, whooping call I did not recognise.

"An' luckily we won that war. And when we won, we put rules 'n' regulations over there. We fought Korea; won that one too. United States put rules 'n' regulations down over there – they had to abide by them. Then we fought Vietnam. I still don't know what the hell went on there!"

There were a few snorts of agreement.

"An' the Native American also fought a war." Tom's voice quietened again. "An' he lost.... I told my people we were very fortunate, for the white man could've just lined the Native American people up along them banks," he indicated the shore of the lake behind him, "an' just shot 'em all. Just mowed 'em down. The only thing left would've been just like the story of the dinosaur: just what you read in books.

"But I take my hat off to that white man, that he said, 'Let's let them live, but let's put them on a Reservation.' He gave me my life. And therefore it's up to me to work alongside of him. Not behind him; try to work with him. An' with that, an' my talks, I go around the country. I might not see it in my time, but maybe in my grandkids's time, that once again this whole land will not see colours anymore. They will not see the white man. They will not see the black man. They won't see the yellow man. They won't see the red man. They'll just see human beings."

Tom had once said to me, "We can choose to be chosen." At the time I hadn't understood, but was beginning to see that while he represented and furthered the Native American way of life, he was actually going beyond tradition, moving toward a creative sea-change that will strengthen Native people's role in society. It is a courageous and controversial undertaking, for he often faces negative criticism and judgement for working with "outsiders" and sharing what some Native people still consider to be secret knowledge.

For a few moments, Tom let his words sink in, then resumed: "Then, an' only then, will I be able to stand up on White Mountain and look in all four directions and see one powerful great nation, as we once had. Took people like us to destroy it. An' we're not happy yet." The mournful horn of the returning ferry almost drowned out his next words, softly spoken: "We still take from Mother Earth. She's the one that provides for all of us. Not only me, not just the Native American, but for ev'ry one of us. I know you buy your food at Safeway, same's I do. The corn, peas, potatoes – all come from Mother Earth.... But who could care less about what's happening?" His voice roughened. "Just flat go out an' rape. Took all the damn timber off'n her, dug holes in her, ripped her breasts out, blasted rock, an' mined. Done all these things, the whole nine yards, an' we're still not satisfied. We're still after progress." His tone curled sarcastically around the word. "An' why? Because our power's not the Great Spirit. Our power's not the Creator. Our power's that almighty dollar.

"When we get done poisonin' this land, where nothin' is edible." He indicated the waters of Columbia. "You can't even eat the fish out of that river now. The poison that's comin' into it, comin' from Castlegar, from Trail – all the stuff that's dumped into that river.... When we get done," his voice rose strongly, "that damn dollar bill's gonna make the poorest soup you've ever had in your life!"

There were nods and grunts of agreement.

"I think it's about time people start wakin' up," he calmly resumed. "An' the reason this ground's so sacred to us here: we've been havin' gatherin's here for fifteen years, me 'n' my brother. Because we give a damn about our people. We care. We put our first gatherin' on here, we had fifty dollars-worth of hot-dogs, ten dollars-worth of hot-dog buns an' fifteen people. Ten of 'em were family, five of 'em were friends.

"Last year, we had over three thousand people. The things, the stories that we have to share; our sweat-lodges, our songs, our prayers, we share with one another. The understandings that we have, that if we give this up...." A sweep of his arm encompassed the splendour of nature all round us. "If we keep destroying what we're setting on, ain't none of us gonna live. Lot of us could care less; we're up in age, we ain't got far to go. Soon we'll be at the end of the road." His next words were spoken so quietly I had to strain to hear: "If nobody stops, what about them li'l ones?" He pointed at Nick and Victor, who were skipping stones across the water. "What the hell are we gonna leave them? They ain't gonna have nothin'. They ain't gonna have a chance. That's about the power we put on the almighty dollar.

"When I used to log, I had an outfit just like that one over there." He pointed to a logging truck, parked near the ferry terminal. "An' I had a loader, four logging trucks, three cats, a skidder an' a crew bus. I had seven pick-ups, two two-ton trucks. My take-home pay was three grand a day. I had fourteen people workin' for me. But my health went all to hell. I couldn't log any more. My loggin' outfit went, my wife went. She divorced me. That's when I woke up. I coulda had all the money in the world, but my health went – I couldn't enjoy that money. Couldn't go anywhere. Couldn't do anything. But once I traded all my money, all that stuff there for what I have today, I became one of the richest blanket-asses that ever walked!

"My spiritual walk.... I have the love in my heart for my people. I have the love in my heart for you. I have the knowledge, the power, and the thanks that I know that the power the Great Spirit gave me is up here." He touched his hand to the centre of his chest then brushed it across his forehead: a man who chooses to live in the way of his spiritual teachings as given him by the Creator. "The power to make a choice, to be where I'm at, to be where I wanna be, to do the things I wanna do. An' the things I like to do is goin' to places, gatherin's; talkin' to people, havin' people talk to me. I like the honesty of people. I like to be down-to-earth.

"An' that's why I was so proud an' honoured, when the gen'leman right there mentioned yesterday, about the smoking. I honour that, give thanks to him. Sure, I coulda talked to Bill, talked to Dave an' said, 'Oh maybe I'll go out back, go up on top, when I want a smoke.' But that's not what it's all about. If what I do, if my habits are gonna bother somebody, then the best thing to do is just to remove myself. It's just like alcohol in my life. I know what it done to me, know what it was doin' to me, so I just removed it. Don't need it.

"An' after I met you people...." Tom's voice softened as he continued: "An' I won't get to know you as well as I wanted to get to know you. But it sure did something an' you can hear it from me: it gives me a whole big lift that there's people still around the country – might not be many of us, but there's people out there that care. People that think back to what it was like, what it used to be.... But what it is like now today," his voice was almost a whisper, "an' this scares the hell out of me, to see what tomorrow's gonna bring. Right now, I wouldn't have any one of these young people here...." Again he indicated Nick and Victor. "I wouldn't put one of them in Seattle, to walk down the street. I wouldn't put one of them in Portland. I wouldn't even put one of them in Spokane. There's no safe place there for them.

"But maybe if we wake up an' start doin' somethin' about it now; maybe our great-grandkids – maybe one day they can walk down the streets in Chicago on a rainy night or somethin', an' a black man'll open the door an' say, 'Hey, you kids, you better come on in, get outta the rain, spend the night in here where it's warm and continue on tomorrow', without havin' to fear. They won't see colours no more. They won't have all this prejudice in their hearts, all these bad feelin's."

Reminded of a time spent back-packing in Europe and the Middle East, and how generously and hospitably treated I had been by complete strangers only twenty years previously, it hit me how people then had been much more open and trusting, unlike in today's climate of uncertainty and fear.

Tom shifted his weight from one foot to the other, looked around the group and grinned. "But what I was suppos'd to talk about, was the sweat. The sweats are going down there." He pointed down to the lakeshore. "There's a man an' his wife, I asked 'em to put twenty-eight rocks in the fire, if you want to sweat. Dave's gonna sweat an' I know Bill's gonna sweat an' I will sweat. It's up to each individual whether you want to sweat or not. An' on the other side over there, is where my sister-in-law an' her friend's gonna sweat, if there's any ladies that wanna use the sweat.

"The sweat was taught to me – it can be used in two ways. The sweat can be used for just cleansin', like a sauna, an' it can be used spiritual. To me, my sweat is very spiritual. My grandfather, he said to me, 'When you have hard times, bad luck, go to your sweat-lodge.' The one time in my life I thought the world was comin' down around my ears, I went out there and was standing in the water, praying to the power of the water, because the water is so powerful. Look where it comes from, it never empties; to where that water goes, it never fills up. It never stops. Without the power of the water, nothing would survive. Not the tiniest insect or the biggest, meanest animal. Without water, without that power, we wouldn't exist.

"An' I was standing in the water, an' I was asking the Great Spirit to help me, because things wasn't goin' the way I wanted 'em to go. An' I ask my grandfather ev'ry time I need help. 'I need a sign, something for you to tell me, just what the hell am I doin' wrong?! Show me a direction to go, show me somethin', show me anythin' that I can understand!'"

Remembering my prayer on Hayes Island, I had to smile.

"An' when I turned round an' was gonna come back, I looked at the sweat-lodge an' it come to me: just like I was comin' out of the womb, I just come out an' been reborn, an' I was standin' in the water, cleansing myself, just like when a baby comes from the mother an' is new an' cleansed. Pure, clean, fresh.

"An' I stood there an' looked at that, it was comin' into my mind: reborn from Mother Earth an' I'll travel all through this life an' when I get to the end, I'll give my body back. What a way. What a blessing. Then it's like the Great Spirit says, 'Tom, I can do no more for you. I've gave you ev'rything I can possibly give you. I gave you a body, an' I gave you two legs an' two feet for that body so you can't be stuck in one place, you'd be able to travel on Mother Earth. I gave you a mouth, the voice to sing, an' I gave you two arms, two hands, so you can pick food up an' nourish that body. An' I gave you two eyes so you can look an' see the beauty that I've left. An' I've gave you two ears to where you can hear the beautiful songs that is created out here. Then I gave you a spirit an' a heart an' soul, so you can feel. I can't do no more for you, I've done gave you ev'rything.... I gave you Mother Earth. She's the one that takes care of you. You get all your medicines from Mother Earth, you get all your food, you get all ev'rything. An' I gave you the sun, that gives you warmth, makes things grow. I gave you Grandmother Moon; the whole universe. I gave you ev'rything. I can only do so much, Tom, so you're gonna have to get off your ass an' start in a direction. You're gonna have to do somethin' for yourself.'"

He sighed deeply. "Just like each 'n' ev'ry one of us: we're all lookin' for somethin'. We're looking for something out there. We ain't gonna find it settin' down. Have to get up, look in a direction 'n' start walking. Look under logs, rocks, behind trees. Maybe you're like me: I was out there a long ways an' I thought, 'Hell, I'm goin' in the wrong direction. Turn round, go back to Go, but do not collect two hundred dollars!'" He laughed briefly. "Then I turn round, go in the other direction....

"Once I found out, that once I got up an' started movin' around – it was there, what I was searchin' for." He lightly touched his chest. "This is the answer I got in my sweat-lodge. Gives me a lot of answers. Takes away a lot of heartache that I have."

Again the drawn-out lonely wail of the returning ferry dramatically punctuated his words.

"An' I know that each an' ev'ry one of us has these heartaches. We have a lot of loneliness, a lot of emptiness. We don't have to. It wasn't meant for us to have these. So many things out here we can live for. So we use the sweat-lodge to purify ourselves. I'm not saying the sweat's gonna help you, gonna zap you, an' Indian songs are gonna come to you an' that ev'rything you touch's gonna turn to peaches an' cream. We have a job to do, each an' ev'ry one of us. An' I know that ... I can go on an' on all night!"

With a grin, Tom introduced Mike, but before the other man could speak, Tom flowed on, proverbial waters without end, spilling out an issue close to his heart.

SPIRIT ɪɴ ALL THINGS

The lake had stilled to a mirror-smoothness, perfectly reflecting the sere, yellow-ochre slopes of the far shore. Shoulders hunched, hands in his pockets, the lean, white-haired pipe-carrier resumed: "Last year, they were gonna develop this whole area. They were gonna put in sixty, eighty houseboats an' I don't know how many ski-boats; this was gonna be a resort, clear down from the ferry to the other cove." He gesticulated to the south. "There'd be a big condominium sittin' right here, a big gas-station, a golf-course, cabins 'n' ev'rything." He was pointing to the earth under our feet. I thought of another sacred place, the devastating intrusion of bulldozers, trucks and scrapers, trees pushed over and ripped out, earth torn and compressed.

"We went to our Tribal Council," Tom was continuing. "We were but only three, an' said: 'Why are you gonna develop here? Other people come here to pray, they come here to sweat, they come here to share.' An' they said: 'Oh, we need progress. Without progress, we can't survive.' An' I said: 'You know, it sure seems funny to me. Ever since I went to school an' read those geography 'n' history books, it's always the Indian that had to move. From the stories that I heard, it was the white man pushin' the Indian around. Now it's gettin' so bad, it's the Indian pushin' the Indian around!'" He waited for the sympathetic chuckles to subside. "'An' all for progress,' I said. 'You're tellin' us that these houseboats is gonna benefit my people. All of what's going on here, this big development, how is it gonna benefit my people? It's gonna benefit five, maybe ten at the most. Because that's all the jobs they're gonna have here, 'cause that's all the sober Indians you're gonna find here. To have somethin' work, you've gotta have the people to work it. You've gotta have sober people that can be responsible for these jobs. If you're gonna be out there meetin' the public, you can't be three-quarters shot. You know,' I said, 'first of all you gotta work on the people, you gotta fix the people first. The only one that's gonna benefit from that progress is the company that puts it in an' the people they put in there. It ain't gonna benefit my people at all.'

"It's just like these houseboats," Tom indicated the boat on the shore behind us. "You know, people had a great write-up on 'em: they'd make 'x' amount of dollars. But I have yet to see a cheque come in my mailbox. They say in ten years that these houseboats are gonna be a great turn-over. You bet, 'cause in ten years, they're gonna need replacements. Look at how they're made. It's not gonna benefit our people.

"So I said: 'On this sacred ground here, we're gonna make a stand. We're not against progress. We want jobs for our people, but we just don't want it here. We got a hundred sixty-three miles of lakeshore on the Columbia River – you could put it anywhere.' An' they said: 'Well, where would you suggest?' An' I said: 'Way down by San Diego!'" There was a ripple of laughter. "But we were losing ground, me an' the two other brothers that were working with me. We come back from a meeting in Nespelem an' we were gonna have to do something, because they were gonna take it. They were gonna develop it. How could we hold on to such a little piece of land? Then I said: 'Well, we've tried to go to their meetings, to do their things, an' we're gettin' beat. Bein' Indian people like we are, an' believin' in our songs an' our sweat-lodges, let's all go to our sweat-lodges an' we'll ask the Great Spirit to help us. We're outnumbered. They got much more education than we do; they know how to use these words, get around us.'

"So we went to the mountains an' to the sweat-lodge, an' we seen one animal. One animal says, 'Look at me. I am the answer.' And that animal was Luk'nux, the bald eagle.

"So with that we turned round and went back to the Council. An' I told the Council: 'You know, I've always wanted a full regalia of eagle feathers. An' if you develop this land, on the south end there's four eagle nests. That's supposed to be a sacred bird to the Native American people. An' you, as our leaders, if you say go ahead and develop that, then it's open season on these buzzards 'cause nobody cares about 'em. Then I will have my full dress regalia, because this is what you're tellin' me: that these sacred birds have no more meanin', no more value to the Native people.'

"That was what saved the camp. But we know we're not gonna keep it." Shaking his head, he sighed. "We're gonna lose it. They're gonna develop it. They're gonna put the marina in here. We know that just as well as I know I'm standin' here. But at least I had a lotta fun, holdin' 'em back for a while!"

The ferry sounded a mellow tone. As Tom turned away, it struck me that it was the fourth time, like four rounds in the sweat-lodge, completed. Laughing and chatting, people got up to stretch and fetch coats and jackets; the air was swiftly cooling. Until now, Mike had been sitting on the ground by the fire with his partner, a non-Native woman, nodding occasionally in agreement with Tom's words. He stood up, and I was impressed by the way the group immediately returned to their chairs.

A small, compact man, his sleek black hair pulled back into a ponytail, Mike's round, kindly face was concentrated in seriousness, his voice gentle but clear: "Eagle inspired me. The message of Eagle inspired me to consecrate a Medicine Wheel on these gathering-grounds, to act as a sacred seal. Because the Tribal Constitution protects anything that is sacred.

"It's only fairly recent that we've opened up spiritual ceremonies, after years of secrecy an' bein' hidden away in enclosures because of the judgement of the missionaries, the Jesuits, the priests. My instruction was to keep 'em hidden until this time, but now we can invite all peoples to see what they're about, what we do, what these practices were, an' share in them."

It felt good to know Tom's was not a lone walk.

"Last winter," Mike was continuing, "I held my first Winter Dance outside under the stars, the way it used to be – at last I can openly practise my ceremonies on these sacred grounds. Some of my work's for the environment. My major concern's the destructive effect of pesticides on medicine plants. I'm tryin' to share the knowledge of the plants' uses in such a way that others cannot capitalise on it. That's the reason that although medicine people share a lot of things, they also hold back a lot. Including a cure for cancer."

Not one snort of disbelief challenged the claim of this unassuming man, dressed simply in dark pants and a jacket, a baseball cap pulled over his brow.

"I'm also concerned," he went on, "with the difficulty of teachin' that most vital element of culture, the language, on the Reservation, since thirteen different tribes were placed together here.

The conflict of two educational systems is another problem, because the thought-processes of the Native American culture are quite different to those of the educational system. It teaches that the individual is important, whereas the Native way teaches that the group is important. This comprises not only men, women and children, but also animals, fish and plants: the whole eco-system.

"It's through ceremonial practice, however, that we're gettin' more and more answers how to help people understand these things, although it's a long road, with no instant results, no short cuts. The songs, the chants – the ones without words," he explained, "they're given when we go out into the mountains, never coming all at one time, but just in little pieces until there's a whole, a powerful tool to use to help people. Each one deals with a specific thing, a special area of life, an' helps bring a person back into balance with the natural harmony of life. The medicine plant works that way – it's not about treatin' the person, but about its spirit bringin' him back into balance, even if that may be death."

This understanding flooded my being with light. For one who believes that death is but one step on a long journey, it made a profound sense.

"In a similar way," Mike continued, "the Medicine Wheel's a visual prayer, showing a person the areas where they're lackin', the places or issues to pay attention to, that need to be taken care of. An' since it's a circle, a person will never reach the end of the Wheel. There's always another spoke to watch out for, another direction to move to, until in the end you get to the centre of the Wheel, the place of balance where the Creator sits.

"Prayer items're another symbol...." He shifted his position, which made me realise how still everyone else was. "In some cultures, a person might be given a bandanna, a reed, a corn husk, or a feather. You'll find the eagle feather in every Native culture. It's very important in this way: prayers are laid on it an' it's presented to somebody, so it's a physical prayer that can be looked at, touched an' felt.

"Likewise, each item of regalia is prayed on, an' in return it continuously prays with and for the person that wears it. A relationship's built up with the spirit of the animal, or bird, or any medicine item, an' then that spirit can be called on to assist – in life, in medicine work.

"This's my partner, Amber," Mike laid a hand gently on the shoulder of the dark-haired woman sitting by the fire, which spat and crackled as she added pieces of kindling to it. "Sharin' my life with a white woman's part of what I'm tryin' to teach: that two cultures can agree an' get along together, that their visions are similar."

A rainbow-bridge dream-vision, like Tom's. Quietly-spoken and modest, Mike had great strength of personality; he had spoken briefly but something about him affected those who had not taken to Tom, as I later discovered. Between them, the two men touched the heart of each and every person there.

Mike's words also helped me to a deeper understanding of the mythical contract with allies in the natural world that Coyote had forged on behalf of the two-leggeds: that the plant- or animal-spirit, if petitioned with humility, might "take pity" on a medicine person and reveal its specific power or impart its particular wisdom. The meticulous care of regalia also honoured this relationship.

The sophistication of traditional Native American beliefs was naively misinterpreted by early Europeans. There was no worship or concept of an animal god; Native people talk about the power of a certain animal, bird, plant or fish, or the water or wind, because they all have an energy, a quality that a person can discover within him- or herself: the Sumix. The Native American way is to believe in the Creator and in all things provided, all of which can help people. It is not a religion, but a way of life.

The Church has divorced the spirit-world from the physical; science denies spirit. In contemporary western society we have knowledge about nature, but not nature's wisdom; knowledge about the world, but not ourselves. We know how, but not why. By ignoring the spiritual foundation, we destabilise the world we are building.

Reminded of the legend of Frog Mountain – Frog stole the Fire from the people and when the mountain (Frog) crumbles, Fire will be returned to the people – I saw it could have another level. I had originally thought fire meant power but it could just as easily mean Spirit, and mountain could be a symbol for the material plane. Symbolised as renewer, Frog could be a force for the positive; the lesson being that the material plane cannot exist without the foundation of the spiritual. In our madness, believing we can be separate from Spirit, we are destroying our world and ourselves. The two-hearted people spoken of in the Hopi prophecy are those who have petrified themselves into believing that duality is all that is; when All That Is, is Oneness.

END OF A RIVER

After spending the night at Tom's, Nick and I were taken back to the houseboat at sunrise. It was another clear, windless day; under a cerulean sky feathered with free-floating hanks of angel-hair, the bite of early autumn clouding their breath, David and Bill worked their way through the early historic period: the incursion of the military, the great battles and wars, the eventual dispersion and relocation of the tribes onto Reservations. Using the video recorder and new tapes Tom had bought, I found it difficult to pay attention. Or perhaps it was a period I just didn't want to hear about.

Reaching the confluence of the Spokane and the Columbia at noon, we disembarked to visit a designated heritage site from the period just covered. The sun blasted like a furnace on the top of my head as we climbed a steep, twisting, sandy pathway up to a bench of grassy land at the foot of a shadowy mountain-shank. Surrounded by broken-down palisades, a scattering of ramshackle, long, low wooden buildings was all that was left of Fort Spokane. Despite the sun and heat, a dark, desolate feeling hung over the whole place. Leaving the group, I went inside one of the smaller buildings. Hazy with drifts of dust-motes, weak shafts of sunlight rayed through windows clouded and streaked with dirt and cobwebs. Spindly, yellow blades of grass poked weakly between creaking, rotting floorboards; a faint smell of fungus and aged wood tickled my nose, making me sneeze and reminding me of a story Bob had once told.

"Why go live in a cave," the Native grandmother had spat when told to leave her "primitive" tipi and move into a cabin, "where Grandfather Sun cannot touch me; where the air is dead?"

Feeling increasingly nauseous, I tried an adjacent building, bigger and in a better state of preservation. On the back wall was a display of faded sepia photographs, but what they portrayed was not what I expected: no soldiers and their wives but regimented lines of Native children, herded together for the occasion outside this very building. They all looked disturbingly the same: girls with tightly-braided hair, wearing ill-fitting, dark and heavy Victorian clothing; boys with short, cropped haircuts and dressed in what appeared to be a military uniform, with high collars. The blankness of their round little faces, the down-turned mouths and sad eyes told the whole story.

A powerful upwelling of emotion – combined anger and outrage, sorrow and pity – made me hurry outside again. The bright sunlight did not help; my head hurt – a strange feeling, like my skull was shrinking. The rest of the group was gathered round David, but with a sudden internal vehemence, I knew I could not stand to hear any more of this history, nor stay another moment in this terrible place. Glad that Nick had not felt like coming, had not had to suffer the anguish that still lingered here, I scrambled back down to the houseboat where I spent the rest of the day trying to quell a feeling not unlike acute car-sickness, and rid myself of the strange compression in my head.

Despite what the others said about my pale face when they returned, I knew it was not heat-stroke. I had lived in the Middle East for years and never experienced anything like this.

What I did not say was that I was sure the place was riddled with the psychic imprint of decades of oppression, violence and suffering, which I had picked up.

That evening, we moored in a small sandy cove Tom had recommended and to which there was no road access. Nick and I put up a little tent on a sandy area among the great piles of beached driftwood, and after the evening meal, joined the group for a story-telling session around the "white-man fire" blazing on the beach. Coyote danced his way into our company as the central character of Native American legends or poems that were read out, and I found myself thinking of Tom. Bill was the only one who did not need the written word for either of his vividly-related Native American stories.

I waited till last; when it came to my turn to stand by the fire, a story probably triggered by what I had sensed at Fort Spokane came to mind: "In the early days of creation, at the place where the two rivers meet, a beautiful place where the air was sweet and the waters cold and clean, where the tall standing brothers and sisters gave shelter, where plant-people provided abundantly, lived many four-legged and winged ones, finned and crawling ones. For the newcomers, the two-leggeds, it was a paradise: forest and river filled with game, plants to eat, plants for medicine; there for the taking, as they needed.

"The two-leggeds had been taught how to live in balance by the animal- and the plant-people, but they grew lazy and, taking it all for granted, began to forget what they had been taught. One day, two brothers were fishing at the place where the two rivers joined. On the bank with their spears, so intent were they, that they did not notice the bear until there was a great splash." I deepened my voice for effect: "Fisher-chief, bear was standing in the middle of the waters. She scooped a large, silvery fish onto the bank, easily as plucking a blade of grass, gobbled it up and went back to get another. Many fish were taken in this way – a big bear, this, with an appetite to match.

"After a while, one of the two-leggeds, disgruntled by his lesser skill, grumbled: 'No wonder we're not having any luck. That bear's taking all the fish. If it wasn't for that bear, we'd be able to catch plenty.'

"His friend agreed; so busily did they grumble and complain to each other that they caught no fish at all that day. By the time they got back to the village, the bear had grown to mammoth proportions: 'It took all the fish. That bear is so huge, there'll not be enough for us, if it goes on like this. Just think how much more we'd have, if it wasn't for that bear. It might even eat up all the fish and there'll be none left for us and we'll starve.' Like a disease, disgruntlement spread through the little village: 'It's the bear or us! The bear has to go!'

"They tracked the bear, found her lair in the mountains; and being crafty, waited till it was the depths of winter. Then a group of hunters took their spears and made their way up the mountain. Swiftly and silently, they stuffed the mouth of the bear's cave with sticks and branches and lit it with some dry kindling they had brought from the village, then hid among the rocks and waited.

"For what seemed like a long time, nothing happened, but the fire smouldered and smoked, gradually doing its job.

"There was a snuffling ... a coughing ... a shuffling. The two-leggeds crept forward, spears at the ready. Suddenly, with a smashing and a crashing, the bear came trundling out from the cave, flinging aside the smoking faggots." Planting my feet firmly apart, I raised up my arms, and swayed. "Up she reared, with a mighty roar. And a great bear she was, with legs like tree-trunks. The two-leggeds fell back in shock as she charged among them, her great paws flailing, knocking one away like a broken branch...." Acting out the great she-bear in the firelight, I felt myself huge and fearsome. Peripherally, I was aware of Nick, racing round the outside of the circle in the shadows beyond the reach of the firelight. "Then another ... and another, tossing them away like twigs before the storm....

"But it was winter," my voice dropped soft and cold as snowfall, "and she had been in the long, deep sleep, and the smoke had made her groggy and slow, polluted her nose and blurred her vision. The two-leggeds were many; they danced forward and back, ducking and thrusting and stabbing, weakening her until her strength gave. She fell, and was finished.

"But there was no feeling of triumph. Three men dead, another mortally wounded, others torn and bleeding. A loud wailing greeted their return to the village. So many dead and wounded hunters – husbands, fathers, brothers – a great price to pay for one fish-hunter, even if she were a giant. But there would be an even greater cost....

"Distraught by the damage and loss, the hunters had not noticed the two young bear-cubs in the cave. Motherless, the little ones were left to fend for themselves; in the depths of winter, they would have little chance of survival. And none of this had gone unseen.... So incensed were the spirits of the place by the greed and selfishness and callousness of the two-leggeds, that they descended from the high places" (again I noticed Nick, a blur speeding through shadows) "and swooped down upon the mourning village, covering the place with a leaden feeling of despondency. The hearts of the two-leggeds were heavy with a weight that would not lift, and they were forced to leave the village." Sighing, I folded my arms. "The two-leggeds could not forget the place where the two rivers met, a place of beauty and bounty. When the waters were high with ice-melt, they returned, and again lived there, and hunted and gathered. But once the leaves began to fall and the nights lengthened," my voice quietened, became menacing, "the gloom returned, covering them with feelings of depression and desolation, and they had to move on. Never again were the two-leggeds able to settle in that place."

Nick skidded to a sand-spraying stop beside the campfire. There was a short silence, then one of the party, a little worse for spirits himself, lurched out of his chair and towards the water, and had to be rescued.

The following morning, we moored in a cove Tom had suggested and hiked up the mountain. The eventual view back down revealed the scale of everything: the houseboat, centre of our world for the past couple of days, was an insignificant matchbox in a vast, watery landscape. Back on the shore, Bill came over to me. "Good story last night. But did you notice your boy?"

Had he been annoyed by my son's weird behaviour, racing round like that? "Um ... what about him?"

"When you started the story, he was playing by the water. Then when you got into the telling, he began to run around the outside of the circle."

I started to apologise but Bill stopped me with a shake of his head, and continued, "The weird thing was, his speed matched the intensity of your story. He'd go faster, or slower; and at the climax, when the bear was being killed, he was fairly flying round – his feet were barely touching the ground," he stressed. "I've never seen anything like it, it was surreal in that flickering light." He turned to Nick. "These're for you," he said, giving my son two small feathers, which glinted, blue-on-black, in the sunlight. "Picked 'em up when we were up there, on the mountain. They're blue-jay. Knew they were meant for you. Add them to your regalia."

Nick accepted them in his usual philosophical manner and Bill climbed back onto the boat, leaving me wondering about the sensitivity of this enigmatic historian. Tom later told us that according to Lakes tradition, a gift of Kwa'sis'ke energy is a great compliment.

In the early afternoon, I noticed that everyone stopped talking as we approached Whitestone, and we passed by the great outcropping in silence, faces upturned to the immense feature. Clearly, they all sensed something. Nothing was said, however, not even once we had left it behind. But what could have been said? Historically, there was nothing and even though they had somehow been affected, it didn't seem these people were willing to risk speculation on other levels. I wished I could make some sort of contribution, but the Coyote stories from the area that Tom had told me at the time hadn't stayed with me.

Reaching the area known as Hell's Gate, for the powerful rapids that had once churned and roiled through a great chasm far below, David passed round a set of photographs from the early 1900s. Features of the landscape through which we were now passing were disconcertingly discernible: we were more than halfway up the mountains we were examining. While we marvelled – or were saddened – David brought us through the last sixty years and the history of the greatest change wrought to the area since the end of the last ice age.

A Depression-era dream-come-true, the building of the Grand Coulee Dam had attracted thousands into the area. Like the river, this dam was big; in the mid-thirties, the largest man-made structure in history. It generated masses of cheap electricity – during World War Two, almost one third of the nation's aluminium was produced by electricity generated by the dam – and irrigation for agriculture.

What it meant for the Native people was what David made his central theme, however. Apparently, none of them remembered being told what would happen to the salmon, around which their existence revolved. According to accounts by Verne Ray, an anthropologist who lived in the area in the 1920s, Native people ate over a pound of salmon a day. The salmon harvest at Kettle Falls – presaged at the time of the laughing thunder, I recalled – had been the most intensive time of the year and the major social gathering, with feasting and celebration. Then the massive white-water falls, thundering over outcroppings of quartzite for as long as memory held, had disappeared under a hundred-and-fifty-mile lake; the salmon came no longer; and over twenty-one thousand acres of prime bottom-land was drowned: the traditional fisheries, trails, hunting-grounds, root-gathering grounds, tribal settlements and burial-grounds of a people who had passed this way for millennia.

Added to the attrition by disease, the legacy is one of horrendous statistics, at rates up to six times the national average: depression, unemployment, alcoholism, drug-addiction, fatal car accidents, suicide, divorce, death by house-fire.

By a political sleight-of-hand, none of the revenue generated by the dam was allocated to the Colville Reservation.[31] The Native people were promised free electricity which they never saw, nor was any of the irrigation water directed onto the Reservation, much of which was without drinking water and electricity for the first thirty years after the dam was completed.

---

31   In 1994, after a delay of sixty-one years, a federal appeals court in Washington DC negotiated a settlement with the Colvilles regarding revenue from the dam.

Since 1942, the Grand Coulee Dam has provided cheap electricity at incalculable cost, and water in the desert – although most people who live in the Columbia Basin do not understand how they are able to live there – and spawned a seethe of polluting industrial complexes, and Hanford Atomic Works.[32]

David's account was a chilling conclusion to the three-day seminar. As we docked at Keller, my mood was despondent. I helped clean up the houseboat, wondering how Nick and I were going to get back to Inchelium. Then, just as the participants were beginning to go their separate ways, Tom drove up – Indian time – in a brown Chevy van, with Nadine and her son.

---

32   Producer of the Nagasaki atomic bomb, and America's largest nuclear dump. High in radiation – the aquifer which discharges into the Columbia will not be safe to drink for about a quarter of a million years – it is ironically the least-disrupted section of the river and a haven for wildlife.

WALKING THE RED ROAD[33]

Instead of taking the usual route back, the Lakes pipe-carrier chose to return to Inchelium using the highway that skirted the eastern bank of the lake. It was longer, a three-hour drive; there was plenty of time to tell them about the seminar, and eventually raise the question that had haunted me for the past four days: "So, Tom, what is it about Whitestone?"

There was a long silence. I began to wonder if I should have waited and let the information come in its own time.

Eventually Tom sighed. Eyes on the narrow, winding road, he said, "Sure makes me wish I paid more attention to my grandfather.... My grandfather, K'soo-soos – that means 'the ugly one', because the spirit-power he called on was ugly, vicious-lookin', an' he was such a fine-featured man."

I remembered Auntie Vi telling me about Tom's grandfather. "The greatest Indian Doctor in living memory," she had said. "A very handsome man, he stayed young-looking his entire life. He was kind and modest; he never accepted payment for healing work. Why, he could even cure cancer; I once saw how he 'sucked' it from a woman's body.[34] It was ugly," she had grimaced, "twisted, a crab-like thing. He sealed it in a glass jar and buried it."

"That's why," Tom was continuing, "I wish I could film the handin' down of teachin's, grand-father to grandson. These things're better understood if they're seen. Not go back to the writin'. That's hearsay, an' it's dead on the paper." He fell silent. I waited, knowing the Native American way is not the most direct but the most relevant.

"My grandfather told me what would be comin'," he eventually continued. "An' even though I don't remember much of what he told me – there's so much I can't recall – what I do remember him sayin' would come to be, has come to be. Everythin' that he said would come to be, did come to be.

"An' he said in 2000, we'd be havin' the Great Heat. That'd destroy all the pesticides and herbicides, all the chemicals that've poisoned our Mother Earth. Then there'll come a Great Cold, to kill all the viruses and germs that make us so ill an' sick an' weak. An' at that time, people will gather. They'll come to the gatherin'-places. One of these places is Whitestone." His voice dropped: "This's not the only one. There's other gatherin'-places...."

Every hair on my body was standing to attention; several miles passed in a blur.

"When that time comes," Tom said quietly, as if there had been no gap, "go up into the mountains."

"Don't even take your coat," I said, almost to myself, recalling something I had read in the Bible. This was the Sinixt version of the Mayan and Hopi prophecies, an echo of the warning of the

---

33 An intuitive understanding of how to act and what to do in response to all situations is one definition of "walking the good red road".
34 Telekenetic transmission of negative energy.

Kogi, a remote South American tribe untouched by western civilisation that had recently emerged from their rainforest home to warn "Little Brother" that he was on a path to oblivion. I was thrilled: never had I imagined I might hear the message so close to source.

The "Great Heat" Tom's grandfather had been predicting had to have been global warming, which in the early nineties was just beginning to declare itself to the general public but forty years earlier could only have been seen by a visionary. As for a "Great Cold", it was being mooted that the planet's climate been stable for a relatively long time and changes were long overdue. Ice-caps were apparently beginning to melt; subsequent significant alterations in the composition of the ocean-waters could bring about another ice age. Some argued this to be a natural cycle, but like many others, I felt that if this were true, at the very least we were speeding up and significantly adding to it in our madness of nuclear testing, burning of fossil-fuels, unprecedented deforestation and general interference with the natural balance of the planet.

For me, the tragedy was that it was the greed, selfishness and blindness of the spoiled children at the top of the global pyramid that was affecting life on the entire planet; that humanity, individually and collectively, yet again seemed intent on learning the hard way. Much as I did not want to see the suffering that would result, a sense of inevitability seemed to hang over it all.

On the subtle level, was Gaia – according to the Lovelock theory, an entity with her own planetary consciousness – responding to an irresistible galactic shift, astrologically labelled in the west as the changeover from the age of Pisces to Aquarius? A stellar cycle: a global rite of passage as the planet moved into another level of dimensionality, with the potential of an accompanying raising of human consciousness. And were we exacerbating planetary throes of transition? A menopausal Mother Earth, experiencing hot and cold flushes (mirrored by the fact that something like fifty million women will have achieved menopause by 2013[35]), did not need the further irritation of having her skin burned and flayed.

Whatever was happening, the global prophecies rang true for me: great changes were imminent and humanity was facing perhaps its greatest challenge yet. We had a responsibility to the planet, to each other and ourselves, to try and make the change positive and uplifting. Only if we failed, I imagined, would certain people be called to the gathering-places; that was, as prophecies tend to envision, the worst-case scenario. I remembered Tom saying that we could choose to be chosen. Yet it seemed arrogant to believe that any one person could affect such an immense happening: ego, clamouring for survival.

Recalling the mystical feelings of awe and power sparked by the two places, I asked Tom: "Do you think Vallican and Edgewood are gathering-places?"

"Last summer, that was the first time I seen Edgewood," he said by way of a reply.

I would never forget: coincidentally on the gate when he and Louella had arrived, I had been able to introduce him to the organisers as an Arrow Lakes pipe-carrier. But he had kept a very low profile throughout the weekend.

"You know," I told him, "a huge rift opened up following the decision to give you Red Cloud's jacket. Sort of like what happened when you gave Nadine the healing stick." Turning round, I grinned at Nadine, who also tended to keep a low profile. She smiled back, her hazel eyes innocently wide. "In fact, the two of you've got a way of sorting out the sheep from the

---

35 Susun Weed, *Menopausal Years.*

goats, and you don't hardly lift a finger! That weekend, Tom, despite having the founder's jacket and being the Lakes pipe-carrier, you didn't even lead a pipe ceremony, or a sweat."

"I can't simply walk in an' take over, start to move things round from where they was put." Tom shrugged. "It'd be wrong to even turn over the stones or move 'em into different places. It'd be an intrusion to get out my pipe an' start layin' my ways down. I wait. Four turns of four seasons. Till the land comes to know you, an' you come to know the land.... Then I can begin with my ceremonies."

Four turns of four seasons. That meant four years. In his own ancestral land. Deeply impressed, I thought about the egos who rushed in, blinded by clouds of smoke. Then it struck me how much respect this showed for Mother Earth and an analogy sprang to mind: how beautiful (and unusual) it would be, as a woman, to be sensitively courted and wooed for four years. A feat of endurance somehow deeply attractive (and nowadays highly unlikely), it would give the woman time to know the man; knowing him, to trust him; trusting him, to love him....

Tom broke into my thoughts: "I felt much more power at the gatherin' grounds at Edgewood than at Vallican."

"Yes," I recalled. "I read in the ethnographical record" (which I knew Tom had never seen nor would be interested in) "that there's three recorded burial-grounds there. It was considered to have been one of the most significant spiritual sites of the Arrow Lakes people. You can sense it ... something extraordinarily powerful, supernatural."

Out the corner of my eye, I saw Nadine nod.

"But I have to say," I continued, "that ever since that one where I met Bob and my life took off, those gatherings have become a sort of trial for me. By the end of the first evening, I start to get a headache, which grows and grows throughout the weekend until it's so bad I say I'll never come back again. But I always do!" I laughed. "Maybe that's why it's called the Rebirth gathering: we get reborn there, in our heads, and in the same way a woman forgets how bad labour was till she's doing it again, we come back for more! In some ways I prefer Vallican; despite all the pain there, that place is lodged in my heart."

Tom smiled gently. "For me, the foundation's at Edgewood. When people there've really learned how to work together, the doubt, the anger, the resentfulness will settle down. Then Red Cloud's vision will be fulfilled. The motivation of those present at these gatherings are many: some're there for what they can get, some for what they can share.... In time, all this political action, like at Vallican – the spirit of the bones, the remains an' stuff – it'll kinda heal over. Mother Earth and the spirits can start takin' care of it.... When that time comes, these people will drift on, to new bones an' new sites an' new excitement an' new things. That's when that ground there at Vallican'll be strengthened by the spirits, an' there'll be a homecomin'. There'll be gatherin's there."

Was he saying that it was the negative energies that caused my headaches, and not my own tension? "Hope I'm still around to see it," I said.

"That time when we was asked to come there, I was asked," he said, emphasising the last word, "to say a prayer at the site, at that altar. An' I went to the altar an' I told the people the story of the Native American prayer. 'You know,' I said, 'years ago, that the Natives were so spiritual, the only teachin's they had – put yourself back there – the only teachin's they had were of Mother Earth. The only way they could communicate was by sign-language. They had their sign-language an' they had the things that were given to them that they could hear. The rippling of the waters. They could hear the wind in the trees; they could hear the roll of the thunder. They could hear these birds singing; they could hear the cayote, wailing.... They could hear the calling of the wolf. They could hear the warning, the screams of the hoopoe. They could hear the grunts, the communication between the bears. They could hear the squeals of the rabbit an' the squirrel. An' these were their teachers. So from their teachers, they learned how to communicate: through song. An' when they felt good, they sang. An' when their heart hurt for loss of a loved one, they sang. They sang with the power, the spirit.... They sang just as loud as they could, like the rolling of the thunder, an' they could be heard miles an' miles away. They sang, before the language.'

"This is what I told 'em: 'An' this is why I'm gonna pray. 'Cause these ancestors – I don't know, you don't know, them people that found these people, where they had 'em in the museum, they absolutely don't know, how old they are. So to make my best, ever,'" he stressed, "'to pray for these people, I'll sing. I'll sing a song.'

"An' I sang, an' when I had sung, then I come back down here. Well, word was already down here before I even got home. An' they were sayin', what right do I have, to go out and speak to the people in this way? This is how it was done; this is how it's put down in books an' this is how it's recorded.

"I told 'em: 'Not the way I heard it. We all have the right to voice our own education, how we was brought up. I'd had one of the greatest teachers: that was my grandfather. An' my father, to verify what my grandfather told me.'

"So then I was asked to come up back up to that meeting they had, about gettin' the bones back, an' I said: 'For a matter of fact, I think them bones are better off, right where they're at. At least them people over there will know that these bones that they have in these boxes in the basement of this museum, at least they were known while they were there. When you bring these bones back to Vallican, these people are just gonna want this recognition of what they've done. Then once that is done, the remains of the ancestors are gonna be forgotten. It's just like a hunnerd-dollar bill. You take a hunnerd-dollar bill; once you have it, you're so proud to have it. Once it's spent, you're lookin' for another one, an' then another one.'

"An' to me, that's what I see in the heart of them people that's involved at Vallican, an' this is why I don't get involved myself. 'Cause I don't consider myself a spiritual person; I'm a Native American, knowledge an' wisdom, one step in front, one step behind from me. An' this is not one of 'em."

It was a perspective that gave me masses of food for thought. Now I knew why he had been at only one Lakes Band meeting, and had not been involved in the repatriation of the ancestral remains. It reminded me of the way Lynne and James had viewed the unfolding.

"One of these days," he continued, "they're gonna ask me to speak up there in front of all these people, an' hopefully all my councilmen'll be there. Hopefully all them people from the Okanagan Band will be there. I have some very strong roots, an' if I think I'm on their shit-list now, wait'll I get done then!

"But that's the way that it was given to me: to help others, sometimes you have to rattle their chain an' sometimes you have to pull their rope pretty hard!

"A few years back, I used to go to Alcoholics Anonymous [AA] meetings. I was wrapped up in AA an' culture for a while. My partner that died here a few years ago, John, he was the one that pushed me an' pushed me an' pushed me to sober up. He tried an' tried an' tried, he never gave up on me. Then we started goin' to AA. An' I felt so good to where I was at, I'd go in these bars an' shake these people up." He laughed. "Try to help 'em sober up! Got in fights over it! John had to say: 'You don't work the program that way. You don't go in there an' beat the shit outta somebody, then drag 'em to AA an' tell 'em how much you love 'em! You don't do things this way!'

"So I started searchin'. But even then, all the literature, all the brochures, all the books they gave me at AA, I never had time for them. Never read a one of 'em." His voice lowered. "I know why now but I didn't know then, but it got so close that at the last, when I 'bout quit goin' to AA an' I was goin' to pick up John – no, it was John comin' pickin' me up – I said: 'Let's go to Olympia, let's go to an AA meetin' there. That's the real big meeting.' An' he says: 'Yeah, I'll go on one condition.' I said: 'What's that?' He says: 'That they ask me to speak.' An' I said: 'Why?' An' he says: 'Because they're not ready for you yet!'" Tom laughed, shaking his head. "So when I got back into my culture, I sacrificed all these things out there. I already had a lotta tools; I just had to clean 'em up. An' when I started going, an' really going to my sweat-lodge ... really going back to my grandfather an' going back to the Winter Dances then. Well, that's the way it was handed to me, that's the way it was given to me from my grandfather. He didn't say: 'Here, this is how you do it.' But by going and participating, being there an' learnin', that was the best thing.

"When I started, it wasn't right. Two dances I was at, the alcohol was there. At the dances, I couldn't help it; I had to open my mouth. An' I challenged all the old people, all the elders, all of them. Ev'ry dance I'd go to. Any dance I'd go to. I don't care how many people, the minute I'd hit that hallway, it was like I drew a blank on 'em. Ev'rybody that was talkin' would get quiet, an' I'd stand there for a few seconds, an' start.

"But I even had to quit doin' that. The only way to do it was to put my own dance on. An' if I put my own ceremony on, then I can do it the way that I see, the way it was handed to me. That way I can know, what's in store. Like I shared with Nadine, what to expect...." He turned and smiled briefly at his new partner, then shook his head gently. We had reached the ferry-landing at Gifford just as the boat was approaching. "But I couldn't do it here. I couldn't do it in Spokane. Because if I done it here, the first thing people would say is: 'The only thing Tom's dancing for, is he's runnin' competitions, with his father, with his brother.' They'd have never seen the positive.

"I've waited a long time. I wanted to dance four, five years ago. But I just couldn't. I need the confidence of the people. It's like Sam's old car," Tom grinned as he banged his hand on the steering wheel of the mutual friend's van in which we were riding, "it needs shocks. An' they definitely need shocks."

Smiling, I found myself wondering what kind of shock it would take. What was needed, to instil confidence in such people?

"Maybe this is about waiting," I offered. "About prayer, and patience. Hard lesson for some of us, patience."

Nadine nodded, but I wasn't sure Tom had heard. Nor did I think about the mirror, or the larger picture: that the whole world was lining itself up for a shock.

THROUGH A GLASS, DARKLY

Week by week, the snow crept down the mountain-slopes white as lamb's fleece, but there was no word from Tom. There was no point in fretting; I had to trust Indian time. It made a kind of sense: just as Bear hibernates winter away, perhaps the cultural projects needed to go underground, allowing a period of introspection while the roots of confidence invisibly took hold. But it was like riding a see-saw: one moment thrilled by what I was involved in; the next, uneasy at how it seemed like yet again I was waiting in a kind of limbo. And at the back of my mind, like the whine of a mosquito, the question persisted: were they right, the increasing amount of friends advising me to move on from this involvement with the Native people?

The most recent was an American artist in her sixties who had recently moved to the Valley, and whom I had met in a powerfully synchronous way.

Shortly after I had first moved to the Valley, a small acreage down the old back road from the log-house in Vallican had gone up for sale. Lightly wooded, with a clear view of Frog Mountain, it had an inexplicable attraction – not in the sense of déjà-vu but in that it fit me, somehow. It swiftly became a favourite picnic and meditation site, filled with my fantasies of the kind of house I would build, the garden I would create, someday, when the capital turned up. For over two years it waited, but then a "sold" notice appeared, nailed to a tree, almost crucifying me. In next to no time, a small log house was being erected.

Yet the land had not let go of me. A series of serendipitous events led to my becoming not only a friend of the new owner, but a sort of pupil. Elder, theosophist and insightful observer of human behaviour, Nancy had swiftly taken me under her wing: "When I first met you, you were like a jangling bell! Energy was shooting all over the place. I had to get to know you." I hadn't been so sure; she had appeared formidable in much the same way as Tom once had. A gifted landscape painter, she favoured mountains: not the misted blue-greens of the land where I sometimes imagined she had come to live in a kind of exile, but the burnt-orange, carnelian and carmines of the Grand Tetons – a powerful, dramatic mountain-scape which hinted at the dynamics of her personality. I liked her but she made me uneasy: the directness; the deeply-embedded crease in her brow. I felt she would cut through the chaff, that knowing her might be painful, but I was swept along on a tidal wave of warmth and care as much as Nancy's conviction that our meeting had been destined.

Over the next couple of months, besides being directed in esoteric studies of the western tradition, I was encouraged to move on: "Working with the Indians will bring great comfort; it is a tie from the past. You feel a 'comfort zone', an ego-stroke, with the Native people, as more than one embodiment was among this race. A spiritual thread from the past is romantically what you want to be involved with. This has no bearing on your spiritual direction, which is not with or through the Native people. However, working with them can contribute to your growth.... Don't mix up conscious mind promptings with the subconscious mind. Revert to what you were taught initially; put things in their proper context."

What's wrong with wanting to be comfortable? I wanted to say. And as for what I was "taught initially"; hadn't I been down that route? Once I got over the ego-clamour, I reflected on her words. I didn't totally understand, but they rang true.

On another occasion, she explained: "Those headaches you said you get when you're on the Reservation. It's not that you're tense; it's your sensitivity to the depressed situation of life there, to the underlying currents of grief, anger and desperation. Negative energies and thought-forms are magnified in enclosed spaces, and in groups, they mass and bounce around. Until one has learned how to shield oneself, they can readily land on an open, sensitive person, leaving them to hold the baggage, so to speak."

Like in the sweat-lodge; like what Tom had said about negative emotions at the gatherings. And Auntie Vi had spoken of the many old, hidden rivalries and feuds, not at all obvious to an outsider, acted out at pow-wows. So nothing had necessarily been "thrown"; it was about a sensitivity of which I had limited awareness.

Troubled and haunted by Nancy's perceptions, although it went deeply against the grain, I followed her advice that winter of "going-within", staying away from pow-wows and dropping Native spiritual practices such as burning sage and sweetgrass. I even put away my drum, and absented myself from Northern Lights. Going into a kind of hibernation within the cave of myself, I found a sort of peace in working with clay, creating weird, hybrid dragon-dinosaurs; perhaps, in hindsight, accessing an inner connection[36] down the ancestral time-line, to a racial memory and "initial teaching" of which I was not yet consciously aware.

Towards the end of winter, with still no word from Tom, an opportunity arose to take part in a local weekend workshop. Initially I turned it down; an "Adamic" workshop called "Beyond the Garden" (the point of which I did not understand) seemed a far cry from the Native American fold. However the words of the woman who had first informed me of it made me change my mind: "Whatever you do, examine your motivation. Always be clear about why you do what you do."

Clarity: that I needed. Perhaps, I thought, with Biblical intimations, this workshop would help me access what I had been "taught initially". Still it was with some reluctance that I went to the Heritage Hall in Vallican, where meetings with the Archaeological Society, Bob and Manny had been held.

Where another switch would now be thrown.

The catalyst came in the guise of an exercise in focussing attention: participants had to gaze steadily into a mirror, eye-to-eye with the self, for a full five minutes. It was a greater challenge than I anticipated; as in meditation, the thoughts crowded in, and the gentle movement of birch-leaves in the window reflected by the mirror were far more interesting. Taking myself in hand, I had just focussed when a grey squirrel scampered down a branch, again distracting me.[37] On the next attempt, however, after barely a minute, something strange started to happen.

It was as if my face were slowly being erased: part of my forehead, then half my face, then all of it was gone. I could actually see the part of the room that had been hidden by my head. It was so odd that I lost focus. Immediately my face was back in place. The next time, I managed to stay with it.

---

36   The dynamic alter major chakra (see Ruth White, *Working with Your Chakras*).

37   Squirrel carries the message to honour the future by readying the self for change, as I later discovered.

It was the most eerie process: my whole face gradually being blanked out. But this time, a face began to appear in its place. And it was not my face. Not the one I wear in this life, at least.

Retaining my focus – a glazed, almost mindless stare; an occasional blink – I watched as deep-brown eyes appeared in place of blue-grey ... dark, well-defined, provocatively-arched eyebrows ... pale, porcelain skin ... high-boned, rosy cheeks ... a blossom of deep red, pouting lips ... a heart-shaped face framed by a cascade of luxurious, dark and curling hair. At the periphery of my attention, I felt an erotic blush of warmth.

A sophisticated Jezebel, wryly commented an inner voice. Immediately the sensuous face faded away and another began a slow slide into focus. Wizened, wrinkled, this face; small, rounded head; thin, pudding-bowl-cut, black hair; eyes dark, beady-bright; mean slash of lips.

Mediaeval; not an attractive fellow.... With the thought, he was gone. Two Native American-featured faces flickered in and were gone, one after another, so swiftly that it was impossible to discern much about either. Spontaneously I leaked in a brief thought: "I know there's a Viking lurking in there somewhere. Show me."

To my utter astonishment, he obligingly revealed himself: large, wide, crude features; skin florid, roughened and reddened; thick, dirty-yellow, greasy tangle of hair, untidily braided; grubby, corn-coloured, bushy moustache; fleshy lips. Eyes, a flinty gleam; the whites, yellowed and bloodshot.... He faded away, and another face, pale and pinched, began to emerge, but my eyes were watering and stinging and I was beginning to feel dizzy, and had to break off.

Afterwards, sharing our experience (nothing like this had happened to anyone else), the workshop leader commented: "You're fortunate to have the ability to access past lives at the drop of a hat."

Although I had a sense that this was what had been happening, I had never before heard nor even thought of such a possibility. While on the one hand part of me wanted to dismiss it all as a vivid imagination, the ugliness of the Viking seemed to bestow validity on the experience. Surely I would have conjured up a more romantic figure, if it were all make-believe?

"The answer lies in the mirror." Aunt Aggie's words seemed to carry a new relevance. I determined to explore further.

Reading up on the subject – scrying past lives – I bought a mirror and a white candle, to be used only for this purpose, and developed a prayer for protection.[38] Alone in a darkened room, I watched an interracial parade of faces passing through so swiftly it was difficult to ascertain race, age or sex. Although it was fascinating, after a couple of sessions like this I began to wonder what was the use of such an ability. If I accepted having lived many lives, what was the point in looking down them? It was like being a voyeur.

On the next occasion, as part of my prayer for protection, I asked whether there was any point in continuing.

Yet again I watched my face fade away and another slowly coming through in the candle-lit semi-darkness. This time it was the face of a very handsome Native American, in what I guessed to be his early thirties, that proudly stared back at me. Amazingly, he stayed in place and I could study his features: eyes of dark velvet; generous nose, not classically-hooked but rounded; jaw deeply-creased; a glory of long, thick, shining black hair hanging down over a naked, broad,

---

38   DO NOT TRY THIS AT HOME! Like a Ouija board, a mirror used in this way can act as a gateway for entities from the astral realms, who may choose to wreak mischief, or worse.

well-defined chest. His skin was dark and he was well-built, the kind of build to which I am attracted. But the way my heart went out to him was beyond fancy or attraction, beyond words, beyond any kind of empathy I had ever experienced. Tears pricked at my eyes, sending him swimmingly on his way.

It was several days before I could return to the mirror; when I did, there was no other face but his. It was weird, seeing him again and only him, but weirder still was the dawning realisation that his face was not unfamiliar. Getting out the scrapbook I had made during the confrontation at Vallican, I found the sketch of the Native man I made during the strange experience of automatic drawing when we lived at the Lodge.

The two men were uncannily similar.

Now I was really confused. Was the man in the mirror not a past life after all; had the husband-guide figure Lynne had told me about sort of "come through"? Yet while it was comforting to think of this powerful, attractive Native American as my guide, when he reappeared the next time, with still no sign of any other face, the powerful, strange feelings which accompanied him made me feel distinctly uneasy. I put the mirror away, resolving not to play round like this again.

Whatever was at work was not going to let go that easily, however; something from the "other" side (or in-side?) was determined to make itself known.

Shortly after, visiting Ratna, I happened to mention the experience. Without blinking an eye she said: "It sounds to me like a 'carry-over'. You ought to do a past-life regression."

The only "carry-over" I knew about was in relation to income tax. Unwilling to display my ignorance, I said nothing and a few days later synchronously came across the concept in a book:[39] just as a departed soul might haunt the earthly plane to which it had a strong emotional attachment, something powerful left unfinished during a past life (most probably the immediately-previous incarnation) can "carry-over" and haunt – directly influence – the present life. Under a trance-like or hypnotic state, it is possible to regress and uncover what these influences might be, as well as how to deal with them.

Having got as far as accepting that we may live many lives, I was not sure I could stretch so much further. Accounts of regressions seemed remarkably glamorous: Atlantean or ancient Egyptian royalty, priests or priestesses; North American shamans or chiefs; historical aristocracy of note and influence. Suspecting that the concept of regression was a New Age fad born out of a combination of wish-fulfilment and an inferiority complex, when Ratna offered to facilitate a regression for me, I declined. Rebirthing hadn't made any difference as far as I could tell, so why should this idea of regression?

Later, however, on reflection, it came to me that my refusal had stemmed from a desire to protect deeply-personal inner terrain. Trying to sort out my mixed feelings, I thought I could detect a great resistance to what seemed like an invasion of the core of my being.

Or perhaps more cogently, of what might transpire as a result of letting inner walls be breached.

---

39 Mary Summer Rain, *Phoenix Rising.*

COYOTE STIRS

There was another, deeply-disturbing new element that had crept into my life, about which I had told no-one, however. Blessed (although I don't always think of it that way) with an acute sense of smell which seemed to have gone into overdrive, I was finding that being in the proximity of almost any man – passers-by on the streets of Nelson, browsers in stores, passing acquaintances – had become unbearable, because of the way they stank, literally: a nauseating, warm, musty sourness, putrid, like old cheese. Nor could I look at them; their skin, not white but a sickly, mottled, pink-purple-blue-orange-yellow, shadowy with a prickle of stubble, turned my stomach.

Strangely, men who were close friends – such as Yellow Bear, Tipi Doug, Al (another member of Northern Lights who had helped me with the preparation of the paperwork for the cultural projects), did not affect me this way; and never a Native American; nor any woman.

Added to this was a deep reluctance to attend any kind of gathering or even go into town. In a way, it felt like I was turning into a heavy, leaden creature that only wanted a shell to wrap herself up in, and forget everything; hibernate forever.

Winter turned on its hoary head. For over two months I had heard nothing from Tom about either project. Then came a further shock: the house I was renting had been sold and I had to move out. Deeply upset – it had a wonderful, haven-like atmosphere – I reverted to what Nancy had condemned as "suffocating comfort": smudged myself and my hand-drum with sage and went down to the river, listened to the water and once again sang the old, familiar Native chants.

What did I care if it were a step backwards? It was as powerfully evocative as ever and I was again in touch with what had to be the most powerful and essential part of myself. Calmed, my mind clear, I could see that the generous three months' notice to move had to be because within that time-frame I would be working on the projects and would need to move south. The river was telling me that life flows on, powerfully, relentlessly; why be upset about having to move? I could not stay circling in this pool forever; like Salmon, I had to ready myself for the next leap which would take me further along the journey of self-discovery ... back to my true self.

Which, I was sure, would be in connection with the Native American people.

At the end of February, Tom dropped by. I had been right to pick up the threads; we were back on track. He had met with Tribal Council-member Doll, who had told him of the many grants available for a project like the cultural encampment; then out of the blue, Skip, head of the rehabilitation branch of the Tribal Agency, had informed him that it qualified for a small cultural grant for equipment.

"Just enough for three tipis and some kitchen equipment.... Ain't much, but it's a start." The lightness behind Tom's voice fed my own blossoming euphoria. Coyote Dreams was beginning to manifest. They were wrong, all those well-meaning friends. Tom's next words lifted me even higher: "I want you with us when me 'n' Skip get the tipis from that outfit over near Creston that's run by the Kutenai. You meet us at Colville, leave your van there an' drive over with me in the pick-up. You hafta be there for this."

"Wow, thanks, Tom," I said breathlessly, then wondered: "But I'm sort of surprised. The Kutenai? Isn't there anyone Stateside who makes tipis?"

He shrugged. "Ain't about sides. It's about gettin' the right people involved. I know the guy, Wilf, that runs the outfit."

"Oh, I've met him. Back in '89 at Vallican, right at the beginning of the confrontation." The memory came flooding back: a small, dark, wiry man with short grey hair and strong glasses, wearing a pale shirt, he had been driving away from the Indian village as I arrived. For some reason he had stopped his car when he came level with me, and introduced himself. Surprised that a visitor of such note – a Kutenai spiritual leader – should be leaving after only a couple of hours, I had asked whether he was coming back, but he shook his head and told me that this was not the way he went about these kinds of things.

Nor, I knew now, was it Tom's way. Nor mine.

The trip to the Kutenai Reserve passed in a heady blur. All I could think about was the unique historical event that was transpiring: Coyote Dreams' first material transaction – an Arrow Lakes descendant buying tipis from a traditional neighbour[40] whose comprehensive land-claim ironically encompassed the Lakes' ancestral land.[41]

After cups of coffee and a long social exchange, the tipis were loaded onto Tom's pick-up. Freshly-sewn and sweet-smelling, the heavy-duty, ivory-coloured canvas was spotless. It seemed a shame that it would soon be blotched with mould and mildew, and blackened with smoke.

"Openin' ceremony's scheduled for summer solstice," Tom told Wilf as we prepared to leave. "Anyone's welcome. 'Specially them as are willin' to get off their backsides and do some work! Like harvestin' lodge poles-"

"Don't put that on the invitations," laughed Wilf. "Nobody'll show!"

"A fair number is already involved," said Tom. "Moccasin telegraph's done its work. Arrangements for the ceremonial feast are already underway."

This was new music to my ears, but on the way back to Colville Tom told me of the differing levels of interest: while there had been many offers of help, there were also those who were affronted at not having been consulted or included sooner, and yet again criticism of my involvement was flying around on the wings of gossip. Butch's words at the Agency meeting, long relegated to the dusty back-files of my memory, were proving prophetic. Having anticipated that my function would eventually be taken over by a Native person and appreciating that it was only right (while another part of me kicked and screamed), I offered to back out.

"No," said Tom firmly. "You're my co-founder an' you're not goin' to just be cast aside. I told you, a major part of my vision is that the encampment'll reflect the ability of the two races to work together toward somethin' for the good of all. That don't start with kickin' out the person that done so much good, white or whatever."

Our hopes and plans reached a zenith several days later, when Tom dropped by to tell me he

---

40   Traditionally, the two peoples apparently had little contact. As languages, Salish and Kutenai are unrelated; Kutenai is a linguistic isolate. Historically, there was at least one battle between the two peoples, over salmon-fishing rights near Nelson, B.C., which may have been a result of the encroachment of settlers.

41   One of three, the other two being the Okanagan to the west and the Shushwap to the north.

had received word that the Navajo Nation had sent a formal request to attend the opening ceremony, in order to review Coyote Dreams as a model for something similar on their Reservation in Arizona.

How had they heard about it? Neither of us knew. Moccasin telegraph, magical as ever. Nor could I find the words to tell Tom that a deep part of me was not surprised at all; it was another piece, clicking into place.

When I had first come across photographs of the austere, arid, starkly-sculpted redlands that was home to the Dine, and read about the Beauty Way and seen examples of their striking art, a deep chord had been struck. But because of my experience at the Indian village at Vallican, the powerful attraction was tempered by a reluctance to see it through, only too aware that I would appear as yet another gawking, pale-face tourist. Under the umbrella of Coyote Dreams would be another story, however. Once Tom left, I fantasised about how, with any luck, I would go to their Reservation with him as a representative of Coyote Dreams. Perhaps the enigmatic sense of connection was not from a past life, as I had imagined, but a kind of precognition, and I would at last be in the place I was meant to be, the Slocan Valley a stepping-stone left behind.

This was what it meant to be truly alive: before me a newly-opening door, the bright promise of a fresh tapestry of adventure, of experience; a sense that this journey was destined and would reconnect me to something I had lost, some essence of myself I was at last re-collecting.

When I was visited by the handsome beast himself, tawny winter-coated, trotting perkily through the melting snow in our back garden and stopping to stare back at me when he glimpsed movement at the kitchen window, I knew it was a sign: Coyote was fully present in my life. After all, wasn't this how the flow worked: surely it wasn't by chance that my contract for the tourism project would end just as Coyote Dreams was taking off?

It was about this time, however, when I reckon Old Man Coyote, lying on his back with his mouth open, dreaming his dream, snored loudly a couple of times, half-woke himself, sleepily scratched some unmentionable part, turned over and began a new dream.

A TWIST in COYOTE'S TALE

Even though it had been my idea, using the trickster's name to head our vision had made me uneasy from the outset. Since Tom seemed happy with it, I said nothing, but every time I said, heard or read the words "Coyote Dreams", I could not help but remember how, according to legend, anything connected to the trickster had a way of turning upside down or twisting inside out, leaving the animal people and often as not Coyote himself, scratching their head in bewilderment and rubbing some sore place. The trickster's visions might be real or just as easily false.

The only obvious part that did not seem to fit in with the flow was having to go through all the throes of moving only six weeks before the opening ceremony. Why was I not allowed to stay in place until my role was clearer? The search for a new home brought swift results, however: a small, quaint log-cabin a few miles north of Winlaw on a private small-holding. Everything fell into place then. Practically the last home on an unpaved back road two miles from the highway, it was so small that half our worldly goods had to go into storage, and would be difficult to access in winter without a four-wheel drive. Next winter, I would be in the sunny south, of course. And with a creative adjustment of the interior, the cabin would provide a sort of vacation hideaway and simplified life, an ideal interim solution until Coyote Dreams got going, along with the next part of my life and all that would entail.

Whoever had come up with the name Harmony Gates had struck a true chord: situated on the side of a mountain, facing the rising sun and surrounded by hundreds of acres of forest, it was a peaceful, idyllic paradise. Only yards from our door, a small creek tumbled down to the Slocan River, twenty minutes' walk away, and sandy beaches, a stretch of backwater and the use of the owner's canoe. It seemed the perfect place to bide my time.

Then a not entirely unexpected turn of events threw me into confusion.

Disenchanted with North American newspapers, I rarely bothered reading them but preparing for the move to Harmony Gates had used some for packing. A small notice in a Nelson edition had caught my eye, inviting applications for a new B.C. Housing [42] complex in Nelson. Despite knowing it would be a situation not too different from the housing cooperative in Vernon – a life-style I had gladly left behind – and my mind was set on Coyote Dreams and the Navajo, for some reason I found myself (in a detached, robotic sort of way) filling out an application form and subsequently attending an interview. Even as I sat answering questions, feeling as if I was speaking for an absent third party, I could sense what was coming. Because of my "situation" – the children, the size of the cabin, its remoteness – within a couple of weeks I was offered first choice at the complex. Move-in date was scheduled three weeks before the summer solstice and Coyote Dreams' opening ceremony.

---

42   Provincially-subsidised rental accommodation.

Berating myself for ever having begun the process, I wanted to turn it down but the pragmatic part of me reasoned madly. During the last five years, we had moved so many times I had lost count; we had been homeless; lived in a motel. The children's needs were changing: wanting the stimulus of the big city, Sivan had already left to live with her father in Vancouver; the other two, now ten and twelve, needed more than nature and my nurture.

Torn, and with mere days to decide, I went to take a look. With the complex close to completion, the builders were willing to let me into the unit I felt would be the most bearable: on the edge, next to the forest, with an awesome view encompassing the west arm of Kootenay Lake, and Kootenay Glacier just visible beyond the peaks of the Selkirks. It was roomier than I anticipated, I would have heat at the turn of a switch, it took just fifteen minutes to walk to the city-centre and Nelson was an attractive little city with an active cultural life. Yet to accept seemed like a betrayal: coming full circle and returning to square one, back into the kind of little twentieth-century box from which Bob had "rescued me", five long years ago.

Why not stay in the Valley until Coyote Dreams spirited me away? If I signed the dotted line (just in case), was it admitting a smidgen of doubt which would compromise the vision? Could I have a foot in two camps? Knowing better, I signed anyway, thinking I would simply tear up the contract when the time came.

The days lengthened, warming. My tourism contract was winding to an end and the children and I became intimate with this part of the Valley, exploring old logging roads high up into the forest and along the uninhabited, unfrequented side of the river as far as Slocan Lake. As always, no matter where I lived or for how long, I worked on the area around our little home, clearing away years of neglect and the tangle of undergrowth that almost obliterated what had once been a garden. Opening up access to the little creek, I found a level area large enough to create a small pool, which gave me the idea that this was the ideal place to cleanse my crystals, something I had been meaning to do for some time.

It was an intensely personal collection: a precious, jagged tooth of dark amethyst, gifted by a teenage friend who had found it on Frog Mountain; a palm-sized chunk of unfinished rose quartz from a Native American friend; a long, slim wand of clear quartz fastened with a hide thong to a magnificent eagle pinion feather, a gift from Nadine. From Tipi Doug, a heavy slab of gleaming coal-black obsidian;[43] from Bryan, a large triple-pointer of clear quartz and a massive, double-headed amethyst. Another amethyst, a multi-pointed cluster, had been gifted me at a pow-wow giveaway. There were smaller tumbled pieces of hematite, Apache tears, turquoise, tourmaline, peridot, and a garnet I had found at the Rebirth gathering grounds.

Ratna had taught me that crystals need to be brought into resonance with the self and also periodically cleansed of static, of energy contamination which can accumulate and "muddy" their function – not that I knew how to use them – and that one of the most effective ways to do this is to immerse them in running water for twenty-four hours. I took the crystals down to the creek, held each one between my palms for a few seconds, then put them into a net bag which I secured with a couple of rocks in the little pool, directly below a small waterfall.

---

43   Judy Hall, astrologer and author of *The Crystal Bible*, left a note for me on this page: "Did you know slabs of obsidian bring things up from the depths, very quickly indeed? They absorb negative energy, but attract it too."

It was early May, a still, hot day. After several days of relative isolation (I worked from home), we were all in need of a change and some company, so I suggested french-fries for lunch at the Duck Stop in Winlaw, fifteen minutes' drive away.

Surprisingly for the time of day and year, the little restaurant was crowded, with not a table to spare. An unexpected but familiar, friendly face beamed at me from across the room. I had never seen Ed – Native ferryman to Hayes Island – up this way before; with him was his slight, pretty, blonde Norwegian wife, Inge, and a grey-haired figure whose back was towards me. Ed waved us over to join his table.

"What are you doing in the far north?" I asked, sitting down opposite him once we had ordered. The children had gone outside to the picnic tables behind the restaurant, where some of their friends were playing.

"On a healin' trip, the hot-springs circuit. Brought the old lady along for a treat." He indicated the third person at the table, a Native elder who seemed fast asleep. Crowned with a thick swatch of grey hair pulled back into an untidy knot, her head was sunk into the collar of her threadbare coat. The folds of her face, exaggerated by her position, hovered mere inches from the few remaining crumbs on her plate. Her wrinkled features and blunt beak of a nose put me in a mind of a snoozing turtle. In a whisper, Ed added: "She's taught me many things.... Yesterday, we were at Ainsworth. We camped out there last night. This mornin', we went to the wild ones north of Nakusp."

"The ones in the forest, or overlooking the Arrow Lakes?" I asked.

"Up a trail by the lake."

"That'd be Halcyon." I could not resist adding: "That's a real power-place. The Lakes people's name for it translates to 'Great Medicine Waters'." Telling this to a Spokane was not like telling a Lakes person, who might resent my knowledge. In any case, talking to Ed – about anything – had always been easy. "The archaeological record notes one pit-house there, so it wouldn't have been a camp or a settlement but a place to go for healing. There's a record from the earlier part of this century, 1926 I think, that tells of crippled members of tribes who'd sojourn there for months.

"Even today, when people go there, well, it's healing, like a sweat. Stuff comes bubbling up and out." I laughed wryly at some personal, painful memories I would probably never share. "But I'll never forget the first time I went there. It was about three years ago, the first full moon after winter solstice. A clear night, and the moon-light made it magical: the lake looked like mercury and the trees were silvery-edged and ghostly with snow. There was no wind, not at ground level, anyway, although clouds were racing across the sky, shadow on pewter, rimmed with silver. It was so beautiful. We had to park on the side of the highway because the snow was too deep to drive up. But the trail was clearly lit by the moon and I could see there wasn't a footprint on it. No-one had been up since last snowfall. And although I didn't know the way, I went ahead 'cause I liked the idea of laying the first footprints, breaking trail.

"I'd taken only four or five steps when I got the hugest fright: a great white explosion erupted out of the ground, right at my feet, without a sound. I fell backwards, snow showering down over me, my heart somewhere in my mouth, and just caught a glimpse of this great, pale phantom, silently winging off into the darkness." The memory of the experience, the shocking eerie nature of it, was still strong. "I'd never seen a snowy owl before, nor since, but I felt there was something, some incredible portent I never really understood."

Ed nodded. "Feminine energy. Remember that owl feather you gave me?"

I remembered: as thanks for his support of Northern Lights.

"Snowy Owl's the most potent and pure symbol of feminine energy," he added, glancing at the old lady, who still seemed to be asleep. "Owl medicine, it's the way of seein' into the darkness, seein' beyond."

"I sure could use some of that right now!" I said, thinking of Coyote Dreams.

Al, a friend and another member of Northern Lights who also knew Ed, turned up then and joined us, and for a while the conversation turned to Ed's work of reconnecting young Native people with their culture and heritage. After a while I asked if he intended to visit the Lakes people at their village in Vallican. His noncommittal shrug made me wonder why I brought it up; most likely what was going on there was no more Ed's way than it was Tom's.

"I haven't been there for a long time," I said sheepishly, trying to wrap it up. "But at least the ancestors have been taken care of."

The old lady's eyes suddenly opened and her head poked forward from the threadbare collar of her coat, swift as a snapping turtle from its shell. "An' who're you?" she barked at me.

It was far from the first time I had been barked at by a Native elder but I still felt a lurch of trepidation. It was as if she had not been asleep at all, but waiting like a fox in the undergrowth for the next dumb rabbit to come along and walk into her jaw. Telling her my name, I felt a need to add: "I met Ed at a Salmon pow-wow, when he took me across to Hayes Island, traditional fishery of the Lakes people-"

"Bet you never heard of my people!"

It wasn't a question. Impaled by the compelling stare of those obsidian eyes, I waited.

"Not many as know 'bout my people," she continued, a proud note in her voice. "Mid-Columbia, we live on the mid-Columbia. Ain't too many of us left, neither. An' we wouldn't move to no Reservation. When they came, we just said 'No' an' stayed put where we was. We weren't havin' no Reservation. Never needed one, never wanted one, wouldn't have none of it, not then, not now. We had our land where we was put by the Creator long before any white man come along. Made of it, put there to care for it. No upstart white man gonna tell us where to go."

I thought she was magnificent; the dishevelled appearance belied an incredibly powerful, authoritative personality.

"Who are your people?" I asked tentatively.

"Weren't you listenin'?!" she snapped.

Rabbit's foot in Fox's mouth. "Uh, yes, but I'd like to know the name of your people, in your own language. If that's alright."

"Ha!" she snorted. "If'n I told you, you won't know to say it!"

"Let me try," I insisted.

But she was right. Just like the word "Sinixt", which has been represented over thirty different ways because of its pronunciation, I could only manage a distorted shadow of the word she gave me.

"You won't 'member it, neither!" she laughed at me.

Oh, but I will; I'll show you, I thought. And I'll do it orally. Over and over in my mind I repeated the word.

"We kept most our ways," she resumed. "I know all the traditions, an' about tannin' hides, makin' dyes from plants, an' the med'cines. Now there's university people got interested, comin' out to talk to us."

Ignoring everyone else, she held me there, filling my ears, my mind with a steady stream of information about their tradition. It was like when Bob had sat me down that first time and told me about his people, their ways. But this time, inwardly, I was frantic. How would I remember all this vital stuff she had suddenly decided to tell me? She had said there were hardly any of her people left. This was precious. Where was my tape-recorder when I needed it? And why was she telling me? Was it a new direction; a new door opening? But she had said there already were academics who would be making a record. And I was not giving her my full attention, but letting silly, useless thoughts fill my mind.

She ended her mini-lecture, quite gently: "You keep in touch now."

Thinking this meant she wanted me to follow through after all, that I would go down and visit her and write up whatever she chose to tell me (things which would elude the academics, of course), I got out my address-book.

Yet there was something about the way she gave me her address.... As soon as I finished writing, her skinny, mottled, sinewy hand, surprisingly strong, took the little book from me and pushed it roughly back into my bag. "Wherever you are, you keep in touch – but not that! An' don't you fret yourself about the old ways. They won't be lost."

Everything went deathly quiet. It was not that the packed restaurant was actually silenced, but suddenly it seemed like there was no-one else there but the two of us. Her voice softened, so I had to lean forward to hear her: "Spirit's never lost. Truth can't be lost, it can't be forgot. Maybe it goes under awhiles, but truth'll always come through." Her hand described a graceful circle in the air above her head then made a movement as if catching and bringing down a gossamer thread. I could almost see it, bright amid the gathering gloom. "Only when the time is right, when the openin' is made. So don't you go worryin' yourself now. Nothin' is ever lost; when the time's right, it's there agin," she emphasised, even more softly.

My mind in a whirl, it dawned on me that that was what the traditions represented: universal truth. Like spirit, it was an energy that would organically grow as consciousness was raised. Form changes, as it must to be able to hold increased energy; essence cannot be lost. From the back-files of the Vallican experience, a memory surfaced: "Don't worry about the ancestors, they can take care of themselves. It's the descendants that matter."

At that moment, a sudden flash-crack of lightning and simultaneous great crash of thunder shook the little building and the lights momentarily flickered. In shock, I looked around. The lights were on in the little restaurant, in the middle of the day. I hadn't noticed them being switched on.

Another searing flash and rolling crash heralded a literal opening of the heavens: rain pounded on the roof and within seconds the children came rushing inside, soaking wet and bright-eyed with excitement.

When I turned to her again, the elder's head was sunk back onto her chest, her eyes closed as if she had never woken, nor spoken. Turtle, withdrawn into her shell, leaving me stunned. Why had the Thunder Beings chosen that exact moment to make their dramatic contribution? What was it about Native people, this incredible tuning into the elements? Reminded of a Stoney spirit-walker and of a Sinixt journeyer, I found it impossible to think.

The immediate violence of the storm was over within seconds but the downpour continued.

Suddenly my crystals came to mind: would they be safe? There was no way I could tear myself away however, at least not until this encounter was over. But the elder said nothing more, not even when we parted company on steaming tarmac under a clear blue sky. Bundling the children into the van, I raced back home.

Somewhere en route, I realised the name the elder had given me was gone. Or had she taken it with her?

As for the creek, it had tripled in size, was an unrecognisable, frothing torrent. Stones and rocks had been tumbled and rearranged, creating a totally unfamiliar waterscape. Until darkness fell and my hands and feet were frozen, I combed the waters but found no trace of the net bag or any crystal.

Nor did I have any success next morning, searching until interrupted by a surprise visit. Preoccupied with my loss, I made coffee for Tom and Tipi Doug, sitting down with my own cup only when I had finished my tale.

"How long you had them crystals?" Tom asked.

A lesson was coming, I could tell from his tone. Soon I would be wishing with all my heart that that was all there was to it. "Oh, different. Some a couple of years; some three or four maybe."

"Been usin' 'em?"

I shrugged and shook my head.

His eyes crinkled. "No wonder the waters took 'em – you had 'em way too long, sittin' doin' nothin'!" Then he added, more seriously: "Crystals got work to do, they gotta move round. I seen a lotta these New Age people, just have 'em for decoration. No use keepin' 'em on a window-ledge lookin' pretty; they gotta work. These crystals, they went where they was needed." Pausing, he looked reflectively out of the window. "An' I guess that river needs all the help it can get."

"Not only the river!" I said, chagrined. There was a long silence, during which it dawned on me that Tom looked more reflective than my loss warranted.

Something was wrong.

"Celia, you must get on with your own life," he began slowly, looking down at his coffee cup. My stomach tightened. Here it came: time for the white woman to back out. I began to feel nauseous. But what came next was not what I expected at all: "There never was any Tribal grants writer told to research for a grant for the River project. An' the Council won't give no response 'bout the Tribal houseboat." He sighed heavily. "Neither's there been any further action on the encampment. An' there's been another blow. The land up at Twin Lakes; well, it's ironic, but Eagle put paid to that. There's a nest or two up there. You remember what happened for us to keep the gatherin'- grounds?"

In a numb state, I nodded.

"An' the Council won't agree to any other piece of land." He shrugged. "It's like they're just turnin' their backs on the whole deal. Even them that wanted to get involved with the camp – there's just arguments 'bout one thing after another. No-one seems to want to do any real work for any of these things but you an' me, an' we don't have the resources to go off an' do this on our own, an' I'm not ready to stretch my limited funds.

"I don't know why it's gone like this. It's come to a dead end. I guess they just ain't ready, it ain't time yet. I'm gonna step back an' put it in the hands of the Creator. You go ahead, get on with your life. You take that trip to England you was talkin' about."

My stomach was somewhere on the floor and my heart was thudding in my rib-cage so heavily I thought my chest might crack. My eyes grew hot; I couldn't move or speak.

On one level I wasn't surprised; by now I knew something of the sensitive, complicated nature of Reservation politics. Not only that, but there had been hints, messages.... The voice of rationality did nothing to quell an up-welling of anger and frustration.

Unbearable, cruel Coyote, pulling the proverbial rug out from beneath our feet. Was this it then: another dream, lying in shards at my feet? But Coyote Dreams had not been just a dream, it was a vision with enormous potential, to which we had committed ourselves. We had done a lot of work, and not for our benefit but the benefit of all: to help people live more fully; to make life better, not only for people, but for all life. And it had begun to manifest. It was not just the waste of our time and energy, but the loss of a far greater opportunity.

"Everythin' happens at the right time, you know that, Celia," Tipi Doug said gently. "Guess the people ain't ready for somethin' like this yet."

There was nothing more to say. As soon as they had gone I went back down to the creek. Getting frozen searching for crystals was better than sitting with this pain.

Yet again I had given myself wholeheartedly to a vision, seemingly the answer to a heartfelt prayer, only to see it evaporate. Why was it like this? Why should I even care about indigenous knowledge? What did it mean about prayer, about faith? Fourteen months, chasing a fantasy. Cruel, cruel Coyote. But I knew better than to blame; especially a mythical Other, an archetype. And I had to remember that no matter how many times the trickster got himself deep into trouble, he always picked himself up again and carried on; even when he was killed, someone was always around who could bring him back to life. Although his tendency was to walk right back into the same situation.

"If Coyote met a steamroller," Tom had told me on the houseboat, a chuckle behind words which brought Coyote into the present, "he'd have to inspect it. An' of course get run over. Mole, his wife, she'd bring him back to life. But you can be sure the next time he saw a steamroller, he'd have to check it out again. And get run over again.

"That Coyote's a survivor; he always comes back."

But I'd had enough of getting run over. I didn't want to go through anything like this, ever again. What was the lesson? I had been following my heart, so what went wrong? Crouching down by the little pool I'd cleared, I splashed my face to cool it and rinse off the tears, and saw what I thought was a piece of white tissue-paper. I reached to pick it out, annoyed at such thoughtless pollution and wondering how it had got there. Instead of a flimsy softness, however, my fingers encountered hard, sharp angularity.

The quartz crystal, the triple-header. Except it now had only two heads.

"Two heads are better than three!" said a voice in my head; despite myself, I had to smile. What a miracle to have found it. But why now, and why in this altered form?

Colour caught my eye. Nor was it pink tissue-paper: the rose quartz was returned to me. And then, as if my sight had suddenly been restored, I found the double-headed amethyst, almost totally submerged in grit. Excitedly, I poked around looking for the rest of my treasures but found nothing else.

Three crystals, caught in the pool of my own making and returned. It seemed weird that I hadn't noticed them before. My mind calmed as I clutched the precious little messengers. I knew I had to let go, let things take their own course. When a situation moves steadily forward, is full of potential and is challenging and exciting, then one is moving naturally with the energy flow of life; if it appears confused, chaotic or difficult, then one is resisting the Dao, the Chinese concept of the natural flow of life, about which I had recently learned. Although if Tom hadn't been so clear about stepping back, I probably would have stubbornly persisted, opening myself up to greater difficulties and further pain: the greater the resistance to the flow, the harsher the ultimate lesson.

I could only fish for the reason why these specific crystals had been restored; letting go of the Coyote- and Navajo-dream and accepting and making the now-inevitable move into a townhouse in Nelson was enough to work on.

As for the trip to England, it was over six months since the invitation to take part in another Gatekeeper Trust pilgrimage in England, organised by some of the same people I had met two years previously. This time it was an exploration of the thirteenth sign of the zodiac in the sacred landscape of Northumbria, which the previous leader, Anthony, had somehow worked out. The concept of a mystical, lunar zodiac had intrigued me; I had seriously contemplated taking part but the opening ceremony of Coyote Dreams had clashed with the date, putting paid to the idea.

It did not seem likely that I could make the move into Nelson, and get myself and the children organised so that I could go to England within a week.

COYOTE GIVEAWAY

The final night in the Valley, Al and Tipi Doug cooked up a feast of bison-meat, and in his own Indian-time style, Bryan showed up with his guitar.

Everyone was long gone and I had been asleep for two or three hours when the beat of the drum seeped into my consciousness. Thinking it had been a dream, I looked outside. It was barely first light, the tree-tops beyond my open window shrouded in mist.

Magically, unbelievably, the drum-beat recommenced and an old Native chant began to drift up from the track below. The voices were two, and familiar: Tipi Doug and Al had sneaked back. If they had even left. Lying back, I listened to "Red Earth", my mood grey as the pearly sky, so moved that I was barely able to hum along with two such precious friends.

Then, magically, in the valley below there began a yipping, which swelled to a singing-howling: a coyote-pack, picking up the chant, adding their voice.

Tipi Doug and Al fell silent; the Snpakcin chorus was joined by another, further up the valley, and the wild ghost-song echoed back and forth, gradually ebbing until the valley was again silent.

Wrapped up in my disappointment, I barely noticed how easily everything – the move, the arrangements to go to England – fell into place. The weekend before leaving, I made a spontaneous trip down to the Reservation to ask Tom's permission to take and share a couple of his songs. He knew I had been invited to create a Medicine Wheel in England on the summer solstice and planned to link with a ceremony taking place on Moses Mountain and one in the Slocan Valley, led by Yellow Bear.

Arriving at his home mid-afternoon, I found the Lakes pipe-carrier in the company of a local elder. Not having much time, against my better judgement I made my request in front of her. Immediately she became extremely agitated: "Don't they have their own songs over there?! They stole our land, they stole our children, they took away our language, our culture, our whole way of life. Will they never have enough? What do they want with our songs, anyways? Don't they got none of their own?!"

Embarrassed, I recalled the criticism Tom often faced for sharing his culture with non-Native people. Afraid to offend further, I waited, but he just slid the pouch of tobacco I'd put on the kitchen table back and forth across the formica. In a way, it was like he wasn't even there. The long silence and charged atmosphere were making me uncomfortable, and I asked: "So, do the songs belong to the land where they sprang from? Is it not right to sing the songs from this land in another land?"

Her mouth a thin, tight, disapproving line, the elder frowned at Tom, who pulled out a cigarette from the pack lying on the table, lit it and leaned back, exhaling a long steam of smoke. Looking at me through the haze, he said, in a gentle, dreamy way: "The songs belong to the

Creator. This's the way I see it: if a man wants the land I walk on, he can have it. If he wants the shirt on my back, I give it to him. If he wants my way of life, he's welcome to it. If he wants the songs I sing, I'm happy to give them. If it's my life he wants, I'll lay it down at his feet.

"All that I have, I was given by the Creator. None of it belongs to me. This is the Indian way."

The only discomfort I felt now was for the other elder. In the golden silence that followed, I remembered Al admiring Tom's ribbon-shirt at the last sobriety camp-out and immediately being the embarrassed recipient; the coyote-pelt, now part of Nick's regalia; the many songs, given Tom by the wind and water in the Slocan Valley, now part of Northern Lights' repertoire. Ever since we had come to know him, Tom's actions had taught the art of giving and receiving gracefully and gratefully, whether it was material items, the time to be at a ceremony, the singing of a prayer-song or listening to another's difficulties.

The giveaway is a scared act, originating in Coyote's mythical contract with the First People, the animals, birds, fish and plants, who agreed to sacrifice themselves so that the two-leggeds – the humans – might live. Everything consumed and used is therefore sacred, and traditional people remember the sacrifice of the community of life in its giveaway of its own body to help others. In this way, nothing is a resource that can be exploited. A conscious spiritual act, the giveaway implies an obligation to help the giver, who sacrificed in order to give.

In the time before European contact, the great gateways in life – birth, marriage and death – were celebrated by a partial or total giving-away of possessions. A mark of a person's wealth was how little he or she owned, because of generosity in giving. This organic redistribution of wealth, a central premise of Native American tradition and one of the primary foundations of a harmonious way of life, was found so outrageous by our forebears that they put it outside the law.

Our forebears had been arrogant and blind; it seemed to me that the vast majority of their descendants had not progressed. The more I learned – although it was more like things slotting into place than a new education – about the traditional Native American way of life, the more I wondered how I could have agreed to any soul-contract about being in a white skin.

Now I was on my way back to where I had begun in this life, having thought I was done there, with no idea of what might follow on my return. I could make no sense of what was going on.

344

DELIVERANCE[44]

Within days of moving into Nelson, instead of opening Coyote Dreams and meeting the Navajo at summer solstice, I was taking part in a "Silver Wheel" pilgrimage in England. Despite what I was learning about moving naturally with the energy flow of life, not once, even on the long flight over, did I appreciate how easily the whirlwind of arrangements had fallen into place; even the money, a surprise gift from a distant relative.

With its origins in a moon-cycle count – in use millennia before the concept of a solar-oriented calendar – like the thirteen-month Jewish calendar, the lunar zodiac consists of thirteen signs. It was not just the profoundly feminine nature of this zodiac, however, but an intriguing personal synchronicity that caught me up and for a while eclipsed the clinging presence of Coyote.

According to our pilgrimage leader's model, the thirteenth sign making up the lunar zodiac is Arachne, the Weaver, represented by the Great Wheel constellation of Auriga, which lies between Taurus and Gemini. It seemed more than a coincidence that not only did my birthday fall within this newly-recollected sign, but the star of first magnitude in Auriga is Capella, which mean "little she-goat". Eighteen years earlier, the Hebrew name I had adopted on conversion to Judaism was Yael, which means "little goat". A name that had somehow chosen me; and I had not been put off by its meaning (I have since come to love goats) or learning that the Biblical Yael was another in a long line of Hebrew heroines who liberated her people by becoming the lover of a tyrannical foreign ruler and driving a nail through his head while he slept. As for the Weaver, according to Hopi mythology, it was Spider Woman who created the First People in the image of the Great Spirit and gave them life. Metaphysical ears pricked, I joined with the pilgrimage more whole-heartedly than I might have otherwise.

My knowledge of astrology was rudimentary, but the landscape zodiac Anthony had demonstrated on the pilgrimage two years previously had been compelling. Over seven days, he led us on a magical journey across desolate, windswept moors to disintegrated Neolithic earthworks, along ancient track-ways and through time-distorted layers of place-names. Only recently had Arachne revealed herself in the Cheviot landscape zodiac: weaving between the Bull and the figures of the Twins, a natural half-circle of streams and rivers, completed into a whole during some forgotten time by a series of man-made ditches now known as the Catrail. These ditches, some of which have been ploughed over or appear as mere depressions, make little practical sense, in that some of them cut across the tops of ridges. But in the springtime, they would fill with water and the great Silver Wheel would come into manifestation, visible in its entirety only from the heavens. The speculation sparked by the phenomenon kept us occupied in the evenings.

44   Less than a month earlier, my close friend Anne had given me a birthday gift I knew to be synchronous. A Hamilton collectable plate taken from the "Mystic Warrior" collection, it is a painting of a Native warrior astride a pinto pony in misted forest, head tipped back, arms open to Father Sky. It is called "Deliverance".

Why should our Neolithic ancestors – if that's who it had been – have created a mirror of the heavens on earth, an astronomical reflection? Why go to so much trouble to create something we doubted they might ever see as a whole? Was it something to do with harmony; with creating heaven on earth? I wondered if the Silver Wheel was a sort of Medicine Wheel, turning the Great Wheel of existence, here, in the land of my origins, and then a thought struck me: was this what Nancy had meant about returning to what I was originally taught? Part of me, a powerful part, shied away from that train of thought.

One of our journeys took us to the henge at Duddo, a small circle of rainwater-furrowed, hunched stones about the height of a tall man. Isolated in the middle of a wheat-field on the crest of a small rise, the site was lonely, exposed, yet hushed and heavy with the raw, powerful, subtle energy of the Northumbrian landscape. Feeling overwhelmed and unable to pay attention to any prehistory of the area, I wove my way in and out of the stones, completing a circuit by the time we were to leave. One of the organisers, an artist with an angelic singing voice, was sketching a monolith and had not quite finished, so I said I would wait for her. As the others headed back to the vehicles, Alma decided we should "tone" together.

Another new concept for me, toning is a creative act that has restorative values and stimulating qualities; not only is it a means to release tension but it is an expression that can create harmony and balance.[45] According to the Hopi legend, it was Spider Woman who appealed to the Great Spirit to give the First People a voice, to give them the ability of creative expression. "In the beginning was the Word" implies vibration as prime mover.

Still within the henge, we began a toning progression. Reaching the highest note, I felt it begin to reverberate strangely inside my ears, my head, then it was suddenly, shockingly amplified. Holding the note for several elongated moments-out-of-time, Alma and I stared at each other in wide-eyed amazement while in the distance, almost a half-mile away, our fellow-pilgrims stopped, looked back and waved. If they called or toned in response, neither of us could hear. Twice more we toned the progression and each time we returned to the note, it sounded more powerfully and we held it until it seemed as if the resonating stones would shudder themselves free from the long grass and nettles twined around their base and, black loam crumbling from long-buried, scarred hides, levitate and fly away in mystical formation.

Had we chanced upon the frequency of the stone circle; the stone itself? Had we, as I fantasised, touched upon some arcane ability, an esoteric method by which in some long-ago, forgotten time, the ancestors moved great blocks of stone into place? Not by ropes and pulley and sweat and blood, as is now speculated, but by "toning the stones"?

Despite such bone-rattling understanding and experience, however, I still felt like an observer, an outsider, wondering why I had to be here and not where I felt my heart lay. Only the creation of the Medicine Wheel seemed of any real consequence. Anticipating that the site would present itself, each day I carried my drum, growing increasingly agitated until the final evening, when we were due to visit a remote site aligned to the solstice. Since it was the last opportunity, I decided this would have to be the place. At least we were close in time to the ceremonies happening thousands of miles away.

---

45 "In the end, we become the words we speak." Laurel Keyes, *Toning*.

A long, ankle-twisting, uphill hike through wiry heather and the bones of the land brought us to a windswept ridge on Simonside, where among the grasses and the bracken lay a confused jumble of huge boulders and rocks. If they had made up a henge, it was long fragmented.

All the more reason to create a new one.

Our pilgrimage leader showed us one of the biggest boulders, a great cube some ten feet across, through which an aperture the size of a man's palm had been cut. I could not imagine how this had been accomplished. Several feet away lay another stone with a cup-shaped depression just large enough to accommodate a chin, in perfect alignment with the hole in the great stone and the setting sun. It was positioned so that a fiery laser of dying solsticial sun would strike the brow chakra, or the third eye, with a specific energy that had to be affected by passing through the stone: surely an ancient ritualistic initiation site.

Then Anthony showed us a long, hand-carved notch in the rock-face above the site, almost completely hidden by overhanging shrubbery. He had deduced its presence through intuition and measurement: it was aligned to the equinox. This had been a site of extraordinary significance.

We lit candles and toned, watching the sinking, reddening sun. It had been a clear-skied day but as we waited, the bank of cloud that had appeared on the western horizon as we climbed expanded and it became evident that the sun would disappear behind it before the alignment through the stone was possible. In disappointment we watched a fiery light suffuse the cloud like a massive, distant forest-fire, a great conflagration that had to still carry energy. One by one, we cupped our chins on the stone and received the muted solstitial brow-blessing.

Then I drew the group into a circle to prepare the Medicine Wheel. But my drum was cold, the beat leaden; a fresh, biting wind that had sprung up as the sun set snatched the chants – which felt alien here – from my lips and whipped them away. Trying to imagine a rainbow bridge connecting with friends an ocean and a continent away in fading light under darkening skies seemed stupidly futile. The stones were placed, but I felt weak and exposed; lost, somehow.

And the entire time, another part of me – a part I hardly dared acknowledge – was thrilled to be back among the soft-breasted hills and secret, clefted valleys of my rootland. The empty, windswept wilderness of purple-heathered moors and great, unpopulated sweeps of a coastline punctuated with tiny villages and crowned with ruined castles and monasteries; the ancient, hidden stone circles and other places of power; all spoke to me in a way I could not deny. Not once but several times, an unbidden, startling, clear thought came to me: what I had found in North America was also here.

But to be free of past ties and truly rooted in British Columbia, birthplace of my children and grandchildren-to-be, was what I wanted: the super-natural beauty; the wild, fjordic, forested coastlines, majestic mountains, massive lakes and wide rivers; the vast, unpopulated space; the sense of a great wilderness; the poetry and harmony of the traditional Native American life-way: this was what fed my heart and soul.

Free of past ties. Be careful what you ask for....

Invited to join another Gatekeeper pilgrimage in neighbouring Cumbria a couple of weeks later, I immediately and gratefully accepted. While it was good to spend time with my mother and sister again, I was missing my kids and my "real" life, and had been wondering why I had decided to stay so long.

Early each morning, a dedicated little group consisting solely of women drove through winding country lanes to Castlerigg stone-circle, where we danced paneurhythmy, a form of circle-dancing, among the monoliths, often as not in misting rain. Situated on a hilltop, with far-reaching views of lakes and mountains (if the weather allows), Castlerigg is one of the crowning glories of the Lake District; the inevitable coach-loads of tourists must have seen a group of women singing and dancing in the rain as part of eccentric local English colour.

The Cumbrian landscape seemed to me like a miniaturised British Columbia; when a participant who was researching Native Americans asked me if she could record some Native American chants, I was glad to be able to reconnect. On the final evening, my drum warm, my voice strong, I lost myself singing every song I knew.

The following day, Alma, who had also joined with this pilgrimage, gave me a ride back along the Borders. En route, we visited another stone circle, Long Meg and her Seven Sisters. Again a fizzy sensation in my adenoids and temples informed me of the power of this place, or perhaps of the presence of ley lines. I decided I would have to learn how to refine whatever it was I was sensing; or at least find out what it was. As we drove away, Alma announced; "Right, you need a partner. Let's tone for a partner for you!"

"What are you talking about?" I retorted, surprised at this bald, out-of-the-blue statement. "I like my single life well enough."

"No you don't. Everyone needs a partner. And just as toning can be used for healing, it can also be used to manifest. Come on." She launched into a long, clear note, and, in and out of harmony, laughing and with the occasional reminder (Alma by this time knew me well) that I should not put a face on this man – and certainly not long black hair and a copper skin – we toned for about twenty minutes while I visualised swirling mists slowly parting to reveal a shadowy, masculine shape. It was a battle to keep him as a silhouette.

Despite the new experiences and wonderful personal connections, I yearned to get back to North America. Even bringing the ley-line information I had gleaned about the West Kootenays to a local couple compiling a record of the planetary grid was like fulfilling a duty. Of course, I also brought along my drum and was only too happy to comply with their request for a chant. Heart and soul I threw myself into the songs; when I ended, a little stunned by my own intensity, Anthea, a sensitive, commented: "Very powerful. And interesting: you sort of faded away and a Native American began to appear."

Intrigued, I asked: "What did he look like?

"Old, grey-haired, his face lined."

Feeling somehow gratified, I did not mention that after my drumming session in Cumbria, a reserved, white-haired, Japanese fellow-pilgrim had told me the same thing, word for word.

Little did I know how close to the mark the perceptions of these sensitive people were, for rising within me and sort of vying with my personality was a force, an energy which was by now close to the surface. Not that I was directly conscious of it, but I was fully aware how selectively sensitive my sense of smell had become, and how I sometimes found myself adjusting the way I walked and how I carried myself, and taking what seemed like an extreme, sensual pleasure in the feel of my long hair brushing silk over my bare shoulders. It was even weirder to realise that it seemed like I was emulating the character played by Graham Greene in the film "Dances with Wolves": Kicking Bird, the Lakota medicine man; and specifically, the scene when he walks with Dunbar and Stands-with-Fist, silhouetted against the evening sky: long hair flowing free, his bearing erect, the medicine man strides with a light, masculine grace and gestures eloquently.

Striking some deep chord within me, the image had imprinted in my mind, a fabulous metaphor for the Native American spirit; but somehow seemed to be manifesting in my body

Things were coming to a head, had I but known it: barely able to tolerate men of my own race; walking in the image of a Hollywood construct; sensitives perceiving another in my place; feelings of being somehow separate, other....

Perhaps Eileen, the Jungian analyst who had taught me so much and introduced me to the Gatekeeper organisation two years before, had been aware she might prove cathartic; perhaps some part of me had suspected. Certainly, I knew I had been avoiding her. After the Silver Wheel pilgrimage I had lunched with my friend and mentor but had not contacted her since. It was not that I did not want to see her, but that I did not want to deal with what had happened when she heard about the Native man in the drawing and the mirror, and Ratna's interpretation. Her bright-blue eyes had widened and her face lit up: "I do past-life regressions. And I'd be delighted to do one with you!"

"If there was anyone I would trust to do this with, it'd be you, Eileen!" The words had come out before I thought; since then I had not been able to "find" the time, not even to ring her. I knew it was avoidance; I didn't need Eileen to point out there was a part of me that was afraid. Which didn't make sense, since I didn't really believe in the concept anyway.

Knowing only too well that avoiding, denying or burying a personal issue invariably leads to it sooner or later resurfacing, often as not in a more challenging or difficult manner, sort of like quietly brushing dirt beneath the carpet until the lump has become so big that you trip over it and come down on your face with a crash, I eventually took heart in the part of me that was intrigued and challenged,[46] and arranged a time with Eileen, three days before returning to Canada.

Appointment with a past-life. It seemed ridiculous.

Phone off the hook, curtains drawn, in a strangely subdued and apprehensive state, I lay on the couch in, of all places, my mother's living-room. At least it was a known and safe place: my home, after all. Or one of them, at least.

Eileen was sitting in an armchair to the side. With no idea of how things would go, whether I would consciously know what was going on or if indeed anything would happen at all, with her agreement I set up my little tape-recorder with a ninety-minute cassette, and pressed the record button when she said we were ready to begin.

"Close your eyes," she said softly. "We will synchronise our breathing."

Slow and steady; calming, centring.

"Now you will go to the special place where you commune with the sacred," she instructed. "Your personal temple, so to speak."

It was a new idea to me but my powers of visualisation have always been strong. Concentrating, I mentally scanned the darkness. Sacred space, temple.... I waited, the words a mantra going round and round in my mind.

Gradually, to my surprise, in my mind's eye formed a vista of undulating, dusty-pink sand-dunes. Before me lay my shadow, elongated; in the distance, a range of jagged mountains, misty-blue-tinged-violet, melded into a hazed, cloudless sky. Not far away lay a pyramidal

---

46   Two years earlier, as part of a decision to give up anything to do with mediumship, I had given up use of the Tarot. Ritually thanking my handmade major arcana, I dropped each card into the flames as it randomly came up. At the end, something strange happened: the last three cards were stuck together and accidentally dropped in as one and freakily, one of them leapt back out and landed on my lap. It was the golden-haired goddess with the tawny-maned lion: Key 8, Strength.

shape: an actual small pyramid of pale, pinkish-grey stone that blended into the desertscape. Over it, like a protective arm, curved a lone palm-tree.

A pyramid? I had been anticipating a tipi, an earth-lodge; never a pyramid. Nor a desert.

"Approach this edifice." Eileen's voice gently entered the picture.

How had she known it was a building?

My thoughts dissipated like a mirage but the faint sense of surprise at my "choice" of sacred place – I had no interest in Egypt, ancient or modern – accompanied me as I projected myself towards the little pyramid, imagining the soles of my bare feet being warmed by the desert sand. I even made myself aware of a coarse, scratchy texture.

"And when you are ready, go within."

The pyramid was only about twelve feet high; the entrance a dark rectangle in the middle of the side facing me. I noticed engravings around the doorway and stopped to examine them. Ankh; spiral; crossed circle; yantra; hexagon; swastika; pentagram; others I could not name. Between each universal symbol were patterns which seemed to be constellations; each one had a point from which emanated fine lines, suggesting the head star. Impressive; not something I would have thought to make up....

"You are now inside this holy place."

Irritated by the intrusion hurrying me along, I nevertheless could not resist and took what turned out to be two shallow steps down into darkness. Underfoot, marble flagstones, cool and smooth, glowed with a soft, greenish light, like Chinese jade illumined from below. To my left, near the wall, stood two small earthenware jars which I somehow knew contained cold, fresh spring-water. Above, the shadows tapered into a velvety darkness.

"Make yourself comfortable in this place. Perhaps others are here with you: your guides or helpers."

I noticed a simple rush mat in the middle of the floor, a folded pad at one end, and lay down on it. My awareness expanded to perceive the benevolent presence of two indistinct robed figures, standing, or maybe hovering, near my feet.

"Now I am going to count backwards from twenty," murmured Eileen after a long period of deep, slow breathing. "With each count, I want you to descend step by step into the place you need to be. Twenty ... nineteen ... eighteen...."

Visualising an opening in the floor, I approached it. It was actually quite weird, because the "me" in the pyramid was aware of the "me" lying on the couch, while the "me" who began the gradual descent into the darkness was aware of leaving behind a reclining self on the rush mat.

The steps were wide and shallow; towards the end of the count, I imagined them becoming increasingly steep, narrow and uneven so that I had to steady myself with my hands. The walls were cold, rough and damp.

"Two ... one ... zero.... You have arrived. Rest awhile. This is the place where you need to be in this journey. Take some deep breaths...." And after some moments: "Begin to take your bearings. Is there anything you can see?"

My eyes closed, I waited as if expecting them to become accustomed to the darkness. But there was nothing but inky blackness and the abstract patterning inside my eyelids.

"Nothing," I said eventually, my voice strange in my ears, distant.

"Wait. Something will show."

I waited. And waited. There was nothing. It was all a waste of time. Part of me felt triumphant, vindicated; there was no substance to this process. Impatiently, I burst out: "It's all a blank!"

Eileen was unrelenting: "Then tell me. Can you describe what you are wearing? What is on your feet? Are you wearing a robe, perhaps?"

The suggestion irritated me. A robe? Did she think I was some kind of priest? That's what she would probably like. But I would dress how I chose. Feeling like a rebellious teenager, I began imagining: "Um ... moccasins, moulded to my feet like a second skin. And leggings, a deer-hide tunic, fringed, decorated with a star of porcupine quills." Recalling the delectable smoky-tangy scent of the hides Tom prepared and how sensuous they felt against the skin, I really got into it: "Soft, supple; wood-smoke-scented."

Perhaps this is all this process really is, I was thinking: a free-flight of the imagination. So let's go for it.

Remembering a dream, and a Native man in a mirror, I continued: "My hair is long, sleek and black, my skin smooth, my body, strong...."

There was some kind of shift or change: with a sort of peripheral sense that was not quite sight, I became aware of something above my head and interrupted my imaginings to tell Eileen: "Oh, above me: it's like a faint light. It's reflecting off something sort of shiny...." Focussing my attention, I "watched" a curved roof of stone gradually come into relief. A runnel of wetness, one of many, picking up light was what had caught my eye. "Stone, around me.... It seems like, like a cave," I muttered as more detail came into sight. It was a relatively large area, the walls irregular with the occasional ledge; the ground packed earth, dusty.

It was one of the eeriest experiences I had ever known, my inner eye sweeping round, distinguishing more and more detail, seemingly independent of my imagination.

A sudden, rank smell stopped everything in its tracks.

Following the involvement of this sense, it was as if the process took me over. Words rose out of me like shimmering bubbles rising from a deep pool: "Ughhh, what a smell. It's like, I dunno, something burned ... old grease ... old sweat. Oh, foul!" My nose wrinkled involuntarily in distaste and I tried to track the stink, a foetid warm cloud.

"It's me!" I realised in disgust. "God, I smell awful!"

Part of me was registering puzzlement at how this could be when I became aware of another sensation: a feeling of something rough at my groin area.

No soft, tanned, wood-smoked deerskin tunic this, but a filthy, stiff piece of I knew not what, not much more than a scrap, and it scratched and chafed. Then from the corner of my eye I caught a glimpse of not a sleek fall of black hair but twisted, matted grey ropes: filthy, tangled dreadlocks, stiff over a knob of a bony naked shoulder and skinny chest; skin dark, coppery, smeared with dirt, soot; filthy, stinking....

Fury rose from somewhere deep within me, rising like lava, burning in my chest. I felt cheated; this was a far cry from the image I had thought to call up. Then the hot anger was gone and I was filled with cold despair at how everything seemed beyond my control. Like a twisted mouth, a bright slash of light leered from the far side of darkness.

"I'm in a cave! And I'm an old man! Dark-skinned, an old, dirty man." Again a warm wave of the smell, my own foul smell, hit my nose. "Oh, how I stink!"

This was how I imagined it must feel to be schizophrenic: looking through the eyes of a person while simultaneously speaking of him, as him. Hot, cold, my emotions were in chaos. Eileen's voice floated in from somewhere above me, calm, detached: "What else can you see? What else is in the cave?"

"Nothing!" I cried out, before I even looked. I would not look, I did not want to know, did not want her to know.

Which was ridiculous.

Yet there was something in the cave. Something some part of me did not want to even consider.

Exactly like eyes becoming accustomed to the dark, otherness awareness was steadily increasing: "I" was sitting on bare ground at the back of the cave, cross-legged. In front of "me" were the charred remains of a small, long-dead fire.

"What else is there?" Eileen persisted. I reported the details, increasingly aware of something directly behind me. A dark, lumpy shape on a ledge. I knew what it looked like, even though I had not turned to look, did not want to think about it.

"The bundle's behind me." Irrepressible, the words fell out of my mouth. I could have kicked myself. This was too personal to share. In the shadows behind me, I could feel it: hide-wrapped, bulky, odd-shaped, a somehow ominous presence.

Eileen sensed relevance. "What's in the package?"

"It's not a package!" I retorted, deeply affronted by her speaking of it as if it were some inconsequential, brown-paper-wrapped, shelved Post Office parcel. "It's a bundle!"

There was a world of difference. This was infinitely precious; sacred. And I could not bear to think of the reason for that preciousness.

"So this 'bundle'," resumed the disembodied voice patronisingly, annoyingly persistent. "What is it?"

"It's not...." In turmoil, I was fighting within myself and coming close to tears. "I can't.... I don't...."

Something caught in my throat, jamming it. The words wouldn't come out. In any case, they sounded strange in my head, as if I was trying to wrap my tongue around something unfamiliar. Or unspeakable.

Nausea filled my gut; my chest tightened. Sucking in a great, shuddering breath, I forced it out.

"It's the bones!"

My heart gave a massive thud. (What bones? another part of me whispered.) I had not wanted to say it; did not want to own this reality. It was as if I was being dragged out of a dream to suffer the most unbearable agony, which so far I had managed to contain.

Cool, dispassionate, came the voice: "Whose bones are they? And why are they here? What do they have to do with you?"

A great anger suffused my body. Mentally I thrashed, only just managing to keep myself from telling the stupid, nosy old woman to go away. Robot-like, I found myself responding: "I brought them here." My voice dipped and softened: "The little ones...." Suddenly it came clear: my grandchildren, who had been in my care.

A sharp, hot lance of pain pierced my gut and a wave of grief welled up, a great surge that rammed up into my throat. Tears ran hot over my temples.

"Why are you here with them?" Disembodied spirit; irksome, persistent.

"Waiting."

"Waiting for what?"

"I don't know!" Oh, I did not want to know; did not want to speak. But could not resist. More calmly: "I don't ... I don't know what to do." Yes, I did know: "Their spirits, they must be freed."

Among the extremes of emotion, the extraordinary scenario, part of "me" was holding back, watching this unfold in amazement. Where was it all coming from?

Again the relentless, disembodied voice: "How do you do that?"

"Sing the song!" I bellowed, appalled at such ignorance. Although "I" was just as ignorant.

"Then sing it."

This was even worse. "I can't. I don't ... it's not my place to sing the song."

"Who should sing it?"

"Grandmother!"

"Then tell her to sing it."

A bright knife-edge of pain twisted in my gut, making me wince. Softly: "She cannot."

"Why can't she sing it?"

A yawning sense of loss threatened to swallow me up. It was not that she was not here. She was.... My awareness rested on the other bundle, beside the first. This was what remained, of my wife. Choking, I whispered: "She cannot, because she's gone."

"Then, you sing it!"

My inner being seemed to curl in upon itself. What she was saying was impossible, unthinkable. It was not for me – a man – to sing this song. It was for woman, for the Old Ones. That was the Way. But there were no women. There was no-one else; only one stinking, filthy old man, sitting here, alone, waiting, waiting for release.

Waiting for death.

The pain in my solar plexus intensified. My head began to spin and I sucked in another shuddering breath.

Suddenly it happened: the song burst out of me, a keening, wailing lament, torn from my gut, ripped from my heart with a power that astounded the "me" observing this incredible unfolding. My whole body seemed to wrap itself around the energy, project itself inside-out through the immense, raw power of my voice: a voice I had never heard myself use before.

No sooner had it ended than a second round commenced.

With stars before my eyes, pinpricks of light spinning, whirling as if in a vortex, I sang four rounds of the song on which souls ride; sang them through the Great Gateway to the river of stars....

Enthralled by the heart-wrenching beauty of the chant, the "me" sitting now way in the background registered gratification that "I" would have a recording of this above all.

Song completed, my voice fell away to ring and echo in my head. Then I became aware of a strange sensation. It began in my head, a warm prickling feeling, like a grainy waterfall, and fed into my neck, throat, shoulders. It faded, then began again in my head, hotter and more intense this time, progressed down to my shoulders and chest, and faded away. Then it picked up again in my jaw, even more intensely, coursed down into my chest and back, and again faded.

Wave after wave of cold-hot, grainy pins-and-needles, overlapping, progressing downwards, tingling through my belly and into my thighs, which grew hot and heavy.

My voice distant, unreal, I described the sensation to Eileen.

"You know what to do, don't you?"

"Yes," I replied, not knowing how I knew. "Just let it go down and out through the soles of my feet and into Mother Earth."

Gradually the odd sensation decreased, draining out through my hot, leaden feet. Limp and exhausted I lay, like beached flotsam after a storm-driven journey. Then the most urgent need to pee pressed in. I told my guide, who gently counted me back to the pyramid and the present by reversing the initial process.

Dizzy and disoriented, as in a dream I stumbled to the washroom. Everything seemed odd, alien: sitting down on hard, cold plastic; the concept of plumbing; the excruciatingly loud noise of the flush. Returning to the couch in a daze, I was glad to lie down again and close my eyes. Again Eileen synchronised our breathing and I was returned to the pyramid, then she began to count me back down the steps.

I didn't really believe it would be possible to go back, or that it was necessary. The song had been sung. But as she reached mid-count, I caught a glimpse of the side of a small, grassy, sunlit hill and the dappled shade of cottonwood, and then the silhouette of a man with a furred hat, sighting down a long-bored musket. With the strangest sensation of floating downwards, I "arrived" among the remains of a devastated encampment. Charred poles, still smoking, were all that remained of three lodges. Objects were scattered round, among them huddled shapes I knew to be bodies.

Immediately I understood: wherever this was, "I" had come back from perhaps a hunting trip, to find my family murdered, my home destroyed. My wife and both grandchildren, slaughtered. Devastated by my failure to protect them, I had wrapped up the remains of my little family and brought them to the cave.

Excitedly, I told Eileen but instead of being impressed she simply said: "You are done here now. You have sung the song, you have set the spirits free. It is finished. Now you can leave."

"No!" The strength of my refusal shocked me. "I'm not going out there!"

"But you have sung the song, you can leave now."

"No! There's nothing out there! There's nothing for me to go to." The red-hot anger was back, filling my body.

"Pray. Speak to the Great Spirit, or the Creator, or whoever you pray to. Make your peace, and go outside."

Whoever I pray to.... The cave-mouth sneered back at me. Stupid old woman, knowing nothing! "Pah! I have nothing to say to the Creator! There is nothing left." A determined finality sealed the next deathly-quiet words that hissed from my lips: "There is nothing for me out there. It is over. It is finished."

Underneath, there was a sense of something. I fished: something off-balance ... guilt.

Eileen persisted: "At least get up and go to the cave mouth."

"Never!" White-hot fury twisted in my gut. Something sort of snapped, and the cave, the smear of light were blotted out; were gone. Somehow I knew, irrevocably.

Opening my eyes to the dim light in my mother's living-room, I felt strangely light and dizzy, and had not the slightest reservation about what I had just experienced.

It had been the end of the bloodline; there was nothing to go out to, or for. Momentarily I wondered about the parents of the grandchildren; "his" own children. There had not been any sense of them being present. Were they away, or had they passed over before this disaster? The latter, I sensed. To the grandfather, it was the end of the trail. Stubbornly he had sat in the cave, unmoving, till he died. And somehow I knew that by discarding the gift of life in this manner, a kind of suicide, he had stepped off the Way of his people. I felt an echo of pain in my chest and tears pricked at my eyes. Closing them, I dwelled on this powerful personality, wilfully ending his life in bitterness and torment, turning his back on his Creator; powerful, negative emotions dominating an aborted life.

Eileen's opinion was that the experience had all the hallmarks of a successful regression: the carry-over had been accessed and its release facilitated.

Her voice was still irritating, distant. My own was loud in my head, as if my ears were stuffed with cotton wool. I did not have the energy to ask her what such a release might mean; part of me was not even sure I was happy about it.

One thing I was sure of: this had not been simply the product of a powerful imagination. So much of it had unfolded in a way that had been outside – or inside – of myself, beyond my conscious control; words and images had surfaced seemingly of their own accord; the stink, not present now, had been all too real. Then that chant, the fabulous spirit-freeing song. I had never heard anything like it; could never have made something like that up.

I rolled over to pick up the recorder. The cassette was wound to the end; automatic reverse had taken care of the turn-over. Apart from a faint hiss, however, the cassette was blank. Devastated, I inspected the little machine, which seemed to be working fine. The batteries were new. I remembered switching it on, as did Eileen. She shrugged: "It's not the first time that something like this has happened."

Trying to mask my deep disappointment, I joked: "Coyote's finger sure can reach a long way."

Like the memory of a dream, the extraordinary chant was gone. Yet I sensed a certain appropriateness: a sacred song – the sacred pathway on which souls travelled to the next realm – was not something to be played with, or exhibited.

Now I had to look forward. If this personality had been "riding" me, perhaps it was his unfinished business that was holding me back. Anticipating that my way forward would now be cleared, I returned to Canada.

GIVEAWAY

Despite being new and a security I hadn't known for years, a city townhouse and the immediate proximity of neighbours was a difficult adjustment, but at least my kids could begin to develop their own social life. It was a relief, not long after I came back from England, to go down to Inchelium for the annual sobriety camp-out and be back among the mountains, the golden grasslands, the steely-seethe of the Columbia; to breathe in the sweetly-resinous scent of the gathering-grounds and feel the yield of the sandy earth underfoot. With the faint hope that the Creator's hands might have fashioned some further development in the cultural projects, I looked out for Tom, but the pipe-carrier seemed preoccupied, looking over my shoulder as we exchanged excruciatingly inconsequential pleasantries and excusing himself before I could ask.

Nonplussed, I joined with Northern Lights, but even at Grandmother Drum odd feelings dogged me. Tom had brought his medicine staff to this year's gathering, and tied it to the central pole. Decorated with feathers and crowned with the gleaming-white skull of a mountain-goat, it seemed to glare balefully at our drum, malevolence dripping from the tip of its great, yellowed, curling horns.

Tom had told me how a total stranger had turned up at his home one day and endowed him with the staff. I knew from the Lakes' ethnography that a mountain-goat staff was a traditional form of crest to identify the Arrow Lakes people at all their meetings, but its glowering presence in Tom's home seemed to cast a shadow from the corner in which it was standing. It was not the skull of itself; I had always been partial to their subtle energy. The deer-skull I had come across with the archaeologist on our first foray together into the Vallican site had been with me ever since, a constant reminder that gentleness of spirit is the way to heal all wounds.

Strangely enough, that skull had only recently "discharged its purpose". I had been putting away a glass jar of lentils when it slipped through my fingers and smashed, spraying its contents all over the kitchen. Then I thought I heard an odd noise in the downstairs hallway. Beginning to pick up the shards of glass, I had just cut a finger quite badly when Natalie came in and told me the deer-skull was lying on the floor in the hallway with an antler broken off.

Happening to drop by, Nadine had suggested a double-sacrifice (deer-energy and food) and a blooding – a threefold initiation rite – but neither of us was able to take that further.

When I asked her if she knew why her partner had brought his medicine-staff to the gathering, Nadine just shrugged. Its presence seemed to haunt me, and I noticed that no-one, not even one of the many children freely running round, went anywhere near it. Later in the day, I came across Tom again and was relieved when he stopped to talk, seeming his old, familiar self: "So how was it, over there in England?"

"Oh, really good. Some very interesting experiences, and people. But I was really happy to get back here." It was Coyote Dreams I wanted to talk about, but could not frame the question.

There was a long, to me awkward, silence then Tom said, his eyes narrow, as if looking down at me from a great height: "You're changed, Celia. You've changed somehow...." He sort of chuckled and cleared his throat at the same time, gently shaking his head. "Like you've put up a wall ... or left some part of yourself behind."

My gut churned, cold and heavy. What was he seeing, sensing; or not seeing any more? He was still talking, but of nothing in particular and I could not listen. When he said he had to get back to the gathering, I stood rooted to the ground, watching him walk away, my mind in turmoil. I hadn't breathed a word about the regression experience to anyone; had barely given it a thought since. Could it be that Tom sensed the absence of an anguished soul, sitting in the cave of my being with the bones? Now that he had been "freed", what did that mean in the bigger picture? I couldn't bear to think about it.

Back with Northern Lights, I couldn't rally any enthusiasm for the drum. A strange tension seemed to hang in the air; behind me, I could feel the dark, empty eye-sockets of the mountain-goat skull, boring into my back.

What was I doing here? But where else could I be?

We had just finished a chant when I became aware of raised voices across the other side of the arena. It wasn't possible to see exactly what was going on but there was a flurry of movement and gesticulations that may have been fists flying. None of us had experienced anything like this among the Native people; tight-lipped, eyes downcast, we stayed with the Grandmother until the storm seemed to have passed.

When I turned around to see if things had settled down, my blood ran cold. The medicine-staff had moved. No longer was the mountain-goat facing our drum but the direction where the fracas had taken place. Somehow, it had made a forty-five degree turn.

Silently I pointed this out to the others. We agreed that no-one had been near it. Nor was Tom anywhere to be seen. Nothing more was said, but I felt increasingly uncomfortable and left the drum and the arena.

What was going on? There was meaning here, but an inner voice kept urging that it was none of my business, and then, for the first time: You don't belong here. Torn, I could find no-one to talk to about any of it but Nadine, who said: "Your own fears have more power to affect you than anything else."

That was true, but didn't seem to have much relevance. Yet somehow her words settled something within me. If there was a lesson here it was the straightforward one of the Medicine Wheel: not to remain stuck but move on. I packed up and went home. All the way, round and round in my mind flew the question: after such intensity of involvement, what could follow?

If I was going to make changes, I thought I might as well start with "normalising". With few decent job opportunities in the area, I embarked on the necessary courses to reactivate my teaching qualification and persuaded the children to enter the local elementary school, only a playing-field away. Then it struck me that if I volunteered as an assistant in my son's class, it might ease his transition and give me some useful experience.

Finding out that the Social Studies component at Grade Four level was Native Studies and that they would study the Coastal Salish and the Inuit, I was certain it was no accident that things had unfolded this way. I submitted a proposal to teach an experimental curriculum focussing on the people indigenous to the local area, which I could enhance with personal experience, artefacts and contacts.

Perhaps because I was prepared to work on a voluntary basis, my proposal was immediately accepted and one morning a week made available. I was thrilled. It was a chance to fulfil another long-held dream: free rein to develop an experiential module which could be tailored to the response of the children. Nor would it be difficult; as I knew from the Whole School, most children love the Native American, whose traditional way of life resonates powerfully with their innate earth-connectedness and sense of fairness and harmony. I even dared hope for the long-term: if these children could consciously embrace some of the traditional teachings, in their future hands would be the power to make the world a better place.

Discovering that the school was on the site of the only known Arrow Lakes settlement within the city-limits, I couldn't help wondering whether the ancestral spirits were again at work. Perhaps I had found my vocation: if this was successful, I could offer it to other schools in the area, not only giving myself meaningful employment but keeping the Native life-way central to my life by sharing what I had learned with children of my own culture. The future was suddenly full of promise.

"What day is it today?"
"Today is a good day!"
"What time is it?"
"The right time!"

Once a week, we gave thanks for a new day and smudged with sage or sweetgrass, each child meticulous about this spiritual cleansing, down to the soles of their feet. After a while, of their own accord, some of them requested a prayer for a sick relative or friend. Everyone we prayed for recovered.

We listened to cassettes of Native chants, chewed chips of bitter rat-root and took turns with Little Drum, a hand-drum made by Tipi Doug. Eventually the chants they learned were accompanied by their own handcrafted drums and rattles.

The many artefacts and wealth of cultural knowledge I had acquired over the years and the stories of our adventures were put to good use, enlivening the experience. Nick was persuaded to display his dance-regalia, and loaned it to another boy to try on. One entire morning was spent on the intricacies of the stick-game, which made its way into the playground at lunch-time. To me, this was education: hands-on, creative, experiential, but I also made a point of including some expected formal, written work.

One of the high points was the frosty morning we went out to build a Medicine Wheel: the hushed forest, rimed with crystals, ground hard as iron; the quiet excitement of the children, searching for a suitable clearing; their natural reverence as the Wheel gradually took form. Some had brought Grandmother and Grandfather rocks from home, or from places where they had been on holiday; others searched till they found the stone that "spoke" to them. All that winter, I was later told, on their own or in small groups, some of them often went back to visit it and tidy up any wayward stone-people, becoming Keepers of the Wheel.

It dawned on me that these children's lives were being touched with a sense of the supernatural, of the sacredness of nature, of the land and all of life. To me, this was the most meaningful part of the whole experience. Aware of their place in the world, perhaps they would be spared the desperate, subconscious seeking that too often leads to the abuse of chemical substances.

Tom offered his unconditional support. Bringing his traditional regalia and many handcrafted items, the Lakes pipe-carrier spent a morning with the children, filling their ears, minds and hearts with drumbeat and songs, traditional tales and stories of his childhood. Watching the rapt children, I thought how fantastic it was for a descendant of the indigenous people of this area, so terribly lacking in Native presence, to be educating them in this way and doing a far better job of it than a white newcomer, no matter her motivation and how much she thought she knew. The children loved him, swarming round him when it was time to leave, and often asked when he was coming back.

In turn, Northern Lights drum group shared a morning with the entire school. The children in Grade Four opened with the songs they had learned, drumming and singing so intently that they brought tears to my eyes. Gifted in interaction with children, Yellow Bear soon had everyone, pupils and teachers, dancing and singing. Many of the children had an opportunity to sit at the Grandmother. It was an unforgettable experience.

Another person I hoped might take part was Auntie Vi, who had planned to come up with a couple of her friends to demonstrate beadwork and bring some traditional foods, but unfortunately she was never quite well enough. It distressed me how her health seemed to be steadily declining.

I kept meticulous notes: what we were doing; whether it worked; how it might be done better in the future. Eventually I understood I was synthesising and passing on the essence of most of the things I had learned over the last five years. Unbidden, the thought came: this is a giveaway. Yet it was no sacrifice, only a joy to see it so well-received. It was just that if it were an emptying, there was nothing I could imagine ever filling me to quite the same degree.

After five months, quite organically, the experience came to an end. In review, there was little to change. The curriculum could be worked through in half a school-year; the balance of the Social Studies curriculum could be taken over by the class teacher. Given the interest of other elementary schools in the area, a three- or four-day working week was a possibility. But while the "experiment" was regarded as a success by teachers and parents, some of whom told me it was the only school-day in the week about which they heard anything, it soon became clear that in the light of prevailing market forces in education, the study of the indigenous way of life offered scant return.

It was not unexpected; I was not really disappointed. I just felt compelled to take the experience through to a logical conclusion, an outcome already made clear by the children's response to Tom: my giveaway of the Native American way of life was a pale-face version.

Competition for teaching jobs in the area was fierce, and in any case, I knew I could not handle teaching in the mainstream system. Half-heartedly I began to look further afield and applied to a couple of remote northern Canadian Reserves.

There was no response. It was chilling: I could see no way forward and felt stuck again, directionless. Only it was worse now: I had finally moved on from something that meant more to me than anything I could imagine, and was left facing a void.

I had forgotten that the Wheel never stops turning; that one can only get stuck by holding onto that which has served its purpose. What I felt as a void was but the space between the spokes.

ARACHNE RISING

Carried across the Atlantic from Old World to New, the concept of a lunar zodiac had caught the interest of the new man in my life, Sam, the esoteric astrologer I had known for several years, and inspired the creation of a mystery play invoking the thirteenth sign. Not street- but forest-theatre, Arachne Rising took place on a sacred seven-acre site my friend Danette had set aside specifically for purposes such as this. Timed for Hallowe'en – Samhain in the Celtic calendar, the dark hours when the veil between worlds is at its thinnest; a time of endings, a time of beginnings – it was a colourful, masked performance, with twelve teenagers representing the Celtic tree-calendar and eight adults, the eight divisions of the year. Amethyst and quartz crystals were used, the Celtic year was ritually affirmed and the thirteenth sign was seeded into the earth. Finally, we danced, a ritual dance that demarked an arcing geometric shape. It was a powerful experience, inspiring the core group to a commitment to nurture newly-seeded Arachne through a full year's Celtic ritual cycle.

It seemed a sea-change was upon us, for some of these friends, mostly first- or second-generation natives of North America with European roots, had been involved with Native Americans for years but were also feeling an inner impulse to move on. Or return to "what we were originally taught". But was a Celtic worldview any more valid? They were but one of the great waves of migrants that had swept across Europe. Within six months, differences of opinion and personality clashes were breaking up the group, nipping my new relationship in the bud at the same time as the teaching experience ended.

Furious at myself for yet again repeating my pattern, I promised myself to remain single until something changed. (What that something might be, I had no idea.) As one last gesture to round things off, I made a new list of all the qualities I wanted in the One (the perfect man for me – I'd done this before but it seemed I missed out too much) and burned it with a prayer that Spirit would know what I'd omitted. In any case, I decided, once my kids had flown the nest I'd be happy enough living out my life in a little log-cabin facing the Pacific, with dogs, beach-walks and writing for company, and frequent visits from any eventual grandchildren.

Letting go. Little did I know that was the most important thing at this point.

In an American store, I'm buying a guitar and putting in an order for a piano. Which is strange, because I don't have room at home for a piano and hardly play guitar. Accompanied by my friend Anne, I return the guitar to the store and cancel the piano. As we leave, two blonde men are walking towards us. Both are extremely good-looking: beauty rather than handsomeness.

"One of them is highly eligible," Anne nudges me and whispers. "His last name is Tyr-lee."

Recording the vivid dream, I could think of no-one by any name like that except for Tyler, the son of a neighbour. He was good-looking. And eighteen years old.

The Weaver's silver-stranded web was trembling with connection, but not once did my mind make the leap to the last name of the English pilgrimage leader who had divined the Silver Wheel, who by that time would have received a copy of the script of Arachne Rising. A gifted wellspring of information about sacred geography – prehistoric, historic, astrological, arcane and esoteric – Anthony had begun a sporadic correspondence with me when his marriage had ended, about six months after the first pilgrimage. By the time of the Silver Wheel, however, the contact had lapsed. I had only sent him the script because in the midst of the preparation for Arachne Rising, Sam had casually remarked it would be a shame if "such a valued mentor" didn't know what had been done with his inspiration. The way these things work, it is quite possible he was reading it round the time of the dream.

What unfolded over the following months was an unforgettable, fairy-tale romance, long-distance, crowded with synchronicities and incidences of telepathy. Within three months it was clear that this was a re-connection of twin flames, so deeply and powerfully connected in love that we wished for nothing more than to walk together through the rest of this – and any other – life. It was all the more incredible for the fact that we had never felt anything more than an easy friendship on both pilgrimages.

The other weird thing was a prediction I had made for myself but forgotten in the interim, and did not even remember until well down the line. Taught how to dowse by the couple who had been preparing the record of the planetary grid, when I came back to Canada, I had asked if I would ever meet the man with whom I would spend the rest of my life.

"Yes," my little pendulum – bobbin on silk – had replied.

"Do I already know him?" I had been inspired to ask.

"Yes."

"Will it happen in the next six months?"

"No."

"The next twelve months?"

"Yes."

When Sam had appeared on the scene, I'd forgotten about the time-scale and dived prematurely into the wrong frying-pan. Anthony resurfaced in my life in the next six-month period.

This tale could well end here: a sort of "happily ever after". Mixing metaphors, Coyote survived yet another "lesson" and picked himself up again, to set out on a new adventure. But I was the child who could not just let things be, who always asked what happened in the "happily ever after", so for those other children-at-heart who do the same, here is what happened after the princess, asleep for a hundred years, was finally kissed awake.

CLOUD-SPEAK

Thousands of miles, an ocean and a continent lay between: my own words, back to haunt me. Neither of us could breach the question of who was going to make the move: Anthony's children were adult but he was in a complicated personal situation that would take months to resolve and had just launched himself into a new aspect of his medical career. Nor would his qualifications be valid in Canada without re-sitting some major examinations. But I was happily – and securely – ensconced in Nelson with two children who would be living with me for at least another ten years. Anthony arranged to take three weeks off work at the end of summer to come over for a visit.

Wanting to surprise me, Anthony has arrived unexpectedly early. I take him on a tour of the area.

The car is difficult to control; for some weird reason I am on the passenger-side and have to lean across him to steer. It is awkward and uncomfortable. "I don't know why I'm doing this."

"Then let's switch sides," he says.

We are high on the mountains, arriving at a ghost-town; once a mining-town, from the greyness and desolation around us: ramshackle, rotting wooden buildings; rutted dirt-roads; scarred granite mountainsides denuded of trees; patches of dirty snow.

The view is magnificent, however: sharp peaks scraping heavy-bellied oyster-shell clouds; velvet-green forest cloaking distant sharp-toothed mountain ranges; jade-bright patches of alpine meadow.

The feeling between us is of closeness, warmth, increasing mellowness.

"I love the mountains," Anthony says, "but I need a more accessible landscape."

Dream-state, indicating what must be. I was fully aware that in essence he was what I termed a "stars-and-stones man": a diviner of the correspondences between Mother Earth and Father Sky whether natural or man-made. My subconscious was making it clear his place was in England and that the most pertinent common ground we shared was there, too. But I had made my home in Canada; my children were Canadian. To leave the beauty, the great wilderness that spoke to the essence of myself to return to live on a crowded little island seemed unthinkable. Perhaps, I reasoned, given his professional expertise and experience in addictions, the Native people would snap him up in some sort of administrative position in rehabilitation. A whole new vista of sacred landscape could open up here for us.

Three steps forward; two back. When people now ask me what on earth made me leave Canada to come back to England, it amuses me to reply: "A man with his head in the stars. And a cloud."

Once you know who you want to spend the rest of your life with, you just want to get on with it. With less than a month to go until Anthony's visit, the dilemma of how that would transpire was reaching crisis-point. On yet another in a long line of still, hot days, having promised the children a cooling swim and since it was already late afternoon, I decided to take them to Nelson's lakeside park. Once they were in the water and I was alone again, sitting on a blanket in the shade, the same monologue going round and round in my head for the umpteenth time, I suddenly had enough. Exasperated, I looked up and cried out to the sky: "What should I do? How can Anthony and I be together? I need a sign! Please, give me a sign!"

I closed my eyes. In the distance, I could hear the faint cries of children at play, the distant hum of city traffic. A sound close by made me open my eyes again.

A small boy, blonde-haired, in blue shorts, two or three years old, little fists clenched, his face puckered in concentration, was running round me in a tight circle. Faster and faster he raced, whizzing round and round.

I remembered a story of Bear – strength – and another small boy running round me so fast he was a blur; Blue-jay, winding a cone of energy; the pure spirit-connectedness of the child. Something was happening.

"I am the perfect manifestation of the feminine in my relationship with Anthony." Well-taught by Nancy, three times I repeated the affirmation and lay back, eyes closed, arms spread-eagled, heart-centre open. Then, remembering the sometimes quirky nature of the spirit-world: "Please make right action totally, utterly clear!"

As ever, emptying my mind proved impossible. Uncertainty crowded in; I was glad no-one else was nearby. Taking a peek, I saw the little boy, my supposed medium, was gone. I closed my eyes again, beginning to feel ridiculous. What would lying here accomplish? What did I expect to happen? I opened my eyes again.

And there it was, the answer, directly above me, filling the space between the evergreens. A massive cloud in the exact shape of the British Isles: crown of Scotland; great bow of Northumbria; rounded bulge of Norfolk; heel of Kent; long pointed toe of Cornwall; belly of Wales. Floating alongside, diaphanous, ephemeral, mystical Ireland, riddled with holes. In awe, I lay absolutely still as the incredible sight sailed out of view, and for several minutes was unable to move, thrilled and chilled and aware of a curious sense of lightness, of relief.

Now all I had to do was put it to him. And then my children, which thought chilled me through. The time-difference meant I had to wait until the next morning, which made for a very long night and a lot of time for reflection.

It was almost six years since I had cried for help and been given another cloud-vision, one profoundly connected to this land, its people and myself. Was it somehow the power of my subconscious or emotional promptings that was manifesting these "signs"? I had initially seen Sky-Wolf as something external but learned it was actually part of a symbolic representation of myself. So what about this cloud-kingdom? I still felt like I was on the edge of cliff, except with the potential of not falling but flying.

ROOTS

It is a measure of twin-flame connectedness that Anthony not only immediately accepted what had happened (and my interpretation) but had been asking the same question at an earth-dedication at about the same time. A couple of weeks later he arrived in British Columbia, and any concerns I might have had about "chemistry" (nothing between us but friendship on both pilgrimages, after all) were laid completely to rest. Knowing I would soon be following him back to England made his visit somehow more real; with a sense of taking leave, we visited the many significant places and people in the Valley – including a session with Northern Lights – that had been so much part of my life over the past six years. Except for the Indian village at Vallican; it felt unapproachable.

We visited Tom and his new partner in Inchelium, and camped for a few days at the sacred gathering-grounds. Empty of people, the area spoke with its own, powerful energy; when soft evening breezes stirred the pines with a susurrus of ghostly whispering, it seemed the ancestral spirits were fully present.

Blessed with a mellow, golden Indian summer, for three days we camped at Wellpinit on the Spokane Reservation for Spokane Indian Days, the grand Labour Day pow-wow. Our first dance together was an Owl Dance, and, returning by way of Inchelium, we ate at Steem'as Spa'uss. My only regret was that I was unable to get hold of Auntie Vi before we had to return to British Columbia to pick up the children from their father's in Vernon.

It was there, in the same city where my van's transmission had fallen apart, obliging me to be at home for a visit that changed my life, that the spirits took Little Drum.

Knowing only too well the problems an eagle feather could create at the border, I had left my Medicine Wheel drum at home and brought Little Drum on the trip. The morning after we arrived in Vernon, I found the hide of Little Drum split along one side. It was a shock; I believed I had taken care of it. Deeply upset, and with Tom's story of Ed's drum ringing in my ears, I guessed the spirits were making sure I understood I had to move on, and was thankful they had not taken the Medicine drum.

Now four, we looped over the lonely beauty of the Monashees and down to the site of the Rebirth of Mother Earth Medicine Wheel gathering. The gift of an Indian summer was in retreat: heavy clouds were massing at the north end of the Arrow Lakes, adding to the moody atmosphere of the place where a great episode in my life had been sparked. Anthony could feel it, too: the powerful energy of one of the most sacred places to the Arrow Lakes people; one of the gathering-places of which Tom had spoken.

Acutely feeling the lack of a drum, I meditated for a while at the great Medicine Wheel, made an offering and sang a traditional chant. Then I went to the site of the moon-lodge and sang a traditional women's song, and finally sat on the ridge beside which a red-jacketed Native elder had warmly embraced me, and exactly where another handsome Native man had told me about his people and touched upon something deep within me, beginning a home-coming journey I would never forget. Nostalgia crept like a chill into my bones, and I wept silently for a while.

Yet how could I be sad? Again I was being called, this time perhaps the final calling, back to my origins in this life. And I was choosing to respond.

Barely six weeks later, after a whirlwind winding-up of eighteen years in Canada, on the day before Samhain – when the veil is thin; time of endings, time of beginnings – we joined Anthony in England. Not until we arrived, however, did it dawn on me exactly where we had landed: among the great, empty sweeps of Salisbury Plain (which eased the transition from the vastness of British Columbia), four miles from the mystery of Stonehenge and close to the epicentre of the intriguing phenomenon of crop formations and the great sacred goddess-complex at Avebury.

The leap across an ocean and a continent had brought me to the ancient kingdom of Wessex, spiritual heart of Britain, bonded to my twin flame, a stars-and-stones man. It was clear that any void was about to be filled; how that would unfold would be the next great adventure.

REFLECTION

Mind may perceive, but heart still has to undergo. Despite finding bliss with my new partner, the pain of separation from Canada hit me unexpectedly hard. Through that first winter, I grieved amid clouds of sage-smoke, chanting the old songs, tears running down my cheeks. I cut my long hair into a bob which didn't suit me at all, only later realising I had unconsciously acted out a Native American tradition.

In January I heard that Auntie Vi had passed over. I knew I should not be sad for a beloved friend and mentor who was now free from pain and with her beloved Jesus; who believed as much as I that we would see each other again on the other side, but the grief broke through when I received her rosary with a poignant message from Carly, her granddaughter: "My grandma would have wanted you to have this. She loved you very much."

Then I heard that Ed had followed her over. It seemed like the end of an era.

Like the memory of an intense love-affair, the anguished, bereft Native American grandfather still lingers in my mind and heart. Often I wonder whether it was his torment, the faint scent of an incomplete past-life trail, that lay beneath my feeling of rootlessness; whether he and his family's bones were the fundamental reason I had been drawn into the story of the Arrow Lakes people. A soul-contract, that was also a karmic balancing of a past, deeply-wounded "me", stuck in some kind of limbo, who "bled" over to affect the present.

Did this explain my strength of feeling about the traditional Native American way of life, about figures such as Tonto and Chief Joseph? Had it been a subconscious factor in my eventual migration to North America?

Red Cloud's personal greeting; had it been some kind of recognition? And Bob: what had he perceived, to take me apart and tell me so much about his people, their tradition; to affect my life so powerfully and fundamentally? The strength of the outrage that had welled up in me when he told me about the disinterred ancestral remains: had that come from a distraught spirit-within?

Was it this same personality who manifested in the automatic drawing, during the rebirthing experience and eventually in the mirror; timeless, rising again and again to the surface of my consciousness, feeding an antipathy to men of my own race; affecting the way I walked; at least twice glimpsed by sensitives?

At the outset, I felt I had been drawn in to help the Sinixt, but in reality it was I who was helped. A lost soul, I had been drawn into an epic story. Faced with the grim reality of the contemporary life of the Native American and the truth of their greatness of heart, I began to see that what I had thought was strength in myself, was a hardening heart. To protect myself from the pain of life, I had built a wall around my heart which was disconnecting me from my true self, de-sensitising me, stultifying my growth as a human being. That wall had to be knocked down, and the heart set free: I had to learn that tears are not an indication of weakness but a necessary expression of pain; that experience must be allowed to touch the heart so that the response can come from that place, tempered by the mind so one does not fall apart in empathy: what the Tibetans call "ruthless compassion". An integral part of this process was learning to drum and chant the Native American way: drum resonating, like the heart, with the beat of life; the chants demanding a surge of power from the solar plexus that acted on the subtle levels to clear the pathways of the heart. Yet even that process may have been facilitated by the presence of an inner, broken-hearted elder. Freed, he took something with him: never again did I sing Native American chants with such power, such confidence.

Once the heart began to be cleared, the gifts I brought into this life were able to find expression. In a way, it was like starting over again as a new-born: it would take practice to sift through and understand what I was picking up as an empath and an earth-sensitive, and articulate the cosmic insights that occasionally flash through.

My friend Celina, Strong Standing Woman, had often teased me that I would be tested by contact with her people, the red-blooded people, the people of the earth. I think it is no accident that an anagram of "earth" is "heart."

A fabulous painting of Frog Mountain, snow-capped and brooding in the misted dark-greens and grey-blues of early winter, was Nancy's parting gift. Her teachings about the power of the will and the mind served to enrich my experience of the earth-centred spirituality of the Native American way, a way not of superstition, but super-perception.

As for my "marathon moccasins", as Uncle Chuck had taken to calling them, I eventually realised they had been a metaphor: it had never been my destiny to walk the Native Way.

It is a great privilege to live a personal mythology. The long walk of six Arrow Lakes ancestors back to the dust from which they sprang, so that their spiritual walk could be continued, was reflected in the microcosm of my own internal drama: an emotional ebb that took me down to the "bare bones" of psychological near-collapse so I could clear my way back onto my spiritual path in this life. The spirit of the angry, grieving Native grandfather may have been freed, but Wolf – essence of myself – dogs me. For the past nine years, we have lived near the beautiful city of Bath, site of the world-renowned Oracle of Sul, founded by the legendary British king, Bladud, whose name apparently means Wolf.

It was here that the great eye of Horus, which brought me peace and comfort during the prayer-circle of six Arrow Lakes women, came to fulfilment: a presentiment of an on-going exploration of the hermetic history of Ancient Egypt, which in turn illumines the path Anthony and I walk together, down our ancestral time-line and deep into the sacred geography of Albion and beyond, into the stars.

ALL MY RELATIONS

In 1995, during a personal voyage of discovery in Scotland, Anthony and I visited Rosslyn chapel near Edinburgh, built in the early 1400s by Scottish families carrying the tradition of the powerful Order of Knights Templar. Carved into the stone columns are images of maize and cactus, plants known only to the New World at a time when "official" history relates that the Americas were still undiscovered.

At the Gunn clan museum in Caithness, we learned that since 1954, archaeologists and historians have been preoccupied with the mystery of the "Westford Knight": a six-hundred-year-old image of a Scottish knight, etched in stone, found on a quiet roadside in Massachusetts. The knight's shield depicts the distinctive three-masted ship of the insignia of the head of the Gunn clan, and his sword is broken. Evidence points to the armorial effigy as commemorating the death in battle of Sir James Gun of Clyth, who accompanied Henry Sinclair, Earl of Orkney, on an expedition to the west. Both knights carried the spirit of the Order of Knights Templar, who, discouraged in their efforts to survive in a hostile Europe, sought to found a New Jerusalem in the New World, a hundred years before Columbus "discovered" America. For a time, these men and their retinue lived with the Micmac Indians on the eastern coast of what is now Canada, and showed them how to fish with nets. Apparently this is still remembered today by the Micmacs during their annual celebration of Glooscap.

I also inquired about any recorded connection to the Arrow Lakes Band. At one of the early Band meetings, Bob and Uncle Charlie had shown me recently-discovered tribal enrolment lists from the turn of the century, vital to help establish present-day Band membership. Chuckling, Bob had flipped over the pages, past columns of his last name and Auntie Vi's, to show me the long list of Gunns.

That same summer, Auntie Vi had taken me to an all-Indian rodeo in Nespelem where the MC had explained for the benefit of the "newcomer from Canada" the significance of each event. Towards the end of the day and the final heats, I heard the name "Gunn" coming up more and more often, and identified two handsome, tall and lanky young Native men and a girl, who seemed to be carrying off more than a fair share of the prizes. Then eight, Natalie ingenuously asked: "Mum, why don't you go down? You might find some long-lost cousins!"

Auntie Vi had laughed. "Now you know why we accepted you so easy from the outset. When Bob told us about you, we thought you were one of us! It sure was a shock when you appeared: blonde, with an English accent, driving an old hippy van!"

Perhaps not so different to the horrors suffered by Native Americans during the 1800s, as a Glaswegian visitor to the Indian village had told me, the story of the ignominious dispersion of the Gunn clan is one of the most tragic of the Highland Clearances. Completely ousted from their traditional lands at Caithness, some of them had to have made their way to North America, where the hardy, forthright and fiercely proud and independent nature of the Scotsmen, their tribal tradition and their closeness to the land would have meshed well with the indigenous peoples; apparently, intermarriage was often successful. But there was no mention of any Native American Gunn at the museum, nor did anyone seem interested, not even when I mentioned they were prize-winning bull-riders, horse-racers and mud-wrestlers.

One more for the blood: according to the Icelandic records, almost a hundred years before Erik the Red reached the North American continent, it was visited in 900AD by another Viking: Gunnbjorn.

Uncovering bloodline connections was thrilling, but also made me consider the concept of a past-life in another light, and the information that lay in the parts of DNA labelled "junk". Had I been treading in the footsteps of my ancestors in ways I had never imagined?

Finally, what if the concept of a past life is a delusion of linear-consciousness? What about the concept of restless spirits stuck in the astral plane and an opening on the earth-level being a potential not necessarily to wreak mischief or havoc, or to take possession, but to fulfil something left undone? Some might speak in hushed tones about infringement of free will, but I do not see it this way. I had come through an experience I would not have foregone for the world and that brought me great personal growth. And if truth be told, I miss the old Indian.

All my Relations.

ENVOI

February 23rd 1997

Natalie and I are standing on the crest of a high, grassy sand-dune. Stretched out before us, steely-grey, white-capped, the sea roars and crashes onto the shore. The spiky sea-grasses are whipped into a frenzy.

The feeling is of end-times.

Below, I see my dog Guin, only instead of being white and tan, she is pure black. She's inside a dry-stone walled enclosure, being chased by three Highland cattle, also black. I call her to safety; she wriggles under the gate and I see the other animals that harmlessly follow her are only dogs after all; a terrier, a Labrador and an unknown.

We assist three old ladies over a steep, grassy dune. Below is a pocket of sand filled with little crabs. I know we have to meet Anthony and Nick, soon.

My daughter and I sit down together on the top of the dune. Watching the wild sea foaming, hearing its roar, a song takes form in my mind. I start to hum it.

"It doesn't go like that!" Natalie interrupts. "It's like this, and it's the Finishing Song."

She chants in a soft melodious voice that rides above the phantom moaning of the wind, the thundering seawaters. And I remember, and sing it, too....

Opening my eyes to the dark and a howling gale outside, barely awake, I said to Anthony: "Listen to this. It's the Finishing Song."

Like a zephyr, it flowed from my consciousness, over my lips. For years, I had listened to the wind, the water, waiting for a song; it had come at last, in the land of my roots: a Native American chant, nine bars long.

Nine: number of completion.

The Finishing Song.

GLOSSARY

Sinixt words which appear in this narrative (author's spelling).
[h as in the Scottish "loch"]

For further material on Sinixt place names, see Bouchard & Kennedy, 1985.

Ah-sq´eest	I am called
Al´t´as Steem´as Spa´uss	Don't bullshit your heart [thanks, Manny]
Heha-aykin	White Wolf – sacred name of Frog Mountain
H´woy! / Wye!	a greeting
Kay-pe-out	Patches of Snow (Tom's Indian name)
Kee´ha-hes´ke´	Laughing Thunder (Bob's Indian name)
Kin-sin	I am
Km´kmeena	? Indian name of hereditary chief John
K´soo-soos	the ugly one (spirit-guide of Tom's grandfather)
Kum-sin´kin	clan
Kuskanux	? settlement north of Nakusp, B.C.
Kwa´sis´ke	blue-jay
Luk´nux	bald eagle
N´chaliam	hits the water – original settlement, now inundated, below present-day Inchelium on the Colville Confederated Reservation
N´kusp	meeting-place – present-day town of Nakusp, B.C.
Nkweio´ten	? settlement at Vallican, B.C.
Qepi´tles	? settlement at the mouth of Kootenay river, B.C., near present-day Castlegar
Quillque´alx	? Auntie Vi's Indian name
Qu´il-tsin	sweat-lodge
Sinixt	Dolly Varden char; for which the people and language central to the narrative are named
S´ink´leep	Old Man Coyote
Ska-ool	the wind in the trees
Slo´heen	pierced in, or through, the head; from which the name of the Slocan Valley is derived
Sna-mut	? mountain on the Colville Confederated Reservation
Snpakcin	First Light (Martin's Indian name)
Steem´as Spa´uss	what's in your heart? (name of the restaurant at Inchelium)
Sumix	the sacred power, spirit, energy of plants, animals
Swar´ah´ahin-shw´il-shw´al	Frog Mountain
Ti-tigh	salmon

ABOUT THIS BOOK

In 1989, descendants of the Sinixt [SNGAYTSKSTX] First Nation or Arrow Lakes Indian Band living on the Colville Confederated Reservation in Washington State USA rallied to request the repatriation of disinterred ancestral remains, removed in 1981 during archaeological investigation from a 3000-year-old ancestral site in the Slocan Valley, in the West Kootenay region of British Columbia, Canada, heart of their people's traditional lands. This action spearheaded the Sinixt renascence as a sovereign nation.

For almost six years, I was unwittingly caught up in something which both occupied and preoccupied me in a way I never thought possible, becoming for a while the most powerful experience in my life. Moving through it and detaching myself before it suffocated me, turned out to be a journey of personal understanding and growth that has led to a profound appreciation of earth-centred spirituality and knowledge of an inner peace I could only have guessed at. An innate interest in the concept of other dimensions underpinning daily reality may have predisposed me to be immersed in the magic of a world where nothing happens by chance, where everything – the elements, the animate and the inanimate, dreams, the concept of time – has spirit and carries message and meaning. This is what I believe living life to really be about, but in my own culture so much of this experience is fundamentally denied. We don't look and we don't see. Nor are we encouraged to do so.

During this intense, unforgettable period, I was awakened into a super-natural reality where everything has significance: a dream, a cloud, a car-breakdown, a breath of wind, a feather, an owl, a mouse. Taken on a journey that taught of power of place and synchronicity and carried me deep into my shadow-side, ultimately I was enabled to reconnect with the being the Creator meant me to be in this lifetime: an inner bone-journey that danced a subtle counterpoint to the outer bone-journey of the Arrow Lakes ancestors.

In Europe, the body has come to be regarded as little more than a shell. All earlier – and uncannily similar to Native American – beliefs about burial were swept away with the advent of Christianity; by the Middle Ages the deceased were regarded as a species of trash to be discarded, and the dead were often pushed aside to make room for the living. However, much like the ancient Egyptians and Celts, Native Americans have an ongoing relationship with those who went before. Settlements existed side-by-side with burial-grounds; the dead watched over the living, who took care of their ancestors' resting-place. Death was an acknowledged and accepted step on the path of the spirit-journey. However, for the spirit-journey to proceed, the bones of the dead must return to dust in the place from which they sprang; if they are removed or displaced, the spirit is bound to the earth and wanders aimlessly, ever seeking restoration. In this tale, the influence of a powerful, super-natural force becomes evident, shaping events and changing lives irrevocably.

An Interior Salishan group named for their major resource, the Dolly Varden char which inhabit the high mountainous lakes of the area, the Sinixt were ethnographically listed under a multitude of name-representations until anglicised as the Arrow Lakes Indians, for the lakes which were part of their traditional lands on the Columbia River. In the 1840s, these lands were bisected by the creation of the International Boundary so that the northern two-thirds lies in Canada in an area now known as the West Kootenays and the remaining one-third in Washington State, America, reaching south of Kettle Falls.

Centuries of systematic programs of cultural genocide carried out by Christian Churches and the government, who forbade the Native people their rituals and forcefully took away their children to residential schools where they were punished for speaking their own language, broke the continuity of tribal life. For over a century, the Arrow Lakes people were increasingly marginalised until in 1956 the Band was deemed extinct by an Order-In-Council of the Canadian federal government, and their small Reserve on the Arrow Lakes in British Columbia reverted to the province.

In the 1970s, descendants of the fragmented Band living in Washington State USA began to ask pointed questions about their ancestral lands in Canada but it was not until 1989, when a 3000-year-old ancestral village and burial-ground in Vallican, British Columbia, came under proposals for development that their continuing existence was publicly brought to light. Both the provincial and federal governments have yet to acknowledge what the law-courts officially recognised that year.

Coyote in the computer!

Originally begun as a novel (third-person with all the names changed), when I reached page seventy a strange lancing pain in my stomach caused me to double over and strike a key which erased everything. At precisely the same point in my second attempt (wiser now and backing up) the floppy disc proved faulty and contaminated the hard drive. Everything I had written was either lost or gobble-de-gook.

Nothing happens by chance. I got the message. The third attempt was first-person with everyone named, telling it exactly as I remembered. There were no further problems.

Filled with an amused tolerance and genuine affection, Native American tales of mythical trickster-teacher Coyote illustrate the ambiguity in the world. As a symbolic representation of man and his dual potential for good and evil, Coyote holds up a mirror to human nature to show people their own foolishness. When he uses his ingenuity and craftiness to help others, there is no retribution for his tricks, but if he tries to outwit his fellows or satisfy his own greed, lust or idle curiosity, he only succeeds in tripping himself up. By demonstrating what not to be, what not to do, the stories strengthen social harmony and moral values. Despite never seeming to learn from his lessons, Coyote's gullibility is matched only by his indestructability. Like the Fool in Tarot, Loki in Norse mythology or the jester at court, Coyote represents the primary aspect of universal consciousness: the superconscious.

The title of this books reflects a powerful slice of life that points, as Coyote tales always do, to the magic of an immediate, personal connection with the natural world, to the joy and pain of learning to live with the weaknesses inherent in being a two-legged creature and to the ability to laugh at and with events in life. The fullness of the many wry, earthy Coyote tales I leave for the reader to discover elsewhere from books, or, infinitely more preferable, directly from Native American story-tellers.

Written over the last ten years, this account is not an attempt at a historical record, an anthropological study or an academic interpretation. It is a phenomenological account intended as a reflective narrative of an intense, tumultuous and extraordinary personal journey as it interweaves with the return of a disinherited people to their ancestral lands, the repatriation of ancestral remains and efforts to preserve a way of life. It also offers a window onto the predicament of Native North Americans at the closing of the twentieth century. Loss of heritage and identity are evident in the grinding poverty, addictive and violent behaviours evident on the Reservation, yet the traditional spirit of hospitality and generosity are still very much alive, as is a wry, dry humour.

Of mixed British and European descent, I was born in the United Kingdom and had no direct connection with the Native peoples of North America before this period. Taken from personal notes and journals, transcriptions and manuscripts, a couple of cassettes and a memory that has unfailingly surprised me with its insistent accuracy and rich detail, everything I have written is the truth as I remember it. All the people are real, no names have been changed and I take full responsibility for any errors of fact.

My purpose is to share and reflect on the profound effect of contact with a people and a way of life tragically misunderstood, wrongly feared and almost totally destroyed. Like many others born in the post-World War Two period, since the 1960s I have been searching for something more meaningful than contemporary aggressive, capitalistic Western values. My hope is that others will see that the teachings of the traditional Native North American way of life have an incalculable value and timeless validity as to the meaning and direction of life, for ourselves, personally and collectively, and our planet, as we proceed into the twenty-first century with such a sense of foreboding.

Celia M. Gunn
Bath, England 2006

CLARIFICATION OF TERMINOLOGY

1. Calling themselves variously the Sinixt, or Lakes Indians, the Native American people central to this tale are also referred to as Arrow Lakes.

2. At the time, the term for the indigenous people of North America considered acceptable by liberal-thinking people was Native North Americans. The Arrow Lakes people speak of themselves and their language as "Indian". More recently, Native activists such as Russell Means have reinstituted the term "Indian" (derived from "In Dios"; Sp.: "in God").

3. The Canadian term for a Native American grouping is Band or Nation and the land allotted them a Reserve, while in America the terms are Tribe or Nation, and Reservation (the "Rez").

4. The prehistoric ancestral Sinixt settlement at Vallican, B.C., is variously called the Vallican Archaeological Park (VAP), the heritage site, the ancestral site and the Indian village.

5. Formed in 1984, the Vallican Archaeological Park Society (VAPS) consisted of a group of local people who voluntarily gave of their time and energy to uphold a mandate to "protect and preserve" the heritage site.

6. B.C. Heritage Trust manages and develops designated heritage sites and is an arm of the Ministry of Housing, Recreation and Culture, Canada.

7. The elected Confederated Tribal Government on the Colville Confederated Reservation is variously called the Colville Business Council, the Tribal Council, the Council, the Tribal Agency, and the Agency.

8. Oral accounts I personally heard indicated that Native Americans had a civilisation on the continent for tens of thousands of years before scientific/orthodox dates and that they did not come to the continent over the Bering Strait.

9. Personally, I prefer the more fluid and holistic term "way of life", to "culture".

ACKNOWLEDGEMENTS

I cherish the memory and wisdom of two dear friends and mentors: Sinixt/Arrow Lakes elder, Violet Desautel of Nespelem, Colville Confederated Reservation, Washington State, USA; and English mystic, Eileen Churchill of Whittingham, Northumberland, UK.

To Grandmother Dorothy, I extend my gratitude for the seed-idea of writing this book. And for making me believe it would be worthwhile, my thanks to David H. Chance, ethnographer.

I am greatly indebted to all the Lakes people who shared their homes and lives with me, and thank them for believing in me, especially: Bob; Tom; Manny; Uncle Charlie; John; Eva; Jim; Junior, Carly and James; Gilbert and Lucetta; Doll; Charlie; Uncle Archie; Pierre; Aunt Tootie and Jenny; Jacqueline and Babe; Aunt Mary and Butch; Aunt Mary; Michael; Francis; Robert; Karen, Patti, Earl, Gary and Victor.

To the following Native Americans, I also extend my gratitude: Uncle Chuck and Aunt Aggie; Ed; Celina; Michael; Shirley; Leo; Louise; members of Little Falls Drum.

I also thank my friends and mentors in British Columbia for their various and vital contributions, especially: Ken and Sue; Leo; Mabel; Nancy; Bryan; Lynne and James; Al; Tipi Doug; Yellow Bear; Linda; Nadine; Hetty; Anne; Shelley; Danette; Walter and Marilyn; Rubiyah Ratna; Sam; and all those others who know.

I am deeply grateful to my children, Sivan, Natalie and Nicolas, for generously bearing my absences and preoccupation.

As ever, I thank my dear Mum, whose life-time of loving care and generosity has helped me realise my hopes and dreams.

Thank you to Judy, Moyra, Siggy and Larry for your kindness, and editorial assistance.

My deepest appreciation is extended to my beloved twin flame, Anthony, whose loving support and encouragement made this book possible.

RELATED READING

Abram, David, *The Spell of the Sensuous – Perception and Language in a More-Than-Human World.* Vintage Books 1996.

Arguelles, Jose, *Surfers of the Zuvuya.* Bear & Co 1989.

Baker, Marie Annharte, *Being on the Moon.* Polestar Press 1990.

Beal, Merril D., *I Will Fight No More Forever.* Ballantine Books 1963.

Bouchard, Randy & Dorothy Kennedy, *Lakes Indian Ethnography and History.* Unpubl. report prepared for B.C. Heritage Conservation Branch, Victoria, B.C. 1985.

Caldecott, Moyra, *Guardians of the Tall Stones.* Celestial Arts 1986.

Caldecott, Moyra, *The Winged Man.* Headline 1993.

Carey, Ken, *Return of the Bird Tribes.* Harper Collins 1988.

Chance, David H., *People of the Falls.* Kettle Falls Historical Center 1986.

Curtis, Edward S., *The North American Indian.* Taschen 1997.

Delehanty Pearkes, Eileen, *The Geography of Memory.* Kutenai House Press 2002.

DeVoto, Bernard, editor, *The Journals of Lewis and Clark.* Houghton Mifflin 1953.

Dickson, Lovat, *Wilderness Man: the Amazing True Story of Grey Owl.* Pocket Books 1973.

Grim, John A., *Renewing the Earth: Religion and Ecology in the Winter Dance of the Kettle Falls People.* Unpubl. ms. 1990[?].

Hall, Judy, *Deja Who?* Findhorn Press 1998.

Hall, Judy, *The Crystal Bible.* Godsfield Press 2003.

Harden, Blaine, *A River Lost: The Life and Death of the Columbia.* W.W. Norton & Co. 1996.

Henry, Will, *From Where the Sun Now Stands.* Random House 1960.

Hill, Ruth Beebe, *Hanta Yo: An American Saga.* Doubleday 1979.

Hungry Wolf, Adolf, *Teachings of Nature.* Good Medicine Books 1989.

Hungry Wolf, Adolf, *A Good Medicine Collection.* Good Medicine Books 1990.

Keyes, Laurel E., *Toning.* DeVorss & Co. 1990.

Lane, Belden C., *Landscapes of the Sacred.* The Johns Hopkins University Press 1988.

Layman, William, *Native River: The Columbia Remembered.* Washington State University Press 2002.

Layman, William, *River of Memory: The Everlasting Columbia.* University of Washington Press 2006.

McLuhan, T.C., *Touch the Earth.* Pocket Books 1972.

Mourning Dove, *Mourning Dove: a Salishan Autobiography.* Ed. J. Miller. University of Nebraska, Lincoln 1990.

Pryce, Paula, *Keeping the Lakes Way.* University of Toronto Press 1999.

Relander, Click, *Drummers and Dreamers.* Pacific Northwest National Parks and Forests Association 1986.

Sams, Jamie,   *Earth Medicine.* Harper 1994.

Sams, Jamie and David Carson,   *Medicine Cards.* Bear & Co. 1988.

Screeton, Paul,   *Quicksilver Heritage.* Thorsons 1974.

Stray, Geoff,   *Beyond 2012: Catastrophe or Ecstasy: A Complete Guide to End-of-Time Predictions.* Vital Signs Publishing 2005.

Summer Rain, Mary,   *Phoenix Rising.* Schiffer Publ. Co. 1987.

Sun Bear and Wabun,   *The Medicine Wheel.* Prentice Hall Press 1986.

The Sacred Tree,   *Four Worlds Development Project.* University of Lethbridge 1988.

Turner, Nancy, Randy Bouchard and Dorothy Kennedy, *Ethnobotany of the Okanagan-Colville Indians of British Columbia and Washington.* B.C. Provincial Museum. No. 21 occasional papers series 1980.

Twohy, Patrick J.,   *Finding a Way Home.* University Press, Wa. 1983.

Wa´na´nee´che´ & Timothy Freke,   *Principles of Native American Spirituality.* Thorsons 1996.

Weed, Susun S.,   *Menopausal Years.* Ash Tree Publishing 1992.

Weyler, Rex,   *Blood of the Land.* New Society Publishers 1992.

White, Ruth,   *Working with Your Chakras.* Piatkus 1993.

Zimmerman, Larry J.,   *Native North America.* Macmillan 1996.

A NEW ARROW LAKES COMMUNITY PROGRAM

ST´AL-SQIL-X-W

"OUR PEOPLE COMING BACK TO LIFE"

The Inchelium Wellness Center

St´al-Sqil-x-w, a residential treatment centre for youth and adults, is entering Phase One at Inchelium on the Colville Confederated Reservation. The project aims to provide culture-based addiction treatment services, and is also organised to provide charitable, professional and educational services to North American Aboriginal Peoples focussed in the Pacific Northwest, with an emphasis on building community bridges for cultural restoration.

Financial contributions would be most welcome.

Details can be found at: www.stalsqilx-w.org

Or write to:

Lou Stone, MSW
Founder, Chief Executive Officer
PO Box 282
Inchelium
Washington 99138
USA
Phone/Fax: 509 – 738 – 6441
Email: admin@stalsqilx-w.org

IRS Code 501 C 3 nonprofit charitable organisation

MAPS

Endpaper rear: South-eastern British Columbia/north-eastern Washington State (modern), with overlay: Teit/Ray delineation of Arrow Lakes/Sinixt ancestral territory (early 1900s).

Opposite page: Vallican, B.C., showing the Arrow Lakes/Sinixt ancestral village (the Vallican Archaeological Park heritage site) and proposed and eventual road alignments (1980, 1989).

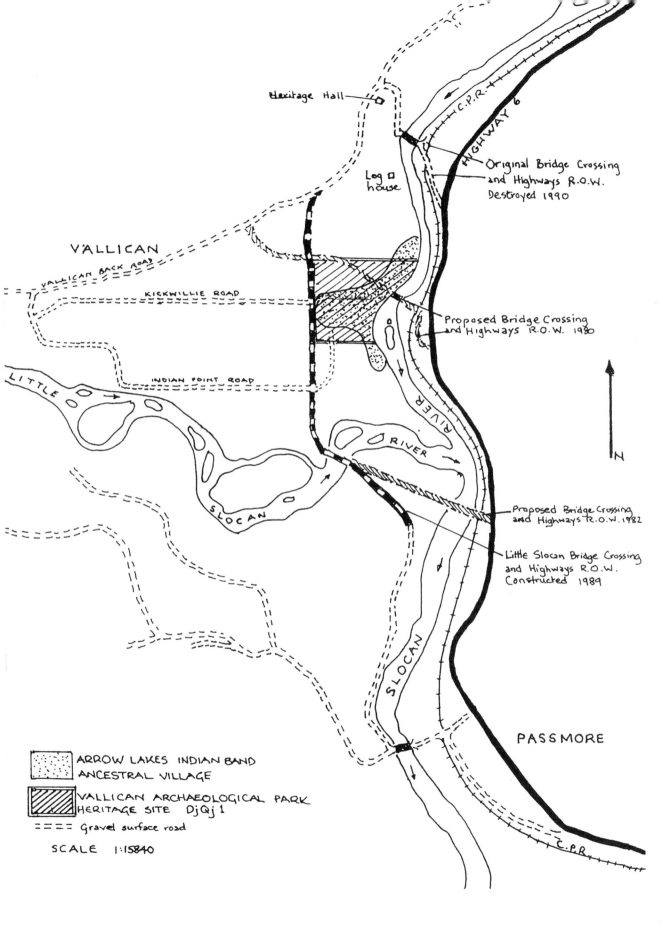

Heritage Hall

Log house

VALLICAN

VALLICAN BACK ROAD

KICKWILLIE ROAD

INDIAN POINT ROAD

LITTLE

SLOCAN

RIVER

RIVER

SLOCAN

C.P.R.

HIGHWAY 6

Original Bridge Crossing
and Highways R.O.W.
Destroyed 1990

Proposed Bridge Crossing
and Highways R.O.W. 1980

Proposed Bridge Crossing
and Highways R.O.W. 1982

Little Slocan Bridge Crossing
and Highways R.O.W.
Constructed 1989

PASSMORE

C.P.R.

N

ARROW LAKES INDIAN BAND
ANCESTRAL VILLAGE

VALLICAN ARCHAEOLOGICAL PARK
HERITAGE SITE DjQj 1

==== Gravel surface road

SCALE 1:15840